THE HANDBOOK

The Unofficial and Unauthorised Guide to the
Production of *Doctor Who*

Volume Two

THE HANDBOOK

The Unofficial and Unauthorised Guide to the Production of *Doctor Who*

David J Howe
Stephen James Walker
Mark Stammers

Volume Two

First published in England in 2005 by
Telos Publishing Ltd
5A Church Road, Shortlands, Bromley, Kent, BR2 0HP
www.telos.co.uk

Telos Publishing Ltd values feedback. Please e-mail us with any comments
you may have about this book to: feedback@telos.co.uk

This edition 2016

ISBN: 978-1-84583-942-0

Previously published in a different form in seven volumes
By Virgin Publishing Ltd, 1992, 1993, 1994, 1995, 1996, 1997.
And in one volume by Telos Publishing Ltd, 2005.

Text © 2005, 2016 David J Howe, Stephen James Walker & Mark Stammers

The moral rights of the authors have been asserted.

British Library Cataloguing in Publication Data.
A catalogue record for this book is available from the British Library.

This book is sold subject to the condition that it shall not by way of trade or otherwise, be lent, resold, hired out or otherwise circulated without the publisher's prior written consent in any form of binding or cover other than that in which it is published and without a similar condition including this condition being imposed on the subsequent purchaser.

Dedication

The seven volumes that comprised the original Handbook series were dedicated to a number of people. We feel it is only right to repeat those dedications here. So this book is dedicated to:

Ian K McLachlan, David Auger, Tony and Nikki Jordan, Martin Wiggins, the memory of Jon Pertwee, Ted, Sheila, Alan, Robert and Caroline, Alison, Anita Cotis, Mark Stammers, Andrew Pixley, Susan, Julie, Teresa and Kimberlie, everyone who ever contributed to *The Frame*, Nicole Adams (aka Suki), Claire.

Acknowledgements

Fourth Doctor: Sincere thanks to Justin Richards and Peter Anghelides, editors of the *Doctor Who* reference work *In-Vision*, for permission to quote from their releases. Also to Andrew Pixley for assistance above and beyond..., Guy Daniels and Richard Bignell of *Private Who*, John Freeman and Gary Russell of *Doctor Who Magazine*, Gary Leigh of *Dream Watch Bulletin*, Christopher Barry, Barry Newbery, Terrance Dicks, Jack Weller, David Auger and Rosemary Howe. Thanks also to all those unsung *Doctor Who* fanzine editors and writers for providing many happy hours of entertainment and education.

Fifth Doctor: For help in delving into the era of the fifth Doctor we are grateful to, as always, Andrew Pixley, and also to Martin Wiggins, David Auger, Jon Preddle, the *Skaro* Team, Jan Vincent-Rudzki, Peter Moffatt, John Brace, Mark Stammers, Patricia Holmes, Richard Hollis, Johnny Byrne, Richard Bignell, Anthony Brown and *In-Vision*, Gary Russell, Simeon Hearn and all *Doctor Who* fanzine editors everywhere.

Sixth Doctor: We are indebted this time around to: Colin Baker for his support and enthusiasm, Richard Bignell, John Brace, Austen Atkinson Broadbelt, Nicola Bryant for her long-distance assistance, David Auger, Pat Godfrey, Graeme Harper, John Nathan-Turner for all his help in the past, Barry Newbery, Alister Pearson, Andrew Pixley for again allowing us to draw on his encyclopaedic memory, Jon Preddle, Gary Russell of *Doctor Who Magazine*, Eric Saward, Paul Scoones, Alan Spalding, Patrick White, Martin Wiggins for supplying us with so much helpful reference material, and Graeme Wood. Thanks also to all those unsung *Doctor Who* fanzine editors and writers for providing many happy hours of entertainment and education.

Seventh/Eighth Doctor: Our thanks go this time first and foremost to our good friend and fellow researcher Andrew Pixley, who has selflessly offered advice and shared his incredible knowledge with us throughout the preparation of this series of Handbooks.

Special thanks to those few knowledgeable and generous souls who have provided sections for the 'Selling the Doctor' chapter: Ian Wheeler, who took on the bulk of this work, and Michael J Doran, Robert D Franks, David Robinson, Richard Prekodravac, Paul Scoones, Damian Shanahan and Dallas Jones. Thanks too to Rosemary Howe, who spent many, many hours spent reading all seven Handbooks in order to create the incredible (and hopefully useful) index that appears herein.

A big thank you to Sophie Aldred for the introduction and for her help in general.

Thanks also to Mark Ayres, Jonathan Blum, David Brunt, Mary Carroll, Michael J Doran, Gary Gillatt and *Doctor Who* Magazine, David Golding, Susan James, Misha Lauenstein, Lance Parkin, Gary Russell, Philip Segal, Mark Stammers, Martin Wiggins and all *Doctor Who* fanzine editors past and present.

For the corrections to earlier volumes, we are grateful to the following people: David Brunt, Michael J Doran, Chris Fieldhouse, Rosemary Howe, Dan Kukwa, Steve Manfred, John Molyneux, Paul Scoones and Martin Wiggins.

Finally, we would like to raise our collective glasses to our editor-in-chief at Virgin Publishing, Peter Darvill-Evans. It was he who encouraged us to submit ideas to him back in 1990, and this series of seven Handbooks would never have happened, and may never have been completed, if it had not been for Peter's faith in us and in the show that we all love.

To Peter, and also to Virgin editors past and present Rebecca Levene and Simon Winstone, we say, thanks for your advice, for your enthusiasm and for your trust. We hope we've repaid it.

CONTENTS

AUTHORS' NOTE TO TELOS EDITION	9
Doctor Who Story Checklist	11
THE FOURTH DOCTOR	**17**
Foreword	19
Tom Baker – In His Own Words	21
Character – The Fourth Doctor	45
Rewriting the Myth	54
Production Development	67
From Script to Screen – *The Brain of Morbius*	79
Effectively Speaking	104
On Location	111
Selling the Doctor	129
THE FIFTH DOCTOR	**147**
Foreword	149
Peter Davison – In His Own Words	151
Character – The Fifth Doctor	170
Rewriting the Myth	184
Script Editing	195
Production Development	209
From Script to Screen – *The Five Doctors*	221
Selling the Doctor	267
Afterword	284
THE SIXTH DOCTOR	**287**
Introduction – Colin Baker	289
Foreword	293
Colin Baker – In His Own Words	295
Character – The Sixth Doctor	331
Rewriting the Myth	342
Production Development	348
From Script to Screen – *Revelation of the Daleks*	358
Cancellation Crisis	387
Being the Companion	406
Selling the Doctor	418
Afterword	435

THE SEVENTH DOCTOR	437
Foreword	439
Introduction – Sophie Aldred	441
Sylvester McCoy – In His Own Words	443
Character – The Seventh Doctor	460
Rewriting the Myth	468
Production Development	474
From Script to Screen – *Dragonfire*	481
THE WILDERNESS YEARS	499
THE EIGHTH DOCTOR	515
Paul McGann – In His Own Words	517
Character – The Eighth Doctor	524
Production Development	526
Rewriting the Myth	533
Selling the Doctor	535

Authors' Note
To The Telos Edition

The Handbook series, originally published by Virgin Publishing in the 1990s, was a great success, not only for us as authors, but also for the publishers. For the first time, we had the scope to delve into some of the minutiae and detail of the production of the *Doctor Who* series, and collect it all together in a series of books that, we hoped, would complement our larger format, illustrated volumes, collectively known as the 'decades' books.

In 2003, Telos Publishing released a new and updated edition of *The Television Companion*, a programme guide that collected together as much information about the actual televised *Doctor Who* stories as possible: the plots, the cliff-hanger endings, cast and crew, location and recording information, and review commentaries. Into that volume we added material from the 'Stories' sections of the seven original Handbooks, to make it even more comprehensive. That material is therefore omitted here, to avoid excessive duplication between the two books.

For this book, we have not extensively re-worked the remainder of the material from the original Handbooks; we have presented it in the same Doctor-by-Doctor format as before. Some corrections and updates have been made to the text to remove inadvertent mistakes, small instances of repetition etc. Also, some material cut from the published versions of those earlier volumes for reasons of space has been reinstated here. Most notably, there is the entire 'Script to Screen' section on the first Doctor story *The Ark*, which appeared only in heavily truncated form in the original Handbook. The extensive Production Guide to the first Doctor's era also has several more entries this time, and some of the other chapters have small embellishments to them as well. We have not, however, added large amounts of material to cover new developments that have occurred since the original volumes were written – such as the production of new audio adventures of the fifth, sixth, seventh and eighth Doctors by Big Finish – as these have already been comprehensively documented elsewhere.

At the time of writing this introduction, there is also a new series of *Doctor Who* due for transmission on BBC1 in 2005 ... something we've been awaiting with bated breath since 1989! Again, this book does not cover the production of the new series – look out for another Telos Publishing title, *Back to the Vortex*, for information on that.

THE HANDBOOK: VOL 2

Our aim here is to complete the picture with regard to *Doctor Who* on television from 1963 to 1996, and provide a complement to *The Television Companion* by chronicling the behind-the-scenes history of the first eight Doctors. We hope you enjoy reading, or re-reading, it as much as we enjoyed writing it.

David J Howe
Stephen James Walker
Mark Stammers

DOCTOR WHO STORY CHECKLIST

SEASON EIGHT (1971)

Terror of the Autons (EEE)
The Mind of Evil (FFF)
The Claws of Axos (GGG)
Colony in Space (HHH)
The Dæmons (JJJ)

SEASON NINE (1972)

Day of the Daleks (KKK)
The Curse of Peladon (MMM)
The Sea Devils (LLL)
The Mutants (NNN)
The Time Monster (OOO)

SEASON TEN (1972 – 1973)

The Three Doctors (RRR)
Carnival of Monsters (PPP)
Frontier in Space (QQQ)
Planet of the Daleks (SSS)
The Green Death (TTT)

SEASON ELEVEN (1973 – 1974)

The Time Warrior (UUU)
Invasion of the Dinosaurs (WWW)
Death to the Daleks (XXX)
The Monster of Peladon (YYY)
Planet of the Spiders (ZZZ)

SEASON TWELVE (1974 – 1975)

The Doctor played by Tom Baker
Robot (4A)
The Ark in Space (4C)
The Sontaran Experiment (4B)
Genesis of the Daleks (4E)
Revenge of the Cybermen (4D)

SEASON THIRTEEN (1975 – 1976)

Terror of the Zygons (4F)
Planet of Evil (4H)
Pyramids of Mars (4G)
The Android Invasion (4J)
The Brain of Morbius (4K)
The Seeds of Doom (4L)

SEASON FOURTEEN (1976 – 1977)

The Masque of Mandragora (4M)
The Hand of Fear (4N)
The Deadly Assassin (4P)
The Face of Evil (4Q)
The Robots of Death (4R)
The Talons of Weng-Chiang (4S)

SEASON FIFTEEN (1977 – 1978)

Horror of Fang Rock (4V)
The Invisible Enemy (4T)
Image of the Fendahl (4X)
The Sun Makers (4W)
Underworld (4Y)
The Invasion of Time (4Z)

SEASON SIXTEEN (1978 – 1979)

The Ribos Operation (5A)
The Pirate Planet (5B)
The Stones of Blood (5C)
The Androids of Tara (5D)
The Power of Kroll (5E)
The Armageddon Factor (5F)

SEASON SEVENTEEN (1979 – 1980)

Destiny of the Daleks (5J)
City of Death (5H)
The Creature from the Pit (5G)
Nightmare of Eden (5K)
The Horns of Nimon (5L)
Shada (5M)

DOCTOR WHO STORY CHECKLIST

SEASON EIGHTEEN (1980 – 1981)

The Leisure Hive (5N)
Meglos (5Q)
Full Circle (5R)
State of Decay (5P)
Warriors' Gate (5S)
The Keeper of Traken (5T)
Logopolis (5V)

SEASON NINETEEN (1982)

The Doctor played by Peter Davison
Castrovalva (5Z)
Four to Doomsday (5W)
Kinda (5Y)
The Visitation (5X)
Black Orchid (6A)
Earthshock (6B)
Time-Flight (6C)

SEASON TWENTY (1983)

Arc of Infinity (6E)
Snakedance (6D)
Mawdryn Undead (6F)
Terminus (6G)
Enlightenment (6H)
The King's Demons (6J)

TWENTIETH ANNIVERSARY SPECIAL (1983)

The Five Doctors (6K)

SEASON TWENTY-ONE (1984)

Warriors of the Deep (6L)
The Awakening (6M)
Frontios (6N)
Resurrection of the Daleks (6P)
Planet of Fire (6Q)
The Caves of Androzani (6R)
The Doctor played by Colin Baker

THE HANDBOOK: VOL 2

The Twin Dilemma (6S)

SEASON TWENTY-TWO (1985)

Attack of the Cybermen (6T)
Vengeance On Varos (6V)
The Mark of the Rani (6X)
The Two Doctors (6W)
Timelash (6Y)
Revelation of the Daleks (6Z)

SEASON TWENTY-THREE (1986)

The Trial of a Time Lord (7A/7B/7C)

SEASON TWENTY-FOUR (1987)

The Doctor played by Sylvester McCoy
Time and the Rani (7D)
Paradise Towers (7E)
Delta and the Bannermen (7F)
Dragonfire (7G)

SEASON TWENTY-FIVE (1988 – 1989)

Remembrance of the Daleks (7H)
The Happiness Patrol (7L)
Silver Nemesis (7K)
The Greatest Show In the Galaxy (7J)

SEASON TWENTY-SIX (1989)

Battlefield (7N)
Ghost Light (7Q)
The Curse of Fenric (7M)
Survival (7P)

THE TELEVISION MOVIE (1996)

The Doctor played by Paul McGann
Doctor Who

THE FOURTH DOCTOR

David J Howe
Mark Stammers
Stephen James Walker

Foreword

On Saturday 8 June 1974, at two minutes and sixteen seconds past six o'clock, the familiar features of the third Doctor melted away to be replaced by those of a stranger; the fourth Doctor. As the credits came up signifying the end of the eleventh season of *Doctor Who*, fans were left with a gap of six months to ponder what lay ahead.

If *Doctor Who* had been cancelled at this point, with the departure of Jon Pertwee, it would no doubt have been remembered as a very successful series of its type, which had been fronted by three excellent lead actors, spawned a number of highly memorable concepts and characters (most notably the dreaded Daleks) and given years of pleasure to a generation of Saturday tea-time viewers. As it was, of course, the series did not end there – it was doing far too well for that even to have been a consideration in the minds of BBC executives. Instead, Tom Baker embarked on what was to become an epic stint as the Doctor, lasting from 28 December 1974 to 21 March 1981, a period of six years, two months and 25 days; and during that period, *Doctor Who* would rise to a higher plane of popularity than at any time since its second season.

When asked about his reasons for leaving the series, Jon Pertwee has often cited the slow break-up of 'his team'. His long serving co-star Katy Manning had left at the end of season ten to be replaced by Elisabeth Sladen, and script editor Terrance Dicks and producer Barry Letts had also decided to move on. The tragic death in a car accident in 1973 of Pertwee's friend Roger Delgado, who had played the Doctor's arch enemy the Master throughout the era of the third Doctor, had also resulted in the series losing one of its most popular villains. But the decision whether to leave or stay was ultimately taken out of Pertwee's hands when his request for an increase in his fee was rejected by the BBC's Head of Drama, Shaun Sutton, and he was informed that he would not be required for the twelfth season. The BBC clearly felt it was time for a new Doctor, and the production office wasted little time in setting about the task of finding a replacement. After a lengthy period of searching, Tom Baker was introduced to the press as the fourth Doctor on 16 February 1974.

This new Doctor was born into a Britain emerging from the nightmare of oil shortages, which had led to the rationing of fuel for cars, sent huge numbers of the population's homes into the dark during frequent power cuts, and left more than a few irate young *Doctor Who* fans staring by candlelight at a blank TV screen that should have been filled with the latest adventures of their hero. Where the Daleks and the Cybermen had failed, a group of Middle Eastern countries that comprised OPEC had succeeded in temporarily defeating the Doctor – a dastardly plan of the Master's perhaps? 1974 also saw the departure of Edward Heath as Prime Minister and the return of Harold Wilson's Labour Government. West Germany won the World Cup, and ABBA took the Eurovision Song Contest, and then the pop charts, by storm. Joining the Swedish super-group in the charts were artistes such as Mud, Slade, Gary Glitter and The Bay City Rollers.

With the departure of Jon Pertwee, some TV pundits, and indeed some fans of the series, could have been forgiven for thinking that *Doctor Who* had run its course and that there was little new ground left for it to cover. After all, the series was already eleven years old, an almost unheard-of age for any drama production other than a soap opera. Yet the next seven seasons would see *Doctor Who* establishing itself as a true British institution, and a worldwide hit with a reported 110 million viewers in some 43 countries, making it BBC Enterprises' biggest money-spinner. Its ratings attained their highest ever level and, for perhaps the only time in its history, it came to be accepted as a truly mainstream TV success – no longer could it be dismissed as simply a kid's show or a cult favourite. Tom Baker himself became not so much a star as a national hero.

In particular, this period saw *Doctor Who* break through into the American TV market. By the end of the fourth Doctor's era, it had gained an enormous cult following estimated at around 56,000 American fans, who could turn on their TVs at virtually any time and expect to find *Doctor Who* episodes playing on one or more of the Public Broadcasting Service (PBS) stations scattered across the United States.

One of the main reasons for the success of the fourth Doctor can be simply deduced. It was the enormously exciting and eccentric personality of Tom Baker himself. As well as the character of the Doctor, the style of the programme was very much influenced by its incumbent producer. There were four producers during the Tom Baker years, and they struggled with a variety of external factors that influenced their decisions, especially the growing criticism from and influence of pressure groups like the National Viewers and Listeners Association headed by Mrs Mary Whitehouse, and the newly formed fan group, the *Doctor Who* Appreciation Society.

If the Seventies were the years of your childhood, then this section should jog your memories of the thrill of travelling with the fourth Doctor. If you are too young to have been there at the time, then maybe this will give you a taste of what it was like to watch unfold before you possibly the most exciting era of *Doctor Who*.

Tom Baker
In His Own Words

ON HIS EARLY LIFE:

'I was brought up in the Scotland Road area of Liverpool among Irish pubs and Irish priests, and brainwashed with a preoccupation with death. Which is perhaps why I still wander round graveyards collecting strange epitaphs.'

Quoted in 1979 in Marvel Comics' *Starburst* **No. 10.**

'One of my earliest memories is of my Auntie Chrissie. She was a street bookmaker before they legalised betting shops. She and my Uncle Willy and Uncle Terry took the betting slips on the street corner. My mother would pick up some of the bets standing in a graveyard while I was with her. It was the most discreet place she could think of.

'In those days people used to die of things like 'flu and TB so, as an altar boy, I went to about four or five funerals a week, especially in the winter. The relatives used to give you a sixpenny bit. Once I was standing at a graveside, and on this particular day the wind was biting and I was crying with the cold. This fella looked at my tears, squeezed my little arm and patted my little head, and gave me a two shilling piece. Two shillings! I mean, that was twenty-four ice creams. So after that I began to cry all over the place and I became a highly paid professional mourner, almost.'

Interviewed by William Marshall in 1979 for the *Daily Mirror.*

'I was always looking for a way out, but how was I to manage it? I was from a poor background: from a house with no books, and parents with no experience of how to form one's life. Here was a young man desperate to make his mark, fantasising and dreaming. Not clever at school. Rather overgrown and therefore odd to look at. "Good heavens! Is he only eleven? But he's six foot one!" people said. In addition I was skinny and had a curved back because I could hardly ever stand up straight.

'When people came to the school to talk about careers, I was always intensely interested. Then one day a man came and talked about monasticism. I was interested because having been brought up by a very devout Roman Catholic mother – my father was away at sea all the time – I was very preoccupied with religion. The man warned us that we would have to take a vow of chastity, poverty and obedience, but that didn't matter to me. The chastity was enforced by my age, the poverty was understood, and as far as obedience went – well, everybody kicked my backside. And it appeared that they fed you as well, and you had sheets on your bed. So at 15 I went into a monastery in Jersey, and later Shropshire, as a noviciate. But I must admit that I did it only to get away from my background.

'After six years I left, and six weeks later I was called up to do my National Service. It was in the Army that I gained the conviction that I could act and enjoy it. I had acted at school and had been offered a job at the Abbey Theatre in Dublin when I was 15, but my mother wouldn't let me go. But now I decided, "This is what I want to do." I've had some terrible moments of depression and sometimes I've felt really isolated and lost, but I've never wavered from that feeling.

'I was appearing in a late-night revue in York, playing a dog, when I was spotted by a talent scout from the National Theatre. Lord Olivier interviewed me and gave me a job. My first part was playing a horse. Sir Laurence encouraged me and helped me a lot. He was responsible for my getting the part of Rasputin in *Nicholas and Alexandra*. The film was made in Spain at a time when I was in two plays at the National and rehearsing a third. I was shuttled back and forth to Spain to film my bits. I was whisked about in limousines and first-class plane seats. It was heady stuff. I was asked, "How does a working-class boy like you adjust to an air-conditioned Cadillac?" I replied, "Terribly easily."'

Interviewed by Peter Dacre in 1978 for the *Sunday Express*, 12 March edition.

'Those years with the Brothers of Ploermel were terribly exciting and demanding. I enjoyed the suffering and deprivation and silence, although I haven't stopped talking since. I enjoyed the hysterical self-indulgence of feeling unworthy.

'I am absolutely certain that when men are together and deprived of women, they become homosexual. I wanted to embrace a young brother called Olivier-Jean so much that my bones used to *crack*. When you're young, it's very difficult to think about anything but lust. By the end of the six years, I was absolutely worn out by my sexual urges, and a priest advised me to get out.

'Once I was doing my National Service and encountering girls, I discovered sex, started practising it in a frenzy and rejected the Church very swiftly. It left me with a huge residue of guilt. Sometimes God knocks on the side of my head now and says, "Let's get back together." But I prefer guilt, lust, anxiety, lies and confusion. I prefer the uncertainties of life.'

Interviewed by Corinna Honan in 1992 for the *Daily Mail*, 28 March edition.

'I simply feigned idiocy right through my National Service and got away with murder. In my second year, I was able to turn up on muster parade in red leather slippers. Harmless dementia is considered something sacred as long as there's no violence in the unhingement. I went around saying preposterous things. I'd say, "I won't be shouted at by a bunch of professional murderers," and of course they'd shout at me, so I'd proceed to cry. And that simply unhinged them. Finally, they just left me alone because I was too much trouble.

'I was a terribly withdrawn, pained, skinny man, and the Army released me. I loathed Queen's Regulations. It was the enforced contact with people of disparate backgrounds that did it. I was coerced into a Unit show. When I discovered I could make people laugh, it gave me a new strength.'

Quoted in 1979 in Marvel Comics' *Starburst* No. 10.

ON BEING AN ACTOR:

'When I was starting out in the Fifties, I was anxious to get started and *so* nervous about trying to make my way. Most people will tell you they want to achieve something, learn something, build a pattern; to find a partner, have somewhere to live that's nice and where they can feel a bit safe; to have a couple of children and a car, collect a few books and go on holiday. That's what most people want, I think. And then there are actors.

'Concomitant with being an actor is that dreadful, exhausting state of being self-aware all the time, because you're marketing your appearance, you're marketing what you sound like. You're worried about whether you're ugly or going bald or getting fat. You're worried about dental bills or worried that no-one wants you. In other words you are *ill*. To want to be an actor, especially these days, is to be ill. It's a kind of illness – this terrible pernicious itch to want what threatens you most, which is insecurity. Performers, like other people, are mesmerised by what threatens them most. They have to learn to love it and live with it and create out of it.

'Performers create out of anxiety, they don't create out of jolliness or a happy song. They have to exorcise the most terrible memories of the last effort, to forget past failures and hope all the time that they're going to please someone. Actors are just professional pleasers, like waiters!'

Interviewed by John Freeman in 1991 for *Doctor Who Magazine* Nos. 179-181.

I'm feeling much jollier and philosophical about most things now. You see the other thing was that [*Doctor Who*] weighed on me, because no-one would employ me. I'd like to think that was because I was a huge success and therefore had no credibility as anything else. That's the way actors always justify it. And then the last two years, thanks to the BBC, again, with *The Law Lords* and *The Silver Chair*, and then *Medics* and *Cluedo*, suddenly things have looked up again.

Speaking at a press conference to publicise the release on video of *Shada*, 11 May 1992.

ON FANTASTICAL CHARACTER ACTING:

'Everyone wants to do something amazing and have the funniest lines or the greatest costume or the best exit or entrance. I mean, we adore what's fantastic, don't we? People are obsessed with fantasy, whether they know it or not. Middle-aged paunchy men – I'm well past that! – dream of being the footballer Maradona or the cricketer Viv Richards. I mean, Richards is just forty, and how many forty-year-old men look at him and wish they were him, and wouldn't dare tell their friends. Everyone has a heroic impulse, a desire towards being amazing, towards achieving, towards being heroic.'

Interviewed by John Freeman in 1991 for *Doctor Who Magazine* Nos. 179-181.

ON THE ATTRACTION OF PLAYING THE DOCTOR:

'To be honest, it was nothing about the character that influenced me at all, it was sheer necessity! I was desperately out of work and was terribly depressed by this. Suddenly, along came the possibility of playing Doctor Who. It was just relief to play a major part!

'Because I didn't watch *Doctor Who* much, I had no notion of what this would do. It just so happened that with the new scripts that Barry Letts (and later Philip Hinchcliffe) had commissioned, the directors, costume and set designers who moved in ... well, it all came together. I didn't know what was happening. I just responded to that, which I suppose is the great secret, isn't it?

'I was working very hard on a building site in Ebury Street, next door but one to where Mozart wrote his first symphony, when I got the job. The builders were actually very good to me, and I have a happy memory of that, but of course I didn't *want* to be on a building site, because I hadn't much skill. I wanted to be an actor.

'When I got the part, I had this feeling of just *huge* relief, and also one of great pride. I didn't tell my workmates I'd got the job. I had the day off and went to the BBC, and then it was in the first edition of the *Evening Standard*. I knew they all took that paper – and bang, all was revealed! So there they were, looking over the tops of their papers at me. It was a great moment of pleasure. They were very proud of me – and I was very proud of them.'

Interviewed by John Freeman in 1991 for *Doctor Who Magazine* Nos. 179-181.

ON HIS DEBUT AS THE DOCTOR:

'I didn't know how I was going to do *Doctor Who*. I had no idea at all – not until the very first rehearsal, and even then I didn't know … I just did it. I just played the script and something evolved and the audience liked the way I did it, obviously, so we kept it like that. But sometimes it was funny and sometimes not so funny and sometimes it was thrilling. It was just an accident, really.'

Interviewed by Dave Dean in 1982. Published in *Private Who* Issue 3.

ON HIS DOCTOR'S COSTUME:

'I think that the style of the costume represented my personal style of dress, which is rather casual. I was inspired by a designer called Jim Acheson, who was young and conscientious and very witty, I thought. I met several lovely designers at the BBC. June Hudson, latterly, was a designer I saw a lot of. But Jim Acheson and I went out to play for a few weeks and we gradually got this tatty costume together, which was a mixture of sort of scruffiness and elegance. Scruffiness in the way it was worn but elegance in the cut of the coat – and madness in the size of the scarf. The hat was Herbert Johnson. Yeah, I had some influence in it, but it was mostly Jim's inspiration really.'

Interviewed by Dave Dean in 1982. Published in *Private Who* Issue 3.

'Jim Acheson designed the scarf, bought the wool and gave it to someone's relation at the BBC called Begonia Pope, who was thrilled to be working for the Corporation. She didn't ask any questions; Jim gave her the design and she knitted up all the wool. Jim of course had no knowledge about knitting, except for colour. He bought ten times the amount of wool that was needed, and she knitted the lot! He omitted to say it was just a scarf, like the sort you'd see on the Left Bank in Paris. When I put it on, it was hilarious, and Jim instantly said, "Keep it, it's funny."'

Interviewed by John Freeman in 1991 for *Doctor Who Magazine* Nos. 179-181.

ON BREAKING HIS COLLAR-BONE DURING RECORDING OF *THE SONTARAN EXPERIMENT.*

'When I fell, I banged my head as well, and I wasn't sure when I fell ... how badly I was hurt, because the pain was very bad and it was quite deep. In fact it was just a shock of the collar bone, which is the swiftest bone to mend but when it breaks it made you feel very sick. I thought, am I hurt badly? And it wasn't that I was afraid of dying. I mean I thought, how am I going to get on with the show? I was taken away for investigation, and when I came back, Barry Letts and Philip Hinchcliffe were looking all grey-faced in the pub, and I swanned in and had several large gins.'

Speaking at a press conference to publicise the release on video of *Shada*, 11 May 1992.

ON *DOCTOR WHO'S* UNIQUE FORMAT:

'I think if I bothered about the plots, I wouldn't get much done. The plots won't stand up to severe examination. The mass of our audience is children and they're only interested in the high spots of the Doctor's adventures anyway.'

Speaking on *Woman's Hour*, 12 January 1977.

'Given fundamental expertise from the producer downwards, the real gold of the thing is the formula. Given that you haven't got a bonehead at the top or a powerful subversive somewhere down the line, you couldn't really fail with it. The first reason we are so successful – the very first reason – is that we are incomparable. Nothing admits to comparison with *Doctor Who*. When people try to plagiarise our situations or our attitudes they fall down, because it's obvious plagiarism. They don't really start with this marvellous thing that the character's an alien, and the wonderful heroic comedy-thriller notion that he can travel in this daft box. That's why I think the formula, which is so wonderful, engages such a huge audience.'

Interviewed by John Fleming in 1980 for Marvel Comics' *Starburst* No. 19.

'I think the formula lent itself to Gothic areas, not because science fantasy should do that but simply because we have that long film background of Gothic horror, tension and fantasy, the tragi-comedy if you like. Do you remember the old Hammer films, especially the late-night ones when one had been drinking? You'd get gales of laughter from one particular section of the audience and the rest would be sat po-faced. It's rather like going to a theatre with a lot of actors or musicians, and they're picking up one thing and someone else is seeing it on another level.

'*Doctor Who* was like that. I was always, constantly trying to translate whatever was happening to me and add it to the role, drawing on other experiences. One of the reasons I spent so much time on the road promoting the programme was that I was drawing on the children from the audience. What they told me they liked, I did more of, or else adapted it and did variations. I used to get hints of what they liked. So it might have appeared I was being very nice to them, but actually what I was doing was 'vampiring' them for ideas. It was quite shameless!'

Interviewed by John Freeman in 1991 for *Doctor Who Magazine* Nos. 179-181.

ON THE PLEASURES OF REHEARSALS:

'Most of the time it was a pleasure to get to work, to get off the street and out of the ghastly world of reality, away from the bloody TV news and into Rehearsal Room 603. It was just bliss.

'During rehearsals, we used to mime a lot and pretend the monsters were there. You'd get actors from other shows peeping in through the bullseye windows and laughing at us – not in a derisive way but with pleasure at all this over-acting. They were still enjoying it, and lots of people – lots of very distinguished actors – wanted to be in it and used to tell me so in the BBC canteen, which moved me very much. I remember polished actors like John Woodnutt being killingly funny about it, and there were others, like Bill Fraser, Freddy Trieves and George Baker.'

Interviewed by John Freeman in 1991 for *Doctor Who Magazine* Nos. 179-181.

THE FOURTH DOCTOR

ON NOT WATCHING *DOCTOR WHO*:

'I didn't watch it before I was in it and I certainly didn't watch it while I was in it, because that would only make me unhappy. My reasoning was, "What is the point in watching it?", because we worked under such pressure; I always wished I could do it better, you see, and there was never any time, with a maximum of maybe two or three takes per scene. If there was any doubt, I sometimes deliberately used to blow it out on such a scale that they had to do a retake. Directors know about this!

'Occasionally I might have watched a sequence over which we'd had an argument, but I didn't watch it as a rule, because I would never have been pleased with it. I might watch it now out of curiosity after so long, but generally, if it's marvellous someone will tell me about it and if it isn't so marvellous I'll just be unhappy.'

Interviewed by John Freeman in 1991 for *Doctor Who Magazine* Nos. 179-181.

ON AUDIENCE REACTION:

'One of the surprising things about *Doctor Who* is the range of the audience. Although I have always thought of it as a children's programme – not a childish programme, mind you – we have a big adult audience. And over the past two years, we have discovered that there are a lot of *Doctor Who* fan clubs at the universities. I was astonished to be invited to St John's and Somerville Colleges at Oxford, and I spoke to absolutely packed halls. If I accepted all the invitations, I could be going to the universities three or four times a week.

'Some actors get a bit neurotic when they are approached by people and called by the name of the character they play. I don't mind being called Doctor Who – which I am all the time. I can't tell you just how dull life was when I was just Tom Baker. Simply nobody recognised me.

'I must always remember that I do not have an existence as Tom Baker. Apart from my close friends and colleagues, everybody calls me Doctor Who. Even children in push-chairs point at me in the street. But I am very aware that they are looking not at Tom Baker but at this image they have of this character. It is important to me, therefore, that I never disappoint people, especially children. I would never be seen being raucous in the streets, or plastered, or smoking cigars. When I want to go out to play, I do it discreetly in selected actors' bars or clubs. Even then there is sometimes no escape. A friend once took me to a select West End club. "We won't be bothered here," he said. We had not been there more than a few minutes when a chap raised his glass and said, "My dear

Doctor, how nice to see you here." My friend was astonished, because the man was a judge.'

Interviewed by Peter Dacre in 1978 for the *Sunday Express*, 12 March edition.

'The programming of *Doctor Who*, in my view, is absolutely brilliant, because it follows the sports round-up, the brief news, sometimes a programme like *Basil Brush*, and it's then followed by *The Generation Game* or *The Duchess of Duke Street* or whatever it is; but that time on a Saturday vitally influences the attitude of the audience. I mean, if you pushed it on, rolling back the frontier to half past ten at night, the audience would be drunk! How are they going to follow our script? They can't possibly follow our script when they're stone cold sober, but if they go out and drink Red Barrel or some inflammatory drink like that, it scrambles people's heads!'

Speaking on stage in August 1979 at the *Doctor Who* Appreciation Society convention PanoptiCon III.

'Sometimes I enjoy being recognised. Especially by children. It gets very debilitating when you're accosted by adults all the time. But *children* – I love it, especially if I'm on the move. Going home from work on the train last night, I made three tube changes, and all the kids were coming back from Hyde Park with their mothers. They were so densely packed and I was threading my way through and, quite often, a child is actually being led towards me and he recognises me and he smiles and then he wonders why he smiled. And then it clicks, but by the time it's clicked, I've gone. It's terrific fun, that kind of contact. Great fun. I love it with the *small* children – it's amazing, that.

'You see, to use a very overworked word, it's a participatory programme. In your average family of a man and his wife and three children, with the children going in age from say nine to three, when it comes to Saturday night viewing it becomes a bit of a charade. Children are very quick to cotton on to some kind of regular routine. So, when they watch *Doctor Who*, several things happen. It's not passive in a two- or three-child family. The older child of nine or ten might be actually following the narrative very carefully and quite critically. His six year old brother, when the monsters come up, is wincing a bit. And the little fellow, getting in on the act, is behind the sofa or he's in the kitchen looking through the crack in the door. Now, the parents notice this and enjoy it. I've talked to hundreds of parents: they enjoy this. The moment you actually give children that attention – just like, indeed, adults – you get this marvellous response. When our music comes up – and the opening music to *Doctor Who* is absolutely *wonderful* – that's the signal for the weekly sit-down and the sharing.'

Interviewed by John Fleming in 1980 for Marvel Comics' *Starburst* No. 19.

'I love small children. By an accident of temperament I get on very well with them. I am perfectly happy to spend a lot of time with them. Wherever I go now, I get enormous attention – from children and adults. Their response is so warm and generous that my life is different from most other people's. I would be lying if I didn't say that it gave me a huge amount of pleasure. I am one of the few men in England to whom "Don't talk to strange men" doesn't apply. When I bump into small children in the park, I can pick them up or embrace them and no policeman will come and move me on. Sometimes I see parents looking a bit anxious, but when they come over and see it is Doctor Who, they are as thrilled as their children. Nothing appeals to me more than *Doctor Who*.

'If I am in a bar alone, everybody feels they can talk to me. Sometimes it gets irritating. I am quite happy to stand alone with my gin and tonic trying to finish a crossword or reading.'

Interviewed by Dan Slater in 1979 for the *Sun*.

'People are quite kind to me; children are always wonderful. But I've had my share of rudeness. The trouble with becoming a "name" on TV is that you are licensed in the public's mind to play just one role. I have to behave like the Doctor. I'll put up with any pathetic, troublesome old drunk, simply because I could not bear the thought of him going home and telling his kids, "I saw Doctor Who today and he told me to sod off." As a viewer, I wouldn't like to see someone from a children's programme behaving badly. It would be like seeing Robin Day dancing on the table in a restaurant.'

Interviewed by Charles Catchpole in 1981 for unknown newspaper, 21 March edition.

ON COMPANION LEELA'S VIOLENT STREAK:

'I've forgotten the details of the character, but I do remember being *appalled* at her aggression, without me having the ammunition to put forward my side of the argument. There was a moral dimension, an ethical dilemma, because she *killed* things. It wasn't just my character, *I* was furious at the beginning. There was some facetious dialogue about it, some claptrap like "I don't really think you should do that." The point is that these gentle ironies are quite inappropriate when life and death are at stake. What I tried to give it was outrage and burning indignation – that if it didn't change, if *she* didn't change, the character would have to go. I don't mean Louise Jameson, but I would have to threaten Leela with this, because I could not coexist with someone whose solution to problems was to kill. So they modified that and Louise was very good and hugely successful. But I was very rattled by it.'

Interviewed by John Freeman in 1991 for *Doctor Who Magazine* Nos. 179-181.

ON THE TARDIS:

'I often felt, myself, that they didn't really pursue the wonderful, cosmically funny aspect of the TARDIS being bigger on the inside than on the outside. I couldn't understand why on the inside of the TARDIS there shouldn't be a whole market town with a cathedral, which we could keep the wellingtons in! Instead it was always just a control room – we occasionally went into other areas – but, in my view, no-one ever wrote a story that suggested the logic of dimensional transcendentalism; that inside the TARDIS is not just a console room but a whole *world*.

'It would be amazing, to go into the TARDIS and have the assistant say, "My god Doctor, look – there are thousands of sheep there!" And the Doctor would say "Good grief, so there are. I remember now ..." And of course he can't remember the exact details, but the sheep would have come in at some difficult time and he'd saved them, intending to transport them somewhere. Why *isn't* a world shown, instead of waving it away with some facetious, smart-assed remark? I mean, who cleans for the Doctor? Why isn't there someone suddenly bellowing, "Where have you been? I've been waiting. Don't you remember you took me on to clean for you?" To which the Doctor would say, "Did I? I really must get a hold of myself ..."'

Interviewed by John Freeman in 1991 for *Doctor Who Magazine* Nos. 179-181.

ON THE DOCTOR'S ROBOT DOG, K-9:

'I don't really have opinions about bits of metal ... I suppose it was a good idea to have K-9. It's an insufferable pun, but it did work. It worked very well, because of what John Leeson, who was the voice of K-9, did in rehearsals, which was much more interesting than K-9 itself. For instance, despite all the money we spent on him, K-9 couldn't run over a matchbox. He could be moved of course from a distance, by remote control, but what

THE FOURTH DOCTOR

John Leeson did was much more interesting than K-9 ever was. So I had strong feelings for what John Leeson did, but not for that dreary metal dog.'

Interviewed by Dave Dean in 1982. Published in *Private Who* Issue 3.

'K-9 was a blasted hard thing to act with! Off-set there'd be John Leeson doing the voice, and because the thing is so small, all the dialogue shots had to be done at its level. We had tremendous technical problems with it as well. It was always breaking down, especially on location when we'd get annoyed because we were always running behind schedule, so that was just another hold-up.'

Interviewed by Richard Marson in 1984 for *Doctor Who Magazine* No. 92.

ON HIS FOUR *DOCTOR WHO* PRODUCERS:

'Barry Letts only produced my first one – although it was he who got me the job. Then Philip Hinchcliffe was with us for quite a while – he was a good, hard-working producer. Graham Williams came on and worked like a dog at a rather trying time for all of us when money was getting scarce and we were behind schedule. John Nathan-Turner did my last year and was very kind to me, very accommodating. I saw a lot of him socially – we were both bachelors at the time. He's good company and he cares so much for the programme. In their own ways, and as far as the series would allow, they were all trying to ring the changes, I suppose. They had their job and I had mine, and we worked quite closely together; the only conflict we ever had was professional, and that kind of conflict is essential.'

Interviewed by Richard Marson in 1984 for *Doctor Who Magazine* No. 92.

ON THE HORRIFIC CONTENT OF *DOCTOR WHO*:

'We often discuss the horror content, and they take it very seriously at our office, because they're experts at it. They're willing to listen to me of course – after all I go out and meet the children. On the other hand, there is often a scene when we're shooting it that looks unbearably horrifying – but that won't be how it's edited. I don't do the editing, that's not my job. That's the director's brief. Then finally the producer and the head of the department decide how far to go. But it is very often an arbitrary thing. Only two people can decide. We've come under a lot of stick from Mrs Whitehouse especially. I understand that she won't even have lunch with me!

'I sometimes think that the stories are very frightening, but the consideration always is that television takes place in a domestic context. And one can go further in terror. Children like to be terrorised. At home, they'll be watching the television and seeing something happening to me, and then they move their eyes through a very small arc and they see their fish fingers, or their mum, or their dad. It's a family event. You have the little ones behind the sofa. I know about this, I've spoken to hundreds of children. Little ones behind the sofa, or looking through fingers, or looking through cracks in doors. And the whole thing in many ways is rather diffused by that, because it is so obviously fictional.'

Speaking on *Woman's Hour*, 12 January 1977.

ON THE DOCTOR'S MORE HUMOROUS STYLE UNDER GRAHAM WILLIAMS:

'I don't know what Graham was told, but although he and I worked together and there were some successes in his time, he and I weren't really all that close. I was just responding to whatever was going there.

'I don't want to try to define what my style was; I just responded to the scripts and finally filtered them through me. As you know – I've been quoted many times – Doctor Who was not an acting part any more than James Bond is an acting part. By acting I mean an actor's definition of an acting job, which is when a character actually develops and discovers something so amazing that there is actually a transformation. Either that or there is a realisation that he has been entirely wrong. This isn't so with heroes. There's an utter predictability about playing heroic parts. Heroes, you *know* what side they'll come down on. Doctor Who isn't suddenly going to become obsessed with sex or money or gratuitous violence – he's predictably good, like an innocent child. Within that predictability, within all that certainty, the fun of doing it was, "How do you surprise the audience and hold them and make them want to watch again and again?"'

Interviewed by John Freeman in 1991 for *Doctor Who Magazine* Nos. 179-181.

ON TENSIONS DURING PRODUCTION:

'One grew to know what the difficulties were for the technical crew who had to realise the story, and one co-operated the best one could. I mean, I was often, I'm afraid, impatient and difficult. Not out of malice or intention, but I'm an anxious sort of actor and I'm easily thrown. I think sometimes I was impatient and difficult and I regret that but, I mean, it was with the best will.'

Interviewed by Dave Dean in 1982. Published in *Private Who* Issue 3.

'I found the schedule very hard, but then I find all acting difficult – it requires a huge amount of work before I'm really happy with my own performance, and on television you never have the time. I used to long for just a few extra days to get it exactly right, but we always had a punishing deadline to work to. As soon as one story was completed, I'd find another wad of scripts to learn for the next week, and so on. I did get tired, but I couldn't stop concentrating, because if I did, it wouldn't have worked at all. By the time I left, I was seven years older and consequently I didn't have the same resources of energy I'd had when I joined.'

Interviewed by Richard Marson in 1984 for *Doctor Who Magazine* No. 92.

'Sometimes things just didn't gel during recording, because I was very possessive and irrational about it. Sometimes I felt that this was *my* show, although when new actors came on it, I wanted to love them, albeit only for the duration of the production. I wanted them to be really *amazed* at this world they came into, so that when we started rolling the cameras, there would be this realistic element of people being constantly amazed by me and by what was going on around them.

'There was tension all the time, which I wanted, but sometimes when it didn't go as well as other times, I became very irascible. I read an article the other day that said how moody I was, and I said to my wife, "Moody? They say I'm moody! Am I moody?" And she said, "Well ..." I cut in with, "Well it's ridiculous, isn't it? *Me*? *Moody*? It's like saying I've got no manners!" So she said, "Well sometimes you're very moody, and often you've got the manners of a pig!".

Interviewed by John Freeman in 1991 for *Doctor Who Magazine* Nos. 179-181.

ON CONTRIBUTING IDEAS:

'The scripts were often dull. I didn't get a buzz of excitement after reading them. I always felt that the series gave you such free rein, such scope for imaginative plots, and that our writers were throwing the chance away with dramatic stereotypes. So I was shamefully badly behaved with the scripts – I maltreated our writers' reputations in rehearsal more than anything else, I found it so frustrating. It's not that they were really terrible scripts, but they weren't great either. We did so many as well; I'd get a huge pile of them to wade through every so often, and it was always the same – a bit of a letdown.

'I was always suggesting this or that – maybe an extra line or a different situation – and the director would say yes or no. Generally they were very kind to me. They humoured some of my extravagances but took me seriously as well. That was nice – it gave us all a working respect for each other. And some of my ideas they kept in!'

Interviewed by Richard Marson in 1984 for *Doctor Who Magazine* No. 92.

'Over the years, I came to understand what the Doctor could and could not do better than any writer or director who has only one story to worry about. I used to spend a long time checking the scripts and dialogue to make sure they conformed to how the Doctor should be played. If I found any scenes that depicted him as being over-emotional or gratuitously violent, then I would argue very strongly for their removal.'

Quoted by Peter Haining in 1986 for W H Allen's *The Doctor Who File*.

'I don't want to give the impression that I claim too much authority. Obviously the writers did try to write for me and the producers did indulge me a great deal, because most of the time I was the one making the contact with the audience. Because I had been doing the thing so long, it became more and more impossible for me to accept any kind of guidance. I felt I knew it all. I was there week after week. I knew the shots, the set-ups; I knew how to do the corridor sequences; I was swift on the words (such as they were); and I knew I had to give the audience a bit of variety.

'So sometimes a director might say, "Tom, I think in this sequence ...," and I'd cut in and say, "No, let's not do that, because we did that last week in an identical situation." Sometimes they'd realise I was only trying to be helpful and we'd reverse it, just to get the variation. So because I was the constant factor, I became more and more proprietorial, and in the end it became obvious I had to go.

'I got more and more irascible, and people seemed to think the programme was me, we became so *utterly* intertwined. This was very bad, and a sign that I had to go. Also I didn't find rehearsals as funny as I had done.'

Interviewed by John Freeman in 1991 for *Doctor Who Magazine* Nos. 179-181.

ON THE SERIES' VILLAINS AND MONSTERS:

'I quite liked the Wirrn, as they were grotesque. But the Daleks and the

THE FOURTH DOCTOR

Cybermen I found, from the point of view of playing the Doctor and beating them, insufferably tedious, because they were utterly predictable and witless and not really ingenious. But never mind – it doesn't matter what I feel about them. Undoubtedly the Daleks seized the imagination of the first generation of *Doctor Who* watchers, and of subsequent generations. I never much cared for them really, but I can see it's what the viewers like.'

Interviewed by Dave Dean in 1982. Published in *Private Who* Issue 3.

'I loved some of our monsters because they were so funny. We used to have a regular set of actors who'd play them, so we were all very chummy. I adored the Krynoid – the giant walking vegetable – and I also liked the Wirrn. They were both fun. Then there was the giant rat in *The Talons of Weng-Chiang* – I thought that looked rather good. We also had some superb villains. Michael Wisher was brilliant as the creator of the Daleks. I remember once he was playing a scene and he was also doing the Dalek voices, and I said, "Can we all go home now?", because he was in total control. Some of our villains were quite chilling – I used to try to believe in them so as to communicate their threat to the audience, and often I didn't have to try very hard, they were so good.'

Interviewed by Richard Marson in 1984 for *Doctor Who Magazine* No. 92.

'I must say I did enjoy Davros in *Genesis of the Daleks*, because Michael Wisher did work so seriously and was unbendingly passionate about the character. He used to make us howl with laughter! He's a very accomplished actor, and he had us gripped from the first rehearsal, he was so unselfconscious. When he used to rehearse with a paper bag over his head, that used to crucify me! I used to yelp. He never relaxed, which is very important for an actor. You must *never* patronise your own character – this is what happens if people stay too long or are recalled into cameo parts. Always play a character from his point of view and never be hard on him, because if you do that, it instantly betrays a lack of commitment. You've got to believe absolutely; never give him or her a hard time. You must play it the way you believe it should be played.'

Interviewed by John Freeman in 1991 for *Doctor Who Magazine* Nos. 179-181.

ON LEAVING *DOCTOR WHO*:

'It was in the works for months before. I struggled with all the arguments for and against staying, but seven years is a long time. I'd given the show all I felt I could give it, but I loved it so much that in other ways I didn't want ever to go. I didn't want anybody to start feeling awkward about me being there, so I had to take the initiative and say, "It's time I did something else and let somebody else come in." I had the happiest years of my life with *Doctor Who* – it was such a thrill to be the Doctor.'

Interviewed by Richard Marson in 1984 for *Doctor Who Magazine* No. 92.

'There was a kind of slight fatigue. And also I was becoming neurotically proprietorial about it ... the signs were that it was entirely mine, so in other words it was really time to go, because that meant that I couldn't be influenced. And when you can't be influenced, then it's time to go to another village, isn't it really, another pub from wherever you are. Because once you're cut off from the influences, there'll be no growth in any direction, however slight it may be. You're not going to have a jolly time.'

Speaking at a press conference to publicise the release on video of *Shada*, 11 May 1992.

ON HIS FAVOURITE STORY:

'I do get asked that question a lot, and I don't really know the answer. I didn't watch them all, but sometimes I do remember them. What I enjoyed about *Doctor Who* was the day-to-day work, the grinding routine of rehearsals and trimming and trying to make it witty televisually. I think I did enjoy one called *The Ark in Space*, because I particularly liked the designs on that. I admired the designer, Roger Murray-Leach, very much, and I think that it was very well realised.'

Interviewed by Dave Dean in 1982. Published in *Private Who* Issue 3.

'I can never remember story titles, and I never watched the series, so all I can remember are the sequences I filmed – which were all out of order anyway – and of course rehearsals, which used to go so quickly. My favourite kind of stories were the "different" ones – and the ones I was happy with for personal reasons, like the Renaissance one. That was a good one; I felt quite happy with that. The one set on the giant Ark was another I liked – it had some beautiful, clever sets and quite a good script. Then there was the one with the giant, man-eating plants, which had Tony Beckley, who was such a fine actor, in it.

'I wouldn't want to give the impression that I didn't enjoy making *Doctor Who*, but sometimes it was very, very exhausting, and occasionally I'd be ill, as I was on my last few stories. But usually I used to have so much fun – I'd never have stayed so long otherwise. I was amazed recently when I saw how many episodes I'd made – I thought, "Goodness, was it really that many?" – and the days when I felt I needed to get out were, happily, few and far between.'

Interviewed by Richard Marson in 1984 for *Doctor Who Magazine* **No. 92.**

ON HIS LEAST FAVOURITE STORY:

'Looking back on it, it would have to be my last one, *Logopolis*. I remember not liking the final shot, because I was leaving by then. I remember I wanted to be gone. I remember thinking the shot wasn't particularly heroic or witty, and they recorded it straight from above with me lying flat. It was very difficult to be heroic in that situation, because, to do that, I should have at least been able to get up on one elbow. But it had to be that way, because they wanted to do that dreary old reverse shot of me looking into a circle of faces. They were stealing the shot anyway, from a film.

'It was all right for them, but not for me, and I went away with that slight niggling disappointment. I can still remember the shot after all these years – I didn't like the images, it wasn't heroic enough.'

Interviewed by John Freeman in 1991 for *Doctor Who Magazine* **Nos. 179-181.**

ON NOT APPEARING IN *THE FIVE DOCTORS*:

'That was a decision I had to think long and hard about. The original plan was to have me with Lis and have us all come together at the end. I finally decided I wouldn't do it because I simply couldn't face the prospect of going back. I was lucky also to have other offers, but when I say I couldn't face the happiness again, I mean it. I went to see John Nathan-Turner and explained all my reasons, and in spite of the difficulties it caused, he was very understanding. The programme is my past now – it would, I think, have been a mistake to try to turn the clock back even for that one story.'

Interviewed by Richard Marson in 1984 for *Doctor Who Magazine* **No. 92.**

'Well, it was too close to my leaving really, and I was very impatient. I didn't want to be seen with either new Doctors or old Doctors. In my own mind, I was the most recent. Thinking about it, perhaps that was another good reason for my leaving. I began to lose that sense of fun and silliness I had. I began to take the Doctor very seriously, and I thought, "Who are these guys?" I didn't know them and I didn't care about them. At first I said I would, and then I read the script and John Nathan-Turner tried to be very accommodating – he always was for me – and he was very disappointed that I couldn't bring myself to do it.

'It was simply that I felt there was a danger that it could be very competitive. I felt it would just be a novelty scheme, and I wasn't interested in novelty at the time. I was looking for good drama.'

Interviewed by John Freeman in 1991 for *Doctor Who Magazine* Nos. 179-181.

ON SPARE-TIME PURSUITS:

'I adore being in pubs – it is my idea of bliss. I spend a lot of time philosophising in ale houses. I go to a pub, and if there are some chums there who are interesting, I stay. If they are not, I just move on.

'I am a joyous drinker. The idea of deliberately going out to get plastered horrifies me. What is the point of doing something that interferes with fundamental functions? I can't bear doing anything that would make me sexually impotent or stop me working or concentrating. I am not saying that from time to time I don't get stinko, but that is an accident – and I love those accidents. You meet a couple of chums, then you meet someone else, and the next thing you know you are as high as a kite. That's lovely.

'I am sometimes unreliable, and my acquaintances know that. People will say, "Come to dinner," and I'll say, "Yes, all right, I'll come if I feel I can contribute, and if you don't like that arrangement, don't invite me." I don't turn up if I suddenly feel on the night that I am not going to make a contribution. Perhaps it is just me licensing myself to be unreliable.

'I like to be in the middle of things. I like to live near enough to the centre of London so that I can walk home from the theatre or a late night jazz concert. I go out to dinner three or four time a week. Recently I had a week off and I went to the theatre every night, saw three movies and read two books.

Nearly everything I do is related to acting. We are professional pleasers, and that works against deep relationships. To spend a lot of time with an actor like me must be boring for people who want to take the relationship seriously. I am not a good proposition when it comes to deep, private relationships, because I am totally preoccupied with work.

THE FOURTH DOCTOR

I live a profoundly shallow life – or a deeply superficial one.'

Interviewed by Dan Slater in 1979 for the *Sun*.

'I read a lot of escapism. I watch very little television: mainly the news or news comment. I sometimes watch Brian Walden at the weekend and have a glass of wine. I read a lot of newspapers every day; I take four so-called serious newspapers and often two tabloids, which I scour. I read some Dickens every day and Shaw.

'I also have a self-appointed job as a churchyard keeper, in which I look after the dead near my house. There are two cemeteries, and I feel very proprietorial about them. I keep them mown and tidy and I know lots of the dead people there, and I know the names of lots of them. I had a pruning session recently. They're full of sinister-looking yew trees. This time of year is the growing season, so I'm kept busy. Yesterday I was in that cemetery for four hours!

'So if I'm home, I go in and do various odd jobs, a bit of mowing or a bit of weeding or just a bit of looking, keeping things in check. It's nice to think about the dead and wonder what they were like and to speculate on so little evidence. The speculation fires one's imagination, because, as you know, on gravestones it doesn't really say what they were like. You don't know whether they were happy or what their last words were, and some of what's written, well it's downright lies! When they say, "Not dead, only sleeping," well! I had my Honda mower near a fellow's head yesterday and he *definitely* wasn't sleeping, let me tell you!'

Interviewed by John Freeman in 1991 for *Doctor Who Magazine* Nos. 179-181.

'I love reading – I simply couldn't survive without books. I appreciate art, music, poetry – I love beauty of any kind. I like people too – there's so much in life to be enjoyed, I can at least say I'm never bored.'

Interviewed by Richard Marson in 1984 for *Doctor Who Magazine* No. 92.

ON LOVE AND MARRIAGE:

'I have no intimate friends. Not one. Fifty or sixty people are acquainted with me, but nobody knows Tom Baker. I am a secretive soul.

'The price of being an unmarried, middle-aged man tearing around the world is that I am so often alone. I consider myself a bachelor and have been now for many, many years. I enjoy the freedom that being unmarried gives me. I can do whatever I'm offered as an actor and go anywhere – which you can't do with the same ease if you are married. I have only myself to think of.

'I envy people with a happy domestic life, wife and children, a house and dogs, but it is a big weight. I choose to be alone and free to go to Brazil or Egypt or wherever I want. I pay the price – you can't have it every way. I don't think of myself as a confirmed bachelor. I am simply an unmarried man. I am not any kind of woman hater. The marvellous thing about falling in love, or getting married, is that reason plays no part in the process at all.

'When I was married to Anna Wheatcroft, I realised that we were two innocent people who got married and who weren't very good together. It wasn't all that difficult to become unmarried. I think it is rare that it is ended by mutual consent, but that is how we ended our marriage. I see my ex-wife from time to time. Being divorced is always a matter for regret when you've got children because, however you look at it, it is a defeat. But I pay my dues, and I am in touch with them in an official way. My sons are grown up now. One is 20, and about to go to university. The other is 17 and not far behind. I was with them when they were very small, and I enjoyed them a great deal.

'I don't think I would like to start all over again having children, although I really adore them. Some men start new families well into their middle age, but that is not for me. *Doctor Who* allows me to have all the pleasure of intimacy with lots of children without any of the anxieties of starting all over again.'

Interviewed by Dan Slater in 1979 for the *Sun*.

'We were incredibly aware of each other from the very first moment when Lalla joined the show. She was in one episode with me, then I went away during a break in the series. We came back to work together again and it happened. We fell in love. I realised that after she left the programme I couldn't envisage living without her.'

Interviewed by Jack Bell in 1980 for an unknown newspaper.

'I know a good thing when I see it. It's a great pleasure to go home now! Lalla's a super cook. She laughs a lot at me – she finds it amusing that I'm so chatty at all hours, even in the morning. Well, I'm not *raucous* exactly, but I'm pretty perky first thing. We're always having meals with her parents. We all get along very well. I'm very confident and happy.'

Interviewed by Maureen Patton in 1981 for the *Daily Express*, 21 March edition.

'I do find co-existence very difficult. Marriage is full of mutual irritations, but the only alternative seems to be this punishing loneliness of being on your own.

'I'm not an accomplished bachelor. I'm quite good at the linen and making beds, but I don't like vacuuming and I can't master ironing boards – vicious things that always collapse on you. One of the prices you pay for being on your own is that very swiftly you can become old womanish and over fussy. I've seen it so often in loners and confirmed bachelors. Luckily I'm very gregarious. I still have my old haunts in Soho: the Coach and Horses, the French, the Swiss and the Colony Room.

'I am still optimistic that Lalla and I might get back together again. This separation is just a period to test out attitudes. Lalla wants my happiness and what is good for both of us. Anyway, actors are prone to making gestures. I still believe in marriage, and there are masses of advantages to being with Lalla. She is extraordinarily well-read, witty, and wonderful good company. The trouble is that it's easier to see all that from a distance, rather than as one of the participants in our relationship, in much the same way that agony aunts can be very rational and philosophical about other people's problems because they're not involved.

'Any marriage is difficult, but two jumpy, insecure, freelance actors, flogging themselves at work and desperately seeking approval all the time, have got less chance of making it than most. I ring Lalla up nearly every day to see how she is and what's happening. I don't do it from emotional dependency, but just as a friendly, civilised, polite thing to do. When you are separated, you can't just excise all the nice things about the other person. When you have been very generous to each other emotionally, you must still remember that. The trouble, when you separate, is that although you may be united in times of happiness, it's rare to be united in times of anxiety. So that just as one person says, "I think it would be a good idea to sever things now," the other is thinking, "I'm sure it's starting to get better." So it's not logical and it's very hard to be reasonable. But I ring Lalla anyway to see how her play is going and to see how the cats are. I do miss the cats ...

'I often wish that Lalla was with me, when I'm alone in the flat. Thoughts of her float about in my head all the time. But even if we don't get back together again, I would never think of our marriage as a failure. We have been very happy together and that's what matters, not how long it lasted. I always remember Germaine Greer, when asked if she regretted her short-lived marriage, saying "No, it was a huge success – for three days!"'

Interviewed by Jenny Nisbet in 1982 for the *Daily Express*, 8 June edition.

'I wouldn't say I'm close to my children. I wouldn't say I'm close to anyone, except my wife, Sue Jerrard. I don't have much capacity for friendship, because of my self-centredness. I'm not generous enough to give to individuals. These things are heightened in actors, when you are thinking about yourself all the time and worrying about where the next round of applause is coming from.

'I've lost my religion and sometimes I think I've lost everything in life, because I'm a great betrayer. The title of my autobiography is going to be *All Friends Betrayed*. That's made me more anxious to hold onto my dear wife. I used to be very fragmented, and I do need to be adored. I feel this overriding security in her affection; she reassures me constantly. Now that I've located admiration, I'm hanging onto it for grim death.'

Interviewed by Corrina Honan in 1992 for the *Daily Mail*, 28 March edition.

'I do adore my wife. I think about her and phone her every day while I'm away filming, and I couldn't exist very well without her. She guards and protects me, because, as you know, I'm not very good at reality.'

Interviewed by Julia Beasley in 1992 for *Woman's Weekly*, 24th March edition.

ON DEATH:

'Must go out and get the papers. Check the obituaries. If mine's in, I can stop worrying. I've always felt at home with the dead. Dear old things.'

From *Just Who On Earth Is... Tom Baker* video released in 1991 by Reeltime Pictures.

'There is a kind of implacable logic in my life. My early memories are of graveyards, I live by a graveyard and I want a good gravestone as a sign that I existed. I might be frightened to die. But if there were two cameras there, I might make an effort. One for close-ups and one for wide angles!'

Interviewed by Corrina Honan in 1992 for the *Daily Mail*, 28 March edition.

'I've always admired the dead. I find them so uncritical. Where I live in the country, on two sides of my house there are churchyards, and when I wake up in the morning, I look out at the gravestones, and no matter how sorry for myself I feel, I think, well, it could be worse. And so I bought myself a second-hand gravestone, in order to give some money to the parish really. Unfortunately, the man who'd had it before me, well, his name wasn't Baker, but I've had it smoothed down a bit, and just on the top of it, being modest, there's a star, and underneath it it says, "Tom Baker 1934 -". I didn't have the courage to put in a second date. As for the epitaph – I'll leave that to someone else.'

From *Myth Makers 17: Tom Baker* video released in 1989 by Reeltime Pictures.

ON FANS:

'I can't imagine life without fans. So when the fans run out, and the fans of the Doctor run out, and the fans of Tom Baker run out, then what we're talking about is when there's no more love left. And when there's no more love left, there's nothing left. And I'd be nothing then.'

From *Just Who On Earth Is... Tom Baker* video released in 1991 by Reeltime Pictures.

'... and I could try, perhaps more convincingly, to demonstrate that I am grateful, and that it all was such fun. And that by and large, if you'll pardon that amazing expression, it goes on being fun. And maybe the fans won't go away, as one of my interrogators suggested so frighteningly a little while ago they would. Perhaps you won't, and if you won't, then I won't. We'll both stay.
    'Good health.
    'Thank you.'

From *Just Who On Earth Is... Tom Baker* video released in 1991 by Reeltime Pictures.

Character – The Fourth Doctor

The character of each of the Doctors has been vitally influenced by the personality of the actor playing the role. As Barry Letts, producer of the series from 1969 to 1974, once put it, 'No actor playing the Doctor should be acting *all* the time. There has to be enough of his own personality showing on the screen. It makes life easier for him, for the script writers, in fact for everybody.' Graham Williams, producer from 1977 to 1980, shared this view, maintaining: 'We are utterly dependent on the individual actor's portrayal of that part.' The casting of a new Doctor is therefore one of the most crucial factors determining how the character will come across on screen.

When the third Doctor, Jon Pertwee, reached the end of his time in the series, it was Barry Letts who had the principal responsibility for choosing the next lead actor. One name he considered was that of 39 year-old comedian and former pop singer Jim Dale, well known for his appearances in the *Carry On...* films; but on the whole he favoured casting someone rather older. Amongst those he approached were: Richard Hearne, whom he eventually discounted as the actor was set on the idea of playing the part in the style of the popular Mister Pastry character he had created in the Forties; Michael Bentine, who was quite keen to take the role but decided against it because he would not be happy working on a series without being able to contribute to the scripting; and Graham Crowden, who was also quite enthusiastic but ultimately decided that he would not want to make such a long-term commitment to one particular series.

Many ideas were considered for the image of the new Doctor, including having him look like Albert Einstein and play a violin in the manner of Sherlock Holmes to emphasise his eccentricity. As Letts told *Doctor Who Magazine* in 1981, 'All of us who were involved in the casting wanted a Doctor who would be radically different from Jon Pertwee's style of portrayal. It was no good just turning out a carbon copy, as that would have given the audience the impression that the new Doctor was a watered down version of the previous one, and that would have been unfair to Jon's successor.'

While Letts was still unable to find a suitable candidate for the role, time was marching on and writers had to be briefed to start work on scripts for the fourth Doctor's initial run of stories. In view of the likelihood that the part would eventually go to an actor of advanced years who would be unable to cope with strenuous physical action, the production team decided to introduce a new, young male companion to undertake any 'rough stuff' that might be called for. So was born the character of UNIT medic Harry Sullivan.

With time running short to decide on a new Doctor, Barry Letts received inspiration from another source, as he later explained:

'Eventually it was my head of department, Bill Slater, who suggested Tom Baker. Now, I'd heard of Tom from such productions as *Nicholas and Alexandra*, in which he had taken on the role of Rasputin, so I invited him along to the production office for discussions. I asked him if he had any video tapes of past things he'd worked on, and he said no, but added that just around the corner was a cinema showing his latest film, *The Golden Voyage of Sinbad*. I duly went along to see it, and was impressed. Shortly afterwards, we asked him if he would like to accept the part.'

Speaking on stage at a US *Doctor Who* convention in 1985, Tom Baker recounted his own, rather colourful version of these events:

'I once wrote a letter to the BBC demanding that I be employed. I said that somewhere there, there was a job for me, and it was disgraceful that I hadn't been given it ... The man I wrote to, Bill Slater, had been to a *Doctor Who* casting session that afternoon – the part just happened to be free, that's the way it happens sometimes – and he'd had no ideas. My letter demanding employment was the last letter he read as he was getting into bed. Now, here is a coincidence. I actually knew his wife quite well. No, I don't mean in the Biblical sense; I was acquainted with his wife. I mean, we had sometimes held hands in various canteens – you know, actors are rather extravagant about those sort of things ... Anyway, he was getting into bed, and he conscientiously read his last letter, with a terrifying sigh, and said, "Bloody Tom Baker, demanding employment." And she said, "Oh really, I thought he was doing rather grand things?" He replied, "No, no, he says here I've got to give him a ..." Then he said, "Do you know, I've just come from a casting session this afternoon, for *Doctor Who*." To which Mary Webster – which was his wife's name – said, "Ring him up now, Bill."

'So at eleven o'clock, I was lying on my mattress on the floor, being rather self-consciously bohemian and feeling tragically sorry for myself, which sometimes can be rather a pleasant sensation, and the phone went. He said, "Bill Slater here, BBC. Come and see me tomorrow." And then my life took another change. That's how it happened. I can scarcely believe it myself. And that's the truth – just imagine if I wanted to elaborate on it!'

With Baker cast as the Doctor, the next step was to decide exactly how he would approach the part. He initially had few ideas of his own, and was happy to be guided by Barry Letts and the series' script editor, Robert Holmes. Letts later told the fanzine *In-Vision* about the preliminary discussions they had:

CHARACTER – THE FOURTH DOCTOR

'Basically, with Tom Baker, we decided to go away from Jon Pertwee. People came up with all sorts of ideas that would have looked like an attempt to duplicate Jon – a poor man's Jon Pertwee. So what we looked for was a strong personality in its own right. We had a meeting in the Balzac wine bar – there was Tom, Philip Hinchcliffe, Bob Holmes and me. This was before Philip took over from me as producer. We discussed the way Tom was going to play the Doctor. The floppy hat and so on was Tom's idea, stemming from me saying that the one thing he mustn't be was a dandy, as Jon had played him that way. And what came out of that conference was fed back to costume designer Jim Acheson.'

Philip Hinchcliffe, *Doctor Who*'s producer from 1974 to 1977, also talked to *In-Vision* about these early discussions:

'I had no hand in casting Tom. He was a *fait accompli*. But I did have a hand in developing the character. Barry was very good about that. I formed a relationship with Tom, and discussed with Barry what the character would be.

'I had quite firm ideas about the Doctor's character. I discussed with Tom what we thought he could do with it. We discussed what he ought to look like. I also did a sort of crash course on the programme – I hadn't really seen that much of it, although luckily I'd seen quite a lot of the Jon Pertwee stuff. That was the first thing I did, in fact. Then I formulated a view of the character, which I suppose was partly from that tradition, and the Sydney Newman 'cosmic hobo' phrase stuck in my mind. I'd read a fair bit of science fiction, not a lot, so I spent my preparation time reading further from writers and authors whom perhaps I knew about but had never really read. I read voraciously throughout the whole genre.

'I got really interested in all sorts of concepts. It was like suddenly discovering a really fascinating area that I had only vaguely known before. Bob Holmes already had a very good background and was very well read. He also had the drop on me, because he could remember all these old movies that I've never seen! So out of all that, we formulated the character. I liked the idea of him being sort of bohemian.

'At the time, heroes were really going out of fashion. Your hero could be a little bit more vulnerable, a little bit more complex. So our Doctor wasn't quite the same moral authority. He was getting a little bit back to the first Doctor – he was irascible, unreliable, and humans were not quite sure whether they should trust him or not. But basically he was an heroic character. He was less powerfully heroic, though. He had to work a bit harder to get out of problems; and we gave him some pretty tough opposition, I think, so he couldn't just "with one bound" be free all the time!

'Tom kept going round saying, "I'm not really human – how do I portray a 500-year-old Time Lord?" And I said, "Olympian detachment, Tom. You're very good at Olympian detachment." So he used to quote this back at me. But basically, the Doctor is a human hero – we all identify with him so easily. He is the ultimate essence of human virtue. But at the same time, biographically as it were, he's got to sort of be non-human. So Tom was quite keen to get some of his "non-humanness" into it. Bob was as well, which is probably why, at times, we showed him being a bit detached.'

Barry Letts' desire to avoid the fourth Doctor being perceived as 'a poor man's Jon Pertwee' was clearly reflected in Tom Baker's debut adventure, *Robot*. Here, the appearance and behaviour of the new incarnation presented a stark contrast to those of the old. Whereas the third Doctor had been the epitome of Seventies elegance in his velvet smoking jacket, bow tie and frilly shirt, the fourth took on the look of a slightly scruffy bohemian eccentric with his baggy jacket, broad-brimmed hat and long, winding scarf. And whereas the popular image of Pertwee's portrayal had been that of a dashing man of action, often using Venusian Aikido – his own brand of unarmed combat – to tackle his enemies physically, Baker's Doctor was introduced as someone whose preferred approach to problems was contemplation rather than action. On the rare occasions in *Robot* when the new Doctor did become involved in a violent confrontation, he seemed to win almost without trying to, his opponents falling over him or tripping over his scarf. Even the scenes immediately following the Doctor's regeneration, as he wanders around in a nightshirt and finds the TARDIS key hidden in his shoe, can be seen as a light-hearted reworking of similar sequences in Jon Pertwee's debut story, *Spearhead from Space* – again emphasising the contrast between the two Doctors.

Comments made by Jon Pertwee and Tom Baker in the numerous interviews each gave while playing the Doctor show just how important the actors' own personalities were in shaping these contrasting interpretations of the role. Pertwee invariably came across as a very active man, often speaking of his love of strenuous sports such as water-skiing and his interest in high-powered vehicles and state-of-the-art gadgetry. Tom Baker, on the other hand, was always reflective and thoughtful, telling of his years as a monk and offering insights of self-analysis.

The script for *Robot* was written by Terrance Dicks, the man from whom Robert Holmes had just taken over as script editor. Talking to *In-Vision*, Dicks confirmed that in his description of the fourth Doctor he had been greatly influenced by Baker's own personality:

'There was very little to go on, except that I had met Tom by then and talked to him, so I had some idea what he was like. And I'd been in on the casting of Tom before I wrote the script. Tom in the flesh does have this type of loony scatter brain, so I played on that very much. I also used the device, which you can always use in the first episode, that the new regeneration is unstable. So he starts off being rather crazy and gradually quietens down and becomes more reasonable by the end of it. So I thought, if they don't like that interpretation, or if Tom doesn't like that interpretation, they could always say, "Well, he was a bit weird then, but he's different now, he's stable." In fact I think they always kept quite a lot of the arbitrary erraticness that I started him off with.

'In any case, the changes are superficial. It's always the same man; his surface mannerisms may change. So the dramatic thing of writing the serious Doctor stuff actually changes very little indeed. The flourishes are different, and the kind of jokes and witticisms.'

The 'flourishes' that Dicks gave the new Doctor included having him, in the words of the script, 'seemingly ignorant of people's conversation, preoccupied with child-like pursuits – although actually deep in concentration.' Another description read: 'He has a general tendency to adopt gawky, sprawling stances. It is characteristic of his new incarnation that he always tends to lie, lean, perch or hang in some unlikely position rather than sitting conventionally.' These characteristics were picked up by Christopher Barry, the director of *Robot*, and faithfully reflected on screen; and, as noted by Terrance Dicks, traces of them were to remain throughout the fourth Doctor's era.

The 'alien detachment' of which Philip Hinchcliffe spoke was also apparent from an early stage. It was highlighted in a speech that Robert Holmes wrote for the Doctor to deliver in his second story, *The Ark in Space*, when contemplating his discovery of a group of humans lying in suspended animation in an orbiting space-station after the apparent destruction of all life on Earth:

'Homo sapiens – what an inventive, invincible species. It's only a few million years since they crawled up out of the mud and learned to walk, puny defenceless bipeds. They've survived flood, famine and plague. They've survived cosmic wars and holocausts. And now here they are, out among the stars, waiting to begin a new life, ready to outsit eternity. They're indomitable ... indomitable.'

It was Holmes again who, in his script for the following season's *Pyramids of Mars*, had the Doctor making specific comment on his alien nature. When his companion, Sarah Jane Smith, chides him on his pensive mood, reasoning that he should be happy to be returning to Earth, he tells her:

'The Earth isn't my home, Sarah. I'm a Time Lord ... You don't understand the implications. I'm not a human being. I walk in eternity ... It means I've lived for something like 750 years.'

In *The Seeds of Doom*, the Doctor refuses to help a group of scientists at an Antarctic base to amputate the arm of a colleague who has been infected by an alien Krynoid. 'You must help yourselves,' he explains, and one gets the impression that he is referring not just to the scientists but to the human race as a whole.

THE FOURTH DOCTOR

It was this other-worldly aspect of the Doctor to which Tom Baker drew particular attention in interviews he gave shortly after winning the role. 'I want to play him in an individual way,' he told *The Times* in February 1974, 'with the suggestion that although he has a human body he comes from somewhere else.'

Baker did not, however, want the Doctor to seem omniscient or invulnerable. As Peter Haining's 1986 book *The Doctor Who File* quoted him as explaining:

'I came to believe that the Doctor should have an air of naive innocence about him to counter his enormous wealth of knowledge and past experience. He had to seem vulnerable, and therefore more interesting to an audience I felt would quickly tire of the Doctor as Superman!

'My basic approach to new situations was to walk boldly into them and say with a broad grin, "Hello, I am the Doctor." Now the audience may be aware, from previous scenes, that the Doctor is going into a situation of dire peril, but their attention is held, subconsciously knowing that, any second now, he is going to get knocked to the floor!'

Giving the Doctor this air of constant optimism and naive trustfulness – unwilling to think ill of any person or creature until presented with hard and often painful evidence of their villainy – was just one of the ways in which Baker sought to keep his portrayal fresh and interesting.

Before long, the fourth Doctor had become, as Barry Letts had hoped, a very popular character in his own right, and a highly identifiable one with his imposing stature, his extraordinary hat and scarf, his rich booming voice, his broad toothy grin, his bag of jelly babies and his yo-yo. This eccentric image was quickly seized upon by journalists in the popular press, whose standard description of the fourth Doctor was along the lines of 'the gangling, 6ft 3in figure in the floppy hat and the long scarf.'

There were however a number of respects in which the character changed and developed as time went by. While his thoughtful side continued to be apparent – one particularly celebrated instance of this being a scene in *Genesis of the Daleks* in which he questions his right to destroy the Dalek race at birth – he also became more physical in his approach to problems, making the Harry Sullivan character partly redundant. He was at perhaps his most aggressive in *The Seeds of Doom*, the story that closed his second season of adventures. In this story, he was seen violently to assault several of his adversaries, breaking a chair over the head of one of them, and even to wield a gun. None of the previous Doctors had ever been quite so unrestrained as this in his use of force to combat evil.

Although the degree of violence in *The Seeds of Doom* was arguably exceptional, this was by no means the only story in which the Doctor was seen to get heavily involved in forceful action. In *The Masque of Mandragora*, for instance, he at one point lashes out with his feet to try to avoid capture and also takes part in a swordfight, as he does again in *The Androids of Tara*. *The Deadly Assassin* and *The Talons of Weng-Chiang* provided further examples of him tackling his enemies physically. On the other hand, where he did employ such tactics, it was almost always because he or one of his friends was under threat or in imminent danger. For the most part, he showed a clear disposition towards reaching peaceful solutions; and he was certainly committed to preserving life wherever possible. He chastised his companion Leela for her tendency to rely on her hunting knife to get her out of difficult situations, and showed a similar disapproval of violent behaviour by others – for example, private eye Duggan's propensity for throwing punches in *City of Death* (although ironically it is with one such punch that Duggan saves the day at the end of the story).

An equally if not more significant development in the Doctor's character was a growing inclination for him to resort to tomfoolery to confuse and outmanoeuvre his enemies, accompanied by his adoption of a generally more outrageous and amusing disposition. His brooding, contemplative moods came to be offset by bursts of manic activity; he began to assail his opponents with flippant retorts and cheeky wise-cracks; and it became increasingly common for him to be seen staring goggle-eyed into camera. All these things helped to give the fourth Doctor a uniquely zany, off-the-wall persona.

This shift of emphasis was born out of Tom Baker's keen determination to keep the character constantly surprising and engaging – an aim that came increasingly to preoccupy the actor, as he told *Doctor Who Magazine* in 1984:

'The Doctor is a moral being – you know exactly what he's going to do and why. There's very little that's unexpected about him. Character development – well, there's no such thing, because the Doctor is a heroic stereotype who conforms to the patterns of behaviour you expect him to conform to. His character basically stays the same. The challenge is to make that character as diverting and as interesting as possible within the given framework. I'd think, "How can this be made different?" or, "There's something new to be exploited here," but it got harder and harder to keep the character fresh. The scripts often didn't help, either.'

Although the fourth Doctor could never have been considered an entirely conventional hero, being – as Philip Hinchcliffe observed – more 'complex' and 'vulnerable' than that, Baker was frequently frustrated by what he perceived to be a lack of imagination and ingenuity on the writers' part in representing the character. While the actor's own natural inventiveness had been held in check to a degree during Hinchcliffe's time as producer, under Graham Williams he came to demand more and more input into the scripting process, using rehearsals as an opportunity to rewrite, sometimes with the assistance of his co-stars, any action or dialogue with which he was unhappy. This gave him the freedom to make the stories, and especially the character of the Doctor himself, much more tongue-in-cheek and exuberant; a philosophy that he carried through into his performance.

This method of working was taken to perhaps its furthest extent after Lalla Ward joined the series as the second incarnation of the Doctor's companion Romana. In Ward, Baker found a kindred spirit – they were later to be married – and together they frequently made radical amendments to the scripts with which they were provided. 'We used to have the most awful problems with our writers,' Ward told *Doctor Who Magazine* in 1984. 'Tom and I used to have to rewrite most of our dialogue with the director, usually because it wasn't right for the parts we were playing. And it happened from the start. Our actual rehearsal time, which was incredibly tight, was reduced still further as a result. So the programme was always a heavy workload – we had this responsibility for the show, and we were doing so many a year against the problems of a small budget and scripts that we wouldn't have done without at least an element of rewriting.'

On screen, there was an obvious rapport between Baker and Ward, and the dialogue in the scenes they shared together was often highly witty and sophisticated. There was even at times a hint of playful surrealism about it, such as in the following conversation as they prepare to descend from the top of the Eiffel Tower in Paris in the opening episode of *City of Death*:

> ROMANA: Shall we take the lift, or fly?
> DOCTOR: Let's not be ostentatious.
> ROMANA: All right, let's fly then.
> DOCTOR: That would be silly. We'll take the lift.

This exchange is given added significance by a scene at the end of the story in which the pair, having returned to the top of the Eiffel Tower, and are then shown back on the ground again only moments later, so that it appears the only they could have got down so quickly is indeed to have flown!

Speaking to *Doctor Who Magazine* in 1991, Baker said: 'Naturalism isn't my strong point – I'm not even good at coming through doors convincingly! But never mind, even if you can't come through a door convincingly, perhaps you can come through a door interestingly or, dare one say, amusingly …'

Baker meant this comment quite literally. Such had been his anxiety not to let his portrayal of the Doctor become stale or repetitive that he had indeed tried to find interesting ways of doing such normally mundane things as coming through a doorway or sitting in a chair. At one point in *The Invasion of Time*, for instance, he had insisted on having the Doctor trip whilst walking along a corridor, for no other reason than that it made the scene more unusual and entertaining. And as was so often the case, it also raised a laugh.

At the time, some critics felt that Baker's performance had gone too far in the direction of humour, making the Doctor appear almost a buffoon – just as, during Philip Hinchcliffe's time, some had felt that too much violence had entered into his portrayal. In his 1984 interview with *Doctor Who Magazine*, Baker explained his attitude both to violence and to comedy in the series:

'I didn't like real violence – the mindless type of thug violence you always get in American police series. I can't say how much that bores me. I always preferred to outwit the baddies – I don't think it's necessary to blow them from here to kingdom come. I mean, it's dull, isn't it? What's new about that? I don't feel we really went too far with the violence in the show. I think if it had been over-the-top, somebody would have said so. The problem in a show where good always wins over bad is how to do it in a new way. Usually our scripts would blow them up.

'As for the comedy, I think a lot of the criticism we got was from people who were used to the old way. The audience expected the old, cliché scripts – the comedy element was only part of it, but I felt it was a wonderful way of winning the children's imagination. I always felt *Doctor Who* was a children's programme, watched by children of all ages. With a comic approach, it was more diverting to laugh our villains into destruction. You can't tell me we lost all our tension – in the comedy there were very serious bits; that contrast is extraordinarily effective. I don't think we overdid either violence or comedy – in fact I think we could have gone further with both elements.'

While the furthest the Tom Baker era went in the direction of violence was probably in his third season of stories, the furthest it went towards comedy was without doubt in his sixth and penultimate season. Baker's final year as the Doctor saw him returning to a predominantly serious characterisation more in line with his original interpretation of the role.

The main reason for this late change of style was the appointment of a new producer in the person of John Nathan-Turner. Nathan-Turner disliked the type of humour that had become a standard feature of *Doctor Who* during his predecessor's tenure and was determined to stamp his own mark on the series – something that initially caused clashes between him and Baker. However, although more serious, Baker's performance in this last season remained as charismatic as ever. It was also, at times, more sombre and brooding than ever before – an impression enhanced by the darker, more subdued costume he was given at this time. This led up to the fourth Doctor's final adventure, *Logopolis*, in which the manifestation of the mysterious figure of the Watcher portended his imminent regeneration. Eventually, in foiling the latest scheme of his arch-enemy the Master, he sacrificed his own life to achieve one last, all-important victory – saving the universe itself from destruction.

Rewriting the Myth

In the fourth Doctor's era, countless new monsters, planets, alien races and other elements were added to the *Who*niverse. Some were so important that they would forever change the nature of the series. Yet continuity would seem to have been fairly low in the list of priorities of the successive production teams making *Doctor Who* in the Seventies, as revealed in an interview with Tom Baker and producer Graham Williams in Issue 19 of *Starburst*:

> **Tom Baker:** I meet people who reel off these titles or ask my opinion about certain things and they obviously know more about the history of the programme than I do. Because I'm not really – except in the informed way of not subverting anything – interested very much in what Pat did or Jon did. We're playing it absolutely from moment to moment, holding on by our fingertips with the pressure of time and money and everything.
>
> **Graham Williams:** I mean, you and I only keep marginally in the back of our minds what we did last year ...
>
> **Baker:** Yeah.
>
> **Williams:** Let alone five years ago or ten years ago.
>
> **Baker:** Not interested in that.
>
> **Williams:** The audience aren't very interested in that either.
>
> **Baker:** What those fans are conceding is they don't understand actors and programme makers. What's in the past is in the past. Each one you try to make history with – 'This one is the best one'.
>
> **Williams:** If we stuck religiously to points of continuity, of what we'd done before, the series would still be exactly where it was 15 years ago. You can't change a programme overnight. I don't think any audience could be expected to wear that – it wouldn't be fair on them.

But, I think, in my years with the show, the changes we've made have been quite significant. It's changed only 15% or 20% a year, so it's still within the acceptable framework of the programme, but nevertheless it's moved on.

Graham Williams seems to have been suggesting that continuity was often sacrificed in favour of good plots, and that this practice of rewriting *Doctor Who* history was acceptable provided that changes were made gradually so as not to confuse the viewer. It would not however be true to say that this was the policy of all the producers of the Tom Baker era, or – perhaps more importantly – of the various script editors who worked under them. Baker's suggestion that what had gone before his era was ignored does not stand up to close scrutiny. Many links with the series' past were apparent during his time with the series. Even if one chooses to ignore the fact that his first story, *Robot*, was a very typical UNIT tale, which could arguably have slotted in at any point during Jon Pertwee's tenure as the Doctor, there is no denying the fact that the remainder of his debut season also drew heavily on the series' past. His third story, for instance, saw the re-use of a monster race – the Sontarans – that had made its own debut as recently as the previous season. This was clearly an attempt by departing producer Barry Letts and the Sontarans' creator, script editor Robert Holmes, to keep continuity between the adventures of the new Doctor and those of the old.

The Sontaran, Field-Major Styre, in *The Sontaran Experiment* appears identical at first sight to the original Sontaran, Linx, seen in *The Time Warrior*. In fact the same actor – Kevin Lindsay – played both parts. A number of minor differences are however worthy of note, especially as they serve to illustrate some of the factors that can underlie departures from strict continuity.

First, although the Sontarans are supposedly a race of genetically identical clones, Styre's facial features are slightly different from Linx's. These changes were the result of a requirement to make the costume more comfortable for Lindsay to wear; the original mask had been made from heavy fibreglass matting coated with a thin surface layer of latex, and had caused breathing problems for the actor, who suffered from a heart condition. The new mask was lighter and better ventilated. This is an example of a departure from continuity caused by a practical necessity.

Secondly, Styre has five fingers whereas Linx had only three. When asked about this discrepancy at a convention, one-time script editor Terrance Dicks joked that Sontarans probably found it easier to break human bones with five fingers! In truth, however, this change was probably the result of a simple mistake or oversight by a member of the design staff. If this change had been carried forward into subsequent Sontaran stories, it would no doubt have become accepted that Sontarans have five fingers, but in their next appearance, in *The Invasion of Time,* they had reverted to having only three fingers, leaving Styre the odd man (or Sontaran) out.

In *The Sontaran Experiment,* it is also revealed that when exhausted, the Sontarans need to recharge themselves. This new fact is introduced as a plot device that allows the Doctor to defeat Styre, and is an example of a deliberate addition to *Doctor Who* mythology.

In terms of character, Styre and Linx are very similar. This is not surprising, as writer Bob Baker recalled in an interview in *In-Vision* that the Sontarans' creator Robert Holmes had given him and his writing partner Dave Martin a very detailed introduction to the monsters:

'Bob had given us the most incredibly deep briefing on the life and breeding systems and defecation systems of the Sontaran (I think he must have met one at some time). We just had to stop him, he was going on so much. It was very funny actually. He was under a bit of a strain, I felt, and this was manifest in the way he was talking about the Sontaran.

'So he said "There's the character, in you go and put the story for two episodes around that." As far as cramping our style goes, it was just a brief – just like the Doctor is already a character. We didn't feel we were being fobbed off with a Sontaran. A story is a story, and we did get our own little monster in it.

'The script was printed, rushed down to the location, and shot. I think Bob changed three or four words – about the Sontaran. "He wouldn't do that. He wouldn't say that." "Oh all right then, change it Bob. It's your monster."'

In the very next story after *The Sontaran Experiment,* the fourth Doctor encountered another old foe, in fact the oldest of all – the Daleks. Dalek history comprises a major part of the *Who*niverse, and in the twelve years prior to their appearance in *Genesis of the Daleks*, their mythology had already undergone a number of subtle changes and developments. From radiation-spawned mutants trapped inside metal casings, powerless to move outside the confines of their metal-floored city, they had been transformed into a space- and time-faring army, sweeping through the galaxy to conquer and enslave countless other worlds.

In *Genesis of the Daleks,* the Daleks' creator, Terry Nation, sought to tell the story of their origins. Naturally enough, he set the action on the creatures' home world, Skaro, which had first been seen in their introductory story, *The Mutants*, back in 1963. In *The Mutants*, the Doctor and companions had learnt from the history records of the planet's humanoid inhabitants, the Thals, that the Daleks had once been a race of scientists and philosophers called the Dals. A terrible nuclear war between Dals and Thals had led to the creation of the horribly-mutated Daleks. This view of Skaroine history is essentially confirmed in *Genesis of the Daleks*, although the Dals are replaced by the Kaleds as the Daleks' ancestors, and a new character is introduced as the Daleks' progenitor. This character, Davros, creator of the Daleks, stole centre stage from the Daleks themselves and would continue to do so in many subsequent Dalek tales long after the end of the fourth Doctor's era.

It was perhaps inevitable that any story about the origins of the Daleks would focus primarily on the situation that had existed before their creation, showing the transition to the state of affairs on Skaro that viewers had seen in *The Mutants*. Davros was the personification of the transition. Half-human, half-Dalek in appearance, he exhibited the evil cunning that he would eventually instil into his creations. Meanwhile, the prototype Daleks appeared almost inanimate, being switched on and off like radio controlled models. It was only at the end of the story that they revealed their sentience, when they apparently exterminated Davros and seized control of their own destiny.

Although *Genesis of the Daleks* appears to fit fairly well into previously-established Dalek history, a few continuity errors do surface. The most obvious of these is the fact that the prototype Daleks are seen to operate outside the Kaled Elite's bunker, far from any metal floors, and even attack the Thal city. Yet in *The Mutants*, which must have been later in the Daleks' time stream, they were unable to leave their city, a disadvantage that the Doctor was able to exploit. Also, the 'prototype' Daleks from *Genesis of the Daleks* resembled those from much later periods of Dalek history, rather than those seen in their debut story.

In *Destiny of the Daleks*, the Daleks' second and last appearance during the fourth Doctor's era, Davros was resurrected. There was of course no overriding need for him to have reappeared for the sake of continuity, as he had already been established to have died at the very beginning of Dalek history. Yet, although *Destiny of the Daleks* is presumably set many hundreds of years after the events in *Genesis of the Daleks*, the character is brought back to aid his progeny in their battle with the Movellans.

The Movellans are humanoid robots, whose thinking is perfectly logical in all respects, including their battle strategy. The Daleks' battle computers are also totally logical, and the resulting impasse sends the Daleks scurrying back to Skaro to excavate and revive their creator in the hope that he will be able to break the deadlock – a hope that proves well-founded, as Davros realises that the required solution is for one of the sides in the battle to make an intuitive, illogical move. This plotline is flawed, however, as the Daleks should have been able to break the stalemate without Davros's help, simply because they are by nature illogical and emotional, conditioned to respond to situations with hate and anger.

Yet the Daleks in *Destiny of the Daleks* are subtly different from the Daleks of old. Several times during the story they are referred to as robots; and at one point the Doctor himself mentions in passing that they were once organic life-forms, perhaps inferring that they no longer are. Is this the 'destiny' to which the title of the story refers – the evolution of the Daleks into the robots that the general public and media have often mistakenly assumed them to be? Whether this suggestion of a radical change in the nature of the Daleks was intentional on the part of the production office is however uncertain, especially in the light of subsequent stories in which the Daleks reverted to their original nature as organic mutations within metallic casings.

Tom Baker's first season ended with a story featuring a race of monsters that had been absent from the series for some seven years. The Cybermen had last appeared in the Patrick Troughton story *The Invasion*. It is perhaps not surprising, then, that many changes were apparent when they returned in *Revenge of the Cybermen*.

For one thing, there were a number of differences in the Cybermen's appearance. This was not an unusual occurrence as there had been some degree of variation in the costumes in every previous Cybermen story. These variations had ranged from very subtle touches to radical redesigns. The introduction of the Cyber Leader into the Cybermen's command structure was another important innovation in *Revenge of the Cybermen*. Previously the viewer had seen only the Cyberman Controller in *The Tomb of the Cybermen*, the Cyber Planner in *The Wheel in Space* and the Cyber Coordinator in *The Invasion*, the latter two of which had been not even humanoid in shape but more like partly-organic computers.

The concept of the Cyber Leader (his rank denoted by the black colouring of the sides and back of his head – an idea drawn from writer Gerry Davis's novelisations of previous Cybermen stories) was an innovation that militated against a view of the Cybermen as being just a horde of identical silver zombies, raising the possibility of Cybermen trained, or rather programmed, for specific tasks. However, it was in the characterisation of the Cybermen that *Revenge of the Cybermen* differed most from previous stories. Before, the Cybermen had not really had individual characters as such. They were merely machine men, without emotions or personalities to distinguish one from another. In *Revenge of the Cybermen*, the Cybermen – and in particular the Cyber Leader – display a wide range of emotions, including anger, pride and fear.

The premise of the Cybermen being vulnerable to gold dust, which plates the respiratory apparatus in their chest units and effectively suffocates them, was an important development in their history. *Revenge of the Cybermen* can in fact be seen as the final end of the Cybermen, their race having been reduced to a mere handful of survivors by an earlier cataclysmic war with humanity. Their plan to destroy Voga, the 'planet of gold', seems born of desperation, and at one point the Doctor taunts the Cyber Leader over his race's depleted state:

REWRITING THE MYTH

> Doctor: You've no home planet, no influence, nothing. You're just a pathetic bunch of tin soldiers skulking about the galaxy in an ancient spaceship.

It is indicative of the level of emotion with which the Cybermen are endowed in this story that the Doctor's goading seemingly causes the Cyber Leader to lose his temper, to the extent that he physically attacks the Time Lord, even though the latter's survival is, for the time being, essential to his plan.

Reinforcing the impression that these were unusually emotional Cybermen was the treatment of their voices. In previous stories, their dialogue had been delivered by a voice artist who, in most cases, used a small electronic palate device inside his own mouth to give the voices a machine-like monotone; a process that effectively removed any sense of emotion from the resulting voice. In *Revenge of the Cybermen*, however, the actors playing the Cybermen provided the voices themselves, with only a slight electronic treatment. The resulting voices were still very human-like, and in the case of the Cyber Leader, played by Christopher Robbie, a slight trace of a South African accent was detectable.

After the death of Roger Delgado in 1973, it seemed unlikely that the Master, the evil Time Lord he had so memorably portrayed, would ever again return to pit his wits against the Doctor's. In 1976, however, *The Deadly Assassin* did see the Master return, albeit in a much-altered form.

The Master had originally been presented as a character with many similarities to the Doctor; he was of the same race, of comparable intelligence and capable of exhibiting equal if not greater charm. Yet whereas the Doctor had always been driven to help the underdog and to combat injustice wherever he encountered it, the Master saw only the possibilities for exploitation and corruption. During the Pertwee era, viewers witnessed the Doctor thwarting many of the Master's evil schemes. Each successive defeat would no doubt have fuelled his adversary's sense of frustration and resentment. It is not surprising, therefore, that by the time of his reappearance in *The Deadly Assassin*, the Master has become clearly unhinged. Although he retains his cunning and guile, and his penchant for the grand scheme, his veneer of charm has gone. Moreover, nearing the end of his natural life, having used up all his regenerations, he is now a twisted parody of his former self. His body is emaciated and blackened, the result of a terrible accident on the planet Tersurus, and he is clinging to life only by virtue of his amazing willpower and his hatred of the Time Lords – and especially of the Doctor.

Writer Robert Holmes included in his script for this story some evocative stage directions for the Master, describing his features as 'the crawling face of death' and his hands as '... belonging to a skeleton, the remaining withered skin hanging in strips.' The fact that the BBC chose to bring the Master back in this deteriorated form is a testament to the strength of the public's association of Roger Delgado with the role of the evil Time Lord. Producer Philip Hinchcliffe could simply have regenerated the character, in much the same way as the Doctor himself had been transformed on three previous occasions, but would the public have accepted a new actor in the part? The idea of depicting the Master in a decrepit state allowed the production team to resurrect the character in a way that would minimise such audience resistance, while at the same time leaving open the possibility of a proper regeneration at a later date. In the publicity material sent out to the press prior to transmission of *The Deadly Assassin*, the BBC went out of their way to stress that this was not the straightforward return of an old foe:

'Although publicity along the lines of "The return of the Master" will help us, please bear in mind that Roger Delgado who formerly played the Master died tragically in a car accident several years ago. The actor playing the new Master, Peter Pratt, is only ever seen wearing a mask.'

It would be another four years before the Master would return in *The Keeper of Traken*, the penultimate story of the fourth Doctor's era. Still initially in his decayed form, he attempts to gain control of the Keepership of the Traken Union and the vast powers that accompany it. His plan is only partially successful, as the Doctor's intervention forces him to abandon the Keepership. However, the residual effects of his time in the Keeper's chair apparently enable him to steal the body of Keeper-elect Tremas, giving himself a new lease of life. (This is not explicitly stated in the story, but if he had already possessed the power to take over another person's body, he would presumably have done so before this point.)

The actor cast as the Master's new incarnation was Anthony Ainley, who had also played Tremas. Whereas each successive incarnation of the Doctor had been given a different and distinctive image, Ainley was intentionally chosen and made-up to resemble Delgado. And in *Logopolis*, the story in which the new Master really established himself, it quickly became apparent that Ainley's interpretation of the role also owed much to Delgado's original. The Master seemed to have regained the calm and self-confidence of his earlier incarnation, albeit now tinged with a streak of pure insanity from his degenerated period.

The Master's plan in *Logopolis* involves disrupting the Logopolitans' calculations, which are holding open a number of Charged Vacuum Emboitments (CVEs) – gateways into other universes. This was in itself a clever piece of story continuity, as CVEs had been previously introduced as part of a linking theme to the stories of season eighteen.

As so often before, the Doctor eventually defeats the Master in the story's closing moments. In doing so, however, he sacrifices his own fourth incarnation and regenerates. And this is by no means the end of his troubles with the Master ...

With such interesting characters as the Doctor and the Master, it is hardly surprising that *Doctor Who* viewers and writers alike were fascinated by the society that spawned them. Of all the new elements of *Doctor Who* mythology introduced during the fourth Doctor's era, those revolving around the Time Lords and their planet were arguably the most important in terms of the series' future development.

When first introduced in *The War Games*, Patrick Troughton's final story as the Doctor, the Time Lords had been presented as a mysterious and rather aloof race possessing awesome powers. Then, in their occasional appearances during the Jon Pertwee era, a little more had been learnt about them and they had come to seem rather less alien.

The first season of the fourth Doctor's era added little to this previously-established history of the Time Lords, although a single emissary did appear to the Doctor at the beginning of *Genesis of the Daleks* to assign him the task of attempting to alter the Daleks' future. It wasn't until the next season, the thirteenth, that any significant new information came to light.

The Brain of Morbius cast still further doubt on the original view of the Time Lords as invulnerable, near-immortal beings. In particular, it revealed their need to use a substance known as the Elixir of Life to get them through difficult regenerations. Something else that became apparent during the course of the story was that Time Lord society might not be as idyllic and well-ordered as had been previously suggested. It was recounted that revolutionaries had in the not-too-distant past attempted to overthrow the Time Lords' rulers and their policies of non-intervention in the affairs of other worlds. Morbius, believing that his race should dedicate itself to conquest, had raised a large following to aid him in his quest for power. He and his supporters had however been defeated on the planet Karn, where he had eventually been tried and sentenced to be vaporised.

Morbius was by no means the first renegade Time Lord to have featured in *Doctor Who* – there had previously been the Monk, the War Chief and the Master, amongst others. The fact that so many Gallifreyans want to rebel against their rulers' authority tends to suggest that there is something rotten at the core of their society. This was certainly the view taken by script editor Robert Holmes, who presented his own interpretation of Gallifreyan life in *The Deadly Assassin* – the first adventure to be set entirely on the Doctor's home world.

Holmes's Time Lords were a race gone to seed, more concerned with etiquette and rituals than with the science that had made them so powerful in the first place. Their superior knowledge in fact appears to have allowed them to slip into complacency, spending their time worrying about petty politics rather than about the affairs of the rest of the universe.

This depiction came as a bit of a shock to many fans who had grown accustomed to the idea of the Time Lords as a race of almost omnipotent beings. The President of the fledgling *Doctor Who Appreciation Society* wrote a strongly critical review of the story, condemning it for not following the established Time Lord mythology. In a letter to the fanzine *Gallifrey*, Holmes explained his reasons for departing so radically from previously-perceived notions of the race:

'I'd noticed that over the years they had produced quite a few galactic lunatics – the Meddling Monk, the Master, Omega and Morbius. How did this square with the notion that the Time Lords were an omnipotent bunch of do-gooders? Could it be that this notion had been put about by the Time Lords themselves?'

Holmes claimed that the main inspiration for the plot of *The Deadly Assassin* was the film *The Manchurian Candidate*, from the novel of the same name by Richard Condon. This told the tale of an American war hero secretly brainwashed by the Chinese and sent back to America to assassinate key political figures, including the President. The mention in *The Deadly Assassin* of a secretive Time Lord organisation known as the CIA (Celestial Intervention Agency) is a clear reference back to Condon's tale of political intrigue. *The Deadly Assassin* also has many plot similarities to the real-life assassination of President John F Kennedy in Dallas on 22 November 1963.

The system of Time Lord government as depicted in *The Deadly Assassin* seems to have its basis both in scholastic and in religious organisations. The Lord President is the figurehead, and beneath him are the Chancellor and the Cardinals, the heads of the Time Lord chapters, three of which – the Prydonians, the Patrexes and the Arcalians – are specifically named in the story. Each of the different chapters is distinguishable by the colours of its ceremonial robes: orange and scarlet for the Prydonians, green for the Arcalians and heliotrope for the Patrexes. The Doctor is revealed to be a Prydonian, and this is apparently the most important and influential of the chapters, having provided more Presidents than all the others put together. The true seat of power on Gallifrey however rests within the High Council, a body on which the most high-ranking of the Cardinals sit.

These facts about Time Lord society are presented to the viewer primarily by way of the dialogue of the character Runcible, one of the Doctor's peers from his days at the Prydonian academy. He is a Commentator for public access video, covering the important Presidential resignation ceremony held in the Panopticon, the central chamber of the Time Lords' city, the Capitol.

Below the Cardinals there are other ranks of Time Lords, including the Castellan, an official responsible for law and order, who is in command of the force of Chancellory guards. There is also the Coordinator, whose duties are akin to those of a librarian, watching over the APC Net and the Matrix – the repository of all the knowledge and experience of deceased Time Lords.

In *The Deadly Assassin*, it is to Coordinator Engin that Castellan Spandrell goes when he wishes to access the Doctor's biographical data.

Engin comments to Spandrell that the Castellan usually deals with more plebeian classes than Prydonian renegades, a remark suggesting that although all Time Lords are Gallifreyans, not all Gallifreyans are necessarily Time Lords. The evidence seems to suggest that the majority of the populace of Gallifrey do not share the great powers of their rulers – a possible cause of the unrest that is hinted at, especially by Cardinal Borusa's insistence that Chancellor Goth's treachery be covered up to avoid the Time Lords being seen in a bad light.

The Time Lords certainly would have looked foolish if it had become commonly known that they had forgotten the true significance of the Sash and the Great Key of Rassilon, which they had believed to be merely symbolic regalia of the Time Lord President. As the Doctor discovers, these artefacts are in truth devices that give access to the Eye of Harmony, a monolith hidden beneath the floor of the Panopticon, which holds stable the core of a black hole and thereby acts as the source of all the Time Lords' power.

Like Omega, Rassilon is described as a legendary Time Lord figure who lived at the dawn of their civilisation. Coordinator Engin reads to the Doctor from the Book of the Old Time, which records that Rassilon was originally an engineer and an architect before the Time Lords abandoned the barren road of technology – a rather strange statement considering that, however ignorant they may be of the workings of the technology that powers their world, they are still very much dependent upon it. It seems odd, too, that although the APC Net supposedly holds the sum total of all Time Lord knowledge, they still have to turn to such obscure texts as the Book of the Old Time to find out about their early history!

Underworld gave viewers a little more information about that history, explaining in the process the reason for the Time Lords' non-interventionist policies. During the story, it is revealed that the Time Lords once aided a race called the Minyans by giving them the technology with which to build an advanced society. The Minyans treated the Time Lords as gods, but were not advanced enough to cope with the new abilities they had been given. They used those gifts to create powerful weapons, and ultimately destroyed themselves in a cataclysmic war. The Time Lords vowed that from that time onwards they would never again interfere in the affairs of other races.

It was in *The Invasion of Time*, the story that immediately followed *Underworld*, that the Time Lords themselves were next seen in *Doctor Who*. This story essentially confirmed the Robert Holmes view of Gallifreyan society, while at the same time adding a number of new elements.

One of those elements was a female Time Lord, Rodan, who – with the sole exception of the Doctor's own grand-daughter, Susan – was the first

THE FOURTH DOCTOR

female Gallifreyan ever to be seen in the series. Rodan was a very junior Time Lord, whose responsibilities included monitoring the approach of spaceships to Gallifrey and controlling the transduction force field barriers that protected the planet from possible invasion.

Another important addition was that of a group of Gallifreyans who had turned their backs on their former comfortable lifestyle and now lived a more primitive existence in the wastelands outside the Capitol. It has often been speculated by fans that these people were the Shabogans, a group of trouble-makers mentioned by Castellan Spandrell in *The Deadly Assassin*, but there is no evidence to suggest that the two groups were connected.

A slight oddity in *The Invasion of Time* is that the rod-like artefact referred to in *The Deadly Assassin* as the Great Key of Rassilon is described here as the Rod of Rassilon, while another Key of Rassilon is introduced that does actually look like a conventional key. The Key proves to be a vital component of the Demat gun, a weapon so powerful that it can remove its target from time and space altogether.

The sixteenth season of *Doctor Who* also introduced a number of important new elements; and the fact that it had an over-arching theme (sometimes referred to as an umbrella theme, or a story arc) was in itself an innovation. The Doctor's search for the Key to Time was initiated by the White Guardian, a being representing the forces of light and order, who was implied to be in an eternal power-struggle with the opposing Black Guardian, representing the forces of dark and chaos. The Guardians were created by *Doctor Who* producer Graham Williams essentially to meet the series' need for a race of powerful, omniscient beings – a role vacated by the now-flawed Time Lords – and they would become an important aspect of the series' development over the next few years.

For one thing, the White Guardian provided the Doctor with a new companion, a female Time Lord by the name of Romanadvoratrelundar – Romana for short. This was the first time the Doctor had had a companion who was his intellectual equal. Romana had in fact gained higher grades than the Doctor at the Time Lord academy! But her aloof nature and her lack of practical experience of the universe outside the transduction barriers of Gallifrey often led her to stumble into dangerous situations.

Romana's relationship with the Doctor was often strained by their competitive natures, and this may perhaps be why, after they had successfully collected all six segments of the Key to Time, she chose to regenerate. This regeneration was quite different from those that viewers had previously witnessed the Doctor undergoing, in that Romana was able to choose her new form. She paraded a number of alternatives before the Doctor, before overcoming the Doctor's resistance to her adopting the likeness of Princess Astra, the living being who had embodied the final segment of the Key. In her new incarnation, her relationship with the Doctor seemed to improve greatly. The Doctor was clearly deeply saddened when she elected to leave him to remain with the Tharils in E-Space at the end of *Warriors' Gate*.

Three stories during season eighteen took place within this mysterious realm of E-Space, a universe smaller than our own, which the TARDIS inadvertently entered through a CVE. It was in was in one of these stories, *State of Decay*, that a further piece of information about the ancient history of the Time Lords surfaced. The Doctor finds himself battling the last of the Great Vampires, the ancient enemy of the Time Lords from the time of Rassilon. It is revealed that the Time Lords formed a fleet of bow-ships to hunt down and destroy the Vampires, but one of the creatures escaped and fled into E-Space. Rassilon then ordered that a special instruction be placed within all time capsules to the effect that the operator should make every attempt to destroy the Vampire if ever its whereabouts were to be discovered.

Further facts would have been added to Time Lord history in *Shada*, but as industrial action at the BBC prevented its completion, it is arguable whether or not these should be regarded as bona fide elements of *Doctor Who* mythology. For this book, we have chosen not to cover anything that was not televised.

The Doctor's TARDIS had played an important part in the series' history from the first episode onwards. During seasons twelve and thirteen, there were actually very few scenes that took place within the TARDIS, but in *The Masque of Mandragora*, the Doctor was seen to take Sarah Jane Smith on a tour through some of the many rooms of his ship, including the enormous boot cupboard. The most interesting discovery is the TARDIS's secondary control room, a wood-panelled affair with a smaller central console on a raised dais, also in wood. This new control room set was used for the whole of the season, and was intended to be a permanent replacement for the now fairly tatty original console and set. However, the panels of the new set warped whilst in storage, and were unusable come the beginning of the following season. Hence the original control room was rebuilt, and made its reappearance in *The Invisible Enemy*.

Another new fact revealed about the TARDIS, in *The Deadly Assassin*, was that it was a Type 40 TT Capsule, and the only one of its type still in operation.

The greatest tour of the TARDIS ever undertaken was during *The Invasion of Time*, when the Doctor and his friends were chased by the Sontarans through the many rooms of the ship. A laboratory and a swimming pool (described as the bathroom!) were amongst the sections shown.

In *Logopolis*, the existence of the Cloister room is revealed. This is a large chamber containing ancient stone work covered in overhanging plants.

Another addition is the Cloister Bell, presumably located somewhere within the Cloister room. The tolling of the Bell indicates the approach of some catastrophe for the TARDIS.

Throughout the fourth Doctor's adventures, new elements were continually added to the evolving myth that is *Doctor Who*. This process of development was the end result of many individual and collaborative decisions by the writers, script editors and producers who worked on the series during this period, each leaving his own personal mark on it. Some writers went to great pains to weave their tales into the existing legend, whereas others ignored the restrictions of established facts in the cause of producing exciting and watchable television.

Doctor Who's strength as a series has always lain in its flexibility. As the Doctor can travel anywhere in time and space, the only limits for a writer are those of his or her imagination. It would be a shame if any writer felt so burdened by the series' past, that he or she could not create new characters and situations because of a fear of contradicting previous stories. If, however, a fact were to be established in one story, only to be contradicted in the next, the viewer would quickly become disorientated and lose interest. As Graham Williams recognised, major changes should be carried out over a period of time to allow viewers to get used to them.

Fans, of course, have a rather different perspective from other, less-committed viewers. They are much more concerned about the minutiae of continuity. However, they themselves have the ability to plug almost any gap, simply by coming up with their own theories to explain apparent inconsistencies. Some even take up their pens to write their own versions of events to link two or more unconnected bits of *Who* mythology. Perhaps if the whole history of *Doctor Who* had been meticulously planned in advance to allow no departures from strict continuity, the series would not still be one of the most exciting to write for, and of course, to watch.

Production Development

The production of a TV drama series relies heavily on teamwork, with many different people – script editor, writers, directors, designers and actors among them – all influencing the form and content of the finished product. Probably the most influential contributor of all, however, is the producer, who has overall responsibility. During Tom Baker's time as the Doctor, *Doctor Who* had four producers – Barry Letts, Philip Hinchcliffe, Graham Williams and John Nathan-Turner – each of whom brought his own particular approach and style to the series.

Barry Letts had been appointed to the producer's job in 1969, and had been in charge throughout all but the first story of Jon Pertwee's successful five-year stint as the third Doctor. In 1974, when he came to cast Tom Baker as the new lead actor, he had almost reached the end of his time on the series; and Baker's debut story, *Robot*, recorded back-to-back with Pertwee's swan song *Planet of the Spiders*, was in fact the last on which he received the producer's credit.

Save for the new Doctor himself, there was little in *Robot* to distinguish it from the *Doctor Who* to which viewers had become accustomed in recent years. It took place in near-contemporary England – the setting used for the majority of the Pertwee stories – and featured not only the Doctor's established companion, Sarah Jane Smith, but also the familiar characters of Brigadier Lethbridge-Stewart, Sergeant (now Warrant Officer) Benton and the UNIT organisation. Interviewed in 1981 for *Doctor Who Monthly*'s Winter Special, Letts explained the thinking behind this:

'Because the audience has not yet accepted the new Doctor, their sympathies are with the characters they know, and they are identifying with these characters as they react to the new and eccentric Doctor. The old characters – the Brigadier, Benton and Sarah – are there to reassure the viewing public that they are still watching *Doctor Who*.'

This was a philosophy that underpinned much of Tom Baker's debut season, season twelve. Although *The Ark in Space*, *The Sontaran Experiment*, *Genesis of the Daleks* and *Revenge of the Cybermen* followed the trend of the latter Pertwee seasons by moving away from the tried-and-trusted UNIT set-up and into more unfamiliar territory, continued viewer reassurance was provided by way of the inclusion of a parade of popular returning monsters – Sontarans, Daleks and Cybermen. Then in *Terror of the Zygons* – planned as the final story of season twelve although ultimately transmitted as the first of season thirteen – the Doctor, Sarah and Harry Sullivan (the new companion introduced in *Robot*) were brought back to Earth for another UNIT adventure.

Speaking in 1987 to the fanzine *In-Vision*, Letts recalled this period of transition between himself and Hinchcliffe:

'The cross-over period was quite lengthy. While I was still producer, Philip hung around; and then, after he became producer, I hung around to hand over. So I was there during *The Sontaran Experiment* and I was there for *The Ark in Space* and made various comments.

'*Planet of the Spiders* was far more my epitaph than *Robot*. I had far more input and directed it myself, and we said goodbye to Jon. With *Robot*, the main thing was to try to get a good, exciting show for the first one of the new Doctor, so that I could hand the success over to Philip Hinchcliffe.'

Although Letts was not physically present for the whole of the season, all the scripts had been commissioned while he was still producer, so his influence continued to be felt. However, much of the responsibility for the content of the season fell to new script editor Robert Holmes, as Philip Hinchcliffe told *In-Vision* in 1987:

'Bob Holmes had quite a large influence. He was very much anti-UNIT – he thought it was all rather silly, running around shooting at monsters. It had had its day.

'When I got there, they'd commissioned a Dalek story from Terry Nation, a Cyberman story from Gerry Davis, and from Bob Baker and Dave Martin they'd commissioned one about a Sontaran – which was a character that Bob himself had invented. Although those stories were not completed – the Sontaran one had been written, and the Dalek one was half written – they were on the go. Bob didn't like the idea of using the old monsters, but he was enough of a showman to know that probably it was a safe bet to beef up the season.'

Despite the presence of some reassuringly traditional elements, these stories contained strong hints that *Doctor Who* was undergoing an important change of style at this time. *Robot*, for all its military hardware, gun battles and explosions, had been essentially cosy, fantasy-based family drama, very much akin to most of the Pertwee-era UNIT tales, but productions like *The Ark in Space* and *Genesis of the Daleks* had a harder, grittier, more realistic quality. *The Ark in Space*, for instance, had a Gothic horror flavour in its portrayal of people becoming physically and mentally possessed by the Wirrn, while *The Sontaran Experiment* depicted what was, in effect, the brutal torture of a group of human spacemen. *Genesis of the Daleks*, with its themes of warfare, racial hatred and genetic experimentation, was even more graphic and disturbing, provoking complaints from some viewers and from TV watchdog Mary Whitehouse's National Viewers and Listeners Association.

PRODUCTION DEVELOPMENT

The new, more adult style was welcomed and actively encouraged by Hinchcliffe, who shared his script editor's view that there ought to be, in tandem with the change of Doctor, a change of direction for the series as a whole:

'Although we'd got these old favourites in the first season – in the bag, as it were – both Bob and I felt that we'd like to move the show away from what had been the "Barry Letts formula". Not because we didn't rate that – I think Barry was a terrific producer of the show, and Jon Pertwee was a very good Doctor ... But I felt that that was now slightly played out.

'I felt that we could move the show in a different direction – more into genuine science fiction and fantasy. We didn't want to be so reliant on monsters in funny masks all the time, but in a way to take the audience on a genuine journey of fantasy by creating an atmosphere in the stories. And that tied in with Bob's idea of not relying totally on monsters that weren't very interesting and didn't have very interesting motives. I thought we could add a bit more power – I was quite interested in doing something in the science fiction area that, okay, would be *Doctor Who*, but we could balls it up a bit!'

The new, more 'ballsy' style was readily apparent in seasons thirteen and fourteen – the two seasons for which Hinchcliffe was fully responsible. The stories of these seasons are generally regarded as amongst the most frightening in the series' history. Incidents often cited as having been particularly horrific include: the dropping of Morbius's brain on the floor in *The Brain of Morbius*; the man-to-Krynoid transformations and Harrison Chase's death in the compost grinder in *The Seeds of Doom*; the strangulations perpetrated by *The Robots of Death*; and the various grim and violent fates suffered by characters in *The Talons of Weng-Chiang*.

The National Viewers and Listeners Association's earlier condemnation of *Genesis of the Daleks* proved to be just the first of many such attacks on *Doctor Who*; and in one instance, when the Association complained about a scene at the end of *The Deadly Assassin* part three in which the Doctor appears to be on the point of being drowned, they even won a written apology from BBC Director General Charles Curran. Curran wrote that the scene in question had in fact been cut down prior to transmission but that, with hindsight, 'the head of department responsible would have liked to cut out just a few more frames of the action than he did.' Although expressed in relatively mild terms, this apology marked a significant change of policy by the BBC, where at one time Mary Whitehouse had been very much *persona non grata*. It represented a minor landmark in the perennial debate about the portrayal of violence in TV drama, and was to have a long-term and arguably damaging impact on *Doctor Who* itself.

In an interview with *Daily Express* journalist Jean Rook, published on 11 February 1977 under the title *Who do you think you are, scaring my innocent child?*, Robert Holmes answered some standard criticisms of the series' new style:

'Of course it's no longer a children's programme. Parents would be terribly irresponsible to leave a six-year-old to watch it alone. It's geared to the intelligent 14-year-old, and I wouldn't let any child under ten see it.

'If a little one really enjoys peeping at it from behind the sofa, until Dad says "It's all right now – it's all over," that's fine. A certain amount of fear is healthy under strict parental supervision. Even then, I'd advise half an hour to play with Dad and forget it before a child goes to bed.

'That's why we switched the time-slot from 5.15 to after 6.00, when most young kids are in the bath.

'When *Doctor Who* started, as a true children's programme, the monsters were rubber and specific and you saw them almost at once. What horrifies far more is the occasional flash of monster – bits and pieces of one. People are frightened by what *might* come round the corner or in at the window.'

When challenged about the portrayal of death in the series, Holmes told Rook:

'They're strictly fantasy deaths. No blood, no petrol bombs, nothing a child could copy. We're not in business to harm children. We learned our lesson years ago, with some plastic daffodils which killed just by spitting at people. We didn't consider that people actually have plastic daffodils in their homes. They caused screaming nightmares, so we scrapped them. You must never attack the security of a child in its home. If you make something nasty, you don't stick it in a nursery.'

In fact, Holmes was slightly mistaken here: seasons thirteen and fourteen did feature both blood and (in *The Seeds of Doom*) petrol bombs. However, it would be wrong to assume that the impact – and undeniable success – of *Doctor Who* under Hinchcliffe and Holmes relied solely on the presentation of a succession of gory or shocking images. Much more important were the chilling concepts underlying the stories and the realistic and frequently Gothic style in which they were produced.

Hinchcliffe explains what he and Holmes were aiming for:

'We'd already decided that we wanted to take the Doctor away from Earth, to go out there to other worlds. So that was one principle. Alternatively, if Earth was involved in some way, it would not be just a case of having a monster invading and then getting the soldiers out to come and shoot at it!

'What I wanted to do were stories that had a powerful concept behind them. Stories that had depth and menace, in terms of science fiction or horror or literature generally.

'We wanted to develop themes – like nemesis, a man trapped in something he doesn't really understand and he's really fighting himself. Those very basic mythic themes were things that I wanted to try and get in.

PRODUCTION DEVELOPMENT

And Bob and I wanted to incorporate them into things we'd either seen before, or that we had read about.'

This deriving of inspiration and ideas from other sources such as popular myths, literature, TV and, in particular, cinema films was another of the distinctive features of seasons thirteen and fourteen. It had been by no means unknown for *Doctor Who* to draw from such sources in the past – some of the early Pertwee stories, for instance, had paid homage to the BBC's science fiction serials of the fifties featuring Professor Bernard Quatermass, while Tom Baker's debut adventure, *Robot*, had been in some respects a reworking of the *King Kong* idea. In these two seasons, however, the practice was taken further than ever before, as Tom Baker recalled when interviewed in 1991 for *Doctor Who Magazine*:

'We used to see lots of movies at that time and often, like actors and directors do, we adapted scenes from films – recalling a scene from a film and doing our version of it. If anyone out there loved the film as much as we did, we wanted to send them a sort of signal. Likewise, when I had to say the co-ordinates of something, I often used the BBC telephone number and the *Doctor Who* office extension, and no-one ever noticed!

'Of course the stories Philip Hinchcliffe and Robert Holmes worked on were all film pastiches, and of course we spotted them. In fact, sometimes I was extremely rude about it if they didn't come clean about where they were nicking the idea from! Like good comedians, you thrash around anywhere for material and steal and adapt, trying to perform that alchemy, transmuting one thing into another.

'If people recognise the influence, it adds a certain pleasure, it's another little level. You don't have to see those things, but there were lots of little nudges and winks that people who were going through time and space were able to send to their watchers, little signals like an astronaut might send, which mean one thing to one listener and something else to another.'

The eclectic referencing of such sources added great depth and resonance to the stories of seasons thirteen and fourteen, and helped to create the suspenseful and often Gothic atmosphere for which Hinchcliffe and Holmes were aiming. These stories also benefited from the fact that they were made during a period now widely regarded as a golden age of BBC drama, with extremely high production values being achieved across the Corporation's entire range of series, serials and plays. Having reached an almost unprecedented level of popularity, *Doctor Who* was at this time regarded as one of the BBC's flagship programmes, and the production team were able to call upon not only the highest real-terms budget the series had ever had, but also some of the cream of the BBC's considerable creative talent to help bring it to the screen.

Contributors included such experienced directors as Douglas Camfield and David Maloney, both of whom had been responsible for many well-remembered *Doctor Who* stories in the past; costume designers of the calibre of James Acheson, later to win Hollywood Oscars for his work in films, and John Bloomfield; and top-flight set designers like Roger Murray-Leach, another subsequent Oscar winner, and Barry Newbery, a BAFTA award winner. Another important contribution to the series' overall style was made by composer Dudley Simpson, who supplied a succession of distinctive and acclaimed incidental scores. Amongst the accomplished writers who provided scripts were Robert Banks Stewart, later to be responsible for such hit series as *Shoestring* and *Bergerac*, and Louis Marks, a playwright and later a distinguished BBC producer.

It is perhaps unsurprising, all things considered, that the stories of this period are now generally agreed to have been some of the most outstanding in the series' entire history. However, the long-term success of *Doctor Who* has always depended upon change and innovation, and as season fourteen drew to a close, another important development was imminent. Having been offered the job of producer on a new, hard-hitting police series called *Target*, Philip Hinchcliffe left *Doctor Who* at this point, handing over the reins to the man who had earlier created *Target* – Graham Williams.

Williams' arrival marked the start of another change of direction for *Doctor Who*. One important reason for this was that he wanted to tone down the level of violence in the series, as he told *In-Vision* in an interview shortly before his death in 1990:

'With Philip Hinchcliffe, Bob Holmes had been spoofing Hammer films for years, and I saw no reason to discourage this practice. Hammer had been going for years in this country and had hardly drawn a breath of comment from the infamous Mrs Whitehouse. I suppose because so much of it was set in the 19th Century and in foreign countries, it was deemed to be the acceptable face of horror – which was as far down that road as I wanted to go. To me, a lot of what Philip had done went too far. When I learned I was taking the show over, I made special efforts to watch it. One of the ones I saw – *Genesis of the Daleks* – had Lis Sladen climbing up a rocket gantry, being shot at by guards with rifles. She almost falls once, and then on reaching the top she gets caught, and is deliberately tripped by her captors and left dangling in mid-air while they laugh.

'I had by then just become father to our first son, and so was more aware that if children were going to be watching *Doctor Who* at 5.25, then a lot of this sadism and deliberate shock-horror, which Bob and Philip took a particular glee in producing, was not very defensible. I did not think Philip was right to let the drowning sequence in *The Deadly Assassin* go through, because the violence was too realistic and therefore could be imitated. Even on *Z Cars*, you did not show a fight using a broken bottle for precisely that reason.'

Even had Williams not wanted to reduce the level of violence, this was an

PRODUCTION DEVELOPMENT

area in which he had little room for manoeuvre, as senior BBC executives were keen for him to 'clean the series up' following the persistent criticisms that had been made during Hinchcliffe's tenure. As he would later reflect, this was the most difficult problem he had to face during his first year as producer:

'I was happy to tone down the realistic horror and gore. But then the BBC told me to go further and actually clean it up. It was over-reaction, of that I am sure, but it did not help that in my first year I was under a directive to take out anything graphic in the depiction of violence.'

While some of Williams' earliest productions, notably *Horror of Fang Rock* and *Image of the Fendahl*, retained the Gothic quality of the Hinchcliffe seasons, it was not long before his new policy took effect. This gradual removal of the series' more horrific elements left a void that was filled in part by an increased use of humour, particularly after Anthony Read succeeded Robert Holmes as script editor mid-way through production of season fifteen. The lighter tone at first manifested itself mainly in the way stories were directed and acted, Tom Baker taking the opportunity to inject a lot of his own ideas and dialogue into scenes during rehearsals to make them more off-the-wall and amusing. Robert Holmes' own *The Sun Makers* however was an exception to the rule in that the script itself had a distinctly humorous slant, with its satirical references to the British tax system; and as time went by, the series' writers increasingly picked up on the new, less serious approach and tailored their work accordingly, incorporating deliberately comedic scenes and dialogue.

This trend gained an added impetus when humorist Douglas Adams, later to enjoy great success with *The Hitch-Hikers Guide to the Galaxy*, took over from Anthony Read as script editor for season seventeen. It culminated in stories like *The Creature from the Pit* and *The Horns of Nimon*, which came complete with ludicrous monsters, slapstick sound effects and scenes of the Doctor giving K-9 artificial respiration and talking directly to camera.

'It was inevitable that the style of *Doctor Who* would change once Tony Read took on the burning torch,' Williams later reflected. 'But of course one can never predict how in advance. In all honesty, and with no detriment implied either to Tony Read or to Douglas Adams, I have to say that I would have been a very much happier chap had I had Bob Holmes as my script editor throughout all my seasons, as Philip had done. I certainly felt I was on more of a wavelength from the word go with Bob than I was with either of the others. It took working towards with the other two, but Bob truly had found the natural slot for *Doctor Who* in the television universe.'

During Williams' time on the series, Tom Baker's Doctor increasingly took centre-stage and dominated proceedings with his wise-cracking, larger-than-life personality. This is not to say, however, that the producer exercised no restraint at all over his lead actor. Baker's more outlandish suggestions –

such as replacing Leela with a talking cabbage perched on the Doctor's shoulder – were instantly discounted, and it was not unknown for major disagreements to occur. Perhaps the most serious of these arose towards the end of production on season sixteen, when Baker threatened to quit unless given script, casting and director approval for the following year's stories – something that Williams, not surprisingly, was unwilling to concede. Fortunately this dispute was amicably resolved when, after high-level discussions and a meeting between Baker, Williams and the BBC's Head of Series and Serials, Graeme McDonald, Baker dropped his demands.

At the time, the change of style that occurred under Williams was viewed less than enthusiastically by some of the series' fans – particularly those who had enjoyed and grown accustomed to the relatively serious Philip Hinchcliffe productions. There were wry suggestions from some quarters that *Doctor Who* ought now to be re-named *The Tom Baker Show*, or even *Tom Baker's Comedy Half Hour*! It would however be a mistake to imply that the stories of these seasons were in any way crass or simplistic. On the contrary, the liberal use of humour often disguised the fact that the scripts were, on the whole, highly literate and intelligent. They exhibited a knowing, postmodern playfulness with the traditional conventions and clichés of *Doctor Who* and of TV drama in general, and were realised with a kind of tongue-in-cheek camp unique to this period of *Doctor Who*'s history.

It is fair to say that the cleverness and sophistication of these stories have become much more widely appreciated in recent years, and that Williams' contribution to *Doctor Who* has been reassessed in a much more positive light. In any case, as far as the general viewing public were concerned, there was never any doubt as to the success of his new approach – they lapped it up!

Although not as consistent as during Hinchcliffe's time, the series' ratings remained generally high while Williams was producer, often breaking the 10 million barrier and, in the case of *City of Death*, reaching an all-time record story average of 14.5 million viewers per episode, albeit with the help of a strike that blacked out ITV. Clearly *Doctor Who* was still very much a high-profile series, and an important element in the BBC's Saturday evening programming.

On the minus side, many critics felt that there was a decline in production values during Williams' three year stint. What they perhaps failed to recognise was that the further the series moved away from the realms of naturalistic drama, the less appropriate it became for it to have 'realistic' sets, props, costumes and so forth. The visual aspects had to reflect the increasingly larger-than-life, fantastical nature of the stories.

Another important consideration is that in those instances where the production did fall short of expectations, this could almost always be attributed to the sheer scale and ambition of what was being attempted.

PRODUCTION DEVELOPMENT

Take, for instance, the case of *Underworld*, in which whole sequences were created through the use of CSO – by far the most extensive use ever attempted in *Doctor Who* of this electronic effect. These scenes have been widely dismissed as unconvincing, but they could equally well be viewed as a praiseworthy effort to push back the frontiers of the series' visual effects work. During its long history, *Doctor Who* has often been at the forefront of technical advances in television, and if the experiment had proved successful, it would no doubt have been hailed as a great triumph.

A further example is provided by the brick-walled TARDIS interior as seen in *The Invasion of Time*. Again, some have cited this as a lapse in production standards that undermined the credibility of one of the series' most important icons. Looked at in another light, however, Williams' decision to have these scenes shot on location could be regarded as a daring innovation, creating the opportunity for an exciting chase sequence that would have been impossible to achieve within the confines of the television studio. If anyone was at fault here, perhaps it was those critics who were unable to suspend their disbelief during the scenes in question. After all, if the TARDIS's chameleon circuit can change the outer shell of the ship into a mundane, everyday object like a police box, why shouldn't it also change the interior to give it brick walls?

One thing that can certainly be said is that throughout his time as producer, Williams consistently pushed the series to the limits of what could be achieved, striving to make it as good as possible given the various difficulties with which he was faced. A particular problem, as he later reflected, was a shortage of money:

'During those three years, inflation was running at breakneck speed. We were almost hourly being told that costs had just gone up by another ten per cent. The knock-on effect was like compound interest, with everything spiralling up into quite lunatic sums. I had several long and very severe conversations with the bosses upstairs, to the effect that they didn't care how I spent my money, as long as it was money from that year. Once that was gone, there was no question of over-funding. I would just lose episodes – end of argument. Philip Hinchcliffe had not left me with too much of a reputation, because so many of his *Doctor Who*s had gone massively over-budget on scenery.'

Another stumbling block Williams had to face right at the outset was the loss of the story that should have been his first production for the series – Terrance Dicks' vampire tale *The Witch Lords*. This had to be dropped at virtually the last minute on the insistence of Graeme McDonald, who thought it might be construed as a send-up of a prestigious BBC adaptation of *Dracula* that was then in the pipeline.

The loss of *The Witch Lords* not only necessitated the hasty commissioning of a replacement script, which Dicks himself provided in the form of *Horror* of *Fang Rock*, it also completely disrupted the production schedule for the early part of the fifteenth season. *The Invisible Enemy*, which should have been second into the studio, had to be recorded first, and consequently ended up looking rather rushed. *Horror of Fang Rock* then followed, but had to be recorded at the BBC's Pebble Mill studios in Birmingham – making this the only *Doctor Who* story of the original series to have had its studio work done outside London – as it transpired that no studio space was available at the usual Television Centre facilities on the dates when needed. All in all, as Williams put it, this was 'a punishing baptism of fire'!

Williams' headaches did not end there, either. Throughout his time on the series, he was dogged by problems arising from industrial action within the BBC. Although *Doctor Who* had been affected by such action even as far back as the Sixties – the 1968 story *The Wheel in Space*, for example, had been hit by a scene-shifters' strike, necessitating several last-minute changes of studio – never before had it suffered to this extent. Inevitably this also had an impact on the stories as transmitted.

'On each of the three years I did *Doctor Who*,' reflected Williams, 'at exactly the same point in time (which was about mid-November), we had the *Crackerjack* Clock dispute. *Crackerjack* Clock is the generic title for a dispute, in those days of some fourteen years standing, about demarcation as to whether it was the props department or the electrics department who turned on the clock to start the children's programme *Crackerjack*.'

It was one such dispute that resulted in the cancellation, only part-finished, of what should have been Williams' swan song production, *Shada*; and the preceding story, *The Horns of Nimon*, was also badly hit, making for a somewhat unsatisfactory conclusion to his producership.

Such were the difficulties involved in making *Doctor Who* at this time that Williams had repeatedly requested the appointment of an associate producer to help ease his burden. Although this request had been turned down, Graeme McDonald had instead given former producer Barry Letts a 'watching brief' over Williams' final season. When Williams left, to be succeeded as producer by the inexperienced John Nathan-Turner (formerly Williams' production unit manager), Letts was officially appointed executive producer for season eighteen. His role was however largely advisory, fulfilling a function usually performed by the head of department, and he has since confirmed that Nathan-Turner was fully responsible for the day-to-day production of the season. Letts therefore had only a limited influence on the style of the stories made at this time.

Nathan-Turner later recalled his aims in taking *Doctor Who* into the Eighties:

'I think you really have to look at the expectations of an audience. The late Seventies and the early Eighties, and indeed the late Eighties, have seen a level of sophistication in television and the movies that no-one could have foreseen. Children particularly now, possibly due to the advent of computer games and so on, have very high expectations of television programmes in our genre. My idea was simply not to attempt to compete with the likes of *Star Wars*, but to use the resources that were available to us to the best possible effect. In that way, we would appear to be moving with the times.'

The resources available for season eighteen were in fact greater than for season seventeen as Nathan-Turner was able to win a modest increase in budget. This meant that he could improve the series' production values and give it a noticeably more polished, up-to-date look than in recent years. One aspect of this was his commissioning of a new title sequence and a more modern arrangement of the theme tune. He was also successful in arguing for an extra two episodes to be added to the season – making it the longest since the Sixties – so that he could schedule seven stories at what he regarded to be the optimum length of four episodes each. The direct responsibility for the form and content of these stories fell however to the new script editor, Christopher H Bidmead, who took over from Douglas Adams at this point.

Interviewed by *Doctor Who Monthly*, Bidmead recalled his initial discussions with Nathan-Turner and Barry Letts:

'I had to confess to both John and Barry that I didn't actually want to do *Doctor Who*, as it had got very silly and I hated the show. They agreed with me – Barry wanted to go back to earlier principles and to find a way of familiarising children with the ways of science. You can understand how deeply that idea had been subverted.

'Two things were going wrong, as we saw it. One was the pantomime element and the other was the element of magic that had come in. Magic is entirely contrary to science, and to my mind the Doctor's view of the world is that he looks at a problem objectively and then tries to apply laws derived from experience to reach a scientific solution.

'So often in the past, it had been a case of the Doctor effectively waving a magic wand, which amounted to teaching children that the scientific way of looking at things was nonsense. It was a sort of infusion of late Sixties hippie ideas that derived from Third World cultures, which had filtered its way down into *Doctor Who*. Now, John liked the idea that it was going to be as different from the previous era as possible. In other words, I got the job on the premise that we would go back to basics.'

In line with this approach, and drawing on Bidmead's own writing experience in the scientific and technical fields, the stories of season eighteen had a much firmer scientific basis than those in the earlier part of Tom Baker's era, dealing with such ideas as tachyons, charged vacuum emboitments, E-Space, block transfer computations and, perhaps most significant of all, entropy. *Doctor Who* at this time was certainly more science-fiction than science-fantasy. This season also had an unusually high degree of conceptual and thematic coherence and a greater level of complexity in its plotting than had others in the recent past, suggesting that the series was being aimed at a more adult audience. Consistent with this, K-9 – originally intended to appeal to the younger child audience that Graham Williams felt had been lost as a result of the horrific nature of many of the Philip Hinchcliffe productions – was now written out.

Another feature of season eighteen was its generally sombre mood. The Doctor himself was considerably more subdued than before, and the stories – particularly towards the end of the season – had a dark, brooding atmosphere. Events such as the reappearance of the Master, the destruction of Nyssa's home planet Traken and the manifestation of the mysterious Watcher in *Logopolis* created an air of impending doom. This was in fact quite appropriate, given that they led up to the Doctor's 'death', his latest regeneration.

Although well-received by the series' fans, season eighteen was apparently less popular with the general viewing public: it was by some margin the lowest-rated of the Tom Baker seasons, averaging only 5.8 million viewers per episode. A new era was however just around the corner, which would see *Doctor Who* being moved to a twice-weekly time slot; enjoying a significant ratings revival; and, of course, featuring a new lead actor in the person of Peter Davison.

From Script to Screen
The Brain of Morbius

INTRODUCTION

This chapter presents an in-depth look at just one of the fourth Doctor's stories. In doing so it reveals the process of creating a *Doctor Who* story at this point in the series' history, and some of the behind-the-scenes discussions and thought which go into a production, a factor common to every story.

The production chosen for this case study is *The Brain of Morbius*, the penultimate story from the thirteenth season, first transmitted in 1976.

To take our view of the story we are grateful to several people, in particular the director Christopher Barry and the designer Barry Newbery who recalled, scene by scene the work that went into it.

THE SCRIPTS

The original idea for *The Brain of Morbius* came from producer Philip Hinchcliffe.

Hinchcliffe had mentioned to his script editor, Robert Holmes, that there had not been an attempt at a serious robot story in *Doctor Who*, and he was keen to try a story that treated the human/robot relationship seriously. Holmes took this basic idea to writer Terrance Dicks, who had been script editor of *Doctor Who* during the Troughton and Pertwee eras and the writer of several previous stories for the show, and discussed it with him.

Terrance Dicks takes up the story: 'We'd been talking about various myths, and one of them was the Frankenstein myth of a man making a monster. I came up with the idea of a galactic super-criminal who has a super robot assistant – a sort of devoted robot Jeeves. The criminal, Morbius, is fleeing from his enemies, and his spaceship crashes.

'Morbius is smashed up to the extent that the robot can save only the head. And having been saved like this, he demands a new body. The robot is well-intentioned, but limited as robots are. Now for some reason, spaceships do crash on this planet. So the robot goes out, scoops up the remaining bits of alien life forms and whacks them together into a roughly-functioning body, onto which he puts Morbius's head. But as Morbius has always been something of a handsome Greek God, he is far from pleased.

'That was the story – it is gruesome, macabre, and funny. But it is also logical: the robot would do that. Bob and I worked out the story, and I wrote a set of scripts which he seemed happy with.'

As Dicks was such an experienced contributor to the series, the usual requirement placed on writers to submit a formal story synopsis, possibly followed by a detailed scene breakdown, before moving on to the scripting stage, was dispensed with on this occasion.

Some of the ideas used by Dicks were actually lifted from his script for the 1974 stage play *Doctor Who and the Daleks in Seven Keys to Doomsday*. These included the name of the planet Karn, together with images such as a single-clawed creature, a brain in a tank, a mind battle and a desolate citadel clinging to a windswept cliff. What happened next was something that, perhaps surprisingly, had happened only once before in *Doctor Who*'s history: the scripts had to be re-written without the writer's consent or input, and the writer objected to the re-writes to the extent that he asked for his name to be removed from the transmitted episodes. The previous time this had happened was on Mervyn Haisman's and Henry Lincoln's story for *The Dominators*, then under its working title of *The Beautiful People*. The disagreement over this story back in 1968 had caused Haisman and Lincoln to forego any further work on *Doctor Who*, but in Dicks's case, the disagreement was short-lived with – eventually – no bad feelings on either side.

Dicks: 'The mistake I made was in delivering my final scripts on the day I went away on holiday! During subsequent discussions, I was out of the country and could not be contacted. And Philip Hinchcliffe turned against the robot. I can sympathise with him more now that I'm a producer than I could then. He thought that the robot would be too expensive to realise. So Bob was instructed to remove it from the story.

'Now, the robot is the whole core of the story. Poor old Bob, in a state of some desperation, he came up with a mad scientist instead. It was not the most original idea in the world, but it was the only one available. He invented Solon.'

What remained after Holmes had removed the robot was the basic idea of creating a body. He couldn't just replace the robot with Solon, as they would not have had the same motivation. Holmes had to go through Dicks's scripts and re-write every scene in which the robot appeared. This involved a total change of dialogue as well as shifts in characters and plot to keep the whole thing hanging together.

Terrance Dicks was less than pleased when he returned from holiday and eventually received the revised scripts. 'I rang up Bob and shouted at him down the telephone. He was apologetic, but asked what else he could have done. Eventually I said "All right. You can do it, but I'm going to take my name off it." (This was the ultimate sanction!) "Not because it's a bad show, but because it's now much more you than me."

'He asked: "Well, what name do you want to put on it?" I said: "I don't care. You can put it out under some bland pseudonym," and slammed the phone down.

'Weeks later, when I saw the *Radio Times*, I noticed it was "*The Brain of Morbius* by Robin Bland" – that's Robin Bland's only existence in life. By then I'd cooled down, and the joke disarmed me completely.'

PRE-PRODUCTION

While Dicks may not have had much to do with the scripts as they finally appeared, Holmes certainly did, and it seems that he even carried the mythical Robin Bland into the production meetings, as director Christopher Barry remembers:

'The scripts were all there and available by the time I joined the team. And as for Robin Bland; Holmes said: "Oh, well, he's the scriptwriter." As a director, I seldom met the scriptwriters, particularly on a show like *Doctor Who*. On *The Dæmons*, Barry Letts was the scriptwriter as well as the producer, again hiding under another name [Guy Leopold – a pseudonym for Letts and co-writer Robert Sloman]. But the scripts had to be written and virtually finalised long before the director joined, and so generally you didn't get to meet them.'

The director would normally be one of the first people to join the production team for a *Doctor Who* story, but often the producer would have previously sent out scripts to the various design departments for them to be able to allocate resources and to get started on the creative process. Usually the producer would have checked with the intended director to see if there were any specific people he or she wanted to work on the show, and then tried to arrange for them to be available. In the case of *The Brain of Morbius*, Hinchcliffe wanted an experienced director and designer to work together to bring the challenging script to life on a studio-bound production, as there was no location work budgeted for.

Barry Newbery certainly recalls that, 'I was told! I had no choice in whether I wanted to do the show or not, and the gentleman's agreement of the producer, director and designer talking at an early time didn't really come about until later.'

Once the director was appointed, his job initially would be to liaise with all the other departments, as Christopher Barry explains: 'As a director joining, it's really a question of you working out your need to get in touch with all these people with their need to get in touch with you. By the time the director joins the programme, he's one hundred per cent committed. But all these other people are working on other programmes, finishing them off, and like as not, you ring them up and say you need to have a chat and they say they haven't had time to read the scripts yet but they'll look at them over the weekend and see you on Monday for a preliminary check. It really was a case of you having to fit them in when their schedules allowed. Therefore, although it would be sensible to talk to the designer first, it often turned out that this was not possible.'

With all television being made to a strict deadline, both Christopher Barry and Barry Newbery found their work cut out for them from the start.

'Working in the Series and Serials Department,' says Barry, 'we always used to complain about the Plays Department having so much time to put on a play; they seemed to have weeks to rehearse. However in Series and Serials we never had enough time.'

Newbery agrees: 'The usual time given at that point to design the settings for a thirty minute recording was nine days. There would be extra allowed for any filming. This is the time in which all tasks have to be completed if settings are to be created and ready in studio for rehearsal and recording.

'This particular *Doctor Who* story was four episodes without any film. I therefore had just thirty-six days – four of which were spent in the studio – to complete my work. Thinking about all the things that had to be done before the first studio, that is in four weeks, I find it incredible now that I managed to do it. But of course, that goes for everyone else as well.'

Christopher Barry certainly agrees with this view: 'If we'd had filming, things would have been even more difficult.' In fact, *The Brain of Morbius* was atypical in that it had no filming or OB work. Almost every other *Doctor Who* story up to this point had featured some material shot either on location or at the Ealing Film Studios (normally modelwork or sequences calling for fire or water or where the story required sets that were either larger than normal or with other specific requirements – for example in *The Creature from the Pit*, Ealing was used for all the forest scenes and those involving the top of the pit into which people were thrown).

If there was to be some location work, then this would normally be completed prior to the studio recordings. Because of costs, the location filming tended to be within easy travelling distance of London, but occasionally would be further afield (for example to North Wales for *The Abominable Snowmen* and to Paris for *City of Death*) where the additional costs could be contained.

Even though *The Brain of Morbius* did not have location filming, there was still a great deal of work to be completed before the show was ready to be recorded. Christopher Barry recalls putting incredible pressure on Barry Newbery as a result: 'I needed to know all his design thoughts, sizes of sets and complete floor plans in time to do my preparation work: prepare a camera script; prepare for planning meetings, meaning that I had to have the production visualised in my mind: how I was going to shoot it; every effect; everything I wanted to discuss at the planning meetings. Ultimately I needed to produce a pro-forma camera script. I always went into rehearsal, unlike most younger directors, with a camera script that could work if I suddenly fell ill. The reason for this was that I had started my training in live television. If something happened to me, then my production assistant could step in and put the show on. We used to go into rehearsal with a camera script and be utterly willing to adapt that to the exigencies of the rehearsal. If an actor didn't like something for any reason, then you resolved the problem. You'd explain the effect you were after, why people were positioned as they were, and then either arrive at a compromise or change your script. In order to do that effectively, you had to have worked it all out beforehand.'

As part of the process of working out who would be doing what and by when, a planning meeting per episode would be held between all the departments that would be contributing to the show.

These would include the designer (in charge of the overall look of the show, together with all the sets), the director (who has to pull everything together to come up with a transmittable production), the costume designer (responsible for every costume seen), probably make-up (designs and executes all the make-ups on all the cast), the visual effects designer (handling explosions, special props, models and other effects that must be achieved 'live' during the recording), electronic effects designer (looks after Colour Separation Overlay (CSO) and other effects produced electronically rather than on the studio floor), lighting (works out and arranges all the studio and location lighting requirements), sound (handles the sound recording of all the scenes), the technical manager (basically in charge of the studio), the production assistant (secretary to the director, looking after the typing of scripts and continuity), assistant floor manager (another of the director's assistants, supervising the special effects and hand props, the artistes, and generally in charge of the rehearsals, including responsibility for marking up the outline of the sets with coloured tape on the rehearsal room floor, using a different colour for each set) and production manager (acts as a deputy to the director and looks after the studio floor during recording); but not the producer at this stage, unless it was the first episode of a completely new show or there was some specific reason for the producer to be there.

All these people would meet to listen to the director outline his plans for the show and to discuss how to achieve the various things that he wanted doing. Often ideas would be changed and expanded upon as each person was able to suggest other ways of getting the production to meet the

THE FOURTH DOCTOR

director's standard.

Following the planning meeting, the next stage was the outside rehearsal, which took place at the BBC's rehearsal rooms in Acton.

Christopher Barry recalls the process: 'The normal procedure was that about two days before you went into studio, there would be a technical run-through at the rehearsal rooms. All the people who attended the planning meeting would come along, as well as the senior cameraman (responsible for the cameras and their positionings based on the director's plans), the whole camera crew if you could get them, the scenic supervisor (ensures the sets are available when required for studio) and the prop buyer (looks after everything that appears on the set that is not a part of the constructed set or a visual effect). This was to allow everyone to see how the programme was shaping up, and to ask any questions. There would be quite a crowd at the rehearsal rooms, and they would all be wandering around with huge floor plans in their hands, on which all the sets were overlaid. Another point is that you would usually have been rehearsing the show in scene order, but at this rehearsal you may well have put everything into recording order for the first time. This could cause problems, but generally it was very useful and a lot of work got done and time was ultimately saved in the studio.

'About the same time, although not necessarily on the same day, the producer and script editor, and possibly the writer [although, in the case of *The Brain of Morbius*, the writer was not available], would come to see a run-through of the episodes at the rehearsal rooms. This was in story order and would give the actors a chance to show the producer what they could do. The prime purpose from the producer's and script editor's point of view was to check that the performances and story points were being brought out, and to discuss with the director how he or she was intending to shoot certain sequences. From the director's point of view, although some of the comments made could be niggly, this run-through was extremely useful, as it gave the opportunity for someone (the producer) who had been at arm's length on the production to see if things were going right. Often the director became too close to the production to see the overall picture.'

IN STUDIO

Eventually, the programme would go into the studio, and would be recorded over a number of days and a number of recording blocks. *The Brain of Morbius* was recorded in two, two day blocks on 6-7 October 1975 in TC1 and 20-21 October in TC3 respectively, with an additional one and a half minute scene for part four between Solon, the monster and Morbius's voice recorded on 24 October. Recording would be done in an order worked out by the director based on which sets would be available for use in each studio. All the scenes that used one particular set would generally be recorded together, and then the crew would move onto the next set and record the scenes there, and so on. In this way, an actor could find himself performing his big death scene before he had even recorded his entrance. There were two alternative ways of recording in studio. First was the rehearse/record method, where the director would rehearse each scene immediately before recording it. The other involved all the rehearsals being carried out in studio during the day, and the evening then being spent recording them. The method used was generally up to the individual director, depending on the facilities available.

The actual recording of a story was always a very time-restricted process, with much being achieved by all the creative staff in getting the material required by the director actually committed to tape. Recording had to stop in the evening at ten o'clock sharp, and unless the director had sanction to go into overtime (an expense that had to be agreed), at ten o'clock the studio house lights would go on, even if the cast were in the middle of a scene, and the cameramen and other technical personnel would leave for the night. Unless all the sets were required in studio the following day, then the scene-shifters would come in and take down (strike) those sets that were not required, and erect those that were, ready for the following day's work.

To indicate some of the considerations involved in making a *Doctor Who* story during the Tom Baker era, what follows is a scene-by-scene summary of *The Brain of Morbius*, taking in comments from Christopher Barry, Barry Newbery and the costume designer L Rowland-Warne as appropriate.

PART ONE

We open on an alien planet where an alien, insect-like humanoid (John Scott-Martin) is crawling over a hexagonal rock formation as thunder and lightning crash and flash around. The creature is being watched by Condo (Colin Fay), who rises up from behind the rocks. Condo's left hand is missing, replaced with a metal hook. Raising a small machete knife in his good hand, he falls upon the alien creature, whose screech of surprise and pain is abruptly cut off.

Christopher Barry: 'The insect alien was an old Mutt costume from *The Mutants* back in 1972, which Jim Acheson had designed and I had directed.'

L Rowland-Warne: 'We found the costume in stock, and the Visual Effects Department did quite a few repairs on it for me.'

Inside his citadel, Solon (Philip Madoc) is admiring a bust of Morbius when Condo arrives with his prize – the head of the alien. Solon berates Condo, as the head is not

THE FOURTH DOCTOR

suitable; he needs a warm-blooded humanoid to complete his work.

CB: 'I'd not worked with Philip Madoc before, but I'd seen him in a black and white series, a BBC Sunday afternoon classic serial, probably *The Three Musketeers* or something. I know he was playing a French d'Artagnan-type character. He had a slightly manic quality but didn't overact doing it. It's in his voice and his eyes, a certain intensity. He really is magnificent; I can't think of any other actor who could have played that part so well.'

Barry Newbery: 'I hadn't really paid much attention to Philip Madoc until I worked on this. I'd seen him on films and things, and you're used to a certain competence on television, but with this, I became a fan of Madoc. I think he's terribly under used as an actor.'

CB: 'Colin Fay was an opera singer; he just happened to write in for a job at about the right time. He said he was over six foot, and I wanted a big fellow to play Condo. He hadn't done any television, so he was cheap. He was a huge man, and like so many big men, was incredibly gentle. Yet he played this backward creature who could be both fearsome and vulnerable.'

Elsewhere on the planet, the TARDIS arrives, and the Doctor emerges, shouting angrily to the skies at the Time Lords, who appear to have pulled him off course. Sarah (Elisabeth Sladen) determines to explore and sees a graveyard of spacecraft off in the distance, lit by the flashes of lightning.

BN: 'That shot was comprised of a number of elements. The background was a cyclorama skycloth and a cut-out of the mountains in the distance. In front of that was a four foot stretch of plain, dotted with model spacecraft from other productions, which I obtained from Visual Effects. The plain was seen as middle distance, the nearer part being hidden by foreground rocks and plants on the set.'

The Doctor feigns complete disinterest and Sarah goes off to explore further. When she cries out upon discovering the beheaded alien, the Doctor comes running. Looking about them, they see a castle atop a mountain in the distance illuminated by a flash of lightning.

CB: 'It's a lovely shot, but it's not there long enough ... it's under three seconds ... it could have been twice that!'

BN: 'The castle was not a model, nor was it painted on the cloth. It was done as a cut out, so that it could be silhouetted against a bright sky.'

FROM SCRIPT TO SCREEN: THE BRAIN OF MORBIUS

CB: 'We could have lit it a bit better – we should have had a tiny spotlight on it or something, just to pick it out. It's such a fine structure, and it helps justify the interior architecture that we're going to see.'

The Doctor and Sarah make their way up to the castle. It starts to rain torrentially, and standing watching their progress is Ohica (Gilly Brown), one of the red-robed Sisterhood of Karn.

CB: 'That's not real rain. We hired a six foot film loop of rain and ran that superimposed onto the main picture.'

In his laboratory, Solon is experimenting on the Mutt head when the generator blows and the lights go out. He calls for Condo to fetch lamps.
  Maren (Cynthia Grenville), the leader of the Sisterhood, is informed of the Doctor's and Sarah's arrival on Karn. Maren fears that they may have arrived to take the Elixir of Life from the Sisterhood. She shows Ohica that the sacred flame that they tend is growing weaker by the day. Soon there will be no flame and no Elixir. The Sisterhood will be no more.

BN: 'Maren's chair had Genoese velvet draped over it. It was actually a curtain pelmet, and I wrapped it around the chair, which had been hired in.'

CB: 'I don't remember any discussions about the colour scheme of the Sisterhood being all red: the girls are dressed in red and the decor is all red too. I don't think it was a coincidence, somebody must have said something.'

LR-W: 'The Sisterhood had hats that were made very cheaply and decorated with coloured latex. The skirt fabric was in two layers, and made ragged and sprayed with wood dyes to give it texture. They wore bodices that were fabric covered in latex, with plastic tea-spoons from Winnie the BBC tea lady, laid into it.'

BN: 'The inspiration for the Sisterhood's flame room came from China. I was working from Chinese wall and panel decoration, and that was where the predominance of the colour red came from. The basic idea derived from the design in Buddhist temples.'

CB: 'The bit when they reveal the sacred flame received its share of criticism, I gather, but it's due as always to the lack of man hours to get the perfect finish. I think the sacred flame needed to be low, as at this point you're trying to show that this fact is desperately dangerous for them.
  'I cast Cynthia Grenville as Maren for her wonderful lined, craggy face and for her strong, but old, voice. She seems to be timeless, and that was the

quality I wanted to bring over. Gilly Brown I liked for her suppressed nervous energy, suggestive that she is realising the critical situation that she is in. The other members of the Sisterhood were cast as being good looking women with dancing experience. Janie Kells was brought in by Geraldine Stephenson, who supervised the movement and dances of the Sisterhood, because she was a professional dancer. This comes down to cost again. Because dancers cost more to hire than extras or walk-ons, we had one real dancer and the rest copied her.'

In the main hall of the citadel, Solon finds Condo looking for his missing arm. Solon tells him that he will get the arm back once his work is finished.

BN: 'I decided that the formal structure of Solon's citadel would be unlike traditional Gothic structures, in that it would have supports on the inside instead of buttresses on the outside. Hence the radiating pattern of struts – the sloping columns that leaned towards the walls. I intended it to look as if each had a gigantic steel ball-and-socket joint at their base to allow for movement of the structure.

'It has been said that I based the designs on the work of Antonio Gaudi, but that's not so. I didn't use Gaudi at all – although I did look at his buildings in my research. The only place in which that influence did perhaps show through was in the shape of the window in Solon's laboratory.

'My starting point was to try to think of ways in which a civilisation parallel to that on Earth – one that had the same genetic make-up and lived on a planet nearly identical in its circumstances – would develop at the same rate but solve its problems differently. So the architecture was inside out.'

CB: 'I can remember talking to Barry about it and saying I didn't want Gothic in the terms of ecclesiastical architecture, I wanted Gothik with a k. I thought something like that would have a macabre quality, something out of a Grimm fairytale, or a drawing by Arthur Rackham; that kind of atmosphere.'

The Doctor and Sarah arrive at the citadel, where Solon greets them enthusiastically, commenting on the Doctor's magnificent head. After Sarah has warmed herself at a blazing fire, they sit at a table and Solon orders Condo to get the wine.

CB: 'This time, as they stood outside the door, we used "fully practical" rain – water falling from pierced "sparge-pipes" rigged up over the doorway. They result in a lot of unwanted rainwater noise, because it is uncontrollable, unlike rain noise off disc, and much mess on the floor, and as a result they are commonly resisted by all concerned.'

FROM SCRIPT TO SCREEN: THE BRAIN OF MORBIUS

BN: 'Those chairs were originally made for the designer Norman James, for a television production of *Canterbury Tales* back in 1959.'

CB: 'Designers always give you a table bigger than you want, because they want you to get back wide enough to see the whole set!

'The shot from behind the fire appears very self conscious. But I wanted to get behind the fire to establish it, firstly because it goes out in a minute, and I also wanted to show warmth and hospitality. It wasn't just done to be clever.'

BN: 'Note that Chris wanted to give a feeling of warmth and hospitality because that was the only thing the set deliberately didn't have!'

Back at the Sisterhood's headquarters, the Sisters are chanting and gesturing as Maren concentrates on the Doctor's TARDIS, transporting it to their throne room.

CB: 'The Sisters' movements came in discussion. I remember talking to Geraldine about this and saying I wanted a sort of ritual. The words "Sacred flame, sacred fire" were in the script, but it was my decision to have them delivered as a chant, overlapping the sounds and also overlapping the visuals, cross fading, making it more mysterious.

'The TARDIS's appearance was not achieved with CSO. The camera pulled back and then was fixed in position (locked off) and then we did the superimposition on the side of the shot.'

Having confirmed that the TARDIS is a Time Lord vessel, Maren decides to locate its occupant. The Sisterhood form a circle and begin to chant again.

CB: 'Directing scenes that involve a number of people can be difficult, as you have to work out the positioning. While they're moving there's no problem, as you have choreographed them and it's just a question of where you cut your shots. But when you get to a static position with lots of people, it's then a question of how to make the most of it. You've paid for them to be there, so you don't want the characters to be hidden either by each other or by the scenery and props. That takes time in rehearsal to get the artistes to hit their marks and to be seen. This planning is dead easy with one camera, but when you are involved in a multi-camera shoot, as with all the *Doctor Whos*, you've then got to ensure that all the camera angles are correct.'

Back at the citadel, the Doctor has recognised the bust that Solon was working on as being Morbius. The Sisterhood pay a telekinetic 'visit', making the doors fly open, the fire snuff out and a chandelier fall from the ceiling.

CB: 'I'm rather ashamed of that shot of the chandelier. It wasn't actually dropped, it was run through a gloved hand with baling rope so it wouldn't break itself on the studio floor. Once it hit the ground, they didn't even let go of the rope, so the rest of the chain doesn't come down. In retrospect, I should have cut the shot a few frames earlier.'

The Doctor falls down unconscious; the wine was drugged. Sarah pretends to succumb as well (she had not been drinking). Solon and Condo take the Doctor to Solon's laboratory, where Solon examines him prior to the operation to remove his head.

CB: 'As far as I recall, Solon's laboratory was to be a mixture of what you would find in a fairly well equipped medical laboratory and in a museum. Old and new together. It's plainly a cod laboratory, it's just got a few pipes and tubes bunged in. It's not a physician's lab, nor a physicist's nor a chemist's, but a bit of everything.'

BN: 'Yes. Basically, as a scientist, I saw him as a bit of a wally.'

When Solon and Condo leave to repair the generators, the Doctor is transported to the Sisterhood's headquarters in the same way as the TARDIS. Sarah enters the room just after he vanishes. She notices the curtained-off bed and assumes that the Doctor is on it. She pulls open the curtain to reveal a monstrous headless body (Alan Crisp), which twitches and tries to sit as she stares in horror.

End of Part One

PART TWO

CB: 'The intention here was to show the monster as late as possible. It's rather like in the first Dalek story: just show a little bit of it, but hold back from revealing the whole thing. All monsters are better if you only suggest them; let the viewer's imagination build a picture of what it looks like in its totality. Look at Ridley Scott's *Alien* for example.

'The design of the monster came from the script. I think it described it as a potpourri, a hotch potch. We came up with the idea that it would be built from bits and pieces of other creatures, but that became rather difficult to realise. Rowland-Warne thought we could have panels of flesh without being specific as to their origin. What we specifically didn't want to use were any metallic or non-organic panels, because the only thing we wanted to look false and inorganic was the head that gets fitted later.'

FROM SCRIPT TO SCREEN: THE BRAIN OF MORBIUS

LR-W: 'We cut up lumps of foam and stuck them onto a cotton jumpsuit, which had been layered with textured latex and foam rubber. We then covered the foam with terylene wadding dipped in latex. We built muscles down the spine – which in fact were to conceal the zip – and I used real surgical clips on the body, and also coffee beans to give the skin the right texture.'

Solon and Condo return to find the Doctor missing. Realising that the Sisterhood must have taken him, Solon determines to get him back.

The Doctor awakens in the Sisterhood's throne room to find himself tied up. Maren informs him that he will die at the next sun and that he should confess his guilt. The Doctor realises that Morbius is still alive, but Maren says this is impossible as she saw him die, and that the Doctor will soon join him.

A pyre is prepared, and the Doctor is placed in its centre as the sun bursts through the window.

CB: 'That light flare is a deliberate light, that's the sun coming in and hitting the Hele Stone, like at Stonehenge. It comes through a hole in the set and hits the post where the Doctor is tied. It was a difficult effect to get right.'

The Sisters dance around the Doctor, leading up to his sacrifice. As they dance, their torches spring into life. The ceremony is interrupted by Solon, who first offers Condo in exchange for the Doctor and then pleads for the Doctor's head to be spared. Maren dismisses him. The sacrifice continues, but this time the dancing Sisters have been joined by Sarah, who followed Solon and Condo. She releases the Doctor's hands before the pyre is lit, and, as the flames leap higher, the Doctor seems to vanish from within them.

CB: 'There's a procedure laid down at the BBC that you must inform the fire department through the studio manager if you will be using any form of flame in the studio. It goes for smoking, too: if someone's going to light a cigarette, it has to be down on paper and agreed. If a fireman hasn't been notified and he happens to be on the set watching somebody light up a cigarette, then he can step in and stop the rehearsal. Studios are strictly non-smoking, cast, crew, everybody.'

BN: 'Because we had fire in the studio, and I was fairly worried about it, I took into the studio a number of those big, black, carbon dioxide fire extinguisher cylinders. The scene boys were standing by with these, and the fireman came in and told us to take them away, as only he was allowed to use extinguishers!

'The fire was designed and built by the visual effects designer John Horton on the scenery podium provided as part of the set. The lower platform was six feet in diameter and the upper central platform three feet in diameter, giving enough room for the Doctor to stand tethered to a central post.

'The flames came from self igniting burners within the brushwood, to which gas was fed through hidden pipes. And of course everything had to be very heavily fireproofed.'

CB: 'Tom was in the middle and there was a gap at the back because Sarah had to come up to cut the Doctor free. There had to be a place where she could crawl up and get close to him.

'In the end, we had to go for two takes on it, because it got out of hand. The flames leapt so high that Tom had to get out early, but not without reason!'

LR-W: 'I wasn't told before we got into the studio that the Sisterhood were going to carry genuine burning torches. So, I had to fireproof their costumes on the day with a substance that could have caused skin irritation.'

As the Doctor and Sarah run from the Sisterhood, Maren fires her ring at Sarah, which blinds her.

CB: 'I wasn't happy with the effect of the ring firing. I would have preferred it to have been more directional, rather than an uncontrolled blast.'

Solon has returned to his citadel, where Condo threatens him with death unless he gives Condo back his good arm and takes the hook away.

CB: 'Colin Fay had quite a lot of make-up on to play this part. He had things behind his lips to plump them out, and I think there was probably a bit of collodian (latex) pulling his eyes down at the sides. He was given big, bushy eyebrows, and I think his nose was slightly disfigured too.'

The Doctor discovers that Sarah has been blinded and realises that the only person to whom he can go for help is Solon.

CB: 'Acting blind is a very difficult thing to do, it's terribly hard to be convincing. Some of it I think Lis (Sladen) does well, some isn't so good. The difficult thing is to not use your eyes. If you watch people who are really blind, like for example David Blunkett, the MP, they're always blinking. But that's somebody who's congenitally blind. Sarah is just temporarily blind, and I thought it would be similar to staring at the sun for too long. You get an after-image burnt on your retina, and I think it makes you stare a bit.'

FROM SCRIPT TO SCREEN: THE BRAIN OF MORBIUS

Solon has descended into a basement laboratory, where he is speaking with an unseen person, eventually identified as Morbius (Michael Spice). Morbius is impatient to be free again, but Solon is reluctant to proceed.

CB: 'I chose Michael Spice to play the voice of Morbius as I'd met him previously when he was working on radio. He had a good, strong voice, and radio actors are used to doing all their acting through their voice. Peter Hawkins, who provided the Daleks' voices for me, was again primarily a voice-over actor.'

Solon returns to the main hall when Condo announces the arrival of the Doctor and Sarah. Solon examines Sarah's eyes and tells the Doctor that there is no hope. He suggests, however, that the Elixir of Life could help, and the Doctor leaves to obtain it. Solon sends Condo on ahead of the Doctor with a message for Maren.
    Meanwhile, Sarah, left alone, hears Morbius calling from below. She heads in the direction of the voice. She stumbles down the stairs into the underground laboratory, where she advances on the source of the voice – a flashing brain, bubbling in a tank.

End of Part Two

PART THREE

CB: 'The brain in the tank came about because I wanted this Grand Guignol feel. It was partly the settings, the visuals from Barry's design, but wherever I could extend the feeling through details, I did.
    'That's one of the things I think is so astonishing about this programme, we always managed it on such a small budget.'

Solon enters behind Sarah and throws her out of the room. She listens while Solon outlines his plan to use the Doctor's head to complete his body for Morbius.

CB: 'This idea of a brain in a tank had featured in another *Doctor Who* before this [*The Keys of Marinus*]. I'm just talking of sources and unoriginality, because this reminds me of the Steve Martin film *The Man With Two Brains*.'

When Solon comments that he has sent the Doctor into a trap, Sarah pulls the door shut and locks it, trapping Solon. Sarah hurriedly makes her way up the stairs and out the main door to warn the Doctor.

CB: 'That is total rubbish! She's never been there before, yet she knows how to shut and lock the door, and she's blind! That's my fault, that's bad direction. Often you get the script and find inconsistencies like this in rehearsal. You stop and discuss it for five minutes, but time is pressing, and eventually you just have to accept it and move on. Either that or you get in touch with the script editor and explain the problem – I've had to do that on occasion as well.

'If you were worried to the point that you couldn't continue rehearsals if it wasn't resolved, then you would telephone the script editor and explain the problem. The script editor would either settle it himself in discussion with the producer or, if he felt it was of prime importance and needed referring to the writer himself, he would get in touch with him and finally let you know. In the meantime, you carried on rehearsing the rest of the scenes. This procedure was used throughout BBC Drama, particularly in Series and Serials.'

Five of the Sisterhood are ritually sipping the last of the Elixir. Maren denies herself the liquid despite Ohica's concern about what will ultimately happen to her.

BN: 'This ritual is fairly typical; many religions have this kind of thing. But look at that! Maren tips that empty cup into the Sister's mouth ... Now she does it to the next one, and she doesn't get any either!'

CB: 'The idea was that there's a sticky liquid in there and there's so little of it that they're supposed to put their tongues in and just touch it.'

BN: 'When I first came into television I wondered why they never ever put any liquid into teacups or mugs or whatever. They were either empty or else just had a token amount inside.'

CB: 'Apparently it's because the artiste's hands shake when they pass the saucer! That said, I should have had more liquid in the chalice than I did, but it's the pressure again. Unless you have been there, you just don't appreciate the pressure! I think I'm known as a director who stops for most details, but you simply cannot cover everything all the time.'

Solon's message arrives, and Maren prepares for the Doctor's arrival.
 Sarah stumbles through the rocks on her way to warn the Doctor.

CB: 'This is highly unlikely. I'd have loved to have been able to shoot this from very low, looking right up so it would look like she's really up high. Had we had some location budget, I would have shot it outdoors with the sky behind her to make it feel high, but you can't shoot upwards in the studio, because there is no ceiling to the sets – all you would see would be the lights and gantry above.'

The Doctor arrives at the Sisterhood's domain and asks for Maren's help. Maren explains that the blindness is not permanent and that Solon knew this. The Doctor explains that he believes Morbius still lives, and discusses Morbius's crimes with Maren.

BN: 'I have been thinking about the colour of the flame room and Maren's chair. The fact that the chair was also in red was not planned. It was sheer serendipity that on one of my buying trips I found such a chair in red velvet and the cut velvet Italianate pelmet I used to dress it.'

CB: 'The scene of the Doctor and Maren walking round the flame-room whilst talking was difficult to shoot. This whole story is very static, with long dialogue scenes. There are some nice opportunities in that subterranean vault at Solon's citadel: I use the set twice to give movement. Solon walks all the way round the columns and back, and later the Doctor does the same thing. On this scene, I decided to have Maren and the Doctor walk round, complicated by the fact that it's in procession, and additionally complicated by a cutting point in the middle of the scene. What I've done there is to jump frame. The Doctor is on the left as they start the walk, and we left the cut until as late as possible. If you look closely, you can see that one of the Sisterhood masks the Doctor on the cutting point, and what has happened is that Maren and the Doctor have swapped positions. Luckily it works, and you get away with it. I was trying to find movement, because otherwise this whole scene would be completely static, as it is all dialogue.'

The Doctor offers his help to the Sisterhood, but there must be no more drawing of ships down onto Karn to their doom.
    Sarah is found by Condo, who picks her up and takes her back to Solon.
    The Doctor checks the sacred flame, as he thinks he might be able to solve the problem of the lack of Elixir. He realises that the flame heats the rocks, which produces the Elixir. The Doctor takes from his pocket a small firework, which he lights and inserts into the crack from which the flame emerges. The flame dies, but then there is a small explosion and the flame bursts out anew, higher and stronger than before.

CB: 'That was a firework, an ordinary sparkler, the sort you can get in a Christmas cracker, but Visual Effects produced the little bang at the end. Then there's the big flame, again produced from a gas jet.'

BN: 'The walls of the sacred flame's niche were made from fibreglass, which had been fireproofed pretty heavily.'

Solon secures Sarah in his laboratory and returns to the cellar to inform Morbius of the impending operation. He lets slip that the Doctor is a Time Lord. Morbius is horrified and suggests that the Doctor has been sent by the Time Lords and is working with Maren to destroy him. Morbius insists that Solon gets him into the body as soon as possible, using an artificial brain-case that Solon had earlier constructed and rejected. Solon reluctantly agrees.

BN: 'All the bubbling vials and equipment were provided by John Horton. The bubbles in the bottle were done with air jets, with the air lines out of sight somewhere, controlled by the effects team. John had two assistants, one of whom was John Brace, who later became a designer in his own right, and there was also someone else there who I think was more like a visual effects operator than an assistant.

'The walls on this set were textured with sawdust taken off the workshop floor and mixed in the paint. Another way to create texturing, which I didn't use on this occasion, was to spray glue over the wall and then throw sawdust and Polyfilla at it, painting it once it had dried.'

CB: 'I decided that the brain was going to flash just to indicate that it was talking; a little like the lights on the Daleks flashing for the same reason. I know a flashing brain is crazy, but I'm not a rational man!'

The Sisterhood carry an apparently dead Doctor up to the citadel. Meanwhile, Solon and Condo carry the tank containing the brain up to the laboratory. Condo sees the patchwork creature that Solon has built and recognises his own arm attached to it. Condo attacks Solon, who shoots him in the stomach. They struggle and the brain is knocked off the table onto the floor. Solon carefully picks it up and places it into the artificial brain-case.

CB: 'Now this is the scene that I, in retrospect, regret. I don't regret it for the same reasons as Mary Whitehouse, but I can see what she was getting at. It was in the era of the bloody Sam Peckinpah films, and I knew what Sam Peckinpah was getting away with and I didn't feel that this *Doctor Who* scene was violent at all. But seeing it again, I can see why it is totally wrong, because it suddenly ceases to be science fiction and becomes naturalism. It was an error of judgment. I think somebody explained about Solon having a gun, and then someone else probably suggested seeing a red splat when Condo is hit by the bullet. I agreed without really thinking about it. If the producer had questioned this, then I probably would have argued with him for a moment and then given in. Watching it today, I don't like it anymore, and it does seem wrong.

'On the other hand, I have no regrets about when the brain falls to the floor. I loved the effect.'

Solon unties Sarah and forces her to operate a pump while he performs the operation

FROM SCRIPT TO SCREEN: THE BRAIN OF MORBIUS

to connect Morbius's brain to the body.

The Sisterhood arrive at the base of Solon's citadel and carry the Doctor up the steps. Thunder and lightning crash about.

CB: 'This is one of my favourite shots in the show. Flashes of lightning can be done various ways. It used to be with two poles and a carbon arc across them, but here it was an electronic flash.'

In his laboratory, Solon finishes connecting the brain-case to the body when he is called away to greet the Sisterhood, who have arrived at his door. Remaining in the lab, Sarah finds that her eyesight is returning as the creature on the operating table (Stuart Fell) begins to stir. It lurches to its feet behind her and moves towards her.

End of Part Three

PART FOUR

CB: 'That claw really is monstrous. Stuart Fell, who played the creature, was marvellous. I always used him for stunts, and he's worked with me on numerous occasions.'

The monster chases after Sarah, knocking over a bunsen burner and setting fire to some liquid and its claw in the process. The creature comes across a mirror and smashes it in frustration on seeing its reflection.

CB: 'The floor was coated in preparation for the flammable liquid spilling on it, and just out behind the camera there are three firemen with extinguishers. After the sequence with the claw alight, we stopped to put out the fire before proceeding with the rest of the scene. You can see the claw still smouldering in the next shot.

'That was real glass in the mirror. Usually you don't have real glass, for obvious safety reasons.'

BN: 'I would probably have had three more mirrors off set, ready for any re-takes.'

Solon enters, and the monster crushes him unconscious before lurching out of the room. The Doctor and Sarah meet it, and it knocks the Doctor down before chasing Sarah again. The wounded Condo comes to her aid, and she falls down the stairs to the basement lab as Condo fights off the creature. It grabs Condo by the neck and throttles him before leaving the citadel.

BN: 'To shoot the scene where Sarah falls down the stairs, we had a crane set up to follow behind her as she fell. The landing at the top of the stairs was twelve feet high, and because there was no handrail around it, the fireman stopped us shooting until one was fitted!'

CB: 'Lis's stunt double, Jenny Le Fre, was at the top of the stairs without handrails, ready to fall down, and the fireman was saying that it was not safe up there.'

BN: 'So many things have to be done even during camera rehearsals to make the sets ready for recording. This was one of those occasions when we didn't actually get it all done in time – the chippy was supposed to have put the handrail in but probably was not allowed time to do it because of other priorities. In the end, we had to wait until the chippy had fixed the handrail before we could continue.'

CB: 'Condo's death here is like opera, and Colin understood the basis – you go on dying for half an hour after you have been mortally wounded. That's straight out of *Rigoletto*, an operatic death!'

Solon recovers, and loads a dart gun with tranquilliser. He recruits the Doctor to help him stop Morbius. They find and immobilise the creature, but not before it has killed Kelia, one of the Sisterhood. The Doctor tells Solon that the brain must be detached and returned to the Time Lords. He picks the creature up and returns to the citadel.

CB: 'This scene is interesting. There is a very slow pace here, long pauses as we see first Solon and then the Doctor, building deliberately until the monster appears, and then a pause as it attacks the Doctor, before Solon comes to the rescue. I love the sequence where Solon is only concerned about his creation, not whether the Doctor has been hurt!'

Back at the laboratory, the Doctor gives Solon five minutes to disconnect the brain, and leaves to check on Sarah in the basement. Solon follows and locks them in. The Doctor explains Morbius's history to Sarah and discovers too late that they are locked in.

CB: 'The Doctor walks around the set again here – I should have had him go the other way round from Solon. This sort of sequence can pose problems for the sound people. They may well have asked me to arrange for Tom to pause behind the column so they could pick the sound up from a microphone on that side, and then pick up the sound on another microphone from the other side, otherwise there would be a dead patch on the soundtrack.

FROM SCRIPT TO SCREEN: THE BRAIN OF MORBIUS

'The columns in Barry's set were a great bonus; you get all sorts of interesting angles and compositions to shoot through and around.'

BN: 'In this instance, it wasn't something I'd consciously thought of. I was simply trying to make the structure of the room echo the constructional principle of internal buttressing. However, Christopher looked at it visually, and two lines at an irregular angle are always going to make the picture look more interesting than two parallel ones.'

CB: 'In terms of past *Doctor Who*, on *The Romans*, the set was full of columns, which gave me ample scope for using them to shoot round and behind. Often in the preliminary discussions about sets with designers, you ask for items to be placed in the foreground, some columns or things like that.'

Solon repairs the brain connections, while the Sisterhood discuss what should be done. Ohica persuades Maren that they should go to the citadel to help the Doctor. Trapped in the basement, the Doctor creates a cyanide gas, which he wafts up a duct to Solon's laboratory. The gas affects Solon just as he puts the finishing touches to the creature, but the creature itself survives, as it has specially adapted lungs. It heads off to the basement as the Sisterhood climb the steps to the citadel.

BN: 'Those poor girls! They all climbed up the steps, but there was nowhere for them to go when they reached the top!'

CB: 'I had to cut the shot before they started backing up on the stairs.'

Morbius arrives in the downstairs laboratory and faces the Doctor and Sarah. The Doctor baits the creature and challenges him to a mind bending contest. They take their places, and the battle commences. As they fight, we see all the past incarnations of, first the Doctor, and then of Morbius, appear on a screen.

CB: 'We got into trouble with Equity, because we used photos of non-Equity people for the images in the mind bending sequence. The photos are of George Gallaccio (production unit manager), Robert Holmes (script editor), Graeme Harper (production assistant), Douglas Camfield (director), Philip Hinchcliffe (producer), Christopher Baker (production assistant), Robert Banks Stewart (writer) and me. The picture of Morbius was a photo of the clay bust upstairs, which was then re-touched. Basically we couldn't afford to hire actors to do it, so we tried to get away with it. In the end, we had to give a fee to Equity's benevolent fund.'

There is a small explosion inside Morbius's brain case, and he staggers out of the room. In the citadel's main hall, he encounters the Sisterhood brandishing flaming torches. *They herd him out onto the mountain, where he falls from a cliff and plummets to the ground far below.*

CB: 'This fall was quite a remarkable thing for Stuart Fell. He actually fell about eight feet onto mattresses. You see him take one look round to see where he's got to go, and then over he goes! He actually hits the camera, which is why the picture bumps as he goes out of shot, but I didn't mind that. The shot of him falling away into the distance was just one take. We put him on a blue turntable, with a high camera looking down on him, zooming out, so he appears to get farther and farther away, then that image is inlaid on a photograph from the BBC's slide library of a high shot of a canyon somewhere in California.'

Back in the Sisterhood's flame-room, the Doctor is given the few remaining drops of Elixir to prevent him from dying. Maren, having denied herself the Elixir for too long, enters the flame, and as she dies, she appears young again.

The Doctor and Sarah enter the TARDIS, leaving Ohica with another two fireworks. The TARDIS vanishes in a flash of light and a cloud of smoke.

CB: 'I read somewhere that we used a double for this because Maren couldn't get in the flames, but she didn't need to get in the flames, it's a superimposition. What they mean is that the younger girl replaced Maren as her younger self.

'The TARDIS's dematerialisation in a puff of smoke was my little joke. We were using pyrotechnics in the story, the script had the Doctor reciting what was written on the firework – light the blue touch paper and stand clear – and off goes the firework. It was a joke that may offend *Doctor Who* purists.'

POST-PRODUCTION

If one considers that the period from the time a writer first submitted his or her scripts to the time the story was transmitted could be many months, and that the actual recording took about one day per episode, it is clear that the proportion of time spent in studio was very low indeed compared with all the work carried out both before and after that.

The early part of this chapter covered the pre-production work on *The Brain of Morbius*. Now Christopher Barry describes the post-production process: what actually happened once the programme had been recorded.

'While we were in studio recording the scenes, the production assistant, Pauline Silcock, had been keeping a log of every take and re-take and had noted where the best takes were and where the faults were. All the recorded tapes were then put onto a Japanese machine called a Shibaden, an early form of helical scan video recording machine, which could be stopped and started at random and which displayed a time code on the picture. We would go into the Shibaden Room in Television Centre, play through the tapes and note down where the edits needed to come. In those days, this was called Shibadening, but nowadays it is called off-line editing. You basically construct your finished programme as a sort of rough-cut. It wasn't as accurate as cutting on the exact frame; you tended to cut within a second of where you actually wanted.

'With that as your guide, together with all the notes made whilst doing it, you would go in to do the final edit knowing exactly what you were going to do, how all the scenes and takes fitted together, and the exact frames for editing it all together. You might even change what you had previously edited on the Shibaden, because the Shibaden showed the pictures in black and white on a tiny screen and you might have missed small details that rendered a take unusable – say a microphone boom was slightly in shot. You could decide on balance that one of the other takes was better than the one previously chosen.

'Once you had constructed a good edit, time was also a factor. The show had to run for the required time, twenty-five minutes in *Doctor Who*'s case. Therefore you logged where you could make cuts, and you had to offset one cut against another. You traded and juggled your cuts until the running time was as required. That was then the final edit.

'Another Shibaden copy was then run off and given to the composer, Dudley Simpson. I would have talked to him beforehand about where I wanted the music to fall, and as I was preparing the preliminary Shibaden, I would have been noting down the time codes of the sequences where I wanted music. Sometimes specific to the frame. Dudley would then come in to the BBC, because Shibadens were huge machines and were not very portable, and he would play it through and get his exact timings from a new time code that was put on the tape after editing. He would then go away and write the music.

'We would then have a recording session to record the music, at which the director would be present; we'd record each piece, and after each piece we'd play it back. I would make any comments, and so we carried on until all the music was complete. There was always the pressure of time, because of the musicians. You would try and record the score in a three hour session. If you went a minute over time, the musicians would want twice the money.

'Once the music had been recorded, the tape would be given to the sound and grams operators, who would arrange a pre-sypher session. (Sypher stands for *SY*nchronous *P*ost dub with *H*elical scan and *E*ight-track *R*ecorder.) This involves putting the music and other sounds onto the final edited visuals. They would get Dick Mills's special sounds, which had been worked on separately by Dick in the same way as Dudley. The pre-sypher session would probably take place in the morning in a small studio containing tape decks and a monitor, and they would look through and log everything that needed doing in the way of adding music, effects and special sounds. We would then go into the proper sypher suite for probably six or eight hours for one episode. It was a rock and roll procedure, like film dubbing: you'd go backwards and forwards through the story until you had everything right. This process has steadily become more and more computerized over the years, and is now very sophisticated indeed.

'Out of all this work would come your final programme.'

TRANSMISSION

The Brain of Morbius was eventually transmitted on consecutive Saturdays from 3 to 24 January 1976, and was well received by the general public. It received an average rating of 9.7 million viewers per episode (compared with the season average of 10.1), which was very respectable, and its position compared with the other BBC and ITV programmes on at the time was on average 28th in the weekly chart.

Complaints were levelled at the show by the National Viewers and Listeners Association (NVALA), in particular because of the scene in which Condo is shot by Solon with an old fashioned pistol and blood is seen to fly from his stomach. *Doctor Who* was always subject during this period to close scrutiny by the NVALA, and there were several instances when their complaints were taken further.

The Brain of Morbius was popular enough to warrant a repeat on 4 December 1976, but rather than repeat the whole story, the BBC edited it down into a one hour omnibus version (thus removing a quarter of its original running time). This edit was done without the participation of the director, and both he and the fans felt that it did not do the story justice, as it lost much of the depth and characterisation of the original.

When *The Brain of Morbius* was chosen as the second *Doctor Who* release from BBC Video in 1984, they decided to use the cut down version. The story was subsequently re-released complete (save for a short piece of incidental music as Sarah enters Solon's laboratory at the end of part one) and unedited in 1990.

The only other area of contention surrounding this story has already been touched upon above. The BBC were taken to task by Equity for their use of photos of non-members during the mind-battle sequence. The BBC had to make a special payment to Equity as a result.

FROM SCRIPT TO SCREEN: THE BRAIN OF MORBIUS

CREDITS

Writer	Robin Bland (pseudonym for Robert Holmes from an idea by Terrance Dicks)
Director	Christopher Barry
Producer	Philip Hinchcliffe
Script Editor	Robert Holmes
Designer	Barry Newbery
Assistant Floor Manager	Felicity Trew
Costume Designer	L Rowland-Warne
Incidental Music	Dudley Simpson
Make-Up	Jean McMillan
Movement	Geraldine Stephenson
Production Assistant	Carol Wiseman
Production Unit Manager	Janet Radenkovic
Special Sound	Dick Mills
Studio Lighting	Peter Catlett
Studio Sound	Tony Millier
Theme Arrangement	Delia Derbyshire
Title Music	Ron Grainer and BBC Radiophonic Workshop
Visual Effects Designer	John Horton

Effectively Speaking

Doctor Who has always put a great deal of emphasis on its special effects. The creation of the numerous monsters, space craft, explosions and futuristic weaponry has taxed the ingenuity of the programme makers from the series' beginnings. During the latter part of the Seventies, *Doctor Who* benefited not only from an experienced, talented and enthusiastic team of behind-the-scenes technicians, but also from the burgeoning of television technology. This allowed ever more complex effects to be achieved in ever shorter spaces of time. *Doctor Who* was, indeed, at the forefront of these developments, as it was seen by many within the BBC as an important proving ground for new techniques and ideas.

With colour television firmly established in Britain by the mid-Seventies, the BBC's technical staff, having got used to the technology, began to experiment with the possibilities of the medium. It was felt that the area of electronic effects – producing something electronically from the images relayed by the TV studio cameras and recording it directly to tape rather than achieving it through a physical prop or model – was one that could benefit from a greater investment of time and money.

Responsibility for producing the early electronic effects at the start of the Seventies was held by a small group within the BBC called inlay operators. There were only three inlay operators at any one time, and the posts were held by cameramen seconded for a three month period before returning to the main camera department. An inlay operator's job was to combine images from two or more video sources (camera or pre-recorded tape) to create a single, combined image. Traditionally, the technique was used to provide the opening and closing titles for programmes, as well as more elaborate effects when images of models or paintings were combined with live-action.

Many cameramen seconded to the position found the job highly tedious and were only too happy to move on once their allotted time was up. However, particularly with the advent of colour, ever greater demands were made of and expectations placed upon the inlay operators. One of the cameramen seconded at this point was A J 'Mitch' Mitchell, who spent much of his three month stint in the department working on *Doctor Who*'s eighth season. Mitchell remembers this period as chaotic, due to the fact that there was no one person overseeing the production of the electronic and photographic effects and this often led to productions over-running their allotted studio time.

Mitchell became so interested in the possibilities offered by electronic effects that he extended his stay in the department to six months. By the end of his time there, he and his fellow inlay operators had begun to plan out the effects, and things were slowly becoming more efficient. Mitchell eventually returned to his job as a cameraman, but his interest in electronic effects did not end there. He submitted a report suggesting that the BBC create the role of special effects cameraman. Four years later, the post was indeed created, although with the title electronic effects operator. Into this embryonic department came Mitchell, together with Dave Jervis and Dave Chapman. The first *Doctor Who* work credited as being performed by the Electronic Effects Department – as opposed to inlay operators – was on *The Seeds of Doom*. Since then, electronic effects have become a staple part of *Doctor Who*'s creative arsenal.

During the Sixties, most effects seen on British television were achieved either through inlay or overlay or were of a mechanical nature, being based on the types of trickery the film industry had been using for years. These included glass paintings, mattes, scaled down and forced-perspective models and other forms of trick photography. Some of these effects relied on the nature of celluloid film, which meant that in order to use them for television, the sequences had to be shot on film rather than recorded on video. By the early Seventies, in addition to these mechanical effects, experimentation in the field of video had given rise to a bag of tricks unique to that medium.

Perhaps the best known video effect is Colour Separation Overlay, or CSO, which was used extensively in *Doctor Who* during the Tom Baker era.

CSO, or Chroma-key as it is known by ITV companies, allows one picture to be inserted electronically into another. A colour (usually blue, but any colour can in theory be used) is chosen as the key, and this is used for all the areas of the first picture that are to be replaced with the other picture. If an actor stands on a full CSO set (usually just a large, coloured curtain hung behind and extending over the floor, covering all areas of the image to be recorded) he can be electronically superimposed against a different background provided by any other video source.

The colour information from the camera recording the actor is matrixed to produce a black and white key signal to be fed to a video switch. The nominated CSO backdrop becomes black and all the other colours in the picture become white. This key signal is then used to combine the original CSO camera's picture with any other background, whether it be video of a model, a painting or photograph or an image being taken by another camera. Of course, the actors and any props that are to remain in the combined image cannot contain any of the selected key colour, otherwise they would disappear. This is partly the reason why blue is often chosen, as it does not feature in most human skin tones.

The earliest use of CSO in *Doctor Who* can be found in the 1970 story *Doctor Who and the Silurians*. Subsequently during the Seventies, it was used increasingly as a way of combining monsters and models in scenes with actors, and of creating fantastic landscapes. In *Robot*, it was employed to achieve the effect of Kettlewell's creation growing to mammoth proportions, and this was just the first of many examples from the Tom Baker years. It became the standard way of realising effects involving monitor screens and spacecraft, and was used particularly effectively in a number of stories such as *The Robots of Death*, where it was utilised to provide a buzzing 'live' pattern on the active Laserson Probes and to make the Robots' eyes glow red when they were converted to the cause of Taren Capel. Generally speaking, however, the electronic effects operators were happiest when their work went unnoticed by the viewers, as this meant that they had achieved what they intended – the creation of a totally realistic effect.

In *The Deadly Assassin*, some very clever combinations of camera work and video effects were used to populate Gallifrey, and particularly the Panopticon set. The impression was given of a far greater number of Time Lords than the story's budget could actually stretch to, by mixing together a number of recordings of the same scene with the twelve extras standing in a different area of the set each time. The apparent size of the set was also increased by a similar effect. The upper galleries were a repeat of the lower ones, recorded separately and then electronically grafted on in the appropriate place. More traditional uses of CSO in this story included the inlaying of images onto the Time Lords' wrist communicators.

Video effects were also used for the scene where the TARDIS is transducted to the museum. A pattern generator, originally created by the effects staff for the Saturday morning children's show *Multi-Coloured Swap Shop*, was used. A shot of the TARDIS was fed through the device, which broke the image up into many little squares in primary colours. The police box was then removed and the signal from the pattern generator faded out, giving the impression that the TARDIS had been converted into some form of digital pattern, which had then been transmitted elsewhere. To make the TARDIS appear in the museum, the process was simply reversed.

CSO was a cheap and relatively simple technique, but was also fairly inflexible. It could not be used for panning shots, for example, as anything that had been superimposed onto the picture would remain static. The only way to achieve good results was to have all the cameras locked in position.

This limitation was one of the main reasons why the most ambitious use of CSO in *Doctor Who*, in the season fifteen story *Underworld*, was largely unsuccessful. All the chase and fight scenes had to be recorded with locked-off cameras – there could be no pans, zooms, tilts or tracking shots – and this resulted in a very static production. Added to this, the sheer quantity of CSO used, and the tell-tale blue outline it often left around the actors (a result of interference between the signals from the two camera sources), resulted in highly unconvincing images. *Doctor Who* relies on the suspension of disbelief of the viewer, and in this case that suspension was very difficult to achieve. CSO generally works best when used subtly and sparingly.

These restrictions were later partly overcome with the introduction of a technique that the BBC called Scenesync. This was first used on the *Doctor Who* story *Meglos*, for the CSO-created scenes set on Zolfa-Thura. When General Grugger and his band of Gaztak mercenaries emerge from their ship and walk between the giant screens on the planet's surface, the camera follows their progress – even as they pass behind one of the struts supporting the screens.

The principal of Scenesync is quite simple. There are two sets. The first is a model onto which the actors are to be placed via CSO. The second is the studio set through which the actors will walk in real life. The studio set must match exactly the architecture of the model set, with one important exception – it must all be in the CSO key-colour. The movement of the camera focused on the actors is electronically linked to that of the camera focused on the model, so that they will move in unison. Thus, for the scene in *Meglos*, when actor Bill Fraser, playing Grugger, walked under the blue mask of the screen's supporting strut on the live action set, the camera on the model followed exactly the same movements, providing an overlay image of the model strut.

Ironically, at about the same time as solutions were being found to the problems posed by CSO, the whole process was about to become virtually obsolete.

New developments in computers and in digital technology had resulted in electronic equipment capable of creating effects similar to those achieved through CSO, but without the use of blue screens, and without any of the problems associated with that technique. An added advantage was that digital images could be manipulated in any way conceivable. They could be flipped, reversed, broken up, re-formed and generally tailored to whatever the director wanted. This new technique was called Quantel Image Processing and, once again, *Doctor Who* was one of the pioneers of its use.

In *The Leisure Hive*, Quantel was used to create the effects of the Tachyon Recreation Generator in the scenes where characters are seen to break into several pieces. A far more subtle use of the technique, however, was witnessed in the scenes where Mena speaks to Brock via an apparently holographic image floating in the centre of a table. Not only did the camera pan past the image as the scene progressed, but people and objects could be seen through the image too. This was a good example of something that worked so well that the viewer could easily forget that it was an effect. Another of this story's claims to fame is that it was the first in which the

THE FOURTH DOCTOR

camera moved during the TARDIS's materialisation – the effect likewise achieved using Quantel.

Tom Baker's regeneration scene was another that benefited from digital effects. As actor Adrian Gibbs, playing the Watcher, moved towards Baker's prone body, the image was distorted to make it appear as if the two figures were merging together. An overall glow was also added to the scene, in which the image of Baker's face slowly dissolves into that of the Watcher's, then blends into a shot of Peter Davison wearing Watcher-like make-up, and finally mixes into Davison's true features.

The advent of video effects might have made life a lot easier in some respects, but for the Visual Effects Department, responsible for all the series' mechanical effects work, the Tom Baker era was very much business as usual. The basic tools of their trade remained essentially the same, tried-and-trusted techniques that they had always used. Apart from advances in film cameras and the increasing miniaturisation of electric and electronic components, the visual effects in *Logopolis* were produced in pretty much the same way as those in *Robot* over six years earlier.

By the mid-seventies, the Visual Effects Department boasted a team of highly-skilled individuals, who were responsible for the great variety of effects seen during the Tom Baker era. Many *Doctor Who* scripts called for spaceships to be seen in flight, including sequences of the TARDIS spinning through space. Visual Effects were also called upon to produce any special props that could not be obtained from stock or brought in from outside the BBC. These included laser guns of all types, communicators, and even futuristic coinage. If weapons had to be seen to cause damage, controlled explosions would be placed to provide the desired effect without endangering the actors involved. Most often, these pyrotechnics would be combined with a ray or pulse of light created via electronic effects to give the ultimate appearance of a laser rifle that really did fire bursts of energy and that could, say, burn a hole in a door.

The contributions of some of the visual effects designers are particularly noteworthy. The stunning model work in *The Invisible Enemy* and *City of Death* came courtesy of Ian Scoones; the numerous effects showcased in *The Stones of Blood* – spacecraft, mobile stone aliens, a flashing wand and a futuristic beam machine that made the first major use of microchip technology in *Doctor Who* – were all provided by Mat Irvine, as was the filmed model sequence of the destruction of the Gateway in *Warriors' Gate*; while arguably *Doctor Who*'s most well-known effect of all was the creation of a designer called Tony Harding. This was K-9, the Doctor's robot dog companion, which was originally built for the story *The Invisible Enemy*. One condition of K-9's continuation as an ongoing character was that Visual Effects had to be able to supply a prop that would function well enough to be used regularly and that would survive the rigours of television production.

When first introduced, K-9 suffered a few teething problems. Difficulties arose because the radio control frequencies used to control the dog interfered with the operation of the television cameras, and vice versa. This led to K-9 going haywire on set and crashing into things. Further problems surfaced when K-9 was taken on location. Camera cables and door sills had been difficult enough for the robot to get over in the studio, but the rougher terrain of grass or quarry floors proved completely insurmountable. In many cases, K-9 was pulled along on a piece of carefully concealed twine, or else wooden boards along which the dog could travel were laid on the ground out of shot.

Following *The Invisible Enemy*, several modifications were made to the dog. The first was to change its drive from rear-wheel to front-wheel. The introduction of newer cameras in some of the studios also coincidentally resolved the problems over the radio control frequencies. However, it is to the credit of the various visual effects designers, and the talents of a radio-control specialist, Nigel Brackley, who was brought in specifically to look after K-9, that it was able to appear in as many stories as it did.

The next major overhaul came during the eighteenth season. Following *The Leisure Hive*, which saw K-9 conveniently write himself out by going for a dip in the sea off Brighton beach, the dog was completely stripped down and re-built internally by a designer called Charlie Lumm, who specialised in mechanical effects work. The wheels were enlarged, with those at the front given independent drives to achieve greater power and control, and the radio control was updated from the AM frequency band to newer FM frequency models.

The first story in which the new, improved K-9 appeared was *State of Decay* – but despite all the time and money that had been invested in the prop, the character was then written out in the following story, *Warriors' Gate*.

The introduction of K-9 coincided with the release of a film that was to have far-reaching repercussions for *Doctor Who* and for television science fiction in general. George Lucas's *Star Wars* redefined the audience's expectations of what could be achieved on screen. With its spectacular visuals and breathtaking dog-fights in space, *Star Wars* made almost everything else pale by comparison. The problem was that, in terms of effects, this film set the standard for all that was to come after it, and to try to match that standard required far more money and resources than the BBC could muster. The effects staff at the BBC did their utmost with the materials and budgets at their disposal, and achieved some remarkable results. The space scenes in *The Invisible Enemy*, *Underworld* and *The Invasion of Time*, and the creatures created for *Full Circle* and *Warrior's Gate*, were arguably every bit as good as those presented by George Lucas's film. However, the advantage of powerful computer control was not available to the BBC at this point, and *Doctor Who* had to wait until technology could provide a cheaper counterpart. This was not to happen until the early Eighties.

It was not only the visual aspect of *Doctor Who* that changed as the series progressed. Technology also improved in other areas, most notably in that of radiophonic sound and music. *Doctor Who*'s signature tune had been realised by the BBC's Radiophonic Workshop back when the show began, but during the Sixties and the early Seventies only a very small proportion of the series' incidental music had been electronic. Rather, it had been realised mainly by freelance composers using traditional instruments and methods.

Although Carey Blyton (*Revenge of the Cybermen*) and Geoffrey Burgon (*Terror of the Zygons*, *The Seeds of Doom*) also provided some scores, Dudley Simpson was the principal composer for the fourth Doctor's stories, and his music came to epitomise the feel of *Doctor Who* during this period. For the eighteenth season, however, incoming producer John Nathan-Turner wanted to get away from the traditional themes and to update the show for the Eighties. One of his decisions was to allow the Radiophonic Workshop to handle the incidental music as well as the special sounds. Therefore the orchestral arrangements of Simpson gave way to the electronic compositions of Peter Howell, Paddy Kingsland and Roger Limb. Their music was generated on the latest synthesisers and complemented the more glossy and hi-tech look Nathan-Turner gave the series.

Another change for the eighteenth season, again intended to update the show's image, was the altering of the title sequence. Ironically, the new titles, showing the Doctor's face being formed from clusters of stars and then disappearing, used a technique that was actually far older and less innovative than that of the version they replaced.

Bernard Lodge's 'tunnel' graphics, first introduced for the eleventh season in 1973, had been completely unlike anything else that the BBC had produced up to that time. Lodge had created the patterns using a version of the technique pioneered by Douglas Trumbull for the film *2001: A Space Odyssey*. This process, called slit-scan, was very time consuming, but gave excellent results. The titles for the eighteenth season, created by Sid Sutton, were simply animation. Numerous cels (sheets of plastic) were created, each showing an advancement of the image from the previous one, and when viewed together they formed the completed title sequence.

The fourth Doctor's era came to an end just as computer technology was revolutionising the creation of both electronic and other effects on British television. The effects created for *Doctor Who* during the fourth Doctor's era were however the most innovative of their time. Without programmes like *Doctor Who*, which has always encouraged innovation, it is doubtful if television as a whole would now be reaping the benefits from ever-more sophisticated technology as it becomes available.

On Location

There are a number of common misconceptions concerning the physical media upon which television programmes are actually made. During the Sixties, *Doctor Who* was recorded on videotape in an electronic studio, with a small proportion of 16mm or 35mm film inserts generally copied onto the tape during the studio day. These inserts would consist of stock footage; model or live action work specially shot at Ealing Film Studios; or material filmed on location. As the series moved into the Seventies, it started to benefit from more advanced technology. By the time Tom Baker took over as the Doctor, it was possible to record onto video on location (termed Outside Broadcast or OB) as well as in the electronic studio. Despite this, up until the Eighties, it was still normal to take film cameras on location and then transfer the film to video to produce the final programme.

The decision to take a programme like *Doctor Who* on location can be made for a number of reasons. There are artistic considerations – that to try and achieve, say, a forest or a cave system effectively in the studio would simply not work, and that to go to a real forest, or to descend into a real cave, would give far better results in the final programme. There are also budgetary considerations – that studio recording and location filming have different costs, and therefore it can occasionally work out cheaper to go on location than to stay in a studio. This however is the exception rather than the rule, as location costs usually far exceed studio costs.

Of course, on a science fiction production like *Doctor Who*, it is not always possible to find what is required within easy reach in the real world – there are not too many underwater Zygon spacecraft, for example, and snow-blown, bleak ice plateaux are not the most hospitable or accessible of places to travel to in real life. Occasionally, however, an alien planet or citadel can be created from the most mundane of settings, and the humble quarry has become one of the most versatile and popular locations for planets from Gallifrey to Skaro.

When *Doctor Who* started, back in 1963, there was hardly any location filming done. The first season had just a few short sequences filmed for *The Reign of Terror*; but following that, the amount of location work steadily increased.

Part of the problem in the Sixties was that the technical equipment required for filming was big, bulky and expensive to move about, therefore

THE FOURTH DOCTOR

it tended to be far easier to create what was wanted in the electronic studio through clever and imaginative sets and effects. As *Doctor Who* moved into colour at the start of the Seventies, so location work increased, but the locations always tended to be fairly close to the BBC's London base, with only one or two longer journeys made, such as to Cornwall (*The Smugglers, Colony in Space*), Wales (*The Abominable Snowmen, The Green Death*) and Cheshire (*The Time Warrior*).

SEASON TWELVE

The fourth Doctor's debut coincided with the first use of OB cameras for the series' location work. For *Robot*, director Christopher Barry had the use of an OB unit, which could record everything straight to video. One of the major advantages to this was that the whole story could have a uniform look to it – a switch from film-originated material to material recorded directly to tape is always accompanied by a noticeable change in picture quality.

Aside from the more practical advantages of OB over film, that it is cheaper and the results can be viewed immediately, another advantage to using all-video for this particular story was that the script called for the eponymous robot to grow to giant size and go on the rampage. Obviously this could not be achieved in reality, and the use of video enabled the effect to be achieved through Colour Separation Overlay (CSO).

The need to use CSO on *Robot* was, according to departing producer Barry Letts, why a bid was put in to use the OB facility in the first place. The sequences were recorded first on location without the robot present. The actors had to pretend that they were shooting at and running from a rampaging behemoth without it actually being there. Then that video material, some of which had been taken from the giant robot's point of view, was married in studio with the robot, played by Michael Kilgarriff, performing in front of a blue screen. Some scenes also called for a further CSO pass to be done, when the giant robot was in the distance and some foreground action was required. Christopher Barry remembered the set-up when interviewed for *The Frame* in 1987: 'One big advantage we had was that all the backgrounds had been shot on video rather than film, which meant that the colour balances were good and the horizontal hold was absolutely rigid, so the background and foreground fitted together better than usual.'

The only problem with the CSO was that the metallic robot reflected the key-colour from the CSO back-cloth, and occasionally parts of the creature were therefore inadvertently replaced by the background video image.

The location used for *Robot* was the BBC's engineering training centre at Wood Norton near Evesham. It was chosen, according to Christopher Barry, 'because there is an underground bunker there, which I thought we could use as the entrance to the underground area in the story. But suddenly somebody at the BBC clamped up and said, "Sssh, you can't have that seen, it's secret". This was despite the fact that if you drive down the road, you can see it! But we couldn't show it on television. So we had to build a rather unconvincing entrance into the side of a hill, rather similar to what we had done with the tumulus in *The Dæmons*, as a way into the underground area.'

Co-incidentally, *Robot*, the first story to be originated entirely on video, was shortly followed by *The Sontaran Experiment*, the first story to be recorded entirely on location, again using OB cameras. The reason for the move to complete location in this instance was that *The Ark in Space* required a high design budget, as the ambitious sets that comprised the Ark had to be created from scratch; to keep costs down, it was decided to make *The Ark in Space* and *The Sontaran Experiment* almost as one six-parter, with the former all in studio and the latter all on location. Another factor was that usually a six-part story would have just one week of location filming, and so *The Sontaran Experiment* had to be completed in that week. The use of OB cameras allowed the necessary versatility and speed in the recording process. Because this situation was recognised early on, script editor Robert Holmes was able to ask *The Sontaran Experiment*'s writers, Bob Baker and Dave Martin, to keep the costs down and to set it all on location.

The location used, at the writers' suggestion, was Dartmoor. In story terms, it represented Piccadilly Circus in the far future, returned to grass and moorland, as they explained to *In-Vision* in 1988: 'We chose Dartmoor because the cast and crew could travel and stay and shoot it there – keeping the cost down to a minimum and therefore invention up. We'd been there many times.'

Although Dartmoor may have been an ideal location from the setting point of view, recording in October did not guarantee the best of weather, as actor Glyn Jones, who played Krans, recalled in the fanzine *Tardis*: 'Filming on Dartmoor in October was enough to freeze the proverbial brass monkey. Looking at it on the small screen, one doesn't realise that, for the most part, the sleet and rain were pelting down. And I wondered why I looked so large until I realised that, under my spacesuit, I had enough tracksuits and sweaters to fit out the entire crew of an oil rig.'

The only other major location shoot during the twelfth season was for *Revenge of the Cybermen*, as the location work for *Genesis of the Daleks* had been restricted to a few scenes shot in a Fullers Earth Quarry near Reigate.

Revenge of the Cybermen made use of Wookey Hole, the world-famous cave system in Somerset. This is the only time *Doctor Who* has been to this particular location, which is perhaps odd as it offers a remarkable variety of backdrops and tunnels that it would be difficult to reproduce within a studio. A story such as *Underworld*, which ended up through budgetary

THE FOURTH DOCTOR

problems being recorded against CSO models of tunnels, would certainly have benefited greatly from use of such a real location. Michael E Briant, the director of *Revenge of the Cybermen*, told *Doctor Who Magazine* an interesting story of one of his visits to check out the location site: 'I wanted to spend about a day in the caves where we were going to film, but the authorities weren't keen on me being down there while they were showing guided tours around. They asked if I would mind going down after closing time, about seven o'clock. I said "fine", but pointed out that I'd have to be there until midnight at least. They agreed, saying that they'd lock both entrances as normal, giving me a key. With my wife, I duly set off into the caverns, and after about two hours of wandering about, taking notes, somebody came up. I thought at first he was a security guy, but then I saw he was dressed in a wet suit. I asked him how he had got in and he said, "Oh, I always come in. Can I borrow your torch?" I refused, because I needed it to see with, and the man said, "Right you are," before going off into the gloom. Shortly afterwards, we heard a little Irish tune whistling from the shadows, and both my wife and I began to feel a bit scared. I decided to call it a night, even though I hadn't finished, but first I asked the caretaker who the man had been and why he had been let in. I was told, "We didn't let anyone in. He was an Irishman who died down there pot-holing, three years ago." Of course I couldn't tell anyone, because my film unit would never have worked there.' Later, during filming of the story, a number of other strange incidents would occur, which some members of the cast and crew would attribute to supernatural causes.

AT-A-GLANCE SEASON TWELVE LOCATIONS

Robot	BBC Engineering Training Centre, Wood Norton Hall, Wood Norton, Evesham, Worcs
The Sontaran Experiment	Hound Tor, nr Manaton, Dartmoor, Devon Headland Warren, nr Postbridge, Devon
Genesis of the Daleks	Betchworth Quarry, Pebblehill Road, Betchworth, Surrey
Revenge of the Cybermen	Wookey Hole Caves, Wookey Hole, Wells, Somerset

SEASON THIRTEEN

The thirteenth season's opening story, *Terror of the Zygons*, was supposed to be set in Scotland, around Loch Ness and the mythical village of Tullock. It had originally been intended that some filming would actually take place in

Scotland, but this was eventually ruled out on cost grounds, so director Douglas Camfield had to find some Scottish-looking locations closer to home.

The place chosen was the small, picturesque village of Charlton, near Chichester in Sussex; and further scenes were shot on a small stretch of beach and sand dunes south of Climping, between Bognor Regis and Littlehampton on Britain's south coast. Charlton was ideal for the village of Tulloch, and Camfield elected to retain the name of the village pub, 'The Fox Inn' (later renamed 'The Fox Goes Free', presumably when the pub became one of a chain whose trademark was names ending in '...Goes Free'), rather than change it as Christopher Barry had done in a similar situation in *The Dæmons*.

The other major location was yet another quarry, at Storrington in West Sussex, this time with a large lake in it that doubled for the shores of Loch Ness for the scenes of the Zygon spaceship emerging from the water. Actor John Woodnutt, who played the dual roles of Broton, the leader of the Zygons, and the Duke of Forgill, recalled for the fanzine *Shada* his work on the story: 'It was shot just outside Bognor, and in fact one village was very cleverly adapted by the scenic designer, who just stuck bits on that looked Scottish, just on the outsides of buildings. We took all the Sussex signs down and stuck up odd things that made you think of Scotland. It's not a bad location for it, in fact, because outside you do have quite a lot of conifers, which look awfully like those in Scotland. One conifer looks very like another, and when you put a bit of bagpipe music in the background, everyone assumes you're actually in Scotland.'

Another real pub was featured, and retained its original name, in *The Android Invasion*. This was the 'Fleur de Lys' in the picturesque village of East Hagbourne in Oxfordshire. The village and its surrounding countryside became the Kraals' duplicate English village, while the National Radiological Protection Board buildings nearby in Harwell became the base on Earth infiltrated by androids at the story's conclusion.

Both *Pyramids of Mars* and *The Seeds of Doom* called for a large country house to be used. For *Pyramids of Mars*, a private mansion house near Newbury called 'Stargroves', a residence of rock star Mick Jagger, was chosen by the director Paddy Russell. This had the additional benefit of a stable block, which doubled for Laurence Scarman's cottage.

The Seeds of Doom used Athelhampton House, which is about six miles east of Dorchester in Dorset. Again, this is privately owned, although it is open for public viewing. Yet another quarry made an appearance in this story, too. This time, it was a sand and silica quarry near Dorking. Another well known building also featured – surprisingly, one not often used as a location by the BBC, their very own Television Centre in London. The script called for short scenes of characters entering and leaving the headquarters of

THE FOURTH DOCTOR

the World Ecology Bureau, and rather than travel miles, the crew simply used one of their own side entrances.

AT-A-GLANCE SEASON THIRTEEN LOCATIONS

Terror of the Zygons	Climping Beach, Climping, West Sussex
	Ambersham Common, South Ambersham, West Sussex
	Hall Aggregates Quarry, Storrington, West Sussex
	Charlton, West Sussex
	Furnace Pond, Mill Lane, Crabtree, West Sussex
	Millbank Tower, Millbank, London SW1
Pyramids of Mars	Stargrove Manor, East End, Hants
The Android Invasion	National Radiological Protection Board, Harwell, Oxon
	Worsham Quarry, Witney, Oxon
	Tubney Wood, Tubney, Oxon
	East Hagbourne, Oxon
The Seeds of Doom	Buckland Sand and Silica Co Ltd, Reigate Road, Buckland, Surrey
	Athelhampton House, Athelhampton, Dorset
	BBC Television Centre, Wood Lane, Shepherd's Bush, London, W12

SEASON FOURTEEN

The fourteenth season contained more filmed location work than *Doctor Who* had ever had before, with every story bar two (*The Face of Evil* and *The Robots of Death*) featuring a large proportion. The season started with one of the most impressive UK locations used on *Doctor Who*. Portmeirion in North Wales is very well known both as a tourist attraction and as a television location, as the Patrick McGoohan adventure series *The Prisoner* was filmed there during the Sixties. Sir Clough Williams-Ellis's baroque mock-Italian village, opened in 1926 and based on the Italian village of Portofino, is situated on a forest-covered headland, which also overlooks the wide expanse of a river delta fed by the Trawsfynydd Lake and the river Glaslyn amongst others, east of Porthmadog.

Designer Barry Newbery recalled working in Portmeirion during the making of *Masque of Mandragora* for *Doctor Who Magazine*: 'I was disappointed when I discovered we were to film in Portmeirion, mainly because I was looking forward to doing some filming in Italy! But I fell in love with the place when I got there, and it approached how I imagined parts of Italy would look. Since then, I've been to Italy and realise now that it doesn't look like that at all. We built the remains of a temple close to one of the lakes, and Williams-Ellis actually asked if we could leave it there when we finished. We couldn't, because it was stock scenery made of light-weight jablite – if there had been a strong wind, the whole thing would have just blown away.'

Sir Clough Williams-Ellis died in 1978, but Portmeirion remains open to the public, and, as it is a holiday village, one can stay and live in what really is a remarkable place.

For *The Hand of Fear*, a power station was required, and the writers, Bob Baker and Dave Martin, as with their previous story, *The Sontaran Experiment*, had already decided on a place that could be used. In this case, they had even gone there to scout it out before writing their scripts. The location chosen was the Oldbury Nuclear Power Station on the Severn Estuary in Avon.

The Deadly Assassin's location footage is well remembered, and so it should be, for over nineteen minutes of part three's twenty-five minute running time was given over to location film. The reason was that Robert Holmes, the writer and script editor, wanted to present: 'a technically innovative script with subjective and surrealist sequences that I felt widened the vocabulary of the programme.' Therefore part three was written as a nightmare dream experience for the Doctor. Sequences at the close of part two, featuring the Doctor falling off a real cliff-edge, a Samurai soldier, a man in surgical gowns holding a huge hypodermic needle, and soldiers on railway lines, were all filmed at Betchworth Quarry and its adjoining goods yard. All the material in the jungle and river was filmed in the gardens of the Royal Alexandra and Albert School, with a short sequence in the school's swimming pool for the scene when the Doctor's face is held under water. Finally, the filming of a bi-plane attack was achieved using miniatures at Wycombe Air Park. It took five full days to film all the required material for this one episode – compare that to the six days it took to shoot two complete episodes' worth of material for *The Sontaran Experiment*.

As previously mentioned, there was no location work for *The Face of Evil* or *The Robots of Death*. However, the production team again pushed the series' resources to the limit to create a gloomy, fog-bound, late 19th Century London for the season's final story, *The Talons of Weng-Chiang*. Wapping and Southwark were lovingly taken back in time and dressed in Victorian style, as director David Maloney remembered in *Doctor Who Magazine*: 'We were due to film in and around a set of Victorian houses in Wapping. We had posted letters to all the owners of the houses, asking them if they'd all please remove their motor cars, because we wanted to bring a carriage through the square. When we got there, there was a Porsche still parked in full view, and it was really going to ruin everything we wanted to do, so Roger Murray-Leach, my designer, had the very clever idea of putting a tarpaulin over the car and covering it with hay.' Other scenes involved the Doctor and Litefoot heading down the Thames in a rowing boat. All the material outside Litefoot's house was filmed in Twickenham.

As well as using film for all this location footage, director David Maloney decided to use OB cameras to record on video the remaining location work, all of which took place indoors. The first port of call was the Northampton Repertory Theatre, which was to become the inside of Henry Gordon Jago's Palace Theatre. This was chosen by Maloney 'because it's still got the original Victorian flying area above the stage, and we had a big chase there.' Philip Hinchcliffe was also impressed by the results achieved in his final credited story as producer: 'All that behind-the-scenes stuff looked really classy, because it was obviously not a studio.' From there, the OB cameras moved to St Crispin's Hospital, where Litefoot's mortuary was set up, as well as the Palace Theatre dressing room where Chang leaves a hypnotised cleaning girl who is found by Leela.

AT-A-GLANCE SEASON FOURTEEN LOCATIONS

The Masque of Mandragora	Portmeirion, Penrhyndeudraeth, North Wales
The Hand of Fear	Cromhall Quarry, Cromhall, Wootton-under-Edge, Gloucs
	Oldbury Power Station, Oldbury Naite, Thornbury, Gloucs
	Stokefield Close, Thornbury, Gloucs
The Deadly Assassin	Betchworth Quarry, Pebblehill Road, Betchworth, Surrey
	Royal Alexandra and Albert School, Rocky Lane, Merstham, Surrey
	Wycombe Air Park, Clay Lane, High Wycombe, Bucks
The Talons of Weng-Chiang	Ealing Film Studios
	Wapping Pier Head, Wapping High Street, London, E1
	Clink Street, Southwark, London SE1
	Ivory House, St Katharine's Dock, East Smithfield, London, E1

ON LOCATION

St Mary Overy's Wharf, Cathedral Street, Southwark, London, E1
Bridewell Place, Wapping, E1
Bankside, Southwark, SE1
Broad Oak, 24 Cambridge Park, Twickenham, Middx
East Dock/Centre Basin, St Katharine's Dock, East Smithfield, London, E1
Northampton Repertory Theatre, Swan Street, Northampton
St Crispin's Hospital, Duston, Northampton
Empty Rates Office, Fish Street, Northampton

SEASON FIFTEEN

Compared with that of the previous season, the fifteenth season's location work seems positively frugal. Only one story, *The Invasion of Time*, made major use of location filming, some of it pre-planned but some because a strike at the BBC forced it out of the studios.

Image of the Fendahl was, like *Pyramids of Mars* and *The Seeds of Doom* before it, set in and around a large country house, and the production team returned to 'Stargroves' to carry out the location work required. One particular problem was that *Image of the Fendahl* required a lot of night-filming.

Whereas filming during daylight often requires only a minimum of additional lighting (spotlights for artistes' faces, white boards to reflect the sunlight and so on), when night-filming is called for, the lighting of all the scenes becomes particularly crucial, and the time required to set up each shot is increased accordingly. Elmer Cossey, the film cameraman, recalled for *In-Vision* an incident that occurred while the crew were setting up to film for *Image of the Fendahl* at two o'clock in the morning: 'The Doctor and Leela were running down through this wood, with mysterious lights in the background. We got it all ready to go, and one of the dressers came up and said, "Your generator's on fire." The gaffer said, "Oh don't be silly, a joke's a joke." And the dresser said, "No, honestly, your generator's on fire!" I said, "Hang on a moment," and we looked round. Over the top of this hill was a red glow and smoke. Suddenly there was a bang, and all the lights went out. There were frantic 'phone calls back to London to the lighting company – a little difficult at two o'clock in the morning. But by about 4 am, we had another generator down, and fortunately there was still plenty of darkness.'

THE FOURTH DOCTOR

The Sun Makers posed its own problems for director Pennant Roberts and his team in scouting out the locations. The scripts called for lengthy corridors along which protracted chases in electric buggies could be staged. Roberts knew that Camden Deep tunnels, which connect various ducts, tunnels and passages between North and West London, would be suitable, as they were far cheaper to rent than London Transport-owned tunnels. However one of the buggies required for the chase scenes was too large to fit through the access doors, so an alternative had to be found for that scene.

The script also called for scenes set on the roof of the Company Megropolis on Pluto, and the production team had assumed that they could use for this any high building in London. However, the script also specified that no other buildings were to be visible, and in London this was impossible. Roberts had almost resigned himself to using CSO to get around the problem, when one of the production team came to the rescue, as Roberts explained: 'My production assistant brought a copy of *The Architectural Review* into the office, with illustrations of the new Imperial Tobacco factory in Bristol. Not a very high roof, but the size of two football pitches. Enormous.' When they scouted the location, they found an unexpected bonus that resolved the problem of getting the large buggy into the Camden Deep tunnels: the cigarette factory had a three hundred foot long underground tunnel, which ran between two halves of the facility.

Underworld has been mentioned previously as having been sorely in need of a decent cave location, but overspending on other sets for the story meant that it had to resort to the less than satisfactory medium of CSO. This left just *The Invasion of Time*, which ended up with more location work than had been originally planned.

The story was already well behind schedule, due to an original story by David Weir (concerning a race of cat-people living on Gallifrey) not working out and a substitute having to be written by producer Graham Williams and script editor Anthony Read. Then, one of a series of wildcat strikes hit *Doctor Who*, causing the loss of some studio time. The only solution was for much of the material to be recorded on location, using OB cameras, rather than in studio. Luckily a partially disused hospital in Redhill was found by the production assistant Colin Dudley, which provided the mixture of required settings, from rooms and corridors for the TARDIS interiors to a boiler room for the control centre of Gallifrey's transduction barriers. There was even a convenient quarry nearby for the filming of the sequences on outer Gallifrey.

This location did not, however, satisfy the requirement for the TARDIS to have a swimming pool, and so the pool at the British Oxygen Headquarters was used, together with the changing rooms. Stuntman Stuart Fell, who was playing one of the Sontarans, remembered the locations in an interview for *Doctor Who Magazine* in 1989: 'We used two contrasting locations; a cold, damp, disused mental hospital in Reigate, and a luxury swimming pool in

ON LOCATION

Hammersmith. I suggested leaping over the corner of the pool, jumping onto a chair, which collapsed, and then doing a roll.'

AT-A-GLANCE SEASON FIFTEEN LOCATIONS

Image of the Fendahl	Stargrove Manor, East End, Hampshire
The Sun Makers	WD & HO Wills Tobacco Factory, Hartcliffe Way, Hartcliffe, Bristol, Avon
	Camden Town Deep Tube Shelters, Stanmore Place, Camden Town, London, NW1
The Invasion of Time	Beachfields Quarry, Cormongers Lane, Redhill, Surrey
	St Anne's Hospital, Redstone Hill, Redhill, Surrey
	British Oxygen, Blacks Road, Hammersmith Broadway, London, W6

SEASON SIXTEEN

The Pirate Planet was the first story of the sixteenth season to require locations, and production assistant Michael Owen Morris found all that he needed, including a power station, fields and meadows and caves, in Gwent, South Wales. The power station was used as the engine room of the space-hopping planet Zanek, while the fields and meadows were used for scenes where the Mentiads advance on the Captain's bridge, the entrance to which was a disused railway tunnel. The Abercrave Caves at Dan-yr-Ogof became mineshafts deep inside Zanak, the large Cathedral Cavern being used for most scenes.

For the following story, *The Stones of Blood*, a rather unusual requirement had to be met. Rather than needing a location to act as some alien planet, or to give the impression that it was somewhere other than where it really was, the story called for a circle of standing stones that was to be used in the story as precisely that – a circle of standing stones.

The circle used was the Rollright Stones, which can be found just off the main A34 road in Oxfordshire. The circle in real life is small and insignificant-looking, and, as visual effects designer Mat Irvine explained to the fanzine *Temporal Limiter* in 1983, it had to be augmented: 'The stone circle we used was a real one and, as a stone circle, fairly boring. We wanted to make it more interesting, so we added a trinithon [two standing stones with a third stone laying across them] in the middle and things. In a lull during shooting, a party of school kids came round, and we let them through. They were going round counting the stones, and counting our dummy ones as well as the real ones. It wasn't until one of the teachers went up and touched one of them that they realised it was a polystyrene one.'

The Stones of Blood's director Darrol Blake also recalled working on the show for *Doctor Who Magazine*: 'I remember we had K-9 running on ploughed fields and various other places. Dear old Mat Irvine said it couldn't be done, so we put planks down and we shot the field through some grass and weeds, which masked the planks the tin dog was on. We got him travelling quite fast to rescue Romana, which took quite a bit of ingenuity.'

One of the most impressive castles in the south of England, Leeds Castle in Kent, was used as the main location for *The Androids of Tara*. Paul Lavers, who played Farrah, remembered the storming of the castle when interviewed for the fanzine *Web Planet*: 'It was about two o'clock in the morning, a night shoot with lots of lights. Just before we were about to start, Michael Hayes [the director] came over with a bottle of whisky to give us all a shot, because it was quite cold by then, and coming across the car park to the castle, [Simon Lack, who played Zadek] slipped, and this bottle of whisky smashed all over the place. Then Michael came up to us and said, "Listen, I know you've got to storm the castle, but could you do it quietly, because there are people inside sleeping."'

The final location used in the sixteenth season was for *The Power of Kroll*, and this time the crew travelled up to Suffolk to a section of flat marshland around Iken. One of the requirements was for the horizon to be flat and low, to facilitate the appearance of the giant Kroll creature in the sky above, and the marshes provided such an environment. Effects designer Tony Harding, interviewed for the fanzine *Fendahl*, remembered the location: 'We were working in a tidal marsh alongside the Maltings in Suffolk. You can imagine the problems this presented. At the beginning of a sequence we would be on dry land, and at the end up to our necks in water. Because of this, there were great problems with continuity, and it just so happened that we chose the few days of the year when the whole area was affected by spring tides. The tide came up twenty or thirty feet further than it normally would have done.' Mary Tamm, who played Romana, also remembered the mud when interviewed for *Doctor Who Magazine*: 'Tom and I got totally stuck in the mud, we just couldn't move until we were rescued. We were miles from anywhere, and it was so bleak. There was absolutely nothing to do between takes, because if you'd wandered off, you'd probably have been swallowed up!'

Terry Walsh, who played the green-skinned Swampie Mensch in the story, also recalled for *Doctor Who Magazine* the location work: 'We were running around in the marshes, and had to wear green waterproof make-up, which had been specially ordered from Germany. At the end of the first

ON LOCATION

day's filming, they told us that they had forgotten to order the special stuff needed to get the make-up off. They sent us down to an American airbase to shower, and we arrived looking like a group of jolly green giants. There were all these black American airmen playing baseball, shouting out, "Hey, now you know how we feel!" We got in the showers, and it still wouldn't come off. We were using brushes, and still nothing happened. We ended up back at the hotel at two o'clock in the morning stark naked in the kitchen, with a group of very embarrassed make-up girls trying to get it off with Ajax. The hotel bedsheets remained green for weeks!'

AT-A-GLANCE SEASON SIXTEEN LOCATIONS

The Pirate Planet	Disused Railway Tunnell, Daren-felen, Gwent, Wales
	Big Pit, Blaenavon, Gwent, Wales
	Coity Mountain, Gwent, Wales
	Monmouthshire Golf Course, Llanfoist, Gwent, Wales
	Bwlch y Garn, Ebbw Vale, Gwent, Wales
	Cathedral Cave, Dan-yr-Ogof Showcaves, Dan-yr-Ogof, Powys, Wales
	Berkley Power Station, Berkley, Gloucs
The Stones of Blood	The King's Men, Rollright Stones, Little Rollright, Oxfordshire
	Reed Cottage, Little Compton, Warwickshire
	Field belonging to Manor Farm, Oakham Road, Little Rollright, Oxfordshire
	Little Rollright Quarry, Oakham Road, Little Rollright, Oxfordshire
The Androids of Tara	Leeds Castle, Nr Maidstone A20, Kent
The Power of Kroll	The Maltings, Snape, Suffolk
	Iken Cliff, Iken, nr Snape, Kent

SEASON SEVENTEEN

The first time the fourth Doctor visited Skaro, he found himself in Reigate Quarry, and for his next visit, in *Destiny of the Daleks*, yet another quarry was used, this time Winspit Quarry near Swanage. The fanzine *Oracle* covered the location filming of this story in 1979 through an interview with visual effects designer Peter Logan. Logan had to build a model that matched the location for the scenes where the Movellan spacecraft landed and then burrowed into the earth. Between the choosing of the location and the taking of the background photograph for matching with the model work, a heavy rainstorm had created an artificial lake just alongside the place where the spaceship was supposed to land. The main problem with the model lake was not the difficulty caused by water's refusal to miniaturise well, but its tendency to seep through sand. Since the lake was always as still as a millpond, and muddy because of the sand, there was no difficulty in making the model look like the real thing. In any event, in many of the model shots, the lake was partially obscured by a strategically placed bank of sand.

The feature went on to reveal that when the TARDIS was buried under rubble at the start of the story, it wasn't the weight of the rocks that was the problem, as they were made of polystyrene; rather it was that a half mile walk around the cliff was necessary to get to a position above the TARDIS in order to drop the rocks. Two or three journeys were necessary for each re-take, as there were so many polystyrene rocks to be dropped.

Destiny of the Daleks was also the first *Doctor Who* adventure to make use of a Steadicam. This is a lightweight, single-operator video camera, finely counter-balanced, giving its operator precise control over the image being recorded. It also allows for smooth tracking shots to be taken over bumpy terrain. Previously, camera tracks had to be laid on the ground, and even then the smoothness of the shot depended on the care of those pushing the camera-dolly along the tracks. With a Steadicam, all these problems are removed, and fast, smooth camerawork is the result.

The next story, *City of Death*, took *Doctor Who* overseas for the first time ever, and the only way that producer Graham Williams managed it was to keep the costs involved down to a minimum, as he explained to *Doctor Who Magazine*: 'No sooner had we settled on Paris [as a setting] than I decided to cost out the script. I felt that we could actually go to Paris at no extra cost, as long as we were clever about it. I gave John Nathan-Turner, then my production unit manager, the list of the cast that I intended taking over and the time we'd be there, and he returned me a costing that was to within about fifteen pounds of what we'd have spent going to Ealing Studios to shoot it.' The reason that this worked out was that at Ealing there would have been the costs of designing and building the sets, buying in the props and other hire charges, whereas by taking a minimum of crew over to Paris – just a film cameraman, a sound man, the director and producer – the costs were minimised on the location. This was the reason why K-9 was written out of this story, as taking him out to Paris would have involved more people in the form of operators and visual effects technicians.

Lalla Ward, interviewed in the fanzine *Eye of Horus*, remembered filming in Paris: 'Tom was a bit annoyed that the French were more interested in me and my schoolgirl outfit than him and his long scarf. Of course, *Doctor Who* isn't shown over there, so the French didn't take too much notice of us. I remember on one location we were to film at the top of the Eiffel Tower, but we couldn't as it was so misty and there was four inches of snow on the ground. We couldn't see a thing!'

As it turned out, this was the last location work seen on screen from the seventeenth season, as both *Nightmare of Eden* and *The Horns of Nimon* were studio-bound stories (although *The Horns of Nimon* was originally planned to include some location work), and the season's final story, *Shada*, was not completed, due to another strike, and was therefore never transmitted.

The location filming for *Shada* was done in and around the streets of Cambridge and Grantchester. Footage was also shot of the Doctor punting on the River Cam. Assistant K-9 Operator Stephen Cambden spoke to *Private Who* fanzine about this sequence: 'Tom Baker, very much a land lubber at heart, managed to move the punt in every conceivable direction except the one indicated by the director! He spun it, pitched it and even jammed the pole into the river bed, while Lalla Ward, a nervous passenger, prayed for deliverance. On the one occasion Tom did steer the punt in for a perfect landing, the cameras were not rolling!'

AT-A-GLANCE SEASON SEVENTEEN LOCATIONS

Destiny of the Daleks	Winspit Quarry, Worth Matravers, Dorset
	Binnegar Heath Sand Pit, Puddletown Road, Wareham, Dorset
City of Death	Eiffel Tower, Parc du Champ de Mars, Paris, France
	Duplex Metro Platform (line 6), Rue August Bartoldi, Paris, France
	Trocadero Metro Platform (Line 6), Place du Trocadero, Paris, France
	Avenue Kleber (Boissiere Metro and Entrance), Paris, France
	Rue de Rivoli (Louvre Museum), Paris, France
	Le Notre Dame Brasserie, Place du Petit Pont, Paris, France
	Place de la Concorde, Paris, France
	Denise Rene Gallery, Boulevard St Germain, Paris, France
	Avenue des Champs Elysees, Paris, France
	47 Rue Vieille du Temple, Paris, France
Shada	Emmanuel College, St Andrews Street,

THE FOURTH DOCTOR

Cambridge;
The Backs, River Cam, Cambridge;
Botolph Lane, Cambridge;
Trinity Lane, Cambridge;
Garret Hostel Bridge and Lane, Cambridge;
Portugal Place and Portugal Street, Cambridge;
King's Parade, Cambridge;
St Edward's Passage, Cambridge;
Blackmoor Head's Yard, Cambridge;
High Street and Grantchester Meadows, Grantchester

SEASON EIGHTEEN

Tom Baker's final season reverted to all-British locations. The opening scenes of *The Leisure Hive*, the only location work in that story, were all filmed on Brighton beach, and whereas the script had called for the weather to be dull and overcast, in fact it was bright and pleasant – something of a novelty for *Doctor Who*, as most location work seems to have taken place either in wet, windy and cold conditions, or at the height of a heat-wave.

Black Park near Iver was the location used for two of the stories, *Full Circle* and *State of Decay*. *Full Circle* made use of a lake in the park, as well as some of the forest surrounding it, and director Peter Grimwade told *Doctor Who Magazine* about the alterations the crew had to make to the location: 'The huge, coloured lights taken on location, which made Alzarius seem as though it had a strange sun, were not conceived at an early stage. That came along when the cameraman suggested lighting the foreground as we were setting up the forest scenes. It worked especially well after the designer, Janet Budden, had made the set look even more exotic by dabbing powder paint all over the foliage and trees. It kicked back off the lights and gave a very garish feel to the setting. The only problem was that the stuff got everywhere and we were continually having to clear it up, because the park was National Trust property.'

State of Decay concentrated on Burnham Beeches' forest areas in Black Park. Due to the park's location close to Bray House, the former home of Hammer films in the Sixties and early Seventies, it was also used in many of their horror films. For *Doctor Who* to have filmed sections of its vampire story there seems somehow fitting.

Logopolis, the final story of the eighteenth season and Tom Baker's final story as the Doctor, made use of a number of locations in central London, and also a lay-by and fields lying alongside the A413 road in

ON LOCATION

Buckinghamshire. The production team had originally wanted to use one of the few remaining police telephone boxes still in existence, located along the Barnet bypass, but the box was vandalised in between their taking of reference photos and arriving to film, and so a prop was used instead. Shortly after this, the genuine box was dismantled and removed altogether.

AT-A-GLANCE SEASON EIGHTEEN LOCATIONS

The Leisure Hive	Brighton Beach, Fish Market Hard, Brighton, East Sussex
Full Circle	Black Park, Fulmer, Bucks
State of Decay	Burnham Beeches, Burnham, Bucks
Logopolis	43 Ursula Street, Battersea, London, SW11
	Albert Bridge, Kensington and Chelsea, London, SW3
	Cadogan Pier, Chelsea Embankment, London, SW3
	BBC Receiving Station, Crowsley Park, Blounts Court Road, Sonning Common, Berks
	Lay-by, Amersham Road (A413), Denham, Bucks

The era of the fourth Doctor had seen technology advance by leaps and bounds, with better, lighter cameras, and ever-more realistic effects being achieved through digital technology. Although the budget had not increased to the extent that regular overseas filming was possible, through careful use of resources the production teams were able to make the most of what was available in Britain.

The filming of *City of Death* in Paris proved that locations could be found further afield, as long as the schedules were carefully prepared, and this paved the way for several more trips abroad in the following years. Some lessons were also learnt: K-9 was never successfully used on location, despite having his wheels modified for the eighteenth season, and his appearances were therefore limited mainly to studio-bound stories.

Other stories looked as though they had used locations, but had in fact been made all in studios. *Planet of Evil*, *The Creature from the Pit* and *Nightmare of Eden* all featured realistic forests that had been artificially created. Even *Horror of Fang Rock*'s effective lighthouse interior was a set, created by designer Paul Allen up at the BBC's Pebble Mill studios in Birmingham.

As technology progressed and *Doctor Who* utilised what was available, so the quality of the finished product improved. *Doctor Who* at the end of the

THE FOURTH DOCTOR

Seventies was very different from what had been produced a decade before, and the use of location work more than ever augmented the final product as the integration of film, OB recording and studio recording became flawless.

Selling the Doctor

Television is the biggest and most popular form of mass entertainment, and a whole industry exists to try and capture and market something memorable, something that will make one particular product or person stand out from all the others. As often as not, it is the unlikely that succeeds, and some products that are hyped up through expensive campaigns fall at the first fence.

When discussing *Doctor Who*'s impact on popular culture, it is impossible not to mention the Daleks, the first great marketing success of the series. Like other cultural icons of the same period, such as Superman, Batman, the Beatles and International Rescue's Thunderbirds, the Daleks were not planned to be a rip-roaring, money-spinning success. Quite to the contrary, the metal monsters from Skaro had been created by an author who conceded to write the story in the first place only because he was strapped for cash at the time; and their look came about through a logical progression by the designer thinking about how best to achieve the effect required on screen. The final element was the voices, and these came about as simply a desire to get away from a human voice.

Three disparate elements: the character, the look, and the voice, but together they captured the imaginations of a generation of children.

If the Daleks were *Doctor Who*'s first commercial success, then its second was the fourth Doctor. This is not to say that the previous three Doctors had been unpopular, but none of them had captured the imagination of the viewing public to the extent that the fourth Doctor did.

While the first three Doctors all had strong characters, and enjoyed a variety of entertaining and memorable adventures, their impact – at least as far as commercial prospects were concerned – was lessened by the far greater impact made by the Daleks. In 1965 and 1966, the Daleks ruled both the television and the toyshops. The other elements that made up the television series in which they appeared were relegated to the background, and so the Doctor, his TARDIS and the many other creatures he met were not given a look in. The manufacturers saw that the Daleks were popular, and if they couldn't have Daleks, then they weren't interested.

One consequence of this was that when the Dalek boom tailed off in late 1966, those responsible for exploiting them commercially moved into other areas. *Doctor Who* had been mined, had been successful for them, but now they wanted another major success, and the Daleks and the Doctor were perceived to be rather old hat. This resulted in a lack of media coverage, made

THE FOURTH DOCTOR

worse by the fact that the second Doctor, Patrick Troughton, rarely gave interviews to the press and kept personal appearances to an absolute minimum. With little backup from the BBC, it was better from the manufacturers' point of view to let *Doctor Who* lie and to try elsewhere.

When Jon Pertwee took on the role of the Doctor, all the elements required to make a successful impact on the media appeared to be there. Pertwee had the look: a frilly shirt, velvet jacket and swirling cloak. He had the gimmicks: a sonic screwdriver and his old Edwardian roadster, Bessie. It wasn't that the actor was shy and retiring. Far from it: Jon Pertwee was a true showman and threw his all into promoting the series and the Doctor. While he was playing the Doctor, there was interest in the show, but despite the fact that Pertwee stayed in the part for four years, the popular memory of his era focuses not only on the Doctor himself but also on the other elements that made the early Seventies so successful in *Doctor Who* terms: the Master, the Brigadier and UNIT.

When Tom Baker arrived, it coincided with the phasing out of UNIT and the re-establishment of the Doctor as an enigmatic traveller in time and space. The focus of the programme returned to its central character. What is more, the new Doctor was more instantly recognisable than his predecessors, due to his distinctive looks and his trademark hat and scarf. The highly memorable costume, combined with Tom Baker's eccentric portrayal, helped to fix the character in viewers' minds. The third Doctor had become somewhat predictable and staid, played seriously and with conviction by Pertwee, but Baker's fourth Doctor was an unpredictable maverick. One could never be quite sure how he would react in a situation, or what he would do next. At times the character seemed so packed full of suppressed energy that he would explode at the merest provocation, and at other times he could be so mellow that nothing could perturb him.

Each of the actors who has played the Doctor over the years has brought a little of himself to the part – Pertwee's love of gadgetry being a good example. With Tom Baker's Doctor, there was more than just a little of the actor on show. Baker's unpredictable nature, his tendency toward self-contemplation, his immediate and tangible charisma, all overspilled into the fourth Doctor. Tom Baker was a larger than life character himself, and that quality reinforced the role he played, creating a truly memorable Doctor.

MEDIA

Tom Baker was a godsend to the media, and his characterisation of the Doctor resulted in more coverage than any other – including pastiches.

There had been the occasional pastiche based around *Doctor Who* before Tom Baker came along, for example newspaper cartoons in the Sixties, a sketch ending with an appearance of a Dalek on *Crackerjack*, and even pop star Cliff Richard including a spoof of the series in one of his BBC variety shows in the early Seventies. However, the real proliferation of *Doctor Who* parodies on TV started with Tom Baker's immensely visual Doctor. There were a number of parodies during his tenure, and many others followed, so that a *Doctor Who* inspired sketch could be found on the TV shows of most popular comedians.

One of the earliest parodies was presented by *Crackerjack* toward the end of 1975, when Don MacLean played the fourth Doctor, Peter Glaze portrayed the Brigadier and Jacqueline Clarke played Sarah. Set in the control room of the TARDIS, which had landed atop the Post Office Tower, it featured the Doctor knitting his scarf throughout.

Another celebrated example was the 1979 *Doctor Eyes* item featured in an edition of the LWT sketch show *End of Part One*, written by Andrew Marshall and David Renwick. In this, actor Fred Harris wearing an exaggerated version of Tom Baker's costume – complete with huge, bulging 'eyeballs' fixed over his own eyes – romped across a tacky alien landscape accompanied by a female companion, Gloria, played by Sue Holderness and based on Mary Tamm's Romana. Gloria was periodically prodded with a stick from out-of-shot to make her scream on cue, and was preoccupied with when in the script she was supposed to scream or sprain her ankle. The Doctor was forced to regenerate (the new version played by Tony Aitken) because his previous incarnation was getting far too expensive. The regeneration was triggered when a Dalek-like monster shot him through his contract. The skit was set on the planet Chromakey 5 and also featured the Doctor's computerised companion, 'plastic-thing-that's-meant-to-look-like-a-dog'.

Other pastiches around this time were seen on *Emu's Broadcasting Company* and Spike Milligan's *Q6* – a classic 'Pakistani Dalek' sketch. Another example from the realms of TV, although this could hardly be classed as a bona fide pastiche, are the series of tongue-in-cheek futuristic commercials that Tom Baker and Lalla Ward made in 1979 for Prime Computers in Australia, wearing their original *Doctor Who* costumes – something they would never have been allowed to do in Britain!

Another notable *Doctor Who* parody of the period appeared not on TV but in print, in *Mad* magazine. Interestingly enough, although *Mad* originates from America, this was at a time when *Doctor Who* was almost entirely unknown in the States, only a few of the Jon Pertwee stories having been shown on PBS stations. Presumably, then, the *Doctor Ooh* feature that appeared in Issue 161 was for the British edition only.

Mad magazine regularly features accurately caricatured parodies of topical films and TV shows, well drawn but usually with somewhat leaden text. The five page *Doctor Ooh* spoof, written by Geoff Rowley, was no exception. Heavily based on *The Ark in Space*, it had characters similar to the fourth Doctor, Sarah Jane and Harry arriving in a remote, deserted spaceship where, as the Doctor puts it, 'a handful of the chosen few are hovering in suspended animation.'

The strip illustrations by Steve Parkhouse are well-observed, although they obviously owe much to stock photos of the regular cast and the sets used in *The Ark in Space*. What wit there is relies heavily on the well-known limitations of the show's budget – "Doctor! There's a plastic bag full of ping-pong balls crawling towards you!" – and the by-then-established characteristics of the regular cast (re-named Dr Ooh, Squarer and Hairy).

Squarer spends the entire strip snivelling and having her clothes removed, rather like Carol Cleveland in the *Scott of the Sahara* sketch from *Monty Python's Flying Circus*. Hairy is bold, forthright – and transformed, frame by frame, from naval surgeon into full blown, Robert Newton-style buccaneer. The bulk of the humour, though, relies on Tom Baker's scarf – which proves to be his undoing – and incidental appearances by everything from Cybermen to Peter Cushing. Devices that work well are Squarer being eventually reduced to a sniffle emanating from a Kleenex box, appearances by the first three Doctors, and a Dalek using its eyestick as a watering can!

Elsewhere, in the mass-market press, journalists were finding tags for the Doctor: 'the curly-haired Harpo Marx with his wide-eyed projection of the Doctor,' reported one newspaper in 1975; 'intellectual, eyeball-rolling,' said another in 1977.

All through Tom Baker's time as the Doctor, and even after he had left, the press headlined features about him with puns and wordplay such as: 'Who's next as 007?', 'Doc's dilemma', 'Who goes hairless', and 'Yo, ho Who!'. Baker loved to promote the show, and was interviewed many times on television, including on *Nationwide* and *Pebble Mill at One*, discussing his past and his approach to playing the Doctor. The coverage was certainly helped in the latter part of the Seventies by the start of Saturday morning kids TV shows, with Noel Edmonds's *Multi-Coloured Swap Shop* featuring many *Doctor Who* celebrities over the years. Other notable appearances included Tom Baker presenting *Disney Time* in August 1975. This was done in character as the Doctor; at the end of the show, he leaves saying that he must get up to Scotland in time to help the Brigadier – a direct link into *Terror of the Zygons*. There was a specially recorded trailer for the seventeenth season, in which the Doctor is awakened from sleep to hear a warning from the continuity announcer that he will be up against the Daleks again. After the announcer tells him to forget the warning, the Doctor returns to the TARDIS, placing a 'Do Not Disturb' sign on the door. Another in-character appearance was on Johnny Morris's *Animal Magic*, where the Doctor speaks about some of the animals and creatures he has met on his travels. This sequence was shot during the filming of *The Creature from the*

Pit, on the forest set at Ealing Film Studios, and the Doctor is seen wearing the portable stocks placed on him by Lady Adrasta.

At this time, *Doctor Who* had an especially large adult following, and the press interest reflected this. The press seemed to delight in asking Baker about his private life, and he seemed equally to delight in revealing very little to them, with the result that what little they did know (his failed marriage to Anna Wheatcroft, his romance with Lalla Ward) was pounced upon eagerly in practically every interview and feature about him.

Further proof of Baker's incredible popularity came when he started writing a regular column in a weekly newspaper, *Reveille*. The column ran for some nine months from March to November 1975, and was written in a chatty, friendly style, with a very broad range of subject matter. There were stories about Tom's fight against chicken bones that kept getting thrown into his front garden; faces in tree trunks; sponsorship of mountain rescue dogs; people with their heads stuck in pots; a visit to the zoo; Peter Pan; not talking to strangers; a dream in which Tom tap-dances in a London museum; and many, many more.

To give some idea of the scope and style of the writing, here are some examples.

'Last week, dressed as an Egyptian mummy, I bumped into 36 schoolchildren. We were filming in Berkshire. They seemed very intrigued, then nervous, then vastly amused. We finally had a picture taken. The next day, in regular costume, I went to the school. The children were delighted. They all looked so well and cheerful. During the conversation, which was mostly about monsters, the excitement grew and the children teased each other and boasted of fantasy exploits. One lad, all of five, said he liked nettle and snake soup. During a lull, I heard a six-year-old singing: "Whistle while you work, Hitler bought a shirt ..." "What's Hitler?" I asked him. "Oh, he was a German, nasty too," he replied. I wondered what programme he watched on television. Could it have been *Colditz*?' (6 June 1975)

'Trees have faces. You didn't know that? But you can find them if you just bother to look. Tree faces aren't like human ones – stuck at the top end and at the front. Sometimes they are halfway up, hidden under a branch. Often they are clown-like with big noses or funny staring eyes. So next time you go for a stroll in the park or through the woods, keep your eyes open and you should spot a few faces looking at you.' (27 June 1975)

'At rehearsal last week, the director asked me if I could do a double loop with my yo-yo. I said: "Of course, watch this." When I swung my yo-yo back it came and hit me between the eyes. Everybody was very amused – except me.' (7 November 1975)

The latter is one of a number of occasional anecdotes that were included about the making of *Doctor Who*, although these were usually very watered down – tending to concern encounters with children or animals while away filming on location.

Other notable press coverage was generated when the production office decided to get rid of K-9. A 'Save K-9' campaign was even waged through the pages of the *Sun* newspaper. This was the first of new producer John Nathan-Turner's many ways of getting additional press coverage for the series, and it worked a treat. The *Sun* had readers writing in with protest letters, and ran a follow up article featuring some of those who wrote in. There was even one girl who had written to the Queen on the subject, but the article did not reveal what her reply said.

Right up until the end of his era, the press followed the fourth Doctor, and when Baker finally hung up the famous hat and scarf and left, John Nathan-Turner, always keen to maximise publicity, arranged for him to 'let slip' that the next Doctor Who might not be played not by a man, but by a woman. This masterstroke ensured banner headlines the following day, as Baker was hounded by the press and TV for interviews. After all, he had played the Doctor for close on seven years, the longest continuous run of all the Doctors to date.

COMPANIONS

It was not only Tom Baker who was subject to the tender attentions of the press, but also the actors and actresses who portrayed his companions. During the tenure of the fourth Doctor, the press developed a near-obsession with the Doctor's travelling companions. No-one had ever made a secret of the fact that this mysterious man travelled with a succession of pretty young girls, but neither had anything been made of it. Throughout the Sixties, the press had reported when companions joined and left, but this had always been done in a serious, news-reporting style. Even in the early Seventies, there had been little fuss made when Caroline John (Liz Shaw) joined and left, and even Katy Manning (Jo Grant) was treated with some respect until her decision to reveal all in a set of nude photographs for a men's magazine called *Girl Illustrated*, the cover of which featured Katy with a Dalek.

All this was to change as, in line with general trends in the British tabloid press, reporting became less and less news and more and more sensationalism. When the 'good girl next door' Sarah Jane Smith decided to leave the Doctor and his new travelling companion was announced to be a half-naked savage girl played by the attractive Louise Jameson, reporters pounced on the story eagerly.

'Dr Who's tough new Lady' screamed one headline, accompanied by a press-call photograph of Leela on the set of *The Face of Evil*, brandishing a knife in a very aggressive pose. 'A cave girl with a killer touch' was the description given, and when Tom Baker was asked what he thought of his new assistant, he apparently said, 'You know the Doctor. He doesn't have a sex life.' One can only surmise that the question actually asked was rather different from the one that appeared in print. As usual, it was the *Sun* that made the most of the situation, going as far as to ask, on its TV pages, 'Is sex about to rear its irrepressible head in that most adult of children's shows, Dr Who? I'm getting worried about the Doctor's attitude to his new assistant, Leela (Louise Jameson). It does not fit the pattern.' The writer went to describe the first three Doctors' attitudes to their assistants, and ended: 'But the present Doctor, Tom Baker, is definitely on the dishy side. And while he was purely avuncular towards silly Sarah, he seems to see Leela in a different light. I'm sure I detect the stirrings of something sexual. Perhaps he is turned on by the wash-leather the strange little creature wears on her bum. But this being a children's show, there won't be any hanky panky, I presume. So will it be Dr and Mrs Who?'

After Leela, the next companion to join the Doctor was Romana, played in her first incarnation by Mary Tamm. The press were in their stride by now, and the standard headlines, such as 'Who's next' and 'Who's in Luck', all appeared. This time, the papers had even somehow got hold of several modelling shots of Ms Tamm, one with her hair blowing in the breeze, another with her hair pinned up, wearing classy clothes, holding classic modelling poses. These photographs were featured alongside stories claiming that glamour was boarding the TARDIS, and that as well as being glamorous, Romana was – gasp – intelligent. Obviously a concept that the papers found hard to take, as the introduction of Romana generated a lot of coverage along these lines.

Lalla Ward was the next companion, taking over the role of Romana from Mary Tamm. This time, the *Daily Express* saw fit to give a large centre-page spread to a round-up of all of the Doctor's 'sexy assistants', describing Lalla Ward as the latest 'teatime sex symbol' and encouraging readers to draw their own conclusion as to whether being Doctor Who's assistant was a passport to stardom or a one way hop to obscurity. At the time this article appeared (1979), only Jean Marsh (the first Doctor's short-lived companion Sara Kingdom) had gone on to greater things, and since then, only Louise Jameson, possibly the most stereotyped of all the female assistants in the press, has continued to carve out a high-profile acting career for herself through numerous roles in popular series.

Lalla Ward went on to hit the headlines again when she and Tom Baker announced plans to marry in 1980, apparently confirming to the tabloids that their suspicions had been correct all along and that there was hanky-panky in the TARDIS. The marriage lasted only sixteen months, and the break-up was again the subject of much press coverage.

Pretty much the same level of coverage occurred when Sarah Sutton and Janet Fielding were announced as joining the TARDIS crew towards the end of Tom Baker's tenure. In Fielding's case, the situation was similar to that in Mary Tamm's, in that the papers got hold of some glamorous photographs and ran those, presumably in preference to the BBC supplied photographs.

During the seven years in which Tom Baker played the Doctor, the role of the assistant had been redefined by the popular press, from being a simple acting role, to that of some sexy bimbette cavorting through time with the eligible and desirable Doctor. Certainly in the eyes of the press, *Doctor Who* was no longer an educational tea time series for children and adults alike, but a light-hearted space series, aimed firmly at kids, but with a pretty girl on board to keep the dads interested.

OVERSEAS

Doctor Who had been sold outside the UK since shortly after it started in 1963, but at the time Tom Baker took over the lead role, all that viewers in the USA had seen were occasional re-runs of a range of thirteen Jon Pertwee stories from *Doctor Who and the Silurians* to *The Time Monster*. These were not particularly well received, despite a fair amount of trade advertising, and it wasn't until 1977 that the BBC decided to sell, through its overseas agent Time Life, a new package of Tom Baker stories to that market. This amounted to ninety-eight episodes featuring the fourth Doctor, perceived by the BBC as being marketable as his Doctor was far more eccentric than the serious Pertwee image, and the American market tended to favour eccentrics. In February 1978, there was a press call to announce that the package of episodes was available. Photos were taken showing the Doctor and a variety of alien monsters supposedly waiting for visas outside the American Embassy in London.

What the American audience were faced with when *Doctor Who* Tom Baker-style first hit their screens was a very doctored and Americanised version. For a start, all the episodes had been given a new voice-over introduction by veteran actor Howard da Silva, which often blotted out dialogue to tell the viewers what they already knew or to give away vital plot twists before they were revealed in the story.

Other changes included the addition of a montage of clips from the forthcoming serial at the start of each part one, and a 'next episode' trailer at the end of all bar the final episode of a story – again with narration from da Silva. As the running time had to be around half an hour (including three commercial breaks and all the montages listed above) the actual episodes themselves were also trimmed down to ensure that they didn't overrun.

To give an example of the style of introductory voice-over, the opening episode of *Robot* was accompanied by Mr da Silva saying: 'Doctor Who's face is transformed as his friends watch – instant plastic surgery. But the change goes more than skin deep. The Time Lord, on the brink of death, is inducing a complete physical metamorphosis ... Recently returned from a distant planet where he was exposed to deadly radioactivity, Doctor Who enters into his fourth incarnation, thus saving his own life. But his new personality is still erratic and in transition, so the Brigadier has no alternative but to place him in the hands of a mere Earth doctor.'

Another example, which shows how inaccurate the voice-overs could sometimes be, is from *Revenge of the Cybermen*, where 'The Cyberscheme unfolds as a plot to take over the galaxy, but the metal men can succeed only if they regain control of their home planet in order to blow it up. Its core is of pure gold, alluring to human kind but fatal to Cybermen.'

Doctor Who was seen in this form via the Public Broadcasting Service (PBS) stations in America for many years, and despite the detrimental impact on the stories, it quickly became a cult favourite, thanks in part to almost continuous transmission of the stories. Eventually Lionheart, the successor to Time Life, distributed *Doctor Who* in its original, unadulterated episodic form, and also as movie-length story compilations. Fan groups sprung up all over the country, and Tom Baker was being hailed by science fiction writer Harlan Ellison in his introduction to a range of *Doctor Who* novelations published by Pinnacle in 1979 and 1980 as: 'The one and only, the incomparable, the bemusing and bewildering Doctor Who, the humanistic defender of Good and Truth whose exploits put to shame those of Kimball Kinnison, Captain Future and pantywaist nerds like Han Solo and Luke Skywalker. My hero! Doctor Who!'

Tom Baker made his first appearance at a fan convention in America in 1979 when the cancellation of *Shada* meant that both he and producer Graham Williams were free to attend. The event did extraordinarily well, and even after he had finished playing the Doctor on television, Baker remained in great demand to attend further American events. Because of the importance of the American sales to the BBC, Williams' successor, John Nathan-Turner, encouraged this attention, and even arranged whole plane-loads of guests to travel out to attend the events. The same attention was not given to Britain, and fan conventions in this country often lost out, as the British organisers simply did not have the cash to compete with the fees offered by their American counterparts. While *Doctor Who* fandom was at its peak, British fans could forget about any reunion of Doctors in this country – every anniversary, all the actors were in America; and Troughton and Baker, along with some of the companions, were not keen to attend British events anyway.

Meanwhile, in Australia, where *Doctor Who* had been screened since 1965 by the Australian Broadcasting Commission (ABC), Tom Baker's debut season coincided with an attempt by the ABC to stop screening the show as the ratings were poor. Australian fans didn't think much of this, and lobbied the ABC to continue with the show. Luckily they got their wish, and also got a fan organisation, the Australasian *Doctor Who* Fan Club, which was created as a means to get the programme back on the air.

One of the problems *Doctor Who* has had to contend with outside its home territory are stricter rules governing what can be shown at particular times of the day. In Australia, adventures like *The Deadly Assassin* and *The Brain of Morbius* were rated as being for an adult audience, and deemed unsuitable for transmission in a 6.00 pm time slot, while others were edited to remove any material that the Australian general public might have found offensive – for example, two sequences from *The Talons of Weng-Chiang* were cut: one in part three when the giant rat appears to bite Leela, and the other in part four when the rat appears to bite Chang.

NEW ZEALAND
By Paul Scoones

The first three Tom Baker stories were initially aired on Saturday evenings at 6.30 pm on the second television channel, South Pacific Television (SPTV), from 4 February to 8 April 1978. The stories were screened in production order, so *The Sontaran Experiment* preceded *The Ark in Space*.

After a gap of four months the series resumed with *Revenge of the Cybermen* through to *Pyramids of Mars* from 12 August to 25 November 1978. *Genesis of the Daleks* was not screened, and the stories were again aired in production order, so *Pyramids of Mars* preceded *Planet of Evil*. The series again screened on Saturdays on SPTV, but at the earlier time of 4.30 pm.

After a month long break, the series returned on Fridays at 6.30 pm on SPTV, with *The Android Invasion*, screened from 29 December 1978 to 19 January 1979. *The Green Death* followed this, which was one of many stories that had been omitted in the initial run of Jon Pertwee stories.

The series resumed several months later with *The Brain of Morbius* screened from 12 May 1979. SPTV screened every story, in order, up to *The Invisible Enemy* except for *Horror of Fang Rock*, which was omitted. The episodes were once again on Saturdays, but at the earlier time of around 4 pm, though advertised start times varied from week to week, from 3 pm to 4.10 pm.

On 18 February 1980, following a major revamp of the schedules, and a channel name change from SPTV to Television Two, the series moved to Monday evenings at the regular time of 6 pm. *Image of the Fendahl* was the first story screened in this new timeslot, followed by *Underworld*. Both *The Sun Makers* and *The Invasion of Time* were omitted. All six Season Sixteen stories were screened in their correct order, however the first three stories of Season Seventeen were then screened in production order so viewers saw

The Creature from the Pit, followed by *City of Death* and then *Destiny of the Daleks*. *Nightmare of Eden* and *The Horns of Nimon* screened in January and February 1981, after which the series went off air for four weeks.

Season Eighteen was acquired by Television New Zealand between 12 March 1981 (for *The Leisure Hive*) and 12 April 1981 (for *Logopolis*). Tom Baker's final season was launched on a new day, channel and timeslot. From 23 March 1981 the series aired on Tuesdays on Television One with an earlier start-time of around 5.30 pm. Most of Season Eighteen was screened in this position, but came to a premature end on 1 September 1981 with the final episode of *The Keeper of Traken*. At this point, New Zealand was just one story short of catching up to the UK, but viewers were then left waiting for just over a year to see *Logopolis*, which finally screened from 20 September to 18 October 1982, with a week off midway through the story to accommodate Commonwealth Games coverage, on the same channel, day and timeslot as the rest of Season Eighteen. TVNZ had held on to *Logopolis* for a year, and their rights to screen Season Eighteen episodes expired 31 March 1983.

The first repeats of the Tom Baker era took place several years later. Following on from a run of Jon Pertwee stories, *Robot* was screened from 30 December 1986, marking the beginning of a run of the entire Tom Baker era, including *Genesis of the Daleks, Horror of Fang Rock, The Sun Makers* and *The Invasion of Time* which had all been omitted during the initial screenings of the Tom Baker stories. *Genesis of the Daleks* was screened out of sequence in May-June 1987, located between *The Seeds of Doom* and *Masque of Mandragora*, but otherwise the stories were transmitted in the correct sequence. The episodes were initially broadcast on TV1, twice a week on Tuesdays and Wednesdays at around 5.30 pm. In February 1987, midway through *Revenge of the Cybermen*, the series moved from TV1 to TV2 but otherwise continued unchanged. In December 1987, *The Ribos Operation* was screened as two double-length episodes from 5 pm. For the last two stories of Tom Baker's era, the series moved to Thursdays and Fridays, and *Logopolis* ended on 19 August 1988. The episodes screened at this time were supplied by the Australian Broadcasting Corporation and consequently in many cases exhibited cuts that had been made by the Australian censor.

Viewer ratings for the 1986-88 period reveal that *The Hand of Fear* Part Four, with a rating of 18.5% (of the potential viewing audience) was the Tom Baker episode with the most viewers, and this episode was placed 45th on the top 50 most watched programmes chart in the first week of July 1987. Part Three of *Horror of Fang Rock*, seen by 15% and charting in 49th position for the third week of September 1987, was second equal with *The Hand of Fear* Part Three. The five top rating stories were: *The Hand of Fear* (14.1%), *The Robots of Death* (13.4%), *The Deadly Assassin* (12.4%), *Horror of Fang Rock* (11.3%) and *The Face of Evil* (10.9%). The time of year would appear to have had an influence on the viewer ratings, with all of the top-rated episodes screened during New Zealand's winter months when television viewing figures are typically higher than in warmer months and correspondingly the lowest rated episodes – including *The Stones of Blood* Part Two (3%), *The Ark in Space* Part Three, *Robot* Parts Three and Four (all 4%) and *The Invasion of Time* Part Six (4.5%) – all screened in December and January, which is New Zealand's summertime.

A further run of Tom Baker era repeats commenced on 9 February 2001 with *Robot*, following on directly from a run of all complete Hartnell, Troughton and Pertwee stories on the UHF and satellite digital channel, Prime Television. The Tom Baker episodes were screened six days a week (Sunday to Friday). Initially two episodes were played each day back-to-back at 6 pm, running until *The Sun Makers* Part One & Two on Friday 30 March 2001. Thereafter the schedule changed to single episodes at 6 pm from *The Sun Makers* Part Three on Sunday 1 April 2001. The run ended with *The Horns of Nimon* Part Four on Thursday 7 June 2001. For the first time on New Zealand television, all of the stories from Seasons Twelve to Seventeen were played in the correct sequence. Prime planned to resume the series with *The Leisure Hive* from Monday 7 January 2002 but around this time the channel changed owners and a major change to the schedules meant that *Doctor Who* was dropped from Prime's programme line-up.

FANDOM

The BBC had for many years acknowledged that *Doctor Who* had a fan following, and the first fan club had been set up and run in 1965 as the William (*Doctor Who*) Hartnell Fan Club. This had survived, following a change of name and several changes of organisers, into the Seventies, but had then folded.

The BBC continued to cater to the wide-ranging interest in the series with numerous competitions, normally of the 'draw a monster' type, with first prize being a trip to the BBC to see *Doctor Who* being made. There seemed to be many of these competitions, with visits made to the sets of *The Masque of Mandragora*, *The Deadly Assassin*, *The Face of Evil* and *The Stones of Blood*. Fans too were invited along to watch the proceedings (usually from the studio gallery, but occasionally from the studio floor), and news of forthcoming stories became much easier to obtain when some fans started working for the BBC and therefore had almost unrestricted access to the observation galleries and other areas of the production process, depending on where in the Corporation they were working – some even worked on *Doctor Who* itself. When John Nathan-Turner arrived as producer in 1980, he was concerned about the fan 'grapevine' and started taking steps to withhold information, leading to his closing the public viewing galleries and stepping up studio security, as well as logging in and out all the copies of the scripts each day when particularly newsworthy stories were being recorded. *Logopolis* was the first story on which the galleries were closed in an attempt to keep the fans away, and to keep the circumstances of the Doctor's regeneration secret.

Backtracking to 1976, this year saw the establishment of probably the most effective, and certainly the best-run, *Doctor Who* fan group in Britain. The *Doctor Who* Appreciation Society began life as a group at Westfield College in London, but the organisers soon realised that there was a potential wider appeal to be had, and so opened their doors to the rest of the country.

From mid-1976, the Society provided a monthly newsletter (*Celestial Toyroom*) and a magazine (*TARDIS*, which had actually been instigated earlier and was adopted as the Society's publication from issue 7) as well as pooling the respective resources of a number of fans to provide various departments like Reference, Art, Fiction, Photographic, and so on.

Those who ran the DWAS were given information about the stories in production, which was relayed to the members via the newsletter. They were also supported in other ways by the BBC, who generally helped with any photographs, interviews and information the group wanted. When producer Graham Williams commented that they ought to check into clearing the copyrights on what they were doing, they did so and were able to negotiate a deal with the BBC for the reproduction and sale of photos to the Society members. When K-9 was announced as joining the TARDIS crew, Williams was careful to maintain the secret, and would not allow photographs or information out. The Society, however, managed to obtain a photograph, and arranged for an artwork rendition of it to be used on the cover of *TARDIS* to coincide with the transmission of *The Invisible Enemy*. Williams never asked how the Society came by the information, but this incident helped to show the production team that the Society could be trusted to keep secrets. The DWAS was also asked to provide assistance with putting together the first ever *Doctor Who* documentary in 1977, a *The Lively Arts* production presented by Melvyn Bragg and called *Whose Doctor Who*.

The DWAS also organised the world's first *Doctor Who* convention, held on 6 August 1977 at a church hall in Battersea, south London, and it has followed this up with numerous events – almost one a year – ever since.

The original organisers of DWAS decided, almost unanimously, to throw in the towel at the end of 1979, and it was left to a handful of other fans, who had joined the Society and had helped out with the organisation in one way or another, to pick up the pieces and restructure the fan club for the Eighties. The fact that the DWAS has survived to date and is still going strong is down to the hard work and dedication of all the people who have helped in its organisation and running over the years.

The DWAS was not the only British fan group operating, but it was by far the biggest. Perhaps next in line, certainly as far as enthusiasm went, were the Friends of Tom Baker, or FOTB for short.

The FOTB was formed in 1976 as a focus for fans of, naturally enough, Tom Baker, and published a bi-monthly newsletter that contained a multi-part interview with the actor, reports from watching the recording of *The Hand of Fear* and *The Face of Evil*, news, reviews, items on Baker's other roles, transcripts of interviews with Baker from television, and really anything and everything to do with him, including some FOTB members' breathless accounts of fleeting meetings with their idol.

There was also some poetry, and even Baker's horoscope appeared, painstakingly worked out by one of the group's members. It is quite apparent, looking back at the newsletter, that the FOTB's predominantly female membership were far more besotted with Tom Baker as a person than interested in any of the roles he had played, and the mix of material tended to reflect this.

It was not only Tom Baker who attracted fans; Elisabeth Sladen, who played Sarah Jane Smith, also had her own fan club called the Elisabeth Sladen Friendship League (ESFL). This club was launched in October 1976, and it too produced a newsletter very similar in format to the FOTB one but lacking the personal 'trembly-kneed' descriptions of encounters with the members' heroine. One disappointing thing for the ESFL was that in their first issue, they had to announce that Sarah Jane Smith was leaving *Doctor Who*. This did not daunt them too much, however, and the newsletter continued regardless. It certainly looks today as though the ESFL was run more out of sheer enthusiasm than anything else, and much of the news and comment contained within the newsletters is of a superficial, rather than informative, nature.

MERCHANDISE

Even before the twelfth season started, there was interest from the merchandisers. It takes anything from six months to several years to get a new product off the ground, and as there were several fourth Doctor-related items on sale in late 1974, early 1975, one can only surmise that the interest had been there almost as soon as Jon Pertwee hung up his cloak.

These early items included a set of photographic jigsaws, the photographs taken during location recording for *Robot*; a series of painting by numbers kits featuring the fourth Doctor; and a set of four pencil sharpeners.

As the Seventies progressed, so more and more merchandise was produced by manufacturers eager to tie their products into the series, and into its star. The Daleks had been supplanted by the Doctor, and although there were a few Dalek items available, the vast majority used other aspects of the series as well.

The *Doctor Who* novelisations published by Target books (an imprint of Universal-Tandem initially in 1975, then of Wyndham Publications, and finally of W H Allen) still formed the backbone of *Doctor Who* merchandising, and with the adventures of the fourth Doctor being novelised, starting with *Robot* in 1975, Tom Baker undertook a great many country-wide signing tours, promoting both the books and the series. As well as the shops, these tours took in schools and hospitals. Baker was often reported in newspapers as being incredibly touched and moved by some of the children he had seen, and he regarded it as part of his job as the Doctor to try to bring a little happiness and wonder into their lives.

As well as the novelisations, there were a great many other books published. World Distributors continued with their *Doctor Who* Annual, and also published a *Terry Nation's Dalek Annual* for four consecutive years. In 1976, Target released an updated version of Terrance Dicks's and Malcolm Hulke's *The Making of Doctor Who* and published the *Doctor Who Dinosaur Book*. Then, the following year, they explored other avenues with a series of titles under the *Doctor Who Discovers ...* banner. They released a second *Doctor Who Monster Book* (1977), two *Junior Doctor Who* books (1980), a *Doctor Who Quiz Book* (1981) and *The Doctor Who Programme Guide* (1981). From other publishers came *Doctor Who and the Daleks Omnibus* (Artus 1976); two Dalek activity books (Childrens Leisure Products 1978); *A Day With A TV Producer* (Wayland 1980), which looked at the making of *The Leisure Hive* in the company of producer John Nathan-Turner; and four titles for young children featuring K-9 (Sparrow 1980).

Aside from the books, many other items were produced. These included a fourth Doctor scarf (Today Promotions 1976), *Doctor Who* underpants (BHS 1981), milk chocolate bars (Nestlé 1975), Candy Favourites (Goodies 1979), two poster magazines (Legend 1975 and Harpdown 1976 respectively), numerous free promotions – including two with Weetabix breakfast cereal (free stand up cardboard figures), and one with Ty-phoo tea (a set of twelve cards to collect, plus a poster and hard backed annual-type book to send away for). There were several records, including a new *Doctor Who* adventure, *The Pescatons* (1976), starring Tom Baker and Elisabeth Sladen; a *Doctor Who Sound Effects* album (1978); a *Genesis of the Daleks* soundtrack album (1979); and several versions of the theme music, one of which – *Doctor Who* by Mankind – even got into the pop charts in 1978. There was bubble bath (Water Margin 1976); colour-in posters (Salter 1978); greetings cards (DAP 1979); a fourth Doctor costume and mask (Berwicks 1976); transfers (Letraset 1976); jigsaws (Whitman 1977/78, World Distributors 1979); bagatelle (Playtime 1978); TARDIS tin (1980); Viewmaster slides for the story

THE FOURTH DOCTOR

Full Circle (GAF 1980); two board games, *Doctor Who* and *War of the Daleks* (both Strawberry Fayre 1975); a talking Dalek (Palitoy 1975); and a range of Action Man-like figures of the Doctor, Leela, the Giant Robot, a Cyberman, a Dalek and the TARDIS (all in 1976) and K-9 (in 1978).

This burgeoning of interest in both the series and its star continued into the Eighties, providing a media boost to the show, something it had been looking for since the Daleks took off in the Sixties.

RATINGS

Part of the success of any television programme depends on the ratings it receives. It is always dangerous to draw conclusions about a programme's popularity from its ratings alone, as there are many different reasons why these can fluctuate. What the weather was like can affect them, as can the time of year, what was on the other channels at the same time, and the pulling-power of other programmes placed before and after it in the schedule. In some cases, other channels might even have been blacked out by a strike, as was the case during the ITV strikes of the late Seventies.

In the case of *Doctor* Who during the fourth Doctor's era, stories from the first three seasons mostly received over ten million viewers on average; then, for the next three seasons, the ratings dropped slightly, while still remaining generally high; then for the final, eighteenth season, a dramatic drop was seen.

The stories at the top of the pile, *City of Death* and *Destiny of the Daleks*, were both transmitted during the ITV strike between August and October 1979. Those of the eighteenth season, by contrast, were up against ITV's offering of a glitzy new space series from America, *Buck Rogers in the 25th Century*. The latter season was also relegated to a 5.20 pm time slot, earlier than that of the more successful stories of the thirteenth and fourteenth seasons, which had tended to start transmission at around 5.45 pm for the thirteenth season and after six o'clock for the fourteenth.

In terms of *Doctor Who*'s popularity relative to other TV programmes at the time, it leaped about a great deal. The highest placed episode in the weekly TV chart was part two of *The Ark in Space*, which came in fifth, with parts two, three and four of *The Deadly Assassin* next at positions 11, 12 and 12 respectively. The lowest placed was part two of *Full Circle*, which was almost at the bottom of the barrel at position 170, with part three of *State of Decay* at 145th and part two of *Meglos* at 139th.

As previously stated, it is very difficult to draw firm conclusions from ratings, but it certainly seems that during his seven year run as the Doctor, Tom Baker took *Doctor Who* from being one of the top rated programmes, with over 12 million viewers, to one struggling near the bottom of the pile, with around 5 million. The reasons for this appear to be an amalgam of poor scheduling on the part of the BBC, an entertaining American import series showing on ITV at the same time, and perhaps even a general public who were beginning to tire of Tom Baker as the Doctor.

**TOP TEN RATED FOURTH DOCTOR STORIES
IN ORDER OF AVERAGE VIEWING FIGURES
(Figures in millions of viewers)**

1	*City of Death*	14.5
2	*Destiny of the Daleks*	13.5
3	*The Robots of Death*	12.7
4	*The Deadly Assassin*	12.2
5	*The Android Invasion*	11.68
6	*The Face of Evil*	11.2
7	*The Ark in Space*	11.1
8	*The Hand of Fear*	10.95
9	*The Seeds of Doom*	10.9
10	*The Sontaran Experiment*	10.75

**BOTTOM TEN RATED FOURTH DOCTOR STORIES
IN ORDER OF AVERAGE VIEWING FIGURES
(Figures in millions of viewers)**

41	*Meglos*	4.65
40	*The Leisure Hive*	5.1
39	*State of Decay*	5.2
38	*Full Circle*	5.25
37	*The Keeper of Traken*	6.25
36	*Logopolis*	6.7
35	*Warriors' Gate*	7.5
34	*Terror of the Zygons*	7.5
33	*Image of the Fendahl*	7.8
32	*The Invisible Enemy*	7.9

THE FIFTH DOCTOR

David J Howe
Stephen James Walker

Foreword

Television is a medium that seemingly delights in giving people their fifteen minutes of fame. Its very nature is rooted in change, and as the months pass, so new programmes are made and presented, and new stars are born. Some of these shows and individuals go on to win enduring popularity, but far more are never heard of nor seen again.

Since the end of 1974, there had been a single constant for *Doctor Who* viewers across the country: Tom Baker *was* the Doctor.

It had been a period during which the BBC had arguably enjoyed more success with *Doctor Who* than ever before. The ratings had soared to an all-time-high – higher even than in the heyday of the Daleks in the mid-Sixties. The distinctive image of the Doctor – incredibly long, multicoloured scarf, floppy felt hat, bulging eyes, tangled curly brown hair and an engaging and disarming smile – was firmly entrenched in the public's consciousness.

Now, however, after some seven long years in the series, Baker was moving on and a new actor had been chosen to take on the lead role. All those who had watched, enjoyed and indeed grown up with Baker as the Doctor must surely have experienced more than a twinge of sadness at the closing moments of *Logopolis*, the fourth Doctor's final regular story. This truly was the end of an era.

The man chosen to succeed Baker was Peter Davison – an actor totally dissimilar in appearance and temperament. This was nothing new for the series, as each of the previous three Doctors had presented a marked contrast to his own predecessor: Baker's image had been very different from Jon Pertwee's; Pertwee's had been very different from Patrick Troughton's; and Troughton's had been very different from William Hartnell's. There was however a major distinction on this occasion in that Davison, unlike the others, was already very well known to television viewers when he joined *Doctor Who*, principally from his role as Tristan Farnon in the BBC's veterinary series *All Creatures Great and Small*.

This was by no means the only innovation to occur at this time. Davison's era as the Doctor in fact coincided with a significant change of direction for *Doctor Who*, as new producer John Nathan-Turner proceeded to stamp his mark on it. The 20th anniversary was also looming, and the series was taking off in a big way in America. Fandom, too, was becoming increasingly well-organised and sophisticated, and the *Doctor Who* Appreciation Society

THE FIFTH DOCTOR

was losing its virtual monopoly on major conventions and other activities.

Elsewhere in the news, Freddie Laker's airline business fell into a state of collapse; Argentina attempted to reclaim the Falkland Islands, provoking a brief war between that country and Britain; Michael Fagan popped into the Queen's bedroom for a chat with the monarch; the *Mary Rose* was raised from the sea bed; long-time Soviet leader Leonid Brezhnev died and was succeeded by Yuri Andropov, who also died just 15 months later to be replaced by Mikhail Gorbachev; and Stephen Spielberg unveiled his new blockbuster film *ET*.

It was against this backdrop, and the increasing freedom that technological advances like digital processing, fibre optics and microchips brought to television production, that *Doctor Who* marched boldly into the Eighties.

Peter Davison brought a fresh charm to *Doctor Who*. His Doctor was an innocent lost in space and time; an elder brother figure intent on righting wrongs and, if at all possible, getting in a good game of cricket too. His era saw him coming up against a wide variety of foes, both new and old, and travelling with a succession of companions – namely Adric, Nyssa, Tegan, Turlough, Kamelion and Peri. It also saw the series making a successful start to the 1980s, despite a number of factors that were not in its favour, and introducing a new generation to the wonders of the *Doctor Who* universe.

Join us as we revisit the era of the fifth Doctor.

Peter Davison
In His Own Words

ON HIS EARLY ACTING CAREER:

'It's a wonderful thing; you don't actually have to do any exams to go to drama school, and all you get at the end is a useless piece of paper which says you have been there! You don't do a degree, you simply graduate from it, and then it's up to you.

'The first part I got after leaving drama school in July 1972 was in *Love's Labour's Lost* at the Nottingham Play House. I had one line, which changes the whole play, but I can't remember it now.'

Interviewed by Andrew M Smith on 30 August 1983 for *The Cloister Chamber*, **published in October 1983.**

ON HIS ROLE AS TRISTAN FARNON IN
ALL CREATURES GREAT AND SMALL:

'Playing Tristan was a very interesting time for me. I know it's been said to me, so it's obviously in print somewhere, that I think Tristan was the nearest I've ever played to myself, but when I first got the part, I thought I was totally unsuitable for it.

'It sounds a terrible thing to say, but it also helped my role that Christopher Timothy walked in front of a car one Christmas and broke his leg. He couldn't move anywhere for about three months, and that meant that a lot of scenes that should have been Robert Hardy and Christopher Timothy became Robert Hardy and me. So that built the character of Tristan up and did me a lot of good. Poor old Chris.'

Interviewed by Stephen Collins in April 1983 for *Zerinza: The Australasian Doctor Who Fanzine* **Issue 30/31, published in August 1983.**

THE FIFTH DOCTOR

ON HIS ROLE AS DISH OF THE DAY IN THE TV VERSION OF *THE HITCH-HIKER'S GUIDE TO THE GALAXY*:

'My wife, Sandra Dickinson, was doing the series as Trillian, and when they were looking for someone to play the Dish, she suggested me.'

Interviewed by David Hirsch for *Starlog* Issue 62, published in September 1982.

'It involved going down to the Visual Effects Department and having a bucket of dental plaster poured over my head. They let me have a straw in my mouth so that I could breathe! This plaster gave them a "face" to work with, so they went away and made the model around it. I didn't initially know what voice to use, but we had the actor Dave Prowse, who speaks with a wonderful West Country accent, in the same episode playing Hot Black Desiato's bodyguard. Suddenly I latched onto this wonderful sound, and it sort of came out like that.'

Interviewed by Stephen Collins in April 1983 for *Zerinza: The Australasian Doctor Who Fanzine* Issue 30/31, published in August 1983.

ON HIS ROLE AS ELMER IN *THE TOMORROW PEOPLE*:

'It was a fairly silly programme. Very definitely a *children's* programme. I played a space cowboy in a blond wig. My wife, Sandra Dickinson, was in it, too.'

Interviewed by Ben Landman in 1985 for *Starlog* Issue 102, published in January 1986.

'I suppose it was ITV's answer to *Doctor Who*, really, except they tried to get children to relate to it by having children in it, and children are usually terrible actors.
    'I don't know if you saw it, but the story we did was not terribly popular with children because we sent the whole thing up. I remember we had this terrible talking ceiling, and I reached up and tickled it and it let out this booming "Ho-ho-ho"!'

Interviewed by Terry and Andy Kerr for *Skonnos* Issue 10, published in March 1985.

PETER DAVISON – IN HIS OWN WORDS

ON BEING CAST AS THE DOCTOR:

'John Nathan-Turner rang me up one Saturday night and told me that Tom Baker was leaving *Doctor Who*, which I didn't know, and I didn't know why he was telling me that. And then he went on to say, "How would you feel about being the next Doctor?" Well, there was a sort of stunned silence. I didn't know what to say. So I told him to ring me back the next night. I spent 24 hours thinking about it; and also asking close friends, or people whose opinion I respected, what I should do. Then he rang me back, and I still really hadn't made any sort of decision, so he asked me to lunch the following week to discuss it.'

Interviewed by Stephen Collins in April 1983 for *Zerinza: The Australasian Doctor Who Fanzine* Issue 30/31, published in August 1983.

ON FOLLOWING TOM BAKER AS THE DOCTOR:

'Of course I was daunted to be following Tom Baker. It didn't hit me until I sat down and tried to rationalize it. Tom had played the part for seven years and that, I figured, meant that no child under the age of 10 in Britain would ever have known a Doctor other than his. That was one factor. And because he was *so* identified with the role, one tended to forget – even though I had watched *Doctor Who* from the age of 12 – one sort of forgot about the other ones. It wasn't until I sat down and thought that William Hartnell had played it for three years, Patrick Troughton for three years and Jon Pertwee for five, that I saw myself in that context and was able to rationalize it. But it certainly did worry me, yes.

Interviewed by Stephen Collins in April 1983 for *Zerinza: The Australasian Doctor Who Fanzine* Issue 30/31, published in August 1983.

ON RECORDING THE REGENERATION SCENE FOR *LOGOPOLIS*:

'It took about four and a half minutes! It was meant to take much longer than that, but we ran out of time. I had to lie in shot with white goo in my hair. Then I was thrown into the Make-up Department, my hair washed, and given make-up. Then I was put onto the set and told to sit up and smile!'

Interviewed by Ian Atkins for *Wholook* Issue 2, published in April 1986.

THE FIFTH DOCTOR

ON HIS DOCTOR'S COSTUME:

'It seemed to me that in some respects the Doctor is essentially English. So what could be more English than a cricket sweater and a pair of striped trousers like those worn by Victorian cricketers?'

Quoted by Peter Haining in *Doctor Who - A Celebration*, published in 1983.

ON HIS CHARACTERIZATION OF THE DOCTOR:

'Any similarities between my characterisation and Patrick Troughton's have never been deliberate. I would say it has more to do with the fact that I am younger than any of the others. I felt, in a way, I had to be more fallible, because I didn't want to play him as a hero as such - like, dare I say it, a Buck Rogers type figure. I was never pushed towards this, but the implication always is that if you get someone younger to play a lead part like that, you tend to try to make him dashing. I felt he should be a sort of anti-hero - not evil so much, but someone who doesn't go about things in the way a normal hero would.'

Interviewed by Jeremy Bentham for *Doctor Who Monthly Summer Special*, published in June 1982.

'I wouldn't say so much that I'd tried to change the role, but maybe I am now getting closer to what I had originally intended. It's always a dichotomy between what you set out to do and what actually comes over, until you find ways in which to play it to your satisfaction. So I don't think my idea of the character has materially changed, but the way in which it is coming over may certainly have done. Because as you gain confidence and knowledge about the part, you get closer to your ambitions.

'I haven't really explored the character to any great extent at the moment. One season, although it seems long when you set out on it, actually is fairly short as far as making the part your own is concerned. So I feel I'm still only on the surface of it to a large extent. I haven't quite decided in my own head yet how the Doctor's mind works. At certain times I can see the line straight through him and know what I'm doing, but at certain other times you rather have to bluff your way through, because you haven't quite got his thinking worked out. After all, it is such a complex character in relation to any other character you might be asked to play, you do have to start from scratch. So I just find things in different stories, and I say to myself, "I could have done that in the last story, and maybe I'll bring it out a bit more from now on."

'Scripts are always changed slightly in rehearsal – especially in a thing like this, which is written by scriptwriters for a character that is in a long-running programme. I don't insist on any radical changes in which I say, "I think we have to change this otherwise I'm not going to do it." It's very much a case of working through and then you say, "I don't like *this* line. I find it a bit awkward. I think it might be better if it was said this way."

'It depends on how much you believe the actor knows best ... Tom Baker did the Doctor for seven years and by that time he really did know the character inside out. However, when you've been doing it for only eight months or so, you still rely very heavily on the back-up from those more involved with the paraphernalia of *Doctor Who*, who were there before me.'

Interviewed by Jeremy Bentham for *Doctor Who Monthly Summer Special*, published in June 1982.

'In the episodes made before *Castrovalva*, I used a technique of playing so blandly that afterward it can be interpreted as being part of whatever aspect you end up doing.'

Interviewed by Gary Russell and David Saunders in June 1982 for *TARDIS* Volume 7 Issue 3, published in July 1982.

'My Doctor does lose his temper sometimes, but so did the early ones. William Hartnell's certainly did. That's really where I picked it up from. Also, I suppose it was initially a thing to counteract the fact that I was much younger. I think I might have dived in a bit with the losing the temper in the first few stories, simply because I did not want to come over as the sort of jolly ex-public school boy – which I'm not, as it happens. When I was looking at how to play the character, I wanted to pick up pointers from the other Doctors. Also, the companions I was with were rather frustrating, in terms of the story, so it was nice to bring that element into it. Probably, looking back on it, I slightly overdid that bit of it, but when you start off, you're not sure how you're going to do it, so you gradually have to work through it.'

Interviewed by Andrew M Smith on 30 August 1983 for *The Cloister Chamber*, published in October 1983.

'Performance wise, I was never very happy with the second season. I think it got just a bit dull, and the stories a bit over-complex. I didn't feel that I had a lot of room to embellish the character, and I think this is definitely one of the inherent dangers of doing *Doctor Who* – the writers tend to latch onto your first portrayal of the part and stick with that. For me, that presented too limited a challenge. On the other hand, I think there was a conscious effort made during the third season to do something about that, which is why I felt happy about going out on top – or at least at a peak.'

Interviewed by Richard Marson for *Doctor Who Magazine* Issue 106, published in November 1985.

'When I first took on *Doctor Who*, I did a terrible interview on *Pebble Mill at One*, with young children suggesting how I ought to play the part, and one little boy said, "I think you should be like Tristan, but brave". If they want to view my Doctor that way, or Campion as Tristan with funny glasses, in a way that's OK. To me, they're very different parts, requiring very different approaches from me. Fortunately, I started off in a very endearing part as Tristan, but it didn't get me stuck with just that role.'

Interviewed by Graeme Wood, Mark Wyman and Gary Russell for *TV Zone* Issue 16, published in March 1991.

ON THE DOCTOR'S COMPANIONS:

'I didn't think Janet Fielding's character worked, which is nothing against Janet, who thought maybe I did have something against her! We actually got on very well, but I don't think that kind of aggressive person, who's always getting at the Doctor, works. I think there's got to be a feeling that they're on the same side. OK, the companion gets fed up with the Doctor when he doesn't do something right, but they're basically on the same side. With Janet's character and with Turlough, I think you came very close to having two companions who very definitely weren't. I think that was a frustration for Mark Strickson, too; he couldn't do anything.'

Interviewed by Richard Marson for *Doctor Who Magazine* Issue 134, published in March 1988.

'The character relationships were worked out in rehearsal. The Tegan character was meant to be abrasive and a little pissed off at things, not to put too fine a point on it. I think actually the best companions are the ones who scream and say, "Help me! Help me!" There is a danger that if you give the companions too many personal problems, it becomes a bit like soap opera.

'Turlough started off well. John Nathan-Turner is a very good ideas man, and promised Mark Strickson a part with a little more meat to it. Mark was very intrigued with Turlough, but, as it turned out, they kept locking him up so he could do no wrong. Mark would often speak to me about this – he was very worried. That's why he wanted to leave.

'With Kamelion, we had a situation where Gerald Flood would record his dialogue prior to the studio recording of a story, and they'd go away and write a computer program to make the robot's mouth move around the words. We'd have to fit our lines *exactly* into the pauses, otherwise he would start talking over us.

'He was terrible. He couldn't move, couldn't do anything. When I first saw him, at the beginning of my second year, or maybe at the end of my first, he was just a head and shoulders mock-up, and his mouth and eyes moved and he looked quite impressive. But when we got the real thing ...'

Interviewed by Terry and Andy Kerr for *Skonnos* Issue 10, published in March 1985.

'Nicola Bryant was pretending to be American with everybody. I think it was under instructions from John Nathan-Turner – although I haven't got quite close to the truth as to whether it was her idea or his idea actually to pretend to *everybody*. The trouble was that we had two reporters with us the entire week we were in Lanzarote for *Planet of Fire*, and I think she had to pretend to be American for them, so they didn't let the cat out of the bag.

'I knew that she didn't have a very strong American accent, but I didn't find out for ages she wasn't even American. What she was telling us was that her father was American, or that she'd been brought up in America. It was all lies ... under instruction, but nevertheless, complete fabrication!'

Interviewed by Nicholas Briggs for *Doctor Who Magazine* Issue 215, published in August 1995.

ON THE LENGTH OF HIS STAY IN *DOCTOR WHO*:

'It seems to me that you either do it for a substantial but short amount of time, or you stay in it for life, because it does follow you around and you have to get away from it. Now, by that I don't mean that I want nothing to do with *Doctor Who*, or that I'm tired or sick of it, but you do have to work in the future. My job is acting. What happened was that when my three years were up, I had the opportunity then to do it for as long as I liked, but I just felt that as I had given myself three years, I should stick to that, because the

THE FIFTH DOCTOR

temptation is always to do another year, and then another, and another ...

'If you did it for endless numbers of years, you could always be developing the character, but at the same time, there has to come a point when you say that's it.'

Interviewed by Liam Rudden for *TARDIS* Volume 9 Issue 2, published in 1984.

'Doing the first season hasn't put me off doing it for any length of time to which I'd envisaged doing it, but exactly how long I'll do it for, I just don't know. I will certainly give it what I consider to be a substantial time, but I think I can safely say I don't want to break any records for duration. At the same time, though, I doubt I'll be the shortest.'

Interviewed by Jeremy Bentham for *Doctor Who Monthly Summer Special*, published in June 1982.

'I did find it frustrating towards the end of the last year, for various reasons. I would have liked in many cases for things to have been done better. I mean, we ran out of money on lots of stories, and time. That was frustrating, because I don't think the programme is given enough time to do it.'

Interviewed by Jackie Marshall for *Space Rat* Issue 7, published in 1984.

'Obviously concern about typecasting was a factor when I said I wasn't going to do a fourth year – the fact that I felt that period was about as long as I could do it without becoming too fixed as the Doctor in people's minds. The only thing I really did to avoid typecasting was to stop playing the Doctor fairly soon. As it is, Tristan is the part I'll never quite get away from in anyone's mind. I think it's the first part in which you come to the public's attention that stays with you. So, I was "Tristan playing the Doctor"!'

Interviewed by Ben Landman in 1985 for *Starlog* Issue 102, published in January 1986.

'I hummed and hawed for a long time. I had set myself three years, not knowing how I would feel at the end of those three years. It was touch and go – I almost did a fourth year.

'If I'd been offered *Doctor Who* when I was, say, fifty, then I would have gone on for many, many years. The fact of the matter is that I was still fairly young – still am, I hope – and there were just other things that I wanted to do. I used to have enormous fun doing *Doctor Who*. We used to rehearse at Acton, and I'd see contemporaries of mine doing other things as well, and I thought I'd do a nice stint, enjoy it and leave.'

Interviewed by Ian Atkins for *Wholook* Issue 2, published in April 1986.

'I was quite happy with my first and third seasons, but not really with the second. I had to make my decision to leave after the second season, and that was difficult. I had to gamble on the third season being quite good, because I wanted to go out on a high note. And the good thing is that the best story I did was the last story, *The Caves of Androzani*. So, I was pleased with that. I'm sure there are many things I wish I could have done differently, given different conditions. There's an anxious time when you leave, where you wonder if you're going to be stuck with nothing else but *Doctor Who*. I don't think I have been. Since I've left *Doctor Who*, I've been busy doing other things, and that's good, the security of jobs being offered.'

Interviewed by Juanita Elefante-Gordon in 1987 for *Starlog* Issue 127, published in February 1988.

'Another contributing reason why I left was that, for two of the years, I was doing *Sink or Swim* and *Holding the Fort*, and then an *All Creatures Great and Small* special, during the break between seasons, but after they stopped, I knew there was nothing new that someone would offer me in my three months off.'

Interviewed by Richard Marson for *Doctor Who Magazine* Issue 134, published in March 1988.

ON RECORDING THE REGENERATION SCENE FOR *THE CAVES OF ANDROZANI*:

'Of course, this regeneration scene wasn't done in the same way as the one in *Logopolis*. Most of it starred Nicola Bryant's cleavage, as I recall! I had good fun on *The Caves of Androzani*. We had a good time with Colin Baker. It was quite a jovial time, but sad as well in a way. I wanted to keep the whole thing bright but, yes, it was quite sad. Still, I enjoyed the whole thing.'

Interviewed by Ian Atkins for *Wholook* Issue 2, published in April 1986.

ON OVERSEAS LOCATION FILMING:

'We all leave *en masse* as a sort of huge coach party, and drink the plane out of booze!

'You usually get more of a sense of a unit when you're filming abroad, because there is nothing else for you to do. The filming when it's done in England is usually done within striking distance of London, so you all make your own way home, whereas when we were in Lanzarote, there was a very good feeling of being a unit, very much like a company in the theatre.'

Interviewed by Liam Rudden for *TARDIS* Volume 9 Issue 2, published in 1984.

'It was nice to be able to film sequences abroad, because it inevitably added a bit more gloss to the look of the show. I tend to prefer location film for various reasons, because it looks better than studio-shot stuff. I was never entirely happy when we were totally studio-bound, and studio work is much more concentrated, because you're recording a lot of material in the space of a very short time. Filming gives you a chance to think, to catch your breath and go into it all a bit more thoroughly. Woe betide you if you hadn't done your homework before going into the studio, because there just wasn't time for you to stop and have a quiet think about it all. Filming abroad was a different kettle of fish again. When we went to Amsterdam, I got a lot of recognition because they had *All Creatures Great and Small* running over there – but not *Doctor Who*. So I caused a lot of confusion I think, as well as some shock, wandering about with all that decaying face make-up.

'I think, if anything, it's harder filming abroad, because the onus is on the director to make the location work, and make it show on screen. You become very cliquey in your unit, because it's all a strange land. Socialising in the evening is very "in". I think Lanzarote looked great; it gave that story a very polished look, which was something that I felt we could be proud about. In either situation it's hard work, because you've got to get it all done within the imposed time limits. You can afford a laugh at a rubber monster or a silly line in rehearsals, but when you actually do it, if you're not concentrating 100 per cent then, as likely as not, that's what will go on tape and you'll come out of it looking silly. It can be difficult keeping a straight face in some scenes, but you have to make the effort or chaos would reign.'

Interviewed by Richard Marson for *Doctor Who Magazine* Issue 106, published in November 1985.

'Lanzarote for *Planet of Fire* was great fun, and generally worthwhile as far as foreign filming goes. It would have been a lot nicer to have filmed a lot more than we did – we were there for only a week. But Amsterdam for *Arc of Infinity* I had grave doubts about. I think it just interfered with the story. The trouble was that it highlighted the impossible coincidences of the programme. If it had been in London, then meeting Tegan would not have shown up as being so ridiculous as it did. That Tegan was in Amsterdam was just too absurd.'

Interviewed by Ian Atkins for *Wholook* **Issue 2, published in April 1986.**

ON PRODUCER JOHN NATHAN-TURNER:

'He's really very, very good, because, unlike some producers, he's there all the time. He's at every day's filming that there is, every studio recording that there is. He takes a hand in everything. That's the way he wants to operate, as total overlord of everything. His dedication to the series cannot be denied.'

Interviewed by Stephen Collins in April 1983 for *Zerinza: The Australasian Doctor Who Fanzine* **Issue 30/31, published in August 1983.**

ON *DOCTOR WHO* MERCHANDISE:

'Quite frankly, I think it's got a little out of hand! It wasn't really anything to do with me, more with John Nathan-Turner. There's a line to be trod between making available to the public things that they want, and exploiting the public. Some items did step over the line a bit. I mean, there's now a *Doctor Who Cookbook*! It seems that a lot of people are sort of cashing in on the whole thing.

'At least I never got underpants with my face on them, like Tom Baker did!'

Interviewed by Ian Atkins for *Wholook* **Issue 2, published in April 1986.**

ON WATCHING EARLIER ERAS OF *DOCTOR WHO*:

'I was a fan of the *Doctor Who* programme 18 years ago, and it had a very big impact on me. Along with millions of other children, I used to hide behind the sofa every Saturday evening. The stories used to terrify me, and even now I can vividly remember certain parts – in particular, the Hartnell and Troughton eras. For about five or six years, I watched it absolutely avidly.'

Quoted by Peter Haining in *Doctor Who – A Celebration***, published in 1983.**

THE FIFTH DOCTOR

'I had watched *Doctor Who* since 1963, really fairly avidly through the first two Doctors. It had *never* occurred to me, before John Nathan-Turner phoned me, that I might play the Doctor – never in a million years. I mean, it *had* occurred to me that I might one day be in the show, but *never* as the Doctor!'

Interviewed by Ben Landman in 1985 for *Starlog* Issue 102, published in January 1986.

ON PUBLIC RECOGNITION:

'My total view of *Doctor Who* is that I am playing a part. However, I realise that there is a lot more to it than just acting on the screen. You somehow take on the mantle of the Doctor, and a kind of instant charisma goes with the job. You have a responsibility – it is important to be always polite and cheery in public. Fortunately, I'm not a rabble rouser in my private life!'

Quoted by Peter Haining in *Doctor Who – A Celebration*, published in 1983.

'After I first appeared as the Doctor in *Logopolis*, it was ages before I actually appeared in my own stories. I said to John Nathan-Turner at the start that when I did leave, I would much prefer to go so that someone else had taken over, so really that thing of being the current Doctor had been lifted from me before the end of the season. If I left *Doctor Who* at the end of this season in the last story, although I would be doing other things, I would still be thought of as the Doctor until the beginning of the following year. So from everyone's point of view, it's really much better if one Doctor disappears and the new Doctor appears and does at least one story in the same season.'

Interviewed by Andrew M Smith on 30 August 1983 for *The Cloister Chamber*, published in October 1983.

'People in Britain get the wrong idea about *Doctor Who* in the States. It is very big there with fans – there were 12,000 at the Chicago convention last year, too many really – but as it is shown on Public Broadcasting Service channels, not the big networks, it isn't that well known to the general public. They know me better there from *All Creatures Great and Small*, though even then, I can still walk down the street unrecognised most of the time.

'I very much want to keep in touch with *Doctor Who* and all the fans. I'm not going to cut the ties with the character, but at the same time I intend to keep a low profile for a while so that I don't tread on Colin Baker's toes. It is so that Colin can become established to everyone as the Doctor. That is why it was a shame, in a way, that they didn't do the regeneration as the last few minutes of the season, as has happened before. That way, the former Doctor can sort of fade out in the time that passes to the next season, and the new Doctor has a chance to establish himself. Colin has done one story, which isn't enough to establish his Doctor to everyone, and since mine is still fresh in the memory, it is that much easier for comparisons to be made. And I think it might have been fun if they'd done the regeneration by in some way bringing in Colin's role as Maxil, the Head of Security on Gallifrey, who shot and tried to execute me in *Arc of Infinity*.

'So I don't think I'll be at conventions for a while, for Colin's sake, but after that, of course, I will when I can.'

Interviewed by Wendy Graham for *Space Voyager* Issue 12, published in December 1984.

'I couldn't go into a supermarket or walk down the street dressed as you are. At one point, I took to wearing baseball hats and dark glasses. The first time I was recognised, after *Love for Lydia*, it was quite gratifying, but that was one person along a crowded street. When they all start to recognise me, I don't like it. So I look at the ground mainly. People's behaviour is rather strange, because they rarely come straight up to me and start talking. Mostly they stand a few feet away and say loudly, "I'm sure it's him," as if I'm on another planet or something! Even when I am not recognised, the fear that I might be is always with me. It's often said to me, "You'll be sorry when they stop recognising you," but that's not true. I won't. I'll be very happy, in fact.'

Interviewed by Terry and Andy Kerr for *Skonnos* Issue 10, published in March 1985.

'I know people like autographs, but there's something about someone approaching you and saying, "Oh, will you sign this please?" that somehow brings down a barrier between you. And, suddenly, you are "the celebrity" and they are "the fan". I would rather simply talk to people, because it's a whole different thing. You can talk to them like you might talk to anybody, like a friend; and you don't have this barrier of "them" and "us". I can't tell you how much I like just talking.'

Interviewed by Ben Landman in 1985 for *Starlog* Issue 102, published in January 1986.

'Being invited to conventions was a very new experience. It wasn't a total shock, but still very amazing. You have to accept that the fans have probably got more knowledge of the programme than you ever will have, so I never pretended to be a great authority on it, even though I played the part and also enjoyed the series before I was in it. Before I did the first convention, which was in America, I was fairly terrified. But when I got up there and said, "Hello, it's nice to be here," there was spontaneous applause! It was fine after that.'

Interviewed by Ian Atkins for *Wholook* Issue 2, published in April 1986.

'You do have some idea of what it is you're getting into before you take on the part. I think my most immediate problem was that I had about a year before I actually appeared on television as the Doctor, and John Nathan-Turner was very keen to sell me beforehand. It all happened very quickly, and I began to get mail and recognition extremely quickly too, so it didn't really matter that I was doing this personal appearance and promotion bit as well. Even if I hadn't participated, I think press interest was still there, and of course there's always going to be merchandise if the show is successful.

'What I tried to do was strike a balance. I didn't mind doing all the publicity and so on, but I didn't want *Doctor Who* to totally take over my life. I needed time to myself, time for other projects. Besides, if I'd have overdone it, I think the public would have got pretty sick of my face. When I did personal appearances, I wasn't keen on going in costume – I didn't want to go in character. If somebody asked for my autograph, it would always be signed "Best Wishes, Peter Davison", because if you sign yourself as the Doctor, you're insulting the person's intelligence.'

Interviewed by Richard Marson for *Doctor Who Magazine* Issue 106, published in November 1985.

'I was aware of what I was letting myself in for, which is one reason why I hesitated when the producer, John Nathan-Turner, offered me the part. I finally said yes in my agent's office late one afternoon, and it was agreed we could call a press conference to announce the fact in a couple of days.

'However, no sooner had I driven home than it was obvious that the story had been leaked to the press, for the phone never stopped ringing with calls from journalists.

'On the *Nine O'Clock News* that night, the first story was that Ronald Reagan had been elected President of the United States – while the final story was that Tom Baker was going to regenerate into me! Friends who had been watching with the sound turned down told me later that they had assumed when my photograph was flashed up on the screen that I must have died!'

Quoted by Peter Haining in *The Doctor Who File*, published in 1986.

'I'm always getting "Where's your TARDIS?" – all the time. With *All Creatures Great and Small* it was "Would you have a look at my dog?" These things people actually think no-one has ever said before! With the *Doctor Who* fan thing, in a way I find it kind of sad. A lot of the fans are fine – they like the programme, know everything about it – but there's a small proportion of those fans to whom it is like a religion, and who get terribly offended when you're talking about the programme.

'I remember at the first convention I ever did, they asked my philosophy of *Doctor Who*, and I said "I get the script and learn the words", and they thought that was an awful thing to say. They do care about it, as I did when I was doing it myself, but at the same time, you have to laugh at it, too, or it gets very po-faced.

'I do find that with very few exceptions, you can never become friends with fans, because underneath it all, they are still fans and they are in awe. I remember once I got on quite well with a couple in America, and they then asked me to sign an autograph in a particular way, and you think, "Wait a minute, if you're supposed to be friends with these people, and you invite them into your home ...?" It doesn't work, though they're very friendly and very nice and we've all done a lot of conventions in America.'

Interviewed by Richard Marson for *Doctor Who Magazine* Issue 134, published in March 1988.

'I don't mind at all appearing on programmes like *Blue Peter* and *Nationwide*, as long as no-one expects me to be entertaining. I don't mind *Wogan* or anything like that – indeed especially not *Wogan*, as he likes to take part of the entertaining on himself. A lot of actors you see on *Wogan* are helped out by him.

'What I don't like are the ones where you're the one that has to come out with the anecdotes and be funny. I'm not very good at that at all. The worst one was *Boxing Night at the Mill*. It was very much a parade of guests expected to be funny, and it was just terrible. Hopeless.

'Doing *Blue Peter* was very funny, because they always want you to hold the cat. Every time they cut away to something, they'll shove this cat in your lap, and every time they come back to you, the cat will run away. And this goes on and on.'

Interviewed by Richard Marson for *Doctor Who Magazine* Issue 134, published in March 1988.

ON THE DIFFERENCE BETWEEN BRITISH AND AMERICAN FANS:

'There is a difference. Over here *Doctor Who* is an institution, but in America it is a cult. At the BBC's Longleat convention we had something like 35,000 people – I can't remember the exact numbers – but a lot of those were general viewers; in other words, people who watched the programme, whose children watched the programme, and who had come along to see Doctor Who. There were thousands of people who just liked the programme. At events in America, on the other hand, they were all fans. They all knew about the show, as all the members of the *Doctor Who* Appreciation Society do over here, and were intensely interested in it, so they were easier to handle in groups of thousands. Whereas Longleat became impossible, because general fans just aren't prepared to put up with the sort of thing that a DWAS fan would put up with. In America, the *Doctor Who* fans would queue for hours and hours just for your autograph and a word, whereas the Longleat people were not used to it. They could not cope with queuing up for three hours to get just one word, and tempers did get a bit frayed at Longleat. Of course Longleat was badly organised, there's no doubt about that.

'Unfortunately, the actors involved sort of got blamed for Longleat. I received quite a few rude letters saying how dare I be associated with something so badly organised. We tried to explain to them that there was no way 25 actors, or indeed only four Doctors, could satisfy 35,000 people. And the organisers insisted on having autograph sessions, which were just an impossibility. One should have spent the whole day simply walking around.'

Interviewed by Liam Rudden for *TARDIS* Volume 9 Issue 2, published in 1984.

ON HIS 'PUBLIC SCHOOL BOY' IMAGE

'Unless you make a positive move to say, "I will not play any more of these types", you are a bit stuck. It's the luck of the first part that brings you public attention. They kind of label you with that.

'I was never by nature a rebel – I never wanted to offend people, I just wanted to do what I wanted to do, so I'm quite at home being a cosy figure, actually. It's quite nice to be liked by little old ladies. But I do find it disconcerting sometimes when people meet me and they expect me to be wearing blazers all the time.

'I *could* say, "I won't accept any similar parts, I want to play different parts", and I'm sure if I put myself out of work for six months to a year, maybe a part like that would come along. But it wouldn't necessarily be successful, and I wouldn't necessarily be any good at it, and I wouldn't necessarily enjoy doing it, which seems to me to be the most important thing. If I enjoy doing it, I'll do it. So, I've never really had a master plan.

'I find the worst thing about papers is getting them to print what you actually say. Going back to this public school thing, they have this insistence of putting everything I do say into kind of public school language. "Did you enjoy this series?" they'll ask, and I'll say, "Yes", but they'll print it as, "Yes, it was jolly good fun". Loads of "goshes" flow all over the place.

'I'm a bit boring for them really, because they haven't got any dirt at the moment.'

Interviewed by Richard Marson for *Doctor Who Magazine* Issue 134, published in March 1988.

ON THE RELATIVE MERITS OF STAGE AND SCREEN WORK:

'I'm not saying that it's not good to go back to the stage sometimes, but I don't personally feel that the stage is where it's at. I don't see that at all.

'I enjoy doing stage work, but it has tremendous drawbacks. You're doing the same thing several months on end, and you can never quite produce a definitive performance. You think you've done it really well one night – you think, "I've really cracked this performance" – and the next night it's rubbish and doesn't work at all. And of course at the end of it, you have absolutely nothing left, apart from memories. On TV, you've created something that's been recorded for posterity.'

Interviewed by Richard Marson for *Doctor Who Magazine* Issue 134, published in March 1988.

ON *DOCTOR WHO* WITH COLIN BAKER AND SYLVESTER MCCOY:

'I have to say, I didn't really watch the show after I left. I watched Colin's first one, as it was at the end of my last season, but I didn't like it much. I think Sylvester is very good, but I think it would work much better if they went back to the older sort of story, because he is eccentric and kind of wacky, but the stories are wacky too, which I personally don't think works. It's kind of university humour. I think it would work better if Sylvester was the kind of eccentric figure in the middle of a serious story.'

Interviewed by Richard Marson for *Doctor Who Magazine* Issue 134, published in March 1988.

THE FIFTH DOCTOR

ON HIS INTERESTS:

'I read a fair amount of science fiction. Either detective fiction or science fiction; mainly American detective fiction. I like Philip K Dick, when I can understand him! Silverberg I quite like. And English science fiction; the H G Wells and John Wyndham school of science fiction, where it's really based on ... in a way, much more normal, everyday life.'

Interviewed by Jackie Marshall for *Space Rat* Issue 7, published in 1984.

'I don't find acting all-consuming at all. You do take it home with you a bit, in that if you're playing a really depressing part, then you tend to get depressed, but I never sit at home and talk about a part. Most of the friends I have are not in the business at all – most of them are school friends.

'I've never been in love with acting in the way that some people are. They love going to the theatre and seeing various shows, and a lot of it is the whole thrill of show business, which I don't enjoy at all. I don't object to it, but it's not me.

'There's a very stereotyped image of the business, and it's generally wrong. I've never really understood the total inability of television and films to imitate themselves. When you see a thriller set in a TV studio, no-one ever behaves like that in the real thing.

'My interests. Well, I don't go to the cinema much, though I ought to. I tend to watch videos! My greatest joy is actually doing absolutely nothing – not having to get up and do anything. I can just sit there and let an hour go by. Or spend hours just wandering round the house. I used to play cricket, but people expect too much of you and it ceases to be relaxing.'

Interviewed by Richard Marson for *Doctor Who Magazine* Issue 134, published in March 1988.

ON HIS CAREER AFTER *DOCTOR WHO*:

'I did a series called *L Driver* for the BBC, which was in the studio at about the same time as one of Colin Baker's *Doctor Who*s. As a bit of a joke, I went in when they were doing a scene with Pat Troughton and crept up behind Colin to give him the shock of his former lives, so to speak – but he took it all in his stride!'

Interviewed by Richard Marson for *Doctor Who Magazine* Issue 106, published in November 1985.

'Things are done differently on different shows. A lot more trouble is spent on *A Very Peculiar Practice* than on *All Creatures Great and Small*, which suffers as a result. As actors, we're just as guilty as the director and producer of being blasé about it and thinking we can come in and just "do it like that", without really needing a rehearsal. Sometimes it works, but you always come a cropper in the end – there's no real substitute for sitting down and thinking it through.

'It's a question, too, of how right the director wants to get it, and that's not an individual criticism. *A Very Peculiar Practice* is very well written, and that's the difference – there's so much to get out of the script. You want to do justice to the script, so you work extra hard.'

Interviewed by Richard Marson for *Doctor Who Magazine* Issue 134, published in March 1988.

'I'm open to offers. Of the sitcoms I did, I didn't like *Holding the Fort* and I did like *Sink or Swim*, because one was good and one was bad. The biggest thing I'd like to do would be a film – something I haven't done before. You'd think I could get in there somewhere, wouldn't you?'

Interviewed by Richard Marson for *Doctor Who Magazine* Issue 134, published in March 1988.

'Really I guess everything I have done has been fairly visible. I went back to *All Creatures Great and Small*, left it and then went back *again* – Bobby Ewing style, but not via the shower ... I did two series of *Campion* ... I haven't, however, snuck off for years abroad or done great theatre tours.'

Interviewed by Graeme Wood, Mark Wyman and Gary Russell for *TV Zone* Issue 16, published in March 1991.

Character – The Fifth Doctor

The genesis of the fifth Doctor can be largely attributed to John Nathan-Turner, who became producer of *Doctor Who* following the conclusion of work on the series' seventeenth season at the end of 1979.

Nathan-Turner had never been particularly enamoured of Tom Baker's portrayal of the Doctor. Baker had by this point completed some six years in the role, and the producer considered that his increasingly assured and flippant interpretation made the character seem too dominant and invulnerable, detracting from the dramatic potential of the stories. He also greatly disliked the slapstick-style humour that the previous production team had allowed to flourish, and the general air of jokiness that Baker now tended to inject into the proceedings. During the eighteenth season, he therefore took steps to address these concerns, cutting down drastically the level of humour in the series and prevailing upon his directors to keep a much tighter rein on their leading man – a policy that, at least initially, created a good deal of friction between himself and Baker. Nathan-Turner's preferences could ultimately be met only by the casting of his own, completely new Doctor, and so it was that he reached a mutual agreement with Baker that the actor would bow out of the series at the end of that year's run.

Nathan-Turner's principal requirement for the fifth Doctor was simply that he should present a complete contrast to the fourth. (And despite his teasing of the press with the notion that the series' new lead might be a 'she' rather than a 'he', he never actually contemplated casting a woman in the role.) In this, he was motivated not only by his misgivings about Baker's portrayal, but also by the thought that to cast an actor who was in any way similar to the outgoing star would be to invite invidious comparisons (a consideration that had weighed similarly heavily with past producers who had overseen the Doctor's previous regenerations). He had no definite preconceptions beyond this basic desire for contrast, and no particular actor initially in mind. One candidate he thought about but then discounted was Richard Griffiths, a well-established character actor of portly build who is now perhaps best remembered for his starring roles in the series *Bird of Prey* and *The Cleopatras*.

As recounted in his 1985 book *The TARDIS Inside Out*, the producer eventually came up with a 'shopping list' of ideal characteristics that he

CHARACTER – THE FIFTH DOCTOR

would like to see in the new Doctor:

1. Heroism – the Doctor must be heroic.

2. Youthfulness – I wanted a younger Doctor for a more youthful audience.

3. Vulnerability – we needed a Doctor who could get it wrong occasionally. This is something the series hadn't had with Tom.

At this point, I began to see that the task wasn't impossible, and my excitement mounted. Fitting together the pieces of a puzzle like this is one of the real pleasures of being a producer.

4. Straight hair – Tom's curly locks had become so famous. We needed an opposite image.

In the end, only one man was ever seriously considered for the role of the fifth Doctor: twenty-nine year old Peter Davison. Pinned up on the *Doctor Who* office wall were an array of stills relating to productions on which Nathan-Turner had worked, including one of Davison taken at a charity cricket match during his time starring as the country vet Tristan Farnon in the popular BBC series *All Creatures Great and Small*. It was this that brought the actor to Nathan-Turner's mind when he happened to notice it while mulling over his choice of Baker's successor, and the suggestion was quickly approved by his BBC superiors.

'He was my first choice,' Nathan-Turner told Jeremy Bentham in a 1981 interview for *Doctor Who Magazine*. 'I had worked with him on *All Creatures Great and Small*, and he was a very talented and capable actor. He had everything I was looking for in the new Doctor'.

Nathan-Turner had realised that Davison would fully meet his list of ideal characteristics. He was younger and slighter in build than Baker and had straight, fair hair as opposed to his predecessor's dark, curly locks. He was also somewhat more reserved and easy-going in manner, and carried with him a large fan following from *All Creatures Great and Small* – a factor that the producer considered a great advantage, given that Baker had become very closely associated with the role of the Doctor and would consequently be very difficult to displace in the public's affections.

Nathan-Turner phoned Davison at his home one weekend in September 1980, told him that Baker was leaving *Doctor Who* – something that had yet to be announced to the public at that point – and asked if he would be interested in taking over. Davison was astonished, considering himself totally unsuitable for the role, and initially felt inclined to turn the offer down. He asked Nathan-Turner to phone back the following week, and then agreed to meet him for lunch one day shortly afterwards, to give the producer a chance to try to change his mind.

When the meeting took place, Davison was further surprised to learn that Nathan-Turner saw him as a 'personality actor' – someone who drew to a large extent on his own personality in bringing to life the various characters that he played, and who would thus imbue the Doctor with the same boyish charm and enthusiasm as he had Tristan. Davison himself had not previously thought in these terms. 'I'd never seen myself in a million years as a personality actor,' he admitted in a 1994 interview with Nicholas Briggs for *Doctor Who Magazine*. Rather, he took the view that he was essentially a character actor who just happened to have come to public attention in one particular type of part. He also felt that the role of the Doctor was best suited to an older man, and that he was too young for it. Again he was left with the distinct feeling that he should decline Nathan-Turner's offer. After several further meetings and phone conversations, however, he decided to accept, almost on a whim, as he could not bear to think that someone else would be given the job instead and that he would then have to remain silent about the fact that he had been the first choice.

Keen to gain as much advance publicity as possible for his new star, Nathan-Turner ensured that the news filtered out to the press almost immediately after Davison agreed to accept the role – indeed, rather more quickly than the actor himself would have liked. An announcement was even made on the BBC's main evening news on 4 November 1980, and a hastily-arranged press conference was held to give eager journalists their first chance to ask questions of the new Doctor.

Later the same month, Davison made his first substantial *Doctor Who*-related television appearance, on the popular BBC children's show *Blue Peter*. Then, on 3 December 1980, he guested on the lunchtime magazine programme *Pebble Mill at One*, discussing with presenter Donny McLeod a number of costume ideas sent in by viewers, ranging from a 'college boy' look, complete with yellow striped blazer, to an outfit consisting of a 'tin foil suit' and a red bow tie. Davison, although reacting diplomatically to these ideas, found little amongst them to spark his interest. There was however a panel of fans on hand in the studio to offer further advice, and a young man named Stuart Unit drew a favourable response when he suggested that the fifth Doctor should be 'like Tristan Farnon, but with bravery and intellect'. The actor was later to cite this as having been one of the most influential ideas in his early thinking about the role.

Nathan-Turner himself offered Davison relatively little advice or guidance as to how he should approach his characterisation of the Doctor – perhaps not surprisingly, given his view that the newcomer was a personality actor who would bring to the series his own distinctive personal qualities and traits.

'I don't think John had much in mind about what he wanted the part to be,' Davison told journalist Ben Landman in a 1985 interview for *Starlog*, 'except for casting me in it. I mean, he didn't say, "I'm offering you the part, and I want you to play it like *this*." The trick of a good producer is to cast someone who is right for the part in the way that they see it, and then let them do it. Which is really what he did. I was very much thrown in and told "You're the Doctor – now do it!"'

The producer did however have some lengthy discussions with the actor as to the type of costume that he should wear. Both men were agreed that it should have, in the tradition of the previous Doctors' images, an air of old-fashioned and slightly eccentric Englishness about it. A sporting motif was also thought to be a good idea. Polo jodhpurs were at one point considered but, in the end, period cricketing attire was decided upon as being a better choice – a suggestion made by Davison, who was himself a keen cricketer, and possibly again inspired in part by the photograph of him on the *Doctor Who* office wall. A test costume fitting was held around the end of the year, in which Davison tried on various cricketing outfits from stock to assess their effectiveness.

Work was meanwhile in hand on scripts for the forthcoming season. The character summary being sent out to freelance writers in the closing months of 1980 gave a general description of the Doctor's background but offered little hint as to the newcomer's intended personality:

THE DOCTOR

The DOCTOR comes from the planet Gallifrey, in the constellation of Kasterborus. His relationship with his fellow TIME LORDs has been portrayed in contradictory ways during the programme's long history; but the original premise is worth bearing in mind: the TIME LORDs were aloof super-creatures who watched the workings of the universe objectively, building up their store of knowledge without interfering. One of their number, unable to remain detached, plunged himself into moral involvement by 'borrowing' a TARDIS from the dry-dock where it was undergoing repairs. This fugitive was the DOCTOR. Subsequent adventures have had him revisiting Gallifrey and redeeming himself in the eyes of the TIME LORDs. There is, however, evidence that at least some of these stories may be forgeries!

THE FIFTH DOCTOR

Like all TIME LORDs the DOCTOR has two hearts and a normal body temperature of 60 degrees Fahrenheit. He's over seven centuries old, and has the capability of regenerating himself into different appearances – his present form being his fourth regeneration.

Incidentally, he's never referred to as 'DOCTOR WHO' either in speech headings or by other characters. His name is the DOCTOR – 'Who?' is the mystery! The fact that he is always 'DOCTOR WHO' for the purpose of the closing titles is a historical quirk, reminding us that the format has been shaped more by collective intuition than by centralised logic.

The DOCTOR shouldn't be seen as a sort of Superman. He's fallible and vulnerable and only too conscious that life consists largely of things going wrong for well-intentioned people like himself. Note too, that he's only rarely intentionally funny. If many of his responses and solutions make us laugh with their unexpected appropriateness it's because we lack his agility of mind and breadth of experience, and didn't see them coming.

The intention at this point was that the new season should open with a four-part story entitled *Project Zeta-Sigma*, the scripts for which had been commissioned from John Flanagan and Andrew McCulloch on 7 October 1980 under the working title *Project '4G'*, and that this should also be the first of the new block in production order. This would then be followed, both on transmission and in production, by another four-parter, Terence Dudley's *Day of Wrath*. By the beginning of 1981, the writers had been briefed to include cricketing references in their scripts. A considerable degree of uncertainty was still apparent, however, as Flanagan recalled in an interview conducted by John C Smith and Michael McLester in September 1981 for the fanzine *Definitive Gaze*:

'We wrote a scene in which Tegan Jovanka, who is Australian, is saying that the Doctor looks like a cricketer, because of his costume. And Adric says, "That's an Earth insect, isn't it?" "Yes, but it's also a game." "Well, how do you play it?" And we had this thing where the Doctor tries to explain cricket to him. If you've ever tried to explain cricket to an American, you'll know it's virtually impossible, so the more the Doctor explains about it, the more ludicrous it becomes. The whole idea behind cricket is that it's so absurd. We had quite a long section on that. Plus a lot of rather bad punny jokes – sort of like "How's that?" Cricket imagery all the way through.

'Peter had his own ideas, the producer had his own ideas, everyone else had their own ideas. There was quite a lot of discussion about the character, especially the costume. We were phoned up half way through writing the cricket scene and told, "Forget every reference to cricket; he's not wearing cricket gear at all; we're going for something else." Then, later that afternoon, another call came, saying, "Don't scratch it altogether." Two days later, "Look, he's possibly going to wear a morning suit." There was a problem.'

The man charged with the task of giving substance to the costume ideas worked out by Nathan-Turner, Davison and others was Colin Lavers, who had been assigned as costume designer for *Project Zeta-Sigma*. Nathan-Turner gave him the following instructions in a memo dated 10 February 1981:

> Literally about to depart to the USA for a few weeks for a holiday and wanted to give you some information about the new Doctor's image.
>
> As you probably know, Peter Davison and I have been discussing various ideas for several months now, namely as follows:
>
> That the basic costume would be *period* cricket outfit (all the Doctors have reflected Earth's history). I enclose some photos of Peter which we took at a 'stock' fitting some time ago. I do feel the *Doctor Who* shirt with the '?' mark on the lapels is worth hanging onto. Similarly, I am committed to a cricket jersey in terms of *Doctor Who* annuals and other merchandise.
>
> Anyway, here are the latest thoughts – I'm sure you can *vastly* improve them ...
>
> *Doctor Who* shirt, cricket pullover, white cricket shoes, period baggy pants – possibly some colour introduced here, e.g. stripes?, with an optional top coat and hat. One idea we tossed around was a morning suit jacket and collapsible topper.
>
> I shall be returning to the office on 4 March and I wonder if you and I and Peter Davison could have some sort of experimental session on the afternoon of Friday 6 March (Peter Davison is not available any other time and leaves the country around 11 March).
>
> If you would like to come and see me either on 4 or 5 March with any drawings or further thoughts I'd be delighted to see you.

THE FIFTH DOCTOR

A major change of plan for the new season occurred shortly after this when Nathan-Turner, apparently while on holiday in the USA, decided to drop *Project Zeta-Sigma* from the schedule, possibly with a view to moving it back to a later slot. (Ultimately it was abandoned altogether, although some pre-production work had been carried out on it.) A replacement first story was hastily sought from Christopher H Bidmead, who had until recently been the series' script editor – a post now held on a caretaker basis by newcomer Antony Root. An outline entitled *The Visitor* was commissioned from him on 9 March, shortly after Nathan-Turner's return from holiday, and a full set of scripts under the revised title *Castrovalva* on 8 April.

One consequence of this change of plan was that Davison's first transmitted story could no longer be the first into production, for the simple reason that recording was due to start in mid-April and the scripts for *Castrovalva* could not possibly be completed in time. Consequently *Day of Wrath*, which in late February had been retitled *Four to Doomsday*, was moved forward to fill the production slot previously held by *Project Zeta-Sigma*. *Castrovalva* was meanwhile scheduled to be made fourth in line, after *Four to Doomsday* and two other stories, *The Visitation* and *Kinda*, which would be transmitted fourth and third respectively. Making a virtue of this necessity, Nathan-Turner considered it a positive advantage that Davison would now have a little time to settle into the role before having to record the story that would introduce his Doctor to the public – particularly as the plot of *Castrovalva* would see him experiencing a confused state of post-regeneration trauma, presenting a considerable challenge to the actor. This was a view with which Davison concurred. He still felt somewhat unsure about his approach to the role, and continued to seek advice from Nathan-Turner, executive producer Barry Letts and others, including *Four to Doomsday*'s director John Black.

Recording of *Four to Doomsday* began on schedule in mid-April, at which point a photocall was also held to unveil the Doctor's costume to the press – and, through them, to the public. The design drawn up by Lavers and approved by Nathan-Turner had a highly stylised, uniform look. This was something that Nathan-Turner had particularly favoured – in line with the redesign of the fourth Doctor's costume that he had instigated for the previous season – as he considered that it would give the character a readily marketable image and help to boost interest amongst toy and other manufacturers in producing spin-off items. Davison himself was not entirely happy with this aspect of the costume; as he would later admit in interviews, he would have preferred a more 'off the peg' look, giving the impression that the Doctor had simply picked up an assortment of clothes found in the TARDIS wardrobe, much as his previous incarnations had done.

The finishing touch to the outfit (although this was removed for the purposes of the initial photocall) was a prop stick of celery affixed to the lapel of the coat – another idea hit upon by Nathan-Turner, although he has never revealed the inspiration behind it.

For *Four to Doomsday*, Davison adopted a style of performance that he would later describe as 'bland', his intention being to avoid doing anything that could conceivably clash with his eventual interpretation of the role, once he had refined this to his full satisfaction. By this stage, he had already formed some quite firm views as to how he should approach the part, as he explained in an early press interview quoted by Peter Haining in the 1983 book *Doctor Who – A Celebration*:

'For a start, I will be a much younger Doctor and I'll be wearing a kind of Victorian cricketing outfit to accentuate my youth. I would like him to be heroic and resourceful. I feel that, over the years, the Doctor has become less vital, no longer struggling for survival, depending on instant, miraculous solutions to problems.

'The suspense of "Now how is he going to get out this tight corner?" has been missing. I want to restore that. My Doctor will be flawed. He will have the best intentions and he will in the end win through, but he will not always act for the best. Sometimes, he will even endanger his companions. But I want him to have a sort of reckless innocence.'

Davison drew a certain amount of inspiration for his performance from the earlier Doctors – particularly the first and second, as played by William Hartnell and Patrick Troughton respectively. He had been an avid viewer of the Hartnell and Troughton stories as a teenager, and had recently watched a number of them again (along with several Jon Pertwee and Tom Baker stories) after borrowing videotape copies from Nathan-Turner. Some fan commentators would later suggest that his portrayal most closely resembled Troughton's, but he himself felt that it drew more heavily on Hartnell's, as he explained in a 1982 interview with David Hirsch for *Starlog*:

'I was given a completely blank page to do with as I liked. But at the same time, I didn't have the advantage I would have with another part, where I could create the character by saying, "His parents were like this," or, "This is his background". So I thought about what the other Doctors had done and I picked up ideas. I didn't want to dive in with a totally down-the-line character. I think my character has more than I intended to do with that of William Hartnell's Doctor. My Doctor gets cross sometimes, as Hartnell's did. Very gruff. He always has the best intentions in the world but, because of this ... He doesn't always make mistakes, but he sometimes *causes* them. When he gets into a dangerous situation, he gets into trouble.'

Perhaps providing some support for this view, Hartnell's widow Heather would later comment that Davison strongly reminded her of her husband as a young man, and that she saw a number of parallels between their respective portrayals of the Doctor (although she also thought that the fifth Doctor's alien qualities were insufficiently emphasised, making him too similar to an ordinary human being).

One major difference between Davison and his four predecessors was that he was already very well known for other TV work at the point when he first appeared on screen as the Doctor – a fact that in the opinion of some critics made it more difficult for viewers to suspend their disbelief and accept him in the role. Not only was he still recognised from *All Creatures Great and Small*, but he was also gaining exposure in two current situation comedy series: LWT's *Holding the Fort* and the BBC's own *Sink or Swim*. *Sink or Swim* would indeed remain in production during the first two years of Davison's time in *Doctor Who*, obliging Nathan-Turner to release the actor between *Doctor Who* stories to work on that series.

The first televised pictures of the fifth Doctor in costume came not in *Doctor Who* itself but in the BBC's outside broadcast coverage of the annual Lord Mayor's Show in London on 14 November 1981, during the course of which Davison and a group of assorted monsters (fans wearing largely home-made costumes) were seen waving to the crowds from a float devoted to the series. After a further round of publicity appearances, including a guest spot on *Boxing Night at the Mill* when Davison was, amongst other things, required to demonstrate his prowess at making chocolate milk shakes, transmission of the new season began with the first episode of *Castrovalva* on Monday 4 January 1982, finally getting the fifth Doctor's era under way on the screen.

This first story saw the Doctor making a gradual recovery from his aforementioned state of post-regeneration trauma. His behaviour was initially confused and erratic, coloured by occasional reversions to the mannerisms of his previous incarnations – Davison essaying brief impressions of his predecessors in explicit recognition of the inspiration that he was drawing from them. He became progressively more stable, however, as the events of the story unfolded in the supposedly healing environment of Castrovalva and as his true character started to emerge.

Many of the qualities that had led Nathan-Turner to cast Davison were immediately evident to the viewer – particularly his relative youthfulness. One early idea, particularly favoured by Bidmead, was that he should give the impression of being an old man in a young man's body, and this also was reflected in the story. It quickly became apparent, too, that the fifth Doctor was to be a less overtly eccentric and off-the-wall character than the fourth. This was partly a consequence of Nathan-Turner's determination to cut down the level of humour in the series – or, as he put it, to concentrate on 'wit rather than slapstick' – but partly also a reflection of Davison's own natural disposition, in keeping with the producer's appraisal of him as a personality actor.

CHARACTER – THE FIFTH DOCTOR

'I'm not a wacky, eccentric person,' noted Davison in a 1988 interview conducted by Richard Marson for *Doctor Who Magazine*. 'If they had wanted a wacky, eccentric person, John would have cast one. He did not want me to do that. I went along with what he wanted – he was the producer – and he wanted me to play it in a certain way. I'm sure if he had wanted me to be wacky and eccentric, I could have done it, but I could never have played the part in the way Tom Baker did. I'm not by nature like that.'

Expanding on this theme, Davison told Ben Landman in his 1985 *Starlog* interview:

'I don't think you ever think too consciously – especially if you're playing someone from Gallifrey, someone 750 years old – *exactly* what parts of yourself you're putting into it. I wanted to change the direction of *Doctor Who* a bit, to make it more believable. The fact of the matter is that it was *me* playing the part. Therefore, bits that are me came over.'

As Season 19 continued, so further aspects of the new Doctor's character began to become familiar. The heroism that had been one of the producer's original requirements was very much to the fore, as was the vulnerability – a quality demonstrated perhaps most vividly in the fact that the Doctor was unable to prevent the death of Adric in a space freighter crash at the end of *Earthshock* – a story written by the series' new permanent script editor, Eric Saward.

The thinking behind this vulnerability was a subject on which Nathan-Turner elaborated when interviewed by David Hirsch in 1982 for *Starlog*:

'I opted for a more fallible Doctor, a more vulnerable character who wasn't always on top of every situation. I felt that, in the past, some of the Doctors had been too dominant. There really had been no threat. Every cliff-hanger ending had left the Doctor in jeopardy of some kind, and we had all known that he was going to get out of it and be back next week. I think that if the role is played infallibly, then, in a way, that's undercutting the drama. If you've got a Doctor who is fallible, I think, hopefully, the viewers can get more involved and seriously believe he might not be back next week.'

The combined qualities of heroism and vulnerability meant that the fifth Doctor was sometimes seen to act rather recklessly, rushing breathlessly into new situations with an air of innocent curiosity and failing to consider all the risks.

'I think he has a certain amount of tunnel vision!' opined Davison in a 1982 interview with Jeremy Bentham for *Doctor Who Magazine*. 'He's not always the wisest of men. Maybe when he sits back and ruminates on the way things have gone he *is* wise, but I think that he's headstrong and he makes more of a mess of things in the short run until he's sorted out his own problems. He doesn't always act for the best. Quite often he'll land in a certain situation and, obviously, the common sense thing to do would be simply to leave – to get out of there because it's dangerous to everyone. But he doesn't get out, he wants to find out what's going on, he's got to explore … and thus he gets embroiled in the story.'

Like all his predecessors, the fifth Doctor was a resolute champion of the cause of good against evil, invariably standing up for the underdog and combating tyranny and oppression wherever he encountered them. He also had a considerable degree of moral courage, as was well illustrated by the following confrontation from *Earthshock*, when he sought to prevent the Cyber Leader from harming Tegan:

> CYBER LEADER: I see that Time Lords have emotions.
> THE DOCTOR: Of sorts.
> CYBER LEADER: Surely a great weakness in one so powerful?
> THE DOCTOR: Emotions have their uses.
> CYBER LEADER: They restrict and curtail the intellect and logic of the mind.
> THE DOCTOR: They also enhance life. When did you last have the pleasure of smelling a flower, watching a sunset, eating a well-prepared meal?
> CYBER LEADER: These things are irrelevant.
> THE DOCTOR: For some people, small, beautiful things is what life is all about!

Again, there were echoes of the Hartnell Doctor here, as this exchange was similar to one that he had with an earlier Cyber Leader in the Season 3 story *The Tenth Planet*, as also seen in *Earthshock* by way of a flashback extract:

> THE DOCTOR: Emotions: love, pride, hate fear! Have you no emotions, sir?

Davison was considered by BBC management to have made a great success of his debut season as the Doctor. Nathan-Turner's superior, Head of Series and Serials David Reid, wrote to him in glowing terms on 29 March 1982:

> Sadly we have only said a fast 'hello' to each other in the BBC Club but then your schedule doesn't leave you much free time. I wanted simply to congratulate you at the end of your first season of *Doctor Who* and to express my admiration for the way in which you have taken the part and made it your own. I am delighted with the response from the audience and I hope very much that you are.
>
> It is, I know, a very demanding schedule and the confidence and expertise achieved is remarkable – so thank you also for the enormous amount of energy, concentration and work that you

CHARACTER – THE FIFTH DOCTOR

have put into the series.

What more can I say except to say that the season has been a great pleasure and a success largely due to you and I greatly look forward to the next season.

Season 20 revealed little more about the fifth Doctor's character than had been established in Season 19. This may have been due in part to the fact that Saward, although acknowledging Davison to be a very good actor, considered him miscast in the role and consequently, as he would later admit, felt uninspired to devote much attention to the character's development. Davison, for his own part, was understandably perturbed at this situation and felt that he was being less well served than he should be by the series' scripts. One thing that he was especially keen to do was to inject some elements of flippant humour into his portrayal, but any such suggestions were generally vetoed by Nathan-Turner in what the actor regarded as an over-reaction against the perceived excesses of Tom Baker in this regard. Davison was also rather dissatisfied with his own performance during the course of this season.

Quite apart from these concerns about his own role, the actor harboured a number of misgivings about the general direction in which the series was moving at this point. In particular, he thought that the stories were becoming too reliant on familiar monsters and characters from *Doctor Who*'s past; he felt that there was an increasing tendency for stylish production values to take priority over good plotting; he disagreed with Nathan-Turner's decision to have Nyssa written out in *Terminus*, the fourth story of the season, as he considered her to be the companion best suited to his Doctor; and he disliked the producer's policy of casting 'guest star' celebrities, often best known for comedy or light entertainment work, in supporting roles.

'I was actually very unhappy with the second season, script-wise and concept-wise,' admitted the actor in his 1988 interview with Richard Marson for *Doctor Who Magazine*. 'I just felt that it didn't go anywhere and John couldn't quite decide if he was having old monsters back or bringing in new ones. And I wasn't very happy with me in it.

'It was then – in the second year – that I had to decide if I wanted to do a fourth year, because of the way it works. But I just wasn't sure about the programme.

'John and I have always got on very well, but we did have a creative difference over the direction in which he wanted *Doctor Who* to go, and the direction in which I thought it should go. We talked it through, and I decided I would be better off if I left.

'As far as companions went, I thought there should be one companion, who was a fairly nice person, to work with the Doctor – preferably Nyssa, although I wasn't insisting on her. I also thought it needed to get away from turning into a sort of variety show in space.

'If you look back to the very first season of *Doctor Who*, I know it looked very tacky – sets that wobbled and all that – but it had a kind of mystical quality in it, an atmosphere that was disappearing when I did it, and that I think has completely disappeared now. It was that atmosphere that made the need to compete with special effects unnecessary. Certain effects we did fine, but you've got to know your limitations and you can't expect to compete with *Star Wars* in BBC television.

'It wasn't a row at all – indeed, I didn't decide until about two months after our discussion that maybe I should leave. It was kind of frustrating coming to the BBC rehearsal rooms every day as well, and seeing people doing other things.'

'I used to meet Peter from time to time for chats and so on,' noted Saward in a 1993 interview, 'and he always used to have this thing at the end of each season: was he going to come back? I know that he felt a little uncomfortable playing the part, and I think he felt it wasn't working as he would have liked. As I recall, before the end of the second season, he was saying more frequently, "I don't know if I'm going to do it again. I don't know if I'm going to do it again". Really he was just saying out loud what he was feeling. So when John came in and said, "Peter isn't doing it again," I wasn't surprised. I don't think anyone was surprised, as he'd been saying it for so long.'

Davison was in fact much happier with Season 21 than he had been with Season 20, and even had second thoughts about his decision to leave. By this point, however, steps had already been taken to write him out and to cast a replacement, so it was too late for a rethink. Thus it was that the fifth Doctor bowed out with the transmission on 16 March 1984 of the final episode of Robert Holmes's *The Caves of Androzani*, bringing to an end an era of the series' history that, for the actor's many fans, had been all too brief.

'The press were all looking for a behind the scenes row,' recalled Davison in his 1988 interview for *Doctor Who Magazine*. 'Indeed the *Daily Mail* printed that I'd been given the elbow because I was too boring! Unfortunately for them, there was no row – in fact John Nathan-Turner tried very hard to keep me on for another season. However, I remembered, when I joined, meeting Patrick Troughton in the BBC car park, and him saying, "Congratulations. Don't stay longer than three years though." And I think he was right. You see, as an actor, I've lived for a long time with the terror of expecting a day to come when there's no work for me. The temptation with doing *Doctor Who* was that I could just have stayed for season after season. But I was risking an association that could have been very damaging career-wise. It was a decision I made through attempting to further my career. It wasn't a happy decision, as in "Thank god that's over". I just wanted to do other things after my time. *Doctor Who* was a lot of fun to do. We had some terrific guest artists, and I wouldn't have missed it for anything. It was very demanding, and strikes delayed my last story so I was too tired to feel sad when it was all finally over, but, yes, one does suffer the odd pang.'

Rewriting the Myth

None of the three script editors who worked on the fifth Doctor's era regarded continuity with what had gone before as being of overriding importance, particularly where they felt that it would get in the way of telling a good, entertaining story. There was, however, a conscious effort made by the production team to avoid committing any really major errors; and, indeed, the series' mythology was drawn upon more heavily than ever before as a source of inspiration for new plot ideas and elements, giving rise to many continuity developments.

A number of new facts about the Doctor become apparent right from the outset. In *Castrovalva*, the transformation of his physical appearance leaves him suffering after-effects far more traumatic than any experienced by his three predecessors, leading him at one point to think that the regeneration is actually failing. (No reason for this is ever given, but one explanation might lie in the severity of the injuries he sustained in the fall that triggered the process.) As with the regeneration of the first Doctor into the second, the mysterious process has affected not only the Doctor's body but also his clothes – his boots have metamorphosed into shoes, and his scarf is starting to unravel. He quickly decides to discard his old outfit altogether in favour of some period cricketing gear found near a pavilion-like room within the TARDIS. Later in the story, he dons a pair of glasses to read; and in the following one, *Four to Doomsday*, he reveals that he is short-sighted in his right eye and carries a magnifying glass in his pocket.

Also in *Four to Doomsday*, the Time Lord is seen to be able to survive for several minutes in the freezing vacuum of space without the benefit of a pressure suit. It is however possible that the helmet-like apparatus that he is wearing to enable him to breathe is also generating some sort of a protective force field around him. Certainly the cricket ball that he throws during the course of his space walk behaves in a manner that would not normally be expected in the absence of any other forces.

The Doctor's improvised use of a cricket ball reinforces the impression given by his clothing that he has something of an affinity for the sport. This is confirmed a little later on, in *Black Orchid*, when he actually takes part in a match in 1920s England and gives a good all-round performance. As the fourth Doctor was also familiar with cricket (evidenced in stories such as *The Ark in Space* and *The Hand of Fear*) but the first was completely unaware of it (established in *The Daleks' Master Plan*), it might perhaps be logical to assume that the third was introduced to the sport during his period of exile on 20th-Century Earth.

In the Buddhist-influenced *Kinda*, the Doctor appears unaffected by the Box of Jhana, a representation of the power of meditation, suggesting that he is already in touch with his inner self. In its sequel *Snakedance*, however, he is unable to find the 'still point' at the centre of his consciousness without the psychic aid of the elderly shaman Dojjen.

The Visitation sees the destruction by the Terileptil leader of the sonic screwdriver, a multipurpose tool introduced during the second Doctor's era in the story *Fury from the Deep*, moving the Time Lord to comment that he feels as if he has lost an old friend.

In *The Five Doctors*, the Doctor is taken ill and then starts to fade away altogether as his previous incarnations are taken out of time and space by the Time Lord President Borusa, causing him to reflect that 'A man is the sum of his memories, you know – a Time Lord even more so.'

An ability to swim is revealed by the Doctor in *Warriors of the Deep*, when he is knocked into a water tank and forced to make his escape through a hatch beneath the surface. *The Caves of Androzani*, on the other hand, sees two weaknesses disclosed. First, the Doctor confides to his companion Peri that he is allergic to certain gases 'in the praxis range of the spectrum' – hence his habit of wearing a stick of celery on his lapel, as this will turn purple if exposed to the gases in question and so warn him of their presence, following which he will eat the celery. Secondly, he is seen to succumb to spectrox toxæmia after touching some strands of raw spectrox, a substance apparently peculiar to the planet Androzani Minor. It is this that ultimately causes him to regenerate once again, after he selflessly uses the last of the antidote to cure Peri of her similar affliction.

The Doctor's ship, the TARDIS, also gives up a few more of its secrets during this period of the series' history. *Castrovalva* involves the Doctor and his companions venturing into some previously unseen areas of its interior, including the pink-hued zero room – a tranquil environment shielded from all external influences (or supposedly so, at any rate, as an image of the Doctor's young male companion Adric is at one point projected inside). This room is part of the random twenty-five per cent of the ship's interior that the Doctor subsequently jettisons when he adjusts the architectural configuration circuits to provide the extra energy needed to pull the TARDIS clear of imminent destruction at Event One, the primordial hydrogen inrush towards which it has been directed by Adric under the Master's evil influence.

It is another of the Doctor's companions, Tegan, who discovers during the course of *Castrovalva* that the TARDIS has a computerised information system, accessible from the main control console. Although she is later disabused of the notion that she has succeeded in piloting the ship to *Castrovalva* by following instructions from this source, she does manage to initiate a short trip in the following story, *Four to Doomsday*, and proves quite proficient at operating the craft later on, most notably in *The King's Demons*.

In Season 20, *Mawdryn Undead* sees the TARDIS making an emergency landing inside a giant spacecraft after colliding with its warp ellipse field. The same story then brings a reminder of the series' past when the Doctor produces a TARDIS homing device first seen, although in a different form, in *The Chase* during the era of his first incarnation and also used by Adric in the fourth Doctor story *Full Circle*.

Terminus presents further problems for the Doctor when his young companion Turlough, coerced into sabotaging the TARDIS, operates some switches behind one of the wall roundels and then partially pulls out a piece of equipment called the space-time element from beneath the control console. The time rotor starts to jam, leaving the Doctor no option but to operate the cut-out. He then refocuses the scanner screen to show images of the ship's interior – another capability not previously displayed – and discovers that a wall of shimmering light is encroaching on its dimensions. The TARDIS has in fact melded itself to a ship headed for the space station Terminus, and an interface soon appears in the form of a doorway in the TARDIS's laboratory area.

The Doctor completely refurbishes the TARDIS console at the start of *The Five Doctors*, but fails to cure it of its temperamental behaviour. In *Warriors of the Deep*, the ship is revealed to be susceptible to attack by energy weapons fired from a satellite orbiting the Earth around the year 2084, the Doctor being forced to perform a materialisation flip-flop in order to remove it from the area of danger. Then, in *Frontios*, the possibility arises that the ship may actually have been destroyed by the power of a creature called the Gravis and his Tractator drones. In truth, however, it has become fragmented and interspersed with the rock of the eponymous planet's surface, and the Doctor is able to trick the Gravis into reassembling it. No sooner has this crisis been averted than, in *Resurrection of the Daleks*, the ship gets caught in a time corridor operated by his oldest adversaries. Finally, in *Planet of Fire*, the Doctor's short-lived android companion Kamelion resets the ship's destination co-ordinates by plugging himself into the data banks via one of the wall roundels, and Turlough performs some further minor sabotage by pulling out a number of wires from beneath the control console in order to cut off an incoming distress call.

Amongst a host of familiar characters returning to the series during the fifth Doctor's era is Brigadier Alistair Gordon Lethbridge-Stewart. He is first seen in *Mawdryn Undead*, working as a mathematics teacher at Brendon, a boys' public school, after his retirement in 1976 from service in the United Nations Intelligence Taskforce (UNIT). He suffers a nervous breakdown and loses his memory in 1977 as a result of the events of the story, but saves the day after the TARDIS takes him forward in time to 1983, where he meets his future self and, in so doing, inadvertently triggers a release of energy – the Blinovitch Limitation Effect (described in rather different terms in the third Doctor story *Day of the Daleks*) – that enables the Doctor to avoid the threatened loss of his remaining regenerations.

It is also mentioned at one point during *Mawdryn Undead* that the Brigadier's former subordinate Sergeant Benton left UNIT in 1979 and is now working as a used car salesman, and that the Doctor's one-time companion Harry Sullivan has been seconded to NATO and is now doing 'hush hush' things at Porton Down. However, as the dates given in this story are completely at odds with those given during the fourth Doctor's era, from which it was clear that the Brigadier, Benton and Harry were all still serving in UNIT in the early 1980s, it may be that *Mawdryn Undead* takes place in a parallel universe (as did certain of the events of the third Doctor story *Inferno*). An alternative explanation would be that, for reasons unknown, a significant change has since occurred in the course of Earth's history.

The Brigadier's other appearance during the fifth Doctor's era comes in *The Five Doctors*. Here, he is attending a reunion at UNIT's British HQ, now under the command of his successor Colonel Crichton, when he encounters the second Doctor – who has for once been able to steer the TARDIS correctly, albeit at the expense of bending the Laws of Time – and is whisked off with him to the Time Lords' home planet, Gallifrey. At the end of the story, the pair depart in what appears to be an offshoot of the fifth Doctor's TARDIS, presumably on their way to further, undisclosed adventures in time and space.

The Five Doctors sees also the return of the Doctor's other previous incarnations, along with his former companions Susan, Sarah Jane Smith, K-9 and the second Romana – not to mention phantom appearances by Jamie, Zoe, Liz Shaw and Captain Mike Yates of UNIT. The first Doctor and Susan and the third Doctor and Sarah also depart in their own respective offshoots of the fifth Doctor's TARDIS once the crisis is over, again heading for destinations unknown.

It is never stated from what points in their respective lives the Doctor's previous incarnations have been taken by the timescoop device used to transport them to Gallifrey. The fourth could easily have been abducted during the course of an untransmitted adventure from his own era. (In fact, the footage was culled from the abandoned Season 17 story *Shada*, although opinions differ as to whether or not this should be regarded as part of the true *Doctor Who* canon.) Where the first, second and third are concerned, however, this explanation would appear to be ruled out both by their appearance – they all look somewhat older than they did at the end of their own respective eras – and by their circumstances – they are all initially without companions, for instance, and at least two of the three appear to be aware of events that occurred at or after the point when they regenerated into their successors. Another apparent anomaly with regard to the second, third, fourth and fifth Doctors is that none of them has any recollection of having already experienced the events of the story in their previous lives.

Similar continuity problems arose in relation to the Season 10 story *The Three Doctors* (and would arise again in relation to the Season 22 story *The Two Doctors*) and, although various different theories have been advanced by fans as possible solutions to them, it is perhaps safest to say simply that they remain unresolved within the fiction of the series itself.

A further point of note about *The Five Doctors* is that no energy release or other apparent adverse reaction occurs when the different incarnations of the Doctor meet up with one another. Although in line with the events of *The Three Doctors*, this appears on the face of it to be inconsistent with what happened when the Brigadier encountered his future self in *Mawdryn Undead*. It may be, however, that Time Lords are less affected by such temporal displacements than are mere human beings (just as they are less affected by temporal disturbances, judging by events in the third Doctor stories *The Time Monster* and *Invasion of the Dinosaurs*).

The Five Doctors is just one of a number of stories in which the fifth Doctor encounters members of his own race. The Master, having recently taken over the body of Consul Tremas of the planet Traken, makes several return appearances, attempting to ensnare the Doctor in the sophisticated trap of Castrovalva (*Castrovalva*); to gain control of the awesome power of the alien Xeraphin (*Time-Flight*); to prevent the signing of the Magna Carta (*The King's Demons*); and to reverse the effects of an accident that has left him stranded in a miniaturised state on the planet Sarn (*Planet of Fire*). In *The Five Doctors* itself, the Master actually attempts to aid the Doctor – at the behest of the Time Lord High Council, who have promised him a whole new regeneration cycle in return – but is thwarted when his old opponent refuses to trust him.

Even more so than in the incarnation encountered by the third Doctor, the Master demonstrates a remarkable ability to disguise his normal saturnine features, taking on various false identities during the course of these stories. He also makes greater use than ever before of his trademark weapon, now referred to as a tissue compression eliminator, which reduces its victims to miniaturised corpses (as previously seen in the third Doctor story *Terror of the Autons* and in the fourth Doctor story *The Deadly Assassin*). One ability of which he makes rather less use than in the past, however, is that of hypnosis.

Arc of Infinity sees the return of another of the Doctor's old adversaries. This is Omega, the legendary stellar engineer whose work provided the Time Lords with the initial power that they needed to enable them to travel through space and time. In his introductory story, *The Three Doctors*, he was shown to be trapped in a universe of anti-matter beyond a black hole, his physical body utterly destroyed and his existence preserved only by his enormous force of will. In *Arc of Infinity*, he makes a further attempt to escape back to his home universe, and again looks to the Doctor to act as the unwilling provider of the means for him to do so. Enlisting the aid of an Ergon servant (an energy creature presumably similar in nature to the Gel Guards featured in *The Three Doctors*) and Councillor Hedin, a traitorous member of the Time Lord High Council who is apparently responsible for providing him with a TARDIS, he conspires to create a new corporeal form for himself by bonding with the Doctor's. The scheme fails, however, and Omega is apparently destroyed when the Doctor fires a matter converter at him.

The Doctor's old Time Lord teacher Borusa, first seen holding the rank of Cardinal in *The Deadly Assassin* and then that of Chancellor in *The Invasion of Time*, has gone one better and become President by the time *Arc of Infinity* takes place – all three stories featuring different incarnations of the character. Other Time Lords encountered during the course of this latest Gallifreyan sojourn include: Damon (an old friend of the Doctor's, although not previously seen in the series); Chancellor Thalia; the Castellan (either a different incarnation of the Time Lord who held that post in *Invasion of Time* or a different Time Lord altogether); and the Chancellery Guard Commander Maxil (whose physical appearance is subsequently adopted by the Doctor when he regenerates into his sixth form in *The Caves of Androzani*).

Arc of Infinity also involves the Doctor visiting once more the virtual reality of the Matrix – the repository of all Time Lord knowledge – as previously featured in both *The Deadly Assassin* and *The Invasion of Time*. This occurs when, despite capital punishment having been long abandoned on Gallifrey, the Time Lord High Council make an unsuccessful attempt to have the Doctor vaporised in order to prevent Omega from succeeding in his plan.

President Borusa features again in *The Five Doctors* – again in a different incarnation – and it becomes clear as the story unfolds that he has now gone insane. It is he who is responsible for bringing all the Doctors and their companions together on Gallifrey, in an area known as the Death Zone. The grim history of this desolate place and of the Game that was played there is explained by the second Doctor as follows:

'In the days before Rassilon, my ancestors had tremendous powers – which they misused terribly. They set up this place, the Death Zone, and walled it around with an impenetrable force field. And then they kidnapped other beings and set them down here.'

At the centre of the Death Zone lies the Dark Tower – the tomb of Rassilon, 'the greatest single figure in Time Lord history'. Official Time Lord lore maintains that Rassilon was a good man, but the second Doctor recalls many rumours and legends to the contrary:

'Some say his fellow Time Lords rebelled against his cruelty and locked him in the Tower in eternal sleep.'

Later, it is revealed that Rassilon's consciousness does indeed live on within the Tower, although his body lies immobile on a bier, apparently in suspended animation. It transpires however that, in keeping with the official history, he is not a cruel tyrant but a wise and benevolent figure. He set up the Game of Rassilon as a trap for those, such as the deranged Borusa, who would seek immortality. These power-crazed individuals are given what they desire, but not in the way that they expect: they are turned into living statues along the side of Rassilon's bier.

The Castellan puts in a further appearance in *The Five Doctors*, but is killed after being falsely accused of treachery. The Chancellor is now a woman named Flavia, who at the end of the story invites the Doctor to return to the Capitol (which, like the planet itself, appears to be called Gallifrey) as President of the Time Lords. The Doctor, however, beats a hasty retreat in the TARDIS ...

The Black Guardian and the White Guardian, introduced in the fourth Doctor's era as awesomely powerful opposing forces superior even to the Time Lords, are featured again in a trilogy of stories comprising *Mawdryn Undead*, *Terminus* and *Enlightenment*. The Black Guardian is determined to avenge himself against the Doctor after their earlier encounter and, unable to intervene directly in the affairs of the universe, co-opts Turlough as a reluctant pawn to bring about his destruction. Ultimately, however, when faced with the choice of handing over either the Doctor or a huge, glowing diamond that he has been offered by the Guardians, Turlough opts for the latter. The Black Guardian is apparently consumed in flames, but the White Guardian warns the Doctor to remain vigilant: 'As long as I exist, he exists also, until we are no longer needed.'

The fifth Doctor's era also sees the return of a number of monstrous alien races introduced in earlier periods of the series' history. In *Earthshock*, a force of Cybermen under the command of a Cyber Leader is attempting to destroy an interstellar peace conference on Earth in the year 2526. As on a number of previous occasions, the creatures' appearance has quite significantly altered since they last crossed paths with the Doctor. This story also contains the first hint that they may now have acquired a limited time travel capability. Not only do they have visual records of events that took place around the 29th Century in the fourth Doctor story *Revenge of the Cybermen* (as well as of incidents in the first Doctor story *The Tenth Planet* and in the second Doctor story *The Wheel in Space*), but one of their devices causes a spaceship to travel back in time after it is tampered with by the Doctor's companion Adric. Another innovation is their use of two deadly androids to guard a powerful bomb that they have concealed on Earth. The Doctor eventually thwarts the

Cybermen's plans, in part by exploiting the fact that, as established in *Revenge of the Cybermen*, gold dust is lethal to them when forced into their chest unit breathing apparatus.

The Doctor's oldest foes, the Daleks, are back in action in *Resurrection of the Daleks*, attempting to free Davros from imprisonment on board a military space station orbiting the Earth. They have lost their long war against the android Movellans – as seen in the fourth Doctor story *Destiny of the Daleks* – and hope that their creator will be able to find a cure for the deadly virus created by their enemies that is wiping them out. They also aim to usurp the power of the Time Lords by infiltrating Gallifrey with android duplicates of the Doctor and his companions. Davros, however, has plans of his own, and begins to inject Daleks with a substance that makes them subservient to his will. This second faction of Daleks then comes into conflict with the one still loyal to the Dalek Supreme (making its first appearance in the series since the third Doctor story *Planet of the Daleks*), although in the end both groups are wiped out when the Doctor releases some of the Movellan virus. Davros, although himself affected by the virus, apparently reaches the safety of an escape pod.

The Five Doctors features a Dalek, a force of Cybermen and also, from the second Doctor's era, a Yeti (which judging from its appearance is a real creature from Tibet, as seen at the end of *The Abominable Snowmen*, rather than one of the Great Intelligence's controlled robots). These creatures have all been transported to the Death Zone on Gallifrey as part of Borusa's scheme, but little new information is revealed about any of them on this occasion.

The Silurians and a force of Sea Devils warriors – survivors of the reptilian species that ruled the Earth before the rise of humankind – attempt to take over an underwater nuclear weapons facility around the year 2084 in *Warriors of the Deep*. Unlike in *Doctor Who and the Silurians* and *The Sea Devils* – the third Doctor stories that gave them their respective debuts – the creatures are this time identified by individual names: the Silurians are led by Icthar, Scibus and Tarpok, while the Sea Devils are commanded by Sauvix. Icthar is described as being the last surviving member of the Silurian Triad and is already known to the Doctor, indicating that there must have been an earlier, untelevised encounter between them. Like the Cybermen in *Earthshock*, both the Silurians and the Sea Devils have undergone a number of changes since their races last appeared in the series. The Silurians' third eyes – which previously acted as weapons and tools – now flash in synchronisation with their voices when they speak, and their voices are themselves completely unlike those heard in *Doctor Who and the Silurians*. In the Sea Devils' case, however, the changes are confined to their clothing: they now wear Samurai-style armour instead of the blue mesh garments seen in *The Sea Devils*.

THE FIFTH DOCTOR

Other new developments in *Warriors of the Deep* include the Silurians' use of a huge, amphibious cyborg, the Myrka, to attack the humans' base, and the revelation that exposure to hexachromite gas is lethal to all reptiles.

Many new characters and monsters are introduced during the fifth Doctor's era, but few go on to make return visits. The Terileptils, for instance, appear only in *The Visitation* (although they do subsequently receive one further mention, in *The Awakening*, when the Doctor explains that – as indicated in the earlier story – they mine a substance called tinclavic on the planet Raaga, and also a cameo in *Time-Flight*). One exception to the rule is Lytton, an alien mercenary seen assisting the Daleks in *Resurrection of the Daleks*, who turns up again in a sixth Doctor story, *Attack of the Cybermen*. Another is the Mara, which also features in two stories: *Kinda* and *Snakedance*. As explained in *Snakedance*, this evil intelligence, which manifests itself in the form of a snake, originated on the planet Manussa. The Manussan scientists had used molecular engineering to produce a Great Crystal attuned to the wavelength of the human mind and able to absorb its energy; only the evil aspects were absorbed, however, and when amplified and reflected by the Crystal these brought into being the entity that became known as the Mara.

Significant though the many continuity developments were during the era of the fifth Doctor, they would be equalled and indeed surpassed during that of his successor, when the series would come to rely ever more heavily on the rich heritage of its own mythology.

Script Editing

It was in early 1963 that the BBC's then Head of Drama Sydney Newman – one of the creators of *Doctor Who* – set up within the Drama Group a system of production teams, each of which would be responsible for making a particular series, serial or strand of plays. Following the precedent already established in many of the ITV companies, these teams would consist of two permanent staff members, namely a producer and a story editor, along with secretarial support. The producer would be given overall artistic, administrative and financial control of the production, overseeing the work of the different directors who would be brought in to handle individual episodes or programmes, while the relatively junior story editor would have the task of finding and working with freelance writers to come up with the required scripts – a function previously performed by the now-defunct Script Department.

The story editor's role was described in more detail by Drama Group Organiser Ayton Whitaker in a loose-leaf Editors' Guide produced in October 1968 for internal use within the BBC:

> The primary function of the editor is to find, encourage and commission new writers. He should concern himself with the details of television scripts so that his producer's horizon can be kept clear. The editor is the writer's representative in the Television Service and is responsible for looking after the writer's interests right through to the time of production. While encouraging writers to practise their art with as much freedom as possible, it is yet the editor's job to guide them on matters of television grammar and the necessary disciplines of the Service, e.g. timing, number of sets, size of cast, amount of film which can reasonably be used ...

The Guide also set out and codified other aspects of the editor's duties, including the need to follow policy guidance on questions of sex, violence and bad language. It went on:

> The principles underlying editorial control are based deeply on the assumption that the finding and encouraging of all those creative and wayward and surprising talents that go into making television

programmes is a major part of the Corporation's responsibility to the public. But, as every truly professional writer will be aware, it is from the disciplining of creative talent, not from its reckless indulgence, that true art emerges.

Other matters covered in the Guide were: checking names in scripts (e.g. to ensure that they could not be misconstrued as referring to real-life people); preparing scripts for typing; keeping track of amendments; and using the services of the Drama Script Unit (the vestigial successor to the old Script Department) in areas such as copyright, briefing procedures, contractual agreements and staff contributions. Also included were a number of articles written by current story editors, explaining how they saw their own jobs in practical terms.

By the early 1980s, most editors were freelancers working on fixed-term contracts rather than permanent members of the BBC's staff. Little else had changed, however. The Guide was still in use – albeit revised and updated, taking into account amongst other things the switch of formal job title from story editor to script editor that had been instituted in June 1968 – and the basic functions of the job were still essentially the same as they had been back in 1963.

Three different script editors had an influence over the stories of the fifth Doctor. The first was Christopher Hamilton Bidmead, who worked on Tom Baker's last season – Season 18 – and played a major part in setting up Peter Davison's first – Season 19. Having initially studied acting at the Royal Academy of Dramatic Art, Bidmead had since earned his living as a radio and television writer and as a journalist specialising in scientific and technical articles. He had been offered the *Doctor Who* post after being recommended by one of the series' former writers, Robert Banks Stewart, and had decided to accept it after being assured by producer John Nathan-Turner and executive producer Barry Letts that they disliked as much as he did the humorous, fantasy-orientated style that had been favoured by the previous production team.

Bidmead enjoyed the challenge of taking the series in a new direction but found the job a very gruelling one, and it was this that ultimately resulted in him spending only a year on the production team. He told *Doctor Who Magazine* in 1986:

'About seventy per cent of Season 18 was written by me, in two senses. One was quite legitimate: as script editor, I would have brainstorming sessions with each of the writers, and there I would contribute at least half the ideas. The slightly less rewarding side of the job was that far too often writers would come back and, for a variety of reasons, they would fail to achieve what was required, and I would end up working far into the night writing stuff myself. Part of the reason for this was my own failure to communicate to them what was needed, part was that they went away in such a frenzy of enthusiasm that ideas would expand beyond our original strictures. It was also partly through lack of experience. I had to attempt to get writers to hammer the stories back into shape, but we needed to feed the juggernaut of the production schedule, so more often than not, I'd have to do it myself.

'I think the script editor has an impossible job, which is indirectly why I left: I mean, I wanted to stay on, but I also wanted the BBC to pay me the sort of money that recognised the kind of effort I was putting into the show. The BBC didn't feel able to do that, so I left. I think you get what you pay for, and subsequent script editors quite rightly didn't have the time to devote to scripts that fans often rightly criticise.'

Before his departure, Bidmead was heavily involved in discussions with Nathan-Turner about the characterisation of the fifth Doctor and about other aspects of the nineteenth season, for which he commissioned a number of stories. He had by this point prepared a revised format document headed '*Doctor Who*: Notes for New Writers', which was sent out to all prospective writers. The document was updated from time to time to reflect new developments, but its basic contents remained unchanged. The version dated 14 November 1980 began with the following general summary of the series' requirements:

THE NATURE OF THE SHOW

What we're looking for from new writers are *not* complete scripts or even involved scenarios, but fresh and readably presented (i.e. brief) storylines.

We're interested in plots that rise convincingly out of characterisation and well-thought-out situations; in particular, storylines should indicate how the idea fits into the four episode shape in which we (usually) serialise our stories. An example, not intended to be definitive, might be: 1. Exposition, 2. Complication Leading to Crisis, 3. The Real Situation Exposed, Revealing the Awful Truth, 4. The DOCTOR Battles Against the Odds But Finally Wins Through.

This kind of thinking gives rise and fall to the narrative, and should throw up strong cliff-hangers in which characters are forced to deal with changing situations, as opposed to the ad hoc 'in one bound our hero is free' variety.

There is no DOCTOR WHO formula, but experience shows that the format allows for three main kinds of story:

THE FIFTH DOCTOR

a. Space Fiction

Recently the programme has been developing a more solid science-fiction basis, and while we feel this is probably a welcome change we're anxious to avoid importing wholesale the familiar clichés of the genre. Of course it's impossible to avoid the sci-fi icons – exploding supernovae, menacing robots and so forth – but they need to be as far as possible rethought into our unique context.

b. Earth-Bound

The appeal of an Earth-bound story is that it gives both the team and the viewers an opportunity to get out on location for a breath of fresh air. But filming is very expensive, and night filming, immensely appealing though it is as a device to wind up the tension, is almost completely outside the scope of our budget. Writers should try to keep all filming to no more than fifteen minutes in a hundred minute story.

c. Historical

These are probably the most difficult to handle, and new writers are recommended to avoid the genre unless they are particularly sure of their ground. Many new writers seem drawn to Kitsch-History themes (Doctor Who meets Machiavelli), but the result is usually an unhappy potpourri of fact and fantasy.

It's a well-understood convention that a Time-Travelling Hero does not change history; additionally we tend to shy away from the sort of story that 'reveals' that the truth about a particular historical event is different from what we always thought it to be. Thus, unless very carefully handled, a story based on the idea that the First World War was actually triggered off by refugees from a coup d'état on the planet Zorrella, is not going to appeal to us.

SCRIPT EDITING

> Having said this, we are in the business of transmitting 'Science Fiction Adventure Stories', and this element mustn't be overlooked.

The adventures of a time-travelling renegade Time Lord are of course built on a premise of wildest fantasy. But without inhibiting creative ideas, we'd prefer writers to work within this concept in a way that acknowledges the appropriate disciplines. Charged Particle Physics (to pick a topic at random) is mapped territory accessible to many of our viewers (there are *Doctor Who* Appreciation Societies in universities all over the world); and writers who want to bring the topic into the story should at least glance at the relevant pages of the encyclopaedia. History of course deserves similar treatment. Imaginative extrapolation of 'the facts' should be preferred to pure gobbledegook.

I should add that having the DOCTOR go back in time to do a fix that solves the problem by not allowing it to arise is a favourite storyline idea we've had to outlaw. If recursive solutions are allowable, our audience will ask why the DOCTOR doesn't always do this, and there'll never be any adventure.

A WORD ON PRESENTATION

Putting characters' names in CAPITALS makes it considerably easier for the reader to track back on plot. Double spacing with proper margins also improves readability. Four pages should be adequate to put across the essence of the idea you want to sell us. I've already suggested that storylines should show clearly how the material fits into the four-part format; but it's sometimes helpful to lead off with a short preface that sets out the premise on which the story is based.

FINALLY

Notes on the DOCTOR, his current companions and the TARDIS follow.

I'm appending a copy of the Introduction to the US edition of a recent *Doctor Who* novel. While it doesn't necessarily represent our official line in all respects, it does give a good overview of what the show is all about.

I'm also enclosing extracts from 'Guide to *Doctor Who* Storylines', written by Douglas Adams when he was script editor of this programme. I think he makes some good points.

Storylines you send in will be warmly welcomed and read. It's always helpful if the writer can include some brief details about his writing history and aspirations. Obviously previous television writing experience is a valuable asset, but we have in the past produced a number of scripts written by newcomers to the medium. A useful book to put you in the picture is *Writing for Television* by Malcolm Hulke (another former *Doctor Who* script editor [sic]), published by A & C Black.

We'll acknowledge all submissions as soon as we can – though experience shows that due to our heavy production schedule our replies are often far from instantaneous. How we proceed from there will obviously depend on the quality and suitability of the ideas submitted.

The US-derived attachment mentioned by Bidmead had in fact appeared as the introduction to all the editions of the Target *Doctor Who* novelisations issued in that country by Pinnacle Books. Written by well-known science fiction author Harlan Ellison, it explained why he considered *Doctor Who* to be the greatest science fiction series of all time.

The appended extract from Douglas Adams's earlier document, headed 'The Script Editor's Guide to *Doctor Who* Storylines', read as follows:

* *Brevity is the soul of storylines.*

We don't want to plough through 20 pages of closely-typed prose trying to work out what the story is about. At the initial stage of story ideas, we just want to know what the idea is, how it resolves, and whether it promises sufficient area of conflict to sustain a hundred minutes of tension and drama. If that takes more than two or three pages then the idea hasn't been thought out well enough. There is absolutely no point in working out all the complicated details of the plot mechanics – who is running after whom at what time and with which monkey wrench – until the basic plot concepts have been properly hammered out.

A script writer is basically in the business of selling his ideas. Imagine the reaction of a harassed script editor faced on the one hand with a very lengthy and detailed exposition of a complicated plotline that he can't fully understand on one reading, and on the other hand with a short, pithy idea that is irresistibly concise.

* *Daleks*

Don't bother to submit stories involving Daleks. Terry Nation invented the beasts, he owns the copyright, and quite properly reserves the right to write Dalek stories himself. In fact the copyright in all monsters and characters is owned by the writer who invented them. It's far better to invent your own.

* *Whose Story?*

This point seems almost too obvious to mention, but it's surprising how often we get storylines which are quite clearly based on previous *Doctor Who* stories, or at least elements of them. Obviously it's terribly difficult to be thoroughly original after a hundred stories, but no-one ever said that writing *Doctor Who* isn't terribly difficult.

I'm writing these notes on the assumption that most people who submit storylines are seriously interested in tackling the very tough professional job of writing for the programme.

It was not a new writer but Bidmead himself who became responsible for writing the fifth Doctor's introductory adventure when the story originally planned for that slot – *Project Zeta-Sigma* by John Flanagan and Andrew McCulloch – fell through at a late stage.

'With *Castrovalva*,' he noted in his *Doctor Who Magazine* interview, 'it was super to start off a new Doctor. It was written at short notice, because another script had fallen through and it was quite a slow burn. They weren't quite sure how Davison was going to work out, and I was asked to write the script accordingly.'

Following his departure from *Doctor Who*, Bidmead resumed his career as a freelance writer. His successor on the series' production team was Antony Root. Root, unlike Bidmead, was not himself a writer.

'I don't write,' he told Philip Newman in an interview for a 1992 issue of *The Frame*. 'I never write scripts. I suppose I'm one of those old-fashioned script editors who believes that script editors are sometimes better when they don't write, because what they're actually doing is, like a publishing editor, trying to get the best work out of other people; helping them achieve what they want to do. I know *Doctor Who* has a tradition of writer/script editors, but I was not one of those people.

THE FIFTH DOCTOR

'After I left university, I worked in live theatre for five years, initially as a theatre manager and then as a publicist. Then, at age 25, I decided that I didn't want to stay in live theatre any longer and got a holiday relief job for three months as an assistant floor manager with the BBC. I suppose that must have been in the summer of 1979 – and, funnily enough, the show I did was a four-part *Doctor Who* directed by Ken Grieve [*Destiny of the Daleks*]. At the end of that holiday relief period, they advertised some permanent positions. I applied, and became a fully-fledged assistant floor manager, a job I did for about eighteen months to two years I guess. After that, I started an internal training course as a script editor and subsequently went on to do programmes.

'What happened was that I went to Graeme McDonald, the person who was then Head of Series and Serials, and asked him what the opportunities were. He gave me some advice that led me to approach the TV Drama Script Unit, where I got what was called a "training attachment" as a script editor. This involved a period of time – about three months, I think – at the Script Unit, followed by a spell back in the Drama Series and Serials Department as a trainee.

'At the end of my time at the Script Unit, Chris Bidmead decided to leave *Doctor Who* and they needed someone to plug the script editor job for a limited period while they found a replacement. I arrived back with perfect timing and was asked if I would do it – which, of course, I did.'

'Root was only meant to be temporary,' explained Bidmead. 'I was getting increasingly bogged down with unsolicited scripts and he was working at the Drama Script Unit, where I used to send stuff. He knocked me out by coming back with a beautifully argued, well condensed report on one of the scripts. That was how he came to my attention.'

'Oh yes,' agreed Root. 'It was always going to be temporary. I don't think I commissioned any new work; I inherited a lot of it. I think I was around for about two stories with John Nathan-Turner.'

Root had followed *Doctor Who* since childhood, and remembered hiding behind the sofa to watch stories of the first Doctor's era. It was partly because of the series' long history that he ultimately found the process of working on it a somewhat trying one.

'It was one of the worst jobs I could imagine a script editor having to do, because the weight of history was so great that it was actually totally stultifying. I was used to working to a fairly broad brief about what one might do in a script, and I was very excited about the possibilities of doing almost any story one could envisage and shaping it within the mould of *Doctor Who*. But then, within twenty-four hours of arriving there, I was introduced to the *Doctor Who* mail, which would often come to the script editor to advise on what the reply should be. You know, you would look at fifty letters that said something like, "Sprodget No 5 in the TARDIS cannot

SCRIPT EDITING

be pressed to do the function that you think it can!" It seemed to me that the weight of history wasn't working to the show's benefit. So I approached it with great hopes but found it an extremely difficult thing to engage with.

'John Nathan-Turner had seen out Tom Baker and was seeing in Peter Davison, whom he knew extremely well from having been production associate on *All Creatures Great and Small*. I think that any difficulties were to do not with the casting but with the usual thing in TV series, like "the production starts shooting in three weeks' time – which script are we going to do?" But Barry Letts was executive producer at that time, so he was always there to turn to.

'I remember I spent a lot of time with Eric Saward on his Great Fire of London story [*The Visitation*], though I don't know that I made any real contribution to it. The other story I remember, with great affection, was written by somebody called Christopher Bailey and entitled *Kinda*. I thought that was really a very interesting script indeed, because it had shades of Buddhist philosophies as well as being quite entertaining on the surface. I have vague memories of the first one we did [*Four to Doomsday*], by Terence Dudley, and another about a cricket match set in the 1920s [*Black Orchid*], but that one was done mostly after I'd gone.

'My job at the time was basically to firefight and to make sure that there were scripts ready to achieve the production schedule that was set. It was a very, very intense time of sleepless nights – I do remember that. I felt like I'd been thrown in right at the deep end. But, as always with script editing, it was about delivering up to directors and production crews, on the day they were meant to start, material they could use that fitted the brief. And obviously I wasn't working solo, but with John Nathan-Turner on that.

'My attachment expired at the end of the *Doctor Who* period and I was told that I would have to go back to being an AFM because, after all, that was technically what I was, as far as the staffing of the BBC was concerned. I said that I didn't want to do that and that I would be leaving the BBC if that had to be – although I understood the reasons why, if it did. A couple of days went by, and then they called me in and asked if I'd like to work on *Juliet Bravo*. So I went and worked on that for a season under Joan Clark, who was the doyenne of series script editors. I then went on with the same producer, Terry Williams, to do the second series of *The Chinese Detective*. Following that, I worked for a couple of years on various things as script editor to a former *Doctor Who* producer, Philip Hinchcliffe. I finally left the BBC in 1984 to go to Euston Films, where I'd been offered a job as their script editor.'

At Euston, Root worked as script editor and script executive on a number of programmes, including a five-part gangster series called *Fear*, which he also co-produced. A few years later, he moved to a company called Working Title, where he continued to serve as a producer on such projects as

Newshounds (a co-production with the BBC), *Lorna Doone* (a co-production with Thames) and the acclaimed Derek Jarman film *Edward II*. Today he continues to pursue a career in film and television production, having always seen script editing as simply a means to that end.

Root's successor on *Doctor Who* was Eric Saward, the writer commissioned by Bidmead to script the pseudo-historical story *The Visitation*. Born in December 1944, Saward had attended grammar school until the age of 18 and then some time afterwards moved to Holland, where he had lived for three years and been briefly married. On his return to England, he had trained and worked for a short time as an English teacher.

'I had started writing by that stage,' he recalled in a 1993 interview, 'and I decided that I didn't like teaching – in fact, the only reason I had gone into it was that there were long holidays and I could spend my time writing, which was what I really wanted to do. I had just started to sell scripts to radio on a fairly regular basis – always drama – and as I had no family commitments, I decided to have a go at being a full-time freelance writer. I had nothing to lose.

'I was about 30 then, and I always managed to stay afloat through one thing or another. I picked up the odd job. I worked in the theatre briefly as a self-taught electrician, including on *Hair* and *The Canterbury Tales* at the Phoenix in Shaftesbury Avenue. I bobbed along like that for a while, and then became involved with *Doctor Who*. Chris Bidmead approached the senior drama script editor at BBC radio and asked – quite boldly – if he could recommend anybody to write for the series. I was doing very well in radio and so, along with a few others, I was recommended. Chris rang me up and asked if I would be interested, and I said "Why not". I hadn't watched *Doctor Who* in years, so I really didn't know what I was letting myself in for.

'I wrote a storyline, *The Visitation*, which John Nathan-Turner disliked, as one of the characters was an actor – John had a thing about not showing actors on television. That was around the March of 1980, I think, and my reaction was, "Well, that's it, I'll just get on with my life". Then, around the September, Chris rang up and said, "Do you remember that storyline you wrote, that John didn't like? Would you like to do us a scene breakdown?" I was initially inclined to refuse, but Chris said that they would pay me a fee, which I think was about £400, and as I needed the money, I agreed to do it. He liked what I came up with, and I think that by that stage they really had to go with it as they needed to fill a slot in the production schedule. I delivered the full scripts about eight weeks later, in January 1981, and that's how I got started in television.'

It was shortly after this that Saward was invited to join the *Doctor Who* production team.

'I went there originally for three months. Antony Root had been working on the series, but unfortunately knew very little about putting scripts together. That's not deriding him; he was just inexperienced. Even after he had done three months on *Doctor Who*, the powers-that-be still wanted him to do something else before they would offer him a staff script editor post – this was how the BBC viewed *Doctor Who*, which in my own view was the most difficult assignment anyone could be given. So Antony went to work on *Juliet Bravo* and then on *The Chinese Detective*, where I gather that he had a really horrible time as it was written by the very distinguished Ian Kennedy Martin, and the producer, Terry Williams, didn't want his star writer to be criticised at all.

'Anyway, there was a lot of humming and hawing, and they kept extending my contract by a month at a time, as they didn't know if Antony was going to be coming back to *Doctor Who* or what was going to be happening. We had this messing around for about three months, which was really very aggravating. In the meantime, I had written *Earthshock*, which went more or less immediately into production. Eventually they decided that I would be staying, and I was then given a nine month contract.'

Like Root, Saward sometimes found himself at odds with the series' fans.

'I remember that when we killed Adric in *Earthshock*, we had just a short scene at the beginning of the next story, *Time-Flight*, where the Doctor was sort of in mourning. This brought a tremendous outcry from the fans. People were saying "Oh god, he should have been in mourning throughout the *whole* story, and the next one as well." Well no, sorry, it doesn't work like that! *Doctor Who* is about the Doctor going off and having adventures. The dramatic impact of Adric dying had been had at the end of *Earthshock*, and that was it. As in life, you move on.'

On questions of continuity, too, Saward felt that many fans were often overly pedantic, devoting their time to picking up small contradictions in the scripts rather than simply enjoying them as entertaining stories.

'You've got an audience with the fans, you see, who know infinitely more about the series than any person working on it can or perhaps even wants to. That accumulation of knowledge can get in the way of telling a good story; you're so busy trying to get the continuity right that the story goes down the tubes.'

Saward was however keen to avoid making any really major continuity errors, and so he – like Nathan-Turner – occasionally sought advice on these matters from prominent fans such as Ian Levine.

'Ian Levine did a hell of a lot of work during that time, all uncredited. I mean, all the clips that were needed for flashback sequences, he sorted them out all in his own time and without payment. He was very, very useful when it came to continuity. I turned to him lots of times, especially when we were using established things like Daleks and Cybermen. We still made loads of mistakes – for which I don't apologise, as there was never any strict continuity on the series – but we tried not to counter massively what had been previously established. So we didn't suddenly have Cybermen who could fly, for example.'

Another aspect of the script editor's job is to check and approve any changes that cast members or directors want to make to scripts during the course of production.

'You don't sit in your office like some demon king, saying "You can't do this" or "You can't do that" to directors. On the other hand, the script editor is obliged to safeguard the rights of the writers – it's in the agreement that the BBC has with the Writers' Guild. Also, he's an independent person in the sense that he's outside the production of the particular story – he's not at rehearsals all the time. Changes will come out of enthusiasm as much as anything else. I was always very strict about any changes that affected the plot, because if it hadn't made sense when it was all cut together then I was the one who was going to be hounded down the corridors by people demanding to know why I had agreed to changes that had ended up ruining it.

'A director is hired to interpret a story, not to rewrite it. In the same way, actors are booked to appear in it, not to rearrange it. If someone comes up with a brilliant line, though, then obviously it's not going to be refused. Lines will also get dropped, because action takes over or because an actor needs only an expression to convey something to the audience.'

Although vigilant about changes being made to scripts after they had been finalised and agreed with the writer, Saward found that – like Bidmead before him – he was often having to carry out a considerable amount of rewriting himself before that stage was actually reached.

'Script editors are a blessing and a curse. I worked for a long time in radio – I still do – and the fact is that, in that medium, what you write is what goes out. I mean, the director will talk to you, if he or she is a little concerned about something, but it's like in the theatre where the writer is viewed as being a little more important than in television series. I think that's a mistaken attitude on the part of television. If you've got lousy writers you've got lousy shows; that's always been so and always will be so. On shows where there is a well known writer – someone like Andrew Davies, for example – I assume that the script editor just makes the tea, because you ain't gonna be playing with his scripts without an awful lot of discussion and an awful lot of reasons why you want to change things. To my mind, that's absolutely right, and most writers will respond to that sort of treatment. I mean, if they know the thing is all right, why the hell should they change it? On a lot of shows, that works. You don't have script editors rewriting or wanting to change the scripts.

'My attitude towards script editing was that what the writer wrote ought to be, wherever possible, what was produced. But *Doctor Who* is one of those old-fashioned shows that is very difficult to write. It requires strong characterisation, strong stories, action, humour, adventure, thrills; the whole gamut. Other shows like *Casualty*, for example, simply aren't that demanding. I'm not knocking *Casualty*, but it's got a stock setting, stock characters and stock situations. The writers just have to weld on their own idea: a road accident, a schizophrenic on the run with a meat axe, or whatever. Half the work is done for them, because they are using the established elements. In *Doctor Who*, the only ongoing characters are the Doctor and the companion. The rest, the writers have to invent for themselves.

'The problem is that modern television writing makes writers very lazy. Up-and-coming writers are used on soaps like *EastEnders*, which have stock characters, and on shows like *Casualty*, which require, to my mind, a limited amount of characterisation and plotting. My experience – and I tried many, many different writers – was that a lot of them just couldn't characterise to the standard that was wanted. Their imagination wasn't developed sufficiently. I mean, imagination is not a gift one is given at birth; it's something that can be developed. The more one works at it, the stronger it becomes. And a lot of writers never have that opportunity. The reason so much rewriting went on by me and by my predecessors was that it was very hard to find people who could do it well.

'Another problem was getting writers to work within the constraints of what could be achieved on our budget. The first hour of my discussion with any writer would always be about the technical limitations: what could be done, what couldn't be done, the number of sets we could have, the number of talking parts. I mean, we would always try to do whatever the writer wanted, but I would have to say things like, "Never give a creature tentacles, because we can't manage that." There were certain things we just couldn't do, because we didn't have the money or the time. The writers had to be realistic about what could be achieved. I assume that Terrance Dicks, Douglas Adams, Christopher Bidmead and all the other script editors down the decades must have said very similar things to their writers, because it's pointless sending a writer away to write something and then finding out that it can't be done.

'I still carry the *Doctor Who* burden, because whenever I write something, I'm always careful about the number of sets I have. I'm always thinking, "Am I justifying the use of this set?" It's good training from that point of view, because one can easily go into fantasy land and have a set for this, a set for that and so on, and it'll never happen, because television just doesn't work like that.'

Saward would generally have three different types of writer in mind when planning each new season: those who had already established a good track record on the series; those who were successful in other fields but had not previously worked on *Doctor Who*; and those who were complete or relative newcomers to television.

'I never drew lines about choosing scripts – there was no prescribed mix between established writers and new ones. I would always use new talent if I could – it was a BBC policy – but at the same time I obviously wanted to go back to writers who had done good work for me in the past. Most of the time it was a case of writers coming to us with original ideas. Occasionally they would come with a thought rather than a fully worked out idea, and then it would be a matter for discussion. And as with any discussion, the original concept would often change drastically.'

A notable feature of the fifth Doctor's era was that more ultimately unused material was commissioned than during any other equivalent period of the series' history. This included the following:

Title	*Writer*	*Commission*	*Date*
Mark of Lumos	Keith Miles	Storyline	14/03/80
Mouth of Grath*	Malcolm Edwards and Leroy Kettle	Breakdown	18/03/80
Farer Nohan*	Andrew Stephenson	Breakdown	18/03/80
The Dogs of Darkness*	Jack Gardner	Breakdown	29/03/80
		Scripts	11/08/80
Soldar and the Plastoids	John Bennett	Breakdown	10/04/80
Psychrons	Terence Greer	Breakdown	13/06/80
Project '4G'	John Flanagan and	Breakdown	15/08/80
(aka *Project Zeta-Sigma*)	Andrew McCulloch	Scripts	07/10/80
The Torsan Triumvirate	Andrew Smith	Breakdown	25/11/80
Hebos	Rod Beacham	Breakdown	05/12/80
The Enemy Within	Christopher Priest	Breakdown	05/12/80
		Scripts	06/02/81
Title unknown	Tanith Lee	Scripts	06/02/81
Way Down Yonder	Lesley Elizabeth Thomas	Breakdown	23/04/81
Space-Whale	Patrick Mills and John Wagner	Breakdown	07/09/81
(aka *Song of the Space Whale*)		Scripts	02/12/81
Parasites	Bill Lyons	Breakdown	22/09/81
(aka *The Parasites*)		Scripts	16/02/82
			23/04/82
Domain**	Philip Martin	Breakdown	13/04/82
		Scripts (1)	14/10/82

		Scripts (2-4)	27/01/83
Poison	Rod Beacham	Breakdown	27/04/82
		Scripts	27/05/82
The Place Where All Times Meet	Colin Davis	Breakdown	10/06/82-
The House That Ur-Cjak Built	Andrew Stephenson	Breakdown	10/06/82
The Six Doctors***	Robert Holmes	Breakdown	04/08/82
May Time (aka *Man Watch*)	Christopher Bailey	Breakdown	24/08/82
		Scripts	16/09/82
Ghost Planet****	Robin Squire	Breakdown	05/01/83
		Scripts	20/05/83

*May have been initially envisaged for the fourth Doctor's last season.
**Ultimately reworked as *Vengeance on Varos* for Season 22.
***Ultimately scrapped in favour of *The Five Doctors*.
****May have been envisaged for the sixth Doctor's first season. Robin Squire had previously worked as uncredited assistant script editor on the third Doctor's debut season.

Other writers who had discussions with the production team during 1980 but who (judging from surviving BBC documentation) were not subsequently commissioned during the fifth Doctor's era included John Gribbin, Richard Sparks, Ian Marter (who as an actor had earlier played the Doctor's companion Harry Sullivan), James Follett, David Tebbet and Geoff Lowe (who submitted an outline entitled *Romanoids*).

'I was always looking for new writers,' notes Saward. 'The first problem was finding people who were actually prepared to do it, because – in spite of what the fans think – it wasn't considered a great privilege to work on the show. *Doctor Who* was viewed within the Department as something that just sort of happened rather than as a prestigious show worth looking at. Our budgets were awful – we always had problems with that – and, as I've said before, new writers found it very difficult to come up with the strong characters and plots that we wanted. Really what I needed was six Charles Dickenses. That would have been brilliant. But I never found them. I had Bob Holmes and I had Philip Martin, but it took me several years to get that far.'

Although he enjoyed his first year as script editor, finding it a new and exciting challenge, Saward became increasingly disaffected with the job as time went by. This was due not only to the gruelling nature of the work, but also to a widening divergence of opinion between himself and Nathan-Turner as to the direction in which the series should be moving and the manner in which it should be produced. This eventually resulted in his acrimonious and controversial departure from the production team during the era of Peter Davison's successor, Colin Baker. Since then, he has continued to pursue a career as a freelance writer, including for German radio (his scripts being translated into German for production). Of his involvement with *Doctor Who*, he is now left with distinctly mixed feelings.

'There were script editors in the building who used to come in at 10 o'clock in the morning and be gone by 12, and there was I working weekends, working evenings ... My life was just not my own. And I did five years of it. Bob Holmes had done three and a half years back in the Seventies, and he said that he didn't know how I'd managed to get to the fifth year. He was absolutely right. I was knackered. The only reason I hung on was that it was quite well paid. I mean, I enjoyed talking to the writers, I enjoyed getting things going, I enjoyed seeing the programme being made, but it was really too much for one person, in the end, with all the problems and all John's messing around. It all piled on in an unnecessary way.

'Most of the stories had massive input from me. Not out of choice, I might add, but because I had to pull the thing round. I mean, if you've got a director sitting across the hall and the scripts are still in a thousand pieces, you can't say, "Excuse me, we're waiting for the muse to strike". He's got only a few weeks to prepare for production, and he wants the scripts. You have to come up with something. I didn't enjoy doing it a lot of the time. I always feel that if you rewrite something, you don't necessarily make it better, you just make it different, you make it you, or more you. And I can't be brilliant every day of the week. No-one can, alas.

'During the years that I worked on *Doctor Who*, I could have gone up as co-author on almost every story.'

Production Development

The production of a TV drama series relies heavily on teamwork, with many different people – script editor, writers, directors, designers and actors among them – all influencing the form and content of the finished product. Probably the most influential contributor of all, however, is the producer, who has overall responsibility for the making of the series.

During the 1980s, *Doctor Who* had only one producer, John Nathan-Turner, who consequently oversaw the whole of Peter Davison's era as the Doctor. He was initially aided by one of his predecessors, Barry Letts, who had been appointed as executive producer to the series for the fourth Doctor's last season, Season 18, after acting as such on an informal basis during the previous year. However, Letts's involvement was essentially supervisory in nature – commenting on scripts, giving advice and approving major production decisions at a time when the BBC's Drama Group was undergoing a major reorganisation and the new Head of Series and Serials, David Reid, had yet to settle into his job – and it lasted until only August 1981, by which time the reorganisation was complete and it was clear that Nathan-Turner had fully grasped the reins of the series.

One of Nathan-Turner's chief concerns in planning the fifth Doctor's debut season was to retain the loyalty of *Doctor Who*'s regular audience. Davison's predecessor, Tom Baker, had remained with the series for an unprecedented seven years and built up an enormous following amongst the general viewing public, many of whom were no doubt unaware that there had ever been any other actors playing the Doctor. To recast the lead role in a long-running and popular series is always a high-risk endeavour, and Nathan-Turner felt that Baker's successor would be bound to have an uphill struggle to win the acceptance of *Doctor Who*'s many avid followers.

One way in which the producer aimed to smooth the transition from the fourth Doctor to the fifth was to arrange, in addition to the usual summer reruns (which this year comprised *Full Circle* and *The Keeper of Traken*), a season of repeats from earlier eras of the series' history, thus reminding viewers that there had indeed been other actors than Baker in the lead role. Despite the trouble and expense involved in re-negotiating rights on 'out of time' repeat material – that is, material more than three years old – the powers-that-be acceded to Nathan-Turner's request, and a season of five stories – *100,000 BC*, *The Krotons*, *Carnival of Monsters*, *The Three Doctors* and

Logopolis – was transmitted in an early evening BBC2 slot in November and December 1981 under the banner title *The Five Faces of Doctor Who*.

Another strategy developed by Nathan-Turner with a view to maintaining regular audience loyalty was to make Season 18's last two stories – *The Keeper of Traken* by Johnny Byrne and *Logopolis* by Christopher H Bidmead – and Season 19's first – *Project Zeta-Sigma* by John Flanagan and Andrew McCulloch – a loosely-linked trilogy of adventures, in which the Doctor's old arch enemy the Master would be reintroduced in a new physical form. Even after the abandonment of *Project Zeta-Sigma* (in which the Master was to have adopted the guise of an alien scientist named Sergo), this plan was followed through with the commissioning of a replacement Master story in the form of Christopher H Bidmead's *Castrovalva*.

To provide still greater incentive for regular viewers to keep faith with the series, Nathan-Turner decided upon the introduction at the end of Season 18 of two new regulars to join the Doctor and his established companion Adric on their journeys – the theory being that these characters would quickly gain their own respective groups of fans who would want to follow their adventures and see how they coped with the new Doctor.

The first of the newcomers, Nyssa, had originally been created by Johnny Byrne as a one-off character for *The Keeper of Traken*, but Nathan-Turner had quickly decided to keep her on for a further three stories. (Even before rehearsals for *The Keeper of Traken* had begun, actress Sarah Sutton had signed a contract for an additional 12 episodes, with an option on the BBC's part for her to appear in a further 16 out of the following 20 – later reduced to 16 out of 18 after Season 19 was allocated a total of 26 episodes instead of the 28 originally planned for.)

The second new regular was Tegan, who made her debut in *Logopolis*. Created by Nathan-Turner and Bidmead to be a more long-term companion, she was characterised as an argumentative air hostess from Australia – a country of origin chosen by the producer partly in order to break the precedent of exclusively British human companions and partly with a view to increasing the chances of gaining a co-production deal for the location filming of a story in Australia.

One consideration that Nathan-Turner had very much in mind in choosing this mix of regular characters was that it ought to give the series a very broad-based appeal. This he felt was ultimately borne out, as he told journalist David Hirsch in a 1982 interview for *Starlog*:

'The younger viewers have Adric and Nyssa to identify with. Tegan, judging by the fan mail, is very popular with some of the older boys and the dads. Peter Davison is very popular all around, but he has a huge female following. Consequently we have a line-up of people who provide something for everyone.'

There were other reasons, too, why Nathan-Turner was keen to experiment with a three-companion set-up, as he explained to Hirsch:

'I brought in three companions because I liked the original line-up of the first Doctor with the two teachers and the grand-daughter. I thought it worked very well. With four people on board the TARDIS, you can have two storylines going and you can have plenty of dialogue. Or you can have four storylines, with the regulars speaking only to non-regulars. It's a very useful device but, like everything, after a time it begins to bore. Keeping four characters on the air throughout the story can be a difficult responsibility.'

It was partly due to his concerns over the difficulty of ensuring that all three companions were given sufficient to do that Nathan-Turner originally intended to have Nyssa written out in Season 19's second story, Terence Dudley's *Four to Doomsday*. He changed his mind, however, when Davison raised strong objections to this plan. The actor, although sympathising with the producer's desire to dispense with one of the companions and thus make the TARDIS a little less crowded, was keen that the one to go should not be Nyssa, whose pleasant, refined character he considered made her the most suited of the three to accompany his Doctor. Nathan-Turner therefore decided to have Adric written out instead – an arrangement with which Davison was content – and this was achieved in the later Season 19 story *Earthshock*, written by the series' new script editor Eric Saward. Saward himself was similarly pleased to see the number of regulars reduced, as he explained in a 1982 interview with Jeremy Bentham for *Doctor Who Monthly*:

'I didn't like the set-up at all of writing for the Doctor and *three* companions, particularly when they're all together in the TARDIS; it's like doing a crowd scene! All the dialogue seems totally artificial when you consider it's mostly the Doctor who has to come up with all the information and the ideas. The companions are forced more and more to become ciphers – something I totally disapprove of – and I'm pleased that we have in fact now lost one of them. Ideally I think it could come down to just one companion, so we could then take that character and develop a full personality to him or her and not just a stereotype.'

One issue over which Davison and the production team continued to disagree was the relative merits of Nyssa and Tegan. Nathan-Turner's view, as he told *Starlog*, was that Tegan was the stronger of the two characters:

'I think Tegan's one of the most interesting companions that there's ever been. She isn't a typical *Doctor Who* girl. In the old days, they used to say that the two basic requirements of being a *Doctor Who* companion were to be able to run down corridors and to say "So what do we do next, Doctor?" with conviction. Now, here's this bossy lady who stumbled into the TARDIS, who gets irritated by the Doctor, and the Doctor gets irritated by her because she speaks her mind. Tegan, being the outsider, is representing the average viewer's point of view.'

Saward also considered Tegan to be a stronger companion than Nyssa, although he did not always see eye to eye with Nathan-Turner as regards the way her character was used, as he explained in a 1993 interview:

'Of all the companions I was involved with, I thought Tegan was the best, because she was ballsy, she had an energy. There was always a struggle with John, though, because whenever a writer gave her something strong to do, he would say, "No, she's a stupid, dumb Australian". Well, the actress is neither stupid nor dumb, the character she was playing was a strong, independent woman, and I thought it was pointless wasting her as we did. We could have developed her. She could have acquired skills under the tutelage of the Doctor. I mean, we could have taken her wherever we'd wanted.'

Having said this, Saward conceded that there had to be a balance struck between the regulars:

'With Peter Davison we had a Doctor who was a softer, younger, more vulnerable person, so if we'd built up Tegan to be a much stronger, tougher companion, that would have overwhelmed.'

Nathan-Turner explained in the introduction to his 1986 book *Doctor Who – The Companions* why he was wary of making the Doctor's companion too strong a character:

> One of the problems I discovered with companions of my own devising was that the more rounded the character, the more it required development. And development of character takes air-time and this reduces the amount of dramatisation air-time and before you know where you are, a science-fiction adventure series is taking on a soap-opera flavour. So, slowly but surely, writers and script editors *and* producers decide to play down the character development of the companion (in any case after 23 years we know comparatively little about the Doctor) and concentrate on the drama of the story.

Despite Davison's affection for Nyssa, the production team eventually decided to have her written out in the Season 20 story *Terminus*. They also decided to have introduced – in *Mawdryn Undead*, the story immediately prior to her departure – a replacement character: a young, male companion named Turlough. Interviewed by Richard Marson for a 1984 edition of *Doctor Who Magazine*, Saward explained how the creation of a new companion was approached:

'If someone wants to leave or the producer decides it's time for a change, we'll discuss a new companion. Based to a degree on the conversation I've had with John, I'll write an audition piece reflecting the character we want to end up with. Then it's up to the actor in the audition to make it his or her own.

'Turlough in his situation piece was a rather shifty, unreliable young man

PRODUCTION DEVELOPMENT

who at the same time was confused. He was self-centred, but he had reason to be scared. Here he was, stuck on Earth, an alien, and suddenly this hideous creature [the Black Guardian] comes out of nowhere and orders him to kill somebody [the Doctor] in order to return to his own planet. It's going to disorientate the toughest of individuals, and we wanted to explore that through Turlough. That said, we knew he would have to settle down and become enough of a companion – friendly with the Doctor – for it to be credible, otherwise we'd have had a situation whereby Turlough spends umpteen episodes lurking about the TARDIS sharpening his knives and polishing his stun gun. The Doctor has got to buy Turlough for what he is – a rather selfish, uncertain individual who has only thrown his lot in with the Doctor to some extent. Turlough too has to accept the Doctor ultimately for what he represents.

'A lot was left to the actor, Mark Strickson, who always maintained a slight edge. Whatever he was doing and however much he had to do, he always had an air of menace. The viewer could never be quite certain. I thought he was an excellent companion.'

A return to the three-companion set-up came with the introduction of the shape-shifting android Kamelion in Season 20's final story, *The King's Demons*. This proved less than successful, however, as near-insurmountable problems arose with the robot prop that had first attracted Nathan-Turner to the idea of accommodating the character. Kamelion would thus appear in only one Season 21 story, *Planet of Fire*, and at the end of that would be written out. It was decided that Tegan and Turlough should also make their respective departures during Season 21, and that the Doctor should then go back to having just a single female companion – an arrangement that Nathan-Turner recalled having worked particularly successfully during the third Doctor's era.

Davison still felt that Nyssa was the companion best suited to his Doctor, and attempted to persuade the producer to bring her back into the series.

'I thought Nyssa worked best with the Doctor's character,' affirmed the actor in an interview with Graeme Wood, Mark Wyman and Gary Russell for a 1991 edition of *TV Zone*. 'I did tire of the abrasiveness of arguing with Tegan, getting annoyed with Adric. But Nyssa always seemed down to earth and sympathetic, fulfilling those things an assistant has to. It may be demeaning, but the companion is there to help the Doctor, to be "in this thing together" as friends. I did suggest that John consider bringing Nyssa back miraculously from the lazars' planet, but he didn't buy it.'

It was shortly after this that Davison decided to leave the series once his contract expired.

The new companion devised by Nathan-Turner, Saward and writer Peter Grimwade was Peri, an American botany student who was introduced in Grimwade's *Planet of Fire* – Davison's penultimate story.

'With Peri,' recalled Saward in his 1984 interview for *Doctor Who Magazine*, 'John decided we should have an American girl to break away from the stereotype of the English girls. We talked about her background and what she should be like and, as with Turlough, I wrote an audition piece. Nicola Bryant read for us, made the part come alive and turned out to be the most suitable ... Peri is quite a strong girl. She doesn't like to be pushed around, but at the same time she's a gentler character than Tegan.'

Davison had disliked having an Australian on board the TARDIS, feeling that this was simply a misguided attempt on Nathan-Turner's part to increase the series' appeal to Australian viewers, and his initial reaction on learning that her successor was to be an American was one of great disappointment.

'There was the American girl coming in,' he recalled in a 1986 interview with Ian Atkins for *Wholook*, 'which I didn't think was an awfully good idea. I mean, the American aspect; Nicola Bryant was very good, but I didn't feel that the American aspect was a very good idea. Apart from anything else, the Americans like *Doctor Who* because it is *English*, not because it has American elements. I would like to have done more stories with Nicola. I think that if I had made the choice later, then I might well have stayed on, but as it was, I went straight into another series'.

One notable aspect of the fifth Doctor's companions that distinguished them from their predecessors was that – like the Doctor himself – the costumes they were given to wear were essentially uniforms: distinctive, highly stylised outfits that generally remained unchanged from one story to the next. This development was motivated in part by a wish to save money on the series' costume budget. A far more significant factor, however, was Nathan-Turner's desire to help keep the series in the public eye by ensuring that the regulars had recognisable, unvarying images for marketing purposes. This strategy was successful, in that these images – the Doctor in his cricketing gear, Nyssa in her aristocratic Traken garb, Tegan in her air hostess uniform, Adric in his Outler's tunic, and so on – became very familiar to the general viewing audience and often adorned the packaging and contents of spin-off merchandise produced during this period of the series' history. When Tegan and Nyssa did finally have a complete change of costume, in the Season 20 stories *Arc of Infinity* and *Snakedance* respectively, this was actually thought significant enough to be made the subject of a press photocall, and gained considerable publicity.

The same philosophy extended to other aspects of the series. The Master, for instance, generally adopted a disguise in the early stages of each story in which he appeared, whether or not there was any reason for him to do so in plot terms, as this was perceived by the production team to be an established and popular aspect of his character. To many fan critics, however, this new focus on identifiable images had the downside of damaging the series' credibility. Viewers, they argued, found it difficult to suspend their disbelief in characters who never changed their clothes; and the series also took on aspects of the fantastical superhero genre, which had been spawned in American comic books and had since entered popular culture more widely, with its easily recognisable, uniform-wearing characters such as Superman and Batman.

This development went hand in hand with *Doctor Who*'s recent adoption by Marvel Comics in their regular publication devoted to the series, which during the fifth Doctor's era was known variously as *Doctor Who – A Marvel Monthly*, *Doctor Who Monthly* and *The Official Doctor Who Magazine*. Although *Doctor Who* strip stories had been running for many years in titles such as *TV Comic* and *Countdown*, these earlier ventures had been very much a part of the long tradition of British children's comics. Marvel's strips, on the other hand, were principally influenced by the American, superhero-dominated comics genre.

There were other respects, too, in which the Davison-era stories came to resemble aspects of American comic book fare. One of these was their increasing preoccupation with the series' own internal continuity, which manifested itself in numerous continuity references; in frequent return appearances by old monsters and other characters; in 'team up' adventures like *The Five Doctors*; and in plots, such as that of *Planet of Fire*, largely devoted to writing out established regulars and introducing new ones.

This growing reliance on the reuse of popular elements from the series' history was initially discernible in the trilogy of Master stories that saw out the fourth Doctor and introduced the fifth. It was taken to a higher level, however, in *Earthshock*. The Cybermen's return appearance in this story, their first in seven years, was one of the most talked-about and popular aspects of Season 19, and generated considerable publicity – although, in order to preserve the surprise, Nathan-Turner made sure that the Cybermen's involvement was kept under wraps prior to the transmission of the first episode, even to the extent of turning down the offer of a *Radio Times* front cover photograph and article.

The success of *Earthshock* encouraged Nathan-Turner to continue the trend by reviving other popular characters in the following season. Saward would later express the view that the producer was motivated in this regard solely by a desire to appeal to the series' fans. In fact, however, the large amount of press coverage and positive comment generated by *Earthshock* had led Nathan-Turner to suspect that such an approach would be welcomed not only by the fans but also by the general viewing public; and in and in order to test this hypothesis he had gained agreement to the transmission of a further season of largely 'out of time' repeats under the banner heading *Doctor Who and the Monsters* (amended slightly from *Doctor Who Meets the Monsters* in his original proposal). The good ratings and positive feedback generated by these repeats – edited compilation versions of *The Curse of Peladon, Genesis of the Daleks* and *Earthshock*, transmitted on BBC1rather than on BBC2 as *The Five Faces of Doctor Who* had been – had convinced the producer that he was on the right track.

The revival of old monsters was initially welcomed by the series' leading man, too. '*Earthshock* was my favourite story from my first season,' noted Davison in a 1983 interview with Stephen Collins for *Zerinza: The Australasian Doctor Who Fanzine*, 'and one of the reasons for this was that it featured the first old enemy I'd faced, apart from the Master. I think old enemies are good. I think that possibly in my second season there weren't quite enough, really, but that was not the fault of anybody except the people behind the standard BBC strike, which seems to come once a year, usually at Christmas time for some reason. Anyway, we were four episodes short, and they would have featured old enemies. I think it's nice to have old enemies back.'

The strike-hit four-parter to which Davison referred was Saward's *The Return*, featuring the Daleks, which was to have been transmitted after *The King's Demons* as the closing story of Season 20. Despite its temporary loss (it would eventually appear in slightly revised form as *Resurrection of the Daleks* in Season 21), Season 20 still drew much more heavily on established *Doctor Who* continuity than had Season 19, making Davison's expression of disappointment seem somewhat surprising. Indeed, there was at least one element from the Doctor's past in every story – a fact that, after it was pointed out to him by fan Ian Levine, Nathan-Turner used as part of his promotion of the series in its 20th anniversary year. The special anniversary story, *The Five Doctors*, itself afforded still further evidence of the series' increasing reliance on its own mythos to provide the inspiration and substance for new stories.

'We drew on the series' past far too much,' reflected Saward in 1993. 'Again it was a case of John wanting to appeal to the fans. I think *Doctor Who* works best when the production team are going for it and inventing their own things. To my mind, the best period of the series' history was in the mid-Seventies when Philip Hinchcliffe and Bob Holmes were in charge. Bob Holmes was the best writer the series ever had, and when he was script editor he – like many others before him and after him – rewrote a lot of the stories. He made them very Bob Holmes, and because he was very confident and very strong, the scripts were very confident and very strong and very inventive. He had in Philip Hinchcliffe a producer who was new to the job and who would go for it; he would be down in the visual effects workshop, for example, trying to get them to do the best they possibly could. He was doing the producer's job, which is to support the script. He had in Tom Baker an excellent Doctor, and he had in Lis Sladen and Louise Jameson two interesting companions, in their very different ways.

PRODUCTION DEVELOPMENT

'Hinchcliffe and Holmes still used old monsters like the Cybermen and the Daleks, but they also brought a lot of new things to the series themselves. We didn't do that when I was script editor, and I always felt that was a tremendous drawback. We weren't adding to it, we were just living off it. It's always better to invent your own things. That's not just an ego trip; you often do better when you invent your own instead of using somebody else's. Writers shouldn't be told, "I want you to do this, this, this, this and this". They'll say, "No, I'm not interested." They should be given as much freedom as possible. What Peter Grimwade got lumbered with on that awful story *Planet of Fire*, for instance, was utterly lunatic. I mean, I felt embarrassed. Turlough leaving, Peri joining, the Master, Kamelion, the Lanzarote location – it was ridiculous.'

Davison, although more restrained in his comments than Saward, has also in later interviews expressed the view that the series came to rely rather too heavily on its past successes. Despite any doubts that there might have been from these quarters, however, Season 21 saw a continuation of the policy of bringing back old monsters – in particular in *Warriors of the Deep*, which featured both the Silurians and the Sea Devils, and in *Resurrection of the Daleks*, the Dalek story postponed from Season 20.

Notwithstanding Saward's contention that little of substance was added to the series' mythos during his tenure as script editor, the frequent reuse of old characters and concepts in fact gave rise to many new continuity developments. In addition, most of the returning monsters – including the Cybermen, the Silurians and the Sea Devils – appeared in redesigned form. Although many fan critics would later express the view that the new designs were generally somewhat less effective than the originals, these changes were initiated by Nathan-Turner as part of a conscious policy of giving the series a more glossy, expensive and up-to-date look. The phenomenally popular cinema film *Star Wars* had dramatically increased the public's expectations of science fiction in the media, and the producer was keen to counter the commonly-held perception of *Doctor Who* as a cheap series with relatively low production values and substandard visual effects. (The aforementioned reduction of Season 19 from 28 episodes to 26 was made at his request, as he considered that the budget allocated to it was insufficient to support the extra two episodes without sacrificing production quality.)

'Looking back to the time I worked on the series,' commented Saward's predecessor Antony Root in an interview with Philip Newman for a 1992 issue of *The Frame*, 'there was then – and frankly it's still to be resolved – a crisis about what you could actually do with television science fiction post-*Star Wars*. On *Doctor Who*, you used to be able to get away with an exploding wall and a weird monster, but once you'd had the cinema, with its massive special effects pictures, showing people what could be achieved, you had to find something else for the show to do, some other way in.'

Nathan-Turner was expert in budgetary matters – he had been production unit manager, responsible for managing *Doctor Who*'s resources, prior to his appointment as producer – and made it a top priority to ensure that the limited money available to the series was spent in ways that would be readily apparent on screen. This was a policy on which he expounded in his 1982 interview for *Starlog*:

'I removed a lot of the location work, which is very expensive. In a way, it's very restricting, because we try to do it within 25 miles of London, which nearly always *looks* like it's within 25 miles of London! For *Time-Flight*, we had a studio landscape created, which looked absolutely marvellous. Totally alien. Had we more money, I guess we would have gone on location. When you remove the location work, it does put a bit more money at your disposal for things that count. Actors count, designs, costumes, make-up and visual effects. My motto is, "Spend the money where it shows". If it doesn't show, let's stop spending it.'

As one aspect of this policy, Nathan-Turner decided that any major location shoots done for the series should generally be in countries other than Britain, which would automatically tend to give the finished product a more expensive look. Thus trips were made to Amsterdam for *Arc of Infinity* and to Lanzarote for *Planet of Fire*; and both stories featured extensive sequences showing off their respective locations, to guarantee that full value was gained from the money spent.

Another manifestation of the producer's policy was the frequent casting of popular television celebrities in guest star roles, ensuring that the budget allocated to hiring actors had maximum on-screen impact. Amongst the many examples here were Stratford Johns (best known for his work in *Z Cars*) in *Four to Doomsday*; Nerys Hughes (*The Liver Birds*) in *Kinda*; Michael Robbins (*On the Buses*) in *The Visitation*; Beryl Reid (distinguished actress and comedienne) in *Earthshock*; Liza Goddard (*Take Three Girls*) in *Terminus*; and Rodney Bewes (*The Likely Lads*), Rula Lenska (*Rock Follies*) and Chloe Ashcroft (*Play School*) in *Resurrection of the Daleks*.

Nathan-Turner's hopes were certainly borne out as far as press coverage was concerned, as both the overseas location shoots and the celebrity guest stars gained considerable publicity for *Doctor Who*. Again, however, many fan commentators had reservations, feeling that the use of overseas locations was unwarranted by the plots of the stories in question, which consequently had to be adjusted to fit around them, and that the inclusion of familiar television personalities made it even more difficult for viewers to achieve the all-important suspension of disbelief.

Nathan-Turner, in response to the latter criticism, pointed out that the celebrity guest stars, although admittedly best known in many cases for their comedy or light entertainment work, were in fact jobbing actors who had previously played a wide variety of different roles, not only on television but also in radio, theatre and – in some cases – film. He likened *Doctor Who* to *The Morecambe and Wise Show*, in the sense that many distinguished performers were delighted to be asked to appear in it, and prided himself on taking a bold approach to this aspect of his job rather than resorting to typecasting, as was more commonly the case in British television. The critics, however, remained concerned that a higher priority was being placed on achieving a slick, expensive-looking production than on telling well-plotted, convincing stories, and that content was thus being sacrificed in favour of style.

Nathan-Turner was in fact unusual amongst *Doctor Who*'s producers in that he had never been an editor or a writer of scripts and had few aspirations in that direction – a recognition, as he candidly admitted in interviews, of his own limitations. He consequently played rather less emphatic a part than had some of his predecessors in defining the overall dramatic style of the series in story as opposed to production terms, and was more reliant on his script editors to take the initiative in this regard. He did, on the other hand, have strong views about certain aspects of the series' scripting. One example of this was his determination to ensure that humour was used only very sparingly; a point on which he was somewhat at odds with Davison.

'I wanted more humour,' affirmed the actor in an interview with Terry and Andy Kerr for a 1985 edition of *Skonnos*. 'John cut the humour for my first two seasons. You see, prior to that, we'd had quite a lot of humour in Tom Baker's time, and I don't think John quite liked it. Occasionally I'd find the early drafts of scripts, which had a bit more humour in them, and I'd say to John, "I quite like this," and show it to him at the producer's run. Sometimes we'd keep those bits, and sometimes we wouldn't. More often, though, I wouldn't see those earlier drafts.

'I remember watching one of Tom's stories, where the Doctor was about to be executed, and he was laughing and joking and offering everyone jelly babies. I think Tom, Douglas Adams and Graham Williams got together to create this image. I don't think Tom and John saw eye-to-eye about humour.'

When Davison decided to leave the series after his third season in the role, Nathan-Turner again became concerned with the question of retaining audience loyalty over the change of Doctors. The series had done well in the twice weekly weekday evening slot that it had occupied for the past three years, winning very respectable ratings (although more so for Season 19 than for Seasons 20 and 21), and he was keen to ensure that these viewers – many of whom he suspected were fans of Davison from his years in *All Creatures Great and Small* – were given every possible encouragement to 'stay tuned' (a favourite expression of his) for the sixth Doctor's era.

One way in which the producer approached this problem was to introduce, just before the change of Doctors, a new companion character,

Peri, who he hoped would help to bridge the gap between the two eras – repeating the tactic he had adopted on the previous occasion with the introduction of Nyssa and Tegan. This time, however, he decided to go one stage further by bringing in the new Doctor himself for the final story of Season 21, thus giving viewers a chance to get acquainted with the newcomer before the series went off the air for its between-seasons break. Thus, in a departure from recent precedent, Davison would make his exit in the penultimate story of the season rather than in the last.

'That was John's idea,' confirmed Saward in 1993. 'He always felt that he wanted to leave the audience with a taste of what was to come. I thought he was worrying unnecessarily, to be honest, because *Doctor Who* is engraved in everyone's minds, and who's playing the lead won't be the reason why people will tune in; they'll tune in because they enjoy *Doctor Who*, or they have memories of it, or they're getting their kids to watch it or something.'

Davison's last story, *The Caves of Androzani*, marked the return to *Doctor Who* of Robert Holmes, Nathan-Turner having been persuaded by Saward to make a rare exception to his long-established policy of using writers and directors new to the series rather than bringing back those who had worked on it during earlier eras of its history. The result was a story considered by many to be the finest of all those in which Davison appeared. The high production values pursued by Nathan-Turner and the strong scripting sought by Saward came together and complemented each other perhaps more successfully than at any other time during the previous three years, ensuring that the fifth Doctor bowed out in considerable style.

From Script to Screen
The Five Doctors

INTRODUCTION

In many ways, *The Five Doctors* was a typical story of its era, involving location filming as well as studio recording and a large number of complex visual effects sequences to realise. In other ways, it was atypical as, being conceived as a celebration of *Doctor Who*'s 20th anniversary, it had constraints and requirements that other stories did not.

For our view of the production we have turned primarily to director Peter Moffatt and to visual effects designer John Brace, who recall, scene by scene, the work that went into it. We have also incorporated comments from other participants: the producer, John Nathan-Turner; the writer, Terrance Dicks; the designer, Malcolm Thornton; the costume designer, Colin Lavers; the composer, Peter Howell; the sound effects designer, Dick Mills; and some of the cast. The primary source for much of this supporting interview material is a publication edited and published by David J Howe for the *Doctor Who* Appreciation Society in 1984, which looked in detail at the making of this story. We are grateful to Jan Vincent-Rudzki, who conducted the original interviews with Malcolm Thornton and Colin Lavers, for allowing us to reproduce his work here. Thanks also to Patricia Holmes, wife of the late Robert Holmes, for allowing us to reproduce her husband's original synopses for the story.

THE SCRIPTS

The idea of a story celebrating *Doctor Who*'s 20th anniversary originated with the series' producer, John Nathan-Turner. He started thinking about this as early as July 1981, and on 3 August that year sent to David Reid, the Head of Series and Serials, the following memo:

> Further to our conversation of the other week, I should like to request that *next* year's *Doctor Who* season transmits in the Autumn of 1982.

THE FIFTH DOCTOR

We must get back to an autumn transmission in readiness for the 20th anniversary programme in November 1983. (The 10th anniversary programme in 1973 starred all the actors who had played the Doctor up until then (William Hartnell, Patrick Troughton, Jon Pertwee), and if I am still producing the show in 1983, I would like to do something really spectacular!!)

As I have had to release Peter Davison for eight weeks during the current season's production period, it became impossible to transmit this season till Week 1 1982. (In any case Controller of BBC1 did not want *Doctor Who* and *Sink or Swim* to transmit at the same time.) The result of the above is that currently *Doctor Who* is *off the air* for nine months as opposed to the usual six months. As you know, interest has been retained in the programme, as we have a *new* Doctor, in August of this year there are two four-parter repeats on BBC1 and in November of this year a season of repeats – *The Five Faces of Doctor Who* (five four-parters) on BBC2.

I would suggest we capitalise quickly on the anticipated popularity of Peter Davison's Doctor, and have only a six month break between seasons next time.

I am sure I can transmit next year's season from Week 36 1982, *even if the programme remains bi-weekly* – *provided* I do not release Peter Davison for *Sink or Swim* during *Doctor Who*'s production period. *Sink or Swim* could then go into production after my final recording and *still* transmit in Week 1, if required.

To simplify, I suggest next year *Doctor Who* transmits in the autumn, and *Sink or Swim, if required*, in the winter. I do hope this can be achieved, as it would be most beneficial to the programme and its future.

Nathan-Turner's idea was that a celebratory story could be transmitted on the anniversary and within the planned structure of the regular season (something that would happen in 1988 with *Silver Nemesis* for the 25th anniversary).

After discussions with Alan Hart, David Reid replied on 25 August as follows:

Controller of BBC1 is not prepared to change *Doctor Who* transmission to the autumn of 1982. He will think again about 1983 but is not prepared to put undue pressure on Comedy for the release of Peter

FROM SCRIPT TO SCREEN: THE FIVE DOCTORS

Davison. He is concerned that *Sink or Swim* might finish up being off the air for too long.

Alan has, however, suggested that he would be interested in, perhaps, a 90 minute special to coincide with the anniversary in November 1983 to trail the series in the winter. This is not a silly thought and perhaps we might discuss it.

As plans for the special developed, Nathan-Turner and script editor Eric Saward decided that they wanted a production that would feature all five of the television Doctors to date, as well as numerous companions and monsters. One early problem was how best to get around the fact that William Hartnell, the first Doctor, had died in 1975. It was felt that the best option was to cast another actor to play the part. In July 1982, a check was made on the last BBC fee paid to actor Geoffrey Bayldon, who had appeared in the 1979 *Doctor Who* story *The Creature from the Pit* and who was considered by many fans and professionals to be an ideal choice for a new Doctor.

To write the anniversary story, Saward and Nathan-Turner had little hesitation in approaching writer Robert Holmes. Holmes had script edited *Doctor Who* for three and a half years during the Tom Baker era, and had seen several of his own scripts for the series reach fruition, the first being *The Krotons* back in 1968.

Holmes was approached, and, despite many misgivings, agreed to have a think and see what he could come up with. In an undated letter to the production office, he outlined three possible scenarios, one in great detail and the other two only sketchily. The entire content of his five-page note was as follows:

> The main problem we face is to find a satisfactory and plausible explanation for all the Doctors, plus companions, appearing at the same point in the space-time continuum. I feel that this – dramatically – is what our audience will expect. However, the clash of mighty egos has been mentioned and it is possible for them to appear in the same story without appearing together.
>
> The purpose of this discussion document is to survey the various options open to us.
>
> 1) The planet Maladoom. Doctor Will and companion striding across a misty landscape. They've obviously just arrived as he is pointing out various botanical features and making deductions about the nature of the planet.

THE FIFTH DOCTOR

We pull back to see that the Doctor is being watched on video. Voices of unseen watchers comment admiringly – 'Really remarkably lifelike,' etc. – (Eventually, about an hour from now, we shall learn that Doctor Will and Carol Ann are cyborgs, created by cyber-technology. This will explain why the Doctor is not quite as we remember Hartnell.)

Tardis. The Doctor helpless at the controls. Tells Tegan the machine is being drawn into a time vortex. It could mean destruction. Maybe we do some clever mirror-work and show more than one police box whirling down this sudden fissure in the ordered universe.

Maladoom. The Doctor and Tegan arrive. He is now very angry. Some irresponsible idiot must be interfering with the delicately balanced polarity of time and matter. Incredibly dangerous lunacy that could create chaos. Must put a stop to it.

Now, one by one, the other Doctors arrive with their companions. All have approximately the same reactions – although Doctor Tom may speculate that some other race has discovered the power previously known only to Time Lords. But, anyway, all go off to put a stop to it.

The Doctor and Tegan are heading across rough terrain towards a pulsing light that seems to be coming from inside a distant, craggy hill. In the shadow of a low cliff they see, apparently inset into the rock face, a rectangular panel of some shiny black substance. As they examine this curiously, concealed jets puff out vapour. They collapse unconscious. Then the panel begins to open.

One by one the other Doctors are inveigled into other automated traps.

Cryogenic chamber. The Doctors and companions lie unconscious. The Master comes in for a gloat. At last he has all the time entities that comprise the total Doctor at his mercy. If he turns the freezer down a few more degrees he will achieve final triumph over his oldest adversary. So why doesn't he? Probably because he daren't, at this stage, upset his allies, the Cybermen.

Doctor Pat is carried off to the operating theatre. The Cybermen prepare for surgery. An injection revives the patient for preliminary tests. The Cybermen intend to find the organic mechanism that separates Time Lords from other species. When they find it they will separate it and implant it into their familiar cybernetic machinery, thus turning themselves into Cyberlords.

This aspect of the plot is brought out in conversation between the Master, Doctor Pat and the top Cyberman.

As the operation begins the Doctor goes into terminal collapse. Resuscitation procedures fail. The patient is pronounced extinct. The Cybermen aren't too concerned; they expect to lose a few Doctors before discovering the vital organ. That is why, with the Master's help, they have drawn all the manifestations of the Doctor's form from their various time loops.

Doctor Pat is returned to the cryogenic chamber where he recovers from his self-willed cataleptic state. Fighting against the numbing cold, he disconnects the freezer panels. As the temperature rises the Doctors slowly begin to stir.

In the operating theatre the Cybermen are reviewing their techniques before investing in another patient.

In the cryogenic chamber total bafflement at finding themselves all together. An impossible situation which they resolve by deciding they are trapped in a temporal paradox created by the Master.

The Cybermen come to collect Doctor Jon. Docs and companions take them by surprise and effect an escape.

Film. Trial by ordeal. Cybermen hunting Doctors who are all intent now on their original objective – restoring the time-space continuum to its natural order before permanent damage is done to the universe. And to this end they are heading for the shining hill.

Doctor Will – the fake cyborg – tries to lead them into an ambush. But at the last moment he is spotted as a phoney. He bounces down a cliff and all his springs fall out. Carol Ann, too, is shown to be a cyborg. This is tough on Frazer because he was getting to like her.

They struggle on and finally reach the shining hill. Its core is a mass of technology linked to the Master's Tardis, the effect of which is to raise its power a thousandfold. Projected through the space-time continuum this enormous force has created a time vacuum into which all Time Travellers (principally our Doctors) were inevitably drawn.

THE FIFTH DOCTOR

The trouble is that it is now feeding upon itself, like a nuclear reactor running out of control, and in a very short while the whole of this part of the universe will implode into a black hole. Unless they can slow the whirligig down and stabilise matters.

We've all been through this one before. The Master will, of course, turn up to provide some last-moment impediment. But, in the end, the Doctors get the machinery into phase before it goes critical. As it slows they, together with appropriate companions, disappear back into their own sectors of time – the relative dimensions effect.

The Doctor and Tegan are alone at the end.

The sharp-eyed reader will ask what happened to the Cybermen. Well, we won't have that many to start with. Some will be blown up when the Doctors escape because, before departing, they sabotage the operating theatre. Others will be disposed of variously – buried under rock falls, sunk in swamps, pushed off cliffs and so on – during the film chase.

2) The other option. Much the same general shape of story but we open with the present Doctor and stay with him until the operating theatre scene.

The effect of the Cybermen tampering with his metabolism, however, is that he starts to regress through his various phases – i.e. turns first into Doctor Tom, then into Doctor Jon and so on.

While doing this, of course, he is also escaping, combating the Cybermen and trying to reach the shining hill. When he reaches his Doctor Will incarnation he knows he is on his last legs. If he doesn't make it before his time runs out, he will be finally dead.

(This, too, offers a possible explanation as to why he doesn't exactly resemble the real Hartnell.)

The attraction of this shape is that it would allow us to have all the Doctors in the story without having them meet up. Its difficulty is in finding a convincing reason for Tegan also to slip back through various companion incarnations. Maybe mental projection? In each of his forms he would see the companion he had at that time?

3) We might use the Tardis as a kind of tuning fork. We postulate that within its structure lie the echoes or 'vibes' of all who have ever been aboard. Given the right technology, therefore, it is possible to recreate any or all of the former Doctors and hold them in corporeal form as long as the energy supply lasts.

The present Doctor – perhaps finding himself out of action – might be compelled to activate this 'memory function' in order to seek help from his predecessors.

This could be a battle of wits between the Doctors and the exhausted old computer at the heart of a starship that has been drifting for twenty million years. But I see no Cybermen in it.

The substance of these ideas is of interest as, although Holmes was ultimately not to use them for the anniversary story, the suggestion of an alien race trying to find the organic basis for the Time Lords' power was later used by him in his 1985 sixth Doctor story *The Two Doctors*.

On 4 August 1982, Holmes was formally commissioned to provide a scene breakdown for the 90-minute special, now with the working title of *The Six Doctors*, reflecting the idea that the version of the first Doctor in the storyline was a fake.

Because Holmes was very unsure as to whether or not he would be able to come up with a workable scene breakdown by the delivery date of 23 August, Saward and Nathan-Turner decided to ask another writer to 'stand by' in the event of Holmes being unable to resolve the logistical problems presented by the story. This was Terrance Dicks, another ex-*Doctor Who* script editor with numerous stories to his name.

On 24 August, Saward wrote to Holmes thanking him for keeping the office advised of progress on the breakdown, and requesting that he provide the document a day before their forthcoming meeting on 1 September to give himself and Nathan-Turner a chance to digest the work so far. On the same day, Saward wrote to Dicks, apologising for the delay and stating that they would be making a final decision on the story once they had seen Holmes' work. Following the meeting with Holmes, Saward again wrote to Dicks, on 2 September, saying that Holmes had decided to try and write the first 20 minutes of the script, despite the fact that he had huge reservations about whether or not he could make it work.

Ultimately, Holmes delivered his scene breakdown on 13 October, and on 18 October, Terrance Dicks was commissioned to provide a scene breakdown as well. Holmes' version was subsequently dropped. Following delivery of Dicks' breakdown on 1 November, at which point the story had been renamed *The Five Doctors*, Dicks was commissioned on 16 November to write the script, which was formally delivered on 20 December and accepted on 27 January 1983.

'I knew from the beginning that the job was going to be appallingly difficult and complicated and full of the most enormous hassles, as indeed it was,' said Dicks. 'Since I was prepared for that, nothing actually threw me. I knew it was going to be like jumping into a combine harvester from the very beginning.'

Dicks was presented with the same set of guidelines that Holmes had been working to. 'My standing joke about it was that it was like that game where you make up a story about objects that come out of a box. This particular box had an awful lot of objects in it!

'First of all, you knew it had to be *all* the Doctors – they had already come up with the idea of having Richard Hurndall as the look-alike first Doctor – and *some* of the monsters – they already knew that they wanted the Cybermen as the lead monster, and as well as the Cybermen, there had to be other villains and other monsters. It wasn't all one way – obviously they wanted my ideas as well. At first they weren't too keen on having Daleks in, but I told them that they'd *got* to have Daleks, even if it's only one Dalek. They weren't too happy about having K-9 either, but eventually they agreed and said he could put his head around the door.

'There was the problem of the companions – who was going to be in it and who wasn't. Some they were sure of, like the Brigadier, Susan and Sarah, but others kept changing. One of the things that kept happening was that they would ring up and say, "Have you written so-and-so in?" I'd say that I had, and they would reply, "Well, write him out again, he can't do it. You can have such-and-such." There was a lot of to-ing and fro-ing with the companions. In fact, it wasn't absolutely set who were going to be the "cameo companions" until almost the last moment. Those bits where they pop up in the corridors on the way to the tomb were almost the last things to be put in the script. They had to be done very simply, because by that time the budget had nearly been used up. The brief was complicated enough, and I still needed a story.

'The problem was to put all these elements together to make some kind of sense. They didn't want a pantomime, they wanted a story that would stand on its own even if it wasn't the 20th anniversary special. The main problem was coming up with a plot to pull all these elements together. It all began to come together for me when I came up with the idea of the game. Almost before anything else, I had this picture in my mind of a black gloved hand picking up this little figure and putting it on a board. Thinking of it as a kind of chess game gave it a basic shape. But this game was against the people on the board. The Player just sat and watched what they did. Then there was the question of who was the Player? The first thought I had was that it was the Master but, quite rightly, Eric Saward said that was too obvious; it would be an anticlimax. You have, however, got to come up with some type of surprise villain as the sting in the tail. If you are going to do that, then it's got to be someone significant, it can't be the third Time Lord on the left. The only candidate was Borusa.

'This happens very often in story writing; things just fall into place. Of course it's got to be Borusa, who else can it be? The thing about Borusa turning into a villain was that you didn't have a saintly character who suddenly went all bad. Borusa had always been a politician and an autocrat, someone who was prepared to be ruthless. I felt that you could believe that he could take that one stage further and say: "Well, I'm the one who knows what's good for everybody; it would therefore be much better for Gallifrey if I were in charge forever!" So you just have to take the existing characteristics and push them a bit further over the edge into madness. It's very difficult stuff to play. I think Philip Latham did extraordinarily well.

'So that was the structure: it was Borusa manipulating the five Doctors in some way, kidnapping them out of time. That became the overall idea, which is the hardest bit. After that, it's just a question of working it all out.'

In the final draft of the rehearsal script, dated 25 January 1983, Dicks had included a scene involving the third Doctor and Sarah encountering several Auton mannequins in a ruined high street. The copyright clearance for this had been checked by the BBC on 14 December 1982, but ultimately the Autons were dropped, and on 11 February 1983, a sequence already in the script, where the second Doctor and the Brigadier were attacked by an underground monster in the caves, was altered to change the attacking creature into a Yeti.

'There just wasn't time to do it,' explained Dicks about the Auton sequence. 'What all that came down to was Sarah going over the cliff, which was a lot simpler.'

There were other aspects of the script and action that were refined as the director mapped out the various practicalities, and these are mentioned as we go through the televised story later in this chapter.

One of the most distinctive and memorable images from the production is the central tower to which all the Doctors are trying to get. Dicks included it specifically as a symbol of evil. 'This is the central citadel of evil; like in *Lord of the Rings*, where Frodo's going with the ring to the tower where the Dark Lord lives. There's also a poem by Browning, called *Childe Roland to the Dark Tower Came*. It's like a little fragment of a non-existent narrative poem. It describes the knight riding up to the old dark castle. There's a horn hanging outside it, and he raises it to his lips and blows. That's all that happens, and I think it was in my mind as an image. After that, I worked Rassilon into it. Again, it had to be Rassilon who was going to resolve it. There was a time when I wasn't sure whether it was going to be a good Rassilon or a bad Rassilon; I trailed that maybe Rassilon had been a monster of evil and that the Time Lords had covered it all up, which was quite fun, as that seemed to be a very Time Lord thing to do – a Bob Holmes type Time Lord thing to do. I quite liked the idea that the Time Lords had some very shabby episodes in their own history that they were ashamed of and hushed up.'

CASTING

Whereas normally the casting of a *Doctor Who* story would be carried out by the director in collaboration with the producer, in this instance, many of the parts were returning characters from *Doctor Who*'s history, and therefore the question wasn't so much who could play them, as whether or not the required actors were available.

The first problem tackled by the production team was someone to play the first Doctor. This was resolved when John Nathan-Turner remembered an actor called Richard Hurndall. 'I was asked to play the first Doctor,' recalled Hurndall in 1983, 'because John Nathan-Turner saw me as Nebrox in *Blake's 7* and thought I looked very like William Hartnell.

'I remembered William's approach to the part very well, and decided it would be stupid to try and "mimic" him, so I hope I split the difference between his performance – his personality – and mine.'

'He was marvellous,' opined Nathan-Turner. 'I did offer him tapes of Bill Hartnell to look at, but as he did remember Bill, he decided that rather than view the tapes and try to do a "Mike Yarwood" on it, it would be better if he just went for his instinct.'

Peter Moffatt had asked Hurndall to suggest Hartnell's portrayal of the first Doctor with some of his mannerisms, such as holding his lapels and using his vocal 'Hm? hm?' and then gradually moulding this to his own interpretation. 'I really believe he gave us a beautiful performance and one accepted him on his own merits,' said Moffatt. 'I know he was very nervous of the undertaking, as the other Doctors had only to drop back into their old performances, whereas he, as a newcomer, had to create his, and then not in his own mould but in that created by a very celebrated and much loved actor who had made an enormous impression on the public twenty years ago. However, he really did a wonderful job and succeeded in conveying a vivid impression of Bill and making the part his own at the same time.'

Hurndall agreed to play the first Doctor on 6 October 1982. William Hartnell's original costume was not held by the BBC (it had been hired from the theatrical costumier's Bermans and Nathans) and so a new one had to be created for Hurndall. In designing this, Colin Lavers went by photographs in a magazine published in 1973 by the *Radio Times* to celebrate *Doctor Who*'s tenth anniversary. The original outfit had featured a morning coat, for which it was fairly easy to find a substitute, but the original waistcoat had been an authentic Victorian one, so a look-alike was made. The script emphasised the age of the first Doctor, so Lavers used mittens to make him appear older and slightly feeble. The mittens also hid the fact that he wasn't wearing the first Doctor's blue ring, as it was felt that the colour would be too noticeable. There was also a photograph in the magazine of William Hartnell in a hat and scarf, but Lavers considered that the scarf was by this point associated firmly with the fourth Doctor and the hat with the fifth, so those two items were not re-introduced.

Because Nathan-Turner wanted to have something of the original first Doctor in the story somewhere, he decided to use a clip from *Flashpoint*, the final episode of *The Dalek Invasion of Earth*, as a pre-title sequence trailer.

Patrick Troughton, playing the second Doctor, presented Nathan-Turner with a problem of scheduling. Troughton was working on *Foxy Lady* for Granada television during the original proposed location filming dates for the story in April, and so Nathan-Turner, recognising that the inclusion of the other Doctors, and for them to be played by the original actors, was essential to the production, moved the dates forward to March to ensure that Troughton would be available to appear.

Most of Troughton's scenes in the draft script were on location, and Colin Lavers was keen to develop a costume that would keep the actor warm. The fur coat used in *The Abominable Snowmen* was suggested, but the original could not be used as it was made of real fur, and to have two of them (to allow for the possibility of one getting damaged during filming) would be very expensive, so two close substitutes were used instead.

The trousers worn by the second Doctor originally featured a large, inch-square check pattern. The BBC was in the early Eighties trying to establish a new picture clarity for Direct Broadcast Satellites, and some striped and checked materials had become unsuitable for use. Bearing this in mind, Lavers opted for a light plaid pattern for the trousers.

Jon Pertwee's third Doctor was less of a problem, as the actor was available on the required dates and happy to reprise his role. His costume was a variation on that worn by the actor for a photocall to publicise *The Three Doctors* back in 1973.

Tom Baker, playing the fourth Doctor, presented by far the greatest challenge to the production team.

'I think I first approached Tom in April 1982,' recalled John Nathan-Turner. 'Initially he said that he was interested but would like to see a script. Then our first writer fell through, which meant that we didn't have a script within three months as we had hoped, and the time was going on. Eventually, in the December, we were filming *The King's Demons* somewhere down south, and I knew that Tom was appearing at the Theatre Royal in Brighton, and so I sent him the first seventy pages of the script, which was all we had. I met him after one of his shows to talk about it, and at that time he had agreed to do it. We were then able to contact Terrance and tell him that Tom was to be included. Within about ten days or so, he pulled out and changed his mind.

'That was an extremely big hurdle to overcome, because we were saying up front that it's the *five* Doctors, and really it was four and a bit, and one of those was a re-cast, so suddenly it started to look as though it was falling round my ears.'

In order to ensure that the fourth Doctor was represented in the show, Nathan-Turner had the idea of incorporating into the narrative some scenes from the *Doctor Who* story *Shada*, which had been partially completed in 1979 before industrial action at the BBC forced it to be cancelled incomplete. To this end, on 10 January 1983 he wrote to both Tom Baker and Lalla Ward, who played his assistant Romana in the story, requesting permission to use clips from the cancelled story. Both artistes agreed.

'I knew this sort of thing was going to happen, but I don't think that even I was prepared for that!' exclaimed Terrance Dicks. 'At the start, I asked Eric if they were *sure* that they'd got all the Doctors, and he said they were. But apparently there was some kind of confusion between Tom and Tom's agent and the BBC. Tom believed that he hadn't committed himself and the BBC genuinely felt that he had, and it was passed on to me that Tom was definitely going to be in it. I had in fact just completed my first draft, with Tom playing a major role, and the phone rang – this was happening every day, it was like a hotline to the *Doctor Who* office. It was Eric again. He asked how I was getting on, and I told him proudly that I'd just finished the first draft and it was all ready to go to the typists. He said, "Oh my god!" – not the reaction I'd been expecting. I asked him what had happened now. He said, "You know what we said about Tom ..." He explained about this confusion and was very apologetic. I had no choice but to go back to square one again.

'Tom in fact was going to steal the Master's transportation device and go back to Gallifrey, Davison was going to go to the tower and work his way in through the front entrance, and Hurndall was probably going to stay in the TARDIS with Turlough and Susan – all three would arrive with the TARDIS. There was also a sub-plot so you might feel that Tom was the villain or maybe he was going to ally himself with the villain. I felt that the Tom Baker Doctor was the one that you could believe would go bad, he has a darker side to him. Eric told me about the footage from *Shada*, the sequence in the punt, and so I came up with the idea that we could see Tom kidnapped. But that was all we could do with him – we couldn't have him in the story. Once again, it all fell into place. The obvious thing was to have his kidnap bungled. The equipment was ancient and Borusa wasn't all that good at it anyway. So, we had the fourth Doctor trapped in a time warp. This gave me another menace, with the Baker Doctor being like a hole in the dyke. There was a danger that the Davison Doctor, followed by all the other Doctors, would be sucked in, giving a sense of urgency. If the Doctors didn't solve the problem by a given time, they would disappear together.

'My feeling is that it all worked better the way it ended up. Five Doctors were just too many to handle, but four worked very neatly, and you do at least *see* Tom. The other thing that I found quite amazing was how well the scenes from *Shada* fitted in. I'll swear that if you didn't know, you would think it was written for the special.'

With all the Doctors covered, the remaining problem was the companions. Nathan-Turner was keen to include one companion per Doctor, and the original idea was to team Susan with the first Doctor, Victoria with the second, Jo Grant with the third and Sarah with the fourth. However, despite agreeing to take part quite late in the day, Deborah Watling then had to drop out from playing Victoria as the location filming dates clashed with another commitment, on *The Dave Allen Show* (which was subsequently hit by a strike and never made). Katy Manning could not travel from Australia to play Jo, so Sarah was paired with the third Doctor instead, and the Brigadier was put with the second Doctor.

Nicholas Courtney was actually asked whether he would appear in the special while he was recording *Mawdryn Undead* during August and September 1982. 'When I heard that all my old friends were going to be in it; Terrance Dicks was writing it, and he had been involved with so many of the ones I had been in; I was going to be with Pat; I thought I had to be in it. Having been around with the programme for so long, I couldn't miss being in the special.'

As Dicks mentioned, the 'guest star' companions were confirmed at a very late stage, and among the casualties was John Levene, who was approached to reprise his role as Sergeant Benton but unable to make the dates.

As far as the guest characters were concerned, Peter Moffatt was able to engage most of the actors that he wanted, although Charles Grey was originally considered for the part of Rassilon and Denis Quilley was felt suitable to play Borusa. Richard Bonehill was originally going to play a Cyberman in the studio, but he dropped out, to be replaced by Mark Bassenger.

The costume and make-up fittings for the cast took place between 27 January and 28 March 1983, with actor Richard Matthews, the ultimate choice to play Rassilon, having a face cast made on 24 February 1983. This was to allow another actor (identity unknown) to play Rassilon's body lying on top of the tomb.

'I cast Richard Matthews because he's a splendid actor,' explained Moffatt. 'I'd worked with him years earlier in repertory when I was an actor, and had always been impressed by his presence and his voice, rasping and deep and full of authority. He played a judge for me in an episode of *Lady Killers* for Granada TV, and when I first read the script of *The Five Doctors*, he immediately sprang to my mind. He had a difficult scene to play, as he was, so to speak, disembodied. We did have his effigy lying on the top of his tomb, and maybe he could have sat up out of this, but I felt in the end that he would have more impact by suddenly appearing in space above Borusa's head. After all, he had no longer any connection with that tomb, he was an all-pervading spirit.'

PRE-PRODUCTION

Unlike other *Doctor Who* productions, *The Five Doctors* was being produced in addition to the scheduled season, rather than as part of it, and therefore the money with which to finance it had to be obtained from outside the standard allocation of funds to the series. Realising that the show had a very great potential to be aired outside the UK, the BBC approached the Australian Broadcasting Commission (ABC) with a view to obtaining co-funding. After numerous discussions, an agreement was signed on 7 April 1983 by the BBC and 16 May 1983 by the ABC, which brought in $60,000 in Australian currency towards the production budget – although the agreement stated that no credit to the co-funder would appear. The agreement meant that *The Five Doctors* was effectively pre-sold to the ABC for transmission in Australia.

With work on the script under way, there were several areas of concern in getting this particular programme off the ground, and another early requirement was the appointment of a director. John Nathan-Turner's original thought was to return to the very start of *Doctor Who* and to see if the services of the first director to work on the show could be secured. Waris Hussein was therefore approached about directing *The Five Doctors*, but on 20 December 1982 he declined to take part. The directorial duties were eventually taken up by Peter Moffatt, a freelancer who had already directed the stories *State of Decay*, *The Visitation* and *Mawdryn Undead*.

Moffatt recalled being temporarily confused by the script when he first read it. 'Well, to be quite honest, I didn't really understand why the Doctors were lifted one by one in the time scoop and then prevented from doing what was required of them by so many obstacles being set in their paths – they were enticed and then repelled. But as I began to work on the script, I understood more and more. It was a game set for the satisfaction of Borusa, with the Doctors being reacted upon like pawns in a game of chess, and the more times I read the script, the more I appreciated the basic theme. This is nothing unusual for me, I may be slightly blank about the content of the script on first reading and then, as I begin to visualise it all happening on the screen, the whole concept catches fire, my adrenaline begins to flow, my enthusiasm mounts, and the whole script becomes an intrinsic part of me, and for better or worse we march together, as one, towards the final realisation.'

ON LOCATION

For *The Five Doctors*, Peter Moffatt was permitted to travel further afield for location work than might normally have been considered affordable or practicable for a *Doctor Who* production (notwithstanding the recent shooting in Amsterdam for *Arc of Infinity*). He had initially thought that Scotland might offer the various bleak landscapes as described in Dicks' script, but on further consideration felt that this was perhaps too far from London and that travelling time would eat too much into the allocation of filming days. Instead he opted for Wales.

Jeremy Silberston, the production manager, managed to find all the required settings – caves, mountainsides and bleak flat areas – around the Ffestiniog area in North Wales. When Moffatt visited the area with Silberston for a technical recce from 21 to 23 February 1983, everything was covered with deep snow, but when they came to work there, the snow had melted, and in its place were freezing winds, rain and mists, which caused specific problems of their own. Also present on the recce were John Baker (film cameraman), John Gatland (sound recordist), Archie Dawson (lighting), June Collins (production associate), Malcolm Thornton (designer), John Brace (visual effects designer), Pauline Seager (assistant floor manager), Jean Peyre (design effects) and Gavin Birkett (safety officer). A recce of the London locations took place on 24 February.

Following the recce, Gavin Birkett submitted to Jeremy Silberston a report dated 28 February 1983, in which he stated that the 'Wasteland 1' location – Carreg Y Foel Gron – should not present any problems. He also noted the following points with regards to 'Wasteland 2' – the Manod Quarry:

Safety harnesses should be provided for the sequences when the Raston robot fires arrows along lines, and the harnesses themselves should be secured to the ground with special stakes.

Care should be taken with the sequence when a Cyberman's hand grabs the Brigadier's arm through a wall. The production team needed to remove stones from the wall to create a hole large enough, and Birkett noted that the structure should be checked after the stones were removed to ensure it was still stable.

There was a loose slab of stone above one of the caves. This was to be removed and a further inspection carried out to ensure that the cave was safe. A second cave seemed safe, but a further inspection should be made of a ledge above the entrance to ensure that nothing was likely to fall onto the BBC staff working there.

The final part of the report concentrated on the sequences in the caves themselves. Everyone was to be provided with safety helmets. Emergency lighting should be provided, with a separate power supply, and good rechargeable torches should be available. Barrier rope was to be used to cordon off areas not in use by the crew. As radio communication did not work too well underground, a landline telephone system was to be employed to communicate with the outside, in case the walkie-talkie system failed. No gas appliances of any kind were to be taken into the caves, and everyone was to be warned of the dangers of exploring the various sites.

Prior to setting off for the location, there was a read-through of the script for the full cast on Friday 25 February 1983 in a conference room at BBC Television Centre, followed by location rehearsals at the BBC's Acton rehearsal rooms between 28 February and 3 March 1983. Then the unit – comprising some twenty nine cast and crew – set off for North Wales on Friday 4 March 1983, arriving just after midday, so that everything would be prepared and ready for the first section of filming on the following day.

The first location was Plasbrondanw at Llanfrothen, which was to be used for the scenes set at the Eye of Orion and also for the sequence when the first Doctor was picked up by the spinning obelisk from his garden. The scenes with the fifth Doctor, Tegan and Turlough were filmed first, followed by the first Doctor being snatched from his garden.

Filming started on Monday 7 March at Carreg Y Foel Gron, a desolate area just off the B4407 road. This was to become a wasteland area, and the first scenes filmed were of the first Doctor and Susan traversing a rock-strewn area just prior to their discovery of the TARDIS. For this scene, the Doctor had to rest on a rock and, despite the fact that the valley was littered with them, there was not one single piece in the right position for Richard Hurndall to sink upon in an exhausted fashion. Therefore, amongst all the lumps of real rock were two pieces of fake rock supplied by the Visual Effects Department.

The next scene to be filmed was where the fifth Doctor, Susan and Tegan discover the Master and are ambushed by the Cybermen. This sequence was continued the following day, with the Master joining forces with the Cybermen, and finally the scenes where the Cybermen prepare to detonate the bombs they have placed around the TARDIS were filmed. Also on 8 March, a special photographic session for the *Radio Times* took place.

The final filming at this location took place on Wednesday 9 March. The crew had planned to start the day with some glass shots of the tower seen through the mountains, but the bad weather meant that these had to be scrapped. The shots were subsequently created electronically in the studio. The first scenes filmed this day, therefore, were shots of the second Doctor and the Brigadier looking at the tower, as the Doctor realises they are on the Death Zone in Gallifrey. A later scene featuring the second Doctor and the Brigadier was also filmed. Peter Moffatt recalled seeing a wonderful vertiginous view of a mighty cliff face above a rocky path that the two actors had to cross in order to reach the cave mouth for which the characters were heading. 'As the cameras turned over to shoot the scene, down came a thick barrier of mist, blotting all else out of sight. Through the various takes necessary to shoot the scene, there were a brief few minutes when the mist vanished and all was dramatically revealed. Unfortunately the assistant cameraman had been obliged to go back to the car to get a new magazine of film, and though I kept saying to myself, "Come back, come back!", by the time he did (and he could not really have been quicker), the mist had swirled down again and the cliff face was obliterated. It looked all right in the end – bleak, isolated and unwelcoming. But I did miss that rocky precipice!'

The crew then moved to the third location, Manod Quarry, wherein a ruined building would be used for the sequence in which a hidden Cyberman grabs the Brigadier's arm through a hole in a wall. The quarry was also used on the following day to film a sequence set in the caves, where the second Doctor and the Brigadier are attacked by a Yeti but frighten it off with a firework.

By prior agreement, and in order to get all the material they needed to film complete, while Peter Moffatt was supervising the filming of the sequence in the caves, so John Nathan-Turner was elsewhere in the Manod quarry directing a series of visual effects close-ups to be edited into the battle between the Cybermen and the Raston Warrior robot. 'Peter asked me to direct it before we went on location,' said Nathan-Turner. 'It was always scheduled as one day where we had a second unit. Originally Peter had asked me for another day on location, but unfortunately we couldn't run to it, so instead he asked for a second unit and asked me to direct it. I had the most marvellous day, blowing up the Cybermen.

'The night before, Peter and I had sat down with a map and worked out where Jon and Lis would be and which ways all the shots should be and so on. The only real problem with the sequence was that Visual Effects put some substance on one Cyberman's mask to make it smoke, but the smoke blew inside the mask and we had to rip, and I mean rip, the helmet off, as the actor was nearly suffocating. It was almost a very nasty accident.'

The next day, Friday 11 March, Moffatt continued with the wide-angle shots of the Cybermen coming over the cliff edge, the robot materialising and vanishing and then later the moments when Jon Pertwee and Lis Sladen entered the scene and reacted to all that was going on. When edited together, it all worked beautifully, but it had been a close thing, as one day had been misty and the next not, and there was a fear that it might be difficult to join everything up together seemingly continuously. All this unending care over a long period of shooting resulted in about three minutes of final edited footage.

On the same day, some further sequences were filmed with the second Doctor and the Brigadier.

After a day off, the crew returned to the quarry, and on Sunday 13 March filmed the scenes where the third Doctor and Sarah are nearly caught by the Cybermen and become trapped between them and the Raston robot. The following day, and still at the quarry, the scene where the third Doctor and Sarah swing across to the tower was filmed, as well as the short sequence where the third Doctor meets Sarah in the Death Zone for the first time.

The lake Cwm Bychan in Llanbedr was the final Welsh location, on Tuesday 15 March, for the scenes where the Master first appears in the Death Zone and then meets the third Doctor and Sarah.

The shooting in Wales had many problems, not least of which was the weather. Being March, 1500 feet above sea level, it was so cold that, as costume designer Colin Lavers commented, 'teeth hurt and faces turned blue'. Often the crew were working in the clouds, and there was a cutting wind from the sea. As much thermal underwear as possible was worn, and because of the damp, any costumes and props that could get wet had to be duplicated. Obtaining two of nearly every costume caused its own problems. Because of the deepening financial recession, shops were not inclined to stock two items of the same size, and so this dictated in part what could be used. For instance, Lavers found what he wanted for Sarah's costume in John Lewis in Brent Cross, but the shop had to obtain duplicates from branches in Oxford Street and Swiss Cottage.

The amount of water present on the location, both on the ground and in the air, was a constant problem. The Cybermen had to be glued together after they had been blown up with explosive charges. Lavers discovered that no glue would work well in the wet conditions, although eventually one aerosol adhesive was found that just about worked. A large amount of silver paint was used on the Cybermen. The explosive charges would be put on, followed by a quick wipe with the hand, and then the paint spray. By the time the team had finished, they had used four dozen cans!

On Wednesday 16 March, having completed all the filming in Wales, the crew returned to London.

On Thursday 17 March, filming took place at Tilehouse Lane in Upper Denham, Buckinghamshire, for the sequences where the third Doctor is snatched by the time scoop. From there, the crew moved to a Ministry of Defence/YMCA Hostel in Hayling Lane, which was to become the exterior of UNIT HQ, from where the second Doctor and the Brigadier are snatched.

This location was the same as that used for the exterior of UNIT HQ in *The Three Doctors*. It was while the crew were at this location that a final photo-call took place, this time for the benefit of the press. Because of the absence of Tom Baker from the line-up, John Nathan-Turner had arranged for a waxwork effigy of him to be brought from Madame Tussaud's in London, and the other four Doctors dutifully posed with the dummy of the fourth Doctor. This was something of a stroke of inspiration, as it almost ensured good newspaper coverage on the following day, with the papers variously asking readers to spot 'Who' was not 'Who'.

The crew finally moved to outside a house at 2 West Common Road, Uxbridge, Middlesex, where the scenes of Sarah bidding farewell to K-9 and being snatched as she waits for a bus were filmed.

The final day's filming for the production, on Friday 18 March, took place at the Television Film Studios in Ealing, where sets had been erected for the interior of UNIT HQ and for the top of the tower, which the third Doctor and Sarah reach by sliding down a wire. Once all these scenes had been completed, preparation started for the studio recordings, which were, by now, only eleven days away.

IN STUDIO

As soon as they had returned from the location work, the cast were straight into rehearsals for the studio sessions. These took place at the BBC's rehearsal rooms in Acton, up until 28 March.

On 26 March, a technical run-through took place, where any final questions or problems with the technicalities of the studio recording were ironed out and resolved.

Much of designer Malcolm Thornton's planning time before recording was spent in trying to balance only three days of recording with the number of studio settings. There were ten sets to shoot and turn around over the three days – almost as many sets as for a normal four-part story, which would be spread over two studio sessions, one of three days' duration and one of two. The initial studio requirements were: the metal corridors, the Brigadier's office, interior of the tower (three levels), the ante-room with the chequered floor, Rassilon's tomb, the TARDIS interior, and the roof of the tower. The amount of setting and striking overnight dictated how much could be recorded in the time available; this is why it had been decided to do some filming at Ealing in addition to recording at BBC Television Centre.

Another planning problem for Thornton and Moffatt was working out the order of studio recording. All the most important scenes had to be shot early on, so that if anything went wrong, there would be time to correct it. A lot of the scenes in the TARDIS control room with Tegan, Turlough and the

Davison Doctor were left to the end, just in case the studio recording did overrun, as it would have been much easier, and less expensive, to recall these actors than most of the rest of the cast.

Thornton decided to use post-production techniques for various wide shots using mattes, such as the roof of the tower and the ceiling of Rassilon's tomb. This technique had been successfully used on *The Hitch-Hiker's Guide to the Galaxy*, and is a method by which it is possible to pre-record, or pre-film, sequences of action and then electronically reduce that action and expand the surrounding background using painted images and the Quantel electronic image processor, to create a composite picture. Another example in *The Five Doctors* was the front door by which the first Doctor and Tegan enter the tower. (The door opening was achieved simply by moving a piece of flat scenery behind an electronic wipe.)

This technique also replaced the glass shots and model shots that had been planned for filming on location but ultimately abandoned due to the bad weather conditions.

The overall style of Gallifreyan architecture and clothing had been established in previous stories, most notably *The Deadly Assassin* and *Arc of Infinity*, so in designing the sets and costumes, Thornton and Lavers had to consider what had been seen before.

The hieroglyphics included on the obelisk in Rassilon's tomb had originated in Piccolo Books' *The Making of Doctor Who*, published in 1972, a copy of which had been supplied to Thornton by John Nathan-Turner. In the book, these symbols had denoted the Doctor's name, but this was not the specific intention here; Thornton simply used it as reference for Time Lord writing.

Thornton also devised a lightning symbol, which he used on the obelisk and all over the interior of the tomb. He and John Brace had been talking about the model of the tower and had remembered the scene in which the Master nearly gets zapped by lightning bolts in the wastelands; they had thought it a good theme to use as a decorative logo, so the inverted lightning flash was used as a device throughout.

The metal corridors in which the first Doctor and Susan encounter a Dalek were described in the script as 'highly polished'. Some thought had initially been given to filming these sequences somewhere on location, but it had been decided that it would cost too much to dress as required, so they were ultimately scheduled to be done in the studio instead. Thornton decided to make the corridors look as confusing as possible, rather than regularly linear with right angles and square panels. He felt it would be much more effective if any recognisable surfaces were destroyed, so stock flattage was used and dressed up using silver-brushed aluminium, polished mirrors and plastics that reflected into each other. The idea was that when the Dalek appeared, it would have three images as it passed. Thornton worked out carefully which surfaces would play onto others, the reflections that would be achieved, and where they would appear. But, scenery being the way it is, by the time it had been moved around and finally put up in the studio during the first night (in place of the tower corridors set), the optical perfection had been lost. However, once it had been lit and patched up, it did exactly what had been intended. Instead of getting optically pure images, there were extraneous and distorted reflections, which made the whole thing look sinister and even more confusing.

The problem with the tower corridors was that, for budgetary reasons, a single set had to be used to represent all three levels – upper, middle and lower. Thornton designed it so that it would look basically different when shot from three different positions, to give the effect of coming up from below, coming down from above and passing through on ground level. He had a few of the lightning symbols switched around, and subtly changed the lighting and dressing, to help create the illusion of three different areas.

Overnight on the second day of the studio recording, the Gallifrey composite (corridors, game control and conference room) was taken down and Rassilon's tomb was put up. It had been decided to use a post production matte to create a high vaulted roof, so when the scenes were recorded the studio lights could be seen above the set walls. The final set had the tomb in the middle, a series of architectural elements around to define the space, the transmat at one end, and the entrance to the tomb at the other. Because this was a long sequence with a lot of action, the production ended up using the whole width of the studio. After the tomb scenes had been recorded, the central raised tomb was then removed to reveal a painted chequer-board, and the architectural elements re-arranged to create the ante-room where the Cybermen were to be destroyed. While this transformation was being effected, the scene with the first Doctor and Tegan entering the tower was being rehearsed and recorded in another part of the studio.

John Nathan-Turner had commissioned Visual Effects to build a new TARDIS control console for this production, and one of the first re-writes to Terrance Dicks' script had been to incorporate a piece of action of the Doctor fiddling with the new console. Thornton therefore felt that there was some justification in re-vamping the console room interior set as well. This was an additional design requirement, but was something that would be carried forward to and benefit many episodes to come. John Nathan-Turner wanted to keep the wall roundels, but knowing the form that the new console would take, Thornton thought that the set could be subtly made more angular. The new TARDIS walls was thus made symmetrical, allowing for the set to be more easily erected in studio than the previous one.

The new design meant that the console could go in only one position, in that each facet of the console corresponded to a particular facet of the walls. Thornton's aim, which he felt he had achieved, was to get more relief interest in the walls. He used fewer roundels and also restyled the main doors slightly. When both doors were open on the new set, it was now not possible to see outside from a normal cross-shooting camera position.

A variety of external hire companies were used to supply all the props required for the various sets. For the main Gallifreyan sets, the armchairs were obtained from Newmans, velvet drapes came from Old Times, the harp was hired from M Plaquet and its pedestal from Giltspur. The ferns and exotic foliage came from a company called Greenery, and the armourer Baptys supplied armour for wall dressing. Finally, the stones and crystals needed to stud the coronets worn by Borusa and Rassilon, as well as to decorate other props, came from a firm called Farley.

To indicate some of the considerations involved in making a *Doctor Who* story during the Peter Davison era, what follows is a scene-by-scene summary of *The Five Doctors*, with comments from some of those involved in the production. The story was made and originally transmitted as a single 90 minute programme. It was split into four, 25-minute episodes primarily for overseas sales, although the four part version was also shown in the UK in 1984. The episode endings for the four-part version are indicated at the points where they occurred.

PART ONE

In the TARDIS console room, the Doctor (Peter Davison) is flicking and polishing the controls with a duster.

Peter Moffatt: This was a new console room, and that's why Peter is polishing it off, so that we can all see how beautiful it is.

John Brace: The new console was designed and built by a team headed by designer Mike Kelt, who was brought in specifically to handle that task.

Tegan (Janet Fielding) enters, concerned that the TARDIS will now work properly.

PM: I had no say in the short skirted costumes for the ladies. John kept saying, 'Something for the fathers ...'.

The Doctor chides her and tries to open the doors. They don't operate, and he bangs the console to make them open.
The TARDIS is at the Eye of Orion, a tranquil stopover point. Turlough (Mark Strickson) is outside, sketching.

PM: This was a lovely location with this wonderful view. I think the building was a ruined abbey.

Meanwhile, in a hidden control room, an unseen, black gloved person is operating the forbidden controls of a time scoop and homing in on the Doctor's previous selves: the first Doctor (Richard Hurndall) is picked up by a black, spinning obelisk in a garden.

PM: That garden was designed and built by Sir Clough Williams-Ellis, the same chap who designed and built Portmeirion. Williams-Ellis's widow, Lady Annabel, who owned the house, asked John and me to tea, and it was a real old fashioned affair with cake stands and little scones and everything just so. She was a lovely lady. Her house was Elizabethan, not an Italianate mixture as in Portmeirion.

JB: The control consoles were all made from black perspex for the game control room set.

When the Doctor has been snatched, a small model of him appears in a box in the time scoop control room. It is picked up and placed on one of five segments on a games board.

JB: The bulk of the games board was made from vacuum formed plastic, but we had to create the shape of the tower in the middle. It was quite a large model, and it was tricky to tie in all the elements. I think Tony Auger was involved in constructing the model. You always tried to apportion out single items of work to the design assistants and leave them to get on with it, once you had talked with them about the initial ideas and what the prop had to do. This then allowed you to get on with the rest of the work. The game was always seen to be a key element in explaining what was going on, and so we were able to spend a little bit more of the budget on it than on other elements that were perhaps not so key.

PM: Someone outside the BBC was commissioned to make those little figurines, but I don't recall who. I do remember that they were very expensive.

JB: All the miniatures had to be hand crafted and had to be proper caricatures. I remember talking to Julie Jones of BBC Marketing about the models, to see if they could be exploited after the show.

The fifth Doctor suddenly clutches his chest in pain. A twinge of cosmic angst, as if he has lost something.
   The second Doctor (Patrick Troughton) and the Brigadier (Nicholas Courtney)

are snatched from the grounds of UNIT HQ, where the Brigadier was to be guest of honour at a UNIT reunion with Colonel Crichton (David Savile), his replacement.

[In the rehearsal script, it is the Brigadier's last day in office before he retires. The Brigadier is handing over command his replacement, Brigadier Charles Crichton.
  The costume for the Brigadier was fairly easy to design, as he was an ex-army type, but Colin Lavers had to keep in mind that he had to be as warm as possible, as he was going to be on location as much as Patrick Troughton.]

PM: The spinning obelisk was put on in post-production. I wish it hadn't been a black triangle. It looks all right once the pictures get in it, but before, it's just a bit blank.

The fifth Doctor again winces in pain and collapses. Two more figurines are placed on the board.
  The third Doctor (Jon Pertwee) is driving in Bessie, his car, when he encounters the scoop. He thinks he has eluded it, but he is snatched.

PM: This sequence had to take place on private land, as Bessie was not properly registered for public roads at that time. It also meant we didn't have problems with other cars.

[Because Bessie needed an overhaul before it could be used in the production, John Nathan-Turner gained agreement that the production would pay the first £250 of the refurbishment costs, with the remainder to be covered by BBC Exhibitions, who would be able to use the car thereafter.]

Sarah Jane Smith (Elisabeth Sladen) says farewell to K-9 (Voice: John Leeson) at her front gate, despite the robot's warnings of danger.

[For Sarah Jane's costume, Lavers chose something that would suit the actress's personality but would not clash with the outfit worn by the third Doctor.]

PM: I liked the area of water in front of the house, because it adds interest to the location, which would otherwise have been a little dreary.

John Leeson: When I first started doing the voice of K-9, they used to put it through a ring-modulator or some such device to put a very tinny edge on it, but the treatment's been getting less and less and I've been finding myself sort of growing into the voice of K-9. On the filming of *The Five Doctors*, the sound supervisor came up to me and said, 'Look, no, we don't want any treatment; just do it yourself.' So I did!

The fourth Doctor (Tom Baker) and Romana (Lalla Ward) are relaxing on a punt on the river Cam. As they steer the boat under a bridge, they too are snatched.

PM: That was the footage from *Shada* that John provided. I had nothing to do with the selection of material.

As each person is taken from their own times, the black gloved figure places a large figurine of each on a big, circular games board, split into five zones, each radiating from a sinister castle-like structure in the centre. All except the fourth Doctor and Romana, for they have been caught up in a time eddy and are trapped in the temporal void.

JB: I always enjoyed designing consoles and setting up all the lights to flash underneath. On the consoles here, underneath the perspex were lots of square, egg box shaped compartments with the lights in, so that when they lit up in sequence, you got the little cubes of light appearing on the perspex panel.

The fifth Doctor, in a rapidly weakening state, operates the TARDIS controls and collapses.
    Sarah Jane Smith is snatched by the spinning obelisk as she waits for a bus.
    In the TARDIS, the fifth Doctor lies on the floor. As Tegan and Turlough watch, he starts to fade from sight.

PM: We wanted a high camera angle on that shot so that he could disappear without getting Janet's or Mark's feet in shot.

The TARDIS materialises on a bleak and windswept plain. In the distance can be seen the tower, and on the games board, the final three figures are placed.
    The remaining members of the High Council of Time Lords on Gallifrey – President Borusa (Philip Latham), Chancellor Flavia (Dinah Sheridan) and the Castellan (Paul Jerricho) – are aware that there is evil afoot, for all four Doctors' time traces are found to converge in the newly-activated Death Zone on Gallifrey

PM: With regards to the casting of the Council, Paul Jerricho had been in *Doctor Who* previously as the Castellan. I cast Philip Latham as Borusa mainly because of the final scenes. I considered him to be a very thinking actor and wanted someone with a bit of authority. I had worked with Dinah Sheridan years ago at Yorkshire Television, and loved the experience. She's got an elegance, too, and I also thought she looked authentically aristocratic.

[The standard Time Lord costumes were eight years old, as they had been originally made for *The Deadly Assassin*. Fibreglass, however, has a limited life: after a while, it tightens up and becomes very brittle. This made getting into the formal Time Lord collars very difficult, as they needed to be flexed open to get them over the artistes' shoulders. They were also very heavy and tended to fall back, which meant the actor had to keep his arms around the collar to stop it doing so. This made movement very restricted. As most of the time the Time Lords were sitting down, it was decided that the formal collar should be used only at the end of the story for Flavia.

Borusa's costume was a variation of the standard Time Lord costume, using different fabrics. The colour was pale to make it look bigger, and the costume cut square off the body to maximise the shape.]

JB: We designed the little handsets that the Council members are using. They were supposed to be small machines that you rest your palm on and then use your fingers to tap out the digits. They're nice little props to design and make.

There is only one hope of escape for the Doctor, and for this the Council have summoned the Master (Anthony Ainley). In exchange for a free pardon and a new regeneration cycle, he must enter the Zone and rescue the Doctor.

[With the Master, there was again the problem of two copies of the costume being needed for location, so a second black velvet outfit had to be made. The original one had Victorian embroidery on the neck, which had to be copied as near as possible. This was not too easy, as it had oxidised silver in a North African pattern. The embroidery was done by Locks, who also embroidered for the Queen and Queen Mother.]

In a metallic corridor, the first Doctor meets up with Susan (Carole Ann Ford), his granddaughter. They narrowly escape from a rampaging Dalek (Operator: John Scott Martin; Voice: Roy Skelton) by tricking it into exterminating itself. They then begin the long trek towards the tower.

[In an early draft of Terrance Dicks' script, there was a scene where Susan was picked up by the obelisk while she was walking through an outdoor market in London. This was cut at the scripting stage.

Colin Lavers had originally thought that Susan had been left on present day Earth, and so clothed her as a woman of today. As it turned out, the costume could well be suited for the future time she was left in.]

PM: Working with reflecting corridors can be tricky, but as long as you work it out beforehand and don't point your cameras directly into the mirrors, then there are not too many problems. It was very difficult to light, because of the enclosed space, and it was tricky for the sound booms as well.

JB: The moving Dalek was taken from stock, but we replaced the top half with an exploding version for the shot when it blows up. Malcolm James was one of the assistants on this, and I remember practising the explosion in the effects workshop. The top part of the Dalek had to be created with all the insides in place. The explosions were titanium magnesium flash charges. There would have been eight or nine charges in the Dalek's casing, and they were contained in steel mortars. When these went off, they blew the various outer panels off, revealing the pulsating creature inside. There were airlines in the Dalek creature that is revealed, to make its tentacles thrash and writhe using compressed air from a bottle. The wall behind the Dalek was pre-cut, hinged and held together with some fine line, which was broken with a small charge at the appropriate point.

The other Doctors also begin making their way towards the tower, each hampered by different menaces: the second Doctor and the Brigadier are nearly caught by a lone Cyberman (Emyr Morris Jones); the third Doctor meets Sarah when she tumbles down an incline at the side of a road.

End of Part One

PART TWO

PM: There should have been a greater drop there. I think the problem was in trying to find somewhere where the path was on the edge for the car. It would have been better if we had used a stunt girl and a proper cliff. As it is, the Doctor could just have stepped down and helped her up.

JB: We used smoke guns to create some of the mists and smoke that drift across to obscure the roadway. There are a couple of shots here where a smoke effect has been overlaid on the picture afterwards.

The first Doctor and Susan find the TARDIS. On entering, the first and fifth Doctors meet and discuss the situation. The first Doctor suggests that Tegan make some tea while they decide what to do.

PM: Janet nearly had a fit over this. 'Why pick on the woman to make the tea? Why pick on me? Why should I make the tea?' She only agreed to go with the scene when Turlough went with her to help.

[In the rehearsal script, it was Susan who suggested she help Tegan to make *the tea.]*

The Council give the Master their seal, and a recall device that will bring him back to the conference room when activated. He enters a transmat device and is transported into the Death Zone.

PM: In that scene, it's nice that Dinah Sheridan is in shot when the Master disappears. She had to stand very still while it was being done, and it worked very well.

The second Doctor explains to the Brigadier that the tower is Rassilon's tomb, placed in the centre of the Death Zone on Gallifrey, which was used by the ancient Gallifreyans as a source of entertainment. They would kidnap different races and set them to fight each other in the Zone. This barbaric practice was stopped by Rassilon when he became President. The Zone was closed off and the tomb placed in its centre as a warning.

The Master comes across a desiccated corpse lying on the ground. He recognises it as one of the Council who had preceded him. A fire bolt shoots from the sky, and the Master moves off.

[The shot of the corpse was edited out of the American version of the story, as it was felt to be too strong.]

JB: I think the body might have been created by Stan Mitchell, another of the workshop assistants.

In the TARDIS, a meal has been laid out, which the companions help themselves to as the Doctors argue.

PM: I don't know what the idea behind all that food was. I think that nobody ever knows what food they have on the TARDIS. It was sort of like manna from heaven, ambrosia, because the Doctor never eats.

The third Doctor and Sarah meet up with the Master but refuse to believe him when he says that he was sent to help them. They drive off when more lightning bolts crash from the skies. The Master runs off, dodging the bolts. Shortly after this, Bessie is hit by a bolt and is immobilised. The third Doctor and Sarah continue on foot.

JB: What we had there were nice balls of flame. We used small camping gas cylinders with a small charge in the dimple at the top. Usually if you wanted a ball of flame, you'd fill up a polythene bag with gas and then ignite that. Under these conditions, that would have been difficult, and you also wouldn't have got the nice spout of gas that takes the flame up into the air.

FROM SCRIPT TO SCREEN: THE FIVE DOCTORS

The fifth Doctor, having gained strength from the presence of the first Doctor, sets off for the tower, along with Susan and Tegan. When they arrive, they plan to deactivate the force field that is holding the TARDIS in place, so that the first Doctor and Turlough can join them there in the ship.

The third Doctor and Sarah are making their way up a mountain when they see a squad of Cybermen (Lee Woods, Richard Naylor, Myrddin Jones, Gilbert Gillan, Emyr Morris Jones) lower down.

PM: It's sometimes tricky to get the timing right when you are directing a group that is far away from the camera and they have to make timed separate entrances into shot.

[There is a big problem with claustrophobia in a Cyberman costume. It takes ten minutes to get into the suit, two more to get the head on, fastened with two large screws. The actors are very aware that they cannot take off the heads themselves, and so Colin Lavers warned the director that if he saw any sign of panic, he'd walk into the shot and stop it. Panic can spread very easily. The main problem with this was that Colin was always looking at the actors, but was never quite sure what the signs of panic would be.]

The second Doctor and the Brigadier find a cave into the mountain. The Doctor remembers an old nursery rhyme about the tower, which mentions three entrances: above, between, below. They are going below. Beside the entrance, there is a flaming brazier and some torches, one of which they take to light their way.

PM: The torches had firelighters in the top so that they would light easily and flame well.

JB: We had to make these up, and used the lightning logo that Malcolm Thornton had worked out. They had to be safe to transport about as well, and reasonably practical to make.

The fifth Doctor, Tegan and Susan make their way across the wasteland.

PM: Poor Janet. John insisted that she wore these ridiculous high-heeled shoes, but you never see her feet! They sank into the mud because it was so wet, and she walked out of her shoes several times. It was awful. She really was shaking with the cold. I felt so sorry for her.

The Master hails the fifth Doctor from a gully, and he goes to speak with him. A Cyber scout (William Kenton) sees them and reports back to the Cyber Leader (David Banks) and the Cyber Lieutenant (Mark Hardy). The Cybermen go to detain them, but the Time Lords run off. The Cybermen open fire, and the Master gets caught in an explosion and is knocked out.

THE FIFTH DOCTOR

PM: These explosions were tricky to time. Especially the one where the Master was running away.

JB: The action here really gives the whole game away. We wanted it to be very visual, and there is a point when both the Doctor and the Master are looking back at the Cybermen, away from the explosion, and that's when we fired it off. It's the essence of a good explosion. You warn and work with the artistes and tell them what will happen step by step.

The fifth Doctor is trapped as he bends to check the Master's condition. Susan and Tegan run back to the TARDIS, but Susan trips and sprains her ankle. The fifth Doctor takes and activates the recall device that the Council gave the Master, and is transported to the conference room. Meanwhile, the Master recovers and swears allegiance to the Cyber Leader.

The fifth Doctor shows the Council the recall device – it has a homing beacon in it, which is how the Cybermen found them so quickly. One of the Council is a traitor! Borusa orders that the Castellan's office and living quarters be searched.

JB: The homing device had a small but bright LED in it, and it also had to contain a battery.

The Cybermen decide to use the Master. When he is of no further use, he will be killed.

The first Doctor and Tegan have already left the TARDIS for the tower when Susan and Turlough hear sounds from outside – they operate the scanner and see Cybermen.

End of Part Two

PART THREE

In the cave, the second Doctor and the Brigadier are chased by a Yeti (Lee Woods).

PM: There was this incredible great deep lake in the caves, which was difficult to light because it was so vast. You couldn't see very much of anything.

PM: On a location like this, you work out very carefully in advance where you're going to film, as it can be very dangerous and slippery in places.

The third Doctor and Sarah encounter a Raston Warrior robot (Keith Hodiak) on the mountain slope. They freeze – it is programmed to react to movement.

PM: The robot was played by a dancer, Keith Hodiak, and at one point when he was inside the costume he had to go to the toilet. He ended up with this terrible stain on the costume, which wouldn't dry, and so someone had to hold a fan up against him to try and dry it off before the next take. We had hired a dancer for the leaps because he had to be able to jump high enough not to land straight away.

JB: We designed this robot with a smooth, reflective head. It was made from a vacuum formed silver chrome material that, once you thinned it out, you could actually see through, like a half-silvered mirror. Unfortunately it kept misting up on location.

The Castellan is accused of being the traitor after the Black Scrolls of Rassilon are found in his quarters. The Scrolls spontaneously ignite, and he is led off by the guards (John Tallents, Norman Bradley, Lloyd Williams) to be subjected to the mind probe.

PM: The number of times I tried to get Paul to say, 'Not the *mind* probe.' Yet he insisted on 'Not the mind *probe*.' It doesn't sound like English at all somehow. We did about four takes, but he never got it right.

JB: The box was electronically controlled. We had holes drilled through the table underneath to take the control wires. We had to use some hot coils to make it smoke first of all, and then the flames had to come later. It also had to be self-extinguishing. We rehearsed it under studio conditions, to make sure it worked without the pressures of time.

The Castellan is conveniently killed by the Guard Commander (Stuart Blake) 'whilst trying to escape'. The fifth Doctor does not believe this and suspects that someone else is the traitor.

[Eight year old costumes were being used for the Chancellery Guards. The helmets tended to be too large, but were not too much of a problem. However, the original fibreglass knee and elbow patches were tightening up and had become very brittle, so much so that the elbow patches could not be used.]

JB: We designed the guns you see here. The guard has one and there is another lying beside the body.

The second Doctor and the Brigadier move further into the caves. The Doctor finds a narrow cave and they squeeze in. Luckily it is too small for the Yeti to follow.

PM: There was a huge drop down from the walkway, but you can't really see it. We found a whole area with all these locations in, and it was too good an opportunity to miss, really.

[An original Yeti costume, made of goatskin, was found in the stores rolled up in a box and had to be laid out for two weeks to get it straightened out. Colin Lavers got into the costume to try it out and see what size of person was needed. There was only one foot, so a new pair was made. No nose section was used, as the costume was to be worn in a cave with lots of cables and fireworks, and the field of vision would have been restricted too much to be safe for the actor.]

JB: We used lumps of dry ice in the pool to make it smoke and bubble.

The Doctor pulls from his pockets a firework – a galactic glitter – and, after lighting it from the flaming torch, throws it at the Yeti. Rocks fall from above, effectively trapping them. The Doctor notices that there is an air-flow, and they move off deeper into the cave.

PM: The section of cave that they were in tailed off to nothing. The next sequence was in a different part of the caves.

JB: We constructed the firework that the Doctor held. It would have been safe for the actor to hold. When the rocks fall here, you can just see that they are attached to a net. We had to close the way out when the rocks fell, and the only way to ensure that was to have a net, which we threw down over the entrance. Unfortunately you can just see it as the net shudders at the end.

Nicholas Courtney: Pat Troughton took one look at the cave mouth and said, 'You're not getting me in there!' But we did. There was also lots of polystyrene rock as opposed to real rock in the little niche that we hid from the Yeti in, and so we had to be very careful with the flaming torch not to set the rock alight. One had to be sure to hold the torch under real rock and not under polystyrene rock, otherwise the whole place would have gone up in smoke.

They find a doorway across the cave and enter the lower section of the tower.

PM: That was built across an existing tunnel by Malcolm Thornton.

Susan and Turlough watch as the Cybermen outside the TARDIS prepare a coffin-like bomb.
   The third Doctor and Sarah are saved when the Cybermen that were following

them appear. *The robot quickly and efficiently destroys them all, cutting them to pieces with steel bolts and discs (Stunt Cyberman: Stuart Fell, other Cybermen as previously on location). The third Doctor and Sarah take advantage of the diversion and carry on up to the mountain, having taken some of the robot's spare weapons.*

Terrance Dicks: The Raston robot sequence came about because we had reached a point in the story where the Pertwee Doctor and Sarah were going to go through into the tower. We needed one last major obstacle. We didn't want another old monster like a Yeti or a Cyberman as we'd already used them, and so this was the place to come up with something new. The robot was planned to be simple and effective; sometimes you write something regardless, and hope the production team do it as well as they can. But by this stage, everyone was screaming about the cost, and also Peter Moffatt was getting worried about the amount of location filming he had to get through. So we planned something that was both practical and good. Something we knew they could do, that at the same time would be effective. It was a kind of martial arts robot. We worked out this business of the smooth egg face and the silver figure and the gimmick that it can practically teleport: it moves at such a speed that it goes from here to there without being seen, and that was it really. An idea that didn't make it to the final version was that the robot was very tidy minded, and would stack all the bits of Cyberman up into a neat pile outside its cave. One bit that was added was the Cyberman being sick, and another – when it came to the studio work – was when the Dalek exploded. I didn't write all that about the dying creature inside, but I was very pleased when they added it.

JB: We had three or four different things that happened to Cybermen. This one loses an arm, this one's head blows up, and so on. It was quite a challenge to put together a battle sequence in an afternoon, when you have the pressure of the weather and all that. It is all so quickly cut together that you don't notice the individual shots and it just creates the impression of overall carnage.

[From a costume design point of view, as the script required the Raston robot to move its hand over one shoulder, it could not be an armoured type and had to be more flexible and plastic. The headpiece had a mirrored visor. When it was light outside, the actor could see out, but in Wales this was not always the case, and often he was almost blind. With so many loose rocks, that was quite dangerous, and often he had to be led on and off the location.]

The fifth Doctor speaks with Chancellor Flavia. The Doctor does not believe that the Castellan was the traitor, and he decides to speak to President Borusa.
The third Doctor and Sarah arrive on a precipice overlooking the tower. The

THE FIFTH DOCTOR

Doctor starts to unravel the rope obtained from the Raston robot's cave.

The first Doctor and Tegan arrive at the main entrance to the tower. The Doctor activates an electronic bell-shaped device, and the door slides open.

The third Doctor lassos one of the tower's cornices with some steel rope. He and Sarah slide down it, much to the dismay of the Master and the remaining Cybermen, who are watching from further down the mountain.

Terrance Dicks: That was originally a hang-gliding sequence. I thought that we could have the third Doctor turn his cloak into a hang-glider and just fly to the tower. But it wasn't possible to do it in the time, so we came up with them sliding down the wire instead. It's always *Star Wars* on a shoestring with *Doctor Who*, and you are always fighting against what's possible and what isn't. I think it's amazing that they do so well. It's always a part of your brief that you must come up with something amazing, astonishing and cheap!

JB: This was originally going to be a bow and arrow idea to fire something across the gap. But we had a bit of a problem with that and it broke, and I think that Pertwee couldn't use it. In the end, we came up with the idea of a lasso. I remember rigging something up in the film studio, so that we could get them swinging along the line to the top of the tower.

PM: There was an enormous pause in filming during this sequence, for over an hour, because Jon Pertwee refused to do the scene. The Doctor was supposed to build a bow and arrow from the bits he had picked up, and I had kept asking and asking how he was supposed to do this, and how this thing should be made, and everyone said it would be all right. When we got to the scene, Jon couldn't see how it could be done. In the end, while the Cybermen were nearly frozen to death in the valley down below, John Nathan-Turner, Pertwee and I went to a car somewhere out of the cold and worked out a way to make the scene work.

The scene as it eventually appeared was a great mixture of different shots that we were unable to do all at the same time. Jon threw the lasso on a cliff-top in a howling gale in Wales; it landed on a pinnacle on a set in the film studio at Ealing; they slid down the wire at Ealing; the Master looking up at it, surrounded by Cybermen, was at the bottom of a valley in Wales; and the high shot of the tower was matted in afterwards. But when edited together, it all worked like a dream.

The Doctor helps Sarah onto the top of the tower.

PM: Sarah's quite high off the ground there. The parapet was about eight feet off the ground. The composite shot there is really nice. It's the film at Ealing plus the painted tower plus the filmed background.

JB: I know we had to make a bigger version of the top of the tower for that. Jean Peyre got involved with this scene as well, to match all the elements together.

The first Doctor and Tegan have arrived in the entrance hall of the tower, only to be confronted by a deadly floor pattern of electrified squares. They hide as the Master, followed by the Cyber Leader, Cyber Lieutenant and a group of Cybermen (Graham Cole, Alan Riches, Ian Marshall-Fisher, Mark Bassenger) enter. The Master, by crossing the pattern, demonstrates to the Cybermen that it is safe. The Cybermen follow, only to be destroyed by bolts of electricity from the ceiling. The Cyber Leader demands to know the safe route, but the Master turns a cyber weapon on the Cyber Leader as it is following him across.

JB: You can't see any wires trailing from the Cybermen to trigger the explosions, because there weren't any. My assistant on the show, Malcolm James, suggested that to avoid the problem of trailing wires, we got the actors playing the Cybermen to trigger the explosions themselves using small battery packs. This was a great idea, and really worked well in the studio.

[There was almost a problem in the studio when the Cybermen were being sprayed with paint to cover up the various explosive charges placed there by Visual Effects. The spray could all too easily drift into the costume and choke the actor.]

The first Doctor deduces from the Master's comment that it is as easy as pie, that the squares have a safe path across derived from the calculation of pi. He and Tegan follow the Master across.
    The fifth Doctor finds that Borusa, who was in the conference room and has not left through the door, is there no longer. He begins to search the room.
    The third Doctor and Sarah move down through the tower. Sarah is feeling scared, so the Doctor checks ahead. He meets phantoms of Mike Yates (Richard Franklin) and Liz Shaw (Caroline John), which vanish screaming when he realises they are not real.

[In the rehearsal script, there were no scenes present with the phantom companions. Instead, Sarah Jane was physically attacked by a phantom of the third Doctor after the real one has left her on her own.
    Colin Lavers chose present day clothes for Liz; simply something that suited the actress and was comfortable to wear. Yates wore a costume from stock, but to emphasise that he was a phantom, and that the mind conjuring

THE FIFTH DOCTOR

it was not perfect, there were no UNIT insignia.]

The first Doctor and Tegan pass by a flight of stairs on their way through the tower. The Master comes down the steps behind them.

End of Part Three

PART FOUR

The second Doctor and the Brigadier encounter phantoms of Jamie (Frazer Hines) and Zoe (Wendy Padbury) on a flight of stairs leading up. The phantoms vanish screaming when the Doctor realises that the real Jamie and Zoe would not have known who they were.

[Colin Lavers again used the 1973 *Radio Times* special for costume reference for Jamie and Zoe. There were two colour photographs of Jamie, each showing a different tartan, but one had been specially shot for the publication rather than taken from the series itself. The actual McCrimmon tartan was mainly blue, but when Frazer Hines saw it, he commented that it was not the right one. Eventually Lavers hired a red and green 18th Century kilt that had been used in the film *Bonnie Prince Charlie*. For Zoe's costume, Lavers wanted to reflect the Sixties plastic look, particularly as Zoe had tended to wear plastic-looking clothes, and so he used packaging material. If Zoe had had to move around, it would have been far too noisy, but it was quite suitable for the short scene. Actress Wendy Padbury was pregnant when this scene was shot, but not to the extent that it showed. Unfortunately she later lost the baby.]

The fifth Doctor notices the Harp of Rassilon by a wall and realises that a musical key must open a hidden door. He begins to experiment on the harp.

PM: Peter played the harp himself at this point, as he's quite musical.

The first, second and third Doctors all meet up in the main hall of the tower. They translate the hieroglyphs on a small monolith: whoever takes the ring from Rassilon's finger will have eternal life. *The Master steps forward from the entrance to the room – now he will claim eternal life. He threatens the Doctors with his tissue compression eliminator weapon. The Brigadier jumps him from behind, and he is tied up.*

The fifth Doctor plays the correct tune on the harp, read from a painting on the wall, and a door slides open revealing the forbidden games control room.

PM: Peter didn't play that sequence. We had a lady harpist come in for the sound dub to record the music.

In the games control room, President Borusa is dressed in black and is presiding over the game board – he is quite mad. He is after immortality and has used the Doctors to breach the tomb's defences.

[Borusa's black costume was almost an opposite to his normal costume. It was cut to emphasise height and thinness with converging lines. Various different black materials were used as, if only one had been used, this would have tended to appear on screen simply as a black blob.) Colin Lavers had designed a new collar made out of black wire to give the impression of cobwebs and possibly provide the director with interesting shots through it. Unfortunately Philip Latham found it rather inhibiting and couldn't wear it.]

JB: Some of the consoles in the room were practical and some were dummies. The walls were made from those milk crate things. Malcolm was always up against the budgets, and if he could re-use materials then he would. In this case, the walls look really good with the lighting behind them.

The Doctors find a communication and control system in the tomb, and the third Doctor reverses the polarity of the neutron flow, thus allowing the TARDIS to come through the force field.
The Cybermen by the TARDIS detonate their bomb just as the TARDIS dematerialises and heads for the tower on pre-set co-ordinates..

JB: The explosion was done with a locked off camera and a cut immediately before the explosion so that the TARDIS could be removed. There's also another of our small props there, which the Cyberman uses to detonate the bombs.

Borusa is wearing the Coronet of Rassilon, and with his mind enhanced by this, he takes over the fifth Doctor's mind. He and the fifth Doctor then go to the transmat, where the second Doctor is trying to make contact.

PM: The sequences on the monitor with the second Doctor were fed through live from the other set, but the Peter Davison sequence was pre-recorded. You can see that the background is different.

The fifth Doctor and Borusa arrive in the tomb, and Borusa freezes the companions in time. The other three Doctors link minds and free the fifth.

PM: To do that sequence of cutting between the Doctors, we just used the normal number of cameras and changed position if we needed to between shots.

The voice of Rassilon booms out that this is the game of Rassilon.

Terrance Dicks: Having put Rassilon at the end to resolve it all, I envisaged him as a kind of Valentine Dyall type actor; tall and gaunt and impressive. I think in the end it worked quite well, because Rassilon didn't look the way you expected him to. I think I had envisaged a more elaborate projection of the giant Rassilon, you would actually see a giant Rassilon towering above at the end of the story, but again it's a matter of time and budget.

Rassilon's face (Richard Matthews) materialises and asks if Borusa wishes immortality. Rassilon asks the Doctors if Borusa deserves immortality, and they all say no – except for the first Doctor, who has realised what is happening. He says that Borusa should get immortality.
Rassilon agrees, and tells Borusa to take the ring from the hand of his effigy, which is lying on top of the tomb itself. At this, Borusa is immobilised in stone and set in the base of the tomb with other megalomaniacs who previously sought immortality (Johnnie Mack, Frederick Wolfe, Charles Milward). He too is now immortal.

PM: All those actors behind the masks were lying underneath the hollow tomb. We had two versions of the side of the tomb – one with transparent faces and one with opaque faces – and we mixed from one to the other.

JB: I remember doing something with the ring on this. We set up a little rig to fire the ring off his hand, but they've done it with a video effect on the final story. Obviously it didn't work too well and it got dropped.

Rassilon returns the first three Doctors and their companions to their respective time zones and the Master to his. The fourth Doctor is freed from the vortex.
The fifth Doctor is proclaimed as President by Chancellor Flavia when she arrives in the tomb. Taking the initiative, the Doctor orders Flavia back to the Council as acting President until he arrives to take over from her later. He then hurriedly leaves in the TARDIS with Tegan and Turlough – a renegade, just like in the beginning.

POST-PRODUCTION

Once the studio recordings were complete, the next stage was to copy them all onto tape for viewing and later editing by Peter Moffatt. This tape-to-tape transfer took place on 18 April 1983, and took around four hours to complete. The footage filmed on location was transferred to video on 13, 19 and 25 May 1983, and took three hours to rehearse, in order to match the studio conditions to the film conditions, followed by an hour to achieve the actual transfer of material.

The video effects, which included the spinning time scoop obelisk, as well as the various ray gun bursts from Dalek, Cybermen and other sources, were created on 16 and 18 May 1983 by video effects designer Dave Chapman using a Quantel 5000 imaging machine in the gallery of studio TC6.

The opening and closing titles were created on 23 May 1983 for both the single part story and the four part version.

The story was finally edited together by Hugh Parson, who had been requested specifically for the job by John Nathan-Turner, on 23, 25, 28, 29 and 31 May and 2 and 3 June 1983 in editing suite B. The final day had originally been booked as a 'safety day', but it was ultimately needed to complete the work.

Two VHS copies of the edited programme were supplied to John Nathan-Turner, one at the end of Sunday 29 May showing the work so far, and one at the end of Tuesday 31 May. These were viewed by Nathan-Turner on Wednesday 1 June for his comments before the final edit on Thursday 2 June.

The dubbing of sound recorded on location to the transferred video footage took place on 30 May 1983, and lasted from 11.15 in the morning until 11.00 at night.

With the final edited version of the story complete, two VHS copies were supplied to the BBC's Radiophonic Workshop for work to start on the music and sound effects for the show. The tapes were delivered over the weekend of 4/5 June 1983 and were viewed on the following Monday by the studio sound technician Martin Ridout and Dick Mills, who as usual would be creating the special sound effects for the story.

The composer allocated to work on *The Five Doctors* was Peter Howell. 'I was actually very pleased to do *The Five Doctors*, as it was rather an exciting idea,' he said when interviewed in 1984.

The Workshop wouldn't start putting music and effects onto a *Doctor Who* until they received a finished tape from the production office, thus making their task a lot easier, as they were able to time exactly how long scenes were and to compose and place the music precisely.

Peter Howell liked to approach the task by getting a lot of inspiration from various pieces of equipment. 'I always like to take a couple of days just setting up the studio using slightly different pieces of equipment in the sort of style that I think is right for the story. In this particular instance I felt that the story really did divide itself into three sections; the first section was the gathering together of the Doctors, with quite a lot of electronic hardware involved with the games board and all that; having got that part over with, you are then into the adventure story with the Cybermen and so on; and the third part of it was the coming together of the characters with the Rassilon sequence, which was to me much more of an epic legend. I found that in my mind I had divided it into three, so consequently when I started off, I was basically interested in setting the place up to do quite a lot of sequenced electronics and things like that, which I felt was right for the electronic hardware in the picture, and then further on I was using the Fairlight computer more. Much of the music in the later scenes was done using the "Rassilon horn", which by the way is the hooter from the Queen Mary, which had been slid up and down and re-sampled into the computer so you that you could play it. It took about a day and a half to make just that one sound, but I felt it was very important. I wanted to link it with the constant view of the tower, and in fact it was quite useful in the culmination of the story as I used it almost as if someone were playing bagpipes until you couldn't stand it any longer. There came a point when Borusa put his hands over his ears just as he was about to disappear into the stone; in fact he was putting his hands up purely as an artistic device, but it occurred to me that he was putting his hands over his ears as the horn beat him senseless, so to speak.'

'I did suggest to the producer early on that bearing in mind that there were five Doctors in this programme, I would like to use the *Doctor Who* signature tune in the incidental music, as that would be quite a nice way of linking it all together, as if ever there was an excuse to use the signature tune in the incidental music, then this was it. I had done it before (in *Meglos*) and enjoyed it, and it is actually a very adaptable piece of music. As a matter of interest, I sampled the original sounds from the original signature tune onto the Fairlight, and during the opening scenes when the Hartnell character is taken, I was actually using the original sounds, only digitally.

'I also considered using some of Malcolm Clarke's excellent music from the previous Cyberman story, *Earthshock*. I borrowed it, but it is incredibly difficult to get pre-written music to sync in with the actual timed sequences that exist. It was very difficult to get it in, but I did try.'

One very notable aspect of the production was that the closing credits rolled over a version of the theme music that combined the original Sixties and Seventies theme with the then current Eighties theme, which Peter Howell had himself arranged. 'I suggested it to the producer, but added that I had no idea whether it would work or not,' said Peter. 'Once I had done it, he came along and listened to it and decided to use it. I personally was very pleased with it. I felt that because the end of the story was not a cliff-hanger, it was not necessary to have the very strong start to the end music. I do have a version of the music that goes from a sort of twenty year old mono with hardly any frequency response to a classy stereo version, and that really blows your mind. I'll tell you a trade secret here: the old signature tune is in E Minor and the new version is in F Sharp Minor, so the two didn't mix very well as they stood, also the new one is slightly faster, so I had to pass the old one through a harmoniser to jack the pitch up to that of the new, and then I had to do a slight speed change on it so that it would match, and it really was a major task. I did it quite a long time before I saw any of the programme, because I had a couple of days at my disposal and I thought I'd try it to see if it worked or not. Most people thought that it was a nice touch. It's probably the right time to do things like that when you are doing a special, as you can get away with it.'

The other aspect of the production handled by the Radiophonic Workshop were the special sounds, created by Dick Mills. Mills had been with the Workshop since the late Fifties, and had been handling the special sound requirements for *Doctor Who* almost single-handedly since the mid-Seventies.

'As with all programmes,' explained Mills at the time, 'we tend to look at each *Doctor Who* story with a view to its complete form, and so our first concern was to make it "moody" and "mysterious" – the actual sound-making part is easy once you've decided where all the sounds are to go.

'We first discussed with the director where sounds would appear and what they would be like. An early decision was to try and make each sector of the Death Zone have its own wind background, so as to give a different location to each Doctor's adventures there. I'm not sure whether this subtlety came off or not in the final version. Another idea was to back Rassilon's presence with sound. Fortunately, with the amount of film material used, there was not a great deal of special sound required, except perhaps to add to the Raston robot scenes.'

One nod to continuity brought in by Mills was the use of established *Doctor Who* sound effects. 'There were the Cybermen and Dalek guns, and the Gallifreyan stasers, in addition to the Yeti roar (from *The Web of Fear*) and the standard TARDIS sounds.

'There is total liaison with the musician on the show, now that both sounds and music are created under one roof at the Workshop. Discussions usually occur over dramatic matters and/or frequency ranges to be used, to avoid clashing with one another. Often just one contribution from either music or sound is eventually preferred at one point in an episode. I usually insist that all dramatic effects in space are covered musically, except for the final obligatory BANG!

'We generally have a ten day space between episode review and the dubbing session, and we always need all ten days. This is particularly true in my case, where I have to visit studios, do reviews or dubs for other episodes as well, once the season has started. The ten days allows for composition, creation, playback to the director and any remaking to occur before the final dub; plus of course all the necessary paperwork (shot lists, dubbing instructions etc.)'

THE FIFTH DOCTOR

It was during post production that it was noticed that Richard Hurndall had made a mistake in reeling off the numbers that comprised the value pi during the studio scenes set on the ante-room set. The actor was then recalled to perform a short sound recording to be used to overdub the erroneous dialogue. This recording took place on 20 July 1983.

The final sypher dub – the combining of all the aural elements of the programme with the visual elements – for the single episode edition of the programme took place over 14 and 15 September 1983 in the BBC's Sypher II suite. The same suite was used for the final dub of the four-part version, which took place on 22 September and 6 October 1983. This involved the inclusion of several new musical 'stings' created by Peter Howell for the new episode endings.

The final dub marked the completion of production work on *The Five Doctors*, and all that remained was for it to be scheduled for transmission.

With all the work complete, Terrance Dicks was pleased with the final result. 'I was very pleased with it, considering all the obstacles and hassles that had to be overcome. It's difficult to say that without sounding self-praising, but there was nothing that disappointed me, I was very pleased with it; it all worked.

'Having said that, one of the problems with the story was that it wasn't written as four episodes. Normally you only have to hold the viewer's attention for 25 minutes at a time, but when everything is all together, it is very long, so it's much harder to keep it driving along. You have got to have a series of climaxes or at least something happening all the time to keep the viewers interested.'

Peter Moffatt also felt the story worked. 'I think it is a great credit to everybody concerned in the production that it succeeded so well. To John Nathan-Turner for all his encouragement and his ever guiding hand, to Terrance Dicks for his intriguing script, aided and abetted by Eric Saward, to the designers and technicians at the BBC for their wonderful enthusiasm and hard slog of work, to the actors who gave it such life. Everyone gave of his or her best, which is the way that good television is made.'

TRANSMISSION

John Nathan-Turner had initially been hopeful that the show would be broadcast in England on the anniversary itself, but this was not to be.

In response to a letter from David J Howe enquiring why this was the case, David Reid, the Head of Series and Serials, wrote on 1 November 1983:

'Thank you for your letter concerning *Doctor Who*. You should know that the original schedule for *The Five Doctors* was indeed Wednesday 23rd November. However, other problems on BBC1 forced the Controller to move it by two days, by which time we had given permission for other countries to transmit on the 23rd. It was not really possible for us to go back on our word, particularly as other countries had already gone to considerable expense to line up simultaneous networking.

'Naturally I would prefer the programme to transmit on the 23rd, but I do assure you that it is not possible and that hopefully the Friday slot is likely to attract a far larger audience.'

The Five Doctors was eventually transmitted in the UK on Friday 25 November at 7.20 pm as a part of the annual *Children In Need* appeal fronted by popular television and radio presenter Terry Wogan. Because the appeal was geared towards raising money via telephone pledges, in some regions of the UK captions were run across the bottom of the screen during the transmission, giving the status of the amounts raised so far by the regions.

After the story had completed, Terry Wogan was joined in the *Children in Need* studio by Peter Davison. This was a pre-recorded sequence, as the actor was at the time travelling to America, along with all the other major cast members, to attend an anniversary convention in Chicago. Davison donated his Doctor's coat for telephone auction to raise funds for the appeal, but it is unknown how much was offered or who finally obtained the coat.

The Five Doctors was actually premiered in Chicago on the anniversary itself, 23 November.

The press coverage was very strong. The BBC placed the story on the front of their press information pack for the Friday, and for the first time since the start of the eleventh season back in December 1973, the BBC's listings magazine, the *Radio Times,* afforded *Doctor Who* a front cover. This was a painting by Andrew Skilleter depicting the five Doctors and the Master around an image of the Dark Tower. Inside the magazine was an article about all the companions who had travelled with the Doctor.

Despite the twin attractions of the 20th anniversary and the *Children in Need* appeal, the UK transmission managed only 7.7 million viewers, which placed it 51st in the week's top rated television shows. This figure, however, matched the highest rated episodes of the twenty-first season.

When the programme was repeated as a four part story in 1984, it managed only a maximum rating of 4.7 million, with the chart position dropping to 88 for the first episode and then falling as low as 107 for the third episode. This was notably lower than the stories in the surrounding seasons.

The press were less than kind about the special. The *Philadelphia Inquirer*, after explaining why two of the Doctors were not 'the originals', said: 'What's left is a silly, occasionally entertaining story in which four Doctor Whos finally converge to solve a mystery and save their individual lives. Like all TV reunion shows, it falls short of the original – but in this case, the original is still running.'

Closer to home, the *Sunday Times* said, 'Just why, in these days of sophisticated, multi-million pound films such as *Star Wars*, *Doctor Who* still attracts a regular audience of some 8 million remains a mystery even to the BBC. Part of the reason is that the viewing habit passes easily from one generation to the next, though that doesn't explain why, in America, *Doctor Who* has become a late-night cult show for adults.'

The *Yorkshire Post* however was slightly more critical. 'Last night's celebratory adventure on BBC1, *The Five Doctors*, was a partial misnomer, as the longest serving, Tom Baker, made no more than a token appearance. Richard Hurndall gave a convincing impersonation of the original Doctor, the late William Hartnell.

'But it did give the opportunity to contrast the styles of the three remaining, and it confirmed my view that Patrick Troughton had the character assessed perfectly.

'Splendid actor that he is, he was able to bring conviction to his highly eccentric and whimsical professor.

'Jon Pertwee took the eccentricity too far, while the latest Doctor, Peter Davison, was too easily recognisable as himself, and he was also too young, barely older than the obligatory mini-skirted female assistants, included to persuade fathers to join their children watching.

'The programme in which the Doctors were stranded in a death zone, which looked like a cross between a fairground hall of mirrors and a slate quarry, also enabled the suavely villainous Anthony Ainley to live up to his description last night as "my best enemy", playing the Master. The deficiencies of some of the Doctor's past adversaries were mercilessly exposed.

'The Daleks, those rubbish bins on wheels which have inspired thousands of children's games, proved inefficient fighting machines as they blew off their own heads, and the Cybermen, predecessors of the *Star Wars* storm troopers, were massacred by a remarkable Jumping Jack Flash character who fired deadly bolts from his fingertips.'

The fans were, on the whole, positive about the show in the *Doctor Who* Appreciation Society's quarterly magazine *TARDIS*. 'A good, traditional *Doctor Who* story, with an excellent dream-like quality. I would label it a classic, but I think sentimentality made that near-inevitable.' (Saul Nasse); 'The show relied too heavily on old material and ideas.' (Christopher Denyer); 'What we got, as nonsensical as it all was, was entertaining stuff.' (Saul Gething); 'I think it deserves a 9.5 out of 10.' (Ian Massey).

The novelisation of *The Five Doctors* was published by W H Allen in their Target range before the show had even been screened; the first time that this had happened for any story. 'They were very keen to get the novelisation out as close to the show as possible,' explained Terrance Dicks, who adapted his own script for book form. 'I finished writing it before I saw the final playback of the programme, which does explain some of the minor differences between the show and the book. For instance, Patrick's furry Yeti coat, which I didn't know he was wearing until I saw the show. It's that kind of thing. When they get to the caves, they had put a little ceremonial entrance outside, with a torch. That wasn't in the script, but it does give them a torch to carry and explains how they could see where they were going in the caves. It's the Brigadier's cigarette lighter that they use in the book. Other things, like Patrick's talking about Zodin the Terrible, came from a Programme as Broadcast script that I got in the last stages of editing the book, so I knew pretty well every line and interjection – but nobody ever mentioned the fur coat! I wish I'd known; I'd have written it into the book!'

CREDITS

Director	Peter Moffatt
	(Shada) Pennant Roberts
	(Inserts) John Nathan-Turner
Producer	John Nathan-Turner
Production Manager	Jeremy Silberston
Production Assistant	Jean Davis
Assistant Floor Manager	Pauline Seager
Floor Assistant	Chris Stanton
Script Editor	Eric Saward
Production Associate	June Collins
Production Secretary	Jane Judge
Designer	Malcolm Thornton
Assistant	Steve Fawcett
Costume Designer	Colin Lavers
Assistant	Peter Halston
Dressers	Carl Levy
	Philip Winter
	Camilla Gavin
Make-Up Artist	Jill Hagger
Assistants	Naomi Donne
	Fay Hammond
Visual Effects	John Brace
	Mike Kelt
Assistants	Malcolm James
	Dave Rogers
Film Editor	M.A.C. Adams
Film Cameraman	John Baker
Assistant	Nick Squires
Sound Recordist	John Gatland
Assistant	Brian Biffin

THE FIFTH DOCTOR

Video Effects	Dave Chapman
Camera Supervisor	Alec Wheal
Crew	11
Technical Manager	Derek Thompson
Design Effects	Jean Peyre
Graphic Design	Ian Hewett
Videotape Editor	Hugh Parson
Studio Lighting	Don Babbage
Studio Sound	Martin Ridout
Grams Operator	John Downes
Vision Mixer	Shirley Coward
Lighting	Archie Dawson
Grips	Tex Childs
Film Ops	John Rice
	Les Thomas
	Brian Walters
	Eric Levey
Armourer	Tony Chilton
Prop Buyer	Robert Fleming
Film Operations Manager	Graham Richmond
Title Music	Ron Grainer and the BBC Radiophonic Workshop
Incidental Music	Peter Howell
Special Sound	Dick Mills
Writer	Terrance Dicks

Selling the Doctor

MEDIA

During the first six years that Tom Baker had played the Doctor, *Doctor Who* had consistently maintained a very high level of popularity. The ratings had averaged around nine to 11 million per episode for most of the period, and had even risen to an all-time high of 16 million at one point during 1979 – although this record figure had been attributable in part to a protracted strike that had hit the ITV companies and blacked out the third channel for several weeks across the country. In 1980, however, the programme schedulers at ITV came up with a secret weapon: a glitzy new American science fiction series entitled *Buck Rogers in the 25th Century*. With its slick special effects, cute robots and lycra-clad ladies, this show was a big hit with UK viewers and had the effect of splitting the audience. *Doctor Who* was left with only around five million viewers per episode for most of its eighteenth season, and although there was a slight increase to around six million by the end of the story in which Baker left, this was still less than half the number that had been watching the year before.

There was, nevertheless, a large amount of press coverage generated by the announcement on 24 October 1980 that Baker was shortly to leave the role that had made him famous. Even the national news media covered the story, and speculation was rife that the new Doctor could be played by a woman (although this was in fact a publicity stunt dreamed up by Baker and producer John Nathan-Turner).

In the event, it is doubtful that anyone could have predicted just who would be chosen as the next Doctor. One factor that Nathan-Turner certainly had in mind, however, was the need to cast an extremely popular actor whose presence would help to reverse the series' disastrous ratings decline suffered during Season 18.

Peter Davison's accession to the role was announced to the press on 4 November 1980 and, given that the actor was best known for playing vet Tristan Farnon in the popular series *All Creatures Great and Small*, the subsequent headlines were fairly predictable: 'Dr Moo! TV Vet is New Space Doctor', 'Meet Dr Tristan' and 'TV Vet's the New Dr Who' were typical examples.

Davison could already be seen appearing on ITV as a regular in the comedy series *Holding the Fort* and in the children's story series *Once Upon A Time*, and he was also recording for the BBC a new sitcom called *Sink or Swim*. By the time he made his debut as the Doctor, some pundits were suggesting that it was becoming almost impossible to turn on a television set without seeing him.

The actor was even promoting Websters beer in a series of television commercials. After being announced as the Doctor, however, and only one year into his three year contract with the firm, he was replaced. The advertising agency were quoted as saying: 'As star of a children's programme, there's no way he should be advertising beer.'

The press mentioned that Davison was the youngest actor to play the Doctor, and Ian Black in the *Daily Express* wrote:

[Peter] said that as a 12-year-old he sat glued to the box watching the original Doctor Who, William Hartnell. And he declared: 'I'm very happy to accept the part.

'I'm not doing it for the money – in fact I'm getting paid less per episode than I've been used to earning in other shows. But I think it will be enjoyable to do.'

Davison went on to predict that he wouldn't be playing the Doctor for too long:

'I expect a lengthy, substantial time on the programme, but I believe any show needs that bit of regeneration to keep the interest up.'

John Nathan-Turner, who had worked with Davison on *All Creatures Great and Small*, commented:

'Peter is an ideal actor for the role. He has the right combination of light humour, drama and realism, is very popular with children and has a large following with feminine viewers.'

A number of early publicity appearances followed for Davison, culminating in the unveiling of the fifth Doctor's costume at a press call on 15 April 1981, where the actor was photographed wielding a cricket bat in front of a set of stumps painted on the side of the TARDIS police box prop.

The BBC's announcement on 19 August 1981 of its schedules for the forthcoming autumn season again saw *Doctor Who* featuring prominently, Davison being photographed in costume along with Pamela Stephenson and other stars of the shows included in the promotion. This was all the more remarkable given that *Doctor Who* was not actually a part of the autumn line-up: its new season would not begin until 4 January 1982.

One major change when the series did return was the move from its traditional Saturday teatime placing to its new twice-weekly evening slot, where it was in competition with a wide range of ITV fare including initially the soap opera *Emmerdale Farm* and the holiday programme *Wish You Were Here*. It is unknown what prompted this change of scheduling, which appears to have been decided upon by BBC1 Controller Alan Hart, but it may well have had something to do with the poor ratings gained by the previous season.

Whereas Tom Baker had actively courted the press, Davison was an altogether more private person. Although during his time in the series he attended many conventions and made many personal appearances – which he was quoted as saying that he did because they came with the job of being the Doctor – the total amount of press coverage that he generated was not great. When interviews did appear, the actor's primary concern seemed to be the fact that he was recognised wherever he went and was becoming tired of signing autographs and being nice to people. The extent to which this public attention arose solely from his role as the Doctor is however debatable; Davison was such a prominent figure on television in the early Eighties that he would no doubt have been recognised anyway.

Amongst the shows on which Davison guested during his time in *Doctor Who* were: *Multi-Coloured Swap Shop* (9 January 1982, publicising *Castrovalva*); *So You Think You Know What's Good for You* (11 January 1982, with his wife, actress Sandra Dickinson); *Pebble Mill at One* (March 1982, plugging a newly published anthology of science fiction short stories to which he had lent his name for promotional purposes); *This is Your Life* (recorded 18 March 1982 and transmitted 25 March 1982 with him as its subject); a BAFTA awards show outside broadcast (20 March 1983, presenting awards for children's programmes); *Saturday Superstore* (26 March 1983, with companions Janet Fielding and Mark Strickson); *The Late, Late Breakfast Show* (10 December 1983, receiving a Golden Egg award for a humorous out-take from *The Awakening*); and *Harty* (20 March 1984, with his successor, Colin Baker). He also took part in a number of radio shows, including one on BBC radio in May 1981 when he spoke about his interest in cricket.

As he himself had predicted, Davison ultimately decided to leave *Doctor Who* after only three seasons in the lead role. 'There was a danger of becoming stereotyped,' he told the press after the announcement was made on 28 July 1983. 'And I've always done three years of everything else. It's a nice round figure.' Some quarters of the press tried to suggest that his decision to leave was prompted by some 'backstage bust up' but, as this was not in fact the case, they were unable to get very far with that line of reporting.

Nathan-Turner again generated a certain amount of controversy by dropping false hints that the next Doctor might be played by a woman – 'I'm not ruling out the choice of having a lady Doctor,' he was quoted as saying – but the press seemed equally keen to report the recent decline in the series' viewing figures. While Season 19 had averaged over nine million viewers per episode, Seasons 20 and 21 had managed only just over seven million apiece. This was still a respectable rating, but Nathan-Turner no doubt had in mind the possibility of giving the series a further boost in popularity when he came to regenerate the Doctor once again. On the subject of Davison's successor, he was quoted as saying: 'The next Doctor will be older and a little more eccentric. We want to change the style of the Doctor completely. The new character will be vastly different from Peter.'

Just as press coverage of the series' lead actor seemed to diminish slightly after Davison took over from Baker, so the interest in the actors and actresses who played the Doctor's companions seemed to drop a little.

Matthew Waterhouse (Adric), Sarah Sutton (Nyssa) and Janet Fielding (Tegan) had all made their debuts at the tail end of the fourth Doctor's era, so their novelty value had been all but exhausted by the time that Davison took over. Waterhouse's departure did gain a little coverage, having been publicised by way of a BBC press release issued on 3 December 1981, but the production team were probably less than pleased to see that this focused mainly on the actor's displeasure at their decision to kill off his character. The tabloid press had always shown rather less interest in the Doctor's male companions than in the glamorous '*Doctor Who* girls', however, and for much of the fifth Doctor's era, it was actually Fielding who attracted the most attention – especially when she posed on one occasion in black leather gear and on another in a moulded fibre-glass outfit.

Nathan-Turner, well aware of the perceived image of the female companions, contrived to dress Nyssa and Tegan in figure-hugging and impractical costumes throughout their time in the series. Perhaps the most well-publicised event of all, apart from the series' 20th anniversary (of which more below), occurred when the crew visited Amsterdam to do location filming for Season 20's opening story, *Arc of Infinity*, and Tegan was finally given a change of regular costume. No doubt to the delight of the assembled photographers, the new outfit was even more revealing than the old – a pair of culottes and a boob tube.

The recording of *Mawdryn Undead* again saw a number of newspapers running photographs of Fielding and Sutton, although these were rather less glamorous than was usually the case as the pair were showing off the old-age make-up that they were required to wear at one point during the action. The accompanying reports concentrated mainly on that fact that Fielding was getting married that week.

There was little noise made in the press when Sutton and Fielding later made their respective exits from the series. Similarly, the arrival and subsequent departure of Mark Strickson (Turlough) went largely unremarked, in line with the usual treatment of the male companions.

The arrival of Nicola Bryant (Peri) brought something of a resurgence of popular interest in the *Doctor Who* companion. The tabloids went wild, printing numerous photographs and articles about the newcomer, and Bryant made her television debut with an appearance on the BBC's *Breakfast Time* on 6 July 1983. By this time, however, the era of the fifth Doctor was almost at an end. The next story after Bryant joined the series, Davison bowed out, to be replaced by the sixth Doctor, Colin Baker.

THE 20TH ANNIVERSARY

An anniversary is always a good opportunity to make an impression, and with *Doctor Who*'s 20th falling in November 1983, everyone involved was determined to make the most of the occasion – especially as the series had by that point really taken off in America.

A special programme, *The Five Doctors*, was planned to celebrate the anniversary on BBC1. The other major event of the year was a convention organised by BBC Enterprises and held at Longleat House in Warminster, Wiltshire. Longleat had been the home of one of two permanent *Doctor Who* exhibitions in the UK since 1974, and Lord Bath, its owner, was keen to see its profile raised in this manner. The event would be open to the general public and would feature guest appearances by all four surviving Doctors – Patrick Troughton, Jon Pertwee, Tom Baker and Peter Davison – and numerous companions, as well as screenings of rare episodes and displays and talks by some of the BBC departments involved in making *Doctor Who*. Advertising trailers were placed after a number of Season 19 episodes, and other advance publicity for the event included mentions on Ceefax and fliers sent out with specialist publications.

The Doctor Who Celebration: Twenty Years of a Time Lord took place over the Easter bank holiday weekend, Sunday 3 April and Monday 4 April 1983, from 10.00 am until 6.00 pm each day. Admission was £3.50 per day for an adult and £1.50 per day for a child. The main convention area was behind the House, where a number of marquees had been set up. These housed displays by the BBC's Costume, Make-up, Design and Visual Effects Departments and Radiophonic Workshop; a forum in which panel discussions and guest interviews were presented; a cinema in which the complete stories *The Dalek Invasion of Earth* (Hartnell), *The Dominators* (Troughton), *Terror of the Autons* (Pertwee), *Terror of the Zygons* (Baker) and *The Visitation* (Davison) were shown; and a sales area where large quantities of spin-off merchandise were on offer and an auction of *Doctor Who* props and costumes took place – the first time such items had ever been made available to the public to buy. A large conservatory adjoining the House was meanwhile converted into an autograph room.

Everything might have gone smoothly had it not been for the inclement April weather and the fact that far more people than anticipated turned up. The walkways and grass were churned into slippery, mud-caked areas, and queues stretched into the distance as every tent was filled to capacity. The organisers had apparently expected around 50,000 people spread over the two days, but over 35,000 came on the Sunday alone, leading to many disappointed families being turned away at the gate.

The event attracted quite a bit of press interest, and Colin Randall of the *Daily Telegraph* described the situation as follows:

> Long queues formed outside most of the main attractions and senior BBC officials apologised for the delays, saying that the event had proved 'too successful'. Families had to wait up to two hours for autographs from the members of cast, past and present. One visitor, Mr David Southwell, said he had spent more than £20 on the day's outing from Bristol with his wife and two children. 'We have been here over two hours and all we have seen is a couple of sets,' he said. 'It is a complete rip-off and everybody is entitled to their money back.' Others made similar points, though with more restraint.

Bryon Parkin, Managing Director of BBC Enterprises, was reported as saying:

> We have been the victims of our own success. No one could have conceived that so many people would have come so early. There were queues at 8 am and we have just done our best to cope with it.

Parkin went on to promise that any ticket holders who were unable to get in would have their money refunded, and the BBC also made a statement that only ticket holders would be permitted entry on the Monday.

Interviewed from Longleat by BBC Radio 2 disc jockey Ed Stewart, Peter Davison put a brave face on the organisational shambles. Behind the scenes, however, many of the guests were extremely concerned at the poor treatment the public were receiving, and at the damage this could do to *Doctor Who*'s reputation. Particularly vociferous and forthright in his condemnation of the event's organisers was Mark Strickson, and he later admitted in interviews that this had almost cost him his job on the series.

In addition to several new ranges of merchandise launched to coincide with the anniversary (which are covered in a later section of this chapter), some special celebratory items were also produced.

W H Allen, the publishers of the successful range of *Doctor Who* novelisations, had put out the soft-covered *The Doctor Who Monster Book* and its sequel back in the Seventies but had not so far ventured to produce a large-format illustrated hardback about the series. It was therefore something of a bold step when they decided to commission a celebratory volume of this type, *Doctor Who – A Celebration*, from writer Peter Haining. Haining was an obvious choice for the task as he was experienced at putting together overview-type publications. He had already completed books on Sherlock Holmes and Charlie Chaplin, and was also a good friend of W H Allen's managing director Bob Tanner, who would later become his agent. To ensure a degree of authority, the publishers put Haining in touch with Jeremy Bentham, a well-known fan historian of *Doctor Who*, who worked on a chapter chronicling all the Doctor's adventures to date. The remainder of the book looked at each Doctor in turn; gave brief descriptions of K-9, the TARDIS, Gallifrey and the Master; and presented interviews with Barry Letts, Terrance Dicks and John Nathan-Turner.

The other 20th anniversary publication of particular note was a lavish special published by the BBC's listings magazine *Radio Times*. The precedent of the similar title produced to celebrate the tenth anniversary in 1973 had led to a widespread expectation amongst the series' fans that such a special would be issued, but it was only after pressure from Nathan-Turner that the powers-that-be capitulated and set one in motion. Brian Gearing, the editor of *Radio Times*, took responsibility for the project and commissioned one of his regular researchers, Gay Search, to provide the bulk of the text.

The format of the special stuck very closely to that established by its 1973 forerunner. Opening with a spread of photographs depicting the evolution of the series' title sequence, it continued with illustrated text features on: the Doctors; the companions; the Master; the fans; the aliens; some of the creative behind-the-scenes team; and the merchandise. A specially-commissioned short story by the series' script editor, Eric Saward, told of the Doctor's original departure from his home planet Gallifrey, and also featured the Master and the Cybermen for good measure. Rounding off the whole magazine was a piece by 'devoted fan' Ian Levine (who had been recommended for the job by Nathan-Turner) looking at all the Doctor's adventures to date.

All things considered, the special constituted a very effective skim through the series' 20-year history, and was nicely illustrated and put together. Even the recently-announced sixth Doctor, Colin Baker, was included in its coverage, making it as up-to-date as it possibly could be.

Other activities connected with the anniversary included: a visit by Troughton and Davison, along with K-9 and a Dalek, to the 1 March 1983 edition of the BBC's *Breakfast Time*; a major photocall for *The Five Doctors* on

16 March featuring all the Doctors (Baker being represented by his dummy from Madame Tussauds) and many of the companions; an appearance by Troughton, Pertwee, Davison and former producer Verity Lambert on the 17 March edition of the BBC's evening news digest *Nationwide*; and a further photocall, on 24 March, at which Davison appeared with many of the actresses who had played the Doctor's female companions over the years.

MERCHANDISE

The boom in *Doctor Who* merchandise that had occurred in the late Seventies continued into the Davison era.

The range of novelisations published by W H Allen under their Target imprint progressed unabated, with around eight new titles added to it each year. Other publications from the same company included Jean-Marc Lofficier's *The Doctor Who Programme Guide*, which came initially in two hardback volumes in 1981. This book, although containing numerous mistakes in its earliest editions, was to become one of the most influential and popular works ever written about the series; since its original publication, it has been revised and reprinted several times in rather more accurate versions. Peter Haining meanwhile followed up his *Doctor Who - A Celebration* with *Doctor Who - The Key to Time*, a 1984 book that presented a chronological history of *Doctor Who* but unfortunately contained numerous incorrect dates and other factual errors.

World Distributors continued to produce their regular *Doctor Who Annual* during the fifth Doctor's era, and other publishers also began to exploit the potential of the *Doctor Who* market. Alan Road's *The Making of a Television Series* (Andre Deutsch, 1982) provided a case study of the making of *The Visitation* - the first instance of a single story being subjected to extensive analysis in a professional publication. More in-depth still was *Doctor Who - The Unfolding Text* (Macmillan, 1983) by John Tulloch and Manuel Alvarado. This was a university-level media studies textbook, which many non-academic readers and fans not surprisingly found rather heavy going. It looked at *Doctor Who* from a variety of viewpoints and featured much material about the making of *Kinda*, a story with a suitably deep religious subtext.

As previously noted, a large number of new products were launched to coincide with the series' 20th anniversary in 1983. These included: badges and a paper Cyberman mask from Image Screencraft (a commercial offshoot of Imagineering, the effects house that had created the Terileptils for *The Visitation* and the Cybermen for *Earthshock* amongst many other monsters and special props for the Davison era);

sundry mugs, erasers, pencils, bags and balloons produced specifically for the Longleat event; a series of large artwork prints, generically called Profile Prints, showcasing the work of artist Andrew Skilleter (who had provided the covers for many of the W H Allen novelisations) and issued by his embryonic Who Dares publishing firm; and the first in what would become a massive range of *Doctor Who* video releases.

BBC Video had in fact carried out some market research amongst attendees at the Longleat event to discover which titles they would like to see made available in this new medium. The Season 5 story *The Tomb of the Cybermen* had come out top of the poll, no doubt mentioned by many fans as a joke in view of the fact that all four episodes were at that time missing from the archives, but BBC Video reasoned that any other Cyberman adventure would do just as well, and so chose the Season 12 story *Revenge of the Cybermen* to spearhead their range.

Other product lines to start up during the Davison era included a large range of pewter *Doctor Who* figures from Fine Art Castings, and Reeltime Pictures' series of *Doctor Who* interview tapes. Also in the shops were: *Doctor Who* wallpaper, featuring images of Davison, Daleks and Cybermen; a TARDIS tent; *Doctor Who* gloves and tee-shirts; and a Dalek hat. The *Doctor Who* theme record was reissued with a photograph of Davison on the sleeve, and the *K-9 and Company* theme was also released. In addition, the first ever LP of incidental music from the series was put out in the form of the highly-acclaimed, if unimaginatively-titled, *Doctor Who - The Music*.

Marvel Comics' *Doctor Who Monthly* was still going strong, with numerous special publications being produced in addition to the regular monthly magazine; BBC publicity photographs from the series went on sale to the public thanks to a firm called Whomobilia, run by fan John McElroy; and eager fans could even obtain a *Doctor Who* umbrella.

In fact, the merchandise produced during this period almost rivalled that of the Sixties in terms of its range and diversity. There was however one significant difference: whereas in the Sixties almost all the merchandise had been issued by large toy manufacturers, in the Eighties most of the items on sale were produced by small firms acting as cottage industries, or even by fans-turned-professionals. These firms and individuals usually escaped the overheads of the larger companies, but also lacked their sales, marketing and distribution functions. Luckily, the enormous fan interest in the series both in the UK and in America had resulted in a great many conventions being held, newsletters being produced and dealers setting up in business, and this had led to the creation of a ready market on both sides of the Atlantic for all the various items produced.

THE FIFTH DOCTOR

OVERSEAS

NORTH AMERICA

The Peter Davison era saw *Doctor Who* approaching the peak of its popularity in the United States of America, as episodes – albeit mainly those featuring Tom Baker as the Doctor – were shown on an almost daily basis on PBS stations covering over two thirds of the entire country.

Barely a weekend went by, it seemed, without a large *Doctor Who* convention taking place somewhere in America, and the show's stars, both past and present, were in constant demand to attend these celebrations, with large fees and travel expenses being offered to entice them from UK shores. John Nathan-Turner even began to act as a semi-official guest liaison officer for the organisers of these events. The biggest US convention of all, attended by an estimated 12,000 people, was the Ultimate Celebration, which took place in Chicago over the series' 20th anniversary weekend in 1983 and achieved the unique feat of bringing all four surviving Doctors on stage together, along with many of their companions from the series.

The North American *Doctor Who* Appreciation Society, which like its UK sponsor had been run essentially on a non-profit-making basis, now gave way to professional organisations such as Spirit of Light – who staged the Ultimate Celebration and many other conventions – and the *Doctor Who* Fan Club of America. The latter body was set up by two commercially-minded fans, Ron Katz and Chad Roark, after they met Nathan-Turner at BBC Enterprises' Longleat event. Its members, who would eventually come to number some 30,000, received a regular newspaper entitled *The Whovian Times*, which featured interviews and news items and also numerous adverts for some of the masses of BBC-licensed (and, in some cases, possibly unlicensed) merchandise items produced in the States at this time, including tee-shirts, jackets, mugs, key-fobs, pens, model kits and towels.

Elsewhere on the North American continent, fan support for *Doctor Who* remained strong in Canada, where an organisation called the *Doctor Who* Information Network launched a regular fanzine, *Enlightenment*, around the end of Davison's stint in the series. Circulation of this well-produced publication quickly rose to around 400.

AUSTRALIA

Doctor Who also remained very popular 'down under' during this period of its history. The Australasian *Doctor Who* Fan Club continued to publish issues of its high-quality fanzine *Zerinza: **The Australasian Doctor Who Fanzine***, as well as a more basic newsletter, and attracted a large influx of new members. A number of '*Doctor Who* Parties' and other events were held, with guests including former companion actress Katy Manning, who now lived in Australia. Other groups, such as the *Doctor Who* Club of Victoria, produced fanzines and carried out activities on a more local basis.

The public profile of the series in Australia received a considerable boost during April 1983 when Peter Davison and his wife Sandra Dickinson made a promotional tour of major cities to meet the fans and do a number of book signings at stores in the Myer chain, who had sponsored the trip and arranged an extremely hectic schedule for the two visitors.

One unfortunate aspect of the Australian transmissions of the Davison stories was that – as had also been the case in earlier eras – a number of the episodes were edited by the censors to remove material that they considered unsuitable for a family audience. The most badly affected of all was Davison's swansong, *The Caves of Androzani* part four, which lost over two and a half minutes of material.

NEW ZEALAND
By Paul Scoones

Peter Davison's Doctor arrived on New Zealand television screens just over a year after his first story screened in the UK, and as *Castrovalva* Part One screened in New Zealand, Davison's second season was ending on British TV screens.

The series screened on Mondays at 5.30 pm on Television One, beginning 14 March and ending 28 November 1983. This run of episodes covered all seven stories of Season Nineteen as well as the first three stories of Season Twenty. Unusually for New Zealand, *Arc of Infinity*, *Snakedance* and *Mawdryn Undead* were all screened the same year these stories were aired in the UK. After *Mawdryn Undead* ended however viewers had to wait over a year for the series to return but further Davison stories were not seen until five years later.

When *Doctor Who* returned to New Zealand television in April 1985, it was with the Troughton story *The Mind Robber* which launched a long-running series of repeat and first-time screenings. The series reached the Davison era in August 1988, at which time *Doctor Who* was screening twice weekly, on Thursdays and Fridays at 5.30 pm on TV2. Davison's first season, *Castrovalva* to *Time-Flight*, was screened from 25 August to 18 November 1988.

The regular Thursday and Friday screenings were interrupted for one week as Television New Zealand scheduled a 'Silver Jubilee' week of *Doctor Who* special screenings, from Saturday 19 November to Friday 25 November, featuring the first New Zealand broadcasts of five stories. *The Five Doctors* screened Sunday 20 November 1988 at midday, followed by a repeat of the 1965 Peter Cushing movie, *Dr Who and the Daleks*.

Following the 'Silver Jubilee' week, regular screenings resumed. The return was short-lived as just two stories were broadcast before the series took a break. *Arc of Infinity* and *Snakedance* screened from 1 to 23 December 1988.

After three months the series returned 6 April 1989 back on Thursdays and Fridays on TV2, but at the slightly earlier time of around 5.15 pm. The series resumed with *Mawdryn Undead* and then *Terminus*, which saw the regular story sequence pick up where it had left off in New Zealand more than five years earlier. Because it had screened as part of the 'Silver Jubilee' week just a few months earlier, *The Five Doctors* was omitted after *The King's Demons*. *Resurrection of the Daleks* played as a four-part story (as opposed to the two episode format seen in the UK), and the Davison era ended 4 August 1989 with the screening of Part Four of *The Caves of Androzani*.

Many of the Davison episodes screened during 1988 and 1989 were broadcast in a slightly edited form, as the commercial half-hour slot to which they had been allocated allowed for only 23 minutes of actual programme time. Further edits were evident because the episodes had been supplied by the Australian Broadcasting Corporation and cuts had been made by the Australian censor.

The version of *The Caves of Androzani* screened in New Zealand was one that had been heavily edited by the Australian censor to remove sequences deemed too violent, with around two and a half minutes removed from Part Four alone.

Viewer ratings for the Davison era stories screened in 1988 and 1989 show that *Frontios* Part Two was the highest rated episode on 9%, with the first episodes of *Terminus*, *Resurrection of the Daleks* and *Planet of Fire* all rating 8.5%. *The Awakening* and *Frontios* were equally the highest-rated stories, each with a 7.3% average.

UK FANDOM

The *Doctor Who* Appreciation Society continued to be at the forefront of UK fandom during this period, although its dominance was now starting to be challenged by other fan groups and, in the publication field, by independent fanzines.

After its original organisers had bowed out in mid-1980, the Society had effectively been saved from collapse by David Saunders (who became Co-ordinator), David J Howe (who had for some time been running the Reference Department) and Chris Dunk (the editor of the Society's newsletter, *Celestial Toyroom*). Over the next couple of years, the Society's executive body took steps to put its organisation and finances on a sounder footing. Dunk was succeeded as *Celestial Toyroom* editor first by Gordon Blows and David Auger, then by Gary Russell and then, until the end of the Davison era, by Gordon Roxburgh. The Society published much material during this period, including regular editions of the fanzine *TARDIS*, edited by Richard Walter, and the fan fiction periodical *Cosmic Masque*, edited initially by John Peel and then, from early 1981, by Ian K McLachlan.

The Society's membership was boosted considerably by a strong presence at the BBC's Longleat convention in 1983, and managed to top the 3,000 mark for the first time. The Society meanwhile continued to stage its own conventions under the aegis of Convention Department organiser Paul Zeus. In addition to the major PanoptiCon event each year, a number of smaller and more informal Inter-Face and DWASocial gatherings were held. It was however a constant source of irritation to the Society that the PanoptiCons had to be scheduled so as not to clash with major American events, such as the one held in Chicago on the series' 20th anniversary, as with their relatively high fees and travel expenses, the latter would always be more successful in attracting guests. The fact that so many of the series' stars were always overseas on important dates such as the anniversary also meant that numerous opportunities for UK press coverage were lost.

VIEWER REACTION

As previously noted, the Davison era gained very respectable ratings, although they were somewhat higher for Season 19 than for Seasons 20 and 21. One factor that impacted on these figures was the boom in home video recording that occurred in the early 1980s; the ratings system took no account of people who videoed shows to watch later. Another factor was that the UK's fourth terrestrial channel, Channel 4, started transmitting in 1982 and offered people a greater degree of choice about what to watch at any given time.

Further information on viewers' contemporary reactions to *Doctor Who* during this period can be gained from the BBC's own internal audience research reports.

The summary report for Season 19 began by discussing the size of the audience, based on results from the BARB Audience Measurement service:

> Audiences for this series were estimated to range from 16.1% to 20.5% (8.3 to 10.5 million) of the United Kingdom population, giving an overall average of 18.2% (9.3 million). There was no appreciable difference between the Monday and Tuesday audience sizes.

There then followed a section on audience reaction, based on questionnaires completed by members of the BBC's regular Viewing Panel. This recorded that the overall reaction index for the season was 66%.

The report continued:

> Viewing of this 26 part series tended to be rather sporadic although ... the majority of those reporting managed to tune in to at least half ... Fewer than one in ten (8%) reporting deliberately decided to stop watching; frequency of viewing, perhaps predictably, tended to be governed by the convenience of the transmission time to individual respondents ... The timing was only totally suitable for a minority, although only about one in ten (12%) found it completely inconvenient ... Predictably, those who found the transmission time less convenient tended to tune in to fewer programmes. Just under half (47%) of the total sample watched with children under the age of 15, and these viewers tended to find the timing rather more suitable. There were several requests for a return to the old Saturday evening transmission time, albeit from a small minority.

Next came a number of sections relating comments on the actual content of the episodes:

> Although only about one in seven of those reporting found the latest series of *Doctor Who* immensely appealing, the large majority reacted favourably and still enjoy the programme. The episodes in this series were considered well written and not too predictable, and most viewers felt that the storylines had been quite exciting ...

> Reactions to the standard of acting were rather mixed, although still generally favourable ... Peter Davison appears to have been accepted as the new Doctor. Although there were a number of unfavourable comparisons with certain predecessors (notably Jon Pertwee) and a couple of suggestions that he should stick to being a vet, the majority of those reporting clearly feel that he has got to grips with the part and now fits in rather well. There were few comments regarding the performances of the rest of the cast, although these were considered good.

> All aspects of the production were thought to have been of a high standard. A number of respondents did feel that the special effects had been unbelievable and obviously false, but their opinions were heavily outweighed ...

As mentioned previously, just under half the sample audience viewed in the company of children aged 15 or under. Boys were slightly predominant (55% : 45%). The children's ages were fairly well spread; all ages between two and 15 were represented, but there was a marked concentration of children (particularly boys) aged between 6 and 10. In general, their comments were succinct ('great', 'brilliant' etc.) and very favourable. Boys tended to be rather more enthusiastic than girls (although both sexes liked the series) but there was a tendency among very small girls (under-sevens) to be frightened. Several children were rather disturbed by the death of Adric, although these were in the minority.

Interspersed with these comments were a number of tables giving detailed breakdowns of the figures in their respective sections. The report then concluded with a final table that the production team must have found particularly encouraging:

Finally, the sample audience was asked whether they would welcome a further series of *Doctor Who*. They responded as follows:

	%
Yes, very much	36
Yes, quite	42
Not particularly	19
Definitely not	3

The audience research report for Season 20, which was accompanied by a three page computer tabulation of statistics, recorded an average audience of 7.0 million and an average appreciation index of 62. Its text read as follows:

This series of *Doctor Who* received a somewhat mixed but essentially favourable response from the members of the sample audience. Approximately half of those reporting regarded it as an entertaining and enjoyable programme which provided excellent viewing for the whole family. A number of this group thought it especially good for children, whilst others indicated that they had been fans of the Doctor since his portrayal by the late William Hartnell. These reporting viewers (who were most likely to be under 54 years of age) considered the storylines interesting, amusing and gripping, liked Peter Davison's portrayal of the Doctor and praised the other members of the cast.

Another group of respondents (between one quarter and one third of the total sample) liked the series, but were slightly disappointed in it. They tended to criticise the plots ('enjoyable, but stronger storylines needed'), the special effects or the transmission time. Indeed, the time at which the programme was broadcast was noticeably less popular amongst the 35-54 age group.

One in five of those reporting had not enjoyed the series. For 15% this dislike had led them to make a positive decision to stop watching. They were mainly over the age of 55 and criticised the series for being, in their opinion, boring and predictable. They also felt it had weak storylines, poor acting and disappointing special effects. A few ceased watching because their young children had been frightened by the programme.

57% of the sample audience indicated that they wished to see a new series of *Doctor Who*. A further one in three had no strong opinion on the subject. The desire for a new series of *Doctor Who* was strongest in those under 34 and weakest in the 55+ age group.

The average viewer and reaction index figures for Season 21, at 7.2 million and 65 respectively, were both slightly up on those for Season 20, but – although no audience research report is available for this season at the time of writing – it is known that there was a considerable drop in satisfaction levels after Colin Baker took over as the Doctor for the final story. Only 66% of those in the reporting sample thought that the sixth Doctor was a likeable character in this story, and only 54% thought that he was well portrayed by Baker. These figures compared with 73% and 71% respectively for the fifth Doctor and for Davison's portrayal during Season 20. While it was hardly unexpected for a new Doctor to encounter some initial audience resistance, Nathan-Turner must have known that a considerable improvement would be required the following year.

SELLING THE DOCTOR

FIFTH DOCTOR STORIES
IN ORDER OF AVERAGE VIEWING FIGURES
(Figures in millions of viewers)

Black Orchid	10.00
The Visitation	9.60
Castrovalva	9.57
Earthshock	9.33
Four to Doomsday	8.88
Time-Flight	8.88
Kinda	8.80
The Five Doctors	7.70
Resurrection of the Daleks	7.65
Mawdryn Undead	7.28
The Caves of Androzani	7.28
Warriors of the Deep	7.25
The Awakening	7.25
Arc of Infinity	7.15
Snakedance	7.10
Terminus	7.10
Planet of Fire	6.98
Enlightenment	6.83
Frontios	6.80
The King's Demons	6.50

Afterword

Following his appointment as *Doctor Who*'s producer at the beginning of November 1979, John Nathan-Turner set about transforming the series – his intention being, as he put it, 'to bring it into the 1980s'.

The new producer's influence was first apparent during Tom Baker's final season as the Doctor. A glossy new star-field title sequence and neon-style logo were commissioned; a more trendy theme tune arrangement was introduced; Dudley Simpson's relatively conventional incidental music, for so long a staple ingredient of the series, was dispensed with in favour of fully electronic scores provided by the BBC Radiophonic Workshop; the two established companions – Romana and K-9 – were written out, while three new ones – Adric, Nyssa and Tegan – were brought in to take their places; all the regulars, including the Doctor, were given heavily-designed, uniform-like costumes that went unchanged from one story to the next; and finally, of course, the Doctor himself was regenerated.

All these new approaches were carried forward to Peter Davison's tenure in the lead role. With a new Doctor in place, Nathan-Turner was able fully to realise his ambitions for *Doctor Who*, and the production became increasingly slick and sophisticated.

'I hesitate to say this,' noted the producer in a 1989 interview, 'but what happened in some – and I would emphasise not *all* – of the older episodes was very minimal. There were a lot of very long scenes, a lot of exposition, and not a lot of action or plot development. I like episodes sharply cut, with a strong narrative drive. The optimum length for a *Doctor Who* episode is now 24 minutes 15 seconds and, once you take away the titles, you have about 22 minutes to play with. So you really want to get on with a whole lot of story development – not just to hold the attention of the audience, but to make what you are handing them more substantial.'

Critics, however, expressed concern that Nathan-Turner's attentions were focused principally on cosmetic, essentially superficial aspects of the production, rather than on the dramatic content of the stories. Certainly this latter aspect was determined more by the respective interests and preferences of the series' successive script editors, namely Christopher H Bidmead, Antony Root and Eric Saward. An interesting mix and variety of different story types was achieved – even down to the inclusion, in the form of *Black Orchid*, of the first *bona fide* historical adventure since 1966 – and frequently the scripts matched the production in achieving a level of sophistication and slickness previously unseen in the series. One common feature identified by many fan commentators, however, was an increased emphasis on concepts and imagery at the expense of *Doctor Who*'s more traditional strengths of good, straightforward plotting and solid characterisation. In other words, many felt that style was being given precedence over content.

Notwithstanding these common concerns about its artistic direction, the series gained very respectable ratings during the fifth Doctor's era – particularly so during the first of the three seasons, when it achieved a significant improvement on the previous year's unusually poor performance. One important factor underlying this upturn in popularity was the rescheduling of the series away from its traditional Saturday teatime slot, where it had recently been suffering in competition with ITV's imported American science fiction series *Buck Rogers in the 25th Century*. In its new weekday evening slot, with its episodes going out at the rate of two a week in the manner of a soap opera, it reached a whole new group of viewers, many of whom would no doubt not have counted themselves amongst *Doctor Who*'s traditional audience.

Another factor contributing to the series' improved ratings was the high public profile that it continued to maintain. One thing of which *Doctor Who* certainly did not go short during this period was promotion. Nathan-Turner was very publicity conscious, and – working in conjunction with senior BBC press officer Kevin O'Shea – highly skilled at dealing with the media. This contributed greatly to the series generating extensive newspaper coverage, many television guest spots for its stars, copious quantities of spin-off merchandise and numerous promotional events – undoubtedly the biggest of which was the chaotic twentieth anniversary convention staged by BBC Enterprises at Longleat House.

The Davison era maintained *Doctor Who*'s position as an important and highly-regarded element of the BBC's steadily diminishing output of family programming. It did however provide some portents of the coming fall from grace that would see the series just managing to escape cancellation in 1985 and ultimately failing to do so in 1989. The changes in style and dramatic content that had so concerned many fan commentators would be taken still further during the sixth Doctor's tenure, when the overall look of the series would grow increasingly gaudy and stylised and the stories would become steadily more concerned with continuity and less with straightforward, comprehensible plotting.

The move to a two-episodes-per-week transmission schedule meant that the series was now on the air for only three months each year, rather than for six as it had been in the recent past, providing less of an opportunity for it to become imprinted on the minds of the nation's viewers as a permanent feature of the television landscape. This problem would also be carried forward to later years when, although there would be a return to the more traditional one-episode-per-week format, the number of episodes per season would be effectively halved (with double-length episodes for the sixth Doctor's establishing season and standard-length episodes thereafter).

In many ways, the fifth Doctor's era marked the end of the original *Doctor Who* as a series with a wide popular appeal amongst the general viewing public. In its declining years, despite presenting many good stories and ultimately undergoing something of a creative renaissance, it would find itself playing principally to an ever-dwindling audience of cult science fiction fans.

THE SIXTH DOCTOR

David J Howe
Mark Stammers
Stephen James Walker

Introduction
Colin Baker

On 10 June 1983, I went to visit John Nathan-Turner at the BBC at his request, not in any way suspecting that that visit would result in my sitting at this word-processor ten years later reflecting on the fact that the work of this 'jobbing' actor could result in a book containing such meticulous and detailed research as that which follows this introduction.

And certainly when, exactly six months later, I stepped into BBC's Rehearsal Room 202 in Acton, I would have perhaps been a little more unnerved, rather than elated and nervous, had I known the exact course of events that would follow over the next three years, culminating in that 29 October 1986 phone call from John Nathan-Turner informing me of the order from above to 'regenerate'!

Now that the moving finger has written and moved inexorably onwards, it is, I am happy to say, predominantly the happy memories that endure, both in the making of the programme and in the warmth and generosity of many of the people I have met as a result of making it.

Having been a guest actor in other series in the past, I was very aware that the regular performer/performers in a series dictate to a certain extent the working atmosphere at rehearsals and in the studio. I was therefore delighted to have the opportunity of ensuring that the atmosphere during the time of the sixth Doctor should be conducive to everyone giving their best, whilst enjoying themselves at the same time. Arguably we sometimes enjoyed ourselves inordinately, particularly when Pat Troughton and Frazer Hines joined us or when we joined Brian Blessed (it would almost be *lèse majesté* to envisage it the other way round)! But I like to think that the work was enhanced rather than suffered as a result of all the good humour.

I was also extremely lucky in my companion. Nicola Bryant had received a lot of good-natured chaffing from Peter Davison along the lines of 'Colin Baker, eh???' followed by a lot of head-shaking and sucking in of air through the teeth – much in the same way as any *soi-disant* expert does when I tell them what car, computer or lawn-mower I have just bought. (Long suck – 'Oh, I could have got that for you for next to nothing, they're phasing them out because the technology' .... etc .... etc).

So Nicola, whilst being aware that she was being wound up, nonetheless viewed the impending regeneration with a little uncertainty. And, of course, from my point of view, she was the old hand and I was replacing her Doctor! But we very soon realised that we worked well together, after she had discovered that there was a slight difference between the Doctor and the actor. At least I hope there is, even if only in terms of dress sense.

It didn't take long before going to work became like going to another home. There are those, I suppose, who might not find that desirable, but I like to feel surrounded by kindred spirits when working. I found John Nathan-Turner a very supportive producer to work with and whilst he could quite properly crack the whip on occasion, nonetheless he would happily enter into the badinage at other times. He was also very much a part of the team, putting in regular appearances at rehearsals rather than simply turning up for the 'Producer's Run', with that 'Right, let's see you earn your money' attitude, which can be somewhat intimidating when that is the only time a producer puts in an appearance. The crew were also a welcome constant. We developed a great rapport with Alec Wheal and his camera team, which saved a lot of time in the studio and added to the enjoyment.

We had some splendid guests on the show – I have very fond memories of working with Maurice Denham, a gentle and understated genius, and Kevin McNally, with whom we laughed a lot on *The Twin Dilemma*, with the inventive and talented Nabil Shaban, the deceptively effortless Martin Jarvis and the refreshingly charming and unaffected Jason Connery in *Vengeance on Varos*, with Sarah Greene, Faith Brown and David Banks in *Attack of the Cybermen*, the irreplaceable Pat Troughton, the irrepressible Frazer Hines and the irredeemable Jackie Pearce in *The Two Doctors*, with the under-used Anthony Ainley and my former sparring partner from the days of *The Brothers*, the eternally glamorous and versatile Kate O'Mara, in *Mark of the Rani*, with that eschewer of understatement Paul Darrow in *Timelash*, and marvellous William Gaunt, Eleanor Bron and Clive Swift in *Revelation of the Daleks* – not to mention the odd Dalek!

In the Trial season the team was joined by Lynda Bellingham, Michael Jayston and Tony Selby, all of whom became very good friends. I think the memories of Michael's and my attempts to invent rhyming slang to baffle Tony were highlights of my entire time as the Doctor. (As in: 'Me carrots are really giving me gyp today.' 'Carrots?' 'Yeah, carrots and onions – bunions.' Well, you should have been there!!) Michael is one of the great 'twinklers' of this business, with a great talent and refreshing lack of ego combined with a finely tuned humour – *and* he likes cricket! The visiting artists included wonderful Joan Sims, BRIAN BLESSED for whom there are no words that do not draw on the epic, the dashing and perplexed Patrick Ryecart, Trevor Laird with his infectious laugh, splendid Adam Blackwood, the impossibly divine Honor Blackman, the dry and very funny Malcolm Tierney and the ditto Geoff Hughes, who had the added advantage of making me look like a

INTRODUCTION

bantamweight!

And, of course, that season brought Bonnie Langford into the long list of companions. I had worked with Bonnie before in *Goldilocks* at Lincoln, when I could only marvel at her sheer professionalism and all round niceness. In a way, she was an easier companion for the sixth Doctor, because she was in a sense less of a 'woman' than Nicola, so it was easier for the Doctor to be protective, in an avuncular way, which might have been susceptible to misconstruction with the undeniably more nubile Peri. And she lacked her predecessor's advantage of being previously unknown. Everyone knows Bonnie, and so she had a hard task to show us a Mel unencumbered by the baggage of her many outstanding previous roles in many areas of the acting profession. That she succeeded so well is a tribute to her.

I was very impressed by another rare quality of John Nathan-Turner's – he spent a lot of time going around drama schools and spotting and encouraging new young talent, resulting in many new faces that have since become well known, making their first appearance on *Doctor Who*. This was a splendid counter-balance against the fact that very popular and 'name' artists were queuing up to appear on the programme. John also had the happy knack of persuading the best directors to take on the very specialised job of directing *Doctor Who*. In the past, highly respected directors had balked at the challenge of bringing to the screen a programme that demanded so much from what, it must be admitted, was not always an adequate budget. Each director with whom I worked rose to the occasion admirably and I am sure the others will forgive me if I single out Peter Moffatt, who made my first story such a delight to do, by trusting me and encouraging me to be my own Doctor. I think he knows how much that helped me through those first few difficult episodes – I imagine that as an actor of no mean reputation himself, he sensed how best to assist those first few faltering steps! Also I must mention Graeme Harper, whom I knew as a young assistant floor manager on *War and Peace* in 1971. He was an amazingly resilient campaigner in a very difficult, whipping-boy position. I was not surprised to find that his energy and enthusiasm had not dimmed over fifteen years and that his boundless appetite for the job and ability to create on the hoof, as it were, made him a delight to work with. And the end results were original and vital.

I cannot recall once during my tenure in the role wishing that I were doing anything else. In a sense, it was as well that Michael Grade and Jonathan Powell decided that three years was the optimum gap between regenerations, otherwise I might have been sorely tempted to try to match my foolishly declared ambition of beating Tom Baker's impressive seven years as the Doctor.

Given the enduring popularity of *Doctor Who*, it is inevitable, I must concede, that I am frequently and sometimes uncomfortably reminded of the less pleasant elements of my brief time in 'the best role on television'. It is still a great sadness to me that there is a handful of people on the fringes of the programme whose misguided devotion to it has led them to engage in behaviour that can at best be described as selfish and arrogant and at worst pathological and vindictive. Whilst I myself have suffered only slightly from the effect of this blinkered obsession, it pains me to see that others have been hounded quite so mercilessly for that great crime – having a different belief. I would draw the attention of those concerned to the effects of intolerance and vendetta on the world around us today and in our daily news. Whilst the plights of Yugoslavia and Salman Rushdie may seem far removed from the subject of this book, and I have no wish to diminish them by this seemingly banal comparison, it is assuredly from the smallest of such seeds of envy and bigotry that grow the forests of hatred and destruction.

It would be inappropriate to end this introduction without paying a tribute to the many members of the *Doctor Who* Appreciation Society and other unaligned fans of *Doctor Who*, worldwide, who have been kind enough not only to write and tell me that they have found my work not unwatchable, but who have also been warm-hearted enough to take on board a charity that means a lot to me. The Foundation for the Study of Infant Deaths has repeatedly benefited from the generosity and industry of fans of the programme who have pushed Daleks, run conventions, held raffles, made films, sold memorabilia and generally harassed people into giving to this very worthy cause. I know that the recent drop in the incidence of cot-deaths is due in part to money raised in this way to fund the research that led to the recognition that sleeping position, temperature, and cigarette smoking in pregnancy were significant and avoidable contributory factors. For that I will be eternally in their debt.

Finally I would like to commend this book to you. I know the authors. They are honourable men. I may not agree with every opinion expressed herein, but like many others before me, I will defend to their last drop of blood their right to hold those opinions. I am grateful to them for the opportunity to write this introduction and hope that you will be as stimulated and intrigued as I have been to read the results of their endeavours. I am amazed how much I didn't know! I know you will find it fascinating and eminently readable.

Colin Baker 20/05/1993.

Foreword

As the swirling sea of colour dissipated and the burly figure of the new Doctor sat up abruptly on the TARDIS floor, the 21 year-old television series *Doctor Who* was – like its leading character – about to enter the most unsettled and difficult period of its history, which would see changes to its format, weekly slot and season length, as well as the eventual halving of its average viewing audience.

The sixth Doctor in the person of Colin Baker was introduced to the press on 20 August 1983. The event even made the BBC's own early evening news broadcast, which commented on the actor's earlier *Doctor Who* appearance as Maxil in the fifth Doctor story *Arc of Infinity*.

The press quizzed Baker as to how long he would like to play the role, and Baker replied – possibly with tongue in cheek – that as Tom Baker had played the role of the Doctor for seven years, he would have to play the character for at least eight years, as he could not bear the thought of anyone having done it for longer than him.

This statement was ultimately proved to be quite ironic, as events overtook Colin Baker's intentions, and the era of the sixth Doctor turned out to be the shortest of his television incarnations to that date, consisting of only eight individual stories over a period of a little under three years.

After three, fairly successful seasons with Peter Davison in the title role, producer John Nathan-Turner found himself having to choose another actor to carry the programme into the second half of the decade. Davison had decided to leave the series in May 1983 after having asked for an extended period in which to consider whether or not he could accept the offer of a contract for a fourth season. In the meantime, Nathan-Turner had been considering Colin Baker as a suitable replacement in case Davison did decide to leave. Baker's own vibrant and open personality was well suited to the role, and would prove an interesting contrast to Davison's more reserved nature.

Nathan-Turner telephoned Baker directly, asking him to come and see him. The actor assumed he was being asked to open a fête or some-such event, little guessing that he was actually being sounded out for the role that he himself had considered asking his agent to put him up for when the fourth Doctor, Tom Baker, had departed in 1981. Once offered the part, Baker agreed without a moment's hesitation.

THE SIXTH DOCTOR

The new Doctor's era took place in a Britain in the middle of a prosperity boom. House prices were rocketing, and the mobile phone had become the badge of a new social class nicknamed yuppies. In the world at large, the threat of war had receded as the Soviet Union's new moderate president Mikail Gorbachev discussed the end of the nuclear arms race with US President Ronald Reagan. The Conservative Government was into its second term under the leadership of Mrs Margaret Thatcher, *Spitting Image* arrived on television, and the Duke and Duchess of York were married.

During the mid-Eighties the nature of broadcast television in Britain was entering a state of change. Competition for audience share was growing between the independent television companies and the BBC. Technology had altered the viewing habits of the British public. Instead of being slaves to the programme schedulers as to when they could watch their favourite series, they could choose what to watch and when to watch it, by using the video recorders that were becoming common household items up and down the country. This meant that the often-used ploy of scheduling two popular programmes at the same time on opposing channels, forcing the viewer to choose a channel and then stick with it, no longer worked, as one programme could be recorded whilst the other was being watched live. This fact also made something of a mockery of the audience viewing figures that all television channels used to judge the impact of their output, as no account was taken at that time of programmes watched on video.

The BBC needed to modernise its image, as well as increase its activities into new areas such as breakfast television and daytime broadcasting, where it had not previously competed for viewers. Meanwhile, the BBC was also taking its share of the flak arising from the government's apparent obsession with bias against its policies in news and current affairs programmes. This led to a siege mentality developing amongst the top management of the Corporation.

On the face of it, none of these events would seem to have had any bearing on *Doctor Who*, yet indirectly they all played a part in the cancellation of the original Season 23, and to some extent in the eventual replacement of Colin Baker in the lead role.

We have spoken to many different people involved in making *Doctor Who* during the period in question, although regrettably the producer, John Nathan-Turner, declined to contribute to this book, explaining that, at the time we were researching it, he wanted to distance himself from *Doctor Who*. We also received help from many fans of the series, and we hope that this volume presents a balanced and accurate record of perhaps the most turbulent and controversial period in *Doctor Who*'s long history.

Doctor Who in this period was adult in content, and yet featured a Doctor with a heart of gold – and a tasteless coat! Join us as we re-visit the era of the sixth Doctor.

Colin Baker
In His Own Words

ON HIS EARLY LIFE:

'I was born in London – on Waterloo Bridge, which is quite a feat, isn't it? At the south end of Waterloo Bridge there is a hospital called the Royal Waterloo Lying-in Hospital, and in the summer of 1943, I was born in the maternity ward on the top floor of this hospital, during an air raid!'

Interviewed by David Banks in July 1989 for *The Ultimate Interview*, released by Silver Fist tapes.

'I spent the first two years of my life dodging bombs. I was oblivious of the fact, although I do still have a piece of shrapnel about the size of a key, which apparently embedded itself in the back of my infant cot when the house opposite caught a direct hit. But for the six inches by which that missed my head, I wouldn't be sitting here today. Those are the little threads of circumstance that separate life and death. It's quite extraordinary, isn't it? Those little, tiny things.

'When I was two years old, I met my father, who'd been away fighting in the war. He'd come home on leave a couple of times before, which I gather had been quite traumatic for me. At two, I didn't like the idea of this *man* who suddenly appeared and whom Mummy seemed to *like* quite a lot. At least, I've been told that. I don't remember it at all.

'I have an appallingly vague memory of my childhood. I think all the information that I trot out on these occasions is stuff I've been *told*! Memory is half what you do actually remember and half what's been topped up by others through the years.

'When I was two or three years old, after my father came back, he was then moved from London up to Manchester for his work. He was managing director of an asbestos company. So I went up to live in the north of England when I was quite young, and lived there until I was 23. When I said that I wanted to be an actor, that was dismissed by my father as being an unworthy occupation for an intelligent young man, so I was despatched off to law college. I studied law for five years.

'About the time I was due to start practising as a solicitor, I decided I'd had *enough*. It just didn't work. I was anarchic, I'm afraid. I had too exaggerated a sense of justice to work in the law. It's quite interesting, but it does tie in with the Doctor actually. The Doctor isn't about the letter of the law at all – he's about *justice*. Natural justice, intergalactic justice or whatever you like. And I always felt that way. The company I worked for was a big company that always worked for the big man and was always crushing the little man, or so it seemed to me. So I used to be very *unethical*! I used to decide who I thought was in the right and structure the case accordingly! I used to tip people off! I'd ring 'em up and say, "Look, you're about to have a summons served on you – I should make myself scarce if I were you," and things like that.

'I've never regretted studying law, though, because it does mean that, for instance, I can buy and sell my own house without having to hire a solicitor, I can make my own will and I can sue people.'

Interviewed by C L Crouch in 1985 for *Fantasy Empire* Issue 19.

ON HIS EARLY ACTING CAREER:

'I actually made one TV appearance as a child. This was around 1954. It was in a series called *My Wife's Sister*, starring Eleanor Summerfield, Martin Wyldeck and Helen Christie.

'In this particular story, Eleanor Summerfield has met a Frenchman who is very good looking, with a moustache and everything. She then has a dream that she is married to him, and she has three little boys. The viewer then sees the backs of these three little boys gathered around a Christmas tree. They all turn around, and they all have moustaches pencilled on. The middle one, which was me, then says, "*Jolie Noel* Papa."

'I got that part because I came top in French that year! The mother of one of the kids at the school was the casting director at Granada. They wanted three kids, and they asked who was good at French. "Oh, Colin is," came the reply. That set me on the slippery slope.'

Interviewed by Michael Sibley in May 1987 for *The Colin Baker Interview*.

'I got a review in the school magazine that read: "Colin Baker threw himself with verve into the part of Phyllis and rarely strayed more than half an octave from the notes." At the time, I thought that was a good review! Thereafter, I appeared in the Gilbert and Sullivan production every year at school.

'When I left school, I went with my mother to see an amateur production of *The King and I* at the Palace Theatre, Manchester. I said to my mother, "I'd love to do that," and the man sitting in front of me turned around and said, "I'm the president of this society. If you'd like to join, come along next Friday night." So I joined the North Manchester Amateur Dramatic Society, and I got really hooked on it. I was studying law at the time, and after five years I thought, "Blow this for a game of soldiers. I'll have a go at doing what I want to do. I've only got one life, so I'll have a try." So I went to drama school and started acting.'

Interviewed by Paul Duncan in 1984 for *Arkensword* Issue 11.

'On 23 May 1969 I made my first professional appearance on the stage, in a play called *Plaintiff in a Pretty Hat* at the Arts Theatre in Cambridge. This was after completing three years' training at the London Academy of Music and Dramatic Art, or LAMDA for short, which I entered at the advanced age of 23, having already done five years' training as a lawyer and deciding that the law wasn't for me.'

Interviewed by Bob Furnell, Dean King and Janette Taylor in March 1987 for *Time Meddlers of Vancouver*.

'My career stared when I was 26. I did two or three years of repertory theatre, in local theatres all over the country. Then I was quite lucky to get my first television very early on, in a series called *Roads to Freedom*. That set the ball rolling, because the next part I got was in the BBC version of *War and Peace*, with Tony Hopkins as Pierre. It was a 26-part series, but it was stunning. It was beautifully done, and I was lucky enough to play Prince Anatol Kuragin. If you know the story, he's the one who elopes with Natasha. The sort of villain of the piece. That took about a year and a half to do. Then I played Count Wenceslas Steinbock in a thing called *Cousin Bette*, which was a BBC serialisation of the Balzac novel.

'I did a lot of those kind of "classics". Then I did a fair bit of theatre again. I was at the Chichester Shakespeare Festival. I did *Macbeth* and *Hamlet*, things like that. Around 1974, I got the part of a ruthless tycoon, a J R type, in a series called *The Brothers*, which I suppose was a kind of forerunner of soap operas like *Dallas* and *Dynasty*.'

Interviewed by C L Crouch in 1985 for *Fantasy Empire* Issue 19.

'I was brought up in Rochdale and went to school in Manchester. Then, when I was twelve years old, at St Bede's College in Manchester, I was invited to take part in a production of *Yeoman of the Guard*. They did Gilbert and Sullivan each year at my school. So I was in the chorus for *Yeoman of the Guard*. Then, when I was thirteen, for some bizarre reason known only to themselves, they decided I ought to play the female lead. So I played Phyllis in *Iolanthe*.'

Interviewed by Trevor Ramsay in June 1989 for *Time Lord* Issue 4.

ON HIS ROLE AS PAUL MERRONEY IN *THE BROTHERS*:

'I made Paul Merroney totally emotionless and without any sense of humour at all. He didn't drink or womanise, and was interested only in business. He was not an unpleasant person, but if you got in his way he would utterly destroy you – legally, honestly and cleverly, which I thought was a little bit more interesting than the "J R" type. Just by chance, another actor who was playing a pivotal role in the series left, and there was a kind of gap. They thought the character of Paul Merroney was a good one to write up, so they asked me to do the next series, and I stayed for about three series. This got me voted the most hated man on television!'

Interviewed by Michael Sibley in May 1987 for *The Colin Baker Interview*.

'*The Brothers* finished in 1976. We didn't *know* it had finished. What usually happened was that we went away for two or three months and did something else. Then the BBC would get in touch – "OK, we're starting again." This time, though, they didn't get in touch! That's the way they work. No-one says, "We're cutting *The Brothers*." They just don't bother to do anything. That was the end of it.'

Interviewed by C L Crouch in 1985 for *Fantasy Empire* Issue 19.

'I was J R before J R was! In England I was the man you loved to hate, which made me the most unpopular person, but at the same time the most popular.
  'It was a series that was on in England from about 1967 until 1976. Halfway through the programme, I came into it. It was about a haulage company – truck driving – which was run by three brothers. And the three brothers all had their own problems. It was a bit like the *Dallas* set-up, only it was set in London and they didn't sit by the pool freezing to death pretending it was hot. Halfway through the series, the company had to expand, so they had to borrow from the bank, and the bank put in a

chairman at the company. This young guy was Paul Merroney, a whiz-kid banker. He was totally ruthless, totally unscrupulous, but totally honest, unlike J R. He never did anything anyone could send him up for, he just ruined people's lives.

'He was a very interesting character, and he made my name what it was in England, so much so that when the programme ended in 1976, I was out in the cold a bit. I couldn't do any television for about five years. I did stage work. That's the good thing in England; there's a very vital theatre network, and they're very anxious to get people they've seen on television out into the theatres. So you can earn a very good living working in the theatre. But I missed television, so it's been quite nice to get back in again. It did rather typecast me. I've always got villain parts until now. They always cast me as the heartless, stone-blooded type.

'I enjoyed the success of *The Brothers* while it was happening. I went to Israel and was told that the Arabs would have stood a better chance during the Six Day War if they had attacked on the night *The Brothers* was on. I was at a party and I had a phone call from Moshe Dayan, who said how very upset he was at not being invited and how much he enjoyed the programme. It had that kind of impact. It was the same in Sweden as well.'

Interviewed by Jean Airey in 1984 for *Fantasy Empire* Issue 12.

ON HIS ROLE AS MAXIL IN THE *DOCTOR WHO* STORY *ARC OF INFINITY*:

'After *For Maddie with Love*, I guested in three episodes of *Doctor Who* when Peter Davison played the Doctor [*Arc of Infinity*]. I played Maxil, who was chief of security on Gallifrey, and I got to shoot the Doctor. Many people suggested that that was my audition for the part – if you zap the incumbent, you get to be the next one!'

Interviewed by Kevin Taylor in 1989 for *Timelines* Issue 3.

'I played Maxil, aided and abetted by Esmeralda. For those of you who don't know who Esmeralda was, that was the name I gave to the hat that I dragged around with me in the story. It wouldn't go through any of the doors, so I couldn't wear it; I had to carry it.'

Interviewed on stage in 1985 at a convention in Texas, USA.

'I've never been one to regard a small part as a small part. So this guy Maxil struck me as the most important person in the show. I was doing a fair few things during the producer's run, and at the end of it John Nathan-Turner said to me, "Yes, that's fine, but .... This isn't about Maxil the guard, it's about the Doctor." And I replied, "Is it really? Good heavens, I didn't realise that. I thought it was called *The Maxil Show*." He said, "Could you tone down the reactions, please, and the acting in the background." Ha ha! But because of that, when Peter Davison said a few months later that he was going to leave, JN-T thought of me for the part of the Doctor. So it paid off in the end! Purely by chance.'

Interviewed by Kevin Taylor in 1989 for *Timelines* Issue 3.

'A little rider ... is that they asked me to play Maxil again, in *The Five Doctors*, but I couldn't, because I was doing something else. If I had taken the part, it would have been too recent, and perhaps I wouldn't be playing the Doctor.'

Interviewed by Paul Duncan in 1984 for *Arkensword* Issue 11.

ON HIS CAREER AFTER *THE BROTHERS*:

'I did very little TV for five years after *The Brothers*. That's the trouble with TV series: they tend to restrict your future employment. So I did a lot of touring. I went to Leicester and did *Macbeth* there, and I toured with productions of thrillers and comedies and all sorts of things. I was pretty constantly employed, I'm pleased to say.

'The first TV I did after *The Brothers* was, I think, an episode of *Blake's 7*, in which I played Bayban the Berserker, an intergalactic space pirate. He was the second most dangerous man in the galaxy, which caused him great annoyance because he wanted to be the *most* dangerous man. It was a great part, an over-the-top role.

'Then I did a series called *For Maddie with Love*, which was an afternoon weepie with Nyree Dawn Porter and Ian Hendry. I played a character a bit like the one in *The Brothers*; a kind of slightly mercenary but very articulate man. I must have done a couple of dozen episodes of that.'

Interviewed by Kevin Taylor in 1989 for *Timelines* Issue 3.

ON WANTING TO BE CAST AS THE DOCTOR:

'The extraordinary thing is that when it was suggested that Tom Baker was finishing on the programme, I rang up my agent and said, "Look, I want to do that programme, get onto it." And before he could do anything, Peter Davison was announced as the new Doctor. I was really annoyed. I didn't think I had much chance, but I thought it would be nice to have a go. And this time, it happened the other way around. I didn't even know that Peter was leaving when John Nathan-Turner got in touch with me.'

Interviewed by Jean Airey in 1984 for *Fantasy Empire* Issue 12.

ON HIS INITIAL THOUGHTS ABOUT PLAYING THE DOCTOR:

'It's a bit like Biggles or *Just William* or Dan Dare, isn't it?

'I want to continue the tradition of making him as quirky and as eccentric as possible; to inject a little acid humour occasionally, perhaps. I think what the producers try to do with Doctor Who is to use as much of the actor's own personality as possible, because it's such a high-density rehearsal and performance rate that you don't have time to go out on a limb.

'Hopefully it'll be a combination of my ideas and their ideas ... A lot of it depends on scripts, of course. People have to write the scripts before you can do it ... An "edge" is a word that is useful to use.

'It's very exciting. There is no other part like it, because there are no other parts where you can actually play the same part as someone else in a television series that has already been created.

'Doctor Who must be nice. "Nice" doesn't mean, necessarily, soft! I think it's important that Doctor Who can be a bit spiky sometimes.

'It is one of those characters that has somehow got into ... almost sort of current mythology. You do bracket him with the sort of great folk heroes of literature. And it was, I think, the first of the science fiction, if it can be so called, programmes on television. It transcends the age gap: children love it, adults love it.'

Interviewed in August 1983 for BBC1's *Breakfast Time* – his first ever *Doctor Who* interview.

ON THE INITIAL SECRECY SURROUNDING HIS CASTING AS THE DOCTOR:

'It had to be hidden for a long time. In fact, John Nathan-Turner and I were having a sneaky drink at a pub one day when Peter Davison came

THE SIXTH DOCTOR

in quite by chance, and we had to make up stories. He knew he was going, but John didn't want anyone knowing who was taking over until the right moment. So I had to pretend I was there for another purpose. "I come to clean the windows." It's tough as an actor.'

Interviewed by Jean Airey in 1984 for *Fantasy Empire* Issue 12.

ON HIS INTEREST IN SCIENCE FICTION:

'I think I have one advantage that perhaps none of the previous Doctors has had, which is that I have always been a sci-fi fan. Which means that there's more to it than just doing a job; it's something extra. So I think I'll enjoy doing it for as long as it's there.

'Obviously in a science fiction show you have to have some special effects, but I think special effects should serve the show rather than the show be a showcase for the special effects. Particularly in a show like *Doctor Who*. When you're making a big movie like *Star Wars*, the special effects play a much larger part, and quite rightly, too. With a programme like *Doctor Who*, what matter most are the story and the characters and the interplay between the characters. Obviously if someone points a piece of twisted plastic at you, you can't just say, "Bang, you're dead." It's got to look as if something's happening, so the effect is put on electronically as an enhancement rather than as the whole.

'I love special effects. I can sit forever and watch that scene in *2001: A Space Odyssey* where the characters are running around inside the spacecraft, exercising. I adore that film, *2001: A Space Odyssey*. It's wonderful. I love all the *Star Wars* stuff. I love *Battlestar Galactica*.'

Interviewed by Jean Airey in 1984 for *Fantasy Empire* Issue 12.

'I'm not mad keen, but science fiction is what I've read more of than anything else. There are some authors, like Ursula le Guin, Anne McCaffrey and Frank Herbert, whose every book I have got. I've just been reading the Thomas Covenant books.'

Interviewed by Paul Duncan in 1984 for *Arkensword* Issue 11.

ON WATCHING EARLIER ERAS OF *DOCTOR WHO*:

'I watched a lot of Hartnell and Troughton, and some Pertwee. Not so much Tom, and not so much Peter, because I was working.

'The ones I watched were in the days when I was younger, before I was an actor. But I've always watched it when I could. I've enjoyed the series and I have memories dotted all along its twenty-four years.'

Interviewed by Penny Holme in 1986 for *Doctor Who Magazine* No. 118.

ON HIS DOCTOR'S COSTUME

'John Nathan-Turner said to me, "What would you like to wear?" and I found that very difficult. My first instinct, which was wrong, was to wear something like the Master wears, all in black, something quite austere. It would have been wrong, I can see that … it's just that I would like to wear slimming black!

'Nothing in Earth's history appealed to me, and you can't really use something futuristic for the Doctor, it's wrong. Then John said, "I think it should be very bad taste." I thought, "Yes, that is rather a good idea for my Doctor. He would just grab something and not care about it. Then, even though he may have realised that it's appalling, he would never admit it, and therefore he would be stuck with wearing it!

'We gave it to a designer, Pat Godfrey, and said, "Give us something in bad taste," and she came back with an exquisitely tasteful design of lots of apparently clashing colours … It's very hard for a designer to design something in bad taste. We said, "No, too good," and sent her away and away and away, until she came back with the present one, which she hated actually putting together, because it was so appalling. But even so, when you get used to it, it has its own entity.

'The only thing I don't like about it is that it's so hot when we're out filming. When we were filming in Spain, it was a hundred and ten degrees, and a couple of weeks ago on Brighton beach, there was no respite from the sun, and it was horrendous.

'But it's lovely on cold locations, when the companions in their skimpy costumes are all shivering and chattering their teeth. So you can't win 'em all.'

Interviewed by Penny Holme in 1986 for *Doctor Who Magazine* No. 118.

'The only things that changed for Season 23 were the waistcoat and the ties; the trousers and the jacket were the same. We did have to have extra jackets made, because of scenes like the one where I had to be submerged in quicksand.

'I did keep saying that I wanted to change the costume, but it's a large expense, unfortunately. John liked it as it was and so was not prepared to waste money, as he saw it. They did let me have new waistcoats and ties, just in order to make the timescale clear. I had a different tie and cat button in each of the different time zones.'

Interviewed by Michael Sibley in May 1987 for *The Colin Baker Interview*.

ON RECORDING THE REGENERATION SCENE IN *THE CAVES OF ANDROZANI*:

'I'd met Peter Davison before on *Arc of Infinity*, but of course I didn't know then that I was going to be playing the Doctor. I was only slightly involved in *The Caves of Androzani*, because I just turned up on the studio day and did it.

'Peter and I didn't have much time to discuss the role, because he was very busy.

'After the recording, I went home, got out of my car, opened my front door, walked in to where my wife was sitting watching television, and stood there and said, "*I am the Doctor*." She looked at me and said, "Oh yes? Could you take the rubbish out, please."'

Interviewed by Gary Levy in December 1984 for *Doctor Who Bulletin* Issue 17/18.

ON PLAYING THE DOCTOR:

'I believe that Tom Baker was quite right, that whoever plays the Doctor does have a responsibility never to cause any children ever to have the remotest worry about what they see him do in public. So I have no intention of breaking the senses of England as I amble through the streets. I think one does have to be very responsible, one's going into so many homes. To go into someone's home like that is a privilege. To be welcomed as the Doctor in this programme is an even greater privilege.

'I can't get over the fact that there are some actors who say, "Oh, look, this is a real drag, all these people wanting autographs." My answer to that is, "Well, do something else then. Go be a bus driver." If you want to be an actor, you want people to see your work. The more people who see your work, the better you're doing your job. The other side of that is that people are going to want you to sign bits of paper for them. If it makes them happy, why the hell not? It's lovely. What other job do you get where people come up to you and say, "I really like what you do"? The majority of the people around the world never get any feedback on the work they do. They go and they do it nine to five. They go home and nobody says, "You're doing well."

It's wonderful, isn't it?

'I also love being the centre of attention. It's really nice. It suits me.'

Interviewed by Jean Airey in 1984 for *Fantasy Empire* Issue 12.

'I've already found that, like all SF TV, *Doctor Who* is good fun off stage, very light hearted.

'Most of the work an actor does tends to be bread and butter, not *Hamlet*. This combines the best of working, as it is so creative.

'As an actor it is marvellous in another way too, for every story has a new cast of guest stars. And, of course, as a devotee of *Doctor Who*, what could be better for me? A fair few years employment in a role that goes round the world and that I've always wanted to do. Wonderful!

'It was exciting to get the role, not daunting. It's not like playing Hamlet. I used to get recognised from my time in *The Brothers* sometimes, but right from the announcement in August, people have been recognising me as the Doctor, and I'm fully aware that I'm going to be unable to go anywhere without being looked at from now on.'

Interviewed by Wendy Graham in 1984 for *Space Voyager* No. 9.

'The atmosphere is great – we have a good time. We always have the same camera crew in the studio, and I've known them from other programmes – we get on very well. I flatter myself that I'm a fairly easy person to get along with, and I'm not at all autocratic. There are people paid to do jobs: writers to write, directors to direct, producers to produce and actors to act. Of course, we discuss things, but I would hate to be in the position where my power was such that I could say, "No, I want that cut, I want this line in," and all that, because I think when you're this closely connected with it, you are least qualified to know best.'

Interviewed by Gary Russell and Justin Richards in 1985 for *Doctor Who Magazine* Issue 97.

'Being associated with something that has such a grip on the imagination of several generations. It really is part of current mythology.

'It's like playing Robin Hood, or King Arthur. It's one of those characters …

'I was already sufficiently impressed with the fact that I was playing it, but I've had a great many, very respected actors who've said to me, "You've got the best part in television." And in a sense they're right.

'It's given me a more secure life – or rather did give me a more secure life until Michael Grade's intervention last year, when the future of the programme seemed a little bleak. But that's beginning to turn over again, and I think everyone is now aware of the value of *Doctor Who* in people's lives.'

Interviewed by Penny Holme in 1986 for *Doctor Who Magazine* No. 118.

'I want everyone who watches *Doctor Who* not to be disappointed that I'm playing it. I think we all have our favourite Doctor, and it is usually the one who was the Doctor when we started watching it. Each Doctor has left a block of loyalty behind him. There's a huge following for Tom Baker. A strong following for Peter. Maybe in ten years' time, the fans will feel the same way about me. I hope so. That's nice, as long as nobody says, "This is the *only* Doctor," and all the rest of it. That's silly, because they've all brought something to the part. They're all very good actors.'

Interviewed by Paul Duncan in 1984 for *Arkensword* Issue 11.

'The atmosphere is great – we have a good time. We always have the same camera crew in the studio, and I've known them from other programmes – we get on very well. I flatter myself that I'm a fairly easy person to get along with, and I'm not at all autocratic. There are people paid to do jobs: writers to write, directors to direct, producers to produce and actors to act. Of course, we discuss things, but I would hate to be in the position where my power was such that I could say, "No, I want that cut, I want this line in," and all that, because I think when you're this closely connected with it, you are least qualified to know best.'

Interviewed by Gary Russell and Justin Richards in 1985 for *Doctor Who Magazine* Issue 97.

'I felt very positive about what I could add to the programme, and a kind of sense of responsibility. It's like when you take the baton and you've got the next 400 metres to run. You don't drop the baton, you don't throw it into the crowd, you don't stop and pick your nose. You actually do something worthwhile while you've got it; you do your best. I was always aware of that responsibility, and not just as a job; it was more than a job. I wanted to honour the tradition that those other five guys had upheld so marvellously before. I just wanted to add another cherry to the cake.'

Interviewed by Nick Briggs in 1990 for the *Myth Makers 19* video, released by Reeltime Pictures.

'At no stage does one ever really feel *au fait* with any part. There's always something one can learn and there are always further avenues to be explored. But if the question is, do I feel happy in the role?, then the answer is most emphatically yes. Right from the very beginning, I felt that it was a part for which I – in all humility – was ideally suited, by chance rather than by any great skill on my part. And right from the beginning, I've enjoyed doing it.

'I enjoy the totality of it. There isn't an individual aspect that overrides all the others; it's playing the role that I enjoy. I enjoy the day to day work in rehearsal with other actors, I enjoy the studio work, and I enjoy the moment when the next script pops through the letter box and – a little ahead of the viewer – I find out what's going to happen next.'

Interviewed by Doug Smith in 1985 for *Fan Aid* Issue 2.

ON HIS FIRST *DOCTOR WHO* DIRECTOR, PETER MOFFATT:

'As he was directing the first story, *The Twin Dilemma*, he gave me a lot of room to experiment and try things out, and of course the first script was very strong. I'd never previously worked with Peter. We got on together well and very quickly. Altogether, we had seven days' rehearsal in which we kicked certain ideas around, but it was a very pleasant process. It wasn't at all traumatic.'

Interviewed by Bill Baggs in 1984 for *Time Watcher*.

ON HIS MARRIAGE TO ACTRESS MARION WYATT:

'It was a pretty instant thing. I wasn't looking for a serious relationship at the time. I was having a jolly good time by myself, doing all the things that chaps do when they're younger, like swilling beer, smoking too much and being a bit of a slob.

'The thing was that I'd hardly ever lived by myself. I'd shared flats, lived with girls, then married [to actress Liza Goddard]. So I took full advantage of the situation.

'At first I was hesitant about marriage again. Having had one failure, I wanted to be sure I was doing the right thing. But then I knew this wasn't going to go wrong – and it hasn't. I don't think it's a problem being married to an actress, either. There's extra pressure, of course. But it's people who go wrong, not their jobs.

'Marion isn't career crazy and she's not jealous of my current success, either. She loves the country life we lead with our dogs and messing about in the home. She, like me now, knows what comes first.'

Interviewed by Ivan Waterman in 1984 for the *News of the World*, 29 April.

ON THE DEATH OF HIS SON JACK:

'It was like being hit in the stomach by a steam hammer. That's the only way I can explain it. Everything just stood still. It was totally numbing and draining. Marion and I will never, ever get over it. It's not something you *can* "get over".

'It took me twelve hours to get home [from working on *The Mousetrap* in Malmo, Sweden]. It was the longest night of my life. As I waited for a boat to catch the plane, I was plagued by the appalling thought that Marion was having to cope on her own. I felt so awful that I wasn't there to support her. That I'd been out enjoying myself while our son was lying dead. I kept thinking: "I knew him only four weeks. I never saw my baby smile." I kept asking, "Would it have happened if I'd been at home? Was it something to do with the last time I held him? Were we feeding him right? Was the house too big, too small, too hot, too cold? Why? Why? Why?"

'He just stopped breathing. He wasn't in any discomfort. It was just as if the habit of breathing hadn't established itself firmly enough.'

Interviewed by Mary Peplow in 1984 for *Woman's Realm*, 1 September.

'Jack died almost a year ago this week, when I was about two weeks away from starting work on *Doctor Who*. I got in touch with the Foundation for the Study of Infant Deaths as soon as it happened, because I didn't know anything about cot death and I wanted to find out about it. Then a newspaper wanted to do an article about Jack's death, and the last thing I wanted to do at the time, about a week after it happened, was to talk to a newspaper, but suddenly I thought, "Maybe I can use this to help." Out of something dreadful like that, one can actually derive some good, and the good I could do was to make the newspaper pay an awful lot of money to the Foundation, which they did happily – it's terrifying what they'll just shell out, especially if it's for a charity, as they don't want to appear mean. Also the article publicised the cause of raising money for cot death research. I mean, 2,000 children a year in this country alone is a lot to go, and nobody knows why.

'The Foundation were, commendably, reticent to use me at the beginning. They said, "Look, give yourself a few months, you might change your mind." But I'm now on the fund-raising committee.

'When I do fêtes and things, I get offered expenses and what have you, and I feel a bit embarrassed saying, "Yes, it's £7.42 please," so I just ask them to make a donation to the Foundation.'

Interviewed by Dominic May, David Saunders and Robert Moubert in November 1984 for *TARDIS* **Volume 9 Issue 3.**

ON THE LENGTH OF HIS STAY IN *DOCTOR WHO*:

'I'm going to have a smashing time, and I'm going to have a long run!'

Interviewed by Wendy Graham in 1984 for *Space Voyager* **No. 9.**

'My thoughts are long term rather than short term. I am someone who likes to break records, and I understand that someone with a name not dissimilar to mine played the role for seven years. So I'd hate to be known as the second longest-running Doctor.'

Interviewed on stage in 1985 at a convention in Philadelphia, USA.

'I'd like to stay in the part as long as I'm enjoying it and the public want to see me playing it, which may be two years, three years, ten years … I've always stated publicly that it would be nice to equal Tom Baker's number of years and episodes, but that would be quite an achievement, because he did seven years in the show, and made an awful lot of episodes.'

Interviewed by Chris Parnham in 1986 for *The Ribos Operation* **Issue 2.**

'I think it's probably in other people's hands, rather than my own.

'Say the choice was mine; when I started doing this, I said that Tom Baker's record of seven years was awfully attractive. I've done it for three years now, even though we've done only two seasons, and I'm enjoying it. So I see no desire on my part in the near future to stop. Also, I'd like to beat the episode tally! In order to do that at the present rate, I'd take about twenty years, because in Tom's day they were making twenty-six episodes a year, now we're down to fourteen.'

Interviewed by Penny Holme in 1986 for *Doctor Who Magazine* **No. 118.**

THE SIXTH DOCTOR

ON *THE TWIN DILEMMA*:

'*The Twin Dilemma* had the problem of establishing a new Doctor, and the difficulties of regeneration were the prime element of the story. In a sense, the plot of Mestor and Azmael and so on was subsidiary to that. Had the story been too strong, it might have distracted from the main purpose of the first story – that is, to establish that the new Doctor was experiencing problems.'

Interviewed by Doug Smith in 1985 for *Fan Aid* Issue 2.

'When I did it, I had nothing to judge it against. I think first scripts are always very difficult. If you look back at any of the incoming Doctors' first scripts, they tend to be very hesitant, because neither the Doctor nor the writers – nor anybody – knows what is actually going to happen, on the basis that any kind of coming together of talents is an organic process.

'We had made certain decisions about what my Doctor was going to be, and I think they were very brave ones, actually. They weren't just mine; we all agreed that we would go for making the Doctor inaccessible, so that people would think, "This isn't my Doctor. Bring back that nice Peter Davison, who was kind and gentle. This awful man is going around strangling Peri, and being remote and arrogant and conceited!"

'The story itself may well have been a weak one. In retrospect, I suspect it possibly was. In fact, it was one of the weaker stories of the time I was doing *Doctor Who*, and certainly didn't compare with the stories I always remember from the past, such as the great Robert Holmes ones of the Tom Baker era. It wasn't in the same league. But that didn't necessarily matter, because you could actually concentrate on what was happening with the Doctor and Peri, and the whole regeneration thing.'

Interviewed by Nick Briggs in 1990 for the *Myth Makers 19* video, released by Reeltime Pictures.

ON *VENGEANCE ON VAROS*:

'*Vengeance on Varos* is one of my favourite shows out of the first complete season. Like all successful plays – as well as *Doctor Who* stories – there are two elements involved. One is that it's on the surface a ripping good story. It's a good adventure, it's well told and the plot's well developed. It has humour in it and good characterisation. But at the same time, it has an underlying theme, which can be quite simply put as: violence corrupts, and violence as a form of entertainment in the media is not exempt from that corrupting effect.

'It's extraordinary that certain elements of criticism have been levelled at *Vengeance on Varos* because of its violence. That seems to me to have missed the whole point of the show. It's a bit like complaining about *Macbeth* because it glorifies regicide, murder and corruption. And – as a parallel – the whole point of *Vengeance on Varos* is that "video nasties" are not a good thing, any more than manipulation of the population is a good thing. For critics – I use a polite term to describe them – to complain because *Vengeance on Varos* portrayed the very scenes of violence it was condemning, strikes me as faintly ludicrous, quite honestly. It has been pointed out that *The A-Team*, which was shown opposite *Vengeance on Varos* on the other channel, was more successful than *Doctor Who* in terms of viewing figures. That illustrates the point that it's very difficult to cope with that kind of violence. *The A-Team* is surely gratuitous, spectacular aggression, and people find it easier to watch that kind of mindless violence. It's a shame that *Doctor Who* was criticised for making exactly that point.'

Interviewed by Doug Smith in 1985 for *Fan Aid* Issue 2.

ON *THE MARK OF THE RANI*:

'*The Mark of the Rani* was excellent. We had the writers, Pip and Jane Baker, with us most of the time on location. They had to do a lot of rewriting, usually because of the poor weather conditions. We had to kind of scrabble for the last few days, so a lot of cutting and changing went on. Pip and Jane went home of a night and produced another few pages to cope with what we'd had to lose or couldn't cope with the day before. I remember that very clearly.

'The thing I liked about Pip and Jane is that they wrote very well for my Doctor; they understood the sixth Doctor very well.'

Interviewed by Nick Briggs in 1990 for the *Myth Makers 19* video, released by Reeltime Pictures.

ON *THE TWO DOCTORS*:

'I'm afraid Patrick Troughton suffered rather badly at my and Frazer Hines' hands. Frazer is one of the quickest-witted, funniest people I've ever met. I mean, he has a repertoire of jokes that would make Bob Hope's card-carriers worry. A very funny man. I made the mistake of battling with Frazer the first two or three weeks of rehearsals, and then I gave up. I kept saying,

"Frazer, I'm the Doctor, I do the jokes," but it was really he who did them. So we used to play practical jokes on poor old Patrick. For example, setting him off in his wheelchair. I don't mean that Patrick himself actually had a wheelchair, but there were scenes in the show where he was strapped into a wheelchair, and as soon as he was strapped into it, he became very vulnerable. So we used to play chariot races with poor Patrick.'

Interviewed on stage in 1985 at a convention in Texas, USA.

ON THE CANCELLATION OF THE ORIGINAL SEASON 23:

'Michael Grade wanted very much to do things *his* way, and there's an old saying – "A new broom sweeps clean." The first thing he did was to cancel *Dallas*. This brought such a storm of protest that there was pressure put on from above (so I understand), and it went back on again. The *second* thing he did was to say, because the BBC is a bit short of money, "We've got to save money, so what we're going to do is *not* produce *Doctor Who* this year. That will save us money to do new drama, because we want to do new things, and the only way we can do that is by cancelling some of the *old* things." That was his logic, and so *Doctor Who* fell under the axe. What then happened was another storm of protest – headlines in the national daily newspapers ... "*Doctor Who* Axed!" *Thousands* of letters have been carried into Michael Grade's office ... First from British fans and then, of course, once they got word of it, from the *American* fans.

'I was *shattered* by the cancellation. I was very upset. I mean, if you put it in the context of someone who had just taken over the part – and at the end of my first season, the programme's taken off! Now, I hope and pray – I think I *know* – that it's not because they think, "My God, he's dreadful! Let's take him off!" But none the less, it could be *interpreted* that way. To someone who's not even slightly interested in *Doctor Who*, it reads: "Colin Baker's taken over the part. Oh, yeah, now they've taken it off ..." The two things are linked together subconsciously in people's minds, and I don't like to be associated with that kind of failure!

'Also, I was enjoying *doing* it! I was geared up for it! I was ready to go on to the next series. We should have been starting next week on a superb story, which I'd read and which I was really excited about – a really good one. It was harking back to something in the past, but a very clever story. So, yes, I'm very, very disappointed.'

Interviewed by C L Crouch in 1985 for *Fantasy Empire* Issue 19.

'I have been very busy during the suspension. I've been to America many times to conventions over there. My wife and I had a baby last March, and I have been around home for the past few months, which has been very pleasant. I've had lots of work to do with the charity I'm involved with, the Foundation for the Study of Infant Deaths, to which the *Doctor Who* Appreciation Society have very kindly contributed quite a considerable amount over the last year. I've been very heartened by the way in which the members of DWAS have taken on the charity I'm involved with as their charity, and it's been marvellous to see the response from all the members.'

Interviewed by Chris Parnham in 1986 for *The Ribos Operation* Issue 2.

'Michael Grade came in as Controller of programmes, and he didn't single out *Doctor Who* as such. In the same breath that he axed *Doctor Who*, he summarily ended some other programmes. These included *Come Dancing* and *The Hot Shoe Show* and things like that, which had their own aficionados. For some reason, *Doctor Who* always seems to be able to attract the tabloid press to write headlines. It seems there is some knack the programme has of attracting those newspapers. So all the other programmes that were axed as part of the new Controller's clearout were not really mentioned, while *Doctor Who* was. I think – and this is only my assumption – that probably Michael Grade was taken as much by surprise by that as by anything else.

'I saw him being interviewed on TV a long time before he came to the BBC. He was saying in response to a question that he thought the BBC had become very old fashioned and was producing anachronistic programmes that were driving viewers away. "For instance," he said, "that terrible, tired old format *Doctor Who*." I remember thinking – and this was before I played Maxil even – "I don't agree with that. I quite like *Doctor Who*." That's why it stuck in my brain.

'So he had a declared aversion to the show. He came along, presumably with far-reaching powers to reshape the BBC, and admittedly it did need it. To a certain extent he was right. It was becoming a sort of tired old machine, turning out tired old programmes. It's all part of the same attitude: "Right, we've got to go for change, so let's get rid of some dead wood. That's been on for a long time, so has that, and so has that, so let's get rid of them and get something new in." It does make a certain amount of sense. But not when you're dealing with a commodity like *Doctor Who*, which earns more money than it costs to make. For that reason alone, it's worth keeping, quite apart from the fact that it has a very strong adherence from a lot of people.

'Counting viewers is one thing, but you can count ten million viewers who sit and watch a quiz show in a sort of mild apathy, turn it off and never give it a thought again, or you can say that there are five million who watch *Doctor Who* and think about it non-stop, and who absolutely love the programme. I think the latter is the more worthwhile type of programme to be making.'

Interviewed by Gill Green and Dominic May in September 1987 for *TARDIS*, January 1988 edition.

ON MAKING SCRIPT SUGGESTIONS:

'I sometimes comment on something if I think that there is a better way of doing it, or if it is inconsistent with something that has previously been said, or if my Doctor – I feel – would not behave in precisely that fashion. But ultimately the producer and the director are the arbiters of what is best, and my attitude is purely that of an actor who is faced with a problem, sometimes, in bringing to the screen that which is written on the paper. On some occasions the producer and the director will agree with me, and on other occasions they will give a very good reason why my suggestion is not as good as the one of the author. The process of bringing a *Doctor Who* story to the screen is – like all acting – collaborative, so there's very little head-on confrontation. It's basically a question of getting together, working with the material we've got and coming up with the best result.'

Interviewed by Doug Smith in 1985 for *Fan Aid* Issue 2.

ON THE *DOCTOR WHO* RADIO SERIAL *SLIPBACK*:

'I think that *Doctor Who* is ideal for radio, given the fact that a major worry in the making of a series like this is the realisation of special effects and sets and costumes. It was wonderful to be in a situation where that was no longer a problem. We had the best sets, the best costumes, the best-looking actors. My costume was wonderful on the radio – it was a shame you couldn't see it!

'I'd been acting on radio for years. I did quite a lot around 1970 to 1972: several Shakespeare plays, poetry readings, all sorts of things. I do enjoy it. It has that wonderful joy that you don't have to learn the lines. You can have an awful lot of fun doing radio productions. They can be much more imaginative than television or theatre, in the sense that the audience – in this case, the listeners – are much more active participants in the play; they are supplying, with your help, all the things that have been taken away from them because it's not a visual production. Some of my most enjoyable experiences of plays have been plays that I've heard on the radio, in ideal circumstances, very often driving in a car, when you can get really involved in the story.'

Interviewed by Patrick White in 1988 for *Tranquil Repose* Issue 6.

ON HIS SENSE OF HUMOUR:

'There are some people who don't understand my sense of humour. I met someone at a convention recently who told me that I had been extremely rude to her at another convention. What it turned out had happened was that I had been walking through the foyer, seen her standing there wearing a huge Tom Baker scarf and said something along the lines of, "Get rid of that scarf at once! How dare you wear that in my presence?" I think the mere fact of saying that indicates that it's not intended to be serious, but this woman had been distraught for weeks because I had told her to remove the scarf. I would say that was hypersensitivity rather than anything that was my fault.'

Interviewed by C L Crouch in 1985 for *Fantasy Empire* Issue 19.

'I don't think uproarious comedy is a good idea in *Doctor Who*, but I enjoy humour and I always try to put in moments of humour. Sometimes the directors like it, sometimes they don't. I think we have decided that the next season will have more of what you might call comedy in it.'

Interviewed by Chris Parnham in 1986 for *The Ribos Operation* Issue 2.

ON *THE TRIAL OF A TIME LORD*:

'I'm very excited by the new season. The trial has a great many twists. The three stories are all very different, and there are also interconnections between them. There are lots of layers, and it's very, very complicated, which I rather like.

'I like things you can't understand, like *Edge of Darkness*. What I loved about that series was what other people objected to, which was that the viewer hadn't got a clue what was going on. It stimulates your thoughts. It's like doing a crossword. I wanted to make the pieces fit before they told me, and I didn't, but it was all totally consistent.

'There is an awful tendency to let the "game show" mentality take over, which is reducing television to its lowest common denominator ... I think we have to get away from viewing figures. The BBC is about providing television for everyone, but not necessarily all at the same time. You can have seven million people watching one programme and then going off and doing something else, and a different seven million watching the next one. I think that is more important than having fourteen million sitting in apathy watching something with no contact, which only sinks them further into the stupor that we are encouraged to descend into. The BBC has stood for quality for so long, it would be a shame to allow it to be watered down.'

Interviewed by Penny Holme in 1986 for *Doctor Who Magazine* No. 118.

'It is very difficult when you're actually doing something on the inside to be objective about it. I read all the magazines sent to me, if I get the time. Some of the criticisms I think, "Well, that's fair, that's somebody's opinion." Others I think, "Oh, you stupid berk! That's just being petty and unpleasant, or you have missed the whole point of it!" Sometimes I think people get it into their heads that whatever one does, they are not going to like it, and they will look for things not to like. I think that's a shame.

'I suppose I was naive when, before the season went out and after we had finished it, I said, "I'm so confident of the new season that I think the future of *Doctor Who* is secure." I even thought my own job was secure, because the "buzz" when we were doing each separate story was really good. People I respected, like Michael Jayston, were all saying, "This is good, this is working really well." Michael enjoyed doing it, and I thought it was excellent.'

Interviewed by Michael Sibley in May 1987 for *The Colin Baker Interview*.

'I thought it was a valiant attempt, a decision by Eric Saward and John Nathan-Turner to mirror what was actually going on – the series being on trial. Unfortunately, they fell out in the final analysis of the last episodes. Rightly or wrongly, I don't know. But I think Pip and Jane Baker did a brilliant job writing a replacement script.

'I loved all the stuff with the Valeyard. I thought that was very good. But it could equally have been the Master, and I know that Anthony Ainley was a little put out at being supplanted – he thought, "This is a part I could've played," and indeed he could.

'That's the sort of stuff I like: the good versus evil; opening doors and stepping out on to the beach; Popplewick and all that kind of weirdness in the Fantasy Factory.'

Interviewed by Guy Wainer, Greg Jones, Neil John and David Greenham in 1990 for *Skaro* Volume 5 Issue 2.

COLIN BAKER: IN HIS OWN WORDS

ON DOING HIS OWN STUNTS:

'One thing that I have insisted upon, as far as I can, is doing my own stunts. I always object when I'm watching something if I can see that it's a stunt man. In film it's easier to get away with, because they have more money and spend more time on it, so the double actually looks like the actor. But in television, you can see that it's a double; the head turns and you can see that it's not the actor.

'So far, everything that the Doctor has been seen to do, I've actually done. The most painful stunt was one in *The Mark of the Rani*, where I was dangling on a chain above a 150 foot drop – which, I'm happy to say, there was a board across, so that if I had dropped, I wouldn't have fallen 150 feet! It was a very cold day for filming, and my fingers were so numb that I couldn't actually feel them. I was still holding on to the chain while people were hitting me with poles, trying to make me lose my grip, and I got one of my fingers caught in the chain and ripped all the skin off. In fact, it's still bent, as you can see. That was … irritating.

'In the same story, there's a scene where I'm strapped on to a trolley on wheels. Peri supposedly pushes it in the wrong direction and lets go, and I go rolling down a hill. It's shot very well. Actually, everyone's saying it looked very frightening. I found it exhilarating! It was actually great, and I was really annoyed that they got it in the can the first time, because I wanted to go again!

'In *Vengeance on Varos* there's a hanging scene, and the platform on which I was standing collapsed! The rope around my neck tightened a little, but fortunately the bit that collapsed wasn't actually the bit on which I was standing, otherwise I wouldn't be here today.

'There was a lot more uncomfortable stuff, such as a couple of fights in *Revelation of the Daleks* in the snow – it was horrendous snow.'

Interviewed on stage in 1985 at a convention in Texas, USA.

'The scene in *The Trial of a Time Lord* where I had to be submerged in quicksand was brilliant! It was shot at Camber Sands in Kent. The prop boys got there a long time in advance and dug a huge pit. They made two chambers, so basically it was a pit with a wall across the middle. When we shot the scene, we had a couple of guys standing in the first chamber with their arms protruding through a waterproof rubber roof, which was covered with water and had cork etc floated on top of it so that it looked just like sand. That was how the shot was done of the hands coming up through the sand and grabbing my ankles. In the second chamber, which was about six feet deep and filled with water, was a hydraulic lift, with a central pole and a platform at the top. All I had to do was to fall onto the platform, which again was covered with the cork etc to make it look like part of the beach. The lift was then lowered so that it looked as though I was sinking into quicksand. Once my hands had gone under, I had to grab the sides and force my own head down, otherwise I would just have floated. I had to hold myself under for about ten seconds, then come out and do it all over again for a retake. In fact, I had to do it three times, I think.

'The funny thing was, the pit was so well concealed that the sound man fell into it! He was walking around checking the sound with his microphone, and the poor chap fell straight into this thing!'

Interviewed by Michael Sibley in May 1987 for *The Colin Baker Interview*.

ON HIS FAVOURITE *DOCTOR WHO* WRITERS AND DIRECTORS:

'My favourite writer was Robert Holmes, because over the years he contributed more in terms of imagination and depth of writing than did many other writers. All his stories worked on several levels. They worked on the superficial level of a ripping good yarn, but also he always wrote a story that had an underlying, very significant message. He didn't shirk the more thorny problems of violence, or indeed of cannibalism in *The Two Doctors*. That was a fairly nasty subject to tackle, but he tackled it.

'I liked very much working with an awful lot of directors. Matthew Robinson was very good. He directed *Attack of the Cybermen*. Peter Moffatt, who directed my first and *The Two Doctors*, is a lovely director. Graeme Harper, who did *Revelation of the Daleks*, was a great favourite of mine. He had an enormous amount of energy and was a smashing director.'

Interviewed by Patrick White in 1988 for *Tranquil Repose* Issue 6.

ON HIS FAVOURITE ADVERSARIES:

'I have a liking for the Autons from Jon Pertwee's time. They've only ever had two stories. I enjoyed them. They provoked, I gather, a reaction from Mary Whitehouse, who didn't like telephone lines and daffodils killing people, because it made children frightened of everyday objects. I loved their smooth faces. I find the humanoid monsters more frightening than the totally alien ones – the bug-eyed monster syndrome. That's why the Master is so effective, because he's another Time Lord. There are all sorts of things that can go on between the two. There's almost a pleasure at the confrontation. One thing that I see in my Doctor is that even though the defence of the weak and the championship of right against wrong is uppermost, there is a certain enjoyment of conflict. I want him to think, "Hello, there's something going on here. I'd like to get stuck in and see what it is!"

'What other monsters? There are the old classics. It would be nice to meet the Ice Warriors. They haven't been around for a long while, have they? Oh, and Davros. I must meet Davros.'

Interviewed by Bill Baggs in 1984 for *Time Watcher.*

'My favourite enemy is the Master, because Sherlock Holmes has his Moriarty, and while most monsters have no particular desire to destroy the Doctor – they want to get on with whatever it is they are doing that's particularly evil, and the Doctor gets in the way – the good thing about the Master is that it's a personal matter. So there is a great opportunity for confrontation. I would like, and haven't yet had, a really thundering good Master story.

'I would also love to work with the Rani again. She was a wonderful adversary. But after the Master and the Rani, I would say the Daleks and the Cybermen come joint second, along with Sil.'

Interviewed by Penny Holme in 1986 for *Doctor Who Magazine* **No. 118.**

'I rather enjoyed working with Sil, particularly because the actor, Nabil Shaban, is such a nice bloke and such a very good actor. I also thought it was a smashing character, and the relationship between Sil and the Doctor developed quite nicely.'

Interviewed by Michael Sibley in May 1987 for *The Colin Baker Interview.*

'My favourite enemy is the Master. I think he's been underused very much in the last few years, and it's a great shame, because the one-to-one Holmes-Moriarty syndrome is a lot of what *Doctor Who* should be about. The Daleks, they're kind of silly, but they're there and they work, and they terrify everybody! The sad thing about *Revelation of the Daleks* was that there wasn't a lot of contact between the Doctor and the Daleks. It wasn't a full-blown Dalek story, because there was so much going on with Davros, the city and all that. I do like the Cybermen as well. I think it's a shame that they have been reduced in their abilities to an extent over the seasons. I have a slight predisposition towards continuity, wanting it to be good, and once or twice it has slipped.'

Interviewed by Guy Wainer, Greg Jones, Neil John and David Greenham in 1990 for *Skaro* **Volume 5 Issue 2.**

THE SIXTH DOCTOR

ON THE LACK OF HANKY-PANKY IN THE TARDIS:

'I don't think the world is ready for Doctor number six and Perpugilliam Brown and hanky-panky! The rule is that there should be absolutely no possibility of any kind of love interest between the Doctor and his companion. The companion is there for the viewer to identify with, so younger people, children, can imagine what it's like for them to be flying in the TARDIS with the Doctor. The one thing we don't want them imagining is …. well … It's the way the show is structured; that's the way it is and has always been. Mind you … I could make an exception for Leela!'

Interviewed on stage in 1985 at a convention in Texas, USA.

ON HIS TWO TV COMPANIONS:

'One problem with Peri is that the scriptwriters think that they're writing authentic American dialogue, but they're not. Nicola tries to get them to change the script, but bear in mind that it's her first job, and in your first job you don't go around trying to tell scriptwriters how to write scripts! She does say, "This is not the way an American would say it; I'd rather say so-and-so," and they reply, "Could you please say the script as it's written." So don't blame her. Also, bear in mind that the programme is made by the BBC initially for showing on British TV. If you have too many words like "faucet" and "sidewalk" you'll confuse the British viewer.'

Interviewed on stage in 1985 at a convention in Texas, USA.

'I think Nicola encountered the problem that an awful lot of companions have, which is that the character isn't ever properly developed by the writers. All they ever do with her is make her say "Oh Doctor!" and fall over. Then they separate her from the Doctor – have her carried off by the monster or something – so that they can get two different story strands going. It's very, very difficult, and considering that this was Nicola's first proper job out of drama school – she'd not even had any theatre experience when she played *Doctor Who* – I think she did wonderfully. She didn't want to do all the whining; it was imposed upon her by the nature of the scripts. Had she been an actress with fifteen years experience behind her, she might have been able to stand up and say, "Look, I won't have this," but like any newcomer, she basically did just what she was asked to do. She was great to work with; I am very fond of Nicola.

'Bonnie was lucky, because she was a known personality. She's been in the theatre longer than I have! The character of Melanie was very quickly made very specific – she had an interest in keep-fit, she was spunky, she was enthusiastic. The idea was that I would be the one who was always saying, "Hey, let's be careful," because she would always be rushing out and doing things. That's a good, positive thing to grab hold of when you're starting in a role.'

Interviewed on stage in 1987 during a convention at the University of Western Washington, USA.

ON HIS LEAST FAVOURITE STORY:

'I suppose it was *Timelash*, which never quite gelled for me.

'It was actually much better than I thought it was going to be. Pennant Roberts did a good job directing it. There was nothing intrinsically wrong with it, it's just that, of that particular series, it was the one that didn't work for me. I don't think that the Doctor's element was as strong as I'd have liked.'

Interviewed by Penny Holme in 1986 for *Doctor Who Magazine* No. 118.

ON HIS FAVOURITE STORY:

'From the point of view of watching them, I think my favourite would be either *Vengeance on Varos* or *Revelation of the Daleks*, because as complete stories, they stood up extremely well and were different. The one I enjoyed doing most was probably *The Two Doctors*, mainly because of working with Patrick Troughton and Frazer Hines, both of whom are now very good friends of mine. I have a particular regard for Patrick Troughton's Doctor, so it was a great honour for me to work with someone who I believe is a very gifted and versatile actor.'

Interviewed by Doug Smith in 1985 for *Fan Aid* Issue 2.

'Pat I've adored for many years, and I've known him for a long time. I was best man at his son David's wedding, and I shared a flat with David for ten years, so I've known Pat off and on, and always admired his acting, and adored his Doctor, so actually to work with him was a special treat.

'I was a bit in awe actually, but that was dispelled in a couple of days, and Frazer also is a delight. Frazer and I got on extremely well. We larked around a lot, and Pat treated us like an affectionate ... I'd say father, but he'd be offended. No, I'll say father anyway, because he calls me Miss Piggy at the moment (a reference to my weight); I call him Gonzo (which is a reference to his physical appearance)!'

Interviewed by Penny Holme in 1986 for *Doctor Who Magazine* No. 118.

'I think in retrospect I was unlucky in that I never really had any great stories; there weren't any that stood out. I think *Vengeance on Varos* was the nearest in that it was very different. Yes, and that was the one that got all the criticism in Britain. It was violent and it was dark and it was gloomy. I liked that. I enjoyed that a lot. I thought it was a good story, and I enjoyed doing it.'

Interviewed by Bob Furnell, Dean King and Janette Taylor in March 1987 for *Time Meddlers of Vancouver*.

ON SCRIPT EDITOR ERIC SAWARD'S RESIGNATION:

'We had a hiccup towards the end of *The Trial of a Time Lord*. I suppose, like all of us, Eric's a complex man. He used to ring me up late at night and moan on about John Nathan-Turner. I would spend an hour and a half or two hours talking on the phone with him – and he'd ring about midnight, so at two in the morning I would say, "Look, Eric, I have to go to bed, I'm tired." I would calm him down and say, "Look, Eric, I think you are being paranoid. I don't think John is trying to do you down. I think all he's doing is disagreeing with you, which he is entitled to do as producer of the programme." Then suddenly I read the interview that Eric did for *Starburst*, most of which he spent slagging off John. Most of it was unfair, and some of it just his opinion. Some of it I don't know about, as I wasn't present.

'What had happened was that dear old Robert Holmes had died before completing his script for the final episode of the season. Eric had been very close to him. He wanted to stick to the spirit of what Robert Holmes had wanted to do. John asked Eric to write it, even after they had fallen out. I've got a copy of the actual script that he wrote. He seemed to be venting his anger in the writing, and he wrote a very strange ending. John turned it down for many reasons.

'Pip and Jane Baker then had to write a new version of the last episode over a weekend, and I thought they did it brilliantly. I think episodes thirteen and fourteen were the best; the characters of Glitz, Popplewick and the Valeyard were wonderful.'

Interviewed by Michael Sibley in May 1987 for *The Colin Baker Interview*.

'The truth is an awful lot of things: there are no absolute villains, there are no absolute good guys. It's certainly true that JN-T and Saward were chalk and cheese, but in the early days that worked extremely well, because they complemented each other. It's only as both of them – and John will admit this himself – have become a bit jaded doing the programme ... JN-T wanted to leave the show. He announced that he was leaving, he told all the fans this. Then suddenly the BBC said, "We want you to carry on and do more." He replied, "I don't want to. I want to go and do something else, please." And they said, "Either you do more or you pack your bags." Obviously he wanted to stay at the BBC – he's got a living to make – so he had to do what they told him. I mean, all I know is what he's told me. There may be things going on behind the scenes. But it does strike me as ludicrous that when you have an actor who wants to carry on playing the part and a producer who wants to go, you do exactly the reverse: you keep the guy who doesn't want to do it and get rid of the guy who does!'

Interviewed by Bob Furnell, Dean King and Janette Taylor in March 1987 for *Time Meddlers of Vancouver.*

ON THE SERIES' RATINGS:

'Michael Grade said publicly that the ratings for Season 23 were very disappointing. I wrote him a letter in which I said, "Given the fact that you had cancelled us for eighteen months, and given that we were again opposite *The A-Team*, which pulls in 30 million viewers and is the kind of whiz-bang violent programme that you don't want to make ... We came on immediately after *Roland Rat – The Series*, which sadly pulled in only two million viewers. Then, halfway through *Roland Rat – The Series*, *The A-Team* started. To get the five million viewers that we did get, I actually thought was bloody good."

'I suppose we did also go out in the hours of daylight, with good weather. These of course are not the factors that people mention when they say that the ratings are poor. So – scapegoat – change the Doctor!

'I would never dream of wishing my successor any ill, but I hope that if he is successful, it's because the programme deserves it, not because of the schedule. I would feel well peeved if the series was put opposite something kind of flabby, and put out at seven o'clock at night, and therefore doubled its figures. Of course, they would say, "Ah, there you are, told you so! Get rid of Colin Baker and you get 10 million viewers!"'

Interviewed by Michael Sibley in May 1987 for *The Colin Baker Interview.*

THE SIXTH DOCTOR

ON THE SERIES' SCRIPTS:

'Actually, I found there was an awful lot of casual script writing went on during my time in the series. I had terrible trouble with *The Trial of a Time Lord* in particular. I remember that the worst part was the segment written by Philip Martin. I would ask the director, "Is this the Matrix lying, is the Doctor under the influence of the process he's been subjected to, or is he lying for some reason of his own that we'll later discover?" "I don't know," came the reply, "you'd better ask Philip Martin." So I asked Philip Martin, and he said, "I don't know. Eric Saward put that bit in. You'll have to ask him." I asked Eric, and Eric said, "Oh, I don't know. Philip Martin wrote that bit!" I told him, "Look, I need to know, in order to play this scene. When I'm chaining Peri to the rock, is that a Matrix lie or am I behaving like that because I'm being watched?" "Oh, whichever suits you!" The thing is that no-one had ever bothered to work it out. In the end, I decided that most of it was a Matrix/Valeyard lie.

'Small continuity points don't bother me: what bother me are basic mistakes like that, which usually come from a total lack of caring. I wouldn't normally accuse an individual, but because Eric was later so vociferously critical of the programme and of me, I will say this: make sure your own slate is clean before you start criticising other people's dirty slates! He really was very casual about it. You can't blame the writers, because they get given a brief.'

Interviewed by Stephen James Walker, David J Howe, Mark Stammers and Gordon Roxburgh in August 1989 for *The Frame* **Issue 13.**

ON HIS OUSTING FROM *DOCTOR WHO*:

'How do I feel about it as we sit here now? As we sit here now, I feel quite calm and unbothered about it. I suppose if I thought about it for a few minutes, I could work myself up into a bit of a lather again, but I think that's rather a waste of time. When it happened, I got cross. I felt I had been treated unfairly and badly. I thought I was a pawn in a game of publicity and power politics, played by Michael Grade. I thought that he had got to a point where he had criticised the show so much that he had to be seen to do something, and the most overt thing he could do was to change the Doctor, because that's the one thing that would get all the publicity. It seems perverse that the Doctor wanted to stay, so he had to go, but the producer wanted to go, so he had to stay. John Nathan-Turner was very keen to move on to something else and wasn't allowed to. That strikes me as the action of someone who doesn't have the programme's best interests at heart.

COLIN BAKER: IN HIS OWN WORDS

'Having said all that, this all happened six months ago now. I had had a career for fifteen years before I became involved in *Doctor Who*, and I hope most sincerely that I will have one for another fifteen years afterwards. I am enjoying the play I am doing now.

'Yes, I shall miss the programme. But my connection with it will remain, as long as people like you and all the other smashing people I have met through *Doctor Who* maintain an interest.'

Interviewed by Michael Sibley in May 1987 for *The Colin Baker Interview*.

'At the end of *The Trial of a Time Lord*, we left the studio with a party, I had a nice time and we all said, "See you next year." I kept in close contact with John Nathan-Turner because, as you know, we did the conventions and things together. Then when the time came for the option on my contract to be taken up by the BBC, which was the end of October, he rang up and said, "I don't even know if we're doing the programme. They haven't even told me if I'm producing it next year, so I can't take up the option at the moment." So the option lapsed. Then, at the beginning of November, he rang me up and said, "Look, I've got a bit of bad news. The programme is going ahead but Michael Grade has instructed me to replace the Doctor."

'I was quite surprised by this! You know that sort of blood-draining-from-your-veins kind of feeling? John said he had told them that he thought it was a dreadful mistake and he wanted me to play the Doctor, but they were adamant. "Grade says three years is quite enough. He's said nothing derogatory about your performance, he thinks you are fine, but he thinks a new Doctor will give the programme a boost. I have pointed out that you have not done three years, and that you have done only one and a half seasons, but he remains adamant that that is long enough and it's time for a change." So there was nothing much I could do about it.

'Three days later, I got phone call from the BBC asking me to go to America with Grade to publicise *Doctor Who*. I thought that was rather odd, but I agreed to do it on the basis that I might be able to find out some more. However, Grade avoided me very cleverly throughout the whole time I was there. All I've ever got from anybody – and I've seen Jonathan Powell, who is Head of Series and Serials – is that they were happy with my performance but that they had decided that three years was enough.

'It goes against what I was asked to do, when I started the show, by David Reid – Powell's predecessor. He asked me if I was prepared to commit myself to the programme for *four* years. Having said yes in 1983 to four years of 26 episodes a year, I actually did one year of 26 episodes (or the equivalent), nothing at all the next year, and just fourteen episodes the next. Then I was unceremoniously bundled out. So I felt fairly aggrieved.'

Interviewed by Robert Cope in September 1987 for *Doctor Who Bulletin* Issue 48.

'I would be dishonest if I was to pretend that suddenly it wasn't the best job on television, because it was. I had a brief spell when I was allowed to play with the best toy there was. And like any little child that has had his biggest and best toy snatched away from him before he is finished with it, I was a little bit *cross*. But my life goes on. I suppose my feelings about *Doctor Who* remain as they were. I loved doing it. I had a great time. Perhaps it is just as well that it was taken away from me. I have done far better than I thought I would this year with the play I am doing. Maybe somebody's done me a favour in some way. I miss it, though.

'I was very irritated about the treatment I received. I could have done what was suggested, which was to pretend that I was leaving for personal reasons, but I don't like to tell lies. I like to tell the truth. It may have been a mistake, I suppose, as I have to talk about it now.'

Interviewed on stage in September 1987 at the *Doctor Who* Appreciation Society's PanoptiCon 8 convention in London.

'I feel that "unlucky" is the word that sums up my tenure, really. A combination of Michael Grade – who changed the schedules, changed the length of the programme, cancelled it in the middle, then put it on after *Roland Rat – The Series* and opposite *The A-Team* – together with the whole Eric Saward business, the upheaval that the BBC itself was going through at that time ... all those things conspired to make it very difficult. In a way, it was more frustrating than anything else. If someone had said, "Look, we think you're awful and we're replacing you," I would have had to live with that. But when I know it was just a combination of circumstances, and I was powerless to do anything about it ...

'You know, if someone else had been cast as the Doctor in 1984 and I was doing it *now*, I'd still be in that part for years to come.'

Interviewed by Stephen James Walker, David J Howe, Mark Stammers and Gordon Roxburgh in August 1989 for *The Frame* Issue 13.

COLIN BAKER: IN HIS OWN WORDS

ON HIS CAREER AFTER *DOCTOR WHO*:

'The first thing I was offered was a tour of a play called *Corpse* – a brilliant play, set at the turn of the century, in which I got to play murderous twin brothers. It meant a number of quick changes, in that I exited through one door as one brother and, as the set changed, returned as the other. Chaotic at first. That went into the West End for five months and covered the full year after *Doctor Who*.

'Then I did panto at Wimbledon with Dennis Waterman and Rula Lenska. Immediately after that, I did another play, *Deathtrap*, with Anita Harris. Then I did 65 programmes for the Children's Channel, a satellite station. These were co-produced by Longmans, the book publishers, and were scholarly in a *Sesame Street* style, which was great fun. I loved doing that.

'I then did four months of *Run for Your Wife* with Terry Scott, following which I directed a play called *Bazaar and Rummage*. Then it was straight into the *Doctor Who* stage show. So I've been busy!'

Interviewed by Kevin Taylor in 1989 for *Timelines* Issue 3.

ON THE STAGE PLAY *DOCTOR WHO THE ULTIMATE ADVENTURE*:

'Everyone says it must be pretty painful going back as the Doctor after my untimely removal, but it's not, as I never really took personal umbrage at what happened. It was just an irritant in the same way as if a headmaster at school was to say that one's half holiday was cancelled. One feels a bit cross about it.

'My decision to take the part was based on exactly the same criteria as any other work on offer. What else is available? What would be the enjoyment factor therein? What would be the financial rewards thereof? This role had the advantage of my already knowing the character. I'd seen Jon Pertwee in the show and thought it would be fun to do, because the cast were all enthusiastic and inventive. I've been proved right; it is great fun.

'I think my new costume is very successful. I wanted a complete break from the previous image and to have something that was going to be cool on stage *and* say something different: add another layer to the Doctor, if you like. But for very understandable reasons, Mark Furness, the producer, said he wanted a costume as close as possible to the essence, if not the actuality, of the original. They borrowed the BBC costume for the brochure photographs, as they hadn't made the new one at that point.

'The only brief I gave the designer was that it must be lightweight, because of my being two hours on stage under heavy lights. Even now, it's still heavier than I'd have liked, but I think Yvonne Milnes, the costume designer, did an excellent job. The trousers are similar to the ones I wore on TV. I've got red shoes instead of green, and another jazzy waistcoat, this time with pineapple buttons. But the *tour de force* is the coat, which I think is much better than the TV one. It's got blue in it, which I couldn't have for television because of the electronic effects, and I think the colours blend rather nicely. Worth seeing, folks!'

Interviewed by Dominic May in June 1989 for *Doctor Who Magazine* tenth anniversary special.

'Jon Pertwee had been playing the part for ten weeks before I took over, and Terrance Dicks, who wrote the script, wrote it specifically with Jon in mind. So he sent me a copy of the script and asked me what kind of changes I thought I'd want. When I'd read it, I rang him up and – to his great relief, I think – said that there were very few changes I would make. Basically, the Doctor is the Doctor, and it's the mere fact that I'm saying the lines instead of Jon that makes it different. The voices are very different.

'The lines that have been changed are about one or two percent of the script. "Reverse the polarity of the neutron flow," which is a Jon Pertwee trademark line, has been changed, and there are things that've been added in, some by me and some by Terrance Dicks, in consultation with each other. It's a shift of emphasis rather than a change of dialogue. I mean, I'm my usual kind of bumptious, arrogant self, and he was his usual kind of dignified, courteous self, but we're saying more or less the same lines.'

Interviewed by Trevor Ramsay in June 1989 for *Time Lord* Issue 4.

'I saw the show in Wimbledon, shortly after it opened, and I wasn't particularly impressed. Then I saw it again four or five weeks later, in Bristol, and it was much, much better. Even when I saw it the first time, though, when it was a bit of a shambles, I realised – with no disrespect whatsoever to Jon – that it was particularly suited to my Doctor. That's because my Doctor is a "stage" Doctor – he's flamboyant and over the top. Jon's dignified portrayal was brilliant on television, but as the centre of a busy show, he had a problem, and the script didn't serve him as well as perhaps it ought to have done. My Doctor, on the other hand, can rush around and do a few things, and I thought, "Maybe I can contribute something to this." So that was one reason why I decided to do it. Obviously the negotiations came into it too – the fact that I was well paid for it. And it fitted in with all the other things that I wasn't doing!

'When I was rehearsing, we took the opportunity to make a few changes to the script. In the swordfight, for example, I wanted to have the Doctor saying, "Now, if you go over there …" – and as he pointed over there with his sword, he deflected one blow – "Or is it over that way?" – and he deflected another one – so that he was totally oblivious that he was actually having a swordfight. Unfortunately, there wasn't enough time to work that out, so in the end we played it as if I was such an expert swordsman that I could actually have a conversation with somebody while fighting behind my back. I mean, it's a terrible gag, but it was a compromise.

'The other scene I particularly wanted to change was the one with the flying ant creatures. When I watched it, I couldn't believe that the Doctor just walked off, consigning these things to a grisly death at the hands of the Cybermen. So now I play it as if I'm trying to stop them from sacrificing themselves, saying, "No, no." And then, as I run off, I say, "Thank you." Otherwise, it made the Doctor look totally callous, actually asking them to fly down and get themselves killed!

'Since rehearsals, we haven't changed anything, apart from the small variations I put in nightly, which keep the rest of the cast on their toes! I see myself, in a show like this, a bit like a soloist in an orchestra. I mean, I've got to play the tune – I've got to say the words – but I'm allowed a little licence. I think the part, and the show, benefit if the Doctor's slightly unpredictable and does something different every now and again. For instance, the business with Zog has grown tremendously since I started doing it.

'The audiences have varied enormously. Usually, if you open to a certain advance booking at a theatre, you can gauge from that how you're going to do during the week, because you know a certain proportion of people will just turn up on the night. With this show, though, it seems we always open quite low, then gradually build and build and build. By the end of the week, we're doing quite well, because the word's got round, but then we go on somewhere else. We just haven't been able to sell it properly in advance, and I don't know why. The hot summer might have had a lot to do with it, or perhaps people have the wrong impression of what *Doctor Who* will be like on stage.

'I learnt quite quickly that I either spend twenty minutes signing autographs at the stage door, uncomfortably jammed against a brick wall, or I formalise it. So I formalise it, and sit at a table in the foyer to sign a few autographs after each performance. Mums, dads and children come up, and the comment I've had consistently from parents is, "Well, we only came because, you know, little Jason wanted to see the show, but we've had a wonderful time, we've loved it."

'Funnily enough, doing this tour has helped to redress the balance. I've had young kids hugging me, in tears, saying, "Why can't you come back on TV? You'll always be my Doctor." I expect every other Doctor has had the same thing, but I personally had never experienced it before. Families, too, have come up and said, "You will always be our Doctor." OK, that's probably because I just happened to be the one who was in it when they started watching, I realise that. But it's nice to know there are people out there who feel that way.'

Interviewed by Stephen James Walker, David J Howe, Mark Stammers and Gordon Roxburgh in August 1989 for *The Frame* **Issue 12.**

Character – The Sixth Doctor

'The light that burns twice as bright burns half as long, and you have burned so very, very brightly ...'

So says Doctor Eldon Tyrell to his android creation Roy Batty in the classic Ridley Scott film *Blade Runner*. Looking back, it seems that the analogy could apply equally well to Colin Baker's Doctor – the most incandescent of the first seven incarnations, but also the shortest-lived.

Peter Davison, the fifth Doctor, had decided in May 1983 that he would not wish to renew his contract when it expired toward the end of production on the following season of stories, the twenty-first in *Doctor Who*'s history. Thus the producer, John Nathan-Turner, was again faced with the difficult task of finding a new leading man. His first instinct was to go for a contrast – a sixth Doctor who would be as different from the fifth as the fifth had been from the fourth – and he was quoted in the press as saying that he was looking for someone older and more obviously eccentric. 'We do want to make the next one a little more eccentric than Peter's been,' he confirmed at a November 1983 convention in Chicago, USA. 'To make him a little more crotchety and perhaps give him a kind of acid wit, which we think would make a nice change.'

He had in fact had Colin Baker in mind since the previous summer, as he later explained in an interview with Peter Haining:

'I got to know Colin during the time he played Maxil, a Gallifreyan guard captain, in a Davison-era story called *Arc of Infinity*. Then we met up again later when we were invited to the wedding reception of my assistant floor manager, Lynn Richards, with whom Colin and his wife Marion had become very friendly. The *Doctor Who* crowd were sitting together on the grass, having a good time, and for the whole afternoon, Colin kept us thoroughly entertained. Even though I wasn't actively looking for a new Doctor then, I thought that if he could hold the attention of fifteen hard-bitten show business professionals for hours, then he could do the same with a television audience.'

Strangely enough, even though she was unaware that Peter Davison was planning to leave the series, Lynn Richards later went to see Nathan-Turner to suggest that Baker would make an ideal candidate for the next Doctor. Little did she know that he was already the hot favourite for the role!

In an August 1989 interview for *The Frame*, Baker recalled how he had first been approached to play the part of the sixth Doctor, and how the character had then been developed:

'John Nathan-Turner rang me up one afternoon and said he'd like to see me. I went in to the office, thinking that he was going to try to talk me into opening a fête or something, and he said, "I'm not offering you the part, but Peter Davison is leaving and I wondered if you would be interested in playing the Doctor?" So I replied, very casually, "Oh, yeah, I wouldn't mind." He said, "Well, I'm going to give you a few tapes and ask you to go away and watch some of the earlier Doctors. We'll meet again in a week's time, and you can tell me how you think *you'd* like to play him." And that's what we did.

'I can't remember all the stories I was given, but they included *The Space Museum*, *The War Games*, *Carnival of Monsters*, *Pyramids of Mars* and *Warriors of the Deep*. Anyway, I watched them all several times, then I went back to see John. He asked me what I thought, and I said, "Well, I would obviously play the part as a kind of distillation of myself, as all the others have done, but one thing I would like to bring out is the fact that the Doctor is an alien – he's not a human being, even though he looks like one."

'I thought it would be quite nice if sometimes he didn't behave in the way we would expect him to behave. So, on one day, if a person was mown down in front of him, he might just step over them and ask somebody the time; on another day, he might go into terrible paroxysms of grief about a sparrow falling out of a tree. Obviously we'd have to be able to explain why, and what it was that was concerning the Doctor; I just didn't want him to behave in an obvious, sentimental, approachable way. I wanted him to be a little bit unapproachable. He could get extremely angry about something – a build-up followed by a sudden explosion, so that the rage might seem to be about one thing when it was actually about something that had happened two episodes ago, perhaps. I think there's a danger with this kind of programme that it's all too pat, all too obvious.

'Now, John liked this idea, and in the end he pushed it further than probably I would have had the courage to do, by making the Doctor *so* unapproachable in my first story, *The Twin Dilemma*. You had to wait for four episodes before finding out if this person had anything remotely *likeable* in him, and I think that was very brave, especially as it was the end of a season. I like that kind of bravery in television. It's all too easy to play safe all the time.

'So that was one thing I wanted. I also saw the Doctor as being rather austere, dressed in black. I wanted a black velvet costume, but it was pointed out to me that the Master had got in there first, so I couldn't have it. And the one aspect of my Doctor that I suppose I do regret is the costume. It works for me now, but I would have liked it to have been something different. Really, though, the costume was, to me, a very unimportant part of the whole enterprise. This was partly because I was inside it looking out – everybody else had to look at it, therefore it meant a lot to them!

'I also suggested that the Doctor should tell excruciatingly bad jokes – you know, the puns. The idea of using quotes was mine, as well. I wanted to use quotes from the English language – obviously, as we were making the programme in English! – but also I wanted to make things up that sounded like quotes from other cultures. So it might be a Venusian quote, or a quote from Aldarberan 4. I thought that was a nice idea.

'There was another thing, too. I have a little bee in my bonnet about the English language. It's the richest language in the world in terms of the amount of words available, but gradually we're losing most of them. I wanted there to be at least half a dozen words in each episode that viewers would have to rush off and look up, because they didn't know the meaning. If you are really hooked on a character and he uses a long word that you don't understand, then you'll go and find out what it means: it's extending people's vocabularies, which I think is nice.

'All these ideas John Nathan-Turner liked, and we both went upstairs to see David Reid, who was then the Controller in charge of BBC1. Fortunately he was watching a Test Match on TV at the time, and I asked, "How's Botham doing?", or something. He said, "Oh, do you like cricket?" and we chatted about cricket for twenty minutes – to JN-T's total perplexity, because he knew nothing about cricket! After that, we talked about the role of the Doctor for a minute or two, and David Reid said, "Well, I think that's great, excellent." Apparently the fact that I liked cricket did it for me!

'I was then asked if I would sign a four-year option, because Peter had left after three years and they wanted to get a bit more continuity. I said, "I'd like that very much!" – I was thinking, "Four years, 26 episodes a year, wonderful!"

'And that's really how it all happened!'

As is apparent from this account, *Doctor Who*'s then script editor, Eric Saward, made relatively little contribution during the meetings when the sixth Doctor's character was being conceived. He now explains that he did not feel inspired to come up with ideas, as he was unhappy with the casting of Colin Baker as the Doctor, considering that although he was a competent character actor, he lacked the screen presence required.

Saward recalls that he took on board Nathan-Turner's idea of making the new Doctor more crotchety and more at odds with the world than the previous one, and also that an attempt was made to reintroduce more humour into the part. Again, however, he considers that Baker lacked the lightness of touch required to bring the humour across on screen.

'The other thing that we were going to try to introduce,' explains Saward, 'which just didn't work, was a sort of Holmesian ability to make extraordinary deductions. Just as Sherlock Holmes might say something like, "I see that you came via Marylebone Road," and then explain that he had deduced this from the distinctive clay on the person's boots, the Doctor would have this wonderful ability to make sense out of highly improbable things. In the real world, of course, it just wouldn't work – the whole of London happens to be built on clay! But that's the sort of thing we were going to try to do. Unfortunately, because of problems with scripts and so on, there were aspects that just got left behind. It takes quite a lot of time to work that sort of thing out; ideally it should be firmly locked into the story.'

When asked by *The Frame* if he felt that he had been given an unusually large say in the development of his Doctor's character, Baker replied:

'Well, in terms of the shape of my character at the beginning, it's not that I had any say as such, it's just that they asked me how I would play it, I told them, and they liked it. I think you'd have to do that with any Doctor. There's no point in hiring an actor for that part and then telling him to play it in a way that is different from how he would naturally approach it. He's got to play it his way.

'After that, though, I certainly wasn't consulted by Eric Saward about scripts, and if ever I made any suggestions about scripts, he didn't respond very warmly to that. He was of the "writers write, directors direct and actors act" school, which to a certain extent I am myself, but I think that when you've got a long-running programme with a central actor, eventually he's going to have more input potential than new people coming in from outside. I could never make any headway with that, though.'

The sixth Doctor's 'unapproachable' debut in *The Twin Dilemma* came as a shock to many of the series' viewers, who had grown accustomed to Peter Davison's sensitive, charming portrayal. Following his regeneration, the Time Lord was seen to suffer a number of violent fits – at one point actually attempting to strangle his companion, Peri – and even during his more lucid periods he appeared to experience a rapid succession of different moods, ranging from disconsolate self-pity through cringing cowardice to narcissistic bravado. Viewers were left uncertain as to whether these bewildering switches of temperament were simply after-effects of the regeneration itself or whether they would continue to be apparent in later stories.

The sheer unpredictability of the sixth Doctor was, indeed, the quality that Colin Baker often chose to emphasise in his earliest *Doctor Who* interviews. 'He has many facets to his personality,' he told the fanzine *Arkensword* in 1984, 'and, bearing in mind that he is an alien, some are difficult for humans to understand. When he's a little bit curt to his assistant. Impatient. Irascible. I think that these are very important aspects for the Doctor to have. For him to behave exactly the same way as a human behaves would be a shame. It would be wasting the character ... He's not a slavish follower of anybody. He is prone to reacting very differently to exactly the same situation, according to the way he feels. The one thing he'll always do is to champion the cause of the weak. In casual conversation he won't always be polite. That's an Earthly concept. He can't be bothered with the social graces.'

Talking to the magazine *Space Voyager* shortly before starting work on *Attack of the Cybermen*, the opening story of the twenty-second season, the actor drew a contrast between this alien unpredictability and the comparatively staid behaviour of more conventional heroes: 'My Doctor will be insatiably curious, intolerant, waspish, and kind but cruel ... Many times he won't react with the emotions expected. As a rule, the baddies are the more interesting parts. The Doctor is the great exception to that. He is a hero, but not in the bland mould. Baddies generally are best because the writers have found it more interesting to write about people who break the rules, but the Doctor makes and breaks his own rules. He is a galactic buccaneer. Neither good nor bad. A bit of a meddler.'

Not for this Doctor the role of a passive observer, staying quietly in the background until forced to act. On the contrary, as signalled by the garish, tasteless costume that John Nathan-Turner decreed he should wear, he seemed actively to court attention; and the overblown, oratorical way in which he often expressed himself was indicative of an ostentatious, self-important personality.

The mood changes he experienced immediately after his regeneration became less violent and erratic as time went by but never abated entirely, making him a highly capricious character. Flamboyant, pretentious, grandiloquent, overbearing, petulant and egotistical: all these adjectives could be reasonably used to describe typical aspects of his behaviour. With these traits in mind, some critics have ventured the assessment that he was 'unpleasant' and 'unlikeable', but this overlooks the fact that on many occasions he also displayed such admirable qualities as kindness, compassion, humour, courage and moral outrage at the many injustices he encountered. Following the events of *The Two Doctors*, he even became a vegetarian! It could be seen as a tribute to Colin Baker's abilities as an actor that he was able to assimilate so many diverse and apparently contradictory idiosyncrasies and mould them together into a three-dimensional (or should that be four-dimensional?), consistent and believable character.

Another common criticism made of the sixth Doctor is that, particularly during Season 22, he appeared to possess a rather violent streak, frequently resorting to the use of force to resolve problematic situations – for example, shooting Cybermen with a gun in *Attack of the Cybermen*, causing some of his opponents to be killed with poisonous vines in *Vengeance on Varos* and physically tackling and suffocating the character Shockeye in *The Two Doctors*. The introduction of a running thread of black humour was also thought by some commentators to have misfired when the Doctor was seen to crack jokes over the bodies of dead and injured adversaries. Rather than fostering an air of alien aloofness, it was argued, this merely made him appear callous.

Colin Baker was generally unmoved by such objections. 'I personally would probably go a bit further myself,' he said in a 1984 interview for the fanzine *Time Watcher*. 'I'm undecided, to be honest. John Nathan-Turner is very keen that the Doctor should not be a violent person, and of course I agree with that. But I think that it's sometimes naive to expect that one can get out of every situation without being placed in a position where one might have to be violent, or to use violence.

'I think that if one sanitises violence, if one cleans it up too much, it has the effect of conditioning people to it. They become so used to seeing people being shot and falling over and nothing messy happening that it makes violence seem acceptable. Whereas, despite what the critics say, directors who show blood pumping out and severed organs dragging across the ground, things that are horrific and unpleasant to look at, are at least showing what violence really is. Violence is horrible. But it's maybe true that in *Doctor Who* we're dealing in an area that is a bit removed from first-degree naturalism, so it's better if we stay away from showing that kind of direct effect of violence. I think it's always better if the Doctor can get himself out of a situation by using the mind.'

On other occasions, the actor was rather less equivocal. 'I am quite fond of violence,' he told the audience at a US *Doctor Who* convention in 1985. 'I like it a lot. Some people were appalled at the vicious way in which I disposed of the Cyber Controller in *Attack of the Cybermen*. I wanted to go much further, but they wouldn't let me. I wanted to stand over him pumping machine gun bullets into him for hours ... green stuff all over the walls. But they said, "No, that's going too far; three or four will do quite nicely, thank you."'

While remarks like this were made partly tongue-in-cheek, Baker clearly relished the more physical aspects of the role. This was something on which he had commented when discussing his interpretation of the Doctor's character in a 1984 interview for the magazine *Fantasy Empire*:

'Doctor Who is neither a good guy nor a bad guy. He's an apart guy. He has a very strict code. He's always on the side of goodness in the universe, but you couldn't say he was being saintly. He's very rude to people, and apparently quite heartless, although he's not really.

'I think in order to play the Doctor, an actor has to draw on himself very largely. I think the reason John Nathan-Turner asked me to play the part is that he saw things in me that he thought I could usefully bring to it ... An interest in cats, a sense of the ridiculous, a sense of chivalry. I believe in a lot of the great values of chivalry, like a sort of a cross between the Dragonriders of Pern and William Tell ... I hope my Doctor will be cerebral.

CHARACTER – THE SIXTH DOCTOR

I certainly want him to be the brightest there is around.

'When John Nathan-Turner spoke to me, he asked me how I felt about the physical stuff, and I said I loved doing it. I've done stage fighting in Shakespeare and all that. There's not a lot of swordplay in *Doctor Who*. I think it might be nice to have a fight between the Master and the Doctor. I'd like to get involved in one of those. I love the physical stuff, and I want to climb the walls and fight the villains.'

Season 22 was, for *Doctor Who*, unusually grim and downbeat in tone, and the depiction of a somewhat harder Doctor can be seen as merely symptomatic of this more general shift in the series' emphasis, the responsibility for which must rest primarily with the production team. The on-screen realisation of a character such as the Doctor is inevitably a fusion of the actor's own qualities with the writers' conception, as reflected in the action and dialogue laid down in the scripts. As Baker put it in his interview for *Fantasy Empire*, this synthesis of performer and script is 'a sort of marriage, if you like. Your own personality plus the page in front of you that tells you what the Doctor says and what he does. All somehow gradually combining over a period of time into something different.'

It should also be noted that the Time Lord's earlier incarnations had been by no means averse to becoming involved in direct physical action: the first Doctor had gleefully indulged in a bout of 'fisticuffs' with the mute assassin Ascaris in *The Romans*; the third had frequently overpowered assailants using Venusian karate; the fourth had launched violent assaults on a number of opponents in stories such as *The Seeds of Doom* and *The Deadly Assassin*; and there are many other examples that could be quoted. So it can be argued that the sixth Doctor's use of force was not an entirely unprecedented departure from established characterisation. The issue was really one of degree.

Having initially studied a number of his predecessors' stories on video, Colin Baker did make a conscious effort to include some of their traits in his own performance, as he told *Arkensword* in 1984:

'It's a lot made up with ingredients of the previous Doctors. Pertwee's adventure sense. I like that, the derring-do, swinging from ropes, and I want Eric Saward to write in things like that, because I enjoy it. Hartnell's irascibility. Tom Baker's irreverence, up to a point. The one thing I don't want to do is belittle the monsters. I think that if you start joking and clowning around when being threatened by a Cyberman or a Dalek, it's so easy to make them look as though they are not very threatening. When analysed, a Dalek is a very difficult thing to be frightened of, because it can't even climb a flight of stairs. And once you start sticking jelly babies in the end of their nozzles, then it makes life difficult, because it has to work for the audience.'

Another influence was Baker's love of cats. He adopted the cat as the symbol of the sixth Doctor's persona, as reflected in various badges that he wore on his coat lapel, and often quoted Rudyard Kipling: 'I am the cat that walks by himself, and all places are the same to me.' (This is actually a paraphrasing of lines from the poem *The Cat that Walked by Himself*: 'The Cat. He walked by himself, and all places were alike to him.') 'Cats,' said the actor in a 1985 interview for the *Doctor Who* Appreciation Society's magazine *TARDIS*, 'do what *they* want to do, *when* they want to do it, and it may fit in sometimes with what you want to do, but that's never a consideration, and I think that's a bit like the Doctor.'

In another 1985 interview, for the fanzine *Fan Aid 2*, Baker was asked how he saw the character of the sixth Doctor developing in future stories. 'I'm afraid it sounds like a cop-out,' he replied, 'but there is no answer to that question. I see it developing, full stop. I wouldn't wish to prejudice that development by saying how I think it should go, because that would imply that the job of the writer and the producer is merely that of a cipher – which is not the case. We work together in a kind of symbiotic way. Very rarely are conscious decisions about development made. It comes out of ideas and developments of ideas.'

In later years, however, the actor asserted that there *had* been a long-term plan for development of the sixth Doctor's character. Talking to the 1989 fanzine *Kroton* about the irritation he had felt at his premature expulsion from the series, he said:

'It was very frustrating, because we had envisaged an overall plan over a few years of how we could learn more about this Doctor, and didn't want to give too much away in the first few seasons. We wanted people to be a little unsure about this person, and then gradually find out "Ah, he's not really like that, that's because of this." All sorts of things and clever nuances that we never had a chance to explore. That's life though.'

In a 1990 interview for the *Myth Makers 19* video, released by Reeltime Pictures, the actor again spoke of his long-term plan for the development of the character, and gave the following literary analogy:

'I always like to compare the idea to that of the character Darcy in *Pride and Prejudice*. For the first 35 per cent of the book you hate him, then you grudgingly come to like him, and then by the end of the book you think he is the best person in it. That's sort of what we wanted to do with the Doctor.'

A degree of progression in the Doctor's character was certainly apparent between the end of the twenty-second season and the beginning of the twenty-third, when the series returned after the 1985/86 production hiatus with the fourteen-part story *The Trial of a Time Lord*. Apart from during a short period when his sanity was called into question for the purposes of a sub-plot, the Doctor as seen in this season was noticeably mellower and less aggressive than before, again reflecting a more general shift in the series' emphasis (and incidentally providing an effective contrast to the season's major villain, the Valeyard – a character intended literally to personify the dark side of the Doctor's nature.)

To a casual observer, the sixth Doctor might still have appeared to be little more than a rather egotistical adventurer with a poor taste in clothes and a tendency towards over-reaction and brash theatricality. Beneath this facade, however, Colin Baker had by this time succeeded in establishing a deeper level to the character, making him more interesting and agreeable. He was now clearly capable of compassion, whilst outwardly continuing to appear off-hand and detached, as illustrated by his habit of offering allusive quotations rather than making direct statements. A distinction was drawn between his superficial image as perceived by others and his true underlying qualities, which were gentler and more concerned. 'I am known as the Doctor,' he would often announce, whereas his predecessors had been content to say simply, 'I am the Doctor.'

This softening of the sixth Doctor's demeanour was very evident in his relationship with his companion, Peri. Up until this point, their conversations had been characterised by ill-tempered bickering and petty point-scoring, Peri displaying a distinct tendency to whinge and whine – a situation that John Nathan-Turner attributed to a lack of ingenuity on the writers' part, as he told *Doctor Who Magazine* in an interview published in May 1986:

'There is a problem that writers face in terms of the show, which is that the initial TARDIS scene between the companion and the Doctor is inevitably preoccupied with its position in setting out where you're going and why you're going there and so forth, in order to lay the foundations for a particular story. One obvious way of getting out of that is by conflict, and often a writer will lapse into unnecessary conflict in order to get that information over. That is just a dramatic device, and one that I would like to see less of.'

In *The Trial of a Time Lord*, this wish was fulfilled, as the Doctor and Peri appeared to be on much friendlier terms. Interviewed for *Doctor Who Magazine* some years later, actress Nicola Bryant explained how she and Colin Baker had modified their performances, sometimes playing scenes against the way they had been written, to help achieve this effect:

'When we came back after so long, we felt we couldn't have the same relationship. We would have parted company on bad terms – either I would have left or he would have dropped me off. The relationship settled down and we had to establish that although they may have their differences, they still cared for each other. Looking back, I think the constant bickering and fighting was taken too far.'

A further change occurred part-way through *The Trial of a Time Lord* when Peri was written out of the series and Bonnie Langford was introduced as her successor, Melanie. Interviewed during a March 1987 convention at the University of Western Washington, USA, Colin Baker spoke of the Doctor's more demonstrative behaviour towards this new companion:

'One change, which was rather nice, was that I was able to be much more openly affectionate towards Mel than I had been towards Peri. This was because Bonnie was very young-looking and wasn't as voluptuous as Nicola, so nobody could misconstrue my actions as having a sexual connotation. If I had put my arm around Nicola and said, "Come on darling," people would have been very taken aback. Bonnie, though, had a kind of asexuality about her in the character of Melanie. As I'm much older than she is, and she's so very girlish, the relationship was obviously paternal or avuncular. So I was able, especially the way it was written, to give her the odd cuddle. That was always very difficult with Nicola's character, and I was constantly being asked by the directors to tone it down; there might have been some suggestion of hanky-panky in the TARDIS, and we couldn't have that! I think the relationship between Melanie and the sixth Doctor would have worked out very nicely, but sadly it was thwarted in its progression.'

It is perhaps ironic that just as Baker had refined his interpretation of the Doctor and succeeded in winning over many of the viewers who had been uncomfortable with his initial, rather more abrasive characterisation, any further development was abruptly forestalled by the BBC management's decision not to renew his contract. As he recalled in his interview for *The Frame*, he was asked to stay on for just the first four episodes of Season 24 to record a regeneration story, but declined to do so: 'I was offered the chance to do the first four episodes of the following season – that was actually a concession won by John – but I said, "Quite honestly, if I've got to leave, I want to leave now and start making a career." The analogy I've always used is that it's like your girlfriend giving you the push and saying, "But you can come back and spend a night with me next year!" It's just not on.'

This was not quite the end of the road for Colin Baker's portrayal of the sixth Doctor, however, as he returned in 1989 in the Mark Furness Ltd touring stage play *Doctor Who – The Ultimate Adventure*.

Many commentators felt that it was in this production that Baker was at his most assured and engaging yet in his portrayal of the Doctor. As one reviewer put it, 'He gives a great performance, which leaves you yearning for more.' This reflected the actor's own satisfaction with his return to the role, as he explained in his interview for *The Frame*:

'Doing this show has been like putting on a pair of comfy old slippers. I was a little alarmed at how easily I slipped into it again, and how much I enjoyed it, although it's rekindled old sadnesses as well. I won't feel particularly sad when it finishes, mind you, because I've done nearly a hundred performances, and that's enough. But it's been nice to play the part again. In a way, it's laid a ghost, it's added a coda. It's made me believe that my Doctor has a part in the scheme of things.'

In a 1990 interview for the fanzine *Skaro*, Baker looked back on his time in *Doctor Who* and offered the following summation of the sixth Doctor's character:

'I would describe him as embodying all the Doctor's traditional virtues – compassion, kindness, high principles, a crusading spirit and a desire to relieve oppression and deal with the oppressor – but at the same time tinged with arrogance, irritability and impatience, which I got a little bit from the first Doctor. He enjoyed the pursuit of the mind and did not find it necessary to display what he was feeling, and could therefore appear to the Earthling observer to be a little unfeeling. That doesn't mean he *was* unfeeling; he just didn't feel the necessity to display it.'

Controversial though it had been, the era of the sixth Doctor finished all too soon for the many viewers who had come to savour his effulgent, larger-than-life personality – truly a light burning bright.

Rewriting the Myth

Is good continuity important a fantasy-orientated series such as *Doctor Who*? Colin Baker certainly considered that it was, as he told the fanzine *The Colin Baker Interview* in 1987:

'I think it is important not to ignore it totally. I did fall out with the script editor, Eric Saward, on a couple of occasions. For instance, on *The Trial of a Time Lord*, I remember reading the script and saying, "Hang on a minute, Eric. As I recall, from watching the episodes before I came into the series, Peter's Doctor was made the Lord President of Gallifrey at the end of *The Five Doctors*, because of his actions in nobbling Borusa. Don't you think that if you're going to put the Lord President on trial, there should be some mention of that fact? Not only the fans but also the general viewers in this case are going to remember it." Eric's reply to that was, "What do you want me to do then?" I said, "Well, can't we write in a little scene where we explain that he is not the Lord President anymore?" So he put in two lines that short-circuited the problem.

'Yes, I do believe that continuity is very important. In the end, one has to recognise the fact that, of the five million people who watch *Doctor Who*, it is only a thousand or so who are going to examine it in detail, and the remainder are going to be perfectly happy. But I think I would agree with a lot of the fans, because I am often put in the position of going to conventions and having to make up excuses for all these things. Whenever I spotted anything in the script and it could be altered, I would alter it. I did not have as much input on scripts as Tom Baker did, but then he played the part for seven years. Towards the end, though, I was putting a few extra bits in.'

In fairness, it should be noted that the Doctor's status as President of the Time Lords was one of the points on which writers were specifically briefed during the initial planning meetings for *The Trial of a Time Lord*. It was suggested that an explanation might be included to the effect that there had been a change in Gallifrey's system of government during the Doctor's absence, and that consequently he had lost his former position. It seems however that this point must have been lost in the translation of the original ideas into script form.

Continuity was certainly not something which Eric Saward or John Nathan-Turner ignored during this period. On the contrary the sixth Doctor's era is often noted for the unusually large extent to which it drew on the series' own established mythology.

Saward, in common with previous script editors, considered that while continuity should not be accorded such an inordinately high priority that it got in the way of telling a good story, care should be taken to keep faith with the series' viewers by avoiding major discrepancies. Consequently he sometimes consulted on such matters with *Doctor Who* fan Ian Levine – whose input, made without payment or credit, he found extremely helpful – as did producer John Nathan-Turner.

Many new facts are learned about the Doctor himself during the eight stories of his sixth incarnation. His first adventure, *The Twin Dilemma*, shows how extreme and unpredictable the after-effects of regeneration can sometimes be, while his last, *The Trial of a Time Lord*, presents a distillation of all his darker aspects in the form of the Valeyard. In *The Two Doctors*, he is seen to suffer a psychic trauma when his second incarnation is apparently put to death, and later he communicates with his other persona telepathically across space.

Viewers are also introduced to a number of old acquaintances from earlier incidents not seen in the TV series. In *The Twin Dilemma*, there is Azmael, a retired Time Lord with whom the Doctor once spent a pleasant drunken evening beside a fountain on the planet Joconda; in *The Two Doctors*, it is revealed that he first met Joinson Dastari while attending an inaugural function as a representative of the Time Lords, before he fell from favour with them; in *Timelash*, the TARDIS materialises on Karfel, where the Doctor is honoured for having saved the population from a disaster during a visit in his third incarnation with Jo Grant and another companion; and in the Vervoid segment of *The Trial of a Time Lord*, he arrives on the space-liner *Hyperion III* too late to save the life of his old friend Hallet, an undercover law enforcement agent, but still in time to come to the aid of Commodore 'Tonker' Travers, a man for whom he apparently caused some trouble during a previous encounter.

In *The Two Doctors*, the second Doctor and Jamie are seen to be undertaking a mission for the Time Lords – something that surprised many fans as, during his own era, this Doctor had not even admitted his origins until the end of his last adventure, *The War Games*. This is an example of a change occurring as a result of a misunderstanding on the part of the writer. Robert Holmes had always been under the impression that it was the second Doctor who had routinely undertaken missions for his own people, as the price of his continued freedom, when in actual fact it was the *third* Doctor who had done so. Some interesting theories have been advanced by fans to account for the apparent inconsistency that arose from this. One ingenious explanation is that after the momentous events of the 1973 story *The Three Doctors*, it was not only the third Doctor who was rewarded by the Time Lords by being given a new dematerialisation circuit for his TARDIS, but also the first and second Doctors, by each being allowed a completely new lease of life. This would certainly account for some of the developments seen in *The Two Doctors*, and also for some of those in the earlier anniversary story *The Five Doctors*, but it is only one of many possible explanations.

The Doctor's trusty TARDIS features prominently in a number of the stories of this period. In *Attack of the Cybermen*, the ship temporarily discards its familiar police box form after the Doctor repairs its chameleon circuits, appearing first as a decorated cupboard, then as a pipe organ and later as an ornate gateway; in *Vengeance on Varos*, it becomes stranded in a galactic void owing to a fault in the transitional elements, requiring the trans/power system to be relined with zeiton 7; in *The Two Doctors*, viewers learn that a TARDIS's briode-nebuliser has to be primed with the Rassilon Imprimatur – a print of symbiotic nuclei within the physiology of every Time Lord – before it can be used; in the same story, the sixth Doctor is heard to express considerable envy on discovering that his second incarnation is now able to operate his TARDIS with a Stattenheim remote control unit, provided by the Time Lords; and in *Timelash*, the ship is used as a deflector shield to neutralise a Bandril missile.

Along with the introduction of a number of new characters who would go on to become returning characters – the evil arms dealer Sil and his fellow Mentors, the exiled Time Lord chemist the Rani and the intergalactic mercenary Sabalom Glitz – the sixth Doctor's era saw the return and development of a number of well-established adversaries from previous seasons.

Attack of the Cybermen could almost be considered a sequel to the Sixties classic *The Tomb of the Cybermen*, as it sees the Doctor being forcibly returned to that story's setting, the tomb complex on the planet Telos. Here he has a new battle with the creatures' ultimate leader, the Cyber Controller, who has apparently recovered from the damage inflicted upon him at the end of his debut story. This time, viewers also meet Telos's original inhabitants, the Cryons – creatures who can exist only in extreme cold – with whom Lytton, the mercenary first encountered working for the Daleks in the fifth Doctor story *Resurrection of the Daleks*, has now allied himself. The Cybermen's plan turns out to involve the use of a time ship, captured from another race, in order to crash Halley's Comet into the Earth and thereby prevent the destruction in 1986 of their original home planet Mondas, as seen in the first Cyberman story *The Tenth Planet*. In the end, however, their scheme is defeated and the Controller finally destroyed.

It has become traditional over the years for subtle – and sometimes not-so-subtle – changes to be made in the Cybermen's appearance for each new adventure. *Attack of the Cybermen* is one exception to the rule, however, as this time, the creatures' costumes are almost exactly the same as in their previous outing, *The Five Doctors*. The only variations are provided by a black-camouflaged Cyber Scout in the sequences set in the London sewers – the site of the Cybermen's base on Earth, as they were in the 1968 adventure *The Invasion* – and by the Cyber Controller, who looks somewhat bloated in comparison with his underlings and whose helmet is notable for having a domed top and a lack of any side handles, echoing some of the distinctive features of the original helmet as seen in *The Tomb of the Cybermen*. Director Matthew Robinson had also intended that the Cybermen seen on the surface of Telos should wear transparent, globe-shaped space helmets over their heads, but this idea was dropped at a late stage as it was found that the globes had a tendency to steam up and impede the actors' movements.

The Doctor's arch-enemy the Master returned to plague him once more in *The Mark of the Rani* – with no explanation given for his miraculous escape from the apparently fatal predicament in which he was last seen at the end of the Season 21 story *Planet of Fire*. His powers of hypnotism – somewhat neglected during the fifth Doctor's era – are very much in evidence here, as is his familiar tissue compression eliminator weapon, but his characteristically devious scheme is directed towards what seems – for him – a remarkably unambitious end. His main aim is simply to disrupt the course of Earth's history by thwarting the start of the industrial revolution – although in the process he also plans, as usual, to humiliate and kill the Doctor!

The Trial of a Time Lord has the Master setting his sights rather higher as, by revealing to the court the High Council's corrupt deal with the Valeyard, he contrives to bring about their downfall, creating insurrection on Gallifrey and leaving a power vacuum that he intends to fill. He has once again miscalculated, however, and ends up trapped inside his own TARDIS, lodged within the Matrix.

The Sontarans also reappear during the sixth Doctor's era, having their fourth on-screen skirmish with the Time Lord. Little new information is learned about them on this occasion, though, apart from the fact that they are vulnerable to attack with a chemical called coronic acid. They are still as bellicose as ever, still attempting to gain the secret of time travel – something that they were seen to have achieved in rudimentary form in Season 11's *The Time Warrior* and that they tried to take by force in Season 15's *The Invasion of Time* – and still locked in their seemingly endless intergalactic war with the shape-shifting Rutans, described on this occasion as 'the Rutan Host'.

No era of *Doctor Who* would be truly complete without at least one story featuring the series' most famous monsters, the dreaded Daleks. *Revelation of the Daleks* presents viewers with two different Dalek factions: one – with the traditional grey livery – loyal to the Supreme Dalek on their home planet Skaro, the other – with a new, white and gold colour scheme – created by Davros on the planet Necros to do his bidding. Continuity with previous Dalek stories is excellent, the splitting of the Daleks into two opposing blocs being a highly logical development after their earlier clashes with Davros, their progenitor.

The idea of Davros deliberately creating new mutants to serve as recruits for his Dalek army is also a fitting reference back to the creatures' origins on the radiation-soaked Skaro, and provides the opportunity for a particularly memorable image – that of the transparent, partly formed Dalek in the incubation room on Necros. The concept of a transparent Dalek had first appeared in David Whitaker's book *Doctor Who in an Exciting Adventure with the Daleks* – the novelisation of the Daleks' debut story from 1963/64 – but could not have been realised in the TV series at that time, so it is nice to see it reaching the screen here.

Another important development in *Revelation of the Daleks* is the scene where one of Davros's Daleks appears to hover some distance off the ground when exterminating the characters Natasha and Grigory, finally providing the answer to the age-old question as to how the Daleks can conquer a galaxy when they can't climb stairs!

Davros's own evolution is taken a stage further in this story. He is represented for the most part as a disembodied head within a life-support unit, which is actually just a decoy to fool potential assassins – although whether it is a clone or a projection or a mechanical automaton of some sort is never made entirely clear. When the real Davros finally appears, however, it is obvious that he has developed some previously unsuspected powers: he immobilises the assassin Orcini with a stream of blue lightning projected from his forefinger, and – like the Dalek in the incubation room – demonstrates an ability to hover effortlessly in mid-air. A rather more prosaic development occurs toward the end of the story when he has his remaining hand blown off by a burst of gunfire from Orcini's squire, Bostock!

Ever since they were devised in 1969 by writers Terrance Dicks and Malcolm Hulke, the Time Lords have been an increasingly important part of *Doctor Who*. Their contribution to the series' mythology is developed significantly during the sixth Doctor's era, and most notably in *The Trial of a Time Lord*. This is the third time the Doctor has been placed on trial by his own people; in *The War Games* he stood accused of interfering in the affairs of other planets, and in *The Deadly Assassin* he was erroneously charged with the President's assassination.

The trial takes place on a giant space station, into which the Doctor's TARDIS is drawn by the mental energy of the assembled Time Lords, and the evidence is presented on a huge screen linked to the Matrix – the computer that acts as the repository of all Time Lord knowledge, as established in *The Deadly Assassin* and expanded upon in a number of later adventures. In charge of the court is the Inquisitor, and presenting the case for the prosecution is the Valeyard.

REWRITING THE MYTH

At the beginning of the story, the Doctor learns that during his absence from Gallifrey, he has been deposed as President due to his neglect of his duties – the reference that Colin Baker had asked to have inserted, as mentioned at the start of this chapter. At first, he is told that the proceedings are merely an inquiry into his behaviour, ordered by the High Council. The charges are that he is guilty of conduct unbecoming a Time Lord, and that he has broken the First Law of Time – which appears to relate here to interference in the affairs of other planets, although at earlier points in the series' history it was the law that prevented a Time Lord from crossing his own time stream. The Valeyard considers that the sentence imposed upon the Doctor at his last trial – presumably a reference to the one in *The War Games* – was too lenient, and before long, he has had the inquiry changed into a formal trial, with the Doctor's present and future lives at stake if he is found guilty. Later, the charge is changed again, under Article 7 of Gallifreyan law, to one of genocide, the Doctor's own evidence having shown him destroying the Vervoid race in a future adventure. Clearly the Gallifreyan judicial process works rather differently from any here on Earth!

During the course of the trial, it becomes apparent that the Matrix is by no means as inviolable as its Keeper – a figure not featured or referred to in any previous story – asserts. The Master has gained access to it using a copy of the Key of Rassilon and, at his urging, Glitz tells the court that thieves from Andromeda had previously been stealing hi-tech secrets from it for some time, before their actions were finally discovered. The Doctor's trial is in fact part of an elaborate cover-up by the High Council to prevent anyone from finding out about the drastic measures they took to prevent their secrets from getting out; measures that involved moving Earth – the base for the Andromedans' operations – light years across space, devastating it with a fireball. As seen in the opening segment of the story, Earth is now known as Ravolox and inhabited by primitive peoples such as the Tribe of the Free. This continues the trend of previous Time Lord stories in suggesting that their race's hold on power – which the Doctor states has been absolute for ten million years – has had a highly corrupting influence.

Further features of the Matrix are observed in the closing stages of the story as the Doctor, Glitz and Mel enter it through the Seventh Door – a portal, situated just outside the courtroom, which is opened by placing the Key of Rassilon against a sensor pad – and as all three become caught up, along with the Master, in a fantasy domain created by the Valeyard – scenes highly reminiscent of those in *The Deadly Assassin*, also written by Robert Holmes, in which the Doctor battled another adversary within the Matrix.

Considering its relative brevity, the sixth Doctor's era saw some significant changes taking place in, and some important additions being made to, the *Doctor Who* universe: a legacy that would remain with the series and be further built upon in later years.

Production Development

The sixth Doctor's era broke with recent precedent right from the outset, the newcomer's introductory story being placed not at the beginning of a season but at the end of one. This was a consequence of John Nathan-Turner's desire to establish the new Doctor before the series went off-air for the summer. It could therefore be considered rather surprising that the production team then chose to make him mentally unstable in the aftermath of his regeneration, leaving viewers uncertain as to what he would be like in later stories. They took this decision partly with a view to keeping all their options open, but also in a conscious effort to try something new, making the sixth Doctor highly impetuous and unreliable, as Eric Saward explained to *Doctor Who Magazine* in 1984:

'Because the Doctor has always been slightly seedy after regenerating ... and because we wanted to make the sixth Doctor different, we decided to make the regeneration so extreme that it would resemble madness. The swings of mood were amazing – if he had been walking around on the streets, he would have been a strong contender for a psychiatric hospital! So the whole behavioural aspect of the Doctor in *The Twin Dilemma* was quite deliberate – I wanted to explore what happened after the regeneration.'

Saward acknowledges that this idea could not be sustained for long:

'It's an obstacle to developing a story. Personal traits in the way a character approaches a problem are interesting, and a writer can use them, but when a character is utterly unreliable, and one doesn't know how he's going to act or which way he's going to go, it creates endless problems.'

In view of this, the sixth Doctor became noticeably more stable in his first full season, Season 22, allowing the emphasis to be shifted towards the stories themselves. One thing that remained unchanged, however, was his garish, multicoloured costume, the initial inspiration for which had come from John Nathan-Turner.

'John very much wanted to achieve a kind of development from one Doctor to another,' recalled the costume's designer, Pat Godfrey, in *The Frame*. 'He wanted to get the feel of the previous Doctors' costumes by going back to a more Victorian shape, but he also wanted to make the new one look very bizarre, rather fairground and clown-like. He even suggested that I could give the character spotted trousers, but that was a direction we chose not to follow. John wanted a garish costume – his own words were "a totally tasteless costume" – which is actually very difficult to achieve, as one has to be tastefully tasteless.

'The other constraints I was given were that the shirt had to have a question mark on each collar and that there couldn't be any blue anywhere in the costume, as it would have caused problems with the electronic effects.'

This brief continued John Nathan-Turner's policy of giving his Doctors highly stylised, uniform-like costumes, rather than simply eccentric collections of more conventional clothing as had been worn by the Time Lord's earlier incarnations. The very distinctive nature of the sixth Doctor's costume had an obvious impact on the style of his stories, in that it precluded any possibility of him making an unobtrusive entrance into a situation and inevitably meant that he became the centre of attention. It also had another, less obvious repercussion, as Pat Godfrey explains:

'This really arose from a technicality of working in colour television. When colour was first introduced, we were trained in how to design for it. We were shown a scale of 0 to 100, where 0 was black and 100 was white. We were told that the maximum range that video cameras could cope with at that time was only about 30 – in other words, the darkest and brightest colours in the picture could be no more than 30 points apart on the scale. So because the Doctor's costume was very bright, I had to move everything else up the scale accordingly. If the companion's costume had been in very subtle hues, it would have been washed out by the Doctor's, so hers had to be bright as well.'

This knock-on effect extended not only to the series' costumes but also to other aspects of the production, most notably the sets. The end result was that the overall look of the sixth Doctor's stories tended to be very gaudy and unsubtle – a development that John Nathan-Turner later acknowledged to have been to the series' detriment, although he was unaware of it at the time.

Season 22 also saw important changes being made in the style and pacing of the series' scripts. These came about as a direct consequence of the decision – reportedly taken by Alan Hart, the then Controller of BBC1 – to double the length of each episode, with a concomitant halving of the number of episodes per season. The new episode length was originally to have been 50 minutes but was eventually fixed at 45 minutes when John Nathan-Turner pointed out that, with fewer title sequences required, a 50-minute episode would actually have demanded *more* than twice the usual programme content, increasing the strain on the series' budget and resources.

The extended episode length was welcomed by Nathan-Turner. 'I feel that the show lends itself more easily to that formula,' he told the fanzine *Zygon*. 'I know that's a kind of outrageous thing to say, after 21 years of the old format, but it provides an opportunity for us as programme makers to examine the relationship between the Doctor and his companion ... and to find out more about the guest characters, to flesh them out more.'

Notwithstanding this potential advantage, both Nathan-Turner and Eric Saward realised that the transition from the old format to the new would require careful handling. In an interview for *Doctor Who Magazine*, Saward later explained the challenges it had presented:

'It involved, from my point of view, an attempt to talk to our writers about a format of which I had no experience, although obviously I'd written 50-minute things myself for other programmes. While rethinking the format, we were very careful to keep the essence of the show, which is a fantasy/SF adventure story. We couldn't just cobble together two 25-minute episodes, because a compilation of two fast-running parts is very off-putting – it jars. We had time to stop and think a bit more, although we did have to keep on hammering away with the action.'

Saward considered that the transition had been achieved relatively successfully and was disappointed when the powers-that-be decided to revert to the traditional 25-minute format for Season 23, feeling that another season of 45-minute episodes would perhaps have been better. This was a view with which John Nathan-Turner concurred, as he told *Doctor Who Magazine* in the same September 1985 interview:

'Yes, I think it did work. Inevitably when there's a change in something that has been a tradition for such a long time, there's a kind of apprehension from the front office that it won't work. Now we're rethinking again. We've got material that has been written for 45-minute slots and will have to be split up again. Those scripts we do finish up using will have to be restructured. There's more to it than just splitting it down the middle. It would have been lovely to have done one more season in that slot to get it exactly right, but we were both surprised and delighted that we achieved accuracy so quickly.'

Another significant change in storytelling style arose from the fact that, unlike his predecessor, the sixth Doctor had just a single companion. This was a change that Eric Saward actively supported, as he revealed to *Doctor Who Magazine*:

'From my point of view, both as script editor and as writer, you can do much more with just one companion. The Doctor and the companion can have a much stronger, better-defined relationship, and they can relate to each other in a more positive way. When you've got more than one companion, you're farming out lines that could be said by one person. Also, if you've got so many people in a confined space like the TARDIS, it's difficult to give them a lot of positive action. That became very apparent with three companions. It's also a problem to deal with so many sub-plots. Thus the return to the old idea.'

What Saward found rather less appealing was the nature of Peri's

PRODUCTION DEVELOPMENT

character, which he considers to have been weak and 'feminine' in all the worst ways. Neither was he any happier with Peri's successor, computer programmer Mel Bush, whom he recalls to have been conceived purely to fulfil Nathan-Turner's desire to have a companion with red hair – possibly with a view to his intended casting of the part.

The original character outlines for Peri and Mel were both relatively detailed. The former was prepared by Nathan-Turner along with Saward and writer Peter Grimwade, while the latter was entirely Nathan-Turner's work. In his book *Doctor Who – The Companions*, the producer gave his own account of the factors that had shaped Mel's development:

'One of the changes we decided to make [for Season 23] was a change of emphasis in humour. I have always maintained that *Doctor Who* should have a helping of wit rather than slapstick. In order to make this helping more than ample I decided to devise a companion whose basic character gave the writers more opportunity for fun and humour; a character who, by her very nature, placed the Doctor in humorous situations.'

Thus Mel was conceived as a get-up-and-go health-and-fitness fanatic with a mane of red hair, who would rush impetuously into dangerous situations and keep the Doctor on his toes in more ways than one, often chiding him about his tendency towards portliness.

Nathan-Turner did however admit, in his introduction to *Doctor Who – The Companions*, that he was wary of making the Doctor's companion too strong a character:

'One of the problems I discovered with companions of my own devising was that the more rounded the character, the more it required development. And development of character takes air-time and this reduces the amount of dramatisation air-time and before you know where you are, a science-fiction adventure series is taking on a soap-opera flavour.'

When he came to cast the part of Mel in December 1985, almost six months after he had first devised the character (his original outline being dated 5 July 1985), Nathan-Turner made a very surprising choice. He later described to *Doctor Who Magazine* how this had come about:

'I was having a meeting with the agent Barry Burnett, and he said, "Is there any other casting I can help you with; what about the new companion?" and I said, "You have a client who is perfect for it from the way I've described it, but I don't know if she'd be interested, or whether it's really a good idea or not." He said, "Who's that?" and I said, "Bonnie".'

The selection of popular variety artist Bonnie Langford to play Mel was not well received by Eric Saward. In an interview for *DWB* in 1992, he commented: 'Bonnie Langford, I'm convinced, was Nathan-Turner's most cynical piece of casting.' Ian Levine, speaking in the same interview, added: 'I'm not alone in believing he hired her not simply because in his opinion she'd be good for *Doctor Who*, but because he saw her as a big draw for

Teynham Productions' pantomimes.' Teynham Productions was an organisation run by Nathan-Turner and others, which mounted regular Christmas pantomimes during this period.

The casting of Bonnie Langford was also unpopular with many fans, who saw it as an extension of the recent policy of featuring 'guest stars', frequently best known for their comedy work, in prominent *Doctor Who* roles. Examples included comedienne Beryl Reid as captain of a space freighter in *Earthshock*, Rodney Bewes of *The Likely Lads* as an android trooper in *Resurrection of the Daleks* and Kate O'Mara, most famous for her roles in the soap operas *The Brothers* (opposite Colin Baker) and *Triangle*, as the Rani in *The Mark of the Rani*.

As some critics saw it, this influx of 'celebrity' actors damaged *Doctor Who*'s credibility, bringing inappropriate 'light entertainment' connotations to serious roles and making it more difficult for viewers to suspend their disbelief – a vital factor in the impact of any science fiction or fantasy series. The *Doctor Who* audience, it was argued, would be unable to dispel from their minds the popular image of Bonnie Langford as a precocious song-and-dance performer, who had come to prominence as a winner of the *Opportunity Knocks* talent contest and as a child star in roles such as that of the obnoxious Violet Elizabeth Bott in London Weekend Television's *Just William* series.

John Nathan-Turner, however, was unswayed by such criticisms, pointing out that Langford's popularity with youngsters could attract many new viewers to *Doctor Who*. 'Bonnie is a terrific little actress,' he told *Doctor Who Magazine*, 'and anybody who has seen her in the West End in *Peter Pan*, which is something a darn sight more recent than Violet Elizabeth, will realise that. I think of myself as ambitious in casting terms, and I know that Bonnie has the potential to make the part totally unirritating, as opposed to Violet Elizabeth.' Nathan-Turner also rejected the more general criticisms of the 'guest star' policy, arguing that it attracted valuable extra publicity for the series.

Another objection to which the production team often had to respond at this time concerned the increasing level of violence in *Doctor Who*, and particularly in the six stories that made up Season 22. This season was, without question, exceptionally bleak and oppressive in emphasis, dealing with such heavy themes as video nasties, genetic experimentation and cannibalism; and, added to this, the plots themselves became rather more gory and horrific in content, featuring disturbing scenes of torture, dismemberment and suffering.

'I've always felt,' says Eric Saward, 'that if you're going to show violence, you should also show the horrific effects of it. If you hit somebody, it hurts; it hurts your hand, for one thing, and it certainly hurts the person you hit. If you hit them in the face, they're going to get a black eye or a bloody nose.

PRODUCTION DEVELOPMENT

Similarly, if you shoot at somebody's hand, they're going to lose fingers, as Davros did in *Revelation of the Daleks*. That's a terrible thing to happen, but if you present an action-adventure story in which there's no apparent consequence to the violence, then I think you're cheating the audience.

'I'll never understand Mary Whitehouse's point of view. She seems to want a bland, safe little world in which everything is quiet and ordered and the traditional class structure is completely in place. That's simply confirming a stereotype, and is an evil portrayal of society. In the same way, if you offer an audience blandness, it's a corrosive thing. I would argue with anybody on this point. To pretend that there's no consequence to violent conflict is to cheat and to deceive.'

This graphic portrayal of violent incidents certainly brought a greater degree of realism to *Doctor Who*. It is also fair to mention that Season 22 was planned on the basis that the episodes would be going out at around 6.20 pm, and not in the 5.20 pm slot to which they were eventually allocated. These factors were of little comfort, however, to the many viewers who remained concerned at the sheer number of violent incidents presented, and at the depiction of gratuitously unpleasant images such as that of the character Shockeye killing and biting into a rat in *The Two Doctors*. The inclusion of such scenes was generally felt to be quite at odds with the series' traditional 'family viewing' appeal - as was the introduction of a blatantly sexual overtone in the form of Peri's titillating outfits and the recurring subplot of aliens lusting after her body.

Some commentators even went so far as to suggest that Season 22 marked a temporary departure from the strong moral standpoint that had previously been one of *Doctor Who*'s most distinctive and popular features. No longer, it was said, was there any clear delineation between good and evil in the stories. The actions of supposedly noble or heroic characters - such as Lytton in *Attack of the Cybermen*, the Governor in *Vengeance on Varos* and Orcini in *Revelation of the Daleks* - were criticised as being almost as questionable as those of the villains themselves, and even the Doctor's tactics did not entirely escape reproach. Although *The Trial of a Time Lord* saw the production team making a considerable reduction in the level of violence - a response to a specific instruction from Michael Grade, the Controller of BBC1 - many still consider this arguable lapse in the series' basic morality to have been a major failing of the Colin Baker era.

Eric Saward sees these criticisms as naïve:

'There have never been moral absolutes. The Doctor has been responsible for many deaths throughout the series' history. The portrayal of characters such as Lytton and Orcini perhaps reflected a more accurate image of life than had been attempted before. Remember that soldiers honoured as heroes have often killed many people, an activity that would be seen as totally unacceptable in peace time.'

Another criticism often made of the Colin Baker era was that it placed an excessive reliance on *Doctor Who*'s own history and mythology to provide the inspiration for new plots. Examples are numerous; and in this regard, *The Trial of a Time Lord* was so complex that even many fans, with the benefit of repeated viewing on video, found it difficult to follow. Other, less-committed viewers were probably completely alienated – a supposition supported by the season's comparatively low ratings.

Speaking at a convention in November 1985, during the period when scripts were being commissioned for *The Trial of a Time Lord*, John Nathan-Turner gave a dismissive response to criticisms that the series had been drawing too heavily on its own past:

'I don't think it's been drawing too heavily. I think the mix has been about right. Something that has a 22-year history should not dismiss its heritage. At the same time, it shouldn't pander to it. I don't think we've overdone it. There are facts and figures one can produce to show that the popularity of the Daleks and the Cybermen is above that of all the other old enemies, and it would be totally foolhardy to dismiss them. They constitute the majority of our returning villains.'

Eric Saward, however, feels that the series did indeed become over-reliant on its own mythology at this point, and had indicated to *DWB* in 1988 that he was never in favour of such an approach:

'I think that it was John's idea to feature a past element in every story [of Season 20], but it was something I wasn't very interested in. I mean, we had had the Cybermen in the previous season, and that had worked; but personally I wanted us to move on. Looking back, it was a fault both John and I fell into. The season and the celebration failed because of wanting to relive history. I must say that this was done, certainly on John's part, to please the fans rather than the general public.'

Saward went on to say in the same interview that as far as the scripts went, '*Doctor Who* should have the highest rejection rate in the department ... because they are very difficult things to write well. The writers tried their best and were paid for their efforts, but the scripts should nevertheless not have been made.' However, as Saward explained, Nathan-Turner did not like rejecting material.

Accepting that John Nathan-Turner would very often request stories featuring popular monsters such as the Daleks, the Cybermen and the Sontarans, it might perhaps be asked why the writers could not then have made original and inventive use of them, just as their predecessors had done during other eras of the series' history. Eric Saward puts this down to the fact that the concepts were in many cases very dated:

'Attitudes have changed a great deal in the last twenty years: schoolchildren no longer accept as gospel what is said by their teachers; adults no longer become staid and over the hill at 45; and no-one now believes that the police are like Dixon of Dock Green. It's the same with good, imaginative writers: they prefer to invent their own projects – it inspires them – rather than try to breathe life into a tired old concept like, say, the Daleks. When they are asked to use such concepts, their work often reflects the tiredness of the original idea.'

There is no doubt that during the mid-Eighties *Doctor Who* drew on its own mythos to a far greater extent than at any other point in its history. *The Trial of a Time Lord* came in for some particularly heavy fan criticism for this, and indeed for its general incoherence. Philip Martin, one of the writers of the fourteen-part epic, had a number of reservations about it, as he later told *Doctor Who Magazine*:

'It suffered from being simultaneously commissioned. Bob Holmes died after his second draft, there were problems with the final storyline – there were six or seven writers altogether – and we never knew where we were going. Then the script editor left, and when we reached the final episode, it was all so confusing I couldn't follow it. And I had been there at the beginning! The story as it eventually reached the screen seemed to have little left of our original idea.'

Eric Saward admits that almost all the scripts commissioned during the Colin Baker era were heavily rewritten by him – a fact that he attributes to the difficulties experienced by incoming writers in coping with *Doctor Who*'s especially challenging format and budgetary restrictions. Speaking to *DWB* in 1988, he recounted some of the behind-the-scenes problems encountered on *The Trial of a Time Lord*:

'Bob Holmes wrote the first four episodes, which, given the pressures, were okay on paper. But Jonathan Powell didn't like them. We got this memo saying, "Didn't like this, or that, thought this was too silly ..." and all the rest of it. So alterations were made, which he accepted and which went into the final programme.'

The original idea had been that Holmes would also write the final two episodes of the story. These would have ended the season with the Doctor and the Master locked in mortal combat and with a question mark hanging over the outcome. Saward says that this was agreed with Nathan-Turner, and that the writing of the scripts was taken forward accordingly.

A further development then occurred, however, when Saward decided to resign his post as script editor. He had, as the sixth Doctor's era progressed, become increasingly unhappy working alongside Nathan-Turner, rarely seeing eye to eye with him over production decisions, and he decided at this point that it was time he left the series. Despite this, when Holmes fell ill after completing only a draft of the story's penultimate episode, Saward accepted Nathan-Turner's invitation to finish the work on this script and to write part fourteen himself, according to the agreed outline. As Saward recalls, when Nathan-Turner eventually saw the script for the final episode, he reneged on what had been agreed and refused to accept the cliff-hanger ending to the season. Saward consequently withdrew permission for the use of this script – a decision he declined to reconsider, although Nathan-Turner wrote to him in conciliatory terms in an attempt to persuade him to do so. Nathan-Turner then had to commission from Pip and Jane Baker a last-minute replacement.

Following these incidents, Saward gave *Starburst* magazine an interview in which he aired his criticisms of Nathan-Turner:

'I was getting very fed up with the way *Doctor Who* was being run, largely by John Nathan-Turner – his attitude and lack of insight into what makes a television series like *Doctor Who* work.'

He went on to say that his former colleague had, amongst other things, brought pantomime aspects to *Doctor Who*; neglected important tasks in favour of trivial ones, such as making arrangements for and attending fan conventions in the USA and approving merchandise for BBC Enterprises; been reluctant to work with experienced people in case they undermined his authority; taken insufficient interest in the series' scripts; and made poor casting decisions.

As Saward had a day-to-day involvement with the series' production, his comments must clearly be accorded considerable weight; and equally critical opinions of Nathan-Turner's qualities as a producer have been publicly expressed by a number of others involved in *Doctor Who* during the mid-Eighties, including writer and director Peter Grimwade, actor Anthony Ainley (who played the Master) and Ian Levine. It should be noted, however, that Nathan-Turner also has many friends and supporters amongst those who worked on the series at this time. These include stars Colin Baker, Nicola Bryant and Bonnie Langford, writers Pip and Jane Baker, and directors such as Fiona Cumming and Nicholas Mallett, all of whom have given quite the opposite impression of the contribution made by the producer, praising him for his strong support of their work, for his enormous energy and for his fierce commitment to the series. This is not of course to suggest that anyone has been less than truthful in their comments on Nathan-Turner; it is simply a reflection of the fact that there seems to be a very wide divergence of opinion amongst those who worked with him, making him arguably the most controversial figure ever to have been associated with the series.

Despite this divergence of opinion, some fans came to believe that the multitude of problems with which *Doctor Who* was beset during this period were almost entirely the fault of John Nathan-Turner. Whilst it is certainly true to say that all matters pertaining to the production of *Doctor Who* on a day-to-day basis were ultimately the producer's responsibility, it can also be said that some of the difficulties the series faced – the frequent, damaging changes of transmission days, times and episode lengths; the postponement of Season 23; Michael Grade's public attacks on the series and its production team; and ultimately Colin Baker's ousting from the role of the Doctor after *The Trial of a Time Lord* – were matters largely if not entirely beyond the producer's control. While opinions may legitimately differ as to the artistic merits of the sixth Doctor's stories, the vociferous criticisms sometimes directed at Nathan-Turner with regard to scheduling and other decisions taken by BBC management would appear to be unfounded.

If *The Trial of a Time Lord* can be seen as a case of art imitating life – Michael Grade and his colleagues having made it abundantly clear that the series itself was still on trial – then it could be argued that there are certain respects in which, conversely, life imitated art during the Colin Baker era. It was as if the unpredictable, mercurial, explosive character of the sixth Doctor was actually being reflected in the dramatic real-life incidents surrounding the series!

Whatever else might be said, this was undeniably the most troubled and eventful period of production in *Doctor Who*'s long history.

From Script to Screen
Revelation of the Daleks

INTRODUCTION

The production chosen for this case study is *Revelation of the Daleks*, the final story of the twenty-second season, first transmitted in 1985. For helping us to compile our information, we are grateful to several people, in particular the writer Eric Saward, the director Graeme Harper, the designer Alan Spalding and the visual effects designer John Brace, each of whom took the time to speak to us in great detail about their respective contributions, and to costume designer Pat Godfrey, who gave an earlier interview to *The Frame*.

THE SCRIPTS

The initial idea for *Revelation of the Daleks* came from producer John Nathan-Turner, who decided that he wanted a Dalek story with which to close the season. He also wanted Eric Saward to write it, as his previous Dalek tale, *Resurrection of the Daleks*, had been very well received.

'I actually went off contract for six weeks to write *Revelation of the Daleks*,' recalls Eric Saward. 'I went away to Rhodes for three weeks round about June/July 1984, had a nice holiday, enjoyed myself, and wrote the scripts.

'I wanted to do something about a planet that specialised in dealing with the dead. I worked out a rough storyline – and it was *very* rough – and went through it with John, and he said "OK".'

The initial inspiration for the story came from an Evelyn Waugh novel. 'When I was on holiday, I re-read *The Loved One*, which is Waugh's skit on how the Americans view the dead. I had first read it many years before, and I remembered that there is a character in it called Joyboy, who is a make-up artist for the dead. He is a very sad character. He is in his thirties, still living with his mother, and is pursued in the novel by an even more lonely and sad woman. I took the idea of Mr Joyboy and made him Mr Jobel, and the poor infatuated woman became Tasambeker. I really should have killed her in the first episode and put her out of her misery!'

Holidaying in Rhodes while writing the scripts provided Saward with the ideas for many of the character names that he used. 'The local goddess of fertility on Rhodes is called Tsambeker, with a silent 'T', and I just took it phonetically as Tasambeker. Stengos ran the local ferry. Cara was a type of potato that we had fresh from the ground out there – I just changed the spelling to Kara. Orcini was the Grand Master of the Knights of St John, who used to be on Rhodes. He defended Rhodes against Suleiman the Magnificent, the Turkish Sultan, and managed to hold out against 100,000 troops for about six months with only 600 Knights and 2,000 auxiliaries. Suleiman was so impressed by their bravery that, when he eventually won, he freed the Knights that had survived. I took the myths rather than the reality and created my warrior Orcini, who is always looking for the mythical "great kill". Of course, there is no such thing as a "great kill" or a "perfect kill", but in his mind there is, because it's noble, it's honourable. Reaching that ideal is what spurs him on to hunt Davros.'

As Saward recalls, there was no pressure from Terry Nation, the Daleks' creator and copyright holder, to include Davros in the story. Rather, this was an idea that John Nathan-Turner suggested and that he was very happy to go along with:

'Davros was included because I thought someone had to be behind the planet's operations. Davros had decided that he was going to be the self-appointed Great Healer, and I wanted him initially to appear honourable. Kara was meant to be the unpleasant one. But it didn't quite work out in either case.

'The thing about the Daleks is that when you come to write them, they're very boring. They're boring to listen to for any length of time – that stilted monotone. Davros is a much more interesting character. He speaks relatively normally, so he can sustain conversations, which the Daleks can't, and he is therefore convenient to use at the centre of the plot. In which case the Daleks themselves take just a supporting role.

'I believe that nowadays the Daleks can't be taken seriously. They're far too old fashioned to be seen as a deadly and ultimate evil. That's the reality. They're no longer this great, frightening creation that Nation thought they were.

'The plot developed further when I wondered what Davros could be doing running this place. The most heinous thing anyone can do when running a cemetery is to sell the bodies. That seemed obvious, if not particularly original, so I used it.

'The other thing I wanted to do was to take the development of the Daleks one stage further. Their history seemed to me to have been very chequered in terms of what they could and couldn't do. Considering that they're supposed to be so powerful, their early beginnings were very feeble and crude; needing to draw electricity from the floor and so on. I thought that perhaps it was about time for them to be able to reproduce themselves, so that they could go anywhere and be anything that they wanted.'

Perhaps the strangest character in *Revelation of the Daleks* is the DJ. 'The idea for him came about one evening when I'd been out for a meal and was driving back home in my car. I turned on the radio and there was an incredibly boring DJ on the air. Now, prior to this, I'd thought that if one was going to have a super-cryogenic planet, then there would be problems. I've always wondered about the cryogenic idea, because if people could come back after 200 years, imagine what state they would be in! All their technology, their thinking, everything would be redundant. The world would have moved on so far and they would have become so out of touch that they would instantly die of nervous breakdowns! I'd reasoned that there would have to be some way of keeping the frozen people up to date, but hadn't yet decided how. Then, when I heard this lunatic DJ, who was trying to be incredibly serious but at the same time hip, I knew I had to have him! That's how the character was born.

'The DJ is completely at odds with the place. He sits there and plays music and passes on notes from the folks and so on, but he is so cynical about it all. I made him really rather grotesque, and he had to be grotesque.'

Revelation of the Daleks was commissioned to fit the new 45-minute episode format that *Doctor Who* was assigned for its twenty-second season. As Saward explains, this required an approach slightly different from that used in writing the traditional 25-minute episodes: 'A 25-minute episode tends to be rather frenetic, because it's zooming up to the cliff-hanger. The 45-minute ones were paced a little slower. There was never any intention to create an artificial cliff-hanger halfway through. I'm told that *Revelation of the Daleks* was cut up into four parts for sale to America, but I had nothing to do with that.'

Saward recalls that when his scripts for the two episodes were completed and delivered, they were found to be too long and required shortening, but that little other adjustment was called for. 'If the script is there and it's working reasonably well, most of the director's time is spent on the other aspects of the show – casting, designing and so on – and so I didn't have that much to do with the actual process of making it.

'I first saw it performed at the producer's run, and I was in the studio for almost all the recording. The first time I saw it all together was in John's office, when Graeme delivered the rough cut. I thought he'd made a good job of it, and it had come together well.'

FROM SCRIPT TO SCREEN: REVELATION OF THE DALEKS

PRE-PRODUCTION

Once the scripts have been drafted, the first person to be contracted to work on a *Doctor Who* is generally the director. In the case of *Revelation of the Daleks*, which had been conceived as the grand finale of the season, John Nathan-Turner was looking for someone who could not only convey the story effectively but also bring a sense of spectacle to it. The man he chose was Graeme Harper, whose work on the fifth Doctor's farewell story, *The Caves of Androzani*, had greatly impressed him.

'When we'd finished *The Caves of Androzani*,' recalls Harper, 'John asked if I would come back and do one in the following season, to which I replied, "Yes". At that time, he wasn't sure which story it would be, or where or when we would be filming, but I knew that if I wanted to do another, then the chances were that I would be able to.' It was in fact around June 1984 that Harper was approached by Nathan-Turner to direct *Revelation of the Daleks*. 'At first, I wasn't sure how this would fit in with my other commitments, but about three months later, when I knew exactly what I was going to be doing, my agent went back to John and told him the dates on which I would be free. Fortunately they tied in with John's schedules.'

Once Harper was confirmed in November 1984 as the director, the next task was to bring on board the key creative personnel. Most BBC departments at this time operated some form of rota system whereby staff were allocated to shows for a whole year in advance. Occasionally the director, in consultation with the producer, would specifically request a particular designer, in which case it would then be up to the appropriate department head to say whether or not that designer happened to be free, as would occasionally be the case, or alternatively whether or not he or she could be freed up from a pre-arranged assignment.

To handle the visual effects for *Revelation of the Daleks*, Harper asked for and got John Brace. 'John had worked on several *Doctor Who* episodes throughout his career, and we knew each other anyway, so it was lucky that he was available.'

Brace was equally pleased to be returning to *Doctor Who*. 'Working in the Effects Department, a designer got the opportunity to be involved in many different types of programmes, but to be allocated to *Doctor Who* allowed particular scope for creativity. There were spaceships and monsters, there were explosions, it was a fantasy world. So to have a *Doctor Who* was good news, and everyone wanted to do them.'

The first thing the director does when joining a production is to read the scripts.

'I didn't understand one bit of them at first,' laughs Harper. 'They were quite complex, and I remember going through them suggesting where we might be able to clarify the plot. Even with this, the story was very complicated.

'As an overall fantasy, however, it was well written. I remember it being very wordy, featuring some almost Shakespearean characters. This was one of its strengths, and it worked.

'I saw the story as a pastiche on the 1973 Richard Fleischer film *Soylent Green*, in which the problems of overcrowding and starvation on a future Earth are both solved by making food (the soylent green of the title) from the people.'

In reading the scripts, the director gets many casting ideas, and these are next discussed with the producer.

'The first conversations a director would have after considering the script would be about casting: the areas and the kinds of characters involved, and whether or not there were going to be any guest stars,' says Harper. 'While those discussions were going on for *Revelation of the Daleks*, I was also talking with the designer about the look and feel of the production and about how we could realise it.

'Soon into those discussions would come the Costume and Make-up Departments – but not *too* soon unless there was something very special required. Visual Effects would also be involved quite early on, and all the while John Nathan-Turner would be listening in and occasionally asking how much all this was going to cost!'

The production team had approximately six weeks – which included a break for Christmas – between starting work on the story and going away on location. This timescale meant that many things had to be worked out quickly, always with an eye on the budget.

'I remember discussing the concept for the planet,' recalls designer Alan Spalding. 'It was supposed to be a death planet. It contained a modern cryogenic plant, but at the same time maintained a tradition of death similar to that found in ancient Egyptian society. Designing the modern aspects was fine, because I could make them futuristic and different, but the ancient elements we found difficult to resolve because Graeme argued that there wouldn't be Earth-type graves and all the associated iconography. I therefore had to aim for impressive and different visuals with a very low budget.'

The costume designer, Pat Godfrey, also remembers that money was tight. 'I think the costume budget for this story was, in all, about £5,000. This had been worked out at the beginning of the season, before the scripts had been completed, and as it was a Dalek story, they'd thought that they wouldn't need too many extra costumes. Unfortunately, there turned out to be a lot of characters in the cast, so the money was spread very thinly.'

The scripts also presented some unusually demanding effects requirements, ranging from exploding glass Daleks through to simple prop bombs, guns and knives, all of which had to be realised by the Visual Effects

FROM SCRIPT TO SCREEN: REVELATION OF THE DALEKS

Department. To try to get around the budgetary restrictions, John Brace took a somewhat radical step: 'We needed all sorts of Daleks – grey Daleks and white Daleks, Daleks that blew up and crystal-clear Daleks in an embryonic stage – and also a large polystyrene sculpture of the Doctor. I went to BBC Enterprises and explained that there was no way that the production could afford to have all these constructed, but I knew they had in the past taken visual effects props and other interesting items for exhibition, and they may have had some old Daleks that we could modify. As discussions evolved with the production associate June Collins and Julie Jones of BBC Enterprises, we decided that we could make new Daleks and Enterprises would buy them back from the programme when production was completed.

'Enterprises were fine with the idea, but my own Department's reaction surprised me. They didn't think that I should be able to do this. "What are you doing making deals with Enterprises?" they asked. "You're just an effects designer. We manage the Department! If you have problems with your budgets, come and see us." However I *had* been and seen them, and they had looked and said, basically, that I was stuffed! They had said that this was television, not films. That this was the real world, and that I had to work within my budget.'

Graeme Harper's previous *Doctor Who* story, *The Caves of Androzani*, had consisted of four 25-minute episodes. Although the amount of material required to be shot for the two 45-minute episodes of *Revelation of the Daleks* was the same, the new format placed much greater demands on the director and his team. 'There was a lot to do in the studio,' recalls Harper. 'They'd changed to a 45-minute format, but it felt as though we didn't have the time in the studio. Whereas in the 25-minute format it was just about possible to scrape through with an occasional overrun, on *Revelation of the Daleks* I think we worked until eleven o'clock every night. We just couldn't fit it all in.'

ON LOCATION

One way of maximising studio time is to film as much material as possible on location. Like many *Doctor Who*s at this point in the series' history, *Revelation of the Daleks* made quite extensive use of location filming.

Location filming is normally carried out prior to any studio recording and takes place at whatever venue the production team have decided is best suited to the requirements of the story.

It can take many weeks of effort to find a suitable location. The director and the producer will first discuss the most important criteria and then, in conjunction with the production manager and members of the design team, start to think about places where all these can be met. As travelling time must come out of the time allotted for filming, it is usually important that the chosen location should boast all the required features within easy reach of one another, and that it should be fairly close to the production base of Television Centre in west London.

Where *Revelation of the Daleks* was concerned, the team felt that the mortuary complex of Tranquil Repose was the central image of the story and should be the prime location. Alan Spalding remembers that it was quite tricky to find. 'We wanted a building that was very futuristic-looking. Because of the Egyptian death motif, we had in mind something that suggested hi-tech pyramids. We wanted the ancient culture to be reflected in a modern design. We eventually found somewhere by going through lots of books and looking for unusual buildings and architecture. It was the IBM office complex at North Harbour, Cosham near Portsmouth. This fitted the bill perfectly. It had all the right qualities.'

IBM allowed the crew eight hours' filming on their premises and, instead of taking a fee, asked the BBC to make a donation to a local school.

'It was a perfect location,' affirms John Brace. 'It had little tunnel entrances, so that we could establish that the place extended underground, and it was all black glass on top. In our production, the building was supposed to look incredibly nice on top, although underneath it was throbbing with evil.'

The main location having been chosen, all the other requirements were found nearby. The place where the TARDIS lands was represented by a large hill and woodland area of the Queen Elizabeth's Park nature reserve in Petersfield, near Southampton. The scenes when the Doctor and Peri, and later Orcini and his squire Bostock, approach Tranquil Repose, were shot at a disused aerodrome in the Poole area.

The script's description of the planet Necros was quite difficult to realise, as Spalding explains: 'The story was supposed to be set on a bare, stark planet, but we weren't allowed to go too far away to shoot it. It was quite a difficult brief. We couldn't go to the Yorkshire Moors or Fylingdales or anywhere like that, as we weren't originally supposed to have any overnight stays.'

Prior to going on location, a director usually needs to have worked out a detailed schedule for the filming. 'There are some productions on which it's not critical to have worked out all the camera angles and so on beforehand,' says Harper, 'but on something as complex as *Doctor Who*, everything has to be well planned.

'The director is constrained by the requirements of all the various departments – Design, Effects, Make-up, Costume – as to the order in which certain things have to be done, because of construction and setting-up times. Even the availability of certain actors and actresses can sometimes dictate whether their scenes have to be filmed first or last. The whole process must be planned very carefully. You have to know what you're going to do. You have to know all the shots, the angles and how they will develop. This is essential because you haven't got time to try to work it all out when you are already there. It really has to be done in advance.'

With this in mind, the director and his team will normally go on a recce – an advance visit to all the chosen locations – to start working out how the camera will be positioned in relation to the artistes and to any special props or sets required, and also to try to anticipate any problems that might arise.

When on location, the standard method of working is to rehearse each scene immediately before it is filmed, this process being repeated as many times as is necessary until the director is happy with what has been shot. 'I would talk through any major dialogue scenes the night before with the artistes,' says Harper, 'and any changes would be agreed with the writer. Otherwise, it would all have been blocked out and planned beforehand, so I would know what I was hoping to achieve on any particular day.'

The major problem with going on location as opposed to working in a studio is the unpredictability of the weather. In a studio it can be made to rain or snow on cue; gale-force winds can be created, and so can hot, balmy sunshine. Out in the wilds of the English countryside, however, the unit are at the mercy of the British weather, and can encounter considerable difficulties. This was certainly the case on *Revelation of the Daleks*, as Graeme Harper recalls:

'Bearing in mind that we were due to be filming in January, I'm sure we must have wondered what would happen if it snowed. I had never really worried about it, though. Snow can actually give you a longer working day, because it makes things brighter.

'Anyway, we went away on location for four or five days, and the first couple of days went by with no problems at all: everything we had planned to film was done, and all was on schedule. And then the snow came overnight. We were due to film at Queen Elizabeth's Park the next day, and had to try to get there through a foot of snow! In the end, we had to alter the schedule, and as a result we lost one of our major effects sequences.

'At the Park there was a valley where we were going to stage a battle between the Daleks and the two "Don Quixote" characters, Bostock and Orcini. There was going to be a massive gun battle and, as the major feature of this, we were going to prove that the Daleks could fly. This had never been done before, and we had all wondered how they got about so easily over all manner of terrain. During the battle, a Dalek was going to fly up, twenty feet in the sky, and then explode. That was going to be a major effects piece but, once the snow arrived, we couldn't get the equipment up there. It had all been planned and worked out, but the spring-device that was going to launch this Dalek into the air couldn't be set up. I was disappointed to lose that.'

Eric Saward, however, cannot recall this scene at all. 'It might have had something to do with the one in part two where Orcini destroys a Dalek on location, as what was seen on screen was not what was scripted.'

The original script for this scene has two Daleks suddenly appearing on a ridge behind Orcini and Bostock. The mercenaries open fire with bastic-headed bullets, capable of penetrating solid rock, but the Daleks are unscathed. Ducking behind a rock, Orcini manages to blow off the eyepiece of one of the Daleks, which then topples down the bank, allowing him and his squire to slip away.

'I had tried to carry through the idea that Daleks are very difficult to destroy,' explains Saward. 'I had written that Orcini just damaged the Dalek, but this was changed on location so that it exploded.'

Although it caused the abandonment of the planned battle scene, the snow did have certain fortuitous consequences, as Harper notes: 'We had always planned to do the opening sequences of the story at the end of the shoot, and the change in the weather meant that we could have the Doctor and Peri landing in a snowy landscape next to a frozen pond. It really brought over the feeling of icy desolation that we were trying to achieve.'

Mention of the pond reminds Alan Spalding that it had not been easy to find. 'We had decided to use the South Downs area because we wanted the bleakness and the lack of vegetation that you find there. Then we had to try to find a pond, and at first we couldn't, because ponds just don't happen in chalk. Mike Cameron, the production manager, hunted and hunted, but it seemed that there just wasn't one to be found on the South Downs.

'In the end, we found one on a farmer's property. The farmer had built it for his cattle to drink from. There was a little island in the middle and a boat that we used to get out to it. Graeme decided that the boat would be a good place to position the camera for the shot where the alien hand emerges from the water.'

Using a frozen pond in the middle of winter posed particular problems for John Brace and his team. 'There was thick ice all over this pond, and we had to break it up in order to get into the water to set up the effects.

'In view of that fact that we needed to get underwater to achieve the effect of a hand emerging, I asked for my Department's diving section to come out. The diving section was in fact Jim Francis and Dave Barton, two other visual effects designers, and it was difficult to get my management to accept that you could have three designers on one location. I kept explaining to them that it wasn't three designers, it was one designer and two divers.'

The location sequences for *Revelation of the Daleks* were filmed from 7 to 10 January 1985. As a final note, this was the last *Doctor Who* location shoot ever to be done on film. The use of outside broadcast (OB) video cameras had since 1974 become increasingly prevalent, and from Season 23 onwards, all *Doctor Who*'s location work would be done in this way.

FROM SCRIPT TO SCREEN: REVELATION OF THE DALEKS

IN STUDIO

The first studio work to be undertaken for *Revelation of the Daleks* was one day of filming by the Visual Effects Department to create all the model scenes required for the story.

In keeping with the usual pattern at this point in the series' history, the main studio recordings then took place at Television Centre in two separate blocks, the first of two days' duration, on 17 and 18 January 1985 in studio TC1, and the second of three days' duration, between 30 January and 1 February in TC8. Cast rehearsals were held at the BBC's Acton rehearsal rooms from 3 to 16 January for the first block and from 19 to 29 January for the second.

All the scenes involving the futuristic sets were recorded in the first block and all those involving the underground areas were done in the second, this split being dictated by the logistics of the story. Normally, a certain proportion of the studio space would have to be left empty to meet the BBC's strict safety regulations, but for *Revelation of the Daleks*, Alan Spalding got special dispensation to fill the studio completely, so as to fit everything in.

Recording of *Doctor Who* in the Eighties was invariably done out of story sequence. The exact recording order would be worked out by the director based on which sets were going to be available in each studio. All the scenes that used one particular set would generally be recorded together, then the crew would move on to the next set and record all the scenes taking place there, and so on.

There were two alternative approaches that directors could take to studio work. One, known as the rehearse/record method, involved each scene being rehearsed on camera immediately before it was recorded, just as on location. The other entailed all the rehearsals being completed during the day and then all the recording being done during the evening. The method used was generally a matter of choice for the individual director, depending on the facilities available, and for *Revelation of the Daleks*, it was the latter that Graeme Harper chose.

Each day's studio recording would have to end at 10 pm sharp, the only exception being where the director had – as on this occasion – obtained permission to go into overtime (an expense that had to be agreed). The studio house lights would be switched on at the appointed time, even if the cast were in the middle of a scene, and the cameramen and other technical personnel would leave for the night. The scene-shifters would then come in to take down (strike) any sets that were not required for the following day's work, and to erect any new ones that were.

To indicate some of the considerations involved in making a *Doctor Who* story during the Colin Baker era, we now present a complete scene-by-scene

THE SIXTH DOCTOR

summary of *Revelation of the Daleks*, taking in comments as appropriate from Eric Saward, Graeme Harper, Alan Spalding, John Brace and (from an interview conducted for *The Frame*) costume designer Pat Godfrey. Make-up designer Dorka Nieradzik was unwilling to contribute to this book, but her recollections are also reported, based on an interview by Brenda Apsley that appeared in the 1986 *Doctor Who Annual*.

PART ONE

A planet in space. The TARDIS arrives on a mist-blown snowy hillside.

John Brace: 'We used three smoke machines here. The tricky thing about this shot was that we had left the TARDIS's blue lamp behind, and we had to knock something up on location.'

Alan Spalding: 'I didn't want to see any trees, but we had to in the end. I wanted it totally blank, but it wasn't to be.'

Graeme Harper: 'I liked it actually, because it got away from the "Dorset sand pit" look.'

Peri (Nicola Bryant) emerges and wanders down to a large pond. She throws into the water the remains of a nut roast roll on which she has been nibbling. The Doctor (Colin Baker) follows her down. They are both wearing blue – the official mourning colour on Necros – as the Doctor intends to honour local customs. The Time Lord has come here to honour the late Professor Arthur Stengos, one of the finest agronomists in the galaxy. As the two travellers turn away from the lake, an alien hand emerges from the icy water and snatches Peri's roll.

JB: 'The hand belonged to Ken Barker, the stuntman who played the mutant creature.'

Alerted by the splash, the Doctor and Peri turn back in time to see the water erupt in a small explosion.

JB: 'We had to have a woofer [a compressed-air device used for simulating explosions by propelling dust and debris with a blast of air] rigged under the water. We had to rig all that up in one day, although we had already put in an underwater scaffold.'

The Doctor and Peri head away, not seeing a ragged figure (Ken Barker) emerge and start to follow them.

FROM SCRIPT TO SCREEN: REVELATION OF THE DALEKS

In a mortuary complex elsewhere on Necros, Takis (Trevor Cooper) is putting the finishing touches to the burial mask of the President's late wife, currently lying in state in the main hall. Jobel (Clive Swift), the chief embalmer, congratulates him. Meanwhile other workers are putting the finishing touches to the arrangements of small blue flowers – herba baculum vitæ, or staff of life – and peacock feathers that line the hall

AS: 'A lot of actors won't work with peacock feathers, because they're supposed to be bad luck, but we didn't have any problems here. We had a thousand of the little blue flowers specially made.'

Tasambeker (Jenny Tomasin), a dumpy, unattractive attendant, fawns over Jobel and tells him that the presidential shuttle is on the way. When Jobel has gone, Takis and his friend Lilt (Colin Spaull) tell Tasambeker that she is wasting her time – Jobel isn't interested in her.

GH: 'When I read the script, certain people came straight to my mind. I knew that Takis and Lilt were going to be Laurel and Hardy. If you watch them, even though they're sinister guys, they have this sort of double act going. Trevor Cooper, who plays Takis, does all these kind of Laurel and Hardy things and mannerisms.

'When it came to Jobel, I just knew that it had to be Clive Swift playing the part. I knew that if I could get him, then he would bring a lot to the character.'

[Dorka Nieradzik decided to give Jobel an obviously Marcel-waved auburn toupée, which deliberately did not match his own grey hair. The intention was to make him appear quite vain, as if he thought that by putting on the toupée he would appear younger, and that everyone would be fooled into thinking it was his own hair – which of course they were not.]

GH: 'I knew that Tasambeker had to be Ruby from *Upstairs, Downstairs*, played here, as there, by Jenny Tomasin.'

AS: 'There isn't actually any set there in the main hall. It's just done with foreground props and a big arch – which was originally made for *Little and Large*. There's virtually nothing on the sides, just space. The idea was to convey a sort of Egyptian high-tech decor.'

As Jobel and the assistants leave to prepare themselves, two outsiders, Natasha (Bridget Lynch-Blosse) and Grigory (Stephen Flynn), cross the hall and, following a map, enter one of the corridors.

The Doctor and Peri are attacked by the creature that has been following them. It is an horrific mutant, its skin peeling from its body, with broken, yellowing teeth and saliva running from its mouth. Peri beats the beast with a stick until it frees the Doctor.

JB: 'We provided a rubber stick for Nicola to use. It was made to look like a lump of wood from the forest.'

GH: 'When *Doctor Who* went over to the longer, 45-minute episodes, I believe the intention was to reach out to a bigger, more family and more adult audience. With the agreement of John Nathan-Turner, we went as far as we dared with the horror, bearing in mind the time-slot and the audience. The intention here was to be a little more frightening.'

AS: 'The makeup was by Dorka Nieradzik and was excellent. Prosthetics were her speciality.'

GH: 'Dorka was fairly unknown to me before this story. I'd worked with her when she was an assistant, but I'd never really known what she could do: the talent that was about to burst forth. She really is someone very special in make-up.'

[Nieradzik provided the mutant with some false teeth made by specialist dental technicians to look as if they were in the process of melting away. She left some hair on his head to give him a pitiful look, and also to make him less frightening and more humanoid, thereby conveying the idea that Davros had been experimenting on him and that his mutation was the result of the experiment.]

The fight is being watched on monitor screens by a hippie-like character. This is the DJ (Alexei Sayle), an employee of Tranquil Repose, who is narrating events to the other, less active residents.

GH: 'The DJ was a very difficult character to cast. We could have gone for a real disc jockey, someone like Jimmy Savile or Alan Freeman, a "name" whom everyone would know and love, and just placed him in the story. But would we have got a performance or would we have had to rely on that familiar persona? Alternatively, we could have gone for a character actor, but that would have meant losing the value of some good publicity.

'We went through a whole host of names and eventually started thinking about going for alternative comedy or something. Alexei had just made *The Young Ones* and *Whoops Apocalypse* and had been very good in them, so we knew that he was a talented actor as well as being a comic, not to mention being larger than life, zany and interesting as a character. So we approached him with the idea, and he liked it.'

AS: 'We were going to make the DJ very Sixties-orientated and a collector of Sixties ephemera. As we were doing this in the mid-Eighties, it seemed like the past, but it didn't quite work, because we couldn't get the right objects. The trouble with a lot of Sixties items is that, even now, they look quite futuristic. The idea that he collected things from the past didn't quite gel, because they looked like things from the future! We should maybe have chosen art deco or something that was more obvious. The items were very hard to find as well, which surprised me.'

Eric Saward: 'Alexei Sayle turned out to be very good casting. When I saw him at the producer's run, he was very flat, and I thought, "Oh God, what have we done here?" But that is how Alexei works. He is a very shy man and very awkward – until, that is, it comes to the performance, and then the energy comes and suddenly he's away. I thought he did it very well.'

Elsewhere in the complex, there is a life-support unit containing the disembodied head of Davros (Terry Molloy), who is attended on by a white Dalek. Davros has been watching the DJ on a monitor, but now orders him silenced, and the sound is cut off. Davros then sees on the monitor that the Doctor has arrived, and comments that his lure has worked.

JB: 'Davros was supposed to be just a head, with life support systems surrounding him. Because later there would be explosions going on around it, and Terry Molloy was inside, we had to make it practical. We used techniques to confuse the eye, so that it wasn't obvious that the rest of Terry's body was in there. I think the most difficult thing was trying to make his head spin round. Colin Gory was my assistant, and had been working on this problem in the workshop while I was away filming. He decided to put Terry on a swivel chair such that he had to squeeze himself into position from underneath with the full head make-up on, and the rest of the tank was then put on top of him.'

Natasha and Grigory make their way through the complex. On level seven, they kill a guard. Davros alerts Takis that there are bodysnatchers at large.

GH: 'This was Bridget's first job on television, although she had done some theatre. I met her at an actors' workshop. I knew Stephen from a fringe theatre production that I had directed. I wanted to give him a break.'

The Doctor and Peri talk to the mutant. Before he dies, he tells them that he has been conditioned and is a product of the Great Healer's experimentation.

THE SIXTH DOCTOR

As Natasha and Grigory penetrate further into the complex, the DJ reads some dedications and Tasambeker orders Takis and Lilt to find the intruders. Davros orders Tasambeker brought to him.

The DJ, now dressed as a Fifties-style leather-clad rocker, is still reading dedications. He picks up on his screen the picture of the Doctor and Peri coming towards the complex.

Davros overhears Takis and Lilt discussing what might be in the catacombs. A Dalek then announces that Kara is ready to speak with him, and an image of the woman appears on his monitor.

Kara (Eleanor Bron) is an industrialist who is helping to finance Davros's operations on Necros. Davros pleads for more money, and Kara agrees to see what she can do. When the communications link is broken, she is obviously ill at ease. She asks her secretary Vogel (Hugh Walters) if Orcini has arrived, and is told that he has.

GH: 'Eleanor Bron was another immediate casting choice on reading the script. I phoned her up and she said yes. Eleanor had some very strong ideas as to how the part should be played, and she was brilliant.'

AS: 'It was quite deliberate that all the parts of the city that weren't to do with death were white, while the catacombs and corridors of Tranquil Repose were either black or had black elements in them.'

Natasha and Grigory have located the cryogenic storage unit for which they were searching. They open it to find it occupied by a mannequin. The body they sought – that of Natasha's father, Stengos – is missing.

AS: 'That unit opened up and was fully operational, but all the rest were just vacuum-formed repeats.'

The two 'grave robbers' are interrupted by guards, who fire on them as they flee.

JB: 'An armoury called Baptys provided all the working guns. The BBC often uses them.'

The Doctor and Peri arrive at a wall, which blocks their path. The Doctor points out to Peri that the occupants of Tranquil Repose are not dead – they are simply resting in suspended animation. He then helps her over the wall.

GH: 'This was filmed at the Goodwood horse racing ground. When they went over the wall, Nicola accidentally kicked Colin between the legs, so his expression of concern over his broken watch is genuine.'

Natasha and Grigory find themselves at a door leading down into the underground

FROM SCRIPT TO SCREEN: REVELATION OF THE DALEKS

areas of the city. They head down into the tunnels to look for a service lift to take them back to the surface. Suddenly Natasha hears a Dalek approaching, and they press themselves into an alcove.

GH: 'I had made a decision that, although we didn't have loads of money, I really wanted to have great lighting effects, which I got from Don Babbage. The idea was to light it from the floor and make it reminiscent of the style of *Alien*, with the interesting shadows and dark, dingy passageways.'

AS: 'The under-city corridors were based on Highgate cemetery. The idea was that this was an ancient cemetery that had been buried under the new city, but that elements of the new technology were still represented there. That corridor was so tight and cramped. It was actually a circular set so that we could go round and round and make it look as though there were many long corridors.'

The Dalek, leading some guards with a covered body on a trolley, passes by. Natasha and Grigory continue on and stumble into a red-lit room in which a heartbeat sound can be heard.

GH: 'That room was lit with red gels and also floor-lit, which is time consuming to do because of all the potential shadows.'

Davros is following the progress of Natasha and Grigory on his monitor.
  Natasha and Grigory discover a rack of human brains bubbling in liquid and, in the far corner of the room, a transparent Dalek containing the remains of a human head – it is that of Arthur Stengos (Alec Linstead), Natasha's father. Stengos pleads with Natasha to kill him, becoming more and more Dalek-like with every sentence. She finally raises her laser pistol and destroys her father and the Dalek. As Natasha and Grigory flee from the room, they find Takis, Lilt and some guards lying in wait for them, and are taken prisoner.

GH: 'The shot where Stengos opens his eye was meant to be much more frightening than that. I don't know what went wrong, but it was meant to be really frightening. I think he opens his eye a fraction too soon.'

JB: 'To do a glass/acrylic Dalek was going to be very expensive and time consuming, so I took it to a specialist firm, Denny's, down at Shepherd's Bush. They did a lot of the BBC's plastics work. The main reason I sent that outside was that we had so much other stuff to construct that there was just no time to fit it all in. They supplied us with the three sections – top, middle and bottom – all made out of clear acrylic plastic. Other considerations were that it had to be lit, an actor had to be in it, and we had to be able to see him. We raised it on a platform to get the lights under it.

'I was glad that it wasn't seen very often, because as well as being very fragile, it collected dust like a magnet. By the time we had finished recording, it looked very tacky and damaged. Dorka had a lot of trouble fitting in all the prosthetics and make-up, with the tubes and everything.

'We also had to consider that this Dalek was required to explode. Whatever else we did, we weren't going to be blowing up the perspex one, because the material splinters and is sharp and dangerous. We had to construct another Dalek out of lightweight, vacuum-formed plastic just for the shot where it blows up.'

Kara receives Orcini and Bostock into her office. Orcini (William Gaunt) is a Knight of the Grand Order of Oberon, a hired assassin, and Bostock (John Ogwen) is his squire. Kara is hiring them to kill Davros.

GH: 'I chose William Gaunt to play Orcini because I'd worked with him a couple of times and knew what he could do. I saw the character as a sort of Don Quixote figure, and I find Gaunt a very elegant and classical actor. I'd worked with John Ogwen on *District Nurse* in Wales, but he hadn't worked very much in England. I felt it was time we saw more of his talent.'

Pat Godfrey: 'I wanted to give Bostock and Orcini camouflage jackets, but it was decided that they should be more Che Guevara-type characters, so we hired their costumes from a costumier and just added some small details to them.'

[Dorka Nieradzik decided that, as Orcini was a mercenary who had found fame for his bravery and skill, she would make him up with some scars on his face, as the legacy of a former battle. She also gave him long hair tied back in a leather thong, the aim being to achieve a 'Buffalo Bill' look.]

The Doctor and Peri walk through the outer boundaries of Tranquil Repose. The Doctor explains that he was suspicious when he heard the reports of Stengos's death and of his internment in Tranquil Repose, and this is why he has come here.

JB: 'This was done at an enormous disused airport, which I had to relate to some model shots later. There were strange, monolithic lumps of concrete dotted around, and Alan put statues and painted scenery along one side of the runway. It all gave the impression of huge monuments dotted around the approaches to the mortuary pyramid.'

AS: 'Of the statuary and scenery that we brought with us, the BBC scenic

FROM SCRIPT TO SCREEN: REVELATION OF THE DALEKS

artist handled the painted ones and a guy called Derek Howarth worked on the sculpted ones.'

Jobel gives his workers a pep-talk prior to the President's arrival.

Pat Godfrey: 'The mortuary workers' uniforms were all dentist's tunics, which were specified in the brief. We had to send them all out to be dyed professionally, to make sure that the colour was consistent. As these costumes would have been fairly boring on their own, I came up with the idea of a cap with coloured stripes on it, which would continue down on to the face. I had recently read an article about face painting in an issue of *Vogue*, so I worked with Dorka Nieradzik to produce the right effect.'

Kara gives Orcini a box-like electronic device, telling him that it is a transmitter that he should to use to send her a signal when he and his squire have reached the undercity. Unknown to Orcini, the device is in fact a bomb, with which Kara hopes to destroy Davros and his Daleks.

Tasambeker arrives to see the Great Healer. Davros tells her that he is pleased with her work and that he wants her transferred to his personal staff.

The Doctor and Peri finally arrive at the entrance to Tranquil Repose.

AS: 'The entrance to Tranquil Repose was filmed on location with a glass painting of pyramids over the top. There was a decorative pond outside the IBM building, and the statues were recycled from the ones we had used at the airfield.'

A Dalek passes by behind the two travellers as they enter the complex. Peri catches sight of it, but does not know what it is. She and the Doctor go to investigate, but it has vanished.

JB: 'There wasn't anyone actually inside that Dalek – we pulled it along on a wire.'

Takis and Lilt torture Natasha and Grigory to try to gain information about any co-conspirators. They force the alcoholic Grigory to drink from a flask that he has hanging on a strap around his neck.

In an area that he describes as the Garden of Fond Memories, the Doctor has found a giant gravestone carved with a huge image of his face. As he stands lost in thought, believing that he must be destined to die on Necros in his current incarnation, the gravestone topples forward and falls on top of him.

End of Part One

THE SIXTH DOCTOR

PART TWO

JB: 'The gravestone was carved by David Howarth from our specifications. He's a clever sculptor who works with hot wires rather than knives. I would have liked the prop to have been very much thicker, but that would have doubled the price.

'When it finally fell, blood was supposed to come out of the statue's eye.'

GH: 'We did do that but it was cut, I think because it was too grim for the end of an episode. There is a continuity reference to it a little later.'

Peri rushes over to the fallen monument but is intercepted by Jobel, who smarmily tries to ingratiate himself with her. The Doctor is in fact unscathed and pushes his way out from under the lightweight imitation stones. His clothes are marked down one side with fake blood. He determines to find out who had the statue erected.

Grigory is now drunk and Lilt can get no sense out of him.

Inside Tranquil Repose, the Doctor and Peri are met by Tasambeker, who gives them a sales pitch about the facilities it has to offer.

Takis uses a communications screen to find out the ETA of President Vargos's ship. The computer voice (Penelope Lee) tells him that a second ship is also en-route for Necros.

AS: 'The screen was done using inlay rather than overlay, because it was not a blue screen. We just replaced a part of the picture with another image.'

Tasambeker shows the Doctor and Peri a promotional video of the DJ explaining the service he offers of relaying loved ones' messages to the Tranquil Repose residents.

GH: 'The DJ's video was a pre-recorded sequence played in through the small monitor screen on the desk there. It was actually the very first thing we did in studio.'

Bostock and Orcini are nearing Tranquil Repose when they see a white Dalek. Orcini lets rip with his machine gun and the Dalek is destroyed in a violent explosion. Orcini comments with pleasure that the bullets are fitted with bastic heads.

AS: 'This was when we choked everyone as a pall of black smoke from the Dalek blew over the camera crew.'

JB: 'The explosion was rigged up by Jim Francis. As there were other things going on that day, we created the Dalek shell in the workshop and brought it out with us so that we could achieve the effect as easily as possible. However, we had a problem with the wind changing direction all the time, and the smoke from the explosion blew straight at us afterwards. Ideally one would plan the shots so that it blew the other way.

'We had to pre-cut and break the shell of the Dalek. Jim manufactured a number of explosive charges to be set off in sequence: maybe one to lift the thing off the ground, one for light and one for smoke. Sometimes we needed a "pretty" explosion rather than a powerful one. Often, too, when the script said "and it blows up" we had to overstate it, because all you see of an explosion is a subliminal image. The actual effect is always better if it is bigger and more impressive than it would be in real life.'

Davros speaks to Kara via her communications screen and reports that a Dalek patrol has been attacked. He tells her that he is sending some Daleks to 'protect' her against insurrection. Kara thanks him through gritted teeth. Afterwards, Vogel tells Kara he suspects that Davros has realised what they are up to. Kara looks forward to Davros's death so that she will control the provision of food for the whole galaxy.

The Doctor decides to pay a visit on the Great Healer while Peri goes with Jobel to see the DJ. When his companion has gone, the Doctor is captured by two white Daleks and led off.

Fighting off Jobel's amorous advances, Peri slips into the DJ's room.

AS: 'The DJ's studio and Kara's office were slightly expedient, and I wasn't too happy with them. They were actually the same set, just changed around a bit. There wasn't enough money to build another set, so we had to make do.'

The DJ is impressed that Peri is actually from America on Earth. He explains that he has based his style of presentation on some recordings brought back from Earth by his great-grandfather.

GH: 'Some of that music playing in the background is genuine. You can't get permission to use most American music as it would cost a fortune, but there are good cover versions and sound-a-likes that you can use.'

JB: 'The DJ's headphones were specially constructed by Andy Lazell.'

Davros congratulates Tasambeker on a job well done. He quizzes her about her feelings for Jobel, encouraging her to watch him on the security cameras and then see if she doesn't hate him enough to kill him.

The Doctor has been placed in a cell with Natasha and Grigory. As he tries to free himself from his manacles, they tell him what they have seen. He gets one foot free.

In Kara's office, a signal is received from Orcini – he has entered the catacombs under Tranquil Repose. Two Daleks enter the office, and, after exterminating Vogel, order Kara to accompany them back to Davros.

GH: 'That is a standard post-production extermination effect. When things have been established over a period of time, you don't just come along and change them for the sake of it.'

Takis and Lilt talk covertly to Jobel about moving against the Great Healer. Jobel is interested but wary.

GH: 'Although Jobel is a slightly camp character, he's real. All the characters are real to me. He's nicely underplayed and, although he's somewhat outrageous, he's real.'

Davros has been watching the discussion on his monitor and is infuriated by Jobel's duplicity. He offers Tasambeker the chance to become a Dalek, and says that to show her total obedience she must kill Jobel.

JB: 'For that shot of the Dalek eyestalk in the foreground, we couldn't get the Dalek close enough to the lens, because the camera was in the way. So we took an eyestalk off a Dalek and moved it in by hand.'

Orcini decides to release the prisoners and use them as scapegoats to divert attention from his own operations.

Tasambeker tries to warn Jobel that he will die unless he leaves. He will not listen, and cruelly snubs her again. In fury, she plunges a filled hypodermic into his chest and kills him.

GH: 'The hypodermic was filled with liquid, and we originally had a shot of it emptying once it had been stuck into Jobel. Again, that was cut as it was too horrific.'

JB: 'The needle was wired with a spring so that it collapsed into the syringe. Jobel was then fitted with a body plate with a needle already attached to it. With careful camera angles and editing, the whole thing came across as effective and real.'

Tasambeker is exterminated by two white Daleks.

Peri uses the DJ's viewing screen to find the Doctor. The DJ shows her how

FROM SCRIPT TO SCREEN: REVELATION OF THE DALEKS

to speak to him. The Doctor responds by telling her that she is in danger. He instructs her to get back to the TARDIS and to warn the President's ship not to land.

Davros has heard this warning and sends his Daleks to bring Peri to him and to kill the DJ.

The DJ bars Peri's exit, saying that it is too dangerous for her to go. He suggests that she uses his own radio transmitter to warn the President's ship.

The Doctor leaves Natasha and Grigory to destroy the incubation room. When Natasha attempts to fire her gun, however, she discovers that its power pack is exhausted. Davros orders that a specimen be activated, and another transparent Dalek materialises in the room. Grigory changes the controls on the incubator tanks in an attempt to stop the process.

Bostock and Orcini arrive at Davros's base and, killing the guard, burst in. Caught in the crossfire from their machine guns, Davros is killed. Orcini feels it was too easy, however, and he is right. The head in the life support unit was artificial; the real Davros suddenly appears on the steps behind them.

GH: 'The only reason I can think of for my use of close-ups when Davros appears on the stairs is that Terry Molloy might not have been in his base at the time. I suspect, because of time, we just had him standing there, and I took the shots accordingly.'

Bostock throws a knife at Davros, but it thuds into the back of his chair, just missing his neck.

JB: 'We didn't throw the knife, we just had it stuck in there. The cutting from the hand throwing the knife to the knife in the back of the chair gives the impression of it hitting its target.'

Davros's white Daleks enter the chamber and fire at Bostock and Orcini. Orcini's false leg is hit and blown away, and Bostock is winged by an exterminator blast. Davros, in his chair, hovers above Orcini, transfixing him with a bolt of blue lightning from his hand.

JB: 'Gaunt was standing there with one leg strapped up behind him, hopping about, and we rigged a little charge to disconnect his fake leg for the shot where it gets blown off.

'Davros's chair was difficult to recreate. The original didn't exist, so we had to re-build it all without much reference material. It was quite expensive.'

GH: 'The shot of Davros hovering above Orcini was a very complicated one to achieve. We had Davros set up on a block against a black background, and that image was then superimposed on the shot of the room with Orcini down on the floor. The crackling blue light came from a Van der Graff generator, which was also in the studio, and the spark of electricity was added to the main image in post-production, as were the red glow under Davros's chair and the blue glow over the lightning bolt.'

Pat Godfrey: 'Davros's costume was from stock, so we just patched it up and made it re-useable.'

The transparent shell has now converted into a fully formed white Dalek, and it rises up to hover menacingly over Natasha and Grigory. It exterminates them, but then explodes due to Grigory's tampering with the equipment.

JB: 'We got hold of a chap, Stuart Evans, who produced Dalek models commercially, and borrowed one of his kits, so that we could get it up high enough. The problem was that, with the limitations of studio space, we could never have got the depth of field to have had a full-sized Dalek floating up in the air. It wasn't physically possible, because the Dalek needed to be close to the camera. We initially thought that if we went for a model, and put that in front of the camera, it would look as though it was a giant Dalek.'

GH: 'We ended up doing the shots of the model Dalek in an effects studio and then adding it to the main picture in post production. It was simply the best and easiest way of getting the effect I wanted.'

JB: 'The model wasn't actually blown up. The explosion was achieved in post-production by using a video effect.'

The President's spaceship has apparently been turned away by Peri's transmitted warning. The DJ has now rigged up in his studio a large gun, which he describes to Peri as firing a highly directional ultrasonic beam of rock and roll. He hopes that this will repel the Daleks.
 Kara arrives in Davros's laboratory. Davros accuses her of trying to kill him, but Kara denies this. Davros gives back to Orcini the communicator device that he earlier confiscated, and instructs him to operate it. Before the Knight can complete the sequence, Kara admits that the device is in fact a bomb. Orcini knifes Kara in response to her treachery, and she falls dead on the floor.

JB: 'The knife worked in a similar way to the hypodermic in the earlier scene; the blade slipped back into the handle.'

The DJ manages to destroy two Daleks with his gun, but is exterminated by a third. The Doctor, listening over the speaker system in the caverns, hears what has happened. Turning a corner, he himself then runs into two Daleks, who escort him away.

Takis and Lilt monitor the landing on Necros of the second spaceship that was earlier detected approaching.

JB: 'We had a special model filming day to do all these scenes. We built a platform and dressed it with bits and pieces to represent the landing pad, and then the spaceship was built. It descended on an air ram, which was hidden by the tower with the flashing lights.'

The Doctor is taken to Davros, who tells him that he survived their last encounter by using an escape pod. While Davros gloats over his achievements, Orcini and the Doctor have a furtive exchange of gestures, agreeing an unspoken plan. The Doctor then draws Davros's attention, allowing Orcini to retrieve Kara's bomb. When asked about the fate of the Tranquil Repose residents, Davros explains that those whom he considered worthy have been converted into Daleks, while the others have been sent to Kara's processing plant to be turned into a protein-rich foodstuff for sale to the starving masses of this part of the galaxy. When he has created sufficient new Daleks, he plans to invade the neighbouring planets to which the food has been supplied.

JB: 'When we came to get Davros's mask done, we found that the sculptor who had done it the previous time had left, so Dorka took on that responsibility and arranged for it to be re-made.'

Takis and Lilt meet the new arrivals – grey Daleks. Ignoring the two men's attempts to bargain, the Daleks demand to be taken to Davros.

JB: 'Two of these Daleks were originals and two we had built. We got the fibreglass workshop to make up some of the basic components, then the carpenters turned these into final structural pieces and added castors and seats and all that kind of thing. When a designer's got only two or three assistants and so much work to do, then it's useful to be able to get the carpenters to screw and bolt these things together.'

Peri arrives in Davros's laboratory, escorted by a white Dalek. Davros prepares to activate his new Dalek army, but Bostock has revived and manages to shoot his hand off before he can do so. Bostock is then exterminated by a Dalek.

JB: 'We went through a couple of exploding hands getting that shot. The hand was made from brown foam, and we gave him green blood.'

The grey Daleks battle with Davros's white Daleks, eventually defeating them.

They sweep into the laboratory and order Davros to return with them to Skaro to stand trial for crimes against their race. The white Daleks will be reconditioned to obey the will of the Supreme Dalek. Davros draw their attention to the Doctor, but they retort that his appearance does not match their records. They intend to hold him until his identity can be verified.

When Davros has been led away, the Doctor uses Orcini's gun to blind the grey Dalek left on guard. Peri then attaches to it a grenade taken from Bostock's pocket, blowing it up.

JB: 'We always had to be careful not to reveal too much of the insides of a Dalek! All the paper debris that flew into the air after the explosion was deliberate. This was an idea I got from Jim Francis. When you blow something up, it always seems to come down too soon, immediately after it's happened; explosions happen too quickly, and you just get balls of smoke. But if you add these bits of paper, they float down slightly later, and it looks a lot more effective.'

Orcini intends to use the bomb to destroy the complex before Davros and the Daleks can escape, and he tells the others to get out while they can.

The Doctor tells Takis and Lilt that Davros has created a demand for synthetic protein and they must continue to supply it. They can use the protein-rich staff of life plant as a new raw material – there's certainly enough of it about.

As everyone races for the exit, the Dalek ship takes off. Orcini detonates the bomb, just too late to stop the ship. Davros has escaped again.

JB: 'The model, constructed by Bill Pearson from my brief, reflected all the elements from the location and from the glass shots: the pyramids, the pool, the statues, the sky. Freon was used for the smoke coming out of the bottom of the ship as it lifts off. There's an awful lot of work goes into a model like this, and then we blow it up! Explosions are especially tricky to do on a small scale.'

As the base rocks with explosions, the workers mill about in the smoke and confusion.

GH: 'The picture shake was all done in post production. It was Quantel shaking the picture electronically rather than us shaking the cameras physically.'

When the excitement has died down, Takis and Lilt prepare themselves for the task ahead – rebuilding the processing plant.

The Doctor decides to take Peri for a holiday, but the picture freeze-frames just as he is about to state the intended destination.

GH: 'The very last word – Blackpool – was cut because the series had been just put on hold and a decision was taken not to trail the following season.'

POST-PRODUCTION

The early part of this chapter covered the pre-production work on *Revelation of the Daleks*. Now Graeme Harper describes the general post-production process: the work that takes place once all the filming and recording has been completed.

'I would sit down with all the recorded material copied on to VHS tapes encoded with a timestamp [a clock with which each frame can be uniquely identified]. From these, I would be able to work out all the "ins" and the "outs" – in other words, the exact frames on which I wanted to cut into and out of each scene – and the order in which I wanted all the shots to come. In the process, I also selected which of the different takes I wanted to use.

'I can't remember whether or not we did an "off-line" edit on *Revelation of the Daleks*. I seem to think that we didn't. An "off-line" edit is where the director supervises a rough cutting together of the show to see how it all fits. Gaps may be left for any post-production work that is still under way, and certain sequences may later be lengthened or shortened by any special video effects that are to be added.

'I think that in this case we went straight to an "on-line" edit – constructing the show from my notes, cutting it according to how I wanted it to be, and to what would hopefully be the correct length.

'It would generally take about two days of work to end up with a basic edit. That would then be shown to John Nathan-Turner, we would go through it with him in the edit suite, and he would suggest changes depending on how he had visualised the show as looking. Any necessary changes would take another day to make.

'We would have to lift off any shots that required electronic video effects and put them on a tape to go over to the Video Effects Workshop. There we would add in John Brace's model work, the Dalek exterminator effects and so on. These treated shots would then be put onto a tape and dropped back into the master tape containing the rest of the programme.

'In the week's gap that had occurred between the end of the location filming and the start of the studio rehearsals for *Revelation of the Daleks*, I had worked with the film editor (Ray Wingrove) to cut together all the film sequences: the fight with the mutant and so on. Once these sequences had been agreed with John, we did a basic film dub [i.e. added the sound] and transferred them all to video. These were also ready then to be dropped into the master tape as and where appropriate.

'Dick Mills at the Radiophonic Workshop would have got a copy of the original "on-line" edit – the one without all the effects added – together with notes showing where and what all the effects were going to be. This was so that he could start putting a basic track of special sounds together. I would go to the Workshop and sit down with him and the composer, Roger Limb, to go through where all the sounds were needed and what I was looking for in the way of music. Eventually Dick would get a copy of the master tape, and he would then be able to add more sounds to complement the effects sequences.

'Dick and Roger would go away and do all their work for two weeks, and when they had finished, I would go and listen to everything that they had done, before we got to the dubbing session. In that way, we could adjust anything that wasn't working. The next time I would hear their work would be at the dub, when we could again make minor changes if necessary.

'I tend not to give detailed instructions to a composer. I think my direction to Roger was simply to make the music big and orchestral. I know the music is electronic but I wanted something huge and orchestral. Roger Limb managed to give me that, and came up with a stunning, electronically produced, orchestral sound. Dick Mills also composed some "death music" for part two.'

Roger Limb, interviewed for *Doctor Who Magazine*, had the following recollections of working on *Revelation of the Daleks*:

'You sit down first with your director, and your relationship with him is crucial for the whole operation. You don't just decide where the music is going to be and what it is going to do in an emotional sense. You also consider the actual sounds themselves. Graeme Harper was very good like that; he really gave me a lot of help in that way. He bullied me a lot, but he knew what he wanted and made me go for it. He made me look for things that I might not have automatically thought of. He was a good director from my point of view. He didn't know anything about music, but he knew exactly what he wanted the music to do. When I played some music, he knew it was something he *didn't* want. The important thing is to find out what the director *does* want.'

Once all the music and special sounds have been dubbed onto the master tape at the sypher dub session, that is then the end of the director's job. All that remains is for the completed programme to be scheduled and transmitted.

TRANSMISSION

The two episodes of *Revelation of the Daleks* were eventually transmitted at 5.25 pm on Saturday 23 March 1985 and Saturday 30 March 1985 respectively, bringing to a close the twenty-second season of *Doctor Who*. The closing episode achieved a notable success in attracting 7.7 million viewers, the second highest rating of the season, bettered only by the first episode of the opening story, *Attack of the Cybermen*, which had attracted 8.9 million. The average viewing figure for the story was 7.55 million viewers per episode, slightly above the season average of 7.12 million. Although very respectable, this was still rather lower than the series had been achieving in the recent past. The season as a whole also fared rather less well than most previous ones in the weekly television chart – perhaps the best guide to a programme's success or failure – its average position being a disappointing 61st.

One reason for the lower-than-normal ratings was that HTV/Goldcrest's new film series *Robin of Sherwood* was transmitted by ITV in direct competition with most of the episodes. Word-of-mouth publicity for this new fantasy-orientated show was very good and, given the choice between this and the known quantity of *Doctor Who*, many casual viewers opted for the greenwood forests rather than the desolation of Necros.

Revelation of the Daleks was repeated in 1993 as the sixth Doctor's entry in a series of BBC2 repeats to celebrate *Doctor Who*'s thirtieth anniversary. The repeat was of the overseas four-part version, rather than of the original two-part transmission, and it ran on consecutive Friday evenings from 19 March to 9 April inclusive in a 7.15 pm slot following repeats of *Stingray* and *The Man From U.N.C.L.E.*

CREDITS

Producer	John Nathan-Turner
Writer/Script Editor	Eric Saward
Director	Graeme Harper
Production Associate	Angela Smith (replaced Sue Anstruther at late stage)
Production Manager	Michael Cameron
Production Assistant	Elizabeth Sherry
AFM	Jo O'Leary (replaced David Tilley at late stage)
Designer	Alan Spalding
Design Assistant	Adele Marolf
Costume Designer	Pat Godfrey
Make-Up Designer	Dorka Nieradzik (replaced Elizabeth Rowle at late stage)
Visual Effects Designer	John Brace
Video Effects	Dave Chapman
Prop Buyer	John Watts

THE SIXTH DOCTOR

Lighting Director	Don Babbage (replaced Henry Barber at late stage)
Technical Co-ordinator	Alan Arbuthnott
Sound Supervisor	Andy Stacey
Grams	Howard Jones
Camera Supervisor	Alec Wheal
Vision Mixer	Dinah Long
Videotape Editor	Steve Newnham
Floor Assistant	Anna Price
Crew	11
Title Music	Ron Grainer
Incidental Music	Roger Limb
Special Sound	Dick Mills
Film Cameraman	John Walker
Film Sound	Steve Gatland
Film Editor	Ray Wingrove

Cancellation Crisis

Rumours that *Doctor Who*'s twenty-third season had been cancelled by the BBC first began to circulate amongst the series' fans over the weekend of 23 and 24 February 1985, but it was not until the following Tuesday, 26 February, that the first public confirmation came in the form of a report by journalist Patrick Hill in the London evening newspaper, the *Standard*:

> *Dr Who* is being dropped by the hard-up BBC for the first time in 22 years.
>
> It has decided that Dr Who's adventures are too expensive to produce.
>
> BBC1 Controller Michael Grade has ordered the series, which stars Colin Baker, to be suspended for at least 18 months.
>
> *Dr Who* fans have launched a campaign to try to persuade Mr Grade to change his mind.
>
> The series has been seen on TV at least every nine months over the past 22 years and regularly attracts nearly eight million viewers.
>
> A BBC spokesman said: 'We intend to make a lot of new drama this year and cannot afford to do that and produce *Dr Who*.
>
> 'The Doctor is being rested, but will be back next year.'
>
> The last episode will go out on March 30.
>
> Within hours of Mr Grade's decision, some of the programme's 110 million fans worldwide in 54 countries where it is shown, had begun their campaign.
>
> An army of fans began mustering letters of complaint about the series being rested.

One fan said: 'If public opinion can change the BBC's mind over *Dallas*, then we hope we can do the same.'

London record producer Mr Ian Levine, a lifetime fan and member of the British *Dr Who* fan club, said: '*Dr Who* is now more than just a TV programme. For 22 years it has been a way of life. We are calling on all fans to write to Michael Grade to urge him to change his mind.'

A spokesman for the British branch of the *Dr Who* Appreciation Society, which has over 3,500 members, said: 'This news has been a great shock to us. We will be meeting to discuss exactly what we can do to help save one of the country's favourite programmes.'

A spokesman for the *Dr Who* fan club added: 'We want all our members to write to Mr Grade.

'At present 30,000 letters have already been sent. We have got to save this programme and we are calling on members of the public to help us.' '

This short article marked the start of an incredible whirlwind of press coverage and fan activity the like of which *Doctor Who* had never seen before. The first national report came just a few hours later, courtesy of the BBC itself, on the children's news magazine programme *Newsround*, and this was quickly followed by brief items on BBC1's main evening news bulletins at 6 pm and at 9 pm, both featuring a short clip from the most recently transmitted episode, part one of *The Two Doctors*. New developments then occurred daily.

On Wednesday 27 February, the rest of the media eagerly pounced on the story, seeing in it a chance to indulge in their perennial pursuit of knocking the BBC, which had been at the centre of another major furore less than a month earlier when Michael Grade had dropped the popular soap opera *Dallas* and then been forced to reinstate it due to public pressure. David Saunders, the Co-ordinator of the *Doctor Who* Appreciation Society (DWAS), was inundated by phone calls from newspaper journalists, from TV and radio stations – both national and local – and from fans in the UK and in the USA, all desperate for information. Society representatives were even booked to appear on the BBC's *Breakfast Time* programme and on ITV's rival *Good Morning Britain*, although in the event both appearances fell through – the BBC's because Michael Grade, who was to have responded to the fans' criticisms, was on a skiing holiday in France and reportedly could not be contacted.

CANCELLATION CRISIS

On Thursday 28 February, the fruits of all the journalists' endeavours became apparent as the story broke in the national press. Every daily newspaper – not only the tabloids but also the so-called quality broadsheets – devoted space to it, and some – the *Daily Telegraph*, the *Guardian*, the *Daily Express* and the *Sun* – judged it of sufficient interest to merit front page coverage.

The *Sun*'s report, under the banner headline *Dr Who is Axed in a BBC Plot*, was particularly memorable, and was the only one to take a slightly new angle on the story. Wrote reporter Charles Catchpole:

Doctor Who was axed by the BBC last night, and furious fans claimed it was a plot to back up demands for a higher licence fee.

TV bosses say they cannot afford to make any new shows about the famous time-traveller for 18 months.

But even the BBC's own men see the axing of the show – a hit for 22 years – as a cynical bid to whip up support for an increase in the fee.

One official said: 'This is absolute madness. *Doctor Who* is getting around nine million viewers.

'There's a strong feeling that the high-ups are using it as part of their propaganda campaign.'

Actor Colin Baker, who plays the Doctor, said: 'I was staggered. We were all geared up to start work on the next series.'

And sexy Nicola Bryant – his assistant Peri – was said to be 'very surprised and clearly upset.'

Colin said: 'I am contracted to the series, but the decision will mean the BBC probably having to pay off a lot of other people. It doesn't seem good financial sense.'

Patrick Troughton, 54, who was Dr Who in the Sixties, said: 'I think it is just power politics at work. I'm sure the viewers will make their feelings known.'

BBC1 supremo Michael Grade claimed: 'We intend to make a lot of new drama, and we cannot afford to do that and *Doctor Who*.'

But Beeb insiders say each episode of the sci-fi serial costs only

£180,000 – against an average £220,000 for drama.

They claim dumping the Doctor will *lose* the Corporation money from sales to 54 other countries. It has a world-wide audience of 110 million viewers.

With just five new episodes left to be shown, fans were launching a massive campaign to save the Doctor last night.

Jeremy Bentham, co-founder of the *Dr Who* Appreciation Society, said: 'The public won't let it die.'

In America, the show's 40,000-strong fan club pledged themselves to raise one and a half million dollars to keep the programme on the air.

This leader article was followed up by a short editorial comment piece inside the paper which, although written in the *Sun*'s usual lurid style, must surely have struck a chord with many of the series' disappointed viewers. Headed *Who Dunnit?*, it read:

There can rarely have been a more popular children's TV show than *Doctor Who*.

Yet this programme is now selected by the BBC to be shelved for 18 months.

The poor dears say that they cannot afford to make another series. *Dr Who* probably costs less than an average TV drama.

So what cheap rubbish is going to be put on in its place?

The life story of Director-General Alasdair Milne? Or just the station signal?

We can tell the BBC how it can start saving real money.

By sacking the over-paid fat heads who came up with this nasty little stunt!

It became apparent as the day wore on that the BBC was trying to play down the story. This was clearly a case of swimming against the tide, however, as interest from other sources continued largely unabated, one of the most notable cases being an interview with Ian Levine, one of the leading fan campaigners, on ITN's *News at One*.

Friday 1 March saw further items appearing in the national press, most of them concentrating on fans' reactions to the postponement and on the pledged financial support from those in the States. The *Sun* and the *Daily Star* both took the opportunity to launch 'Save *Doctor Who*' campaigns, the latter giving over no fewer than five pages to its coverage of the series. Reports also started to appear about the possibility of a record being produced, along the lines of the Band Aid famine relief single, to publicise the series' predicament.

The BBC had by this time had an opportunity to formulate a considered response to the situation, having been caught completely off guard by the initial outcry. This belated damage-limitation exercise began on the afternoon of 1 March when Bill Cotton, Managing Director of BBC Television, took the highly unusual step of telephoning DWAS Co-ordinator David Saunders to inform him that the BBC was issuing a press statement to clarify its position over *Doctor Who*'s future, confirming that the series would be returning in 1986 and in its original format of one 25-minute episode per week. Further evidence that the BBC was finally getting its act together came when a planned appearance by Ian Levine on BBC1's early evening chat show *Wogan* was called off at the last minute, denying the fan campaign a valuable publicity opportunity.

The press release that the BBC issued that day was a cleverly worded piece of media manipulation that made it appear that the Corporation had in some way capitulated to public pressure when in actual fact its position remained completely unchanged. Headed 'More *Doctor Who* in 1986 – Another Miraculous Escape for Fiction Favourite', the release read as follows:

> As every follower of *Doctor Who* knows ... You can't kill a Time Lord. Today Bill Cotton Managing Director of BBC Television phoned David Saunders, Co-ordinator of the *Doctor Who* Appreciation Society, to explain the BBC plans.
>
> He said: '*Doctor Who* will be on the air in 1986, as it is in 1985, and as it has been for each of the past 22 years.
>
> 'Instead of running in January 1986 we shall wait until the start of the autumn schedule, and then *Doctor Who* will be a strong item in the mix.
>
> 'We are also going to go back to the old tradition and have 25-minute programmes rather than the 45-minute version running at the moment. We think that is what the public wants. So does the

producer, and his team.

'The 45-minute series has been a good experiment, but we need to get back to basics, and to established ways. It also means that with a 25-minute length we can run the series for a greater number of weeks.'

Mr Cotton added: 'We appreciate the passionate support of the fan club in this country, and of fans around the world. We ask them to be a little patient while we get the Doctor back onto familiar rails. I am confident that *Doctor Who* has a great future on BBC1'

The tabloids, perhaps sensing that they had got as much mileage out of the story as they usefully could, seized on this as a chance to claim that their 'Save *Doctor Who*' campaigns had been a success. The *Daily Star* of Saturday 2 March repeated sections of the press release verbatim, and went on to add:

A Band Aid style record has been planned to raise cash for the Save *Dr Who* cause. Fans hope Elton John and Holly Johnson – both *Who* fans – will take part along with the Village People.

It is the second time in 10 days that Mr Cotton has had to calm angry viewers.

He earlier admitted that the BBC had boobed dropping *Dallas* in mid-series and announced that it would be back next month.

The *Doctor Who* news came on the same day it was revealed that the BBC had paid £500,000 – for an American series it hadn't even seen.

Kane and Abel, based on Jeffrey Archer's best-seller, is being made by Embassy Films, which was headed by Mr Grade until 1983.

Mr Grade has a credit on the series as executive producer – but he has no financial involvement in it.

The elusive Mr Grade also entered the fray on 2 March, the *Daily Mail*'s Corinna Honan having actually flown out to the French Alps in order to track him down. His rather brusque comments betrayed a sense of irritation at the sensational coverage given to what he appeared to consider a rather trivial matter:

Of course I care about the *Dr Who* fans, but I'm only thinking about British viewers. Do you know how many watched *Dr Who* last week?

CANCELLATION CRISIS

Six million. Very low indeed. Two or three years ago it was getting 10 to 11 million viewers.

But there's no reason for anyone to make waves. It's not as if I'm cancelling the series. We've got a lot of work to do on it but the show *will* be back. That's a promise. And it will be better than ever.

The BBC is *not* broke. It's just a question of priorities. A lot of drama shows are reaching their natural end. The writers don't want to write. The actors don't want to act. We need new material.

The policy has been for short-run series in the last couple of years. We hope these new ones will run for more than a year or two.

When challenged to respond to the enormous public outcry that the postponement had generated, Grade dismissed the series' fans as a special interest group and asserted that the rest of the world would barely notice its absence. 'Taking *Doctor Who* off the air is a piece of professional judgment. It is nothing to do with the licence fee coming up. We take a million of these decisions every day of the week. It's just an extraordinary storm in a teacup. Anyway, we've just had our best week in a long time on BBC1 and 2 – over 51 per cent of the total TV audience from 6 pm to close down every day.'

Sunday 3 March saw the DWAS's executive committee holding a meeting with other prominent fans to discuss their next steps. They decided on two courses of action: first, to send all Society members a photocopied letter explaining the current situation and, secondly, to write to Bill Cotton in response to his phone call to David Saunders, requesting some more meaningful assurances on *Doctor Who*'s future.

Saunders began the following day, Monday 4 March, by taking part in BBC Radio 4's topical *Start the Week* programme, answering presenter Richard Baker's questions about the fan campaign. Then, in the afternoon, he travelled from Broadcasting House to Television Centre to deliver the DWAS's letter personally to Bill Cotton's secretary.

Cotton's reply, sent the very next day, had little to offer in the way of further reassurance, but was interesting in that it marked the first real attempt by the BBC to suggest that the postponement decision had been taken for reasons other than purely financial. Received by Saunders on Wednesday 6 March, it read in part:

Our intentions are clear. We intend to continue to produce *Dr Who* for as long as we believe the British public enjoy it. There is no decision to drop it after the next series.

As far as money from America is concerned, I regard that with a degree of scepticism, but I will certainly look into it. However the problem is not just financial, it is also about scripts and resources.

The day of the week, the time it is transmitted and the exact number will be decided over the next few months. What is important is that it will be a major offering on BBC1.

On Thursday 7 March and Friday 8 March, recording sessions took place for the much-vaunted record release to draw attention to *Doctor Who*'s plight. Entitled 'Doctor in Distress', it was written and produced by Ian Levine and his song writing partner Fiachra Trench, who together had previously supplied the theme music for the *Doctor Who* spin-off *K-9 and Company*. The reported original intention of using the proceeds to further the campaign for the series' return had been dropped once it was realised that this might command insufficient support. It had since been decided that any money raised should go instead to a charitable cause, the National Society for Cancer Relief. Although the hoped-for participation by major-league pop stars still failed to materialise, a number of artistes were then assembled by organisers Paul Mark Tams, a long-time *Doctor Who* fan, and Jeff Weston, the Managing Director of Record Shack, the label on which the record would be released, and for whom some of the artistes recorded.

Under the group name Who Cares?, four *Doctor Who* regulars – Colin Baker, Nicola Bryant, Anthony Ainley and Nicholas Courtney – performed the song alongside a whole host of other celebrities and entertainers. The full list ran to some 25 names: Earlene Bentley, comedienne Faith Brown, Miquel Brown, Warren Cann of Ultravox, Hazell Dean, Floid of the Hot Gossip dance troupe, Bobby G of Bucks Fizz, Steve Grant, Julie Harris, Justin Hayward and John Lodge of the Moody Blues, Jona Lewie, Phyllis Nelson, Richie Pitts from the cast of the musical *Starlight Express*, John Rocca of Freeez, actress Sally Thomsett, Basia Trzetrzelewska and Danny White of Matt Bianco, David Van Day of Dollar and Music Academy, and the group Time UK, consisting of the Jam's former drummer Rick Buckler with Ronnie Ball, Fletcher Christian, Jimmy Edwards, Ray Simone and Nick Smith.

The record was pressed and distributed as quickly as possible and released a week later, on Friday 15 March, accompanied by a video directed by Reeltime Pictures' Keith Barnfather after pop impresario Mike Mansfield reportedly pulled out at a late stage. ITV's *The Six O'Clock Show* marked the occasion with a short, very light-hearted item featuring clips from the Aaru cinema film *Dr Who and the Daleks* and interviews with fans and members of the general public. The press, however, showed only limited interest in the record's release, and it received scathing reports and reviews in some of the weekly music papers. BBC radio stations refused to play it, claiming that it was too poor artistically, although it did receive quite good air-play on some of the independent stations.

The next development in the saga came when a fan's letter of complaint about the postponement met with the following reply from Michael Grade in the 23-29 March edition of *Radio Times*:

> The response of *Doctor Who* enthusiasts is bordering on the hysterical given the exact nature of the BBC's decision. *Doctor Who* has not been cancelled, just delayed for a year. The ratings for the current season have been disappointing and we need time to consider the reasons for this. The current series is an experimental 45-minute length and this has not proved as popular as we had hoped. We were looking to make some financial savings in the coming year and it seems that after 21 years a short rest would do the Doctor no harm at all.
>
> Long-running television series do get tired and it is because we want another 21 years of *Doctor Who* that we have prescribed a good rest.

This pronouncement, which again sought to shift the emphasis away from the financial reasons underlying the postponement and towards supposed deficiencies in the series itself, triggered a slight resurgence of press activity. Reports of Grade's comments appeared in several newspapers, most notably in the *Daily Express* of Thursday 21 March 1985, but to the fans' disappointment, these merely followed the BBC line, again asserting that the series' future was safe.

At the beginning of April, further rumours began to circulate within fandom, this time to the effect that Season 23, when it did eventually appear, might be reduced from the then standard length of 26 episodes to only 20 episodes. Ian Levine made an announcement about this at a DWAS convention, DWASocial 5, on Saturday 6 April, but John Nathan-Turner, who was next up on stage, angrily denied that any such decision had been taken.

Throughout the period since the news of the postponement first became public, many thousands of *Doctor Who* fans had written individually to the BBC to make their displeasure felt. Most had received just a standard photocopied letter in response, but DWAS member Gavin French managed to extract a personal reply, dated 17 April 1985, from Head of Series and Serials Jonathan Powell. This offered another slightly different slant on the reasons for the BBC's actions:

> We decided to postpone *Doctor Who* for two reasons. Firstly, we have a financial problem on BBC1 and looking at the programmes we decided that *Doctor Who* would benefit from some breathing space. It

seems to me that the show does not work in its new three quarter hour episodes, and would be much better returned to its traditional 25-minute format. To change the format requires time and I believe it to be entirely advantageous that the producer of the programme has some time to consider it in depth.

As yet we have not decided how many episodes we shall make when the show returns. We plan to have it on the screen by Autumn 1986 and the number of episodes will be decided according to our editorial wishes balanced against the financial means.

To add to the fans' bewilderment, Saturday 20 April saw Michael Grade giving yet another explanation, when questioned on the subject during an interview for the Channel 4 chat show *The Late Clive James*. This time, no mention at all was made of any financial problems: 'The truth about *Doctor Who* is that it was a target for a cut, because the show's not doing very well. It's overly violent. It's losing audiences. Its appeal is not what it was. It's not getting new generations of children. We needed time to take it off the air and get it right.'

It was perhaps fortunate for Grade that these statements went unchallenged, Clive James no doubt being unaware that Season 22 had actually achieved quite respectable average ratings of 7.12 million viewers per episode and correspondingly high audience appreciation figures. Nor would anyone with any knowledge of *Doctor Who* have had much difficulty in rubbishing his claim that time was required in order to revamp the series, some quite radical changes having been made in previous seasons without the need for any such delay.

Wednesday 8 June brought further news in the form of a report in the *Sun* stating that Grade, along with Jonathan Powell and BBC Director of Programmes Brian Wenham, had decided to reduce Season 23 to fourteen episodes and subsequently to cancel the series altogether if its ratings failed to improve. The BBC Press Office denied that any such steps were being contemplated, but the fans remained understandably sceptical.

One of the few highlights of this period came with the commissioning of an original *Doctor Who* radio serial, *Slipback*, to go out on BBC Radio 4, in stereo, as part of a new children's magazine programme, *Pirate Radio 4*. Welcome though it was, this was nevertheless regarded by most commentators as being scant compensation for the lack of any new TV stories.

On Saturday 3 August, the *Sun* returned to the subject of the proposed episode count for Season 23, reporting an extraordinary error made by the staff of BBC Enterprises' Sales Director John Harrison:

CANCELLATION CRISIS

A BBC TV boss's blunder has confirmed *Sun* forecasts of *Dr Who* cutbacks.

Beeb chief John Harrison wrote a secret telex message to US distributors, saying next year's series will be trimmed from 26 shows to 14 25-minute episodes.

But someone mixed up the telex numbers – and the message went to the American *Doctor Who* Appreciation Society!

This report was again flatly denied by the BBC Press Office, even though photocopies of the offending telex reportedly began to spread amongst fans both in the US and in the UK.

Having been out of the *Doctor Who* news for a while, Michael Grade returned to controversy in September, using the opportunity of an interview on BBC Radio 2's popular *Jimmy Young Show* to launch another public attack on the series, this time explicitly criticising its production team: 'The people who make it have got rather complacent. The show got rather violent and lost a lot of its imagination, a lot of its wit, and was relying far too much on straightforward on-the-nose violence, and had failed really to capture a new audience. There's no question of it being killed off. There is going to be another series next year. The problem with the programme was that it had been losing its appeal. I decided that it was time to take stock, to look at the show, to rethink the scripts, to rethink the shape of the programme, to think how we might revitalise *Doctor Who* so that it's going to last another 20 years.'

On Wednesday 18 December, the BBC made an announcement finally admitting that Season 23 would indeed be only fourteen episodes long. This time, the disclosure failed to generate any press coverage at all, not even the *Sun* bothering to report the official confirmation of its earlier scoop. It seemed that the phase of media concern over the postponement had finally run its course.

As the glare of public attention moved away from *Doctor Who*, it was left to the series' fans to take a more considered look at the hectic events of this extraordinary ten month period, and to try to assess their long-term implications.

It would later be reported that the original news of the postponement had been leaked to the press by John Nathan-Turner, via Ian Levine.

'The day it was cancelled,' recalled Levine in a 1992 interview for *DWB*, 'John and Gary [Downie, his partner and a *Doctor Who* production assistant] came round to my house and spent the whole evening plotting what to do and how to get the press involved. John got me to phone Charles Catchpole of the *Sun*. He'd told me that there were codenames within the BBC that

Catchpole would know, so I phoned him and said that I worked on the sixth floor [of Television Centre] under Michael Grade and that my name was Snowball. I said that there was a plot to get rid of *Doctor Who*. While I was talking, John and Gary were busy scribbling away telling me what to say. I told Charles Catchpole how the show made profits for the BBC, how the series was being used in a plot to defend the licence fee increase – John was even reeling off figures off the top of his head for the number of countries that *Doctor Who* was sold to, and for the millions of pounds [it made], for me to quote at him! John was pulling the strings and using me, because he couldn't risk being identified as being involved. He knew this whole code thing and exactly what to say. Then we did the same thing with Geoff Baker of the *Daily Star*.'

Had Nathan-Turner and Levine not taken this step, the chances are that the phenomenal media outcry would never have occurred, and that the series could indeed have been cancelled altogether. Nathan-Turner himself has since denied that cancellation was ever a real possibility, but Colin Baker, in a 1989 interview for the fanzine *Kroton*, said: 'Originally it was the axe; it was coming off! Grade back-tracked very swiftly when he found out the reaction was as strong as it was, and it turned into a suspension, which was the only way he could get it back without losing too much face, I suppose.'

One thing on which all parties are in complete agreement is that the postponement decision, apparently conveyed to John Nathan-Turner by Jonathan Powell at a meeting on Monday 25 February 1985, came as a severe blow to the morale of the series' production team and cast. Speaking at a convention in Manchester on 16 November 1985, Nathan-Turner described their reaction to the news: 'It's a horrid thing to happen, to be told that the season you've prepared is kind of pulled from under your feet. I think my feeling was that of the rest of my team and of all the actors concerned, and indeed of all the directors who had been engaged. It's all very well to get your money at the end of the week, but it's far, far better actually to earn it. So I think we all felt fairly devastated.'

Eric Saward recalls that Nathan-Turner was in fact particularly demoralised by the decision. Saward himself remains uncertain as to the reasons for the postponement. 'I really don't know what the thinking was,' he says. 'I'm sure that Jonathan Powell hated the show. He was always very hostile to us at playbacks. Very indifferent, whether the show was good or bad. It seemed he'd really decided that he didn't like us. I think it was entirely his decision. I don't think Michael Grade cared one way or the other.'

Fans have often sought to suggest that the postponement was an act of pure vindictiveness on the part of either Grade or Powell, inspired by their apparent dislike of *Doctor Who*. This analysis overlooks the fact that the series had been unpopular with BBC executives throughout much of its history, without ever before having been dropped from the schedules. Programme planners tend to act not on the basis of their own personal preferences but on that of their professional judgment and expertise, weighing up a whole range of different factors before reaching a conclusion. The weight of evidence now suggests that the postponement came about largely as a consequence of the financial problems to which some of the earlier press coverage alluded – and this is a view to which John Nathan-Turner lent support. Two developments were particularly significant in this regard.

First, there was an enormous outlay involved in producing 104 episodes per year of the new soap opera *EastEnders*, which made its on-air debut in the week beginning 18 February 1985 – the very same week that the postponement decision was taken. The need to finance and support this show, which would soon become the BBC's most successful in the ratings, placed a very considerable strain on the budget and resources of the Series and Serials Department and resulted in a permanent reduction in the number of other programmes that it was able to make.

Secondly, and even more importantly, there was a substantial financial shortfall in the 1985/86 accounting year due to a decision taken by top-level management to bring forward by several months the launch of the BBC's daytime TV service, so as to get it up and running in advance of ITV's rival effort. This rescheduling meant that several million pounds had suddenly to be clawed back from the previously allocated departmental budgets, with cuts being made right across the board. *Doctor Who* was just one of the programmes to suffer, along with others such as *Mike Read's Pop Quiz*, *Come Dancing*, *The Hot Shoe Show* and *Crackerjack*.

It can indeed be considered an astute move on John Nathan-Turner's part to have placed in journalists' minds the idea that there might be a link between Season 23's postponement and the BBC's difficult financial position, as Ian Levine told *DWB*:

'John knew that the story of *Doctor Who* being cancelled alone would not have made the front page, but using the angle that the BBC was axing something popular to draw attention to their efforts to get the licence fee raised was extremely cunning, and it worked!'

A skilled publicist, the producer no doubt reasoned that a fierce public backlash was the one thing that could save the series if Grade and Powell were truly intent on killing it off.

The resulting furore is certainly reported to have caused considerable consternation amongst the BBC's Board of Governors, who saw themselves being drawn into an unexpected and embarrassing controversy. They regarded the postponement as just the latest in a succession of poor management decisions, and apparently took the matter up in forceful terms with Director-General Alasdair Milne. Milne's own view was that Grade, in underestimating the strength of the public's affection for *Doctor Who*, had made a serious error of judgment. On the other hand, however, he admired the way in which his subordinate had coped with the ensuing media circus.

There seemed to be no question of the cancelled season being reinstated, so the production team were left with the difficult task of deciding how to proceed.

The season had been at an advanced stage of preparation when the postponement decision was taken. The scripts for the first story, *The Nightmare Fair* by Graham Williams, had already been distributed to the regular cast and to key members of the production crew, including director Matthew Robinson. This serial, in two 45-minute episodes, would have seen the Doctor and Peri arriving on Blackpool's famous Pleasure Beach (a setting decided upon by John Nathan-Turner after he and Colin Baker made a promotional visit there in 1984 to open a new ride). There they would have discovered that one of the amusement arcades was in fact a deadly trap set by the sinister Celestial Toymaker, a character who had first appeared in an eponymous story in *Doctor Who*'s third season of adventures, way back in 1966.

The second two-parter was to have been *The Ultimate Evil*, written by Wally K Daly and directed by Fiona Cumming. This would have involved the Doctor and Peri arriving in the peace-loving domain of Tranquela with the intention of taking a holiday, only to get caught up in the devious schemes of an unscrupulous arms dealer, the evil Dwarf Mordant, who hopes to provoke a war between the Tranquelans and their neighbouring race, the Amelierons, by causing them to suffer sporadic fits of extreme violence.

Another two-parter for which draft scripts had already been prepared was Philip Martin's *Mission to Magnus* – previously titled *Planet of Storms*. As Martin later recalled in an interview for *Doctor Who Magazine*, this story, set on the female-dominated planet Magnus, would have featured the return not only of a popular character from Colin Baker's first full season as the Doctor but also of a much more well-established foe:

'I was asked to do a script, again with Sil and maybe involving the Ice Warriors. I'd written a first draft, in which I had the Ice Warriors inside a polar ice-cap, because it suited them being so cold. They were burrowing workshops in the ice-cap, which was beginning to flood the planet, and the people couldn't understand why. This ice environment allowed the Ice Warriors to move freely, because I was always worried about how slow they had been in previous stories.'

The season's longest story, a three-parter, had the working title *Yellow Fever and How to Cure It* (shortened in some later documentation to *Yellow Fever*). Written by Robert Holmes, it was to have been set, and filmed, in Singapore and included return appearances by the Autons, the Rani and possibly also the Master. In the event, Holmes had completed only a brief outline of the adventure before the season was postponed.

One of the two remaining two-part slots would probably have been filled by a Christopher H Bidmead story entitled *In the Hollows of Time*. The other would probably have gone either to a story, title unknown, by Bill Pritchard or to one called *The Children of January* by Michael Feeney Callan.

Following the postponement decision, Robert Holmes, Christopher H Bidmead and Michael Feeney Callan were all asked to continue working on their stories, but in the new 25-minute episode format rather than the old 45-minute one – a request to which all three writers immediately acceded. BBC documentation also indicates that Pip and Jane Baker were commissioned as early as 11 March 1985 – less than three weeks after the postponement decision was taken – to write a story, in four 25-minute episodes, with the working title *Gallifrey*. This is believed to have involved the destruction of the Doctor's home planet. In the end, however, these stories were all abandoned, as were those by Graham Williams, Philip Martin, Wally K Daly and Bill Pritchard, the cancellation ultimately being seen by the production team to imply that they had to start afresh with some new writers and some new ideas.

In any event, the production team decided that a completely different approach was called for, after they learned, in early June 1985, that the postponed season was to be only 14 episodes long. Eric Saward suggested having a season-spanning story in which the Doctor would be seen to be on trial, reflecting the fact that the series itself was still in this situation. This suggestion was readily agreed by John Nathan-Turner, and the two men then set about developing a workable format for what ultimately became *The Trial of a Time Lord*.

The basic premise of the story was that the Doctor would be brought back to Gallifrey by the Time Lords to stand trial for his repeated interference in the affairs of other planets. In a conscious allusion to the structure of Charles Dickens' *A Christmas Carol*, the evidence would be presented in three segments – the first concerning an incident in the Doctor's recent past, the second an incident in his present and the third an incident in his future – before the story was eventually concluded in a fourth and final segment. Two pivotal figures in the proceedings of the court would be the prosecuting counsel, known as the Valeyard, and the judge, known as the Inquisitor, for whom John Nathan-Turner and Eric Saward developed the following character outlines dated 5 July 1985:

THE VALEYARD AND THE INQUISITOR

The Doctor is not very popular on his home planet of Gallifrey. Over the years, his independence of mind has made him many enemies who would like to see him dead.

THE SIXTH DOCTOR

So when the Doctor is summoned home to stand trial for crimes that could cost him his life, it is decided, by the High Council, that a judge and a prosecuting counsel must be found who are seen to be both above suspicion and free of prejudice concerning the Doctor.

After close consultation with the KEEPER OF THE MATRIX, the High Council decide to find suitable candidates from their own future.

To avoid any form of prejudicial selection, the Matrix itself is ordered to draw up a list of qualified candidates. To make the selection even more random, the Matrix gives each candidate a code number, and it is from this list that the High Council choose their INQUISITOR (Judge) and VALEYARD (Prosecuting Counsel). This way only the Matrix knows the identity of the candidates concerned.

THE INQUISITOR is female, middle fifties and very learned. She is also a friendly, agreeable soul with a strong sense of humour. (Although it is tempting to parody contemporary judges, I think it would be more interesting and more fun to play against the accepted stereotype.)

THE VALEYARD, on the other hand, is far less agreeable. He is tall and lean with strong angular features, giving him the manner and appearance of a powerful, predatory bird, whose talons are a sharpness of mind and a verbal dexterity capable of dismembering the strongest and most considered of arguments.

As the trial continues, evidence comes to light suggesting that the Matrix has been tampered with and that the list of jurists it produced was far from unprejudiced.

But who has manipulated the Matrix? And who of the two jurists is involved in the deception?

The Doctor has to find out, while at the same time fighting for his own existence.

The intention was that, somewhere around part twelve of the story, the Valeyard would be revealed to be a corrupt future incarnation of the Doctor who had manipulated the whole Trial simply in order to destroy his own former persona. Peri was to be killed off at the end of part eight, becoming trapped in a situation from which the Time Lords were unable to extricate her, and a new companion, Mel, would be introduced in part nine. It was also decided at the outset that the Master should put in an appearance as one of the witnesses in the later stages of the proceedings.

CANCELLATION CRISIS

The original writers chosen to provide the scripts for the season were Robert Holmes, Philip Martin, award winning playwright David Halliwell and the late novelist Jack Trevor Story. The idea was that Holmes and Martin would contribute the first two segments of evidence, each in four episodes; that Halliwell and Story would then write two episodes apiece of the third four-part segment, liaising closely to ensure that their ideas dovetailed and could be realised using the same sets; and that Holmes would then provide the final two episodes to form the concluding segment.

On Tuesday 9 July 1985, all four writers travelled to the BBC's Threshold House offices for an initial discussion with John Nathan-Turner and Eric Saward, who explained the format to them and briefed them on their respective contributions.

Despite having made great play in the press of the need for *Doctor Who* to be revamped, Michael Grade had apparently taken no active interest in the formulation of the Trial idea. The only advice he had given John Nathan-Turner, in a meeting reportedly lasting somewhat short of ten minutes, was that the new season should contain less violence and more humour than the previous one. The production team therefore instructed the four writers along these lines, stressing the need to avoid any graphic violence and to make the stories fun and entertaining, albeit with humour arising organically out of the drama rather than grafted on artificially.

While work proceeded relatively smoothly on the segments commissioned from Robert Holmes and Philip Martin, which were given the final working titles *The Mysterious Planet* and *Mindwarp* respectively, the same could not be said of the two-part contributions by Jack Trevor Story and David Halliwell.

Little headway was made on Jack Trevor Story's segment. 'He came up with an idea for his section of the trial,' recalls Eric Saward. 'He said, "I've got an idea of a man sitting in an empty gasometer playing a saxophone." I told him, "That sounds wonderful, but I don't think we can use it in *Doctor Who*!"'

David Halliwell's script – working title *Attack from the Mind* – progressed a little further. Halliwell later recalled the plot when interviewed in 1992 by the New Zealand *Doctor Who* Fan Club fanzine *TSV*: 'It was set on a planet called Penelope, which was inhabited by two rival races; the Penelopeans who were extremely beautiful and poetic, and the Freds who were extremely ugly and plodding. At first it seemed as though the Freds were the aggressors, but later it appeared that this was not the case.'

Attack from the Mind went through a number of drafts before it was eventually dropped, Eric Saward informing Halliwell in a letter dated 18 October 1985 that it lacked the sort of energy and humour that he and John Nathan-Turner were seeking.

Following this, the production team decided that the four-part gap in the season should now be filled by just a single writer. A submission was commissioned from Christopher H Bidmead on 29 October 1985 under the working title *The Last Adventure*, although this would later be changed to *Pinacotheca*. In view of the urgency, Bidmead completed his scripts at a rapid pace, sending in first drafts of episodes one, two and three in mid-November, early December and late December respectively, and personally delivering to Eric Saward a second draft of all four episodes on 9 January 1986. On 7 February, however, Saward wrote to Bidmead to tell him that his story segment was being dropped, as he appeared to have misunderstood the brief he had been given. The script editor later amplified this by explaining that he had found the scripts dull and lacking in substance from the outset, but that he had been reluctant to pass comment until he had seen the complete story.

With the situation becoming ever more urgent, another writer was then approached to provide the missing four-part segment. This was *Sapphire and Steel* creator P J Hammond, whose attempt, commissioned on 10 February 1986, had the working titles *End of Term* and, later, *Paradise Five*.

A fantasy-orientated piece, *Paradise Five* would have seen the Doctor masquerading as a businessman and Mel as a hostess in order to discover the sinister secrets of a planet supposedly designated as a holiday haven for overworked executives, both human and alien. At first sight, the Paradise would have seemed idyllic, being run by two seemingly friendly characters called Michael and Gabriel with the assistance of a host of beautiful girls with names such as Stella and Bella and, to perform the menial tasks, a race of creatures known as Cherubs. However, it would ultimately have been exposed as a brash, artificial front for murderous money-making schemes. The Doctor's task would have been further complicated throughout the plot by the fact that the planet was plagued by a race of evil, ghost-like entities called Angels.

According to Hammond, Eric Saward liked this idea but John Nathan-Turner did not, and it was consequently rejected after he had completed just the first episode in draft.

On 6 March 1986, yet another four-parter was commissioned to fill the gap, and this one – working title *The Ultimate Foe* by Pip and Jane Baker – would finally be accepted. In view of the shortage of time, the writers were asked to have the first episode ready in draft form by 17 March, less than a fortnight later, and the other three by 7 April. In discussion with John Nathan-Turner and Eric Saward, they decided to make their plot a 'whodunit in space', paying homage to Agatha Christie.

In the meantime, on 4 February 1986, Robert Holmes had been commissioned as planned to write the final two episodes of the trial, under the working title *Time Inc.*. (It is thought that he was also at this point offered the chance to write the missing episodes nine to twelve, but quickly declined.) The intention was that *Time Inc.* would tie up all the outstanding plot threads from the fourteen-part story and provide a dramatic climax to the season. As things transpired, however, Holmes became seriously ill, and subsequently died on 24 May 1986, having completed only a rough draft of part thirteen. Eric Saward himself then took over the task of writing part fourteen, and in order to facilitate this, he also rewrote completely the latter scenes of Holmes's script, introducing a new character named Mr Popplewick.

This was by no means the end of the season's problems as Saward, who had resigned from the BBC after overseeing the first two segments of the Trial, subsequently had a major disagreement with John Nathan-Turner over the way in which the story was to end. Saward decided to withhold permission for his script for part fourteen to be used, and Nathan-Turner therefore brought in Pip and Jane Baker to write a completely new final episode for the story.

With the eventual transmission of Season 23, it seemed that, at least for the moment, *Doctor Who* had been reprieved.

Being the Companion

Doctor Who has always placed a great deal of emphasis not only on the enigmatic Doctor himself but also on those with whom he travels. The companion figures have invariably fulfilled the important dramatic functions of facilitating plot exposition and of providing a point of audience identification, but within these basic parameters have ranged from being well-written and interesting characters in their own right to being little more than pretty girls to keep the dads interested.

As one might expect, the attitude of the Doctor (and, more importantly, of the script writers) to the companion has changed over the years. With the changes that occurred during the Seventies and Eighties in social attitudes towards sex stereotyping, the role of the companion in *Doctor Who* was under pressure to develop beyond that of the helpless screamer.

When the *Doctor Who* production team were planning the series' twenty-first season, they were aware that a number of significant changes would have to take place. They knew that Janet Fielding (Tegan) had expressed a desire to bow out along the way, as had Mark Strickson (Turlough). They wanted to lose the Kamelion robot as well, and to introduce a new, female, companion for the Doctor.

In his book *Doctor Who – The Companions*, producer John Nathan-Turner explained that 'the decision to try one solitary companion with the Doctor was an attempt to echo the Pertwee-Jo relationship of the Seventies, which had been so successful'. Of course, the Doctor-companion relationship had gone through many variations over the years, but it is certainly true that, with the third and subsequent Doctors, the one-on-one format had seemed to work well, particularly from the point of view of the female companion. It had started with Liz Shaw and then developed through Jo Grant, Sarah Jane Smith, Leela and Romana. In fact it was John Nathan-Turner again who had broken the, by then, traditional format by introducing three companions – Adric, Nyssa and Tegan – to see out the fourth Doctor and introduce the fifth.

In February 1985, Nathan-Turner, Eric Saward and Peter Grimwade, the author of the new companion's introductory story *Planet of Fire*, devised an outline for the character:

Perpugilliam (Peri for short) Brown is a wealthy 18-year-old American student studying Botany. She has long blonde hair which complements her attractive looks. She does not suffer fools gladly and her most charming attribute is an acute sense of humour.

We meet Peri for the first time, while she is on holiday in whichever country we decide to film next season's foreign story.

Peri's mother, Janine, has remarried a man Peri dislikes – Howard. Peri still treasures the memory of her father who died when Peri was 13, particularly as her mother appears to care more for Howard's three children than for Peri herself. It is because of her respect for her father that Peri thinks so highly of the Doctor – to some extent the Doctor replaces the gap in Peri's life. When he died he was of the same age as the Doctor appears now. This never develops further than admiration and close friendship. Peri is the kind of girl who is popular – not just because of her looks, but because her warmth and sense of fun make her appeal to people of all ages.

As Eric Saward recalls, it was John Nathan-Turner's decision to make Peri an American. 'John wanted an American,' he says, 'and his brief was simply that: an American.' In Saward's view, this decision was motivated by a desire on the producer's part to curry favour with the American fans of *Doctor Who*. Nathan-Turner has however denied this. According to him, the decision was taken partly because of the popularity of Tegan – another non-British companion – and partly because he wanted to get away from Earth-UK companions in general, as he felt that their former predominance had lacked credibility.

Having auditioned a large number of actresses for the role, Nathan-Turner eventually chose Nicola Bryant, a young woman just out of drama school. Saward considers that the deciding factor for the producer was Nicola's voluptuousness. Having said this, however, he also accepts that she was the best candidate of all those auditioned. Clearly her attractive appearance and vivacious personality were more than sufficient to outweigh the fact that she lacked the blonde hair specified in the character outline. Another respect in which Nicola failed to meet the initial specifications was that she was not in fact an American – although neither producer nor script editor realised this at the time.

Nicola was born in a small village just outside Guildford in Surrey. 'It was the sort of village where everybody knew everybody else,' she explained in a 1992 interview for *The Frame*, 'and you daren't go out and play up because someone would tell your mother what you'd done. My father's central heating company was there, and my mother's family had lived there all their lives. There was no entertainment background at all in my family, except for the fact that my uncle, my father's youngest brother, was very big in amateur dramatics – he actually met his wife while playing in *The Pyjama Game*. I thought he was very funny. I remember as a kid going to see him and thinking "that looks fun", even though I wasn't interested in being an actress at the time. I wanted to be Margot Fonteyn Mk II.

'From as early as I can remember, my very first thoughts were of dancing. I started taking dancing lessons at Bellairs Dance School when I was three, and dancing was all I wanted to do right up until I was eleven, when I told my family that I wanted to go to ballet school. Choosing a career at that age is a very difficult thing to do, and dancing was a very precarious business, so understandably my parents preferred me to stay at my current school, where I could have a better standard of education. This was tough, but they thought it was for the best.

'My mother, being such a wonderful woman, realised that I was very upset at their decision. Having noticed in a newspaper that a local amateur dramatics society were auditioning for parts in *Fiddler on the Roof*, she suggested that I go along, even though you had to be sixteen to join and I was much younger. I went for the audition and when they asked what O levels I was doing, I made them all up. I ended up getting the part of the second youngest daughter, and the lady who played my youngest sister was eighteen! They had absolutely no idea I was so young.

'I took all my O levels and A levels and did well, and my father was very pleased. I worked hard, all through the holidays. Boyfriends used to come round and knock on the door and ask if I could come out, and I'd say, "Oh, not now, I'm doing my Chemistry." I didn't want to go out with boys, I was busy working. I did ten O levels and one O/A level when I was fifteen, then went on to take A levels in Geography, Economics, English and Home Economics.

'Eventually I gave up dancing, because the only classes I could now take were modern dance and tap. I didn't like them very much, as I was classically trained and wanted to be a classical dancer, and as far as I was concerned, anything else was just second best. Either you're going to be Margot Fonteyn or you're not. But I continued to appear in plays put on by the local company. After *Fiddler on the Roof*, I did *The Sound of Music*, *Snow White* ... all musicals, simply because I enjoyed them.

'There was an unwritten agreement in our household that once I had done my O and A levels, my parents would support me in whatever I wanted to do. And what I wanted to do was to go to drama school. I wrote to all the accredited schools and got auditions for everyone, but they were all sneering about my age. They said, "You can't come here at sixteen or seventeen. We want experienced people, people who have been through things in their life." It seemed that they weren't really interested in how good you were, just in how old you were.

'Now, when I went to the auditions I noticed what type of person each school wanted. You're sitting around waiting before it's your turn to audition, and you see the students going past on their way to classes or whatever. You look at the photographs on the wall and can see who has got which part. It's all a case of how observant you are. After I had been turned down, I reapplied to the schools three months later and was accepted by them all. The reason was that, the second time, I acted my interviews. In other words, I acted the part of the type of person I now knew each of them was looking for.

'The two most extreme were Central and Webber Douglas. For Central I frizzed my hair, put on black eyeliner and wore jeans in which I'd slashed holes long before it was fashionable to do so. Throughout the audition, I talked in a really common accent. At Webber Douglas, in contrast, I wore a full length practice skirt, put my hair in a bun, wore no makeup, and was a very classical, serious young lady. When they mentioned my age, I turned to them and said, "I'd just like to ask you ... please don't judge someone by the number of birthdays they've had, but by the events that have occurred between them." And that seemed to do the trick.

'I ended up at Webber Douglas. I'm not sure what drama school teaches you, though. I suppose that if you can survive two or three years there, then you can probably survive anything that gets thrown at you in the business. However, I came out after getting my diploma thinking that if that was what the acting business was like, then I didn't want to go into it. I found it so aggressive and bitchy, and it was very hard to strike up real friendships with people, because everyone was so fiercely competitive. Maybe part of my difficulty was that I came from a very close and loving relationship with my mother, very intimate and supportive, and I was as a result much more sensitive. I pick things up about people and what they're thinking. I have very, very acute hearing. I can walk into a familiar room and tell if the battery needs changing in the clock, because I can hear that the ticking is at a different rhythm from the week before. I actually have to sleep with ear-plugs in, because I hear so many sounds. One benefit of this is that I have perfect pitch and can pick up accents easily. The fact that my mother was deaf probably had something to do with it.

'The end-of-term play in my final year at Webber Douglas was the musical *No, No, Nanette*. A director came in from outside the school to audition us, and we had about a week in which to prepare. I looked at the book and thought that I was ideally suited to the lead role: sweet, innocent – I *was* Nanette! But as far as singing went, I thought "forget it", because I had had no training. My fiancé at the time – Scott Kennedy, a singer who had played the lead in two or three Broadway musicals and who was at Webber Douglas doing a post-graduate course – encouraged me and said that of course I could do it. He coached me for a week, and I just went for it. I auditioned and I read the piece and I sang the song. I didn't really think anything of it, because I didn't think they'd give me the part – but they did!

'I was married to Scott at 18, incredibly young, in my final year at Webber Douglas, and then walked straight into *Doctor Who*. I told John Nathan-Turner that I was 21. I was trying to be older than I was, and I think it was odd for someone who looked even younger to be settled down and married. When I played Peri, I wore my wedding ring on another finger, but I never lied about being married. If I was ever asked, I wouldn't say yes or no, I'd simply say that there was just one person in my life.

'I was very lucky that I landed the part in *Doctor Who*, because it gave me back a sense of family. Colin [Baker] and Peter [Davison] were very nice, and so especially was John. John was very paternal and took great care of me. I had three and a half years to develop a thick skin and to realise that there are lots of nice people in the business. I might come across a couple of right so-and-sos, but the majority are all right. I think I was so lucky, because otherwise I might have given it all up and tried to do something else: married the boss's son or something.

'When I auditioned for *Doctor Who*, John had no idea that I was not really American. I do have dual nationality through my marriage to Scott (although we're now separated), and also my room-mate at boarding school was from New York, so I had picked up her accent. I had been playing an American in *No, No, Nanette*, and an agent, Terry Carney, who came in to see it, assumed that I was American. He called me up and asked me to go and audition for *Doctor Who*. He didn't want to take on someone new out of drama school unless they had a job, so this was in his interest as well as mine. I told him that I wasn't strictly American, but he told me to be American anyway. So I did, and I thought that if they weren't happy with my American-ness, they'd just reject me. There was someone from Denver at the office, and I thought that if I convinced him, then I was doing all right.

'I went through several auditions until it finally got down to a choice between me and one other actress. They decided that they wanted me, but then of course I had to get my Equity card, because they couldn't let me have the part unless I was a member of the union. I had to get all my friends together and do cabaret work around some clubs to gain enough work experience to qualify for membership.'

One aspect of *Doctor Who* that makes it unlike other BBC dramas is the large amount of publicity that it often generates, particularly when there is a change of Doctor or of companion. In Nicola's case, this resulted in her first work being an interview for BBC's *Breakfast Time* programme on 6 July 1983.

'That was really bizarre. The first money I ever earned was from an interview on breakfast television! Funnily enough, Terry Carney hadn't wanted to draw up a contract with me at first, but when he saw me on TV in front of the cameras, he rang me that morning asking me to come in and sign a contract.'

Throughout this first interview for breakfast TV, Nicola maintained the pretence of being American. She used her 'Peri' American accent; she talked about driving, and the difference between the UK and the USA; she said she was 'an American playing an American part,' but added (and demonstrated) that she could speak perfect standard English if she wanted to; she even said that she was 21 years old, and then got into a discussion about early *Doctor Who* stories and what she could remember about them.

At the time the interview was conducted, as the interviewers stressed, she had not actually recorded any *Doctor Who*, nor had she even met any of her co-stars, and all she had to go on with regard to the part she was to play was the original character outline. There was therefore only a limited range of questions that could be put to her. One thing that did come up, however, was the suggestion that she might be typecast as playing only American roles. No doubt this concern was justified at the time, but in retrospect Nicola feels very positive about the high profile she gained as a result of playing Peri.

'When I started in *Doctor Who*,' she told *The Frame*, 'I didn't realise how much emphasis the programme would end up placing on me and on my role in it. It was one of those fortunate – for me – bits of timing that the show went through a period of change just before I joined. There had been five companions – Nyssa, Turlough, Adric, Tegan and Kamelion – all working with one Doctor, and in a very short space of time it was back to just the one. Me. So I didn't have to share my dialogue with several others. My first story [*Planet of Fire*], shot in Lanzarote, represented an obvious injection of money and enthusiasm into the show, and it gained a lot of publicity, most of which featured me.'

In interpreting the part of Peri, Nicola was never in any doubt as to how she should be played.

'I knew exactly who she was from day one,' she explained in an interview for *Doctor Who Magazine*. 'I think you've got to. I don't think it's one of those parts that you can go into thinking, "Oh, I'll see how she comes out," otherwise you can get yourself into all sorts of difficult situations. I started to think that there was a lot of me in the part as it was written. That's why I felt sure I could play her. But in the event, I couldn't say really that there's more than half of me in Peri.'

One of the problems in playing a young, 20th Century girl when you *are* a young, 20th Century girl is this great temptation simply to play yourself. How does Nicola see herself as differing from the character she portrayed?

'If it had been Nicola Bryant travelling in the TARDIS rather than Peri Brown, I would not have been so easily *led* by the Doctor. I would have wanted to establish a different kind of relationship with him, and I would have expected lessons on how to fly and operate the TARDIS, amongst other things. I think when I began on the show, Peri and I shared a similar adventurous quality mixed with a certain naïveté, but that's where the similarity really ends. Many of Peri's reactions were actually based on that American friend of mine from boarding school. She too was away from home, on her own, and insecure – but so full of adventure.'

Nicola had envisaged Peri herself as being 'a naïve innocent; quite a spunky kid, but not really experienced, having a pretty sheltered upbringing, with a domineering mother and a stepfather who wasn't exactly a bundle of laughs'.

What happened in practice was that particular character traits were either emphasised or lost by successive writers on the show – a lack of continuity that Nicola found very off-putting: 'I would suddenly find that a writer had highlighted one particular aspect, which might be one that I had never seen as a major part of the character anyway.'

'The part of Peri was very bland,' asserts Eric Saward, when asked about the way the character was treated, 'and writers will never respond to blandness. We did try to use her, but she was generally involved just in a sub-plot. This tends to happen with companions, because, first, it gets them away from the Doctor, so you don't have a constant inane dialogue going on, and, secondly, it means that they can contribute to the story. Peri was used very much in that way, as Nyssa had been before her. She wasn't really developed, because she wasn't very interesting as a character.

'I personally think that the companion should be strong. Of the ones with whom I was involved, I thought Tegan was the best, because she was ballsy and she had an energy. But John Nathan-Turner took a different view, and I always found it a struggle .... We could have developed her, had her acquiring skills under the tutelage of the Doctor, but we weren't allowed to. The same goes for Peri.'

Speaking to *Doctor Who Magazine*, writer Peter Grimwade confirmed that he had been asked by Saward to make Peri's debut a strong one, but that this strength had been rather lost along the way: 'The first draft I did, I made Peri a bit wimpish and vague, and Eric said, "This is dreadful. I want her hard and gutsy," and I went away and really re-thought it.

'I came back with a much harder character. They actually used her opening scene as the audition piece, which was very pleasing. I felt I'd cracked it. Then this and other areas were shortened and re-written to accommodate different aspects of the location, because they'd found bits of Lanzarote that they liked.'

Nicola was never consulted by any of the writers regarding Peri's character, but she has a fondness for the scripts written by Philip Martin (*Vengeance on Varos, The Trial of a Time Lord 5–8*) and Robert Holmes (*The Caves of Androzani, The Trial of a Time Lord 1–4, 13*). 'They had real drama and strength in their episodes,' she explains. She also has no doubts as to which story she liked least. '*Timelash* was my pet hate. Nice ideas, shame about the constant harping back to the Sixties victim role Peri played. It contained the same *Beauty and the Beast* idea as was in *The Caves of Androzani*, but there Peri wasn't weak; she was sick, naïve and inquisitive, but not pathetic.'

Peri certainly starts out well enough in *Planet of Fire*, the first of her eleven on-screen stories, which provides a good establishing framework and sketches in a character with some potential. She thinks nothing of attempting to swim a considerable distance to shore in order to escape from a boat on which she has been stranded – even if she does ultimately get into difficulty and has to be rescued by Turlough – and she stands up to the Master with bravado and bluster. It is obvious that Peri likes the fifth Doctor, and so it is perhaps unfortunate that *The Caves of Androzani*, their first full adventure together, is the last for that particular incarnation of the Time Lord. Here, Peri is initially quietly confident, clearly relaxed and happy in the Doctor's company. As the story progresses, however, she contracts spectrox toxæmia, and gradually descends into fever and delirium as the illness takes its toll – although she still manages to answer back to the unpredictable and unstable Sharaz Jek.

Following this escapade, Peri is faced with an unpredictable and unstable Doctor in *The Twin Dilemma*, and it is probably here that her character really starts to shine through. Her loyalty is very apparent as she stands by the much-changed Doctor – even when, in a fit of temporary insanity, he tries to kill her – and so is her resourcefulness as she takes the lead in exploring on Titan 3 and ultimately as she is left with Hugo Lang to hold the fort while the Doctor disposes of Mestor.

The problems with Peri's character really come to the fore in the twenty-second season. It seems that, perhaps partly as a result of the switch to the 45-minute episode format, the majority of the writers had little idea of what to do with her. She is at times reduced to a cipher, simply the person to whom the Doctor explains the plot.

She certainly shows little bravado or resourcefulness in *Attack of the Cybermen*; and in *Vengeance on Varos*, she becomes the archetypal damsel in distress when Quillam uses her in his transmogrification experiments. Obvious opportunities for use of the character are missed – for example, it is the Governor who persuades Maldak to free him and Peri from confinement, when it could so easily have been Peri herself – and the story is dominated by the Doctor and Sil, who get all the best lines.

Matters improve somewhat in *The Mark of the Rani*, as Peri is again allowed some independence. She suggests making a sleeping potion to help the afflicted miners – virtually the only occasion on which her experience as a botany student is put to good use – and agrees, albeit nervously, to escort the Master and the Rani as prisoners back to the Rani's TARDIS. She even manages to resist the Master's attempt to hypnotise her – one up to the writers – although she then lets herself down by falling for a rather obvious ploy on the part of the Rani.

Further good material for Peri comes in the next story, *The Two Doctors*, as she has a chance for a fight scene with the temporarily deranged Jamie on board the space station, and later acts as a decoy at the hacienda by posing as a student calling for assistance.

This more effective handling of the character is short-lived, however, as in *Timelash*, it is straight back to the damsel in distress routine. Again, opportunities are missed: Peri simply stumbles upon the Falchan Rocks instead of actively seeking them out after receiving a cryptic message about a rendezvous there; and she has to be rescued by Herbert when it would have been perfectly possible for her to have thought of using a flambeau herself to frighten off the inquisitive Morlox. Perhaps the worst aspect of *Timelash*, though, is the illogical plot point that the Borad falls instantly in love with Peri, and then wants to alter her appearance – the only thing that could have made her attractive to him in the first place, since he had never met her. This whole subtext, that a woman is worthwhile only because of what she looks like, really had no place in a television programme of the Eighties.

The season's final story, *Revelation of the Daleks*, sees some attempt being made to establish a better rapport between Peri and the Doctor. Another plus point is that, as in *The Mark of the Rani*, Peri is not totally the helpless bystander – she beats off the mutant attacking the Doctor, and later manages to elude the fawning Jobel with both verbal and physical rebuffs. Unfortunately, this refreshing self-assurance was never developed further.

What then happened was that *Doctor Who* took an eighteen-month break from the nation's screens, following the decision to cancel the original Season 23. During this longer-than-usual pause in production, Nicola and Colin Baker decided that Peri and the Doctor could not go on as they had been. The whinging American wimp that Peri was becoming was not working, and the two actors decided between themselves that, whatever future scripts be might like, they would do their best to show that travelling in each other's company had changed them both.

The Trial of a Time Lord consequently presents viewers with a slightly mellower Doctor, and with a Peri not quite so at odds with him and with their life together. Peri's final two adventures show her at her best. The first segment of the Trial has her going through some highly emotional situations as she grieves the fate of her planet and then has to face the grim prospect of a life of enforced baby-making at the hands of the Tribe of the Free, while the second gives her perhaps the best characterisation and development she ever had. With the Doctor having apparently lost his mind, it is up to Peri to calm the tempestuous Yrcanos, to talk the strangely bland Tusa around to the fact that they are not his enemies, and to attempt to help her fellow traveller as best she can. For this to be Peri's swan song is fitting, as it illuminates previously unexplored aspects of her character and leaves the viewer wanting more.

The two stories of Season 23 are however overshadowed by the bulk of the previous season, in which Peri was simply a victim to be used in order to generate exciting plot twists as the writers saw fit, or simply as a sounding board to explain proceedings to the viewers. This 'generic companion' aspect of the role is what irritated Nicola Bryant most. 'Having talked to the other girls who had played companions,' she told *Doctor Who Magazine*, 'I realised that we had all had the same problem, that just occasionally we would get a story that didn't really seem to be related to our character, but to the *Doctor Who* "companion of all time".'

Part of the identity of any character, whether on stage, film or television, is established by the costumes they wear. After the departure of Romana in 1980, the *Doctor Who* companions, in common with the Doctors themselves, generally wore 'uniforms' rather than 'clothes'; that is, they tended to wear either exactly the same outfits for every story, or slight variations on a theme. As clothes reflect personality, it is not really surprising that as the clothes became fixed, so did the personalities behind them. Peri was no exception to the rule.

The costumes with which Nicola was presented for Peri were both eye-catching and colourful, but not exactly what she would have chosen herself. The Peri 'look' – generally consisting of figure-hugging shorts and skin-tight leotards – apparently came about because of the clothes Nicola chose to wear to her first photo-call. 'I thought she looked so stunning', relates John Nathan-Turner, 'that I asked our costume designers to echo Nicola's own clothes!'

Nicola, however, recalls that there was slightly more to it than that. 'I was asked to bring several outfits along for the photo call,' she says, 'and "short and very fitting" was the description I was given. I never wore short skirts and clingy-fitting tops myself – all I possessed were a pair of shorts and a leotard. I asked John if this would be okay, and he said "Great!" Unfortunately, he liked it so much that we got stuck with it.'

The result was a succession of costumes that left very little to the imagination, and that were usually wholly unsuited to the weather on location.

'We filmed *The Caves of Androzani* in Devon,' Nicola recalled in *Doctor Who Magazine*. 'But it was very cold, and I had no way of wrapping up, because my costume was in direct continuity from the previous story. I was wearing the same clothes I had worn in Lanzarote. I remember the cameraman saying, "Slap your face, love, you're going blue." I got frostbite, then pneumonia. Then Peter [Davison] fell ill too – it was a pretty rough shoot.

'In *Attack of the Cybermen*, I started out in a shocking pink leotard and shorts, then got into a sort of red jump-suit. In *Vengeance on Varos*, I had a blue leotard and shorts ... They went out first and bought the shorts – pink, turquoise and even a pair in yellow – and then tried to find matching leotards. In *The Two Doctors*, I wore a psychedelic thing that glistened nicely in the sun, but filming in Seville the temperature reached 102 degrees, and it was like a thermal blanket – I felt like a roast chicken! I could have used that in Devon!'

She has a pragmatic attitude towards the costumes, however. 'I think that's one of the unfortunate things that comes with the part. The newspapers always want something extra. There's nothing I could have done to escape it, and I wasn't in a position to do so. Other actresses who came into the show often said, "Why don't you put your foot down and say no?" My reply was, "Look, I'd rather be playing Peri and wear that than not be playing Peri." There's just no point in jumping up and down screaming about it. I hoped that a few people would look beyond all that, at the face and at the acting, and judge me on those things, rather than on just the outward appearance.

'I was a lot happier with the more realistic costumes I wore during my last season. It was a relief – especially in Britain's climate. I think the things I wore in that season reflected Peri's character slightly more as I had originally seen her. I still had no choice as to what they were, though.'

So what would Nicola's own choice of costumes have been?

'*Planet of Fire* was fine by me, but afterwards I would have been in jeans, T-shirts, sweat-shirts and sneakers. That's the way I saw Peri. Back to shorts in Seville for *The Two Doctors*, and then of course period costume for *The Mark of the Rani*. Peri should have worn basically the kind of clothes that real American students lived in – casual clothes of the Eighties. I think to have been in jeans and sensible shoes would have added to that more spunky, independent feel that Peri began with.'

Nicola joined the series not long before her original co-star, Peter Davison, left. 'I first met Peter at the studio when I came to watch an episode being recorded. I was amazed at how long the hours were. I remember that when I started the shoot in Lanzarote, the director Fiona Cumming said to me, "Just watch Peter as often as you can," so I did, and in that way, I learned an awful lot about acting in a short amount of time.'

Nicola recalls that she was initially rather nervous and unsure about the new Doctor, Colin Baker, 'mainly because Peter had been winding me up, saying everything and nothing. He would say "So, you're working with Colin Baker ... Well, if you have any problems, you just call me. And good luck!"

'After a rather bumpy start, Colin and I turned out to be great mates. As actors, we have the same strong feelings about our characters – something that even now, when we work on video projects together, unites us and makes us a strong team. I think it's also to do with the fact that we trust each other on several levels. Colin was really there for me in a very quiet and special way when my Dad died, and that means a lot.'

Nicola decided to leave *Doctor Who* during the twenty-third season, simply because she felt that three years working on one show was enough. 'As an actor I had to say, "Right, okay, I'm going to get out there and see what else there is." I was happy to do so, in that I felt that I wanted to go and do something else, but sad to be leaving such a nice bunch of people behind.'

If she could give some advice now, to herself as she was then, what would it be?

'I would tell myself to have even more fun that I did. I was a little more serious then than I am now, and perhaps if I had relaxed a little more, then I could have enjoyed it even more than I did.'

It is ultimately down to the production team whether a companion works or fails, and certain key qualities must be present if she is to inspire the writers to use and develop her. Eric Saward's concept of a really strong character was not to see fruition during his tenure on the show, and it subsequently fell to his successor, Andrew Cartmel, to create arguably the true 'Eighties' companion in Ace. It clearly helps if the producer and the script editor are in accord as to the treatment of the character, and this appears not to have been the case where Perpugilliam Brown was concerned. However, the fact that she is still recalled with so much affection by so many viewers must surely be a testament to the skills of all those involved in bringing her to life.

Selling the Doctor

MEDIA

During the Eighties, *Doctor Who* enjoyed a healthy relationship with the media. John Nathan-Turner often played the newspapers at their own game, creating 'news opportunities' at every turn and maximising the impact of those celebrity actors and actresses who agreed to appear in the show with strategically arranged press and photo calls.

During the two-and-a-bit seasons that Colin Baker played the Doctor, almost every story received some news coverage, whether it be because of who was appearing in it, or because of the location, or the monsters, or the companions, or sometimes all of these together.

When Baker's appointment was first announced on 20 August 1983, there was a wealth of press coverage, but, strangely, the *Daily Telegraph* and the *Daily Express* made no mention of the fact that not long before this, they had both announced a completely different actor, Brian Blessed, as having been chosen to play the part. The *Daily Express* report, in the edition dated 1 August, had stated unequivocally that Blessed was to play the sixth incarnation of the Time Lord, had given a brief biography of him, and had even pointed out that his appointment quashed rumours that the next Doctor would be a woman, claiming that BBC chiefs had even described the kind of woman that they had been looking for!

The next major press call was on Tuesday 10 January 1984, when Baker's new costume was unveiled to the waiting lenses of Fleet Street. The following day, 'The Tasteless Time Lord' and 'Who's the height of bad taste?' were the headlines, as John Nathan-Turner was quoted describing the Doctor's outfit as 'totally tasteless'. Almost every newspaper covered the story, many of them in colour. Then, not long afterwards, yet another photo-call was arranged, to publicise the first episode of *The Twin Dilemma*. Such was *Doctor Who*'s press potential for the BBC that their Press Information pack for the week beginning Saturday 17 March 1984 even had a photograph of Baker on the front, promoting his on-air debut.

All in all, Colin Baker probably had more press coverage to launch his Doctor than did any of his predecessors.

A part of this interest was a story run in the *Sun* and the *Daily Star* concerning the fact that Colin and his wife Marion had lost their first child,

Jack, to the Sudden Infant Death Syndrome four months previously. Although the *Sun* had run the news of Jack's birth in October 1983, and had also covered the tragic death in November, it considered the story worth repeating, apparently with additional comments from Colin. Colin was determined to use the exposure that *Doctor Who* was to give him to campaign and raise money for the Foundation for the Study of Infant Deaths.

Further media interest was created when John Nathan-Turner 'accidentally' let slip that the Doctor would be getting rid of the TARDIS's familiar shape, as most viewers no longer knew what a police box was. This resulted in a deluge of viewers' letters to the BBC, and in newspapers jumping on the 'Save the TARDIS' bandwagon. One paper even ran a competition to design a new exterior for the Doctor's timeship. In the event, even though the Doctor got the TARDIS to change shape a couple of times in *Attack of the Cybermen*, it otherwise remained in the trusty form viewers knew and loved. The *Sun* claimed that this was totally down to its campaign, proclaiming on 17 November 1983 that it had saved the TARDIS from the scrap heap.

For the twenty-second season, there was press interest a-plenty when Prince Andrew's ex-girlfriend, photographer Koo Stark, was announced as featuring in the opening story. This guest appearance was not to be, however, the *Sun* explaining on 18 June 1984 that Stark had been dropped from the role after a row over publicity.

Despite this setback, *Doctor Who*'s aptitude for attracting top names to its cast meant that the BBC soon had further media personalities to parade before the press. On 3 July, comedienne and impressionist Faith Brown was announced as a forthcoming guest star, and on 15 July, Sarah Berger was reported to be replacing Koo Stark as one of the Cryons in *Attack of the Cybermen*. Another Cryon was to be played by ex-*Blue Peter* presenter Sarah Greene. 'Koo missed out on a lot of fun,' said Greene.

Further guest star names announced in the *Daily Star* on 5 January 1985 were Alexei Sayle, Eleanor Bron, Terence Alexander, Martin Jarvis, Frazer Hines, Jason Connery and Jacqueline Pearce. Colin Baker was reported as having the 'best job on television'. 'It's like being a grown-up who is getting paid to play cowboys and indians, it's great fun,' he said.

As the season progressed, *The Mark of the Rani* received coverage because of the presence of the Master, while *The Two Doctors* made the news because Frazer Hines apparently needed hardly any make-up to recreate his role as Jamie.

Of course, while *The Two Doctors* was part-way through transmission, news of a far more dramatic nature broke: *Doctor Who* was being rested for eighteen months. The full story of this turbulent period in *Doctor Who*'s history is covered in its own chapter.

THE SIXTH DOCTOR

After all the media hype about the postponement had died down, the press turned its attention to publicising the twenty-third season. The series was heralded as coming back 'for a laugh', those anonymous 'BBC chiefs' that the newspapers loved quoting having felt that it was too violent and needed an injection of humour. This approach was apparently confirmed by the casting of *Carry On ....* actress Joan Sims in the first segment of the story. Some interest was also shown because of the Trial theme of the season, which echoed the feelings of those BBC chiefs toward the series itself. The guest cast found themselves the centre of attention, as once again the programme was promoted on its ability to attract star names. This time it was Michael Jayston, Lynda Bellingham, Joan Sims, Tony Selby, Brian Blessed, Patrick Ryecart, Geoffrey Hughes, Christopher Ryan, Honor Blackman and Michael Craig who featured in the reports.

Ultimately, following all the press coverage of the postponement, which included in the *Sun* some damning indictments by Colin Baker of BBC1's Controller Michael Grade, the news broke on 13 December 1986 that Baker had been 'sacked' from the role of the Doctor, reportedly because of these comments. His contract had not been renewed, but Bonnie Langford's had. It later transpired that Baker had been offered four episodes at the start of the twenty-fourth season to make a final story, but had declined them, not wishing to have to forego other work in the interim.

The hunt was now on for Doctor number seven.

COMPANIONS

As always, the press were very keen to feature the Doctor's companions, mainly because they tended to be pretty young women. In the case of Nicola Bryant, the tabloids had a field day.

'Naughty Nicola' screamed a headline in the *Daily Star*, which reported that fans were apparently up in arms because her outfits were too sexy. This outcry came as *Vengeance on Varos* was being screened, and Nicola's tight blue leotard-top and shorts left little to the imagination. 'Red-faced mums and dads want her to wear more modest outfits and hide her ample charms,' said Geoff Baker, writing in the *Daily Star* on 26 January 1985. Sexy the outfits may have been, but the show had again managed to achieve almost a full two page spread, effectively advertising the series, on the day it was transmitted.

When reporting Nicola's departure from the series, some newspapers even found some photographs of her posing with nothing but a smile and a towel. It is perhaps inevitable that the tabloid press will latch on to anything if it is sold to them with a little sex appeal – a fact that the *Doctor Who* production office knew and used to maximise publicity.

SELLING THE DOCTOR

When Bonnie Langford was announced on 23 January 1986 as being the replacement for Nicola, the press were, for once, a little confounded. Here they were presented with a 'name', someone of whom they had all heard, and who was arguably more famous than the actor playing the Doctor. There was also no way they could present Bonnie Langford as a sex object, which, given their established attitude towards 'the *Doctor Who* girl', also caused them difficulties. To introduce Langford to the public, the BBC staged a press call at the London theatre where Langford was appearing in *Peter Pan*. Colin Baker, looking somewhat chubby after five or so months with little work, was squeezed into a flying harness, and the two of them were photographed clowning about against a starry background.

Picking up on Colin's apparent increase in weight, the *Daily Record* provided the news that the first thing Langford would do in the series was to put the Doctor on a diet.

The introduction of Langford's character Mel in *The Trial of a Time Lord* was followed up with another press call, this time with Baker sporting a moustache and a beard, grown following his departure from the series. The pair fooled about on this occasion with a pair of garden shears.

PERSONAL APPEARANCES

While *Doctor Who* may not have been as popular with the viewing public at this point as it had been in the past, the producer and his stars were out and about almost constantly promoting the series.

Prior to transmission of *Attack of the Cybermen*, John Nathan-Turner appeared on the BBC1 children's show *Saturday Superstore* talking to presenter Mike Reid about the possibility of the TARDIS's police box shape being replaced. He said that the office was being bombarded with petitions, but stressed that no decision had yet been taken – he and his team were just thinking about it.

The Kenilworth Agricultural Show over the August bank holiday weekend in 1984 played host to a number of *Doctor Who* stars during its three day run. These included Colin Baker and Nicola Bryant, who turned out to promote both the programme and John Nathan-Turner's forthcoming pantomime production, *Cinderella*, in which they would both appear.

The week before part one of *The Twin Dilemma* was transmitted, Colin Baker appeared on *Blue Peter* to publicise the story. A lengthy clip was shown of Mestor in his throne room speaking to Azmael, and of the Doctor and Peri investigating the wreckage of Hugo Lang's ship. This was followed by a further clip, of the Doctor attacking Peri in the TARDIS. Presenter Janet Ellis explained that both stars would be on *Saturday Superstore* that coming weekend. There, the pair answered questions and took phone calls, including one from 'the Master' (actor Anthony Ainley), who warned that he would be coming from the depths of hell to haunt the Doctor. He challenged the Doctor in his new guise to settle their feud once and forever. Baker (as the Doctor) accepted the challenge, and the Master then rang off.

Later in the programme, Baker's handwriting was analysed by an expert in that field. Not knowing whose it was, she came to the conclusion that he was well travelled, well educated and had a very inquiring mind. She recommended a job in which he could do his own thing, as he was too independent to go along with group decisions. She also felt that he saw his rightful place as being at the top, that he had a great sense of timing and presentation and that he appeared to have an affinity for detailed analytical work. She suggested that he would make a good barrister. She added that he liked to work things out for himself, that he liked to cut a dash, and that his clothing would have a certain panache as a result. Baker felt that this summation was partly accurate.

The same week, Baker, together with Peter Davison, also appeared on *Harty*, the weekly chat show presented by Russell Harty; and, on the actual morning of day of the first episode's transmission, he and Bryant guested on the BBC's *Breakfast Time* show with Selina Scott and Frank Bough.

Take Two, a children's version of the *Did You See* viewers' correspondence programme, spoke to John Nathan-Turner about the series. Children they had interviewed felt that Colin Baker was too young to play the Doctor, and that Peri whined too much and had a disagreeable accent. They didn't appear to be frightened by the monsters, and cited the Daleks and the Cybermen as their favourites. However, the feeling was expressed that *Doctor Who* was shown too early for younger children. Nathan-Turner explained that the show was going out later than it ever had been, and that the intention was not to terrify, just occasionally to scare.

As the twenty-second season got underway, Baker, Bryant, Mary Tamm and Jacqueline Pearce all appeared on the *Saturday Superstore* of 5 January 1985 to promote John Nathan-Turner's *Cinderella* pantomime, which was playing in Southampton at the time. They did, however, find time to answer questions from viewers about *Doctor Who*.

Towards the end of 1985, Lenny Henry turned his satirical eye on *Doctor Who* and presented, in the edition of *The Lenny Henry Show* broadcast on 2 October, a sketch featuring himself as the Doctor. The TARDIS – in fact the Master's TARDIS control room set from *Planet of Fire* – brings the Doctor and Peri to Earth in the future. The planet is now controlled by the most ruthless woman in the universe, Thatchos, who threatens to have them privatised. They escape in the TARDIS, where Peri wants to use the fact that they are no longer on television to get to know the Doctor better.

Shortly after this, on 22 November, the BBC's annual *Children In Need* fund-raising telethon saw no fewer than twenty *Doctor Who* stars presenting a cheque for £1000 to Terry Wogan. The money had been collected earlier in the year at the *Doctor Who* exhibition on Blackpool's Golden Mile, during a special appearance by Colin Baker and Nicola Bryant to sign autographs and meet the fans.

In the studio to present the cheque were Patrick Troughton, Carole Ann Ford, Jackie Lane, Peter Purves, Michael Craze, Adrienne Hill, Jon Pertwee, Caroline John, Nicholas Courtney, Richard Franklin, John Levene, Elisabeth Sladen, Louise Jameson, Ian Marter, Peter Davison, Janet Fielding, Matthew Waterhouse, Mark Strickson, Nicola Bryant and Colin Baker. This was the biggest assembly of *Doctor Who* cast members ever achieved in this country. A cheque for £100 was also presented by Patrick Troughton on behalf of the *Doctor Who* Appreciation Society.

The *Doctor Who* exhibition at Blackpool had been running for ten years, but at the end of October 1985, it closed its doors for the last time. The lease on the building in which it was housed had expired, and many of the costumes and props contained there were needed to fit out a massive *Doctor Who* exhibition bus that was to tour the USA. The new exhibition was contained in a trailer, 48 feet long, that was too large to travel on Britain's roads. It was designed by BBC designer Tony Burrough. Artist Andrew Skilleter created huge *Doctor Who* murals for the sides and interiors, and the whole thing was sent over to America, where, on 9 May 1986, it was launched on its tour by Peter Davison and Michael Grade in New York. The tour was joined at various points by stars from the programme, including Tom Baker and Colin Baker, and was very well received.

Doctor Who appeared on ice in 1986 when, from 14 June until 1 November, an eight minute *Doctor Who* segment was included in the annual *Ice Spectacular* show at Blackpool.

Also in 1986, the French TV network TF1 bought *Doctor Who* to screen in their *Temps X* programme. To publicise the series, they put together a documentary called *Who is Who*, and even arranged for some of the Target *Doctor Who* novelisations to be reissued in French translations, featuring the two presenters of *Temps X* on the covers.

On 25 August 1986, Colin Baker and Lynda Bellingham appeared on *Wogan* talking about Baker's acting career and the new season of *Doctor Who* starting on 6 September. The show also featured a Mandrel (from *Nightmare of Eden*) and a Sea Devil Warrior (from *Warriors of the Deep*) wandering about the studio.

Bonnie Langford made an appearance on *The Saturday Picture Show* on 6 September 1986, primarily to talk about the tour of *Peter Pan*, although *Doctor Who* did get a brief mention. A clip from the end of *Revelation of the Daleks* was shown – strangely, as Langford did not appear in it – leading into a brief clip from the start of the new series.

Colin Baker appeared as the Doctor on 13 September to introduce Roland

Rat at the start of that week's episode of *Roland Rat – The Series*.

The next major *Doctor Who* feature on TV was again on *Saturday Superstore*, Sarah Greene and Mike Reid playing host on 29 November 1986 to a TARDIS full of *Doctor Who* monsters and Time Lords to celebrate twenty-three years of *Doctor Who*. To fill the *Doctor Who* costumes, the producers of *Saturday Superstore* contacted the DWAS, and arranged for a group of fans to come along and wander about dressed as Cybermen, Mandrels, Sea Devils and Time Lords. Colin Baker was also in the studio to talk about the series, and the regular 'pop panel' was enlivened by 'Tony the Cyberman' (played by DWAS Co-ordinator Tony Jordan and voiced by David J Howe) commenting on the videos and attempting to destroy Mike Reid in the process. The programme ended with the cutting of a special TARDIS-shaped cake.

OVERSEAS

AMERICA

In the mid-Eighties, *Doctor Who* was amongst the top ten bestselling British TV programmes overseas, reaching 54 different countries and attaining world-wide viewing figures estimated at 110 million. One of the series' most important markets was the United States of America.

Since the start of the Eighties, *Doctor Who* had become more and more popular with American fans, and this popularity peaked during the period when the sixth Doctor was appearing on British television screens.

As with Peter Davison and Nicola Bryant before him, Colin Baker's first convention appearance was in the USA, at Panopticon West in Ohio in July 1984, and he also guested at the massive annual convention in Chicago in November of that year, organised by the commercial Spirit of Light company. This frustrated and infuriated the organisers of Britain's *Doctor Who* Appreciation Society (DWAS), who felt that their members were losing out to their American counterparts, as had been the case the previous year when no Doctors had been available for the biggest British fan convention to celebrate the series' 20th anniversary, as they were all being paid to attend the convention in Chicago. *Doctor Who* was, as usual, generally not being repeated in Britain – the latest repeats had been *The King's Demons*, *The Awakening* and *The Five Doctors* in 1984, during the break between the twenty-first and twenty-second seasons – but in America it was being shown almost continuously on Public Broadcasting Service channels. The fact that the American fans were now meeting new Doctors before their British counterparts added to the sense of injustice that many of the latter felt.

What British fans often overlooked, however, was the fact that their fellow devotees in the States outnumbered them by at least ten to one at this point. The *Doctor Who* Fan Club of America boasted some 30,000 members, and could reasonably be considered to have been the hub of *Doctor Who* fandom in the mid-Eighties.

The early US convention appearances by Colin Baker – who would later be extremely generous with his time in attending numerous British events – were partly down to the influence of John Nathan-Turner, who had apparently foregone British fandom in his desire to woo the Americans with the programme and its stars. The BBC themselves were certainly not going to object to this, as they were gaining valuable overseas sales of the show, not to mention a sizeable income from the masses of licensed merchandise being produced in the States. By June 1985, *Doctor Who* was being seen in 146 American markets, covering 70 per cent of the country.

NEW ZEALAND
By Paul Scoones

The first the New Zealand television audience saw of Colin Baker's Doctor was nearly two years after the actor had left the role. The first of his stories to be screened was *Revelation of the Daleks*, which was one of five stories all screened for the first time during Television New Zealand 's *Doctor Who* 'Silver Jubilee' week of special screenings in November 1988 on TV2. *Revelation of the Daleks* was broadcast in a four episode format over four nights from Monday 21 November to Thursday 24 November 1988 at 5.30 pm. The story gained the highest viewer ratings of all the *Doctor Who* screenings that week, with an average of 6.9%.

The Colin Baker era proper began with *The Twin Dilemma* on 10 August 1988, following on from the end of the Davison era stories. At this point, *Doctor Who* screened twice a week on Thursdays and Fridays at around 5.15 pm. The Season 22 stories were screened in the 25 minute episode format, and the season was also screened in production order, so *The Two Doctors* preceded *The Mark of the Rani*. The series suffered some disruption when it was moved in the schedules at short notice as TV2 realigned its programming to combat the launch of the rival television channel, TV3. *Timelash* Parts Three and Four, which were advertised as screening on Thursday 2 November and Friday 3 November, were moved to Saturday afternoons at 5 pm, with Part Three playing nearly a week earlier than scheduled on 28 October, and Part Four on 4 November 1989.

Viewer ratings for this period show that of the Colin Baker episodes, *The Twin Dilemma* Part One was the most watched, with 9.5% which higher than any of the Davison episodes screened in 1988-89. Part Four of the same story was the second highest at 9%, followed by *The Two Doctors* Part Four on 8%.

THE SIXTH DOCTOR

The average audience ratings for the first six stories of the Colin Baker era are: *The Twin Dilemma* 8%; *Attack of the Cybermen* 6.3%; *Vengeance on Varos* 6.5%; *The Two Doctors* 6.8%; *The Mark of the Rani* 4.5% and *Timelash* 3.4%.

The series resumed with a repeat of *Revelation of the Daleks* followed by *The Trial of a Time Lord* from 27 December to 22 January 1990. These episodes were screened five days a week, from Monday to Friday on TV2 at around 4.30 pm. No episode was screened on the Monday of New Years Day 1990.

Many of the Colin Baker episodes screened in New Zealand were sourced from the Australian Broadcasting Corporation and were quite heavily edited. Cuts had been made by the Australian censor to remove violence and further edits were made in New Zealand, sometimes just to reduce the running time to fit the timeslot. The most edited episodes included *Vengeance on Varos* Part Three, which lost around five minutes, *The Two Doctors* Part Six (three minutes), *Timelash Part Three* (nearly three and a half minutes) and *The Trial of a Time Lord* Part Nine (two and a half minutes). Worst affected of all however was *The Trial of a Time Lord* Part Fourteen, which lost over eight minutes of footage simply to fit the unusually long episode into the available timeslot.

FANDOM

As already noted, the main *Doctor Who* fan activity during the Colin Baker era took place in the USA. In addition to the numerous conventions, the *Doctor Who Fan Club of America* – a commercial organisation run by Ron Katz and Chad Roark – offered their members, reported to number some 30,000, a regular newspaper, *The Whovian Times*. This contained interviews with the series' stars and columns by John Nathan-Turner and, providing all the latest British news, writer Jeremy Bentham. The pages of the newspaper also featured numerous adverts for some of the masses of BBC-licenced (and, in some cases, possibly unlicenced) merchandise items produced in the States at this time, including tee-shirts, jackets, mugs, key-fobs, pens, model kits and towels. Readers were even given regular invitations to join an organisation called the Gallifrey Beach and Body Club!

In Britain, the *Doctor Who* Appreciation Society (DWAS), the only official fan group in this country, was still growing steadily, following publicity gained at the 20th anniversary BBC convention at Longleat in 1983 and subsequent advertising in Marvel Comics' *Doctor Who Magazine*. The Society's newsletter, *Celestial Toyroom*, continued to appear on a regular monthly basis, and the news, as one would expect, covered all the major events of the time.

Apart from Marvel's official *Doctor Who Magazine*, in which news was scant and consisted mainly of brief details about forthcoming stories, the other main source of *Doctor Who* information was a monthly fanzine, *Doctor Who Bulletin*, edited and published by Gary Levy (who later changed his name to Gary Leigh). Levy had started *DWB* (as it was generally abbreviated) because he was interested in magazines and their production, and also in *Doctor Who*. He was a member of the DWAS and felt that he could improve on the news aspect of their newsletter. In contrast to *Celestial Toyroom* and *Doctor Who Magazine*, which tended to report news and current events without comment, *DWB*'s editorial style was highly outspoken and controversial. Also unlike the other two publications, *DWB* showed no hesitation in printing information before it had been either confirmed or denied officially. *DWB* started out with a fairly positive attitude towards *Doctor Who* and its producer but, following the postponement of Season 23, the fanzine took on a far more critical and negative stance.

The influence of American fandom made itself known to British fans in July 1984, when the planned annual DWAS convention, Panopticon VI, scheduled for 23, 24 and 25 November 1984, had to be postponed, as on those dates all the potential guests were going to be at the huge commercial Spirit of Light convention in America, which had just had its dates rescheduled from October. The British event was eventually moved to 26, 27 and 28 July 1985 and took place at the Brighton Metropole hotel. The event was notable for featuring the first and only British fan convention appearance of Patrick Troughton. While the convention went ahead and was reasonably successful, when it was all over, the DWAS was left with a hefty bill to pay and insufficient funds to do so. The Society's newsletter reported that the convention's finances had been mismanaged by its organisers.

As the DWAS' Co-ordinator, David Saunders, had resigned just prior to the convention, his successor, Tony Jordan, together with the rest of the DWAS Executive, now had to recover the Society from the brink of bankruptcy, while continuing to provide members with a reasonable service. To this end, the newsletter and the Society magazine, *TARDIS*, were merged, and the membership fee increased from six to eight pounds a year. With these measures in place, planning tentatively started towards the end of 1985 on the next big convention, this time with an edict to put the Society back on a sound financial footing, and with a new team doing the organising.

The resultant convention, Panopticon VII, was praised by many fans as being the best the DWAS had ever organised. There was the added bonus for attendees of being able to watch the transmission of the first episode of *The Trial of a Time Lord* live on a big convention screen, along with 500 of their fellow devotees. This screening was for some the highlight of the event, and was described as 'electrifying' by many of those present.

At the end of 1986, after a great deal of hard work, the Society was again financially stable, and Tony Jordan, feeling that he had done what he was brought onto the Executive to do, moved on. He was succeeded by Andrew

Beech, who was to steer the DWAS into yet another new era of *Doctor Who*.

One other UK fan activity of note from this period is Fan Aid. This charitable endeavour was the brainchild of Paul Cornell, who decided to raise money for famine relief in Ethiopia, spurred on by the Live Aid concert and Band Aid record for the same cause. Cornell, along with many other helpers and assistants, organised a very successful convention in Bath, released some interesting and informative fanzines, and managed to raise an announced total of £2,165.

MERCHANDISE

While *Doctor Who*'s popularity might have been slipping somewhat as far as the ratings and the BBC were concerned, from the point of view of the merchandisers, things had never looked better.

There were just over 200 individual items of merchandise issued during the Colin Baker era, which is 100 per cent more than was released in the whole of the Sixties. Whereas in the Sixties, the items were very diverse, in the mid-Eighties, the releases tended to be concentrated in three areas: books, metal miniatures and videos.

W H Allen continued releasing *Doctor Who* novelisations, and when Nigel Robinson took over as editor of the range, he started to look into the past for the stories to feature, as most of the more recent ones had already been tackled. Thus under Robinson's enthusiastic editorship, more novelisations of first and second Doctor stories started appearing, as well as 'gaps' being filled for all the other Doctors.

When W H Allen contacted Baker's agent about using his likeness on the covers of the books, they offered a single fee in lieu of a royalty. Baker's agent asked if a royalty could be negotiated instead, but the publishers refused, and did not contact the agent again. As a result, Baker's face did not appear on any of the first-edition covers of the novelisations of his stories. An illustration of the sixth Doctor that had already been completed for *The Twin Dilemma* was dropped just prior to publication, after proof covers had already been printed up, and artist Andrew Skilleter was asked at short notice to come up with a replacement.

W H Allen, along with all the series' other merchandisers, were reaping the rewards of the increased popularity of *Doctor Who* in America, and all manner of 'factual' books appeared. Some of these had only a very tenuous connection with the series, but this did not appear to matter, as if the product had 'Doctor Who' on the cover, it sold. Hence we saw: the *Doctor Who Cookbook* (recipes provided by numerous *Doctor Who* cast and production team members) compiled by Gary Downie, who had choreographed the dance sequences in *Black Orchid* and had also worked as production assistant on several *Doctor Who* stories; *Travel Without the TARDIS* (an American's guide to visiting *Doctor Who* locations in Britain), written by two American fans, Jean Airey and Laurie Halderman; a number of *Doctor Who* quiz books and similar items; and, perhaps most obscure of all, the *Doctor Who Pattern Book* (knitting and sewing patterns – make your own woolly Cybermat!) by Joy Gammon. Even John Nathan-Turner turned his hand to writing and brought us *Doctor Who – The TARDIS Inside Out*, in which he presented his memories of the actors who had played the Doctor, and *Doctor Who – The Companions*, where he did the same for the companions. While not being as bad as some of the other publications, these volumes were a little slim; and in the case of the companions volume, some additional research on those actors and actresses with whom Nathan-Turner had not worked would not have gone amiss.

There were some highly acclaimed books, too, and top of the pile was J Jeremy Bentham's *Doctor Who – The Early Years*. Published by W H Allen, this told of the design work that had gone into the creation of the Daleks, as well as of other aspects of the early stories, and presented numerous design drawings and photographs from the extensive collection of ex-BBC designer Raymond P Cusick. Bentham had founded and organised the *Doctor Who* Appreciation Society's Reference Department during the late Seventies, and was considered by many to be one of the stalwart historians of *Doctor Who*.

Another worthwhile publication was Mat Irvine's *Doctor Who Special Effects*, published by Beaver Books. Irvine was an effects designer at the BBC and had worked extensively on *Doctor Who*, as well as on many other programmes. This book collected anecdotes and photographs from his own collection and provided an illuminating glimpse into the world of *Doctor Who* special effects.

Lastly on this subject, there were a number of 'game books' released featuring the sixth Doctor. In the US, FASA Corporation in 1986 published *Doctor Who and the Rebel's Gamble* by William H Keith Jr. Described as a 'solo-play adventure game', it involved the Doctor and Peri arriving in the middle of the American Civil War to find that history has been changed. In the UK, meanwhile, Severn House in the same year published six 'Make Your Own Adventure' books. These featured the Doctor alongside a number of TV and original characters in stories written by William Emms, Philip Martin, David Martin and Pip and Jane Baker, all of whom had previously written televised *Doctor Who* stories, and also one by Michael Holt. William Emms's *Mission to Venus* was a particularly notable example, as it was based on a story, *The Imps*, that had been planned for inclusion in Season 4 of the TV series but had ultimately abandoned after the writer fell ill.

The other major *Doctor Who* product type of the mid-Eighties consisted of cast metal miniatures of characters from the series. These were produced by Fine Art Castings out of their small workshop near Andover. The company

THE SIXTH DOCTOR

had previously concentrated on military models, and were keen to branch into another market. There were three basic ranges of *Doctor Who* figures: 80mm figures, 40mm figures and a few 20mm figures, the latter two designed for role-playing games. With the help of David J Howe and Mark Stammers (then involved in running the DWAS' Reference and Graphics Departments respectively), the figures were as accurate as could be represented, given their dimensions. Before long, all six Doctors were available, as well as most of the companions, and a great number of the monsters and villains, from the Daleks and Cybermen right through to the Borad and Drathro.

The company also produced two limited edition bust sets, the first of all six Doctors, and the second of a monster or villain from each of the Doctor's eras. In the three or so years during which Fine Art Castings issued the figures, an impressive total of over 70 different *Doctor Who* characters were made available.

BBC Video decided to release more *Doctor Who* adventures for purchase by the general public, following their successful debut launch of *Revenge of the Cybermen* in 1983. Unfortunately, all the titles from this period presented edited versions of stories. They did however cover a good range of the series' history, even extending back to the black and white Troughton story *The Seeds of Death* and the Pertwee-era's *Day of the Daleks*. Also included were the highly popular stories *Pyramids of Mars* and *The Robots of Death* from Tom Baker's era.

As well as the BBC, another major contributor to the *Doctor Who* video market was a new company called Reeltime Pictures. This was under the aegis of Keith Barnfather, who had previously spent eight years working at the BBC and Channel 4 before leaving to move into business television production for himself. Reeltime Pictures was set up to provide film and video production facilities for corporate customers and, as Barnfather was also a big fan of *Doctor Who*, he decided to put together some video interviews with the stars of that series.

Thus was born the MythMakers range of tapes, which started in 1984 with Michael Wisher (Davros) and John Leeson (voice of K-9) and, when those were well received, continued with such popular actors as Nicholas Courtney (the Brigadier), Janet Fielding (Tegan) and Nicola Bryant (Peri). Each tape improved on the one before as the range became more ambitious in terms of production values, with location recording introduced and limited scope for visual effects. None of the tapes was ever made solely for profit – they were done primarily for fun, and, as the fans seemed to like them, there seemed no reason to stop as long as their production costs were being covered.

Other items of interest released during the sixth Doctor's era included the incredible Dalek hat (a rather sorry felt construction that fell apart rather quickly); the *Doctor Who The Music 2* record, which followed on from the success of the first release and contained incidental music from stories up to *The Caves of Androzani*; more Who Dares Publishing art prints; and, from the same company, a rather nice book celebrating the *Doctor Who* work of artist Frank Bellamy.

There were two sixth-Doctor artwork jigsaws released by Arrow; a set of *Doctor Who* plates from Royal Doulton; and a rubber playmat produced by Sport and Playbase Ltd, which featured a large panoramic illustration of the sixth Doctor and Peri surrounded by Daleks and Cybermen. (As an interesting side note, the latter product was also issued in a slightly different form for the American market, with the fourth Doctor and Leela replacing the then-current UK equivalents.) There were even two computer games – *The Mines of Terror* (Micro Power Ltd) and *Warlord* (BBC Software) released.

Doctor Who merchandise was still selling well and, despite the apparent slump in the series' television ratings, there was no sign of an end to this boom.

RATINGS

During the Eighties, ratings became less and less reliable as a means of gauging the public's reaction to any given television series. For one thing, they didn't take into account the boom in home video that was occurring in UK, as indeed it was across the world. In the past, viewers had only one chance to see a particular programme (unless it gained a repeat), but with a video recorder, they could happily tape their favourite shows to keep, while watching the more transient but still entertaining fare on the other channel.

Towards the end of Tom Baker's tenure as the Doctor, the ratings dropped alarmingly, going from a maximum of 16.1 million viewers in his penultimate season to 8.3 maximum (and 3.7 minimum) in his last. Through the following three seasons – which included the first Colin Baker story, *The Twin Dilemma*, at the end of the Season 21 – the ratings tended to hover around the somewhat lower 6 to 7 million mark.

The twenty-second season, the first full season for the sixth Doctor, maintained this level, receiving between 6 and 7 million viewers per story on average; however, the return of the programme to Saturday evenings with Season 23 proved disastrous in ratings terms.

The main reason for this is arguably easy to identify: ITV had now established an effective and popular line-up of Saturday evening shows, so by the time *Doctor Who* returned to its traditional slot, there was little impact that it could make against this opposition.

The Saturday evening line-up on BBC for the duration of the twenty-third season was: *Roland Rat – The Series*, *Doctor Who* and then *The Late, Late*

Breakfast Show (for the first ten weeks) or a film (a good example being the family offering *One of Our Dinosaurs is Missing*) or *All Creatures Great and Small*. ITV's viewing for the same time period consisted of: *Blockbusters*, *The A-Team* and *Blind Date*.

The average ratings (and chart positions) for these programmes at this time were as follows:

Blockbusters	7.8 (Pos 48.8)
The A-Team	11.8 (Pos 13.8)
Blind Date	14.8 (Pos 3.9)
Roland Rat – The Series	unrated (Pos >100)
Doctor Who	4.8 (Pos 87.3)
*Late Breakfast**	8.0 (Pos 45.4)

*figures include the film and *All Creatures Great And Small*.

As can be seen, *Blind Date* was not only ITV's top-rated show, it was frequently in the top three shows on British television. On some occasions, it was second only in popularity to the BBC's flagship soap opera *EastEnders*, which was pulling in around 21 million viewers. There is no way that *Doctor Who* – or any similar programme, for that matter – could compete with this, and as *Blind Date* followed directly on from *The A-Team*, another high rated show, which started ten minutes before *Doctor Who*, viewers tended to be hooked into to ITV for the whole of the early-evening period. If they videoed *Doctor Who* to watch later, then, as mentioned above, this was not reflected in the ratings.

Doctor Who was also not helped by being placed the *Roland Rat – The Series*, a short-lived puppet show that entered the TV chart only once during Season 23's run, polling 4.8 million viewers and coming 91st in the chart for the week of the final episode of *The Trial of a Time Lord*. As this episode was also the highest-rated *Doctor Who* episode of the season, it could be speculated that the Rat's figures were boosted by viewers waiting to see the climax of the Doctor's trial. It may also be significant that *Blind Date* was not shown on that final Saturday, and whatever was shown in its place did not appear in the TV chart at all.

Another factor contributing to the poor showing of the twenty-third season was that *The Trial of a Time Lord* was one long, fourteen part story. It is possible that viewers who had missed earlier episodes were not be too motivated to watch later ones – particularly if they did not realise that there were more-or-less self-contained adventures within the story. Despite the voice-over explanations that preceded all but the first two episodes of the season, anyone coming into the story part-way through would have had a hard job understanding exactly what was going on.

Overall, despite an eighteen month break, supposedly to put the show back on the rails, little was apparently achieved except for dramatically lowering the series' ratings. The press coverage cannot be faulted – there was lots of it – and many commentators had wished for a return to the familiar Saturday evening slot ever since the programme had been moved from it back in 1982.

It certainly looked, at least from the ratings point of view, as though *Doctor Who* might have had its day.

THE SIXTH DOCTOR

SIXTH DOCTOR STORIES
IN ORDER OF AVERAGE VIEWING FIGURES
(Figures in millions of viewers)

Attack of the Cybermen 1	8.9
Revelation of the Daleks 2	7.7
The Twin Dilemma 1	7.6
Timelash 2	7.4
The Twin Dilemma 2	7.4
Revelation of the Daleks 1	7.4
Mark of the Rani 2	7.3
Vengeance on Varos 1	7.2
Attack of the Cybermen 2	7.2
Vengeance on Varos 2	7.0
The Twin Dilemma 3	7.0
The Two Doctors 3	6.9
Timelash 1	6.7
The Two Doctors 1	6.6
Mark of the Rani 1	6.3
The Twin Dilemma 4	6.3
The Two Doctors 2	6.0
The Trial of a Time Lord 14	5.6
The Trial of a Time Lord 11	5.3
The Trial of a Time Lord 9	5.2
The Trial of a Time Lord 12	5.2
The Trial of a Time Lord 7	5.1
The Trial of a Time Lord 8	5.0
The Trial of a Time Lord 2	4.9
The Trial of a Time Lord 1	4.9
The Trial of a Time Lord 5	4.8
The Trial of a Time Lord 10	4.6
The Trial of a Time Lord 6	4.6
The Trial of a Time Lord 13	4.4
The Trial of a Time Lord 3	3.9
The Trial of a Time Lord 4	3.7

Afterword

The news that Colin Baker would not be returning for the twenty-fourth season of *Doctor Who* was broken to the general public in early December 1986. The press once again took an interest in the series, with the *Sun*'s Charles Catchpole interviewing Baker for a rather sensationalist three-part centre-page special. Fan reaction to Colin Baker's departure was, on the whole, muted. Although there was a widespread feeling that he had been very badly treated, many apparently saw the casting of a new Doctor as a sign of hope for the future and an escape from the troubled times of recent years.

This feeling of a bad time best forgotten has perhaps dissuaded fans from looking back and re-evaluating the eight stories produced during Colin Baker's incumbency. It is often forgotten that Season 22 received an average audience of 7.12 million viewers, with a high appreciation rating. It could be argued that, had Season 23 continued as originally planned, Baker would have settled comfortably into the role of the Doctor and viewers would have become used to this flamboyant portrayal of the Time Lord. It is also interesting to speculate what might have happened with the arrival of a new script editor for Season 24. Under Andrew Cartmel's aegis, the sixth Doctor may have taken on a slightly darker nature, a change in characterisation that Colin Baker has indicated he would have been happy with, had it taken place. In fact, this concept was later taken up by the BBC Film Club in a series of video dramas, produced and directed by Bill Baggs, in which Colin Baker played the Stranger alongside Nicola Bryant's Miss Brown. While having no visible connection – other than the casting – with *Doctor Who*, these tapes presented an interesting counterpoint to Baker's tenure as the Doctor.

It is inevitable to conclude that the eighteen-month hiatus in transmission and the public vilification of the series by the Controller of BBC1, Michael Grade, did immense damage to *Doctor Who*. The changes of scheduling and scripting that were supposed to tackle perceived shortcomings in the series' style and direction and increase its popularity with the general public had precisely the opposite effect, leading to a sharp drop to an average viewing figure of 4.8 million.

It is unfortunate that Colin Baker's departure from the role of the Doctor was the only remaining, and highly visible, action that could be taken to give the viewing public the impression that changes were being made to improve the series for the future. In this way, fan and press attention could be diverted from any other reasons for the falling viewing figures, and instead blame, by implication, the series' lead actor for all its woes. Whether this strategy came about by design or by accident is not known, but it worked.

The beginning of Season 24 saw the arrival of a new Doctor in the earthly form of Sylvester McCoy. As Colin Baker had turned down the option of making a regeneration story, the change-over of Doctors was achieved by McCoy donning a blond, curly wig and lying on the floor of the TARDIS dressed in the sixth Doctor's costume. Baker's understandable decision to bow out when he did meant that the last line delivered by the sixth Doctor on screen was the immortal phrase: "Carrot juice, carrot juice, carrot juice!"

A rather less than fitting epitaph.

THE SEVENTH DOCTOR

David J Howe
Stephen James Walker

Foreword

The era of the sixth Doctor came to an ignominious end. Colin Baker had been fired by the BBC and producer John Nathan-Turner instructed to cast a new actor to star in the twenty-four-year-old series. The problem was that Baker, understandably sore at the treatment he had received, had refused to return simply to record a story in which he would be written out, and so, for the first time in *Doctor Who*'s history, a regeneration had to be achieved without the participation of the outgoing Doctor.

To complicate matters further, the only other regular cast member, Bonnie Langford, was a newcomer, who was still settling into her role as computer programmer and health and fitness fanatic Melanie Bush; and the series' long serving script editor Eric Saward had resigned the previous year following disagreements with Nathan-Turner, leaving that post temporarily vacant.

The actor chosen to take over as the Doctor was Sylvester McCoy. Previously known mainly for children's television work and daredevil comedy stunts – including, famously, stuffing ferrets down his trousers in one particular show – he grasped the opportunity that *Doctor Who* presented him to establish himself in a different kind of role with a higher public profile. For the next three years, the Doctor became a lively fellow with dark wavy hair and a faint Scots accent, sporting a paisley-patterned scarf and a question-mark pullover and brolly. McCoy's was a uniquely different interpretation of the nation's favourite Time Lord. Behind his sometimes clownish façade, this was a more introspected and thoughtful Doctor; a more mysterious Doctor; a Doctor who could take command of a situation with simply a suggestion here and a quiet adjustment there.

In the wider world during McCoy's time as the Doctor, the Archbishop of Canterbury's special envoy, Terry Waite, was kidnapped in Beirut, not to be released until some five years later; a car ferry capsized off Zeebrugge, killing two hundred passengers; Margaret Thatcher was elected for a third term as Prime Minister of the UK; hurricane force winds killed seventeen people and left a £300 million trail of destruction across southern England; and the bottom fell out of the London stock market, wiping ten per cent, or £50 billion pounds, off the value of shares on a day forever to be known as 'black Monday'.

Join us as we revisit the eras of the seventh and eighth Doctors, and bring to a end – at least for the time being – our coverage of the ever developing, ever popular chronicles of that mysterious traveller in space and time known only as the Doctor.

Introduction
Sophie Aldred

Last year I travelled down to Wiltshire to open a small *Doctor Who* exhibition in a museum in Trowbridge. There were all the usual suspects; beautifully crafted Cybermen models, display cabinets stuffed with well treasured boxed sets of monsters, vehicles, Doctors even. And, guarding the entrance to the exhibition, the most menacing and terrifying creation of the lot – poised at the head of the stairs, lethal weapons pointed towards an unsuspecting Mum and her seven-ish year old son who'd popped up from the shopping centre below to see what all the fuss was about.

As I watched, the boy stopped short, pointed and exclaimed; 'Mum, what are those?'

'Daleks, darling,' she replied, 'They had them on telly when I was your age.'

So there we have it. A whole generation growing up without that knowledge we used to take for granted. As I stood there, musing rather sadly, I started wondering how long it's going to take for the *Doctor Who* references to pass out of popular culture altogether. At least at the moment, we can be assured of the odd mention of the TARDIS or Daleks on afternoon game shows and panel games.

But of course there are the fans. You lot out there who keep *Doctor Who* alive by organising and attending conventions, by writing and reading books such as this one, by supporting magazines, keeping *Doctor Who* on the video shelves, introducing new people to the show ... the list is endless. And you're doing it not from a sense of duty or loyalty, though that does come into it somewhere along the line, but because you love this programme and these characters and don't want to see them disappear. There's a growing library full of excellent books like this to remind and inform us. There's a lot of stuff in here that I had no idea about, even after all the trawling through my memory banks for my own book on the subject, *ACE!* All the details you could ever wish for, and a bonus chapter on the eighth Doctor, and hope for the future.

So maybe it's not all doom and gloom. Sylvester and I have recently spent a couple of days working together on a spin off audio project created by one of that band of fans who have grown up to become professional writers, directors, production companies and so on. I wondered how it difficult it would be, almost ten years on, to walk back into the relationship, to remember how it was. I needn't have worried. Something that wasn't quite me and wasn't quite acting took over the moment Sylv and I stood together at the microphone; a voice and an attitude that's not quite mine came back to me, like slipping an arm into a familiar old jacket that has been hanging in the back of a wardrobe for some years, waiting and hoping that one day it'll come back into fashion. It's a bit of a saggy old jacket now, lightly faded from lack of use. But the thing is, it's still there ... and the badges are nice and shiny.

Sophie Aldred, 1998

Sylvester McCoy
In His Own Words

ON HIS EARLY LIFE AND CAREER:

'[I was born in] Dunoon, Argyll, Scotland, on a rainy day, 20 August in the year of our lord 1943 ...

'I was a lively little lad. I'm sure there were times when people thought I should have been put in prison, but I didn't get caught! ...

'I used to go to Saturday cinema and watch those dreadful but wonderful serials like *Flash Gordon* ... I collected jam jars, which were worth a ha'penny each, so I could get in to see *Flash Gordon* for four jam jars. The first horror film I saw was *The Beast with Five Fingers*, which I watched through the buttonhole in the top of my school mackintosh, because I was so scared. I remember Quatermass too, which terrified me.'

Interviewed by Johnny Black in 1987 for *Starburst* Issue 110.

'I was raised by my grandmother and sometimes my aunt ... My father was killed in the War a couple of months before I was born. He was blown up in a submarine. And my mother subsequently had a nervous breakdown. It lasted ... well, it lasted until the end of her life, really. She died when I was twenty-one. She spent most of her life in hospitals.'

Interviewed by uncredited writer in 1988 for *Whovian Times* Volume 17.

'Being a Catholic, I went to the local Roman Catholic primary school, where we used to have vocational talks from people ... We had a priest one day, and they asked if anybody would like to be one. Three of us put our hands up – me, Danny Sweeney and Mary O'Malley. Naturally Mary wasn't called out, but Danny and I were!

'This had never happened before, and we were sent off post haste to see the priest ... When we got there, Danny lost his bottle. Being a cocky little thing, I knocked on the door and said, "I want to be a priest". Next thing I knew, I was on a train to Aberdeen to study for the priesthood. I got so holy, I had housemaid's knee from praying. At first I wanted to be the Pope, then I decided to be much humbler and become a mere monk. I wrote off to the Dominicans, and they replied, a very encouraging letter. When I left [Aberdeen] they all kneeled down and prayed and praised me as a saint, because no-one had ever left to become something even more hard and harsh, a monk.

'Luckily, when I got home, another letter arrived from the Dominicans saying I was too young to start. I was just fifteen. It was the best thing that ever happened, because I had to cram in some education that year, so I was sent off to the local unisex grammar school, where I discovered those wonderful creatures ... girls. I gave up all thoughts of Popes and monks right away.'

Interviewed by Johnny Black in 1987 for *Starburst* Issue 110.

'I worked in the City of London [for a time. It] was much more Dickensian than it is now. It [was] a very uptight place, especially in the matter of attire ... Once I was a trainee executive in charge of the liaison between the computer and auto insurance. In fact, I was more a trainee alcoholic. It was driving me mad. You see, I didn't know I wanted to be an actor. All I knew was that what I was doing wasn't fulfilling, whatever it was. I was very unhappy in that world. You weren't allowed to take your jacket off on a warm day unless you got permission. I knew that this was madness, lunacy, dictatorial and unfair. It wasn't that we were in an office with people coming in to see us. We were just in an office all together, and there was no air conditioning.'

Interviewed by Lou Anders in 1995 for *Dreamwatch* 17.

'I remember once my grandmother – who is Irish – sitting in the bay window of a lovely house we had near the River Clyde, looking out onto a rainy landscape ... Suddenly, in a mysterious kind of way, she turned to me and said I should become an actor. It came from nowhere, and I thought it was a completely barmy, silly idea. But it was there and it took root, I suppose.

'What then happened was that I was working in London for a company that went bust. I ended up working in the box office of the Roundhouse Theatre, and one day Ken Campbell came in. He was setting up the Ken Campbell Roadshow with Bob Hoskins and various others, and someone had let him down. Brian Murphy was collecting the tickets I was selling ... Ken went to Brian and said, "I need someone for this wild show starting in the North of England," and Brian said, "Well, ask the guy in the box office – he's completely out of his head!"

'So he came up to me – and in those days I was a hippie with a moustache, long hair, beads, the lot – and he asked me to join the Roadshow. I told him I wasn't an actor, and he said, "Do you want to be?" I said, "Yes," and he said he'd come back on Monday. He did – and I became an actor!'

Interviewed by Richard Marson in 1987 for *Doctor Who Magazine* No. 130.

'It was supposed to be for one night, but I stayed with the Roadshow for two years. We toured all over Europe, Britain and Ireland and Israel too, and it became a bit of a cult on the fringe. I left there and went to Joan Littlewood's theatre workshop at Stratford East and worked with her for a while, then from there I went to Nottingham Playhouse with Richard Eyre ... and I worked with him for two or three years. At the same time, television started for me, and a kind of parallel career went on. It was about sixteen years ago I started as an actor and about twelve years ago I started *Vision On* for the BBC ... Then every year I did another television series: *Jigsaw*, *Eureka*, *Tiswas*, *Starstrider* ...

'So I had two careers going on: one in the theatre, [where I was appearing in productions of] Shakespeare, Beckett [and] Brecht and ... having plays written for me by Adrian Mitchell, Ken Campbell and Ken Hill; [the other] paying for my mortgage in a sense by doing television and children's stuff. I also did *The Last Place on Earth*, which was a very adult piece for television – seven one-hour films about Scott's race to the Antarctic, which we actually filmed in the Arctic. [I did] *Tiny Revolutions* for Granada, which was an adult film about a professor stuck in prison in Czechoslovakia for telling jokes against the state.'

Interviewed by Gary Levy and Robert Cope in 1987 for *DWB* 50.

'[At first] I had no idea what sort of actor I was. But because of the nature of working with Ken Campbell and Bob Hoskins, who are both physical performers, I started doing very physical theatre. Then people would come up to me and say I reminded them of Buster Keaton, Stan Laurel or Charlie Chaplin. So I thought I'd better have a look at the work of the comedy pioneers – and by discovering them, I also discovered my own acting "self".'

Interviewed by Graeme Wood and Andrew Lennard in 1992 for *TV Zone* Special # 4.

THE SEVENTH DOCTOR

'The name I used at first was Kent Smith – part of a very long name I've got. There was another actor in America called Kent Smith, and I always had ambitions beyond my ... rights. I thought perhaps I might do something in America, not realising I'd end up doing *Doctor Who*. Also, I thought Kent Smith was more of a matinee idol name, and I didn't think I was that kind of actor. I was doing a show called *An Evening with Sylvester McCoy, the Human Bomb*, and in it, we wanted the audience to believe that there was this little man who could do all these amazing stunts. So we printed a programme stating, "Sylvester McCoy played by Sylvester McCoy," and it stuck, really. I thought it was quite a good name, so I kept it.'

Interviewed by Paul Travers in 1988 for *Doctor Who Magazine* No. 142.

ON WATCHING EARLIER ERAS OF *DOCTOR WHO*:

'I started watching *Doctor Who* with Patrick Troughton when I was about 20 odd, then I watched it with Jon Pertwee and Tom Baker, but when I became an actor – because of the nature of the job – I got out of the habit of watching series and serials ... You can never follow them, because you are working. I really didn't see Peter Davison very much, or Colin [Baker].'

Interviewed by Gary Levy and Robert Cope in 1987 for *DWB* 50.

ON BEING CAST AS THE DOCTOR:

'It was a role I had wanted for some time. I remember that three years earlier, when Colin Baker got the part, I heard about it a bit too late, but I still thought to myself, "I wish I'd known about that – I'd quite like to have tried for it". So though I wasn't actually pursuing it all the time, it was a role that I fancied doing. Then when I heard on the news that Colin was leaving, I phoned my agent and told him that there was a job going at the BBC ...

'Actually, what happened was that my agent phoned John Nathan-Turner, and immediately he had put the phone down, [a producer named] Clive Doig also came on the line and told John he should take a look at me. Apparently John said, "Wait a minute, are you and his agent in cahoots?"'

Interviewed by Peter Haining in 1988 for *Doctor Who – 25 Glorious Years*.

'I was at the National Theatre doing *The Pied Piper*, which was actually a very good audition part for the Doctor. Then I had a two and a half hour interview with John Nathan-Turner.'

Interviewed by Johnny Black in 1987 for *Starburst* Issue 110.

'It was two and a half hours of charm, because you go into these interviews and try to be charming.

'I don't know what I talked about, but I kept thinking, "I hope this interview finishes soon, or I'll run out of charm" ... I managed to con my way through that one. Then I went back and did another two hour interview, and then I met the Head of Series and Serials, Jonathan Powell, who gave me only five minutes, thank god! They decided that they quite liked my quirkiness and humour, but they weren't sure I had the seriousness and the power to overcome the many enemies that I would meet in my time travels.

'So we did two screen tests – two scenes – and one of those was overpowering the enemy, and I passed that, so they gave me the job.

'Janet Fielding did the test with me, and she'd rehearsed this stuff on another day with me and a few others that were also up for the part, so I had to hang around quite a lot. At first I wasn't too bothered one way or the other, as you go up for a lot of parts, but then I began to think, "Oh my god! They're serious!"'

Interviewed by Richard Marson in 1987 for *Doctor Who Magazine* No. 130.

ON THE DOCTOR'S CHARACTER:

'He's someone who loves the Earth, and therefore humanity. But he is also a very wise man who sees the follies of man – and also those in himself. Those are his strengths. But he also has his weaknesses, which are equally interesting. Take his passion for minutiae, and innocently wandering into dangerous situations that perhaps he should see: maybe does, maybe doesn't. He's also a rebel and doesn't really like authority, which is something I like in him. Because, you know, authority has to prove its worth – just because it *is* authority, it shouldn't be accepted. It should be questioned – and the Doctor does, and it gets him into trouble. He's also a bit of an anarchist as well! There is even a bit of Doctor Johnson in him – you know, one of those people you admire who stand up and say what they think.

'In fact, he is a mixture of all sorts of things, but at his most basic, he loves the Earth. He is a man who should not use violence, I believe, but his wits and his intelligence to get him out of any tight corner.'

Interviewed by Peter Haining in 1988 for *Doctor Who – 25 Glorious Years.*

ON HIS DOCTOR'S COSTUME:

'The hat emerged because I wore one to the interviews. I did wear a hat just like that [in my private life], but I can't now, really. Sad. They wanted the hat, though. I wanted my costume to be the sort of thing that could be seen on the street, and that there was only something strange about when people get close. Not too alien. I've actually worn it in the street in Wales when we were [on location] and people who didn't recognise me or realise what was going on didn't notice anything odd. One guy came up to me and said, "I like your jumper; very nice that. Where did you get it from?" I said my mother had knitted it!'

Interviewed by Richard Marson in 1987 for *Doctor Who Magazine* **No. 130.**

'I knew I wanted a baggy jacket with lots of paraphernalia in the pockets. I think the Doctor should be something of an Edwardian character, like in those wonderful Jules Verne novels ... It was basically a combination of various ideas put forward, and I'm really pleased with it.'

Interviewed by Gary Levy and Robert Cope in 1987 for *DWB* **50.**

'The jumper is based on a 1930s golfing sweater. We did consider the idea of the Doctor wearing glasses – as I normally do – but it was decided that my eyes could be seen better without them. The umbrella with the red question-mark handle was all my own idea.'

Interviewed by Peter Haining in 1988 for *Doctor Who – 25 Glorious Years.*

'I like the pullover, but ... the costume is too loud for my taste. I'd like to tone it down. As for the question-marks, they're a nice motif. I don't know whether it matters. I'd miss the [question-mark handle] umbrella if it went ... but I think the scarf could be darker, and the hatband too. Perhaps the jacket could be brown.'

Interviewed by Paul Travers in 1988 for *Doctor Who Magazine* **No. 142.**

'I personally would have liked to have got rid of the question marks on the jumper. I thought that was a bit too much, but I think the umbrella is all right, because at first people don't actually notice it. The pullover I would have preferred to be just plain. I tried to get rid of it last year, along with the jacket change, but the producer said no, really because it was his idea, and the umbrella was mine, so that was fair enough.'

Interviewed by Mark Attwood in 1990 *DWB* No. 77.

ON *TIME AND THE RANI*:

'I had to dress up in Colin's costume with a silly wig, and I looked like Harpo Marx. I had to lie down on my face and then turn over. For just an instant I did look surprisingly like Colin, and then the picture went all funny and [when] it returned to normal, I was me – much to my horror when I looked in the mirror! ...

'Right from the beginning there was a good feeling both in front of the cameras and behind them. No-one made me feel I was the new boy and had to prove my worth. The director of that first story was Andrew Morgan, who had done my screen test for the series. And because I sensed right from that initial meeting that he was the sort of guy who would give me a chance, it was wonderful to work with him on the first story. It felt almost like coming home, and I said to myself, "Hey, I belong here." It was very funny – I didn't worry. I felt relaxed. I just had to learn my lines and not bump into the monsters!'

Interviewed by Peter Haining in 1988 for *Doctor Who – 25 Glorious Years*.

ON *PARADISE TOWERS*:

'There seemed to be so much to learn in the way of words! The Doctor had so much to say! Most of the speaking was on one set, and because we taped it in sets, rather than in order, I was on that set talking nonstop. By the end of it, I was completely bored by the sound of my own voice, and exhausted at having to remember all those words. It wasn't all that enjoyable to do, but when I saw it, it really worked. I was surprised by how well it came across, considering the mountain I had to climb.'

Interviewed by Joe Nazzaro in 1993 for *TV Zone* Special # 11.

THE SEVENTH DOCTOR

ON *DELTA AND THE BANNERMEN*:

'It was a fun story to do, and all the people in it were a great laugh. Nobody was trying to act the star – which some of them had every right to do. I was still a bit of a new boy as the Doctor, but they were very welcoming and good fun to be with ...

'We were [recording a] sequence on a rooftop with explosive charges going off all around me. One of them went off a little too early, and this banged my head a bit, but we were able to keep on. Mind you, with the tight schedules we have, we *had* to – and I suppose that I learned right there and then that the one thing one would like more of on *Doctor Who* is time!'

Interviewed by Peter Haining in 1988 for *Doctor Who – 25 Glorious Years*.

ON *REMEMBRANCE OF THE DALEKS*:

'I didn't feel as if I were a real Doctor until I'd worked with the Daleks. But it's incredibly difficult to move them around – it's also very boring hanging around waiting for them. The new ones have these great round balls, you know, like under those wheelbarrows, and that made them wobbly Daleks! It's like a big joke. I said I'd like to work with the Daleks because I'd like to find out what was underneath their skirts – and now I've found out, they've got three balls!'

Interviewed by Mark Attwood in 1990 *DWB* No. 77.

ON *DRAGONFIRE*:

'The bizarre thing was, John Nathan-Turner wanted Bonnie [Langford] to stay on for another two stories in the next season. That way, the first story would have us arriving in the new season, and the next story would be about why Bonnie's character had to leave. Because of her commitments in the theatre, she couldn't say, "I'll give you eight weeks," so she said, "I'll give you four, and do the first story".

'I think John felt, "I don't want to do that with the first story in the twenty-fifth season; having someone leave," so he said, "Maybe you should leave now," and we would start afresh. Originally it was going to be a very quick scene, but I said, "We've got to get more into it". The Doctor had been with this character for two personas, and he was obviously very fond of her, so we should have some sort of goodbye scene.

'I'd done a really lovely goodbye scene with that character for my screen test, which had been written by the script editor, Andrew Cartmel, and I suggested we use that scene to give it more impact. It seemed terribly curt to just say goodbye.'

Interviewed by Joe Nazzaro in 1993 for *TV Zone* Special # 11.

ON *SILVER NEMESIS*:

'If you ever see the [American] documentary made [on *Silver Nemesis*] ... you'll see me sitting on a table, cross legged, with my hair standing up, having a nervous breakdown. The asbestos scare [at the Television Centre studios] had affected us badly. We only had one and a half days' rehearsal left after *The Greatest Show in the Galaxy* to do the story, and we had to make the documentary on the same day. We were just going potty ... I didn't know where I was.'

Interviewed by Mark Wyman in 1989 for *TARDIS*, spring 1989 edition.

ON *THE GREATEST SHOW IN THE GALAXY*:

'We had a very difficult time with *The Greatest Show in the Galaxy* because of the asbestos scare at the BBC – we had to [record the studio scenes in a] tent at Elstree. The cameras broke down, we had to stop every time a car went by or a bird whistled. Amazing.'

Interviewed by Paul Travers in 1988 for *Doctor Who Magazine* No. 142

ON *THE HAPPINESS PATROL*:

'*The Happiness Patrol* was slightly disappointing, because it was done in studio. If think it was a bit over-ambitious.

'If they've got to do a story in studio, it would be better to do something actually indoors. Trying to create a planet, it obviously doesn't work. You have to suspend a lot of [disbelief], especially as the other stories [in the same season] were so successful at creating wherever we were on location.'

Interviewed by Paul Travers in 1989 for *Doctor Who Magazine* No. 154.

'It was a great story, I thought. Really good. It had the underlying theme against the more extreme Thatcherite policies of our time. It had a neo-fascist feel about it as well. The harmonica music and the sense of longing … It would have been great in black and white. Maybe we should encourage everyone to turn their colour off when they watch it and see what it looks like.'

Interviewed by Nick Briggs in 1994 for *Doctor Who Magazine* No. 216.

ON *BATTLEFIELD*:

'To work with Nick [Courtney] was lovely! I've always been a great fan of the Brigadier, ever since I watched it when Patrick Troughton and Jon Pertwee were in it. He's a lovely man, and we got on very well. I'd met him at conventions before, but it's not the same as working with someone.

'Jean Marsh was lovely too! … They're all lovely! I'm a luvvy now! You know how sometimes you just get on with people? The chemistry was great. She could have stayed in *Doctor Who* forever as far as I was concerned. And James Ellis was a great, big-hearted Irishman with all the charm and warmth of that.'

Interviewed by Nick Briggs in 1994 for *Doctor Who Magazine* No. 216.

ON *THE CURSE OF FENRIC*:

'There was a great moment in *The Curse of Fenric* where Sophie [Aldred] and I ran out of a hut and could literally feel the heat of [an] explosion [set off by] the visual effects guys … I enjoyed that!'

Interviewed by Graeme Wood and Andrew Lennard in 1992 for *TV Zone* Special # 4.

'It was very well written. It made sense and there weren't too many holes in it. I liked it, because it was about another time. Personally, I liked to travel back in time … My attraction to *Doctor Who* in the beginning was the fact that we could go back in time. I've always been interested in history, so it was rather nice to go back to the time of World War Two.'

Interviewed by Nick Briggs in 1994 for *Doctor Who Magazine* No. 216.

SYLVESTER MCCOY: IN HIS OWN WORDS

ON *GHOST LIGHT*:

'I'm enjoying [making] *Ghost Light*. I don't like doing studio work, but I'm happy [that] this one's set inside a building. It will give it much more [credibility]. It's got a brilliant cast, and it's a good story ... once we work it out!'

Interviewed by Paul Travers in 1989 for *Doctor Who Magazine* No. 154.

ON *SURVIVAL*:

'We were filming in the deserts of Dorset. There's a big sandpit in Dorset. Vast thing ... It was over 100 degrees in the heatwave, and it was just like doing a spaghetti Western ... It was incredibly hot and all these girls had to be dressed up in catsuits and all this fun fur stuff; I mean it was just too hot for them! Too unbearably hot. But then again, they were very patient, except for one, who suddenly freaked out and ripped all her clothes off and was last seen running for the train. It was a lovely sight though ...'

Interviewed by Bob Furnell, Bonnie Gale, Misha Lauenstein and Pat Burt on 28 January 1996.

'It was lovely to work with Anthony Ainley. It was interesting finding, in acting terms, that he had a way of playing the character. I kept thinking, "Now he's a Time Lord," and so I tried to act similar to him. As Time Lords, when you go round the universe ... you respond differently to different people. But when you meet your own, there would be that kind of similarity of movement, as well as various other things.'

Interviewed by Paul Travers in 1989 for *Doctor Who Magazine* No. 154.

ON HIS DOCTOR'S COMPANIONS:

'Bonnie [Langford] was a specific type of actress, and she was definitely employed to act against [Colin Baker's] coat. It was so colourful! ... You needed a very colourful person there, so there was Bonnie. The pairing was excellent for them, but then I came along. I was a different kettle of fish, and so it wasn't the right kind of pairing. Bonnie and I got on really well, 'cause we're good mates, and we'd worked together before on stage, but it didn't work. It was just the state of play; she didn't have to act against such a colourful coat.'

Interviewed by Darren Floyd, Jeremy Taylor and Huw Griffiths in 1991 for *The Global Times*.

'We are developing the relationship between Ace and [the Doctor] ... I don't know in depth about the other Doctor/companion relationships, but this is definitely different from [the] relationship with Ace last year, or the one with Mel. It's deeper; and we have arguments – strong arguments.'

Interviewed by Mark Wyman in 1989 for *TARDIS*, spring 1989 edition.

'The companion shouldn't be someone who screams all the time, and shouldn't be the token woman. She should be a fully fledged character in her own right. I'm sure that others have been; I'm just going by my own prejudice of what I thought. Sophie [Aldred] is great, and we're great mates.'

Interviewed by David J Howe, Mark Stammers and Stephen James Walker in 1989 for *The Frame* No. 11.

ON THE PLEASURES OF HIS TIME AS THE DOCTOR:

'I enjoyed working on it very much ... Just for purely acting charms, it's a great role to play. You're asked to call upon all sorts of acting in it, from kind of merry to mad, and all the various things in between ... melancholy and manic and murderous ... and all those various things! It's a terrific role and I had a very happy time. I got on incredibly well with all the technicians and the cameramen and also the production staff. My companions were very good friends. One was an old friend, Bonnie, whom I knew before, and Sophie became a good friend ... I felt that our job as the regulars on the show was to make sure that all the other actors who came to it had a very good time, and as far as I know, everyone did.'

Interviewed by Mike Doran, Andrew Gurudata and Kristian LeBlanc in 1993 for *The Chameleon Circuit* Issue 15.

'As we only did five months of the year, I had seven months to go off and do other things. So that made the job even more wonderful, because it afforded me the luxury of experimenting. I went off around England with an Iranian theatre group, doing a play about Iran. Because of the wage from

Doctor Who, I could afford to find out what it was like working in another culture. And, of course, I went back to the National Theatre and did various other things, plays, and *What's Your Story?* for the BBC.'

Interviewed by Nick Briggs in 1994 for *Doctor Who Magazine* No. 216.

ON THE PRESSURES OF HIS TIME AS THE DOCTOR:

'It's exhausting in the studio. The first studio I did was with Kate O'Mara, and ... we were on set from ten thirty in the morning to ten at night, just the two of us doing these scenes. By the end of the day, I couldn't stand up, I was completely shattered!'

Interviewed by Richard Marson in 1987 for *Doctor Who Magazine* No. 130.

'I don't like the loss of privacy. I get lots of letters. I find it a terrible responsibility trying to answer them, finding the time. I'm delighted to get them, obviously. My family would have preferred that I hadn't done [the series]. I've been on television for twelve years regularly ... People are used to seeing me in the street and saying hello and all that. But *Doctor Who* had a different effect. People do invade your privacy a great deal.'

Interviewed by Mike Doran, Andrew Gurudata and Kristian LeBlanc in 1993 for *The Chameleon Circuit* Issue 15.

ON HIS DEPARTURE FROM THE SERIES:

'To be very, very honest, when the third year actually came up, I was thinking of jacking it in then, thinking that this is maybe too long. I also had at the back of my mind that Peter Davison had told me that Patrick Troughton had told him: "Only do three years." But then John [Nathan-Turner] said, sometime during the negotiations for the third year, "You must agree to do a fourth term." So I thought, "Okay, I'll do it," and decided to go for it.'

Interviewed by Nick Briggs in 1994 for *Doctor Who Magazine* No. 216.

'I was upset at the end of *Doctor Who*, but I think, in a way, the fates have taken charge, so perhaps it's right. Otherwise I might have been tempted to stay on for quite a long time; part of me thinks that would have been a bad thing, another part of me thinks I would have enjoyed it. [For my career] as an actor outside ... *Doctor Who*, it's much been much better that I did only three short seasons ... If I'd stayed for a long time, I might ... still be typecast. I don't know yet. I'm not that far away from it.'

Interviewed by Darren Floyd, Jeremy Taylor and Huw Griffiths in 1991 for *The Global Times*.

'It was pretty painful for the first couple of years. I was a bit pissed off, really, at the way it had been handled, which seemed to be unfair, but I got used to it as time went on. You just have to carry on.'

Interviewed by Joe Nazzaro in 1993 for *TV Zone* Special # 11.

ON FAN REACTION TO HIS DOCTOR:

'I was told that there were such things as science-fiction conventions, but that's like saying there are bumps on the moon. I didn't know what they were really. Conventions in Britain at that time were very few and far between. My only knowledge of conventions came from the Laurel and Hardy film *Sons of the Desert*, where they run off; their wives don't want them to go, but they end up at a convention. So I had a sort of comedic view of conventions. I had no idea what they were like. I got the job on Monday, and on Thursday I was flown to Atlanta, and there was a convention. People dressed up as various Doctors, companions and monsters from *Doctor Who*. Such great fun.'

Interviewed by Mike Doran, Andrew Gurudata and Kristian LeBlanc in 1993 for *The Chameleon Circuit* Issue 15.

'It amazed me at the beginning. I had no idea. At first I was a bit scared, frightened of it. I didn't quite know how to handle it. Then slowly I've grown to like it. I would miss it now. I mean, at one time I used to go to conventions more out of duty – but also because they took me to parts of the world I'd never been to ... But now, you get to know people and various faces and I look forward to going back to places I've been before and meeting people I've met before – seeing old friends.

'In the early days, there were some bad moments, because some fans ... especially in Britain ... became very critical ... before they'd seen a shot I'd done. In a way, Doctor Who is a strange role, because normally you don't have that comparison. The only other similar kind of roles are

Shakespearean roles – you [have people talking about] good Hamlets and …bad Hamlets, [saying one's] not as good [as another, and so on]. In television you really never have that, but with *Doctor Who* you do. So that was a bit of a problem to deal with at first.'

Interviewed by Bob Furnell, Bonnie Gale, Misha Lauenstein and Pat Burt on 28 January 1996.

'There was a tour I did that was on a ship that went from Florida to Mexico and back. [It was] a wonderful convention. But one of the fans, she got a bit emotional, in fact she was so happy that she didn't want to carry on living, and we had to talk her down from jumping off the side of the boat, because she was just so happy! That was a bit sad really.

'There was [once] an American guy who stood up and said [something like], "Excuse me, Doctor, but when you were in your third persona, what were you thinking when you opened the TARDIS door onto the planet Skaro?" He believed it, obviously. Then someone else stood up and said, "Excuse me, Doctor, now you're so universally famous, are you worried about being shot?" That was quite an interesting question. I just said, "Next question, please," and hid behind a chair!'

Interviewed by Mark Attwood in 1990 *DWB* No. 77.

ON THE 1996 TELEVISION MOVIE:

'It's wonderful. The only piece of the original costume is the hat, and when I put that on, I felt, "Oh I'm wearing this hat again. How good!"…

'They've treated me wonderfully. They've been very good to me – treated me with a great deal of respect, which is nice …

'There's more time and money to it. It's still very British. The director's British. It's a very calm and happy crew as well, and everyone's very enthusiastic … What is actually lovely is the Canadian crew, who keep saying, "It's wonderful. We're going to get our names up on BBC Television". That's very lovely. They're really excited about it. So there's a great feeling of excitement and joy, and people are really working hard to make it as good as they can, and I'm mightily impressed by the crew. They've been wonderful.'

Interviewed by Bob Furnell, Bonnie Gale, Misha Lauenstein and Pat Burt on 28 January 1996.

THE SEVENTH DOCTOR

ON THE RELATIVE MERITS OF STAGE, FILM AND TV WORK:

'Theatre [is my favourite]. I'm a show-off. I like live theatre. I like standing on the stage and performing to a lot of people. I enjoy it immensely. I like to feel the instant feedback.

'I like doing film. On the stage you paint with a broad brush, and with a film you paint with a minute brush, sort of like little Chinese miniatures ... Television I sometimes found a bit odd, because the multi-camera shoots are very odd. You never quite know which one you're on, and it's like two mediums married together – theatre and film – which doesn't quite gel.'

Interviewed by Bob Furnell, Bonnie Gale, Misha Lauenstein and Pat Burt on 28 January 1996.

ON HIS HOME LIFE:

'I have a family that I love very much, and [mixing private and professional activities] it's like schizophrenia. It's a very schizophrenic profession, and I'm a very schizophrenic person. Someone once read my palm and they said it was the most schizophrenic palm they'd ever seen. I think that's acting all the different parts. I go home and, though I obviously talk about acting, I try to give as much energy there as when I'm working.

'My wife isn't in the business and doesn't really want to be a part of it. She enjoys the fact that I am ... I'm not looking forward to finding a *Sun* reporter in my dustbin. If I do, I'll stick the lid back on and chain it down. I presume people are going to pry, but if they do, they'll get a poke in the eye, or they'll be told in a very Scottish way where to go. They'll no doubt carry on doing it, though, and I'll just have to learn to live with it.

'As for my other interests, I go out to the theatre a lot, I like ballet and I like films and opera.'

Interviewed by Richard Marson in 1987 for *Doctor Who Magazine* No. 130.

'My wife's name is Agnes. We've been married for fifteen years. We have an eleven year old son whose name is Sam and another boy named Joe, who will be ten in November.'

Interviewed by uncredited writer in 1988 for *Whovian Times* Volume 17.

'I like classical music a lot. But I do enjoy all other sorts of music. The other day, I was sailing up the Thames on a barge, and we stopped at this supposedly boring place called Staines. We went into the square [and] there was an opera on at the Town Hall, so I went to the opera ... Then [after the opera I] came out and went across the road ... into [a] pub where they had heavy metal, and I enjoyed that as well ...

'I watch documentaries [and] the news [on television]. I rarely watch series or comedy shows any more. Films if there is a film on. But I have a secret and terrible addiction I must confess ... I don't want anyone to know about it. I watch *Prisoner: Cell Block H* ... I sit there and roar with laughter. It is *so* bad – I love it.

Interviewed by Bob Furnell, Bonnie Gale, Misha Lauenstein and Pat Burt on 28 January 1996.

ON HIMSELF:

'Sylvester McCoy was born at the height of a Scottish summer, i.e. it was raining, it was cold, it was windy. He came out crying. I can't say he's been crying ever since, but he's been trying to make sure that not too many people around-about him cry too much. He's always felt slightly outside society, as if he was looking in and should be commenting on it. He was quite pleased about that. He was delighted to have eventually ended up as an actor, and agrees very much with the idea that actors should be, like gypsies, buried outside the walls of a city. They should not be allowed to be put in consecrated ground. He's delighted by that fact. He finds society comical, cruel, interesting, and he's sometimes incredibly critical of it. He doesn't want to become a knight, because then he'd know that he'd really been bought by society.'

Interviewed by Nick Briggs in 1994 for *Doctor Who Magazine* No. 216.

Character – The Seventh Doctor

Unlike when he had overseen the transition from the fourth Doctor to the fifth in 1981, or that from the fifth Doctor to the sixth in 1984, producer John Nathan-Turner had no opportunity to lay careful plans to take *Doctor Who* through the difficult process of the departure of the sixth Doctor and the arrival of the seventh. The unexpected nature of Colin Baker's exit from the role in October 1986 – Michael Grade, the then Controller of BBC1, having instructed Nathan-Turner to dismiss the actor after the completion of work on the series' twenty-third season – meant that arrangements for the casting, characterisation and introduction of the seventh Doctor had to be made between seasons. This was a task that Nathan-Turner had not expected to have to manage himself. He had acceded to his superiors' request to inform Baker of his ousting from the series only on the understanding that he would then be allowed to move on to a different project – something that he had been requesting for some time. On his return from a period of extended leave over the winter, however, he was informed that if he wished to remain on staff at the BBC, he would have to continue as producer for the following season.

The most pressing problem requiring attention at this time was the lack of any suitable scripts lined up for production. Nathan-Turner therefore set about urgently finding a new script editor for the series (the previous one, Eric Saward, having resigned amid controversy) and, in the meantime, contacted Pip and Jane Baker – who had written for the sixth Doctor's era – and asked if they would consider contributing the new Doctor's introductory story. They agreed, and on 22 December 1986 were commissioned to provide the scripts for a four-parter entitled *Strange Matter* (adapted from an earlier, unused storyline).

The fact that a new Doctor was required for the series had been picked up by many actors and actors' agents, who were eager to put forward suggestions. On 18 December 1986, Nathan-Turner was contacted by Sylvester McCoy, whose agent subsequently sent in a photograph and information about his client. 'I had endless lists of possible Doctors,' recalled Nathan-Turner in a 1988 interview for Peter Haining's *Doctor Who – 25 Glorious Years*. 'I also got lots of calls from actors' agents suggesting their clients. It really is a plum job, you see, even with all the demands on both private and public life. One of these calls was from Sylvester McCoy's agent, who suggested that I went to see him at the National Theatre in London where he was appearing in *The Pied Piper*. It was 6 January 1987 [when I went], I remember. I was very impressed with Sylvester's performance and decided to meet him. He later came in to my office and we sat chatting for about two hours. There is this wonderful, natural, eccentric quality about Sylvester. There is a sort of disjointed way that he speaks – the gestures are never quite in the right place at the right moment. I found myself riveted, and quite happy to go on listening to him.' Nathan-Turner also viewed videotapes of some of McCoy's television appearances and was particularly impressed by a Channel 4 interview in which the actor had spoken about himself and his role in *The Pied Piper* and exhibited the same kind of fascinatingly offbeat quality that the producer had noted in his office. He was keen from the outset to give the part to McCoy, but his immediate superior, Head of Series and Serials Jonathan Powell, asked him to cast his net a little wider and to carry out some screen tests.

Nathan-Turner and director Andrew Morgan, who had been assigned to handle *Strange Matter* (later retitled *Time and the Rani*), eventually came up with a short-list of actors, three of whom – including McCoy – were subsequently screen tested, as Powell had requested, on 18 February 1987. This involved them being recorded on the TARDIS set performing two short scenes written by Andrew Cartmel, the new script editor found by Nathan-Turner for the series, and directed by Morgan. Former companion actress Janet Fielding was contracted to act opposite them, playing an evil adversary in one of the scenes and a departing companion in the other. 'I did the tests with Sylvester and some other actors,' explained Nathan-Turner, 'and – with no disrespect to the others – Sylvester was the Doctor I was looking for. I had always envisaged a Troughtonesque quality, and here it was. Mind you, I don't think Sylvester and Pat Troughton are madly similar, but there are little characteristics that are the same. I also wanted somebody who was much smaller than Colin Baker.' In addition, the producer favoured casting a relative unknown. The final decision to go for McCoy was made by Nathan-Turner in consultation with both Powell and Grade. The actor's accession to the role was officially announced by the BBC on Monday 2 March, although news of it had leaked to the press over the previous weekend as Nathan-Turner had made his own announcement in the USA on the Friday.

Nathan-Turner had briefed Pip and Jane Baker when they started work on their story to make the new Doctor a more humorous character than the old one. He also wanted to have him behaving 'semi-normally' by the time he had his first confrontation with his adversary the Rani (in contrast to some previous occasions when the Doctor had been seen to act in a decidedly erratic manner for an extended period following a regeneration). 'We were well into writing the story when we were shown a video of Sylvester McCoy,' revealed the husband-and-wife writing team in a 1988 interview. 'We had to find a) a way of regenerating the Doctor and b) a character for him. John asked for a pre-credits teaser. All of us felt that we couldn't go straight into the story. If we had to regenerate in this way, we needed to start with it, then have a full stop and then start the story. It would have been impossible to open with Sylvester's title sequence otherwise; it would have looked silly.'

The apparent implication of the teaser as seen on screen was that the Doctor's regeneration was precipitated by nothing more serious than a fall from an exercise bike when the TARDIS was attacked in flight by his renegade Time Lord adversary the Rani – although it is possible that far more momentous events had occurred before this, of which the viewer was simply left unaware.

McCoy himself was very much in sympathy with Nathan-Turner's wish to bring a degree of humour into the portrayal of the seventh Doctor – at his initial press conference, he told reporters that he wanted to play the part with 'more zest' as a combination of eccentric scientist figures Magnus Pyke and David Bellamy; as someone who was 'madly interested' in everything he did and would get enthusiastic about tiny things amidst mayhem. He was inspired in part by Patrick Troughton's approach to the role, which he recalled as being predominantly humorous, and was in any case naturally inclined toward taking a comedic approach in his work, having been greatly influenced by figures such as Buster Keaton, Stan Laurel and Max Wall, and having started his acting career in madcap comedy roles in Ken Campbell's Roadshow. 'I said in my [initial] discussion with [John Nathan-Turner] that I wanted to be a very Troughtonesque type of Doctor and have the contrast between the comedy and the seriousness,' he told Gary Levy and Robert Cope in a 1987 interview for *DWB 50*. 'He accepted that, but there was one time where he came in and said it was too comedic in the first rehearsal. I think the first story was a learning process for all of us, because it wasn't written for me, it was written for an unknown Doctor and by people who had only written for Colin. Some of the lines are just pure Colin's lines – you can *hear* Colin saying them.'

The 'learning process' of McCoy gradually finding his feet as the Doctor and the writers coming to reflect and cater for his characterisation in their scripts was something that continued throughout the remainder of the twenty-fourth season. 'The first season was just a hotchpotch, really ...' noted McCoy when interviewed by Mark Wyman for the spring 1989 edition of *TARDIS*. 'The writers didn't know who to write for, and I arrived not really knowing ... Although I'd said at the interview, "This is how I want to play the Doctor," I was just talking off the top of my head. I hadn't seen *Doctor Who* for quite a few years, and the memory I had of it was what I was vaguely selling. When I came to do it, half way through the season I suddenly thought, "Now I know what it's about", but by then it was too late and we could only carry on.'

McCoy was in fact able to have a limited degree of input into the scripting of the Doctor's character as the season progressed, as he told an uncredited writer in a 1988 interview for *Whovian Times* Volume 17: 'When the opportunity presented itself, I was able to make a few changes. Very few, but important things. I was even allowed to add a few scenes. If I believed in it and I was enthusiastic enough about it and could get them enthusiastic about my idea, they would put it in.' Another way in which the actor was able to bring his influence to bear was by placing an interpretation on the script that the writer might not have anticipated. Sometimes, for instance, he would deliver a line much more angrily than might have been expected from its immediate context – an attempt, as he later explained, to evoke memories of William Hartnell's Doctor, whom he had been told was often irascible. On other occasions he would endeavour to suggest hidden depths to the Doctor's character, such as through his adoption of a melancholy tone and faraway look when commenting 'Love has never been known for its rationality' in *Delta and the Bannermen*. It was only when work on Season 24 had been completed, however, that he had the opportunity to get together with the series' production team for a detailed discussion of how the seventh Doctor ought ideally to be portrayed. 'We sat down and chatted between seasons,' he told Wyman, 'and I said, "I want him to be more mysterious – to show the inner side of him. He's not just clear cut." Of course, he may have been all those things before that I wanted him to be, but it wasn't clear in my mind.'

The standard brief on the Doctor's character that the production team made available to prospective writers at this time was relatively minimal, and read as follows:

THE DOCTOR

The DOCTOR is a Time Lord from the planet Gallifrey which is in the constellation of Kasterborous. He possesses two hearts, has a body temperature of sixty degrees Fahrenheit and is over seven centuries in age. He has the capability of regenerating himself into different appearances – his present form being his seventh guise.

He no longer resides on his own planet due to his boredom with his own super-advanced planet and fellow Time Lords – he roams through time and space in his own personalised ship – the TARDIS.

The DOCTOR himself is not infallible. Part of his appeal is his problem-solving capacity when things go wrong, making do with bits and pieces of electronic gadgetry that just happen to be around.

Cartmel, rather than leaving his writers to rely on these basic notes, preferred to talk through with them the way in which the character ought to be depicted, in line with the discussions that he and Nathan-Turner had had with McCoy. The fruits of these discussions became readily apparent in the transmitted stories. In Season 24, the Doctor had been seen to act – particularly at first – in a quirky, somewhat clownish manner, taking near-slapstick tumbles, playing the spoons (an example of McCoy drawing on his own talents for the role – something that Nathan-Turner was keen to take advantage of) and coming out with scrambled adages and mixed metaphors (an adaptation of his predecessor's trait of offering pertinent – and generally accurate – quotations). In Seasons 25 and 26, however, he was shown to be a far more serious, brooding character. He also appeared more able than in any of his earlier incarnations to influence and control events occurring around him; far from being simply an aimless traveller, doing his best to help the underdog and to fight injustice wherever he encountered it, he was now seen to adopt near-Machiavellian strategies in order to achieve his objectives, leaving his new companion Ace to handle the more physical aspects of his battles.

The idea emerged of the Doctor being a master strategist, manoeuvring his adversaries and manipulating his allies like a galactic chess player – literally so in the case of Fenric in *The Curse of Fenric*, although the chess motif was also made explicit in *Silver Nemesis*. In *Remembrance of the Daleks*, there were suggestions that, contrary to previous indications, the Doctor might somehow have been a contemporary of Rassilon and Omega – the legendary founders of Time Lord society. Then, in *Silver Nemesis*, the 17th Century sorceress Lady Peinforte claimed to be in possession of momentous secrets about his past 'from the dark time', although in the event, she never had an opportunity to reveal what these were. There were even hints that some aspects of the Doctor's established history might have been deliberate fabrications on his part.

'[We wanted] to increase the mystery,' confirmed the actor in a 1995 interview conducted by Lou Anders for *Dreamwatch* 17. 'The only way we could do that was to make the audience uncertain of him, to find out whether he was this loveable character or he was dangerous. [I wanted to toy with the viewer,] to actually open up another area, peeling an onion, another layer. You'd been given the Doctor that you'd known for the last twenty odd years, and all the mystery had been stripped from him. In order to create mystery, we had to peel another layer and invent another dimension, as it were. Perhaps he was one of the three creators of Gallifrey, and where would that lead you? Well, into a whole new sphere [that] the writers could go and explore.

'[The change didn't happen overnight.] It was like turning a great ship in the ocean. It takes a long time to turn it round, because the scripts have already been written for the next season and all that stuff. It wasn't until half way through ... the second season that the scripts started to arrive that fitted the Doctor that I wanted to do; and by the third season, we were getting there. [Had the series continued, the Doctor's character would have become] much darker, keeping the comedy all the time, but in layers. This was part of the defence system of the Doctor.'

McCoy also felt that the Doctor should be a non-violent person who solved his problems through the use of his wits and ingenuity. 'It's a combination of unarmed vulnerability and eccentric imagination that makes the Doctor so appealing as he confronts evil,' he asserted in an interview for the 5 October 1988 edition of the *Morning Star*.

In gaining agreement to all these changes, McCoy found an enthusiastic and like-minded ally in Andrew Cartmel. 'He's played a hell of a big part,' he admitted to Wyman. 'It's often instant agreement between us. I'll say, "What about ...," and he says, "Yes, what a good idea ..." We seem to have agreed a lot ... I'm getting a trifle worried now about the lack of humour. I have to find the humour as well, because I think it's very important that he has that kind of "front". Now and again, he opens a door, and behind it there is great, dark foreboding, or mystery, and anger, really. The Doctor has spent nine hundred years travelling around, and seen such destruction; love and wonders too, of course, but all that terrible destruction. So I want to bring that out.'

'We certainly did want to build up the mystery,' commented Cartmel in a 1994 convention interview. 'Having said that, we had no agenda. I think that we did say on several occasions that we wanted the Doctor to be more mysterious and also more powerful, because he didn't seem to be this huge, dangerous, interesting alien, and I think we managed to recapture some of that with Sylvester.'

The non-violent aspect of the Doctor's character was reflected in scenes such as the one at the end of *Remembrance of the Daleks* in which he effectively talked the Dalek Supreme into committing suicide by convincing it that it was the last of its kind still alive; this was substituted for a sequence in Ben Aaronovitch's original script in which the Doctor blasted the Dalek Supreme with a gun in a pastiche of a Western shoot-out.

Interviewed in 1994 by Nicholas Briggs for *Doctor Who Magazine* No. 216, McCoy described how he had hoped to take the development of the character further, had he gone on to make a fourth season as the Doctor:

'I wanted to bring a much darker side to the character – not all the time, but I was enjoying mining this part of the character, you know? The misery that the man, this jolly person, carried around. So that's what the fourth term was going to be about.

'He'd been around for, they told me, nine hundred and fifty years – it kept changing. I thought about my grandmother, who'd lived for one hundred years and three months. She got to one hundred and then decided that was it. In the three months left, she took up alcohol and merrily knocked herself out, went to sleep one night and didn't wake up. She'd never drunk throughout the whole of the rest of her life. But she used to tell me that she was tired; not so much physically tired – she was incredibly fit, with a very sharp brain – but all her friends had died; her immediate family had all gone before her. There was that sadness of old age, the sadness of longevity.

'I found that interesting, because the Doctor had lived for all this time. I thought of [the Biblical figure of] Methuselah (who was supposedly nine hundred and sixty-nine years old) and the Ancient Mariner [in Coleridge's poem]. These people who lived for so long ... there was a great sadness in their lives. I thought, that ought to be part of the Doctor's baggage. He goes through all these experiences, and although time is relative and all those kind of things, I felt we had to feel those nine hundred and fifty years. He'd lost so many companions, some happily, but generally it was tragically. He'd seen so much violence and misery! So I wanted to bring that baggage with me – to be part of what he was carrying.'

The discontinuation of *Doctor Who* as an ongoing BBC series denied McCoy the opportunity of exploring these ideas. The seventh Doctor did however make a brief reappearance in the 1996 *Doctor Who* television movie, giving the actor a chance to fulfil a promise he had made to the series' fans that he would return for a regeneration story if ever he was asked to do so, and thereby help to give his successor a smoother introduction than he himself had had. Interviewed by Bob Furnell, Bonnie Gale, Misha Lauenstein and Pat Burt on 28 January 1996, while in the Canadian city of Vancouver to film his scenes for the movie, he summarised the development of his portrayal of the seventh Doctor over the course of his three seasons in the role:

'Starting up in an incredibly naïve way, not knowing really anything about it, diving in the deep end, relying on my own kind of natural bent towards comedy and then realising what the job was, then trying to work towards getting it, not quite achieving it – because really I needed another season to get where I wanted to. And in a sense I kind of arrogantly wanted to bring it back to a more mysterious, dangerous Doctor – not necessarily evil, but questionable. To get back that mystery. I also wanted ... I was very interested in the fact of his longevity. I wanted somehow to start carrying that longevity to the screen ... I wanted all that. [I wanted to make him darker, but to keep] the comic facade. You know, that kind of Patrick Troughtonesque quality. My first Doctor was Patrick Troughton, and I always remembered him as light and amusing and still at the same time having the ability to switch back and forth. That was the idea. I don't know if I really ever achieved that, but that's what I wanted. I thought [that] *Ghost Light* [had] the best written part for the Doctor. It didn't work on the screen –

CHARACTER – THE SEVENTH DOCTOR

Ghost Light was a bit confusing, you have to read the book to understand what's happening – but I liked what the writer had done for the Doctor … That was really good. I thought, "Oh good! This is how I want to play him. These are the words I want to say."'

Rewriting the Myth

In the era of the seventh Doctor, the main developments related to the character of the Doctor himself. The revelations were relatively minor to start with. In *Time and the Rani*, the Doctor's age was stated to be 953 – the same as the Rani's. The last mention of his age, in the previous year's *The Trial of a Time Lord*, had put it at 900, but this sort of discrepancy was nothing new: wildly different figures had been quoted during the course of the series' history. More remarkable was the fact that no real explanation was provided on this occasion for the Doctor's change of appearance, the viewer being left to assume that it was brought on as a consequence of the Rani's attack on the TARDIS.

The new Doctor seems to experience far less post-regeneration trauma than on previous occasions. The situation is complicated by the fact that the Rani drugs him in order to increase his confusion, but nevertheless he instantly recognises his adversary and is immediately on the alert – even if he promptly trips over and performs an impressive pratfall in her laboratory. When the effects of the Rani's drug wear off, he seems stable and fully in control.

Certain aspects of the seventh Doctor's character do, however, seem somewhat at odds with what has gone before. During his visit to Paradise Towers, for example, he seems to have no qualms about killing Kroagnon by pushing him into a mined storeroom (although in the event this task falls to the young man Pex). It is hard to imagine any of the other Doctors, except possibly the sixth, taking such an active part in the destruction of a life-form, no matter how hostile. In *Delta and the Bannermen*, he appears not overly upset at the death of Gavrok – in fact he seems more pleased that Gavrok's trap around the TARDIS has been drained of energy as a result. In *Remembrance of the Daleks*, he blows up a Dalek and deliberately goads Davros into destroying Skaro, and similarly, in *Silver Nemesis*, he arranges for Nemesis to wipe out the Cybermen's fleet in space. In the Dalek story he also tells Ace that lives must sometimes be sacrificed for the greater good, suggesting that his justification for his actions is that the end justifies the means – a philosophy rejected by his earlier incarnations.

These glimpses of a darker side to the Doctor's nature coincide with a deepening of the mystery surrounding the character – a considered policy on the part of the series' production team. In *Remembrance of the Daleks*, the idea is introduced that when the first Doctor came to Earth with his granddaughter Susan in 1963, he brought with him the Hand of Omega, a remote stellar manipulator device used by Omega – one of the legendary founders of Time Lord society – to detonate stars. Quite how he came by this device is left unexplained, but he is seen to be in total command of it. (It is this that he ultimately uses to bring about the destruction of Skaro.)

There are however a number of apparent inconsistencies between the events of this story and those of the first ever *Doctor Who* episode, *100,000 BC: An Unearthly Child*. A book about the French Revolution is seen lying in the science lab at Coal Hill School, but it looks quite different from the one on the same subject that was lent to Susan by history teacher Barbara Wright, and the latter book was not left in the science lab. A possible explanation for this is that it is simply a different book, and that its presence is a complete coincidence. More difficult to explain away, however, is the fact that the junkyard at Totter's Lane also looks somewhat different this time around. Quite apart from anything else, the owner's name on the entrance gates is spelt differently – in *An Unearthly Child* it was 'I M Foreman', here it is 'I M Forman'. Then there is a scene in which a television announcer is heard to introduce a new science-fiction series on BBC television. Nothing unusual in this – except that the time is stated to be 5.15 in the afternoon, and yet it is still light outside, whereas if this really is November – and a calendar seen on the wall of the café visited by the Doctor and Ace seems to confirm that it is – it should be dark by this time. More interesting still is the strong implication that the series about to start is actually called *Doctor Who*.

One way to rationalise all these apparent quirks is to assume that the action of *Remembrance of the Daleks* takes place in some kind of parallel universe where it is indeed light on November evenings in England, Davros is the Dalek Emperor and the Doctor is a contemporary of Rassilon and Omega, rather than – as implied in previous stories such as season ten's *The Three Doctors* and season fourteen's *The Deadly Assassin* – from a later era of Time Lord history.

The question of the Doctor's origins is further explored in *Silver Nemesis*, when it is hinted that he might not even be a Time Lord after all, or perhaps not *just* a Time Lord (a suggestion also contained in dialogue recorded for *Remembrance of the Daleks* but edited out before transmission). How and why the metal validium fell to Earth in the first place remains unclear, but the viewer learns that after Lady Peinforte fashioned it into a statue of herself, the Doctor was on hand to send it back out into space. It transpires that validium was created by Rassilon and Omega as the ultimate defence for Gallifrey in the 'dark time', and that while in Peinforte's possession, it told her secrets about the Doctor. What exactly those secrets are, however, is not revealed.

THE SEVENTH DOCTOR

'We all knew that there was a mystery as to who exactly the Doctor was,' noted Ben Aaronovitch, the writer of *Remembrance of the Daleks*, in a 1994 convention interview, 'but we all had different ideas about what it was, so that it remained a mystery. I remember that Kevin Clarke [who scripted *Silver Nemesis*] had a completely different idea as to who the Doctor was, and he wasn't telling! So there were two objectives for me: to get more mystery back, and to get the kids back behind the sofa.'

The idea of the Doctor being 'the Other', a mysterious figure associated with Rassilon and Omega, was indeed one of those discussed by script editor Andrew Cartmel and his writers (and ultimately featured in Aaronovitch's novelisation of *Remembrance of the Daleks*), although at least one of the writers, Marc Platt, took the view that 'the Other' was actually a completely different character. Further, arguably more outlandish, ideas considered at one time or another included the Doctor being twice-born (first as a contemporary of Rassilon, then again in his Hartnell incarnation); being more insane than his adversaries; and even being a Christ figure (the idea particularly favoured by Clarke). As scripted, *Survival* had the Doctor explicitly confirming to his old adversary the Master that he had evolved into something more than just a Time Lord (tying in with the loose theme of evolution that had run through the last three stories of the twenty-sixth season). This however was vetoed by John Nathan-Turner and did not feature in the transmitted story. 'Andrew and the writers had all sorts of sensational revelations as to who the Doctor was,' recalled the producer in 1996 in the book *Ace! The Inside Story of the End of an Era* by Sophie Aldred and Mike Tucker, 'none of which I was prepared to entertain. I was prepared to accept the odd hint, but originally it was spelt out. I think that you have to be very careful with what you say to an audience, especially an impressionable one, and I felt that what Andrew and the writers were going to do went totally against making the Doctor more mysterious.' On screen references to the Doctor's mysterious origins were consequently confined to occasional hints and suggestions.

The idea of the Doctor having had untelevised adventures was nothing new for the series; many references to such adventures had been made in the past, often in the form of throwaway remarks about meetings between the Doctor and famous historical figures. In the McCoy era, however, this plot device took on a particular importance. As well as the revelation of the earlier encounter with Lady Peinforte, there are references to the Doctor's hiding of the Hand of Omega on Earth, past battles with the Gods of Ragnarok (*The Greatest Show in the Galaxy*) and Fenric (*The Curse of Fenric*) and a future encounter with the witch Morgaine in an alternate dimension wherein he poses as Merlin and sides with King Arthur (*Battlefield*).

The Doctor during this incarnation is also revealed to have some hitherto unsuspected talents. He is seen to be a consummate magician and acrobat, able to entertain the three demanding Gods of Ragnarok for some time with a seemingly endless succession of conjuring, manipulation and escapology tricks. He is also seen to be able to incapacitate foes with his fingers, apparently transmitting some form of energy to make them sleep (although this could just be a different utilisation of Venusian akido skills that have lain dormant since his third incarnation). More significantly, he is frequently shown to have a degree of foreknowledge about the situations into which he arrives, as in *Remembrance of the Daleks, Silver Nemesis, The Greatest Show in the Galaxy, Battlefield, Ghost Light* and *The Curse of Fenric*. He tends to keep this information to himself, however, leaving Ace – and anyone else unlucky enough to be around – to get caught up in events and learn from the experience.

'This version of the Doctor, I have a lot more respect for him,' Cartmel told interviewer David Bishop in 1994 for *TSV* 40. 'I always hated it when he was zapped on the head or knocked unconscious and tied up. I always thought that was demeaning to him. If he does get tied up, it should be that it was his plan all along … It all goes back to "Doctor who?" The mysterious, scary, powerful Doctor … It struck me this was the most interesting way to do the show. You could crack on and do some really exciting television.'

These moves toward restoring some mystery to the Doctor's character went hand in hand with a conscious policy on Cartmel's part, already evident in Season 24, to eschew the continuity-heavy approach of the sixth Doctor's era, in which every story had relied to a greater or lesser extent on the series' established mythology. 'We had a conscious junking of the mythology,' confirmed writer Stephen Wyatt in a 1989 interview conducted by Joe Nazarro for *Doctor Who Magazine*. 'Let's forget about the Master; let's forget about the Time Lords; let's get back to the original idea, which was [that the Doctor was an explorer in] outer space … There was a clean sweep. [My story] *Paradise Towers* had no cross references whatsoever to any previous *Doctor Who* adventures or characters, and that was quite a conscious decision.'

Given this approach, it is perhaps not surprising that few stories of the McCoy era add anything to the viewer's knowledge of other previously established elements of the series' mythology. The exceptions to the rule are *Remembrance of the Daleks, Silver Nemesis* and *Survival*.

In *Remembrance of the Daleks*, it is revealed that there are, at this time, two rival factions of Daleks: renegades who report to the Black Dalek – otherwise known as the Dalek Supreme – and imperial Daleks who report to the Emperor. They can control human subjects through the use of electronic implants located behind the ear – perhaps a refinement of the Roboman technology previously seen in *The Dalek Invasion of Earth*. It is also explained that the two factions of Dalek creatures are physically different from each other. The imperial Daleks have proper limbs and are fitted with cyborg attachments, whereas the renegade Daleks are little more than blobs with

THE SEVENTH DOCTOR

vestigial limbs.

The major revelation, however, is that the Dalek Emperor is none other than Davros, now reduced to little more than a Dalek himself (an idea suggested to Aaronovitch by visual effects assistant Mike Tucker). The Emperor had not previously been seen in this form in the series, although it had appeared in season four's *The Evil of the Daleks* as a static creature housed in and linked to the Dalek city on Skaro. No explanation is provided as to how Davros managed to 'become' the Emperor following his capture by the Daleks loyal to the Dalek Supreme at the conclusion of Season 22's *Revelation of the Daleks*, but the splitting of the race into two rival factions is consistent with the events of that story (in which Davros's Daleks had the same cream and gold livery as the imperial Daleks in *Remembrance of the Daleks*) and also with those of Season 21's *Resurrection of the Daleks*. It is also quite understandable that the imperial Daleks are more genetically advanced than the renegades, as Davros would no doubt have been continuing his experiments to make them ever more ruthless and efficient.

Another major development in this story is the destruction of Skaro's sun, and with it, Skaro itself, by the Hand of Omega. No time frame is given for this, however, and a Dalek at one point announces that the Hand is entering Skaro's time zone, which might perhaps be taken to imply that it occurs in the very far future.

One well-remembered aspect of *Remembrance of the Daleks* is the scene at the end of Part One in which a Dalek is seen, for the first time, to ascend a flight of stairs. This did not constitute a particularly major development in the series' mythology, however, as even as far back as Season 2's *The Chase: Journey into Terror* it had been implied that this was within the creatures' capabilities, and Season 22's *Revelation of the Daleks* had actually shown that both the Daleks and Davros could hover above the ground.

Earlier stories had been inconsistent in their indications of the Daleks' vulnerability to attack. In Season 9's *Day of the Daleks*, for example, the creatures had seemed impervious to anything that UNIT troops could throw at them, but in Season 11's *Death to the Daleks* one of them had burst into flames on being attacked by spear-wielding Exxilons. *Remembrance of the Daleks* places them at the more vulnerable end of the spectrum, as they are destroyed by Ace's augmented baseball bat and home-made nitro-9 explosives as well as by rockets fired at them from military rocket launchers.

The implied vulnerability of the Daleks is nothing, however, to that of the Cybermen in *Silver Nemesis*. It was well established in *Revenge of the Cybermen* and *Earthshock* that the forcing of gold dust into the Cybermen's chest units could suffocate them by coating their respiratory systems. Here, however, the creatures seem to have an aversion to gold in any form (as vampires have an aversion to garlic, perhaps), and a number of them are destroyed by gold-tipped arrows and by gold coins fired into their chest units by means of a catapult. Paradoxically, however, the Cyber Leader actually survives having a handful of gold dust thrown into his chest unit.

Toward the end of *Silver Nemesis*, the Doctor arranges for the Nemesis statue to destroy the Cyber fleet, which – as hints have been given throughout the story that this is their last remaining force – could be taken to imply that this is the final end of the Cybermen, or at least that they are subsequently reduced to isolated groups scavenging space, as suggested in *Revenge of the Cybermen*.

The final revelations of the McCoy era occur in *Survival*, when the Doctor and the Master become trapped on the dying planet of the cheetah people. The Master has succumbed to the planet's influence and started to transform into a cheetah person himself. It is established that the only way off the planet is for someone affected in this way to lead others back to his or her home world; thus is Ace able to lead the Doctor and her friends back to Earth at one point. At the end of the story, however, as the Master prepares to deal him a killing blow, the Doctor manages somehow to transport himself to Earth. If one supposes that he too has become 'infected' by the planet, this raises the question why he did not return to Gallifrey or perhaps to the TARDIS interior – the only other place that he could legitimately call 'home' – rather than to Earth. Perhaps, though, the answer is something more fundamental; something unique to the Doctor that links him with Earth in a manner previously undisclosed …

Production Development

John Nathan-Turner had not expected to remain as *Doctor Who*'s producer for the seventh Doctor's debut season – his seventh in that capacity. He was asked to do so by his BBC superiors only at the eleventh hour, and agreed with considerable reluctance. He consequently had less time to prepare for this season than for any other that he had worked on, and matters were not helped by the fact that he had to find not only a new lead actor but also a new script editor for the series. 'With regard to the latter,' he recalled in 1996 in *Doctor Who Magazine* Issue 246, 'I had a stroke of luck. Richard Wakely ... [an agent] I had known from the moment I arrived in London ... asked me to meet a young man called Andrew Cartmel, which I duly did, and found him bursting with many ideas and, indeed, firm opinions about the show. Although we didn't always agree, we instantly struck up a rapport – which I do think is a good sign. I invited Andrew to join the team, and I have never regretted it.'

Cartmel had previously been working for a computer company in Cambridge, but had also attended some workshops at the BBC's Television Drama Script Unit and been taken on as a client by Wakely on the strength of some unproduced scripts that he had written. 'The reason John gave me the job was that we got along,' he said in a 1994 interview conducted by David Bishop for *TSV* 40, 'and I didn't impress him as being an idiot. He'd read a script of mine, and obviously saw qualities in there [demonstrating] that I knew what a good TV script should be.'

Pip and Jane Baker had already been asked by Nathan-Turner to write the season opener, *Time and the Rani*, but Cartmel disliked their approach and found the development of the scripts problematic. To provide the other three stories required to make up the fourteen episode run, he commissioned new writers whose way of thinking was more in tune with his own. One of these, Stephen Wyatt, had contacted the production office and been recommended to him by Nathan-Turner (who had had some discussions with him the previous year when the series was temporarily without a script editor) but the other two, Malcolm Kohll and Ian Briggs, were contacts of his from his time at the Script Unit.

Cartmel was a big fan of contemporary comics, and was keen to bring that influence to *Doctor Who*. Collections of Alan Moore's *Halo Jones* stories from *2,000 AD* consequently became virtually required reading for prospective *Doctor Who* writers. 'Alan Moore's *Halo Jones* showed me you didn't have to write comics in a stylised way,' Cartmel told interviewer Tim Robins in 1991 for *The Frame* No. 19. 'You could actually explore interesting aspects of a character's personality.' Another suggestion the script editor frequently made to writers unfamiliar with the series was that they read the 1983 media studies book *Doctor Who - The Unfolding Text* by John Tulloch and Manuel Alvarado. Nathan-Turner meanwhile had decided that, with the series now reduced to only fourteen episodes per season on a permanent basis, a varied mix of stories should be maintained by subdividing each season into two four-parters and two three-parters in a 'traditional-bizarre-kooky-traditional' pattern, with writers selected to fit these styles according to their perceived strengths.

A significant constraint on the production team at this time was pressure from their superiors to avoid the inclusion of any overtly violent or adult content in the stories – a continuing legacy of the controversy that had surrounded the series during the sixth Doctor's era, when it had at one point been taken off the air for eighteen months. 'My basic idea was that I wanted the show to be quite dark and scary,' recalled Cartmel in a 1994 convention interview. 'When I went in to talk to the Head of Drama, one of the first things that he asked me was, "Who is *Doctor Who* for?" I said that it was for everyone – a diplomat's answer – but he said, "No, it's for children." I nodded, but thought, "No it isn't." I never thought that it should be a show that children shouldn't be able to watch, but I thought it should be an adult [show] that was accessible to children.'

Season 24 as it eventually reached the screen had a relatively light, whimsical quality. This, coupled with an avoidance of naturalism in the production and the casting of numerous well-known comedy and light entertainment performers in guest roles, resulted in it coming under fire in sections of the fan press as a further move toward what some saw as a 'pantomime' style of drama in *Doctor Who*. Cartmel found these criticisms misplaced, as he explained to Bishop:

'If we could have just brought the lighting right down, and got really imaginative, moody lighting, I think the whole pantomime thing would have evaporated. That bright, artificial lighting gives a brashness and a lack of depth. That's what made it look like a pantomime. Shooting on video really doesn't help.

'A lot of the problem with *Doctor Who* is that people will say that they don't like a story, the writing is crap, when what they actually mean is that the studio lighting is bad. Frequently the reasons that stories didn't work related to the costumes or the lighting, but fans don't analyse it that way.'

One aspect of the twenty-fourth season that came under particular fire from critics was Bonnie Langford's larger-than-life performance as Mel. Nathan-Turner, speaking to Peter Haining for his book *Doctor Who – 25*

Glorious Years, defended the actress's contribution: 'Bonnie helped bridge the change-over of Doctors very well. She established a very good relationship with Sylvester; they got on extremely well. Actually, they had worked together before on the stage in *The Pirates of Penzance*. I know there are those who love Bonnie or hate her, but to my mind that is the mark of somebody who is making an impact. I think she has been very good for *Doctor Who*.'

Langford had told Nathan-Turner at the start of 1987 that she would probably want to bow out of the series at some point during the course of the season. The production team decided in view of this to keep their options open by ensuring that the last two stories – the ones written by Kohll and Briggs – each featured a character who could if necessary succeed Mel as the Doctor's companion. There were practical considerations to this as well, as initially it was uncertain in which order the two stories would be transmitted. The potential companion character in Kohll's story, *Delta and the Bannermen*, was Ray, played by Sara Griffiths; that in Briggs's, *Dragonfire*, was Ace, played by Sophie Aldred. Cartmel was particularly keen to ensure that the new companion would be a strong and independent young woman: 'We were going for that sort of sisters-are-doing-it-for-themselves kind of thing, which was not Bonnie,' he told Bishop. 'We wanted a post-*Alien* teenage girl.' Ace was a refined version of just such a character, originally called Alf, for whom Nathan-Turner and Cartmel had drafted a rough description dated 26 January 1987, and it was she who was eventually kept on as a regular. A new character outline for Ace was prepared in August 1987 in view of her confirmed status as a companion, and a more detailed set of notes on her character and background were put together by Briggs two months later for inclusion in the guide supplied to prospective writers for the series. The latter read as follows:

Notes on the character ACE

Name: 'Ace' is her nickname. She's ashamed of her real name, and only told Mel in a moment of intimacy. (I feel that she would only ever tell another girl; not a man or a boy – probably not even the Doctor.) Her real name is Dorothy. I didn't specify a surname; it can be either the surname of Dorothy in *The Wizard of Oz*, or something that works in the context of the story it appears in – or, more likely, she'll just avoid the question and keep it secret.

Age: At the point of her appearance in *Dragonfire*, she was meant to be 16 years and 11 months. In fact, she's based on three girls I know, all of whom are 14, so she has the personality and maturity of a young (rather than middling) teenager.

Home: She comes from Perivale, which she regards as the pits of London. As far as she's concerned, the only good thing about Perivale is that it has two tube stations! (One of the girls she's based on actually said this while watching a recording.)

Family: She doesn't have any brothers or sisters. If she did, she'd have mentioned them in her intimate speech with Mel. Besides, she's too much of a loner inside. She didn't get on with her parents, and she gets angry simply at the mention of them. Sometimes she refuses to accept that she even has any parents; at other times she wants to believe that her 'real' parents – the kind, loving ones – are somewhere else, maybe on another planet. But however bad a picture she paints of them, the truth is that her parents are an ordinary middle-class couple who always kept their feelings hidden, and didn't know how to cope with their tearaway daughter.

School: She enjoyed chemistry and was taking it at A-level – although she would probably have failed because she isn't the academic type. She got suspended from school when she blew up the art room.

History: While she was at school she also had a boring evening job working in a fast-food cafeteria. She also used to do experiments with explosives in her bedroom, and it was an accident with one of these that triggered a time storm and carried her to Ice World – where she again found work as a waitress.

Speech: She uses phrases typical of London teenagers: 'Wicked!', 'Well worth!', 'Naff!', and of course 'Ace!'. I don't care if, technically, she left Perivale in early 1987, and so ought still to be using the phrases of that period; the more current and realistic her speech, the better. She coins nicknames for everybody, such as 'Doughnut' for Mel, and 'Bilgebag' for Glitz. And even though it irritates the Doctor, she can't help calling him 'Professor'. The only time she reverts to using real names is when she's frightened, as when Kane was holding her hostage in *Dragonfire*.

Personality: Typical teenager really. Bright and full of life one moment, spiky and argumentative the next. Even though she likes the Doctor, she's bound to come over all moody and complaining with him from time to time. A particular characteristic is her heightened sense of excitement, which sometimes overrides her sense of danger: her immediate reaction on first seeing the Creature in *Dragonfire* was to yell with delight, and only later did she think to run like hell!

THE SEVENTH DOCTOR

The urgency with which stories had been required to be commissioned for the twenty-fourth season had left Cartmel with little time for reflection. In preparing for the twenty-fifth, however, he was able to take a more considered approach. Acting on a fan's recommendation, he viewed a number of highly-regarded stories from *Doctor Who*'s past, including Season 13's *The Seeds of Doom* and Season 14's *The Talons of Weng-Chiang*, and formed the view that the essentially serious and dramatic style of earlier eras had been rather more effective than the relatively light-hearted and comedic one that had prevailed during McCoy's first season. He discussed this with Nathan-Turner, and they decided that the departure of the somewhat lightweight Mel and the arrival of the strong, streetwise Ace should mark the start of a more general shift back toward that more serious and dramatic approach. There would also be a return to a more naturalistic style of production and an increased emphasis on social comment, both overt (such as in *Remembrance of the Daleks*, with its fascist characters in Sixties London and a scene in which Ace discovers a 'No Coloureds' sign in the window of the guest house where she is staying) and allegorical (such as in *The Happiness Patrol*, with its thinly veiled attack on Thatcherism).

Another move that Cartmel was keen to make, in keeping with McCoy's own wishes, was to introduce a greater degree of mystery into the Doctor's character. He felt that over the years, there had been too much revealed about the initially enigmatic time traveller's background, and that this had considerably lessened the appeal of the character. With Nathan-Turner's approval, he therefore briefed the writers of the twenty-fifth season to include in their stories some elements casting doubt on aspects of the Doctor's established history and on the true nature of his character.

Season 25 was also notable for the high degree of emphasis that it saw being placed on Ace. In the past, it had often been the case that the companion characters had suffered from a lack of development after their initial introduction, but Ace by contrast came to take on an increasingly prominent role. McCoy, interviewed by Paul Travers in 1989 for *Doctor Who Magazine* No. 154, explained how this had come about:

'When we chatted between seasons, I thought it would be good for Ace to be educated between adventures. I would be educating her, pointing things out. Each time we got to a story, she would arrive with new knowledge ...

'It was a good idea, and the writers went further, and John Nathan-Turner too. They decided the Doctor was trying to make her get over her fears, her weaknesses. The Doctor, in a very back-handed and subtle way, is trying to put Ace straight, so that eventually, if he does leave her, she'll come back and be Prime Minister ...!'

Cartmel continued for this season to pursue a policy of commissioning enthusiastic young writers who were new to the series and had little or no previous TV experience; something in which he again had Nathan-Turner's full support, as the producer told *Doctor Who Magazine*:

'I think that the new writers that we have encouraged, whether they're experienced or not, are bringing fresh ideas. They challenge the system, and by the system I include myself.

'We have a phrase here: *Who*ed out. Writers get *Who*ed out, they start going over the same territory. We really needed to get a new band of writers, and, as I've been here a long time, it's more challenging and stimulating to have people say "why not?"'

The newcomers this time were Ben Aaronovitch, who had come to Cartmel's attention when fellow BBC script editor Caroline Oulton had passed on to him a script that he had written; Graeme Curry, who contacted the production office after winning a screenplay competition with a play called *Over the Moon*, later adapted for BBC Radio 4; and Kevin Clarke, who was approached by Cartmel on the strength of a script he had written for a series called *Wish Me Luck*. The remaining story was provided by Stephen Wyatt.

Nathan-Turner had been content to remain as *Doctor Who*'s producer for the 25th anniversary season but had again asked his BBC superiors to make this his last year on the series. They refused this request and persuaded him to stay on for Season 26. Cartmel also remained on the series, for his third year as script editor.

This season continued to show the Doctor acting in an increasingly enigmatic light, manipulating events from the background rather than taking centre stage. Even his costume was changed to reflect the darker quality emerging in McCoy's characterisation; his previous, light coloured jacket was swapped for an identical, dark brown one, and his tie and hat band were similarly exchanged for darker versions. Ace, meanwhile, was accorded an ever greater share of the action. She in fact turned out to be effectively the pivotal character in three of the season's four stories, and Sophie Aldred was given an early opportunity to talk to the writers about the development of the part. This was a consequence of Cartmel's preferred approach of working with his writers as a team and involving them more closely in the production than would normally have been the case in the past. Ben Aaronovitch was particularly heavily involved in the development of the season, acting almost as an unofficial assistant script editor, and in addition contributed its first story. Ian Briggs was also commissioned to provide a further story, but the other two writers for the season were again newcomers. Marc Platt had been a long-time fan of the series who had been submitting story ideas to the production office since Robert Holmes's time as script editor in the mid-Seventies; Rona Munro was an up-and-coming writer who had met Cartmel when attending a training seminar at which he was a speaker and had been invited by him to send in some ideas.

The very positive reception given to Season 26 by fan critics suggests that the process of experimentation and development that had taken place during the McCoy years had resulted in the refinement of a highly effective new style for *Doctor Who*, and one that had just started to bear fruit at the point when the series was taken off the air by the BBC. How that achievement would have been capitalised upon in the planned twenty-seventh season, and what other developments would have lain in store, can only remain matters for speculation.

From Script to Screen
Dragonfire

INTRODUCTION

This chapter presents an in-depth look at just one of the seventh Doctor's stories – *Dragonfire*. In doing so, it reveals the process of making *Doctor Who* at this point in the series' history and – a factor common to every story – some of the behind-the-scenes discussions and thought which go into a production.

THE SCRIPTS

Writer Ian Briggs had been approached to contribute to the series by script editor Andrew Cartmel, whom he had met some months earlier at a writers' workshop at the BBC's Television Drama Script Unit. He had started his career in the theatre after studying drama at Manchester University, and had found work as a script reader – not only for the BBC but also for the Royal Court and some film companies – after several years spent as a theatre lighting and set designer and occasional actor.

Briggs's first idea, submitted in January 1987, was rejected by Cartmel, as the writer admitted to Paul Travers in a 1989 interview for *Doctor Who Magazine*: 'He read it, said it was rubbish, so I started again.' His second attempt – which had the working title *Absolute Zero* and then, when this was deemed too pretentious, *Pyramid in Space* – was judged more promising. 'The first one I'd written had been very old-fashioned, very clichéd SF. After Andrew rejected it, we'd sat down and talked about exactly what he was after, based on [the] new style he'd brought in. *Pyramid in Space* was close, but it went too far. It was too zany, too cartoonish ... A disgusting 14 year old boy who's a financial genius, running [a] huge business empire with an obsequious sidekick called Mr Spewey! Brilliant stuff, but perhaps not *Doctor Who* ... But there were some good ideas in it; the idea of [a] creature living in the cold and itself being the treasure that everyone was hunting for. We hung onto that and constructed another story around it, which was much more serious.'

THE SEVENTH DOCTOR

This more refined idea, which involved a huge pyramid floating through space with a strange creature roaming around its ventilation system, was developed into a detailed storyline bearing the revised working title *The Pyramid's Treasure*. This was commissioned on 9 March 1987, completed on 17 March, delivered on 23 March and formally accepted on 30 March.

The Pyramid's Treasure tells of a villain called Hess, 'whose body temperature is -250° C', running a frozen goods trading centre from a planet-sized pyramid in orbit around a larger planet. The Doctor and Mel arrive looking for refreshment and meet up with 'an intergalactic bounty hunter-cum-pirate called Razorback' who tells them about a treasure hidden in the pyramid, supposedly guarded by 'an ice monster'. The Doctor and Razorback go off to find the treasure, which turns out to be the monster itself, which 'is also the missing component in an opto-electronic circuit – a lens that will focus all the Pyramid's energy and give Hess immense power'. The Doctor realises that Hess's plans for galactic domination will be his downfall. This indeed proves to be the case as, when the pyramid moves out of the shadow of the larger planet, 'the crystalline circuitry ... concentrates and focuses [the heat of the sun] on Hess ..., who melts away'. At the end of the story, Ace, a young human waitress stranded at the trading centre, goes off with Razorback while Mel continues her travels with the Doctor.

On the strength of this storyline, Briggs was quickly commissioned to write the three part story that ultimately became *Dragonfire*. (Briggs's normal preference, as he confirmed in later interviews, was to prepare a scene breakdown between the storyline stage and the script stage, but this appears not to have happened in the case of *Dragonfire*.) The script for the first part was formally commissioned on 2 April 1987 with a target delivery date of 6 April, and those for the other two on 13 April with a target delivery date of 14 April – the closeness of these dates indicating that Briggs had already started working on the scripts, by informal agreement with Cartmel, prior to being formally commissioned. The three scripts were actually delivered by Briggs on 8 April, 16 April and 13 April and accepted by the BBC on 10 April, 22 April and 20 April respectively. A number of revisions were requested by Cartmel, in particular to remedy the fact that Briggs had overwritten, but these initial drafts were quickly turned into polished rehearsal scripts. Later, during the course of the rehearsal process, these were further refined into camera scripts for the studio recording.

In terms of content, the final scripts stuck quite closely to the original storyline. One of the few significant developments arose when Bonnie Langford, who played Mel, decided during the course of production to make this her last *Doctor Who* story. On 3 August 1987, Briggs submitted a new closing scene in which Mel is the one who goes off with the pirate – changed at producer John Nathan-Turner's request from Razorback to Glitz, played by Tony Selby, from the previous season's *The Trial of a Time Lord* –

and Ace, played by Sophie Aldred, who leaves with the Doctor to become the new companion. Sylvester McCoy disliked this version, feeling that the Doctor seemed too unmoved by Mel's departure, and suggested that some lines of dialogue be incorporated from a short scene that Cartmel had originally written for the screen tests carried out in February 1987 for the role of the seventh Doctor. The objection he had raised was recognised to be a valid one, and further work was then carried out on the scene right up until the day of recording.

'Bonnie finally decided that she was going to leave after the first studio recording,' recalled Briggs, 'so that final scene was rewritten during rehearsals for the second studio work. We worked on it ten or twelve times and finally got it right at breakfast on the day it was [recorded]. It's a cliché, but it was genuinely written on a napkin at the breakfast bar in Television Centre.

'I feel it got there, but only by the skin of its teeth. The problem is not so much that it was written at the last minute, but that it could be no longer than three minutes, and it's very difficult to get all the stuff in, that needs to be there, in just three minutes. The biggest problem [was] that it followed straight on from the ... death [of the villain] originally, so that it needed a minute – well, perhaps not even that, probably fifteen or twenty seconds – to wind down from the death to the farewell scene.'

Other, more minor changes made between storyline and final script included the alteration of the concept of the trading centre – called Iceworld in the final version – from a planet to a city-like spacecraft on the dark side of another planet; the renaming of the planet (between rehearsal script and camera script stage) from Tartros to Svartos; and the renaming of the villain from Hess to Kane.

'I [originally] wanted [a name for the villain] with lots of sibilants – "s" sounds – in it,' Briggs recalled in a 1989 interview conducted by Michael Proctor for the fanzine *Private Who*. 'I thought, "Hiss – what sounds like 'hiss'? Hass ... Hess ..." And I thought, "Hess – that sounds okay". A couple of minutes later, I realised it was the name of [a high ranking Nazi in World War Two], but I thought nobody would notice. [The first time we saw] the design of the [character's] helmet was the point at which we actually changed it. We'd been talking about changing it, because ... something had happened – I think the real Hess had written some letters asking to be released or something. When we saw the costume design, we thought "We can't do it," because it looked like a First World War German helmet, and people would [have thought] there was a connection. I was also [conscious] that there were a lot of foreign names – all the baddies had foreign names, which felt uncomfortably racist. It's a cliché as well – something I wanted to avoid – so I was quite happy to change some of them to more English-sounding names like "Kane" and "McLuhan" ... Three quarters of the stuff [in the scripts] had a reason for being there. Names had a reason, but I can't remember all of them now. Once you begin to piece together the big things, you forget about the small things.'

The name Kane was in fact taken from Orson Welles' film *Citizen Kane*; and many of the other character names in the story also had cinematic connections. Belazs for example was named after Hungarian film theorist and critic Bela Belazs; Kracauer after German film critic Siegfried Kracauer; Bazin after French film critic André Bazin; McLuhan (originally to have been named Eisenstein after Russian director Sergei Eisenstein) after Canadian communication theorist and documentary maker Marshall McLuhan; Anderson (Ace's boss, unnamed in the final dialogue of the story) after British film maker Lindsay Anderson; Pudovkin after Russian film maker and theorist Vsevolod Pudovkin; Arnheim after German/American film and art critic Rudolph Arnheim; and Dorothy, alias Ace, after Dorothy Gale, the lead character in the film *The Wizard of Oz*.

One problem that Briggs encountered in writing the story was that he had only a vague idea of how McCoy was approaching the lead role. The sole example he had seen of the actor's work on the series was his initial screen test. He therefore had to rely on Cartmel telling him whenever he went wrong in his characterisation of the seventh Doctor. He later recalled Cartmel describing McCoy as a 'real-life animated cartoon,' but admitted that he had not understood what this meant until he had actually seen the actor in rehearsals.

Of the writing out of Mel and the introduction of Ace, Briggs told *Private Who*: 'There was always the possibility that Bonnie might not want to continue for another season, and a stand-by companion had to be drawn up. The proposed character was a teenage girl called Alf from North London. Then the season was [reordered and *Delta and the Bannermen* was due to be] the final [story], so I was free to make some changes. I moved the character away from North London – because I had worrying visions of some trendy teenager from Islington! – and ... changed the name, because I never did like the idea of calling a woman "Alf". So Andrew [Cartmel] and John [Nathan-Turner] created the original idea for the character (so the BBC owns the copyright), I created the personality, and Sophie brought the character to life. When my story was moved back to the end of the season, and Bonnie decided to leave, Ace became the new companion.

'I fashioned the personality in a way that I found interesting – she's based on three teenage girls I know. I think it was always intended that she was going to be very contemporary. One of the themes of the story is loneliness, ... people who are lonely and don't have a home – a trait that struck me as fairly typical of teenagers. They feel as though they don't quite recognize themselves and everything isn't as it ought to be.'

Briggs was well satisfied with the story as it eventually reached the screen: 'The finished programme can never be as good as the original idea, because what I saw in my mind was absolutely perfect. It took place in hundreds of places on different planets with different coloured skies ... In that respect, every stage in the scripting and production process is a compromise between the vision and the possible. I don't think there's anything in that programme that anybody working on it need feel ashamed of. There are parts of it that are not the same as I envisaged them, but I don't claim a monopoly on creativity ...'

'Briggs is a really skilled writer,' noted Cartmel in a 1994 interview with David Bishop for *TSV*, 'good on construction. I did have to keep hammering away about the thriller thing, because he came from a background of writing non-thriller material. But he's a really good writer, because he gets passionately committed to things and he writes about people's emotions. When he invents characters, they've got something going for them emotionally.

'A problem was he hadn't written science-fiction before, as a lot of the writers hadn't, and I had to keep hammering that too. It's a thriller, it's a suspense story, it's got to have these punches at certain stages.

'I remember *Dragonfire* has got one of my favourite bits of Briggs's writing, where he has the Doctor trying to go into Glitz's spaceship and discussing philosophy with the guard ...

'The thing I liked about *Dragonfire* was that there were a couple of nice revelations, like there's this monster but it's a synthetic monster and inside the monster is this jewel, which is the McGuffin they're looking for. Then that turns out to be the ignition key for the city, which turns out to be a whole spaceship.'

DIRECTION

The director of *Dragonfire* was Chris Clough. Born in the Yorkshire town of Harrogate in 1951, he had started his working life as an accountant, but then decided on a change of career and studied for a degree in English Literature at Leeds University, where he had also staged a number of student plays. In 1974, he had joined Granada TV as a researcher for current affairs programmes. His real interest lay in drama, however, and he had subsequently gained directing assignments on Channel 4's *Brookside* and on the BBC's *EastEnders*. It was on the strength of the latter than John Nathan-Turner had invited him to work on *Doctor Who*. He had made his series debut on the last six episodes of *The Trial of a Time Lord* and then been invited back to handle Season 24's last two stories, *Delta and the Bannermen* and *Dragonfire*, which were made effectively as two halves of a single production sharing mostly the same designers and behind-the-scenes crew.

The following description by Clough of his general approach to directing *Dragonfire*, and all the quotes attributed to him in later sections of this chapter, have been compiled from interviews that he gave to Richard Marson for *Doctor Who Magazine* (1988), Stephen Payne, David Richardson and Lee Matthews for *Starburst* (1988) and Rod Ulm for *Private Who* (1989), and from comments that he made during an on-stage interview at the PanoptiCon IX convention (1988).

'I leapt at the opportunity to return to *Doctor Who*, despite the fact that I didn't see the scripts beforehand. John Nathan-Turner just asks you whether or not you'd like to come back – you leave him and Andrew Cartmel to sort out the scripts. You certainly don't get approval. Basically, John decides which director will be right for which story and then allocates them accordingly.

'When scripts first arrive, I read them very casually – almost just for enjoyment's sake – which allows me to gauge them as if I'm a viewer. Then I start to think about them more, reread them, tinker with a bit here, fiddle with a section there – just trying to get under the skin of the story really. It's a funny thing about any form of communication; the writer can write something with a certain emphasis in mind, and you can read that same piece and get something completely different out of it. So in those very early stages, I like to have conversations with the writers to discover what precisely their thinking is, and to debate whether there are any holes in the plot or whether I'm just being a bit thick and missing the point. From there, it's a question of trying to inject some style into it – you have to consider what it's going to look like. Okay, the writers have given you some clue as to their ideas, but you have to consider not just that, but a whole range of other options.

'You have to have done your homework before you go into the rehearsal stage. You've got to know what you think the actors should be doing at any particular time in the story and where they should be in the set. Otherwise, all you can say is, "Let's just kick it around for a while".

'I start off with little drawings – he starts there and moves to here, the entrances are here, and so on – and I try to prepare my camera scripts – a very boring job – after I've rehearsed everything at least once. If you do your camera scripts too early, things don't work when you come to rehearsals, and it restricts the actors.

'I like to keep the camera moving – there's an awful lot of boring television around, and I try to avoid the "wallpaper" effect.

'*Doctor Who* is the most difficult thing I've ever done! It is on its own; a mixture of action, adventure, fantasy and nightmare, and you are trying to amalgamate all these different areas to make the plausible out of the implausible. The concept of having a police box flying through space is obviously quite ludicrous, but the fun of it is to be able to turn the accepted form of logic on its head.'

CASTING

The casting of any *Doctor Who* story is primarily the director's responsibility. Chris Clough recalled how he went about the task:

'Casting really is a long and complicated procedure. You have to begin by taking the decision to cast one particular part. Then, if that person accepts, it affects who you can offer other roles to. It really is like a jigsaw puzzle – you're constantly trying to mesh together a well balanced ensemble. After all, it's no good having a goodie and a baddie who share similar physical characteristics, because you're in danger of confusing the audience. You have to find a good mix of physical types, so that when any one character comes up on screen, that's that – the audience recognises immediately who it is. You cannot allow for creating shades of, "Is that him, or maybe him …?"; it has to be distinct.

'You have to consider what sort of characterisation an actor will bring to a role, and what qualities he or she possesses. Equally, you yourself have to establish what qualities you perceive within each character – it's no easy task. Whenever I get a script, I go through it and write out a list of casting ideas, which I discuss with John Nathan-Turner. We then see who is available – not everyone is free, and not everyone is willing to do it.'

Amongst the actors considered for the role of Kane were David Jason, who was sent copies of the scripts on 23 June 1987, and John Alderton, who was sent copies on 3 July. Eventually, however, it went to Edward Peel.

'Kane was a very difficult character to cast,' noted Clough, 'but I chose Edward because I thought the physical height would be good, and I liked the overall acting style. I had seen him in *Juliet Bravo*, and also many years before in Hull in a play called *What the Butler Saw*. I was pleased that he had already shaved off his usual moustache, as I would have asked him to take it off anyway. For one thing, you wouldn't have any surplus hair at -200° C; it would snap off. Also, I did think it made him look rather like a second-hand car salesman!'

VISUAL EFFECTS

Dragonfire, in common with most other *Doctor Who* stories, had extensive visual effects requirements. The designer responsible for meeting these was Andy McVean of the BBC's own Visual Effects Department; but, as usual for this period of the series' history, he had the support of a number of the

Department's assistants, including Mike Tucker, Lindsay McGowan, Paul Mann, Paul McGuinness and Jonathan Clarke, and contracted certain aspects of the work out to freelancers, including the team of Susan Moore and Stephen Mansfield. In the following section of this chapter, all quotes attributed to Tucker, Moore and Mansfield are taken from a 1988 interview conducted by David J Howe, Mark Stammers and Stephen James Walker for *The Frame*.

One of the most important aspects of the effects team's work was the realisation of the dragon – the legendary beast hunted by the Doctor and Glitz. Tucker recalled how this had been achieved: 'The script initially said, "a huge, fire-breathing dragon". It turned out in Part Two to be a biomechanical creature with laser beam eyes, breathing smoke and fire. That was handled almost entirely by one guy in the Effects Department, Lindsay McGowan. Andy McVean came up with some initial design drawings for the head, and Lindsay prepared a rough maquette of the creature – a small plasticine model about twelve inches tall – which was approved by John Nathan-Turner and Chris Clough. Then Lindsay sculpted a full size version, which was a latex and polyurethane foam suit and a fibre-glass head. There was also a separate mechanical head, the mechanics of which were done by Paul Mann, which opened up to reveal the dragon's treasure. That suit was then painted up by Lindsay and Paul McGuinness, another effects assistant who in the previous season was inside Drathro. The head was sat on top of a helmet arrangement on top of the actor's head, and he looked out through the neck.'

'The original maquette of the creature was very beautiful, very menacing,' wrote McVean in *Ace! The Inside Story of the End of an Era* (Doctor Who Books, 1996), 'but the actor that they cast was short and fat and we ended up making blocked up shoes for him, to try and get him to look taller. He really couldn't cope at all, because he had a complete rubber body suit on, which was uncomfortable, and because his hands needed to be free and he had to operate the smoke from the nostrils with a blow switch. This meant that when he blew into the mouthpiece, it operated a solenoid, but it also meant that you had to have a battery and a gas canister in the head, so the entire thing was quite top heavy.'

Numerous other creatures were required for sequences set in Iceworld's refreshment bar, where Ace was seen working as a waitress. The intention was that these sequences should be reminiscent of *Star Wars*' famous cantina scene, with examples of a great many different alien life forms gathered together in one place. Moore explained how most of these had been created:

'The make-up designer asked us if we had any off-the-peg masks that had not be used in any other TV or film production. We had a number of bits and pieces that we'd made over the years – masks and puppets and so on – and I took along a whole collection, including a few masks made by another colleague. Make-up chose a selection and used them on the extras in the background. Luckily, the director was there at the same time, and he spotted a half-mask I'd made for a party and thought that it would be perfect for the scene where the child wears a mask to frighten Mel. He also spotted Eric the puppet, and Eric became a legend in his own lunchtime! (For some obscure reason, every creature we make seems to end up being dubbed Eric – it's a silly name at the best of times, and it seems a suitably ridiculous name to give to anything that's an alien, and supposed to be taken seriously.)

'At one point, the producer called down from the gallery asking if it had a name. I just said, "Eric". It was originally going to be in the background, but then they decided to start the scene with Eric at the table with this fish creature that we provided, and they finished the scene off with him snapping at the Doctor as well. Eric was operated by the man in the green fish mask, and everyone was very pleased with it.'

Dragonfire also featured a certain amount of modelwork, all of which was shot on film rather than recorded on video, owing to the greater controllability of the medium. A major aspect of this work was the realisation of Glitz's ship, the *Nosferatu*. 'Basically we knew it had to have an undocking scene, a take off scene, a flying away scene and an exploding scene,' noted Tucker, 'so two versions were made: one for all the flying work, and a breakable version for the scene where it explodes. The feel of *Dragonfire* was that Glitz's ship should be a rusty old tramp steamer, and that is basically what I used as an influence when we designed it. I had this rusty orange colour and a ship-like conning tower at the back and cargo pods. It just seemed to suit the character of Glitz, that this was the sort of ship he would have.' Another model required to feature prominently in the story was that of Iceworld itself. 'Initially what was wanted,' continued Tucker, 'was a planet with an obvious hot side and an obvious cold side, and on that cold side ... an icy, crystalline structure. This would be seen as simply a city, but in Part Three it would be revealed to be a spacecraft. So the initial shots had to disguise the fact that it was going to be a spacecraft, but at the same time it was designed around the fact that it would be taking off into space. Iceworld was designed by Andy and, because of lack of time, had to be made by outside contractors, Derek Hendon Associates.'

The shots in which icy vapour is seen to rise from Kane's hands and from a coin that he places on a desk were achieved, as Tucker explained, by a clever combination of effects: 'When we could, we ran smoke pipes through the costume and out through the cuffs. For the scene where the coin was put down on the desk, we used two chemical substances that, when mixed together, smoke slightly. We sprayed one on the coin, one on the desk top, and when the two were brought into contact, they smoked.'

'The portrait on the coin was meant to be Kane's face,' pointed out

Moore, 'so we modelled a likeness of Edward Peel onto it. I hope it looked like him, because originally we were told it was just going to be handed to people in long shot, and we were surprised when it was seen quite close up.'

One of the best remembered aspects of *Dragonfire* is the horrific final sequence in which Kane's face melts away in the light of the sun – another effect achieved by Moore and Mansfield.

'While we were working on the Chimeron baby for *Delta and the Bannermen*,' recalled Mansfield, 'we were told that there was the possibility of a melting head sequence at the end of the final story. At that time, it was not confirmed that we would be handling the sequence, but we were asked whether or not we thought it was feasible. We had to bear in mind the potential complexity of such a sequence and the limitations of a TV studio recording. There were two major stipulations. As the effect had to be done on a live recording day, it had to melt very quickly. In addition, there were to be no red colours on the underskull or any liquid resembling blood.'

'We went off and did a lot of research,' added Moore, 'and found out how the similar melting effect in *Raiders of the Lost Ark* was done. I spoke to some senior effects people in the film industry. Everyone said that it couldn't be done, not on video and certainly not that quickly. In spite of that, we felt the problems as we saw them could be overcome, and that it was certainly a project worth having a crack at. And, as it turned out, a month later, we were offered the job.'

'Edward Peel apparently wasn't keen on the idea of having an alginate face cast made,' noted Mansfield, 'especially as it would have had to have been with his mouth open, which is doubly uncomfortable for the subject. There wasn't really the time, anyway. Andy McVean arranged for us to meet Edward Peel at Visual Effects during a break in rehearsals. We took instant photos of him in the facial position he would assume at the start of the melting scene. I then took caliper measurements of his face, while Sue took more detailed photographs. We set to modelling the head from the instant photos that same afternoon.'

'The head was sculpted in water-based clay, from which a multi-piece plaster mould was taken,' explained Moore. 'From this mould, six wax outer skins were eventually taken. As the mould was multi-piece, the original clay bust remained intact – just as the inflexible wax casts had to! Using the teeth and the top of the head as registering points, we started cutting away at the face, taking it back to what it would be if it had melted to the bone. A silicone mould was then taken of this new sculpture, and two fibre-glass skulls were cast. The skulls and the skins were then airbrushed.'

'As the melting had to be done very quickly,' continued Mansfield, 'the wax skins had to be very thin. Therefore when they melted, they tended to give off only a very thin dribble of wax and not much else. To overcome this problem, we fitted the under-skulls with various pipes – in the mouth, in the nose and under the helmet – and through these pumped a liquid coloured to match the molten wax, thus creating a more authentic, head-sized volume of wastage.

'Selected areas of the glass-fibre skull were cast in latex and acted as bladders. These sections, when inflated, helped to distort the face, and generally accelerated the degeneration process by pushing wax away from the skull. The whole lot – six skins, two under-skulls, liquid and so on – was finally completed with hours to spare, at about 4 am on the studio day, 29 July 1987.'

'The head had been fitted to a support post in the studio that was the same height as Edward Peel,' added Tucker, 'and Costume had provided a collar section to go around the neck – they couldn't use a real costume, because all the wax and gunge would have ruined it.

'There were four of us operating it in the end. Steve provided the spit and gunge, while Sue, Paul Mann and I all wielded hot air guns and bladders. Cameras lined up on it and told us when we were in shot or out of shot. When we were all ready and out of shot, we turned on the hot air guns and away we went.'

'There was a little bit of improvisation when the instruction came from the gallery to start dropping it out of shot,' admitted Moore. 'As the rig was mounted on a huge baseboard we couldn't literally drop it downwards – so we just tilted it backwards.'

'What they were trying to get,' explained Tucker, 'was the effect of a collapsing man; they wanted to see Kane shrivel and deflate as he melted, and they wanted to match this shot with one we had done of the body collapsing from behind.

'Then the electronic effects designer Dave Chapman, in post-production, actually managed to mix in Edward Peel's real mouth, so that it actually screamed as it melted.

'In the end, we did only one take on it, because it all seemed to go well and the gallery was happy with it.'

'Ultimately it turned out to be quite an unsettling effect, in spite of the lack of red colours,' felt Moore. 'At one stage in the middle of shooting it, all this yellow gunge came out in a torrent because of a blockage in the air pipe. Also, one of the wax eyes that were underneath the skin popped and ran down the face. Not a pretty sight. Needless to say, none of this reached the final programme. We were flattered though to receive a round of applause from the assembled cast and crew.'

'What you saw on screen was a fraction of what was recorded,' reflected Tucker. 'It was shown at about thirty times normal speed, and the melting in real time took about ten minutes, from which they chose a suitable sequence to use.'

'I think on the whole it worked very well on screen,' concluded Moore, 'which is, of course, the ultimate consideration. Apparently it was the first time an effect of that type had been attempted on British television, so it was a first for *Doctor Who* – and of course for us.'

Chris Clough was well pleased with how this effect turned out, as he later confirmed:

'When it came to melting his head, I really did want to make it look realistic, otherwise it would have been awful. At one stage we considered, as an alternative, shooting it from behind Edward, having him pretend to melt, and then cutting to a puddle on the floor. However, that might have looked very laughable, so we decided on going for it, and having the facial close-up, which is what I'd wanted to do from the start.

'For the body, we were going to do a reverse shot. Someone went and bought an inflatable doll from a sex shop, then we dressed it in Kane's clothes [and allowed it to deflate]. However it ended up looking absolutely stupid. Still, there's a lovely photo of it somewhere with its trousers having fallen down, revealing these little [deflated] legs!

'In the end, rather than use the doll, we actually had a shot of Edward Peel sinking to his knees and used that instead, bleached out to give the impression of the blinding sunlight.'

IN STUDIO

Rehearsals for *Dragonfire* took place in the then standard venue of the BBC's custom-built rehearsal block, sometimes referred to jokingly as the 'Acton Hilton', in Acton, West London. Camera rehearsal and recording then took place in two sessions, the first over 28 to 30 July 1987 in Television Centre Studio 1, the second over 12 and 13 August in Television Centre Studio 3.

'I think we had only one week between coming off the OB for *Delta and the Bannermen* and going back into rehearsals for *Dragonfire*,' recalled Chris Clough, 'so everything had to be set up at the same time. I really needed to know that everything was already prepared, so that I could use that free week just to relax and to get my mind clear from the previous story.

'We did have a very tight recording schedule, and fortunately we didn't fall into the trap of letting things drift at the beginning, because if we had fallen behind then, by being too fussy or having things go wrong, it would have been very difficult to make up that time later. There's nothing easy about *Doctor Who* at all. Large chunks of dialogue are very easy to record, but we're dealing with SFX and also a great deal of action, which has to look convincing.

'We did a lot of rehearsal in costume for the scenes involving the dragon – it's unfair on actors to dump them in a costume at the last minute. The worst thing for them is the discomfort, because they sweat buckets.

'With the dragon, I think we had a good design. I tended to put it into half shadow and shoot it to avoid the legs, which never look terribly good on monsters.

'Kane had to be convincing too, without going over the top. That's always the problem with these ultimate foe-type characters – the temptation to go "Aargh!" and all that sort of stuff. And it usually works better if they do less. Then, when they're really angry, they can twitch their eyebrows or something. Edward Peel did that very well.

'And one of the things I enjoyed about *Dragonfire* was having the real cliff-hanger with the Doctor and his umbrella at the end of Part One!'

Not everyone was pleased with how the latter scene turned out, however. 'The worst cliff-hanger we ever had was the one at the end of *Dragonfire* Part One,' asserted Andrew Cartmel. 'In Ian Briggs's script, the Doctor climbs as far as he possibly can along a path in an ice cliff, then he is forced to climb down the face of the cliff itself. This all makes perfect sense in the script – he's on his way somewhere, the path runs out, he has no alternative, he has to start climbing downwards.

'But the way it's shot! He's walking along, then, for apparently no reason, suddenly he dangles himself over the edge. Someone rang me up and said, "Why does he do this?" The problem is, when you've got the script and you know what's supposed to be happening, when it's expressed on the screen like that, you don't question it. But if you're just a viewer watching this, there's no apparent reason for his actions.

'One of the things the director has to bear in mind is that the viewers don't know the script. Something to do with the essential visual grammar of that scene was missing.'

Ian Briggs himself felt that Clough's pacy, action-orientated style of direction was not entirely well suited to his scripts, which he saw as being very much driven by the characters and their motivations and interactions.

For Sophie Aldred, the recording of *Dragonfire* marked not only her debut as Ace but her first ever experience of acting in front of television cameras; before starting work on the production, she had not even known where Television Centre was. The regular costume that she would wear in the role was inspired partly by some clothes of her own and partly by a couple of photographs of teenage girls wearing club gear that she recalled seeing in an issue (July 1987) of the style magazine *The Face*. She and costume designer Richard Croft went on a shopping trip to the King's Road in Chelsea to choose a collection of suitable items off-the-peg. Some of the many badges and patches that ultimately adorned the jacket were obtained on this trip; others were found by Croft in various Oxford Street shops; and the remainder were supplied by Aldred herself.

'I had every confidence in Sophie Aldred's Ace,' wrote John Nathan-Turner in 1996 in his memoirs for *Doctor Who Magazine*, 'but decided to wait and see her good work in the rehearsal room committed to tape before taking up the option on a full contract ... The first studio day went well. Sophie was splendid. I took up the option and, in order to stave off any more leaks to the press, I swiftly organised a press call at TV Centre with Sophie, Sylvester and the TARDIS.'

An interesting contemporary view of the studio work for *Dragonfire* can be gleaned from the following report by *Doctor Who Magazine*'s Richard Marson, who visited the set for the final day's camera rehearsal and recording:

> To an outsider, watching the *Doctor Who* crew at work can be a very frustrating process. Just as a scene gets into its stride, it will either stop, so that [those responsible for] cameras and microphones can ensure their positions are exactly right (according to the director's detailed camera script), or simply because each scene doesn't tend to be longer than a couple of minutes ... With all the stops for effects and added camera angles (which increase the pace and tension), as well as for the inevitable mistakes, one might be forgiven for thinking that the cast and crew would be slowly driven out of their minds.
>
> That this isn't so is generally down to the production manager. It is he or she who acts as the director's assistant on the studio floor and maintains the vital discipline that keeps the show on schedule, without the grind wearing down those who are involved. For *Dragonfire* ... the production manager was Gary Downie ... [who] has captured the ability to have jokes and keep smiling while at the same time letting everyone know what was what and that no slackness could be tolerated.
>
> This discipline showed itself when a confused actor walked off the set before he was cleared to go, and when the busy studio got too noisy ...
>
> Making an ice planet convincing has been one of the principal challenges of this production, especially as it has all been taped in the studio, thus losing the added space that can be gained on location work ... The sets were of necessity quite flimsy, and looking at them close up, it's a wonder that they look so good on screen. Very often television sets look absolutely dreadful and extremely tacky before they are lit, and this was definitely the case with those assembled for *Dragonfire*. However, on camera they looked fine; as convincing as it was possible to achieve and greatly helped by the acting of the cast.
>
> It was possible to view what was going to be seen on screen in the

final stage by looking at one of the monitors carefully arranged around the studio. These are most important to all concerned, and everyone, from make-up and costume [staff] through to lighting men and production manager, [was] glued to what they showed during each run-through of a take. Woe betide anybody who got in the way!

The difficulties of creating a convincing frozen environment in a television studio, with expanded polystyrene 'snow' and sheets of plastic 'ice', were not lost on Chris Clough:

'There is always that problem with something of this nature, but there are no real alternatives to what we used. This was something we gave a lot of thought to in the planning stages, but without the money available, you are always going to be limited to using the same old measures.

'John Asbridge's sets were highly original. We had wanted the cryogenic centre to be very big and very high – an example of pomposity gone berserk – and he did a splendid job. The swirling mists were an absolute nightmare to realise. We had dry ice machines everywhere, but the problem was that the stuff disperses very quickly. We got through literally hundreds of pounds' worth, but it was ultimately very effective. The one real problem though was that we couldn't show the actors' breath. Orson Welles got round this problem by building his sets in a cold storage unit, and Frank Capra put little boxes of dry ice inside the actors' mouths. Others have tried using cigarette smoke, but really, for us, it would have been virtually impossible to show.

'We just had to make sure that the actors kept in their heads the continuity of where they were supposed to be, and didn't start wandering about as though it was the middle of summer. We rationalised it by saying, "Well, it's cold, but it's not *that* cold!"'

Andrew Cartmel also admired Asbridge's sets, but felt that they had been let down by over-bright lighting.

'That's always been a problem in television,' noted Clough. 'Don Babbage, who lit *Dragonfire*, worked with me on *EastEnders*, so we sorted our way through that. He calls me the Prince of Darkness, because I'm always after shadows everywhere and forever shouting, "Turn the bloody lights down!"'

POST-PRODUCTION

'Once you've recorded it, you go into editing,' noted Chris Clough, 'and you have to let the editor have his input, just like you let the actors have their input. One plays and discusses with the editor – I'll say, "I've shot it with this in mind," and he'll say, "Well, that's a load of crap. Wouldn't it be better if ...", and so on and so forth.

'Editing can be a frustrating process. You often find yourself saying, "Why the bloody hell didn't I shoot it from that angle, or go for a close-up there?"

'Boom shadows are very embarrassing, but if there was a choice between a take where the performance was better with the shadow and one where it was worse without it, I'd go for the better performance and try to edit round the shadow.

'In the case of *Dragonfire*, the main problem was that the episodes overran and had to be cut down to the right length. This meant, for example, that we trimmed a sequence where the Doctor gets trapped under a piece of falling ice and has to be freed by Glitz. In editing, you always have to trim the arty bits, which is very distressing.'

Ian Briggs recalled this trimming process in his interview for *Doctor Who Magazine*: 'Because we were trying to get so much in, we had to cut the "wind down" [between Kane's death scene and the start of Mel's farewell scene]. But when Chris had done a rough cut of the episode, we all agreed that there really was too much of a jump ... Tony [Selby] had to come in and revoice something else, so I [took the opportunity to add an] extra linking scene between the [other] two [– specifically the one with Glitz making an announcement along the lines of] "This is your new captain speaking" – using some spare [visuals that had been recorded.]'

'After the editing,' continued Clough, 'there's the sound dub. We have two days for location stuff and a day for studio stuff, which should be fairly simple. Dick Mills, the special sounds artist, adds his splits and splats, and then there's the incidental music. For *Dragonfire*, the composer Dominic Glynn came down to both studios and we gave it a lot of thought.'

Interviewed by Philip Newman in 1990 for *Doctor Who Magazine*, Glynn recalled that his score for *Dragonfire* had represented a significant development in both style and quality of composition over the ones that he had provided for the previous season's *The Trial of a Time Lord*: 'The music for [those earlier episodes] was done purely on a synthesiser, which made it difficult to get certain "warm", "fat sounding" noises. I had to double track everything. But between seasons, I bought a sampler, which made a huge difference to the range of sounds I could use. I could record a second, or a few seconds, of any instrument, sound or noise and then play it back, at any tone or pitch, on an electronic keyboard. So I was able to sample the jingle-bell sound from a baby's toy, and the biggest church organ in the South of England.'

Speaking to Austen Atkinson-Broadbelt in 1993, also for *Doctor Who Magazine*, Glynn elaborated on his intentions for *Dragonfire*: 'I was attempting to get a more orchestral feel in that story ... I tried to give a feeling of being there on that freezing planet. It was a good story. I think I began to feel more relaxed by the time *Dragonfire* came along. I tried very hard to help build up the atmosphere on that one. I loved doing the music for the soldiers. That's all very metallic. Good stuff!'

TRANSMISSION

Dragonfire was transmitted over three consecutive Saturdays in November 1987 as the last story of *Doctor Who*'s twenty-fourth season. Its first episode captured an audience of 5.5 million viewers – the highest individual rating of the season – and it also received good audience reaction figures, reflecting a gradual upward trend during the course of the season. Ace proved to be an instant hit, gaining a higher approval rating than either the Doctor or – by some margin – Mel.

Ten viewers' phone calls about the story were logged at the BBC's duty office. One complained that the story was too childish; six thought that the scene of Kane's face melting was unsuitable for transmission so early in the evening; one considered that the series was great; one felt that the timeslot was wrong; and one was glad to see the back of Bonnie Langford. The production office also received one letter of complaint dated 2 December 1987 from a viewer named Dorothy Barrass, who was upset at a line of dialogue in which Ace had stated that the name Dorothy was 'naff'. John Nathan-Turner replied on 11 December apologising for any offence that had been caused.

'There was something traditional about *Dragonfire* that made me feel it was the right story on which to end the season,' commented Nathan-Turner in his *Doctor Who Magazine* memoirs. 'It was studio-bound, of course, but it also somehow harked back to earlier days of the show, while still using the latest technology. Sometimes innocent, sometimes simple, and yet advanced, moralistic and, hopefully, entertaining. Again, a story of "Hello, goodbye", but with a reasonable degree of optimism for the future.'

CREDITS

Director	Chris Clough
Producer	John Nathan-Turner
Script Editor	Andrew Cartmel
Production Associate	Ann Faggetter
Production Manager	Gary Downie
Assistant Floor Managers	Christopher Sandeman
	Kim Wilcocks
Production Assistants	Rosemary Parsons

THE SEVENTH DOCTOR

	Karen King
Producer's Secretary	Kate Easteal
Designer	John Asbridge
Design Assistant	Hilda Liptrott
Costume Designer	Richard Croft
Costume Assistant	Leah Archer
Dressers	Bob Springett
	Lena Hansen
	Tom Reeve
	Kate Hirst
Make-Up Designer	Gillian Thomas
Make-Up Assistants	Petrona Winton
	Anabela Dellot-Seguro
	Jayne Buxton
Visual Effects Designer	Andy McVean
Visual Effects Assistants	Mike Tucker
	Paul Mann
	Paul McGuinness
	Lindsay McGowan
	Jonathan Clarke
Properties Buyer	Cathy Cosgrove
Sound	Brian Clark
Deputy Sound Supervisor	Mike Weaver
Lighting	Don Babbage
Technical Co-ordinator	Richard Wilson
Senior Cameraman	Alec Wheal
Video Effects	Dave Chapman
Vision Mixer	Shirley Coward
Videotape Editor	Hugh Parson
Film Cameraman	William Dudman
Floor Assistant	Jes Nightingale
Production Operatives	Arthur Stacey
	Dicky Wickes
	Dave Rogers
	Barry Du Pille
Title Music	Ron Grainer, arranged by Keff McCulloch
Incidental Music	Dominic Glynn
Special Sound	Dick Mills
Writer	Ian Briggs

The Wilderness Years

After the completion of work on its twenty-sixth season, *Doctor Who* was effectively cancelled as a BBC production. Unlike when it had been taken off the air for eighteen months in 1984, however, there was no official announcement made to this effect. Consequently there was no press coverage of the series' demise and, at least initially, no concerted attempt by fans to get the BBC to change their minds.

Although *Survival* was the last story to be screened in the ongoing series, *Ghost Light* was the last to go before the cameras, the season having been made out of transmission order. Following its completion, there were just two pieces of additional recording undertaken. The first was of a voice-over by actor David Bingham for Part One of *Battlefield*. This was done on 13 August 1989. The second was a voice-over by Sylvester McCoy, consisting of the Doctor's final monologue for the end of Part Three of *Survival*. Whether by accident or design, this was done on a very appropriate date, 23 November 1989 – the twenty-sixth anniversary of *Doctor Who*'s debut transmission.

The BBC's *Doctor Who* production office had already begun to wind down a couple of months before this, and Sylvester McCoy was reported as telling a convention audience: 'The BBC don't want to make *Doctor Who*. They aren't interested in a series that's lasted twenty-six years.'

There had for some time been rumours circulating that the BBC wanted to farm *Doctor Who* out to be made by an independent production company. (At this point in the BBC's history, there was a general move toward outsourcing as many productions as possible; *Doctor Who* was one of the last drama series to be made in-house, and John Nathan-Turner was the last producer on the staff of the Series and Serials Department, all his former colleagues having been obliged to go freelance.) Bids were rumoured to have been made to the BBC by a number of interested companies, including Cinema Verity (run by former series producer Verity Lambert), Saffron Productions (run by former series story editor and writer Victor Pemberton) and Coast-to-Coast Productions Ltd (who were in fact looking to make a feature film based on the series – a subject covered in a later section of this chapter).

In November 1989, prompted by numerous enquiries from concerned fans and a certain amount of press speculation about the series' future, the BBC's new Head of Serials Peter Cregeen issued a statement in which he claimed that *Doctor Who* could easily continue for a further twenty-six years, but added that the BBC was considering the best way to 'take *Doctor Who* through the '90s'. These words were to ring ever more hollow as variations on the same statement continued to be issued by the BBC to anyone who enquired about the future of *Doctor Who* in the years that followed. Another notable occurrence in November 1989 was that Nathan-Turner officially stood down as *Doctor Who*'s producer after some ten years in that post. He remained on the BBC's payroll, however, and would continue to take an active role as the series' 'guardian'.

The following month, former story editor and writer Gerry Davis and writer Terry Nation confirmed in the fanzine *DWB* that they were interested in making a joint bid to produce the series. This, along with approaches from other sources, apparently forced the BBC to reconsider its attitude to the series, to the extent that senior press officer Kevin O'Shea (who had handled much of *Doctor Who*'s press promotion in the past) made a statement that an announcement on its future was likely to be made soon. Nothing came of this, although two months later, in February 1990, Cregeen was back with another pronouncement, commenting cryptically: 'There will be more changes than people think ...'

1990

The only new *Doctor Who*-related production to be transmitted during 1990 was an edition of the BBC schools series *Search out Science* in which Sylvester McCoy's Doctor and Sophie Aldred's Ace were joined by a John Leeson-voiced K-9 to educate viewers in the wonders of space. There was plenty of old *Doctor Who* to be seen, however, as it became one of the flagship shows on the new satellite channel BSB (which was also available through many cable television suppliers). This began, in April, repeating selected stories from the William Hartnell era onwards; and on 22 and 23 September there was an entire '*Doctor Who* weekend', otherwise known as '31 Who'. This consisted of special screenings, guest appearances and other items put together largely by Nathan-Turner, who had finally left the BBC at the end of the previous month (although he had immediately gained work with BBC Enterprises, producing *Doctor Who* video projects). Nathan-Turner also acted as on-screen co-presenter with Shyama Perera and Debbie Flint.

The stories and individual episodes shown on the Saturday were: *100,000 BC*, *The Mutants* (1963/64), *Inside the Spaceship* (with the second episode accidentally preceding the first), *The Abominable Snowmen* Episode Two, *The Web of Fear* Episode 1, *The Space Museum*, *The Keys of Marinus* and *The Aztecs*. Also shown was the Sixties cinema film *Dr Who and the Daleks*. Interspersed between these screenings were short interviews with: William Russell ('Ian'), Carole Ann Ford ('Susan'), Verity Lambert (producer), Waris Hussein

THE WILDERNESS YEARS

(director), Elisabeth Sladen ('Sarah Jane Smith'), Terry Nation (writer), Raymond P Cusick (designer), Mervyn Haisman (writer), Nicholas Courtney ('the Brigadier'), Sylvester McCoy ('the Doctor'), Andrew Beech (fan), Peter Purves ('Steven'), John Freeman (editor, *Doctor Who Magazine*), Terrance Dicks (script editor and writer), Gerry Davis (story editor and writer), Deborah Watling ('Victoria') and Jennie Linden ('Barbara' from the cinema films). Also presented during the course of the day were a *Doctor Who* 'expert' quiz, a piece on American *Doctor Who* conventions, vox pops of people doing Dalek impressions, an interview with a Cyberman, and the video for the 'Doctor in Distress' single record from 1984.

The stories and individual episodes shown on the Sunday were: *The War Games, The Dominators, The Mind Robber, The Three Doctors, The Abominable Snowmen* Episode Two, *The Web of Fear* Episode 1 and *Inside the Spaceship* (with the episodes screened the correct way round). Also shown, between *The Three Doctors* and *The Abominable Snowmen* Episode Two, was the cinema film *Daleks Invasion Earth: 2150 A.D.*. The interviews this time were with: Wendy Padbury ('Zoe'), Frazer Hines ('Jamie'), Pat Godfrey (costume designer), Brian Hodgson (special sound effects), Dick Mills (special sound effects), Sylvester McCoy ('the Doctor'), Stephen Mansfield (visual effects), Susan Moore (visual effects), Raymond P Cusick (designer), Barry Newbery (designer), Peter Hawkins (voice artiste), Terrance Dicks (script editor and writer), Nicholas Courtney ('the Brigadier'), Bob Baker (writer), Dave Martin (writer), David J Howe (collector), Verity Lambert (producer) and Terry Nation (writer). Additional features this time were a special effects demonstration and a top ten *Doctor Who* monsters compilation.

BSB spent a great deal of time and effort promoting *Doctor Who* generally, but all this came to an end in November 1990, when it merged with the rival Sky and the *Doctor Who* repeats stopped.

Also in November, one year on from the end of the twenty-sixth season and with no signs of the BBC taking any specific action to revive the series, a 'day of protest' was organised by the fanzine *DWB*. The idea was that on this particular day, Sunday 2 November, fans would bombard the BBC with at least twenty phone calls each in protest at the delay in returning the series to production. In the event, however, only 973 *Doctor Who*-related calls were logged at the duty offices of BBC television and radio. This was certainly far more than on an average day (on the Saturday immediately beforehand, for instance, twenty-three such calls had been logged), but it still fell well below the organisers' hopes; and while the great majority of callers were no doubt sincere individuals genuinely concerned about the series' future, the fact that some gave names very similar to those of well known *Doctor Who* characters and production personnel – 'Mr T Jovka', 'John Turner' and 'Alistair Gordon' amongst them – does raise questions about the motives of a minority. A further problem with this well-intentioned initiative is that, far from increasing the chances of new *Doctor Who* being made, it reportedly had the opposite effect of turning some senior BBC executives against the series altogether, leaving them determined not to let the fans dictate their policy in relation a show that they considered dead.

The following month, the BBC stated that a final decision on the series' future would be made in 1991.

The year did end on a relatively high note, however, when *Doctor Who* was the subject of a *Cult Heroes* documentary on BBC Radio 5 on Christmas Eve. This was produced by Anne Hinds, written by Ed Thomason and presented by comedian Tony Slattery, and featured contributions from John Nathan-Turner (producer), Sylvester McCoy ('the Doctor'), John Collins (DWAS Co-ordinator), Verity Lambert (producer), Dick Mills (special sound effects), Jon Pertwee ('the Doctor') and Elisabeth Sladen ('Sarah Jane Smith'). Also included were interview clips of Tom Baker taken from the 1977 *Lively Arts* documentary *Whose Doctor Who*.

1991

February 1991 saw BBC Chairman Marmaduke Hussey, in response to an enquiry from Sir Hugh Rossi MP, stating that the Corporation was looking 'at all possible avenues before making any long-term decisions' on *Doctor Who*'s future. Other senior BBC figures responded to public enquiries with standard letters along similar lines.

There was no further movement until May, when, following questions from the national press, the BBC finally confirmed that any future series would be made by an independent production company rather than in-house. No particular company was named, however, and nothing of substance seemed to be happening. Some magazines picked up the fact that a new science fiction show was about to be made at Shepperton Studios and leaped to the conclusion that it must be *Doctor Who*. It was actually a completely different production.

Arguably the biggest development during 1991 was the launching by Virgin books of their New Adventures range of original novels featuring the seventh Doctor and Ace. Visitors to London's Museum of the Moving Image (MOMI) were meanwhile able to see 'Behind the Sofa', a major exhibition devoted to *Doctor Who*. This opened on 5 July, following a press launch at which three concept models of creatures from the supposed forthcoming Green Light feature film were on show. Jointly arranged by MOMI, BBC Worldwide and Lorne Martin's company Experience (who were hired by BBC Worldwide to manage all the *Doctor Who* related exhibitions), it proved massively popular and was extended several times, finally running until 23 February 1992 before going on tour to regional venues until November 1992.

THE WILDERNESS YEARS

Tying in with the exhibition, a company called Teynham Productions, the directors of which were John Nathan-Turner, Gary Downie, Fiona Cumming and Ian Fraser, staged a series of two-day events at MOMI. These involved people associated with *Doctor Who* giving lectures about their work to a group of paying attendees. The dates and speakers were as follows. 6/7 July 1991: Jeremy Bentham (history of *Doctor Who*), Bernard Wilkie and Jack Kine (visual effects), Colin Baker ('the Doctor'), Carole Todd (director, *The Ultimate Adventure* stage play), June Hudson (costumes), Nicholas Courtney ('the Brigadier'), Fiona Cumming (director), Sophie Aldred ('Ace'), John Freeman (editor, *Doctor Who* Magazine), Dick Mills (sound effects), Sylvester McCoy ('the Doctor'); 2/3 November 1991: David J Howe (collecting), Barry Newbery (designer), Sue Anstruther (production assistant), Ken Trew (costumes), Mitch Mitchell (video effects), Barry Letts (producer), Tony Selby ('Glitz'), Ian Dow (lighting), Kevin O'Shea (publicity), Nicola Bryant ('Peri'), Shirley Coward (vision mixer), Elisabeth Sladen ('Sarah Jane Smith'), Ian Fraser (production manager), Jon Pertwee ('the Doctor'); 15/16 February 1992: Andrew Beech (appreciating *Doctor Who*), Gary Downie (choreographer, production assistant), Keff McCulloch (music), June Collins (production manager), Henry Barber (lighting), Jane Wellesley (production assistant), Tom Baker ('the Doctor'), Stuart Fell (stuntman), Lorne Martin and Martin Wilkie (exhibitions), Janet Fielding ('Tegan'), Graeme Smith ('Jason' in *The Ultimate Adventure*), Christopher Barry (director), Denise Baron (make-up), Terry Molloy ('Davros'). Teynham subsequently organised a number of similar events, some of them lasting only one day, in different locations around the UK.

On 26 August 1991, the series' pilot episode had its first ever transmission, some twenty-eight years after it was made, as part of BBC2's tribute to Lime Grove Studios, which were shortly to be demolished. The same month, Peter Cregeen issued another statement to *Doctor Who* Magazine about the series' future:

'There is no question of *Doctor Who* being abandoned. It is still an important programme, and when the time is right, it should return. However, the show's popularity over the years has waned in the United Kingdom, with an average audience of four million. In a competitive market environment, where BBC TV Drama is required to produce a wide range of programmes at an economically viable price, one cannot continue to support a programme that is not able to achieve a substantial audience.

'A decision was taken to rest the programme for an extended period so that when it returns, it will be seen as a fresh, inventive and vibrant addition to the schedule – rather than a battle-weary Time Lord languishing in the backwaters of audience popularity.

'*Doctor* Who is too valuable a property for us to relaunch until we are absolutely confident of it as a major success once again.'

Confused and angered by what they saw as yet another bland statement from the BBC, a group of fans announced plans in October to take the BBC to court for failing to make *Doctor Who* in the face of massive public demand. The consortium included chairman and legal adviser John Giacobbi, Andrew Beech, Steve Wickham, Colin Griffiths and Jonathan Way from the DWAS, Gary Leigh from *DWB* and historian Jeremy Bentham. This well intentioned but perhaps misguided campaign ultimately came to nothing, as a prize competition intended to raise money received only a lukewarm response and insufficient funds were raised to pursue the matter further.

1992

3 January 1992 saw the transmission on BBC2 of a half-hour overview of *Doctor Who* entitled *Resistance is Useless*. This was put together by the production team of the arts programme *The Late Show* (who had also been responsible for the previous August's screening of the pilot episode) and directed by Archie Lauchlan. It consisted mainly of clips from *Doctor Who* compiled into a number of categories and linked by a mysterious character who appeared to be nothing more than literally a talking anorak – the voice for which was provided by comedian Steve Steen. The clips were selected on the basis of responses to a questionnaire sent to a number of fans and on the advice of John Nathan-Turner, who had been engaged as a consultant. Other contributors to the programme included Steve Roberts (a fan who worked in the telecine department at the BBC) and Ian Levine, who along with Nathan-Turner supplied Lauchlan with lists of what was available to be included. The list of categories was: Resistance Is Useless; Thoughts Of An Anorak; Time And Relative Dimensions In Space; Fab Gadgets; Fashion Victims; Leave It To Me, Dear; The Brigadier's Finest Moments; Doc Fax; Behind The Sofa; Doc Fax (again); Effects (Special); Death By Special Effect; Give It All You've Got; Surreal; and Doctor In Charge.

Transmission of *Resistance is Useless* led on to a season of BBC2 repeats, starting with *The Time Meddler*, *The Mind Robber*, *The Sea Devils* and, in a specially restored recolourised version (combining images from a broadcast-standard black and white print with those from a poorer quality colour home video recorded off-air in the USA), *The Dæmons*. This was the first time that the BBC had screened any complete repeats of *Doctor Who* since *The Five Doctors* in 1984. Satellite and cable channel UK Gold also began transmitting regular repeats of the series, following the demise of BSB.

In February, Dark Light Productions was reported by *Doctor Who Magazine* to be the latest independent company bidding to produce a new series. The producer, Alan Jonns, eventually made a statement in the May edition of the magazine, indicating that no episodes had been filmed, no actor had been cast and no contracts with the BBC had been signed. He revealed that his company had simply been carrying out test work to see if their ideas were suitable. Although this work ultimately came to nothing, some of the monster designs created for the company by the Henson Creature Shop were later seen in relation both to the aborted 30th anniversary special *The Dark Dimension* (see below), one test photograph even appearing on the proposed cover of an ultimately unpublished Adrian Rigelsford book about that production, and to a potential Bill Baggs video drama featuring Cybermen and Ice Warriors.

Other notable events during 1992 included as part of the BBC's ongoing programme of *Doctor Who* video releases the cancelled Season 17 story *Shada*, with the missing scenes bridged by narration from Tom Baker, and in May, the Season 5 story *The Tomb of the Cybermen*, all four episodes of which had been amongst a consignment of film prints recently recovered from Hong Kong after being missing for many years from the BBC archives. In Virgin's New Adventures novels, meanwhile, a new – and ultimately highly popular – companion named Bernice Summerfield made her debut.

1993

The run of BBC2 repeats continued into the early part of 1993 with *Genesis of the Daleks*, *The Caves of Androzani*, *Revelation of the Daleks* (in the edited four part version originally created for overseas sales purposes) and *Battlefield*.

In April, the BBC held a press launch, with Jon Pertwee, Peter Davison, Colin Baker, Sylvester McCoy and Nicholas Courtney in attendance, promoting the package of video and audio releases planned for that autumn to tie in with *Doctor Who*'s 30th anniversary. Tony Greenwood, Director of Home Entertainment at BBC Enterprises, also mentioned that, as had been rumoured since the previous December, a script had been written for a special anniversary production – although he added that it might not actually reach fruition, as the necessary agreements had yet to be concluded. (The original aim of BBC Enterprises in holding this press launch had in fact been to announce the making of the special, but they had had to backtrack as it had yet to be given the go-ahead.)

The following month, it was confirmed that the special, entitled *The Dark Dimension* and intended to feature all the surviving Doctors, would be directed by Graeme Harper (who had made his mark on the series with *The Caves of Androzani* and *Revelation of the Daleks*). Then in June, there came the only official announcement that the BBC ever made on the subject, when a ninety-six minute, 16mm film special, referred to as *Doctor Who: Lost in the Dark Dimension*, was listed in its forthcoming drama publicity press release. The special was written by Adrian Rigelsford and Jo McCaul and a production office was set up with Penny Mills (from BBC Enterprises) and newly resigned Head of Drama Peter Cregeen acting as co-producers.

On 9 July, the special was abruptly cancelled. No official reason was ever given, as the BBC denied that it was ever a finalised project. The Managing Director of Network Television, Will Wyatt, blamed over-eager fans for taking it beyond the ideas stage. BBC Video's David Jackson broke the news by saying: 'Due to the constrictions of our budget and the time available, the production has been cancelled.' It is believed that internal BBC politics and objections raised by Philip Segal, the American-based producer bidding for the rights to make a new series, also contributed to the decision not to go ahead with the project. Rigelsford, who had been trying to get his script produced for two years, was reported by *Doctor Who Magazine* to be 'deeply disappointed'. It was also revealed by *Doctor Who Magazine* that Nick Jagels had been brought on board as production associate and that Rigelsford, Harper and Jagels, together with Alan Jonns, had been the 'guiding force' behind Dark Light's earlier attempts to get *Doctor Who* back on air.

Despite future rumours to the contrary, Tom Baker was the only actor ever contracted to appear in the special (and hence the only one to be paid); no other casting was ever agreed (although the other surviving Doctors – who, with the exception of Sylvester McCoy, would have had much smaller roles – were sent copies of the script); no filming or location work was ever carried out; and, aside from Rigelsford writing a draft rehearsal script (of which there appear to have been several different versions, none of them bearing a co-writing credit for McCaul), the only other production work ever carried out consisted of one or two early 'ideas' meetings drawing together interested parties – including production designer Nigel Jones, visual effects designer Tony Harding and first assistant director Kevan van Thompson – who may or may not have ended up working on the project had it gone ahead. Kevin Davies had also been approached with a view to designing the title sequence, and Mark Russell and Alan Hawkshawe had been under consideration to provide the music.

In August, BBC Radio 5 transmitted a new *Doctor Who* radio serial entitled *Paradise of Death*, written by Barry Letts and featuring Jon Pertwee, Elisabeth Sladen and Nicholas Courtney reprising their roles as the third Doctor, Sarah Jane Smith and Brigadier Lethbridge-Stewart respectively. This had been recorded in May. The serial's producer, Phil Clarke, was also responsible for a documentary, *Doctor Who – 30 Years*, which was broadcast on BBC Radio 2 on 20 November and ran for 55 minutes and 44 seconds. This was narrated by Nicholas Courtney and featured interviews with: Gary Russell (editor, *Doctor Who* Magazine), Katy Manning ('Jo'), John Scott Martin (Dalek operator), Jon Pertwee ('the Doctor'), William Russell ('Ian'), Peter Purves ('Steven'), Louise Jameson ('Leela'), Barry Letts (director, producer and writer), Terrance Dicks (script editor and writer), Terry Nation (writer), Frazer Hines ('Jamie'), Jessica Carney (William Hartnell's granddaughter), John Nathan-Turner (producer), Verity Lambert (producer), Sylvester McCoy ('the Doctor') and Brian Hodgson (special sound effects). Also recorded but unused in the final programme were interviews with Anneke Wills ('Polly'), Elisabeth Sladen ('Sarah Jane Smith'), David J Howe (historian) and Roberta Tovey ('Susan' from the cinema films).

The Season 10 story *Planet of the Daleks* was meanwhile repeated on BBC1 in November and December, with a five minute 'mini documentary' preceding each episode. The themes of these mini-documentaries were as follows: *Bigger Inside Than Out* (Colin Baker narrating a piece on the history of the TARDIS and the police box upon which its external appearance was based); *The Antique Doctor Who Show* (a pastiche of the BBC's *The Antiques Road Show* in which presenter Justin Pressland and collector David J Howe spoke to several fans about their *Doctor Who* collections); *Missing in Action* (a look at the junking of *Doctor Who* episodes and the efforts to retrieve them); *I Was That Monster* (interviews with people who had played monsters); *Crimefile – The Master* (a pastiche of the crime prevention show *Police 5* in which presenter Shaw Taylor warned the public to be on the lookout for the Master); and *UNIT Recruiting Film* (in which Nicholas Courtney encouraged people to join up). At the end of the last of these mini-documentaries was given a telephone number, callers to which could hear Courtney telling them that *The Green Death* was due to be repeated the following year.

Although plans for a proper anniversary story had come to nothing, there was a minor consolation for fans, as the two-part skit *Dimensions in Time* was transmitted as part of BBC1's annual *Children in Need* telethon on 26 and 27 November.

On 29 November, BBC1 also transmitted a more substantial fifty minute documentary entitled *30 Years in the TARDIS* (which was released on video the following year with additional material under the title *More than 30 Years in the TARDIS*). This had suddenly been given the green light in September by the team responsible for the previous year's *Resistance is Useless*. Recorded during October and November, it brought together clips, interviews and dramatic interludes to provide a well balanced overview of the series. Interviews were conducted with: Mat Irvine (visual effects), Mike Tucker (visual effects), Colin Baker ('the Doctor'), Nicola Bryant ('Peri'), Carole Ann Ford ('Susan'), Verity Lambert (producer), Roberta Tovey ('Susan' from the cinema films), Sophie Aldred ('Ace'), Sylvester McCoy ('the Doctor'), Barry Letts (director, producer and writer), Terrance Dicks (script editor and writer), Elisabeth Sladen ('Sarah Jane Smith'), Delia Derbyshire (theme music arranger), Brian Hodgson (special sound effects), Dick Mills (special sound effects), Jessica Carney (William Hartnell's granddaughter), Jennie Linden ('Barbara' from the cinema films), Deborah

Watling ('Victoria'), Frazer Hines ('Jamie'), John Nathan-Turner (producer), Ian Levine (fan), Gary Russell (editor, *Doctor Who* Magazine), Jon Pertwee ('the Doctor'), Eric Saward (script editor and writer), Mary Whitehouse (retired head of the National Viewers' and Listeners' Association), Ben Aaronovitch (writer), Philip Hinchcliffe (producer); Stephen Bayley (academic), Professor Steve Jones (academic); Lowrey Turner (fashion editor); Mike Gatting (England cricketer/celebrity fan), Ken Livingstone (politician/celebrity fan), Toyah Wilcox (pop singer and presenter/celebrity fan) and Gerry Anderson (puppet series producer/celebrity fan). Several of those interviewed were not seen in the broadcast programme, although Davies was able to include some of the unused material in the later video release.

1994

Further repeats – this time of *The Green Death* and *Pyramids of Mars* – were transmitted on BBC2 at the start of 1994. Then, in July, Virgin launched a new range of Missing Adventures books to complement their New Adventures.

On 9 July, listeners to BBC Radio 4 were able to hear *Whatever Happened to ... Susan?*, the fifth in a series of humorous programmes looking at the lives of popular fictional characters, the subject in this case being the Doctor's granddaughter Susan Foreman, played here by Jane Asher after the original actress, Carole Ann Ford, apparently failed to return the BBC's calls. The programme was produced by Brian King, written by Adrian Mourby and, in addition to Asher, featured James Grout (playing Ian Chesterton), June Barne (Barbara Wright), Eva Haddon (Jo Jones, née Grant), Andrew Sachs (Temmosus Skyedron), Peter Woodthorpe (Joey Oxford), Barry Harrison (researcher) and Claire Rayner (as herself).

Following the success of *Paradise of Death*, a further *Doctor Who* radio serial, *Doctor Who and the Ghosts of N Space*, was recorded in November, although its transmission was ultimately delayed until March 1996, when it went out on BBC Radio 2 (Radio 5 having by this point become an all-news station). Like *The Paradise of Death*, it was produced by Phil Clarke, written by Barry Letts and featured Jon Pertwee, Elisabeth Sladen, Nicholas Courtney and new regular Richard Pearce playing Sarah's young assistant Jeremy.

1995

1995 was a relatively quiet year for *Doctor Who*, although UK Gold continued to transmit repeats and there was still a steady stream of new tie-in merchandise being issued, including the first in a range of BBC audio books featuring abridged versions of the Target novelisations of televised stories read by their respective Doctors. By this point, however, the series' followers were becoming increasingly excited by news reports that seemed to suggest that there might, at long last, be a real prospect of new *Doctor Who* being seen on television for the first time in over six years ...

MOVIE HELL

Omitted from the preceding sections of this chapter has been any mention of the numerous unsuccessful attempts to get a *Doctor Who* feature film off the ground during the late Eighties and the Nineties - a subject that merits a section all of its own.

There had been serious talk of a *Doctor Who* movie from as early as 1976, when Tom Baker, actor Ian Marter (who played companion Harry Sullivan) and producer James Hill developed an idea, with the working titles *Doctor Who and the Big Game* and *Doctor Who Meets Scratchman*, featuring 'Scratchman', another name for the devil, as the villain. After much negotiation, BBC Enterprises granted James Hill Productions, with effect from 1 November 1978, a one year option to make the film, with no commitment on their part to renew. The project eventually fell through, however, due to difficulties in raising the necessary finance.

In the meantime, numerous other overtures were made to the BBC by parties interested in pursuing *Doctor Who* film projects. On 4 April 1978, Jill Foster Ltd made contact regarding a Douglas Adams film treatment based on the series. An approach came on 12 May 1980 from producer Brian Eastman of Paramount; another on 23 August 1982 from Anthony Williams of Sandfire Productions, based at Pinewood Studios; and another in May 1984 from American producer Norman Rubenstein, who remained in contact with the BBC until October of that year. These all came to nothing. Milton Subotsky, co-producer of the two '60s *Doctor Who* films, contacted Head of Series and Serials Jonathan Powell in April 1984 to indicate that he would like to do a third. This had the working title *Doctor Who's Greatest Adventure* and would have involved two Doctors teaming up to combat some giant monsters. Powell turned the idea down, and confirmed with Head of Copyright Brian Turner that there was nothing in Subotsky's original contracts with the BBC that gave him any rights in this regard. A proposal that progressed a little further was put forward on 15 October 1984 by Edward Joffe of Multivision Communications Ltd. The BBC stipulated as conditions for granting the film rights to Multivision that John Nathan-Turner would have to be involved in the project; that one of the television Doctors would have to be given the lead role; and that a fee of around £50,000 would have to be paid. Peter Davison was subsequently contacted to see if he would be interested in starring in the film, and Christopher H Bidmead was earmarked as a possible writer. In the end, however, this also fell through. On 7 May 1985, Nathan-Turner suggested that *Doctor Who*'s first producer, Verity Lambert, might be a good candidate to make a film based on the series. Then, on 21 June 1985, producer Michael Bond put forward a film treatment entitled *The Crossroads in Time*. This too came to nothing.

It was in March 1985 that Coast-to-Coast Productions Ltd – run by co-directors Peter Litten, George Dugdale and John Humphreys – first entered into negotiations with BBC Enterprises with a view to acquiring the rights to make a *Doctor Who* feature film, having apparently started discussing the idea the previous month. In November of the same year, Litten wrote an undated letter to BBC Enterprises' Director of Business Administration John Keeble, setting out the company's latest proposals for the film and indicating that the budget and scope had recently been increased in all departments. He stated that: actors Denholm Elliott, Steven Berkoff, Caroline Munro, Tim Curry and Laurence Olivier had all agreed to be involved; composer Mike Oldfield had been approached to adapt the series' theme tune and provide the incidental music; make-up artist Christopher Tucker, whose credits included *The Elephant Man* and *The Company of Wolves*, would be creating the creatures and monsters; John Stears, who had won an Oscar for his work on *Star Wars*, would be in charge of visual effects; Rodney Matthews and Anton Furst would be teaming up to design the sets and costumes; Douglas Adams would be acting as script consultant; Robert Holmes would be providing the screenplay; and Richard Lester, the man at the helm of *Superman 2* and *Superman 3* amongst many other projects, was being considered as director. He also stated that Sun Alliance had undertaken to provide financial backing for the film, and that only the BBC's agreement was now required.

Jonathan Powell, when shown Litten's letter, expressed considerable scepticism. In an internal memo to Keeble he wrote: 'With respect, this strikes me as slightly full of baloney. *No* actors would agree without a script. The technicians mentioned would never agree without production dates. Robert Holmes is not an adventurous choice to write the screenplay. Anyone can *consider* Richard Lester. The statement means absolutely nothing in practice.'

Powell went on to state that he believed that the BBC should keep the project for themselves, and that if they did decide to allow it to go ahead outside, then there should be 'some known factor involved'. He concluded by stating that he was unimpressed by Litten's letter, which made many promises and listed many prospective contributors when 'clearly their statements are absolutely meaningless.' He also asked if anyone had any idea as to what Litten had done in the past, or what his production company had actually achieved.

Despite this unfavourable reception from Powell, negotiations with Coast-to-Coast continued, and were eventually concluded around July 1987, when the company was finally granted the rights to make a *Doctor Who* feature film in return for a substantial fee, reported to be £46,000. It was apparently envisaged that the company would need to raise some £1.6 million in backing in order to proceed with the project.

During the latter half of 1987, rumours regarding the film's casting, content and production started to appear with increasing frequency in newspapers and magazines. It was variously reported that actress Caroline Munro would be featuring in the film as the villain; that £5 million was being spent on the effects alone; that Sylvester McCoy was the hot favourite for the role of the Doctor; that the budget was around £9 million; that Tom Conti and Tim Curry had turned down the starring role; and that Tom Baker was the hot favourite to take the lead.

Stage and Television Today carried a short piece on the film on 8 October 1987, headed by a mocked-up image of Munro as the computerised television host Max Headroom (Coast-to-Coast having previously been involved in the production of Chrysalis's *Max Headroom* show). John Humphreys was quoted as saying: 'We intend to make it a big budget film with extensive and advanced special effects – I can promise you we won't be using the BBC's infamous quarry.' The report went on to suggest that the film involved Munro 'in the title role' as a robot who operates a pirate radio spaceship to beam pop videos down to earth. However, as this sounds suspiciously like a description of *Max Headroom* (albeit that Munro did not star in that series), it is possible that the reporter had his or her wires crossed.

Early in 1988, John Cleese was tipped to play the Doctor, and Dudley Moore was also mentioned as a strong contender for the part. Munro was now apparently in line to play the companion rather than the villain, and it was reported that the film's directors would be Litten and Dugdale. £14 million was the latest figure quoted for the budget, and a script was stated to have been commissioned from writer Mark Ezra. In March, another writer, Johnny Byrne, was reported to be under contract to work on the script, and a release date of Easter 1989 was mooted.

In May 1988, fan Ian Levine was confirmed as a consultant on the project. Then, the following month, it was predicted that shooting would commence in January 1989. John Cleese was at this time still being tipped to play the Doctor, and, in a new twist, it was suggested that there would be no fewer than four companion characters. In November 1988, the *Daily Mail* gave over part of the front page of one of its editions to the news that Dudley Moore was to star as the Doctor in a film with a budget of £19 million – the highest figure yet suggested. The following month, however, Moore was reported to be only one of a number of contenders for the title role, others being Donald Sutherland, Ian Holm and Peter Firth. Filming was still reported to be due to start in January, the chosen locations being London and the Canary Islands, but Munro had now apparently reverted to playing the villain.

In April 1989, with no shooting having actually taken place, it was reported that the film had been postponed indefinitely due to lack of finance. In August of that year, however, it was apparently back on again, with filming due to start in March 1990 in Yugoslavia. On 23 October 1989, a number of newspapers reported that Donald Sutherland was to take the lead role, having been cast in preference to Dudley Moore, Michael Caine, John Cleese and Sylvester Stallone, and that – scandalously – the film would show the Doctor boozing, having bar-room brawls, carrying a gun and making love to his assistant. The budget at this time was claimed to be £20 million, and the makers of the Johnny Byrne-scripted film were said to be Pathé.

By the end of 1989, *Doctor Who* fans who had eagerly followed all these reports were understandably totally confused, and many were starting to become highly sceptical that the film would ever see the light of day. Philip Newman, a fan who wrote regularly for several genre magazines and who had apparently been in regular contact with Litten since December 1987, tried to clear the air by explaining in the fanzine *Proteus* what had been really happening. 'Firstly,' he wrote, 'I think it is most important to get one particular message across: *Doctor Who – The Movie* is *definitely* going ahead, and will go into production once all the financial, distribution and other arrangements have been finalised – probably sometime early in 1990.' On the subject of why it had taken so long to get to this stage, Newman indicated that Coast-to-Coast wanted to keep the film as authentic as possible to the original television series and that, with much of the financial backing coming from America, it had 'been hard to keep control of all aspects of the film's production and, moreover, to keep it British.'

As for the scripting of the film, Newman recounted that Mark Ezra had written a first 'rough framework' in 1987 and that this had since been totally reworked by Byrne into a full length script, which had subsequently been through as many as sixteen rewrites. Levine had checked the script for accuracy in terms of the series' mythology, but otherwise had had no involvement in the project. According to Newman, only twelve actors had ever been seriously considered for the role of the Doctor, and just four of these were still seen as possible contenders. At no point had any of the television Doctors ever been under consideration. Newman went on to add: 'Pre-production work is well underway, with twelve conceptual artists, working from different parts of the country, now engaged on producing preliminary designs and plans for all the sets, lighting rigs, creatures and costumes. Several storyboard artists are currently at work on realising the large volume of special effects sequences that the film requires.'

Jean-Marc Lofficier's book *The Nth Doctor*, initially published by Virgin Publishing in 1997, also gives a description of Coast-to-Coast's abortive attempts to get their *Doctor Who* film off the ground, and in some respects this is at odds with the account presented by Newman. According to Lofficier, Ezra had by August 1987 completed not only a 'rough framework' but a full draft script entitled *Doctor Who – The Movie*. Byrne then worked on several different treatments and drafts during 1988 and 1989, and the story gradually evolved away from Ezra's original. The resultant scripts were retitled *Doctor Who – [The] Last of the Time Lords*. The project was sufficiently advanced for the Coast-to-Coast team, now calling themselves Green Light, to prepare an advertising flier for the Moving Pictures International film conference in Milan in October 1990. This showed a re-worked *Doctor Who* logo along with the tag line: 'The Man – The Myth – The Movie'.

As *The Nth Doctor* tells it, Byrne completely rewrote his script in 1991 while Litten and Dugdale brought to fruition another project: a low budget horror feature called *Living Doll*. Green Light, meanwhile, obtained from the BBC another extension of the time period available to them to make the film. This would now expire on 6 April 1994 at which point, if shooting had not commenced, all rights would revert to the BBC.

In 1992, in a further attempt to gain the required finance, Green Light joined forces with Lumiere Pictures and apparently sold on the *Doctor Who* rights to them. One of Lumiere's first acts was to abandon Byrne's work on the project, and instead to commission a totally new script, first from Nicholas Meyer and then, when this did not work out, from a writing partner of Meyer's, Denny Martin Flinn. Lumiere also approached actor and director Leonard Nimoy (famous for his role as Spock in *Star Trek*), and, after reading Flinn's script, he agreed to produce and direct the film. The actor strongly favoured to play the part of the Doctor at this time was Pierce Brosnan. In the event, however, Green Light/Lumiere were unable to commence filming by the deadline date, at which point Lumiere decided to withdraw from the project.

There is one final development to report in this saga. On 10 January 1996, just as news of the Philip Segal/Universal/BBC Worldwide television movie was breaking, the London *Evening Standard* carried a two page exposé on the problems that had beset the earlier feature film project. The report, by Keith Dovkants, stated that Litten, Dugdale and Humpreys were all 'special effects experts' who had worked on *Doctor Who* (it is indeed the case that Litten and Dugdale once worked in the BBC's Visual Effects Department, and it is known that the Morlox creature seen in Season 22's *Timelash* was built by one or other of them, although neither ever received a credit on the series) and had decided to obtain the rights to make a *Doctor Who* film in the late Eighties (sic) as they 'deplored the fact that no-one was tapping the enormous cinema potential'. The report went on to explain that the three men had obtained finance from a consortium of about twenty individuals (including singer Bryan Ferry and, from the band Dire Straits, John Illsley) and formed a company called Daltenreys to take the project forward, pouring in additional money from second mortgages on their homes in the process. Their deal with the BBC was reported to have been with Keeble, and it was stated that Daltenreys had had meetings with Warner Brothers in America, who had suggested Jack Nicholson as a suitable actor to play the villain – this was at the time when Tim Burton's *Batman*, featuring Nicholson as the Joker, was flavour of the month – and Bill Cosby, Denholm Elliot, Donald Sutherland and Alan Rickman as potential Doctors.

The problem had come, according to the report, when Keeble had resigned from the BBC and BBC Enterprises had become BBC Worldwide, with a remit from new BBC Director General John Birt to maximise profits. Humphreys was quoted as saying that Daltenreys had signed a deal with Lumiere in 1993; that Lumiere had wanted to make three *Doctor Who* films with a budget of more than $30 million; that Leonard Nimoy had been engaged as director and Alan Rickman 'courted' to play the Doctor; and that after they had heard Stephen Spielberg's name linked to a *Doctor Who* film project (as it had been in the press) they had contacted the BBC and been fobbed off: 'We got the run around'.

The report went on to note that Daltenreys had spent the next few months trying to work out what their position was, and that on 4 March, a month before the filming deadline, the BBC's senior lawyer Rowan Vevers had written to them querying their arrangement with Lumiere on what Humphreys described as a 'technicality'. This had apparently been too much for Lumiere, who according to the report had already spent over a million pounds on the project, and they had withdrawn. This had left Daltenreys high and dry and with no other option but to speak to their own lawyers regarding the legality of the BBC's actions.

The resultant legal action was reported by Joanna Bale in *The Times* a year later, on 15 February 1997. Daltenreys were said to be seeking a million pounds in compensation and £21 million in damages against the potential profits from the three film versions of *Doctor Who* that they had planned to make. They were also said to have paid £440,000 for the rights to make the films. In an interesting aside, Bale reported that the BBC claimed to know nothing about any legal action, but that if it was pursued, they would 'vigorously contest it'.

As of writing, nothing more has been reported about the prospective legal action. Nor have any further proposals for *Doctor Who* feature films been made public.

THE EIGHTH DOCTOR

David J Howe
Stephen James Walker

Paul McGann
In His Own Words

ON PUBLICITY

'We've never been Mr and Mrs Showbiz.'

Interviewed by Garry Jenkins for *TV Times* dated 25-31 May 1996.

'I'm fairly private, you know. I don't live in London. I don't do that "showbiz" stuff. I've got family. There's times when I don't want to get involved, and there's times when it's great to be associated with something ... Fame is a double-edged sword'

Speaking in Birmingham after a screening of *Withnail and I* on 22 March 1996.

ON TAKING OVER THE ROLE OF THE DOCTOR

'When I saw the casting agent in Los Angeles I kept saying, "You've got the wrong fella." Other actors seemed to fit the image better, so I turned it down. I said, "This is daft, I can't do it." There was no pressure, it's easy to say no.'

Interviewed by Garry Jenkins for *TV Times* dated 25-31 May 1996.

'I was on the *News at 10*! My mum was ringing me up saying, "You're on tonight!" It's like being an ambassador. That's what it feels like for a Brit. It's an honour, but a responsibility as well, which is the part that's beginning to dawn on me.'

Interviewed by Frank Garcia for *Starlog* dated June 1996.

THE EIGHTH DOCTOR

'Taking on such a key role hasn't really sunk in yet. It is just beginning to dawn on me what all this means. Sylvester McCoy is a friend, so he's told me everything I need to know. I loved *Doctor Who* as a kid. William Hartnell used to terrify me. My favourite villain was the Yeti, but the Daleks never did it for me – they couldn't run upstairs.

'This film will be loyal to the spirit of past series, but will find fresh appeal too.'

Speaking at a press launch on 10 January 1996.

'There was a style to the Doctor that, quite honestly, I didn't think I could live up to. Some of the skills were almost vaudevillian. It was sort of that indoor scarf-wearing, eccentric kind of thing. It wasn't me.'

Interviewed by Mark Nollinger for *TV Guide* dated May 11-17 1996.

'In the past, the Doctors have been rather kooky, manic and zany. I am not a kooky person. When Philip [Segal] initially offered me the role, I said to myself, "What is this person thinking! I'm all wrong for this part."'

Interviewed by Lou Anders for *Sci-Fi Universe* dated December 1996.

'I've signed a contract. I can't go anywhere. I am him. I am Who. He is me.'

Interviewed by Christy Slewinski for the *New York Daily News* dated 14 May 1996.

'I knew I'd have an effect on lots of people, and especially on children. It is a responsibility. But I thought that if I was going to do telly, I may as well do the biggest telly. And there's no doubt the biggest telly is *Doctor Who*.'

Interviewed by Gary Gillatt in 1996 for *Doctor Who Magazine* No. 238.

'It's like a top posting. It's like being the ambassador to the US or something. It's like getting a mega-top job. The Beeb's equivalent of "our man overseas" or something. I'm just realising the size of the job.'

Speaking on the video *Bidding Adieu* produced by BBV and released in 1996.

PAUL MCGANN: IN HIS OWN WORDS

ON THE EIGHTH DOCTOR'S CHARACTER

'He's a bit clean, isn't he, old Doctor Who? There's gonna be some changes ... I might put that out on the internet – "There's gonna be some changes ..."'

Speaking in Birmingham after a screening of *Withnail and I* on 22 March 1996.

'There are elements like the jelly babies. There are little bits that have been carried over that have survived. I can't help thinking of Patrick Troughton or Bill Hartnell, but certainly, I'm doing it *my* way. That's easy. It's the only way I *can* do it.'

Interviewed by Frank Garcia for *Starlog* dated June 1996.

'I have been looking for something more edgy. It's like the vampire. You can't have hung around for three hundred years and not feel kind of bitter. There are darker elements to it.'

Interviewed by Garry Jenkins for *The Times Magazine* dated 25 May 1996.

'Playing the Doctor has been strange, trying to find the right level. I spend half the film not knowing who I am, so the character's not even there. It's a learning process for me. I'd like to do more, so I can get my teeth into it, and work with the Doctor.'

Interviewed by Gary Gillatt in 1996 for *Doctor Who Magazine* No. 237.

'Being British and having grown up in Britain you couldn't see past ... the character as he's been represented – that collective popular understanding of what the Doctor is like. So not only was I not convinced that I could hack it, I also couldn't see how they could make it seem remotely interesting for me. I think it was because the names that were being bandied round, pop stars and celebrities rather than actors, created a certain impression about the type of person who would be playing the Doctor. I didn't see that I could fit in with the expectation that a known eccentric should play the part. Much as I loved *Doctor Who* as a kid, I felt I could no sooner play him than I could play, say, Prince Charles. As I said, it's just not what I do.'

Interviewed by Gary Gillatt in 1996 for *Doctor Who Magazine* No. 238.

THE EIGHTH DOCTOR

'What'll I bring to the part? Youth. Glamour. I was going to say "Scouseness", but I'm following in a long line of Scouse Doctor Whos, because Tom Baker's one, isn't he? I shall bring my usual thing. I just do my thing, whatever it is I do.'

Interviewed by Mark Gatiss in 1996 for *Starburst* Special #28.

ON KISSING GRACE

'There are kisses and kisses. There are kisses that are innocently meant. He doesn't kiss her by mistake. But it is not licentiousness.'

Interviewed by Garry Jenkins in 1996 for *TV Zone* Issue 78.

'I kept my lips together when I kissed Daphne [Ashbrook] because I didn't want the love scenes to be too sexy. It is the first time the Doctor has been seen kissing, and I didn't want to do anything that might upset a family audience.'

Interviewed by Shoba Vazirani for the *Sun* dated 25 May 1996.

'All innocently meant, though, you see ... It's an American kiss, it's not a European one ... no tonsil-tickling.'

Speaking on the video *Bidding Adieu* produced by BBV and released in 1996.

'It's a magic moment.'

Interviewed by Garry Jenkins for *Inside TV* dated 25-31 May 1996.

'This has been a sore point, hasn't it? I wasn't aware actually that there had never been a ... that there was never a ... I mean ... has the Doctor never had a snog? ... So is it going to get the fans' backs up?'

Interviewed by Gary Gillatt in 1996 for *Doctor Who Magazine* No. 238.

ON THE AMERICANISATION OF *DOCTOR WHO*

'We have got mad chases on police bikes – why not? We have had gunfights at the OK Corral in *Doctor Who* before. Who says we can't have *The Streets of*

PAUL MCGANN: IN HIS OWN WORDS

San Francisco?'

Interviewed by Garry Jenkins for *The Times Magazine* dated 25 May 1996.

'This is going off in a new direction. If it goes to a series, I don't know what I'll do, really. It depends whether I've got the bottle to just go with it, embrace it. ... Given that it's pitched deliberately as North American, the remnants of the quintessential Britishness of it will have to remain, because they regard that as commercial.'

Interviewed by Mark Gatiss in 1996 for *Starburst* Issue 214.

ON FANDOM AND ATTENDING CONVENTIONS

'The thought of me going anywhere near a convention at the moment makes my flesh creep! I know I'm going to have to. I'm going to get collared at some point, but I want to die when I think about it. Obviously it comes with the job. I can't run and hide forever. Mind you, I can always send one of my brothers ...'

Interviewed by Mark Gatiss in 1996 for *Starburst* Special #28.

'It fills me *with absolute dread*, to be honest with you. I know I'll do it. I just know I'll end up doing it at least once, because I like to scare myself. That's very Catholic. I know McCoy does the circuit. But he's very gifted. He can simply stand on a stage and entertain two thousand people for an hour. I'm nervous – the thought of standing there – I won't even do the theatre for the same reason. I'm too scared. I suggested to McCoy that I go along with him in disguise, incognito, to see what it's like, and he said there's no such thing anymore. He said, "You would be eaten alive! They can smell you! You don't stand a chance!"'

Interviewed by Frank Garcia for *Starlog* dated June 1996.

'The fans are very understanding. I've been very pleased and surprised to find that the real fans, the people from the magazine and stuff, have the right amount of "tongue-in-cheekness" about it. It's great, 'cause they love it and they're into it, but it's only a game – they're not going to put someone's nose out of joint! They seem to realise that if I don't want to do something, I won't do it. And recognising that is generally the best way to deal with me. I'm the kid that says "no" to something for ages, then eventually knocks on the door and says, "Well actually, can I join in?" – y'know? I'll do it in my own time though.'

Interviewed by Simon J Gerard in 1996 for *Doctor Who Magazine* **No. 246.**

ON FAN REACTION

'Sylvester McCoy put it well when he told me that I was basically on a hiding to nothing. He said that some people would love me and some people would hate me, but everyone has their own views of what the Doctor should be like and you can't please all of them. He told me I can't really win, but I can't really fail either.'

Interviewed by Gary Gillatt in 1996 for *Doctor Who Magazine* **No. 238.**

'There's a lot of people that care a lot – for quite a big group, I'm suddenly the star, there are thousands of people I'm suddenly really important to. But feelings do seem to run very high. People take it all deadly seriously, which is strange, because it's actually quite a light and witty programme.'

Interviewed by Gary Gillatt in 1996 for *Doctor Who Magazine* **No. 238.**

ON THE FINISHED PRODUCT

'I have a good feeling about it. But who knows, who knows?'

Interviewed by Garry Jenkins in 1996 for *TV Zone* **Issue 78.**

'When I saw the finished film, I thought it looked amazing. It looks like a major movie.'

Interviewed by John Millar for the *Daily Record* **dated 25 May 1996.**

'The ratings will be what we're judged by, but the future of the series also seems to be contingent on whether or not the "big cheeses" like it – that's the impression I get. We've been getting good feedback, though; we've been receiving flowers from Hollywood every day, so we must be doing something right. We're getting a good vibe, and we're having a laugh doing it.'

Interviewed by Gary Gillatt in 1996 for *Doctor Who Magazine* **No. 237.**

PAUL MCGANN: IN HIS OWN WORDS

ON THE FUTURE

'I'll stay with it. I've got to. I've signed a piece of paper that says I will'

Interviewed by Frank Garcia for *Starlog* dated June 1996.

'Even if it doesn't go any further and I end up being the George Lazenby of the Time Lords, I'll have had a good time. And I'll still get asked to the *Doctor Who* conventions.'

Interviewed by John Millar for the *Daily Record* dated 25 May 1996.

'Well, frankly, it'll be great if it takes off, because I'll be offered more work. That's the first consideration – I won't be sitting on my arse as much as I used to. As for the type of work ... I don't know, it's hard to say ... I'm not conditioned to think that far ahead. I go out of my mind if I try to do that.'

Interviewed by Gary Gillatt in 1996 for *Doctor Who Magazine* No. 238.

'The situation is that we're doing a TV movie but putatively it's a pilot and it might go to a series. But the fact is that the people who run the series are another department altogether. So who knows. If it was all under the same roof, then probably they'd know by now that it was going to go [to a series] and things would be a lot clearer. What's going to be happening in twelve months ... who knows? It might not go at all. The chances are dead against it, in fact.'

Speaking on the video *Bidding Adieu* produced by BBV and released in 1996.

Character – The Eighth Doctor

It was always the intention of executive producer Philip David Segal to introduce an eighth Doctor in the television movie; no serious consideration was ever given to featuring the seventh Doctor in anything other than a brief appearance leading up to a regeneration. Interviewed exclusively for this book, Segal recalled the qualities that he had been looking for in the new Doctor:

'I don't think my perception ever really changed. I knew the qualities that he had to have. Looking at the series itself, and even at the information gleaned from the books that have been written about it, you can see that a good proportion of what was established with the previous Doctors was stuff that the actors themselves brought to the role. So all we could really do to influence that was to find someone whose appearance and demeanour gave us indications that externally they had the stuff to give us what they might have internally.

'Obviously humour and a dark side and a sort of child-like behaviour along with some alien-like qualities are all important parts of the mixture.

'It influenced the casting in a certain way. I wasn't trying to do anything that I thought was so brilliant that everyone would say it was a work of genius. All I wanted to do was to find somebody who fitted the shoes, so to speak, because whether you like it or not, if you try to go in a direction that moves a long way away from the spirit of who this character is, then I think you're actually damaging the fabric of the franchise. So it wasn't so much that I could bring a unique perspective to this; that wasn't my intention at all. I never felt that I was doing this because I was the one who understood *Doctor Who* better than anyone else in the world. I never felt that way at all. But I was the one who was the keeper of the keys, so I had the opportunity to keep it going, and given that that was an enormous task, I tried to do things that were aesthetically pleasing to me and creatively responsible for the franchise.

'The casting was my responsibility, but I had bosses. I couldn't just wave my wand and have whoever I wanted. Paul McGann was always my first choice, but he joined the project late, and there was a reason for that; it was my responsibility to go out into the field, as it were.'

McGann himself was reluctant to become associated with the project, and in fact initially declined, unable to see himself in the role as it was popularly presented in the media as an outrageously costumed eccentric. In the end, however, he was won over.

Also instrumental in shaping the eighth Doctor's character was writer Matthew Jacobs. 'He had very strong opinions about what the Doctor should and should not be,' acknowledged Segal. 'There was a lot of Matthew's influence in the material ... I specified areas that I felt were very important for us to touch on and that I felt were central to the Doctor's world, and Matthew really ran with it. We had numerous conversations about things that we could and could not touch on. He was terrific, in that he was like a sponge: once he got an idea of the direction I wanted to go, he was very good at picking up the ball and taking it on to the next step. There's very much his imprint on the material. I think he did quite a good job, all things considered.

'When Paul was cast, the thing took on a life of its own. Paul brought his own unique qualities to the role. The first time I saw him on set in his costume, it was pretty uncanny. There was one moment where I didn't think he ever wasn't the Doctor. Once he settled down, I think he felt the same way. I don't know what the general perception was from the audience, but I believe it was fairly positive.'

Any attempt to evaluate the eighth Doctor's character on the basis of just a single adventure is inevitably fraught with difficulty. (To realise this, one need only consider how skewed an assessment would be gained from considering in isolation the debut stories of each of the other Doctors.) Some fan commentators have attempted to do so, however, and a particularly perceptive summation was made by Lance Parkin in *Matrix* Issue 53 dated autumn 1996: 'The eighth Doctor acts impulsively, without planning. He lacks arrogance, instead demonstrating child-like qualities of wonder and boundless energy. Everything is done in earnest, with a passion. He fixes on things and is capable of brilliant improvisation.'

As the Doctor himself says to Grace in the movie: 'I can't make your dream come true forever, but I can make it come true today.'

Production Development

It was in 1994 that Philip David Segal, an Englishman working as head of television production at Stephen Spielberg's Amblin company in the USA, was granted by BBC Enterprises the rights to make a new series of *Doctor Who*. This was an ambition that he had been pursuing ever since the BBC stopped producing the series in 1989, as he explained:

'I wanted *Doctor Who* back. And that took a long time. Simply put, my aim was to rebuild the franchise; that was the object of the exercise, to bring it back. There was a period of time at the BBC where there was a real willingness to do that, so I took advantage of that, and that's essentially how we got *Doctor Who* back.

'That intensified and really became real in 1993; that was when it really became real in terms of actually negotiating a deal with the BBC and wanting to move forward.'

Segal's intention was always to make a television series rather than a feature film, so the fact that the BBC had already granted the *Doctor Who* film rights to the group now known as Daltenreys presented no obstacle. 'We had no interest in making a feature film,' he confirmed. 'That was always the case. I made it very clear from the very beginning that I didn't think that it should be relaunched as a feature film; that there was still a lot of work that had to be done in terms of television; but that ultimately one day it could become the basis of a film ... We had some dialogue with Daltenreys, but nothing that really meant anything significant to me. The sad thing about it is that you don't like to see anyone spend the kind of money they did and not get anywhere, which they did. I feel bad for them in that regard. But it had no bearing on what I was doing.'

The project was initially envisaged as a three-way co-production between BBC Enterprises, Amblin and Universal Television in the USA. Writer John Leekley was commissioned by Segal to put together a 'series bible' – a detailed document outlining, partly for the benefit of potential purchasers, the concept and its intended treatment – and the script for a movie-length pilot episode. The bible turned out to be a lavish affair. Printed on a parchment paper and bound in a real leather cover embossed with the Seal of Rassilon, it purported to be written by Lord Borusa and charted the history and activities of a Time Lord known as the Doctor. By way of illustration, several new pieces of black and white artwork were used (including a sequence of drawings showing some redesigned 'spider' Daleks) along with more familiar (to *Doctor Who* fans) images intended to give an idea of what the characters and settings might look like. To illustrate the section on the Master, for example, Segal used a photograph of Michael Jayston as the Valyard from *The Trial of a Time Lord*, simply because his flowing robes and dramatic appearance matched the style and vision he and Leekley had for the Master. Similarly, to depict an effective alien being, an image was taken from the cover of one of Virgin Publishing's New Adventures novels, *Birthright* by Nigel Robinson.

Leekley's script for the pilot movie featured the Daleks, Davros and the Master in a story set partly on the Doctor's home planet, Gallifrey. Entitled simply *Doctor Who* (although the writer later suggested that *Fathers and Brothers* would have made a good subtitle), it was completed in September 1994, but ultimately failed to find favour. Robert de Laurentis was then commissioned to provide a replacement; his attempt, entitled *Dr Who?*, was completed in December 1994. Segal was at this time attempting to sell the series to the Fox television network, although when problems arose in his negotiations with them, he also entered into discussions with a number of other networks. 'Fox didn't decline it,' he explains. 'There was a situation that happened where there was a distinct split between Amblin and Universal that caused a derailment of the project. It wasn't Fox's fault. But the situation sort of reorganised itself when an executive called Trevor Walton, who is English, came to Fox. We had had serious offers from CBS at that time as well, although they ultimately declined.'

Walton was in Fox's made-for-television movie division, which meant that the project was now seen primarily in that light. 'In our eyes, it was still a pilot for a series,' commented Segal, 'but it was produced through the movie division of Fox and not the TV division. It's not unusual, though, for a two hour movie to be made by the movie division and still end up being treated as a pilot; it's standard in the States. In this situation, you would be canny enough to produce it to look like and feel like and smell like a pilot, so that it had enough story to satisfy a two hour movie audience but at the same time had enough strings so that you could see the character returning. So there were deliberate attempts on our part to package the movie in that way, to give us the basis for hopefully a good series.'

At the Gallifrey convention in February 1995, Segal showed attendees a video featuring some test images of a new computer-generated title sequence (very similar in style to the one used during the fourth Doctor's era) and of a redesigned race of armoured, spider-like Daleks. He also gave a short slide show displaying some early set and prop ideas prepared by one of the movie's production artists.

Segal had always been keen that his version of *Doctor Who* should be true to the spirit of the original, and he found that Walton was much more sympathetic toward this idea than had been his colleagues in Fox's TV division. Walton, for instance, agreed with him that the movie should if possible be explicitly linked to the continuity of the BBC series by opening with Sylvester McCoy's the Doctor and leading up to a regeneration, whereas the TV division executives had wanted it to stand completely apart from what had gone before, to the extent that he had considered having dialogue included in the script indicating that it took place in a parallel universe (drawing inspiration from a an idea presented in the third Doctor story *Inferno*). A new script was thus required and, although established series writer Terrance Dicks was on the short-list of potential writers, it was eventually commissioned from Matthew Jacobs, another Englishman who already had experience of working in American as well as UK network television.

'It was actually Trevor Walton who had worked with Matthew and asked us to consider him and meet him,' noted Segal. 'The networks rarely make demands over things like that. Usually they will allow you to make a case for a particular writer. However, there were reasons why Matthew made sense to me. When I sat and talked with him at Amblin, it turned out that his grandfather had been an actor in the Wyatt Earp episode of *Doctor Who* [Season 3's *The Gunfighters*, in which Anthony Jacobs played Doc Holliday]. His relationship with his father had been an incredibly rocky one, and when his father had eventually died, they had not been reconciled, so there was this real emotional kind of bridge that this script was going to build for him. And I liked his writing style. He's a very colourful individual and brought a lot of colour and passion to the project, so I was very pleased indeed with the choice.'

Jacobs started working on his script around April 1995, and the first complete draft was dated 18 July. Segal recalled the factors that had influenced its development:

'It was a pretty fast track once we got going. There were a couple of glitches in the story as we went though. Some that I thought were good changes and some that I was disappointed with. Ultimately there was more than one voice in that script, so that's the struggle that I had.

'We knew that the Doctor had to have a companion, simply from the mechanics of the franchise. The problem with the Doctor is that unless he has someone to ask what he's doing or thinking, the audience never gets to know what he's doing or thinking. That's just the flaw of the process.

'I think we first set about trying to think where the location should be. We knew it had to be in the United States for identification reasons, but we also wanted it to be a place that had some universal awareness of it. Most people know of San Francisco, and it's my favourite city in America. The last place I wanted it to be was Los Angeles; it would have felt just so clichéd, for some reason. San Francisco didn't seem clichéd. It had a sort of mystique to it that Los Angeles didn't have. It didn't hurt that Matthew lived in San Francisco. We started to formulate the story out of this, and it changed dramatically as we went along. Matthew's first impressions had a lot more emotionality for Chang Lee than we ultimately ended up with.

'The hospital thing was something that we were also playing around with. We didn't really get all the mileage out of that, really.

'There were several companies that needed specific things, and there was definitely a distinct difference between Fox's need for something with an adult appeal and the familiar perception of *Doctor Who* as a family or children's show. The end product was not necessarily what the BBC wanted, but how far they were prepared to go. They were extremely collaborative with me at various points. Alan Yentob was, and is in my opinion today, this project's best friend. That's just a reality from my eyes. This is the man who, through thick and thin, has supported this project and who still believes in *Doctor Who* as a franchise. He's in a very difficult position. One's philosophy has to be to let management manage, so if you hire someone to do a job, you have to stay out of their way and let them do it; he can make suggestions, but he really has to let people manage.'

Amblin (where Segal had earlier been given a co-executive producer in the person of fellow Englishman Peter Wagg) dropped out of the picture in 1995 after Spielberg joined forces with former Disney executive Jeffrey Katzenberg and music mogul David Geffen in a new company called Dreamworks SKG. Segal left the company in September, and went on to produce the movie independently, as a joint venture between the BBC (eighty percent of whose financial input came from BBC Worldwide, as BBC Enterprises had now been renamed, and twenty percent from BBC Television) and Universal. Fox also had a financial input into the movie.

'The production office was located in the Spelling complex. We leased out some space in Barnerby, just outside Vancouver. That was where the stages were. Locations were in and around Vancouver proper. The production itself was housed in Barnerby, and I had an office there. During pre-production, I was moving backwards and forwards between Los Angeles, Vancouver and London. I also spent some time in New York doing casting. But I worked out of my office on the Paramount lot.

'Universal gave me a boss by the name of Alex Beaton. This was because I was somewhat alienated from the studio – I wasn't somebody they had a tremendous love affair with, let's put it that way – and they wanted to make sure their interests were protected. But Alex and I got on very well. His job was basically to manage the money. He never interfered creatively at all with the production – nobody did, I had the final say in all creative matters – but when it came to the financial side of things, and I fought for what I wanted, I won some battles and I lost some battles.

'Then there was a producer by the name of Peter Ware, who basically managed the physical production. There was also a unit production manager called Fran. He was a fabulous guy. It was his below-the-line crew that worked on the movie.

'Richard Hudolin was the production designer, and was first class. He and I got on like a house on fire. I told him exactly what I wanted to do, and it was done.

'The amazing thing about a lot of these people is that they immediately went out and got every *Doctor Who* book that existed and looked at everything that had been done in the past. So many of them were fans. There was a real passion to get everything right, and sometimes they'd go overboard. The funny thing about it, of course, is that as you dip into *Doctor Who*, you're taking from thirty years of mythology. It's interesting to see people's reactions when you take material from different eras, mixing them up and putting them all in one thing. Some fans look at you and say, "You can't do that!" I thought it was wonderful to take from the cupboard of mythology and just paint a new picture. That's what we did with this production to a certain extent. We painted details throughout it that gave you a taste of the traditions of the show.

'Jo Wright from the BBC was ultimately given the title of executive producer in the end credits; she was the BBC's person.

'Each of the organisations involved had to have its own person; that's the reality of life. Trevor from Fox never got a credit; American network executives don't get credits on movies. He was the big boss. He was the one looking over scripts. I must say he was very supportive of me in the process. What happens is that once a network commits to a project, it goes into a slot and the clock ticks. The pressure is to deliver that project for that time slot, because there's nothing else to fill it; they don't double develop and double produce. So once *Doctor Who* had been given a firm airdate, which we knew at the start was 14 May 1996, we were on a runaway train. Five months to make it, with no excuses. Trevor's job became much more difficult, because the studio wanted to cut corners to save money, it had other agendas; the BBC had its own agenda; and BBC Worldwide had its own agenda – although the truth of the matter is that it was not managing anything.'

The completed movie was delivered to Fox about a week before it premiered. It was promoted with the tag-line 'He's Back – And It's About Time,' and US newspaper critics gave it an almost universally positive reception. In ratings terms, however, the movie ultimately underperformed. This was partly due to the fact that it was up against some very strong competition from the other networks, including a much-anticipated episode of the comedy series *Roseanne* in which the title character's husband, played by John Goodman, suffers a heart attack. In Segal's view, however, there were other underlying political reasons why it did less well than it might have:

'When you really go into the mechanics of why *Doctor Who* didn't get a bigger audience, that would require a two hour dissertation on who the Fox network actually are, who their station groups are, what their demographic audience is ...

'If you had put that same movie on a different network, at a different time, with different promotion, away from the sweeps – which is programming designed to hype the network – you may or may not have had a different result. I can't sit here and say to you, "Oh my show would have done a 20 share anywhere else." I don't know that. There may truly have been some problems with the female appeal of the show, the audience awareness of *Doctor Who*, the story itself. There may have been a lot of things working against us.'

In the UK, the movie did much better, winning very good ratings and generally enthusiastic audience feedback. There were over 100,000 copies sold of the BBC's video release of the production, some 55,000 copies of Gary Russell's novelisation and even some 15,000 copies of the script book. Total worldwide sales of the video release were in excess of 150,000 copies. Universal retained an option on *Doctor Who* until the end of 1997, but in the event, did not take it up.

'Several things happened that made it very clear that it wasn't going to be a series,' reflects Segal, 'least of which was the fact that it underperformed. I was also very tired – eighteen hour days, not seeing your family, the stress and the politics, it does take it out of you. There was another regime change at Fox; there were regime changes all the time at the BBC. The movie itself happened for very specific reasons; it wasn't just because I pushed hard enough, there were other reasons, and we got caught up in the tidal wave. All the fans could really see was that it was coming back, but the truth on the inside was that it was a limited time offer – get it now while it's available. But that's another story.'

Even though the movie did not, in the end, lead on to the hoped-for series, Segal was well satisfied with the end product:

'My job as producer is to bring all the elements together. I think it's ultimately a mistake to try to impose your will on people. That's a dangerous thing to do. I think the object of the exercise is to bring together the best people you can get hold of and give them the room and the opportunity to be the best that they can be. That's something that I take a lot of pride in. I'm very strong when it comes to what I want and don't want, but I also feel that once I've had my two cents' worth, it's very important to take two giant steps back and let people do their jobs. If I feel that the wheels are coming off, then I'm quite happy to jump in and to try and fix that.

'I feel that what you saw there was a chorus of very talented people who came together and made something very special, in my opinion. I'm very proud of it. For all its faults and for all the problems and things like that, I think we did a damn good job, given the rules that we had to play by, I think we did the best we could. I feel that everyone did the best that they could do, and I'm certainly very proud of it.'

As for the future, Segal asserts: 'I really believe that *Doctor Who* will be back again. I really do. Whether it's me or someone else who makes it. You can't kill *Doctor Who*. It will never die.'

Rewriting the Myth

Throughout *Doctor Who*'s history, each successive change in the series' behind the scenes team led to a development of its style and content – and of its mythology. Never was this more true than of the 1996 television movie.

The action opens with a seventh Doctor who is visibly older than when last seen. He also seems to have dramatically reconfigured his TARDIS interior, which now has a very gothic, 'Wellsian' look to it – appropriately enough, given that he is seen reading a copy of Wells's *The Time Machine*. The possibility of such reconfiguration had been well established in earlier stories – some of which, including Season 15's *The Invasion of Time* and Season 19's *Castrovalva*, had made explicit reference to it – but the change seen here is the most radical to date. Even more novel is the revelation that the ship contains in its Cloister room an Eye of Harmony. Season 14's *The Deadly Assassin* had suggested that there was just a single Eye of Harmony, the source of all the Time Lords' power, located on Gallifrey; now it seems that every TARDIS must contain a fragment of the Eye. This does make some sort of sense, as it is difficult to see how otherwise the power from a central source could reach the ships, given that they can go anywhere in space and time.

The Eye as seen in the television movie appears to have many properties and functions aside from simply powering the TARDIS. It is somehow connected to the Doctor himself, and can 'see' what he sees. It can also project images of his earlier incarnations and, when correctly set up, can actually transfer one Time Lord's remaining lives to another (as the Master attempts to do here). Perhaps the strangest idea is that it can actually swallow the Master whole, a process that apparently gives the TARDIS 'indigestion'. Also remarkable is the fact that it is able to restore life to both Grace and Chang Lee after the Master has killed them. This could perhaps be viewed as a result of the TARDIS moving back in time to the point before the Eye destroyed the Earth, although an alternative explanation might be that it stored the life essence of the Doctors' two friends when they died and then returned it to them once time had resumed its normal course. The Doctor's own observation is that the TARDIS is sentimental.

The Doctor's regeneration on this occasion is a delayed reaction to him being shot and actually dying on the operating table, his alien metabolism adversely affected by the anaesthetic and by Grace's manipulation of a heart probe. Following the regeneration, the new Doctor goes through the customary period of confusion before recovering fully.

One of the most talked-about aspects of the television movie is its revelation that the Doctor is half-human. This, however, ties in quite well with what has gone before. For one thing, it helps to explain why the Doctor has always seemed to have such an affinity for the Earth and its indigenous people. (The Doctor talks of seeing Gallifreyan skies with his father, and mentions that he is half-human on his mother's side). It could also explain why his grand-daughter Susan wanted to attend school in England. In addition, it provides possible answers to the questions raised about the Doctor's identity in the series' twenty-fifth and twenty-sixth seasons – including the suggestion that he was more than just a Time Lord – and how he managed to return to Earth at the end of *Survival*.

Another fact revealed in the movie is that when a Time Lord reaches the end of his regenerative cycle, he can apparently change species. The Master has become (whether or not by his own choice is left unclear) a reptilian, snake-like creature. With this change, he has acquired the power to change form; to spit a burning venom that can immobilise the victim; and to possess those 'marked' with the venom.

There is arguably only one major aspect of the movie's plot that it is difficult to reconcile with what has gone before. This is the aforementioned idea of the TARDIS travelling back in time to a point before the Eye of Harmony was opened so as to prevent the disaster precipitated by the Master. This flies in the face of many previous assertions made by the Doctor about him being unable to change the course of history – as, for example, when his companion Adric was killed at the end of Season 18's *Earthshock* – and undermines the whole basis of the series' format by raising the question why he does not always simply travel back in time to thwart all his adversaries' schemes before they have even got off the drawing board.

It is a pity that this one less than satisfactory aspect marred what was otherwise an admirable production from the point of view of the use and development of *Doctor Who* mythology.

Selling the Doctor

MEDIA
By Ian Wheeler

Doctor Who has always been considered newsworthy by the British media, who over the years have expressed both love and hatred for the series – often according to the whims or prejudices of the particular journalist responsible. The Sylvester McCoy era was no exception, and in fact proved to be perhaps the most controversial period of *Doctor Who*'s history as far as press reaction was concerned. In 1985, during Colin Baker's time as the Doctor, the tabloid newspapers had campaigned to save the series when it appeared that it was going to be axed. By 1987, it was clear that things had changed, and that the seventh Doctor was going to get a somewhat rockier ride.

On 28 February 1987, the *Sun* was the first to report the identity of the seventh Doctor. Under the headline 'New Doctor Who is the Unknown McCoy', Charles Catchpole wrote: 'A zany Scot who used to make a living by stuffing ferrets down his trousers is the new Doctor Who'. The paper referred to McCoy as 'a shock choice', adding that other hopefuls had included former companion actor Frazer Hines (who had, in fact, never been under consideration).

The *Sun*'s exclusive was followed by reports in other papers on 3 March (an announcement of the new Doctor's identity having been made on the television news the day before). A number were quick to point out McCoy's lack of celebrity status but, more positively, some also reported that the actor had been awarded a three year contract. In *Today*, McCoy was quoted as saying: 'I might not be all that well-known, but that's going to change. People have been telling me for years that I'd be perfect to play Doctor Who, and I'm going to prove them right.'

The launch of the new Doctor was somewhat overshadowed by the news at the end of March that one of his predecessors, Patrick Troughton, had died following a heart attack at a *Doctor Who* convention in the USA.

The first reports of the new season came at the beginning of April, when a modest number of papers featured the new Doctor in costume on location for *Time and the Rani*. Details were sparse, with particular emphasis being given to the fact that Kate O'Mara was also appearing in the story. A more informative item on the making of the story was however to be seen on the BBC's *Breakfast*

Time programme on 5 May. Other TV coverage of the series during this period included items about the location recording of *Delta and the Bannermen* on BBC Wales on 31 July and on BBC1's *But First This ...* on 31 August.

It was in September, with the twenty-fourth season now beginning on BBC1, that the new Doctor really began to make his presence felt. The *Star* promised that the new-look show would be 'the glossiest ever', going 'flat out for fun' with stars such as popular comedy actor Richard Briers. Meanwhile, the 5-11 September edition of the BBC's listings magazine *Radio Times* featured the seventh Doctor in full colour on page three with an additional article included as part of the 'John Craven's Back Pages' feature.

The reviews for *Time and the Rani* proved to be less enthusiastic than the pre-publicity. McCoy was nominated 'Wally of the Week' in the *Daily Express* and described as being 'bland' and 'a joke' in the *Sunday Post*. Paul Mount, television reviewer for the monthly science fiction magazine *Starburst*, also expressed dislike for the new series, but at least admitted to McCoy being 'convincing in a way that neither Peter Davison or Colin Baker ever were'.

October began with the *Sun* reporting that the BBC had axed *Doctor Who* after twenty-four years. This 'exclusive' went on to say that the show was losing viewers every week and that the current series would be the last. Days later, the *Sun* was claiming to have saved the show, adding that a new movie produced by Coast to Coast was set to appear in November 1988.

At the end of October, a more encouraging piece appeared in the *Daily Mirror*. The article focused on the appearance of comedian Ken Dodd and actor Don Henderson in Malcolm Kohll's *Delta and the Bannermen*. According to the report, *Coronation Street* had failed to kill off the Doctor, with the Time Lord attracting 'an audience of more than five million'.

The floodgates really opened in November, the month of the series' 24th anniversary. McCoy gave an interview to the *Daily Express* during which he was quoted as saying 'I believe the Doctor is still valid in the *Star Wars* generation'. The week after, the *Star* printed a disturbing article with the headline, 'Who's a Load of Rubbish?'. Fans were said to be dissatisfied with the series and were calling for producer John Nathan-Turner to be sacked. This was prompted by campaigning reports in the fanzine *DWB*, a source to which several newspapers turned for their more sensationalist coverage of the series.

Later the same month, the *Daily Telegraph*'s Charles Spencer reviewed *Dragonfire* Part One, and was generally supportive, referring to McCoy as 'an appealing Doctor with a genuine sense of wonder and a nice line in irony'. He was, however, not entirely without reservations, and felt that the new Doctor could do with 'a little less whimsy and a shade more authority'.

Following *Dragonfire*'s spectacular climax, in which the villain Kane melted on screen, the *Star* reported that angry mothers had phoned the BBC to complain about the sequence. The editor of *DWB*, Gary Levy, was quoted as saying: 'This new controversy will prove more damaging'.

'The Daleks are back!' was the very clear message carried by most of the national newspapers in the spring of 1988. 'Doctor Who has defeated his greatest enemy – former BBC1 chief Michael Grade,' reported the *Daily Express*, 'and when he returns to BBC screens in the autumn, Doctor Who will take on his other deadly foe – the Daleks'. And according to the *Sun* on the same day, 'The Daleks are as evil as ever, but they have swapped their dull grey metal jackets for a gold and white livery'.

A colour article in the *Radio Times* heralded the return of the Daleks as part of BBC1's autumn season: 'Those evil, heartless, cruel, diabolical Daleks are back – and the latest Doctor Who is rather pleased about it!' John Davies' full page feature included comments from Sylvester McCoy, John Nathan-Turner and writer Ben Aaronovitch. Each had his own opinion on the secret of the Daleks' appeal, with Aaronovitch commenting that: 'They are beings within machines rather than just machines. If they were just robots, they'd be boring.'

Following some glowing reviews of *Remembrance of the Daleks* Part One, *Doctor Who* was the subject of an in-depth critique in the *Listener* magazine. 'Sylvester McCoy, the new and promising Doctor', wrote Mark Ball, 'faces the uphill grind of a series hopelessly locked in repetition, unable any longer to break out of its past.' A letter from Dr David M Duckels in the 10 November edition suggested that 'Sylvester McCoy seems set to establish himself as a vintage Doctor'.

A more controversial piece appeared in the *News of the World* on 13 November. 'Bertie Bassett Takes On Doctor Who' was the headline, following a protest from Bev Stokes, chairman of confectionery manufacturers Bassett's, about the alleged similarity between the Kandy Man from *The Happiness Patrol* and the company's famous marketing character, Bertie. 'We would like the programme to do something to restore Bertie's honour', Stokes commented. The Kandy Man's 'death' in Part Three of the story brought the matter to a quiet close.

The week of *Doctor Who*'s 25th anniversary saw the beginning in the *Radio Times* of a new feature called 'My Kind of Day'. McCoy was the subject of the first piece, and was shown sitting in a tree house. As the year drew to a close, the *Weekend Guardian*'s reference to McCoy as 'one of the best Doctors yet' boded well for the venerable Time Lord in 1989.

In May 1989, the *News of the World* asked 'Who's That Evil Parson?', referring to Nicholas Parsons' guest appearance in *The Curse of Fenric*. The actor commented that McCoy had 'been a joy to work with' and that he had 'never had so much fun in [his] life'. Rather less fun was had by Sophie Aldred in June when, as reported by the press, she was nearly killed in a water tank accident during studio recording for *Battlefield*.

The beginning of the twenty-sixth season in September was met with minimal press coverage, and even the *Radio Times*, once the show's greatest supporter, let the side down by running only a brief black and white article about Ace on the children's page. *TV Guide* was far more generous, featuring McCoy on its front cover and a two page report, 'What's Up Doc?', from the quarry location of *Survival*.

Ever a creature of habit, the *Sun* again claimed that *Doctor Who* had been axed on 21 October. Unfortunately, this time, it was true. 1989 came to a close with the series' future uncertain but, according to the BBC, at least safe.

1990 began with the news, on 5 February in the *Daily Express*, that Sylvester McCoy and Sophie Aldred had had their contracts withdrawn, and that the odds were firmly against them returning to play the Doctor and Ace. The paper claimed that independent companies were bidding to produce the twenty-seventh season, and that Dalek creator Terry Nation and Gerry Davis, co-creator of the Cybermen, were the favourites. Again these stories appear to have been inspired by reports in the fanzine *DWB*.

'Doctor Who could be in for a sex change,' suggested the *News of the World* on 26 August. Ex-companion Mary Tamm, who had been the first Romana during the Tom Baker years, was quoted as saying that she would 'love to play the Doctor'.

An interview with McCoy was published by the *Daily Express* on 9 October under the heading 'Doctor Who's the Real McCoy – by Sylvester'. John Munro reported that McCoy had 'fought his way back to the top in theatre' after his 'high-flying career was brought down to Earth when the BBC axed the show' and added that 'when the BBC mandarins finally get round to launching a new series, its odds on that the flamboyant McCoy will be playing the good Doctor'.

As the years rolled by, there were to be a great number of speculative newspaper articles about *Doctor Who*'s future, many of them bizarre and almost all of them inaccurate. Actors David Hasselhoff, Eric Idle, Pamela Anderson and director Steven Spielberg were just some of the names that were linked with a mooted *Doctor Who* TV series or movie. Fans had to wait many years before concrete news about the series' future was finally to emerge.

THE TV MOVIE
By Ian Wheeler

After years of speculation and many disappointments, the identity of the eighth Doctor was finally revealed to the world on 11 January 1996. All the major newspapers covered the story and reported that a television movie was in production. 'Our man McGann beats the stars to become new Doctor Who,' declared the *Daily Express*, obviously delighted that the role had gone to a British actor rather than an American. Amongst the celebrities whom it claimed had been considered for the part were Bill Cosby, Jack Nicholson and Alan Rickman, while the *Daily Star* reported that Simon Callow and the pop star Sting had both been in the running.

As the first new *Doctor Who* to be broadcast in over six years, the TV movie itself was understandably the subject of considerable media attention. For the first time in its history, *Doctor Who* had the honour of being featured on the front cover of the IPC-published listings magazine *TV Times* (which had at one time covered only ITV programmes). The magazine described McGann as 'the unlikeliest Time Lord – EVER!' and quoted him as saying that he wanted the Doctor to be 'a bit more edgy … a bit darker. It's also important to me that I have a hoot – and this *is* a hoot. I've got a good feeling about it now.' *Radio Times* also ran a *Doctor Who* cover and rewarded its readers with a free, sixteen page *Doctor Who* souvenir booklet. In addition, there was the promise of a new comic strip based on the series, which would begin in the following issue. This was written by Gary Russell and drawn by Lee Sullivan.

Initial press excitement about the Doctor's return was counterbalanced by a distinct lack of enthusiasm once the movie had actually been transmitted. Reviews were mixed, to say the least. Max Davidson of the *Daily Mail* commented that the movie 'was like a bad memory of childhood. I thought this absurdly inflated character had achieved his final resting place as a line in a knock-knock joke. Seeing the TARDIS again, in a vulgar American reincarnation, was too depressing for words. Do we never grow up?' Others were more positive, and the *Daily Express*'s review by Maureen Paton was fairly typical: 'At last we have a grown up hi-tech *Doctor Who* in Paul McGann … Only a low-tech Luddite would miss the endearing amateurism of the old teatime serial format … The makers would be mad not to pursue the option of a series.' Matthew Bond of *The Times* would probably have shared this sentiment, but felt that: 'If the series is to return, it will need stronger scripts than this simplistic offering, which struggled to fill eighty-five minutes and laboured somewhat in its search for wit.'

The general public were also determined to have their say on the movie, and the letters page of *Radio Times* for the week beginning 15 June 1996 was packed with viewers' comments. 'Paul McGann's performance in the new *Doctor Who* film delighted me,' wrote Simon Harries of Dartford. 'He brought an exciting new intensity and intelligence to the character, while still reminding me of Tom Baker at his most "other-worldly" and Patrick Troughton at his most mixed up'. Georgina Scott of Derby was also taken by the new Doctor and claimed that the BBC had given her a 'universally acceptable new sex symbol' in the form of McGann. Sean Coleman of Scunthorpe was more critical. 'The BBC should be exterminated!' he wrote, concluding that the Corporation had 'sold our dear old Time Lord down the Mississippi'.

In the pages of the *Doctor Who* fan press, there was an equally wide range of comments. *Doctor Who* Appreciation Society (DWAS) member Peter Lewis was 'pleasantly surprised and impressed' by the movie, whereas *Doctor Who Magazine* reader Michael Dax found it to be 'a god-awful mess'. Perhaps the best summary was offered in the DWAS's *Celestial Toyroom* newsletter by editor Keith Hopkins, who considered the project to be 'a success ... a qualified success perhaps, but a success nonetheless'. One way or another, the new movie had generated a huge amount of media and public interest, and *Doctor Who* had once again demonstrated its unique ability to make an impact and refuse to go unnoticed.

PERSONAL APPEARANCES
By Ian Wheeler

Of all the actors to have played the Doctor, Sylvester McCoy was one of the keenest to promote and publicise the series. Many people received their first glimpse of the new Doctor on 2 March 1987, when he emerged from the TARDIS on the Monday edition of the children's magazine show *Blue Peter* and chatted with presenter Janet Ellis about his hopes for the role. He also appeared on BBC1's Saturday morning children's show *It's Wicked* on 30 May. When Season 24 began transmission, *Doctor Who* was featured on *Open Air*, the BBC's daytime television discussion programme. McCoy was present, along with companion actress Bonnie Langford and producer John Nathan-Turner, and early viewer reaction to the seventh Doctor seemed to be positive. As his tenure progressed, McCoy was also to be seen on the youngsters' Saturday morning show *Going Live* (in 1987, and again in 1988 for *Doctor Who*'s 25th anniversary), the *Children's Royal Variety Performance* and the 1988 *Tomorrow's World Christmas Quiz*. In 1989, he joined TV presenter Noel Edmonds and comedy actor Jeffrey Holland on *The Noel Edmonds Saturday Roadshow*, and in November participated in the *Children in Need* telethon.

From late 1989 onwards, with *Doctor Who* no longer in production, McCoy tended to avoid wearing his seventh Doctor costume for personal appearances. He did, however, relate a *Doctor Who* anecdote or two to presenter Bruce Forsyth on the ITV game show *You Bet!* in 1990, and briefly stepped back into character for a BBC schools programme, *Search Out Science*, which also saw the return of Sophie Aldred as Ace.

When the ill-fated satellite broadcaster BSB ran a whole weekend of *Doctor Who* episodes and other related material – another first for the series – McCoy was one of the large number of stars to be interviewed about his involvement with it.

In 1993, McCoy joined sixth Doctor Colin Baker and a Tractator (from the fifth Doctor story *Frontios*) on *This Morning*, and the following year he appeared with Baker, fifth Doctor Peter Davison and actors Tim Brooke-

Taylor, Bill Oddie and Graeme Garden (otherwise known as the Goodies from the eponymous cult BBC series of the Seventies), for an item on animals on *Good Morning with Anne and Nick*. McCoy was invariably happy to be seen on screen with his fellow Doctors, and good fun and humour were always evident on such occasions.

Perhaps the most unusual appearance for McCoy's Doctor was not on television, but in the pages of one of the nation's favourite children's comics. In the spring of 1988, he was featured in the 'Strange Hill School' comic strip in *The Dandy*, being pursued, rather appropriately, by hideous monsters.

Advertisers were also amongst those eager to utilise McCoy's talents. He played the Doctor in a television commercial for the *Radio Times* in which he claimed to like the travel section of the magazine. On the radio, meanwhile, he participated in a commercial for batteries, which saw the Doctor up against his old enemies, the Cybermen.

This brief summary has highlighted those personal appearances by McCoy that were primarily intended to publicise *Doctor Who* or had an interesting *Doctor Who* connection. It should be noted that throughout his time as the Doctor, and beyond, McCoy was much in demand as a celebrity in his own right. He was frequently to be seen on a variety of light entertainment shows, his contributions ranging from being a mystery guest on the children's programme *Knock Knock* to appearing as a panellist on *The Holiday Quiz*.

Things changed dramatically when Paul McGann inherited the mantle of the Doctor in 1996. McGann was clearly a much more private person than McCoy, and was unwilling to be associated with the role in terms of public appearances. In interviews, he expressed a reluctance to attend any kind of *Doctor Who* convention, claiming that he lacked McCoy's ability to get up and entertain an audience. Consequently, the only appearance of the eighth Doctor in costume was in the television movie itself, and in related press photocalls, and the only on-camera interviews that McGann gave about the role were for the movie's 'electronic press kit', used by the Sci-Fi Channel amongst others to compile behind-the-scenes reports on the production, and the Bill Baggs-produced video documentary *Bidding Adieu*. It was the end of an era in more ways than one.

THE TWENTY-FIFTH ANNIVERSARY
By Ian Wheeler

1988 was a year of growing optimism for *Doctor Who* fans, and the series' 25th anniversary was celebrated in a quiet but enthusiastic manner. There was no special story reuniting old Doctors, as there had been for the 10th and 20th anniversaries, but the Cybermen were brought back in the three-parter *Silver Nemesis*; and, as Cyber Leader actor and sometime writer David

Banks remarked in his book *Cybermen*, 'It was thought ... that the Cybermen would make it an appropriately Silver Anniversary'. The season opener *Remembrance of the Daleks* also contained nostalgic elements and included a return to the junkyard in Totter's Lane where the Doctor had begun his televised travels in the winter of 1963.

Production of *Silver Nemesis* was covered by a crew from the US television station New Jersey Network for a programme entitled *The Making of Doctor Who* (one of a series of documentaries that NJN had made about the series). This was not transmitted in the UK, but would eventually be made available in edited form as part of the BBC's *Silver Nemesis* video release.

The British press were also keen to publicise the story, and chose to focus on the appearance of actress Mary Reynolds in a cameo as the Queen. Under the headline 'Her Royal Who-ness!', the *Star*'s TV editor Michael Burke reported on 29 June 1988 that 'new locations and a record budget of £1.5 million mean that the autumn anniversary series will be the best ever for fans all over the world'.

Sylvester McCoy, Sophie Aldred and third Doctor Jon Pertwee appeared on *Daytime Live*, a popular BBC interview show, to publicise the anniversary. The three actors stepped out of the TARDIS and answered questions from the audience (a group of *Doctor Who* fans who had been specially invited). McCoy was asked if he had been approached to take the lead role in the mooted *Doctor Who* feature film. He and Pertwee both seemed keen to be involved and expressed the view that all the surviving Doctors should appear in the film. Aldred meanwhile seemed delighted to be taking on the Daleks and the Cybermen in stories during the anniversary season. Clips of each of the seven Doctors were also shown on the programme.

Radio Times celebrated the milestone by running a retrospective article on the Doctor's many companions. There were also a modest number of merchandise items issued to commemorate the anniversary. These included an album featuring various versions of the theme tune and a selection of Keff McCulloch's incidental music from stories such as *Paradise Towers* and *Remembrance of the Daleks*; *Doctor Who – 25 Glorious Years*, a W H Allen hardback book by Peter Haining; a special *Doctor Who* playset from Dapol; a badge from the BBC; and two different 'first day covers' featuring the signature of one of the actors to have played the Doctor.

The first episode of *Silver Nemesis* was transmitted in the UK on the actual date of the anniversary. The night before, Noel Edmonds had mentioned the Doctor's birthday on an edition of his *Telly Addicts* quiz show. A trailer had also been extensively shown, utilising scenes from the new story and old footage of William Hartnell from Season 2's *The Web Planet*, to emphasise the series' longevity.

There was also a press call to publicise *Silver Nemesis*. This was held at Space Adventure, a new 'theme ride' located in London's Tooley Street, which boasted an exhibition of *Doctor Who* costumes and props. A photograph from this event of Sylvester McCoy and Sophie Aldred cutting a TARDIS cake appeared in the national press. Shortly after the anniversary, producer John Nathan-Turner was a guest on the afternoon show *Behind the Screen*, talking about the Doctor's past and future. A clip from the forthcoming adventure *The Greatest Show in the Galaxy* was shown, and when asked if there were any plans for a new Doctor, Nathan-Turner replied that he was perfectly happy with McCoy's portrayal.

THE THIRTIETH ANNIVERSARY
By Ian Wheeler

Doctor Who's 30th anniversary in 1993 was a time of surprises and disappointments. The main event planned for the year was *The Dark Dimension*. When this was cancelled, press coverage focused on the fact that Adrian Rigelsford's story had given the fourth and seventh Doctors by far the biggest slices of the action, with the third, fifth and sixth relegated virtually to 'guest appearances' – something that had greatly displeased actors Jon Pertwee, Peter Davison and Colin Baker when they had received copies of the script prior to any formal contract discussions taking place. A number of reports even suggested, incorrectly, that this was the reason why the special had been abandoned.

The two-part skit *Dimensions in Time*, involving characters both from *Doctor Who* and from the popular BBC soap opera *EastEnders*, was transmitted in November as part of the BBC's *Children in Need* telethon. This was featured on the front cover of the *Radio Times*, making it the first *Doctor Who*-related production to be accorded this accolade since *The Five Doctors* exactly ten years earlier. The BBC's popular science programme *Tomorrow's World* ran a report on the new 3-D process and also acknowledged *Doctor Who*'s anniversary by examining the concept of time travel as part of a special feature.

In addition to the *Children in Need* special, BBC1 broadcast the new *Doctor Who* documentary *30 Years in the TARDIS* and repeated the Season 10 story *Planet of the Daleks*, each episode of which was preceded by a five-minute mini-documentary examining one aspect of the series. BBC Radio 2 meanwhile had its own retrospective, *Doctor Who – 30 Years*, produced by Phil Clarke and narrated by Nicholas Courtney.

On the merchandise front, two commemorative video tins were released by BBC Enterprises. The first featured the Daleks and contained videos of Season 2's *The Chase* and Season 25's *Remembrance of the Daleks*, together with a booklet about the Daleks. The other was a TARDIS-shaped tin containing all fourteen episodes of Season 23's solitary story, *The Trial of a Time Lord*.

Both tins came in a variety of 'editions' featuring different photographs on their bases. Videos of *Resurrection of the Daleks* and *The Two Doctors* also arrived in the shops, having been designated the 'Fan's Choice' following a *Doctor Who Magazine* poll. Virgin released David J Howe's *Timeframe*, a lavish and colourful collection of photographs and artwork from the series' thirty-year history, which went on to become one of Virgin Publishing's best selling *Doctor Who* titles. Marvel Comics meanwhile produced a special magazine, stylistically based on the *Radio Times* publication in 1973 to celebrate the series' 10th anniversary, with Sylvester McCoy replacing Jon Pertwee in a similar cover photograph. The DWAS published their own glossy booklet with contributions from many of the series' stars, and Dominitemporal Services Ltd organised for them a huge convention in Hammersmith, London, with Doctors Jon Pertwee, Tom Baker, Peter Davison, Colin Baker and Sylvester McCoy attending. All but Tom Baker appeared on stage together in front of a delighted audience. Despite the absence of a new series of *Doctor Who* on television, the 30th anniversary was, all things considered, celebrated in fine style.

MERCHANDISE
By Ian Wheeler and David J Howe

During the McCoy years, the range of *Doctor Who* merchandise available continued to grow at an incredible rate. One notable development was the launching by a company called Dapol of a collection of poseable plastic figures, similar in scale to a famous *Star Wars* range. Early examples included models of the seventh Doctor, his companion Melanie, a Tetrap, K-9 and the TARDIS. They would later be joined by Daleks, Cybermen and an assortment of monsters and other characters. Dapol also manufactured children's versions of the costumes worn by the seventh Doctor and Melanie, and an adult-sized replica of the former's pullover, complete with question-marks.

Of the other new items that became available during McCoy's time as the Doctor, the most noteworthy included: a TARDIS telephone (manufactured by Holdcourt Ltd and costing nearly £100), which had the rare distinction of appearing on popular singer and television presenter Cilla Black's *Surprise Surprise* programme; *Doctor Who* bubble bath (also in the shape of the TARDIS); slippers; the initial volumes of a *Doctor Who* encyclopaedia (written by former *Doctor Who* Appreciation Society Co-ordinator David Saunders and published by Piccadilly Press); and a set of *Doctor Who* logo badges, cloth patches and magazine binders (commissioned by John Fitton Books and Magazines). Not strictly a *Doctor Who* item in itself, but still worthy of mention, is a single record entitled 'Doctorin' the Tardis'. This was based on and sampled 'Rock and Roll Part One' by Gary Glitter and was released in

1988 by a group calling themselves the Timelords, later revealed to be an incarnation of cult band The KLF. It eventually topped the UK music charts for one week in June and also appeared in various remixed forms, including most notably 'Gary in the TARDIS' featuring new vocals by Glitter himself.

The discontinuation of *Doctor Who* as an ongoing series in 1989 did little to decrease its popularity, and new merchandise continued to appear. The BBC video releases of old stories were one of the main growth areas. The number of new titles made available each year increased dramatically in the early Nineties, before decreasing again toward the end of the decade. In addition to 'standard' stories, special extended editions of *The Curse of Fenric*, *Silver Nemesis*, *The Five Doctors* and *Battlefield* were released. The BBC also produced and marketed a series of video documentaries, commonly referred to as 'the Years tapes', each of which featured themed clips and episodes and was introduced by one of the actors who had played the Doctor. The titles issued were: *The Hartnell Years*, *The Troughton Years*, *The Pertwee Years*, *The Tom Baker Years*, *The Colin Baker Years*, *Daleks – The Early Years* and *Cybermen – The Early Years*. Other special BBC video projects included: a completed version of *Shada*, the Season 17 story that had been abandoned due to industrial action, with the missing scenes bridged by narration from Tom Baker and a facsimile edition of the original scripts included in the package as a special bonus; and *More Than 30 Years in the TARDIS*, an extended and re-edited version of the *30 Years in the TARDIS* documentary.

The Nineties also saw major developments occurring in the world of *Doctor Who* publishing. With the appearance of John Peel's *The Power of the Daleks* and *The Evil of the Daleks*, the long-running series of licensed novelisations of the televised stories came to an end. (There remained four transmitted stories – *The Pirate Planet*, *City of Death*, *Resurrection of the Daleks* and *Revelation of the Daleks* – that had not been novelised, but these could not be done as the original scriptwriters had withheld their permission.) In their place, Virgin Publishing launched a range of original seventh Doctor novels known collectively as the New Adventures.

The publishers, at that time W H Allen, had first approached the BBC with the idea of presenting 'further adventures' of the Doctor in a letter dated 18 October 1985 from Nigel Robinson, the then editor of the novelisations, but John Nathan-Turner had replied that he was unwilling to consider such a move until January 1987 at the earliest. The idea had then been reactivated in a letter dated 6 February 1989 from new editor Jo Thurm, and again in one dated 30 August 1989 from her successor Peter Darvill-Evans. Following these approaches, Nathan-Turner had eventually agreed to the principle of the original novels being done. Darvill-Evans then prepared a detailed proposal, which was sent to the BBC on 1 February 1990. It was at this point that W H Allen was bought by Virgin Publishing. A large number of W H Allen staff were made redundant, and existing book ranges sold off to other publishers.

THE EIGHTH DOCTOR

The Target range of *Doctor Who* novelisations remained, however, and Darvill-Evans continued working toward his aim of publishing original *Doctor Who* fiction.

On 27 June 1990, Darvill-Evans sent out a press release inviting submissions from authors. One of the first to send in ideas was John Peel, whose work was liked by Darvill-Evans. His *Timewyrm: Genesys* consequently became the lead title in the initial four book 'season' featuring a creature called the Timewyrm. The second book, *Exodus*, was commissioned from experienced *Doctor Who* author Terrance Dicks, while the third and fourth came from ideas submitted by Nigel Robinson and new author Paul Cornell respectively. Robinson's had the working title *The God-Machine* but was renamed *Apocalypse* to follow the Biblical theme now decided upon for the titles of the Timewyrm books. Cornell's, which had the working title *Total Eclipse Rewrite* and was later retitled *Revelation*, was based on a short story that he had previously written for the fanzine *Space Rat*. Nathan-Turner disliked Cornell's submission but, as the television series was by this point no longer in production and the *Doctor Who* office had been closed down, Darvill-Evans decided to publish it anyway. The New Adventures were launched to the public on 20 June 1991. They were initially published at the rate of one every two months, but eventually moved to a monthly schedule starting with Gareth Roberts' *The Highest Science* in February 1993.

In July 1994, Virgin launched a complementary range of Missing Adventures – original novels featuring previous incarnations of the Doctor. The first entry in this range was *Goth Opera* by Paul Cornell, published on 21 July. Further titles followed, again on a bimonthly basis initially but quickly moving to a monthly schedule in September.

Virgin also continued to produce a range of factual *Doctor Who* books. Titles such as *The Sixties*, *The Seventies* and *The Eighties* and the series of Handbooks (of which you are now reading a new, compilation edition!) by David J Howe, Mark Stammers and Stephen James Walker won widespread critical acclaim. *Ace! The Inside Story Of The End Of An Era* by Sophie Aldred and Mike Tucker, which took an in-depth look at many of the seventh Doctor's adventures from the point of view of the authors (Aldred had played Ace and Tucker was one of the BBC's visual effects assistants), was also very popular. Other titles in the range included *The Gallifrey Chronicles* by John Peel, *Monsters* by Adrian Rigelsford, *Companions* by David J Howe and Mark Stammers, *Timeframe* by David J Howe and *Blacklight*, an extensive portfolio of Andrew Skilleter's *Doctor Who* artwork. Jean-Marc Lofficier updated his *Doctor Who Programme Guide* and also produced two further books, *The Terrestrial Index* (which included a chronology of the Doctor's adventures) and *The Universal Databank* (an A to Z of characters and terms from the series). Lofficier also wrote *The Nth Doctor*, a study of several aborted *Doctor Who* film projects; Lance Parkin was responsible for a more comprehensive chronology in *A*

History of the Universe; and, for those eager to see the funny side of *Doctor Who*, Paul Cornell, Martin Day and Keith Topping unleashed *The Discontinuity Guide*, and Chris Howarth and Steve Lyons came up with *The Completely Useless Encyclopaedia*. Virgin also published one unlicensed *Doctor Who* title called, appropriately enough, *License Denied*, a compilation of fanzine material edited by Paul Cornell.

In the spirit of the World Distributors *Doctor Who Annual*, which ceased publication in 1986, Marvel began publishing a series of Yearbooks. This ran from 1991 to 1995. They also launched a *Doctor Who Classic Comics* magazine, which over its twenty-seven issue run reprinted many of the Doctor's comic strip escapades from the Sixties and Seventies (in some cases with added colour) along with related interview and feature material, and a short-lived *Doctor Who* poster magazine.

Virgin's domination of *Doctor Who* book publishing was unsuccessfully challenged by Boxtree, who brought out a number of titles. The *Doctor Who Poster Book* and the *Doctor Who Postcard Book* were straightforward collections of photographs from the series. More ambitious was Adrian Rigelsford's *The Doctors – 30 Years of Time Travel*, which was unlicensed by the BBC and heavily criticised by reviewers for its many factual inaccuracies and major omissions, and its quoting of much interview material of uncertain provenance. Boxtree also published Rigelsford's *Classic Who: The Hinchcliffe Years*, a look at the *Doctor Who* work of producer Philip Hinchcliffe. The 'Classic Who' appellation was adopted in order to avoid the use of the BBC's own licensed *Doctor Who* logo. The BBC was nevertheless displeased that such books were appearing, and brought its weight to bear on the publishers. Consequently Rigelsford's final Boxtree book – *Classic Who: The Harper Classics*, featuring the *Doctor Who* work of director Graeme Harper – although originally intended to be unlicensed, was in fact licensed, and the appropriate credit given to the BBC. After this, Boxtree decided not to continue with further *Doctor Who* titles (four others – *The 500 Year Diary*, *The Making of 'The Dark Dimension'* and similar *Classic Who* books covering the *Doctor Who* work of director David Maloney and producer Barry Letts respectively – having been mooted by Rigelsford).

With no prospect of new *Doctor Who* appearing on television, groups of fans took matters into their own hands by producing on a professional basis a number of independent spin-off dramas designed for video release (although some were subsequently also transmitted on the Sci-Fi Channel, as were various different versions of a video documentary that took its title and cover image from Adrian Rigelsford's book *The Doctors – 30 Years of Time Travel*). The first such project – *Wartime*, starring John Levene as Benton, a character from the third and fourth Doctors' eras – was masterminded by Keith Barnfather and released in 1988 by Reeltime Pictures. Dreamwatch Media followed this up in 1994 with *Shakedown*, featuring established *Doctor Who* monsters the Sontarans and the Rutans. This was scripted by Terrance Dicks and directed by Kevin Davies and starred, albeit not in their familiar television roles, *Doctor Who* regulars Sophie Aldred and Carole Ann Ford and *Blake's 7* regulars Jan Chappell and Brian Croucher. The following year, Reeltime Pictures released *Downtime*, directed by *Doctor Who* veteran Christopher Barry and written by Marc Platt, who had scripted *Ghost Light* for *Doctor Who*'s twenty-sixth season. *Doctor Who* characters featured in this production included the Brigadier (Nicholas Courtney), Sarah Jane Smith (Elisabeth Sladen), Victoria Waterfield (Deborah Watling) and, providing the opposition, the Great Intelligence and its Yeti robots (as seen in the fifth season stories *The Abominable Snowmen* and *The Web of Fear*). 1997 saw the release of *Auton*, written and directed by Nick Briggs and featuring the return of the Nestene Consciousness and its killer plastic Auton mannequins from Season 7's *Spearhead from Space* and Season 8's *Terror of the Autons*. This was produced by Bill Baggs and released commercially by Reeltime Pictures, who also continued throughout the Nineties to add to their range of MythMakers video interviews with former *Doctor Who* cast and crew members.

Other video releases with looser *Doctor Who* connections included, as well as some one-off projects, the *Stranger* series featuring Colin Baker as 'the Stranger' and Nicola Bryant as 'Miss Brown' and several titles about an investigative organisation called PROBE, headed by the third Doctor's companion Liz Shaw (Caroline John), now elevated to the status of a professor. These dramas were produced by Baggs and also starred, in new roles, other well known *Doctor Who* actors including Peter Davison, Jon Pertwee, Colin Baker and Sylvester McCoy.

On the audio front, cassettes and CDs related to *Doctor Who* became more popular. It was possible to buy selected incidental music soundtracks (for *The Greatest Show in the Galaxy*, *Ghost Light* and *The Curse of Fenric* amongst others), talking book versions of certain novelisations, tapes taken from old off-air recordings of television stories otherwise missing from the BBC archives, and even audio equivalents of the spin-off drama videos.

When the *Doctor Who* television movie finally came to fruition in 1996, its transmission precipitated a minor flood of related items. The BBC themselves released a video of the movie (which was actually available to buy about a week before the UK transmission), a novelisation by Gary Russell, and a script book. Other items included posters, a record bag, a watch, a set of postcards and, in 1997, a CD of the soundtrack. This latter item was available only through specialist dealers as it was privately released by one of the composers, John Debney, as a promotional item.

A significant change in *Doctor Who* licensing came in 1996 when, as a direct result of their involvement with the television movie, the BBC declined to renew Virgin Publishing's long-standing fiction licence. This was so that they could take over publication of the range of original *Doctor Who* novels themselves. The switch came in May 1997, which saw publication of the final novels in the Virgin range, Lance Parkin's eighth Doctor New Adventure *The Dying Days* and Gareth Roberts' fourth Doctor Missing Adventure *The Well Mannered War*. The following month, the BBC's range began with *The Eight Doctors* by Terrance Dicks and *The Devil Goblins from Neptune* by Martin Day and Keith Topping. The BBC also released at this time a Paul McGann-narrated talking book of Gary Russell's novelisation of the movie and a postcard book of images from the movie. Further original novels then followed at the rate of two per month, one featuring the eighth Doctor and his new companion, Sam, the other featuring a past Doctor-and-companion team. Virgin, meanwhile, continued their range of New Adventures minus the *Doctor Who* logo (which they had actually dropped some months beforehand in order to help ensure a smooth transition) and with no BBC-owned characters, concentrating instead on the exploits of the Doctor's erstwhile companion Bernice Summerfield, who had been created for the range by author Paul Cornell some years earlier. From June 1998, these Doctor-less New Adventures moved from a monthly to a bimonthly schedule.

While Virgin retained an interest in factual *Doctor Who* publishing, the BBC also embarked on a programme of such books. The first titles to see print were *The Book of Lists* by Justin Richards and Andrew Martin and *A Book of Monsters* David J Howe. These were followed up by *The Television Companion* by David J Howe and Stephen James Walker and *From A to Z* by *Doctor Who Magazine* editor Gary Gillatt.

Doctor Who merchandise continues to sell well and at the time of writing, and there is no sign of the series' popularity waning. There have been many other items released in addition to those mentioned here – everything from calendars, posters and graphic novels to trading cards, playing cards and model kits. *Who's There?*, a biography of William Hartnell written by his grand-daughter, Jessica Carney, has been published; Tom Baker's autobiography, *Who on Earth is Tom Baker?*, was launched with a nationwide book signing tour by the actor and sold very well (as did a talking book version); and *I Am The Doctor*, a memoir co-written by the late Jon Pertwee and David J Howe, has been much sought-after. Other products released in the wake of the television movie include a BBC CD-ROM game called *Destiny of the Doctors*.

THE VIRGIN DOCTOR
By David Robinson and Richard Prekodravac

The sixty-one New Adventures novels published by Virgin took the characters and concepts of the television series and used them as the basis for stories, as they put it, 'too broad and too deep for the small screen'. The seventh Doctor as presented in the first sixty of these novels is a complex individual who is defined by his actions, by his relationships with his companions and by his place in the societies he touches. He is a dark Doctor, a clown, a horrifying alien. He is also someone who changes and matures, evolving from an apparently uncaring manipulator of events to a somewhat redeemed and responsible humanitarian. The novels' numerous authors created and developed not only a multifaceted seventh Doctor but also, along the way, a rich tapestry of new *Doctor Who* mythology, adding to that of the televised adventures.

MYTHOLOGY AND TIME'S CHAMPION

The first layer of mythology to be introduced was generically termed 'the Cartmel master plan'. Set out in a format document dated 9 November 1990, this was developed for Virgin by Andrew Cartmel, Ben Aaronovitch and Marc Platt based on ideas devised by them while working on the series' twenty-fifth and twenty-sixth seasons. It postulated the Doctor's origins and his connection with the Hand of Omega and the Other (a character from Aaronovitch's novelisation of *Remembrance of the Daleks*) and described Time Lord society as developing out of an era of superstition dominated by the powerful matriarchal Pythia (as subsequently featured in the fifth novel, Platt's *Time's Crucible*), whose rule fell with the establishment of a lasting curse that transformed Gallifrey into the society as seen in the televised stories.

The second layer of mythology established here was that of the Gallifreyan gods. These are Eternals who exist only as representations of archetypal ideas stemming from the Gallifreyan collective consciousness. Time, Death and Pain are the main gods used by the Gallifreyans as an aid to understanding the ideas they represent; Pain, for example, acts as a reminder of the sacrifice made by betraying friends (*The Left-Handed Hummingbird, Set Piece, Sleepy*). In order to prevent himself becoming his potential evil incarnation the Valeyard (as seen in season twenty-three's *The Trial of a Time Lord*), the Doctor became Time's champion in a deal with the Gallifreyan god (*Love and War, Millennial Rites*). This idea followed a Western literary tradition established by the classical Greeks: the hero as a champion to one of the gods. In this case it was essentially about the Doctor becoming responsible for the actions of his present and past incarnations. It was this acceptance of responsibility that caused him to become a much darker character. The Doctor would use the role of Time's champion as a technique to rationalise his thoughts and actions. Hence he would take up the mantle of someone who not only interceded in the problems of others but was also responsible for the consequences of his actions.

SELLING THE DOCTOR

THE DARK DOCTOR

The seventh Doctor in the novels was initially the character as presented on television. This had been firmly established in season twenty-five's *Remembrance of the Daleks* and perhaps best demonstrated in season twenty-six's *The Curse of Fenric*, where the Doctor defeats Fenric by betraying the trust of his companion, Ace. The first twenty-three New Adventures novels concentrated on this dark aspect of his character. He was someone who made deals with Death, Time and Pain and would ride roughshod over the feelings of his companions and friends in order to win the greater battles. Often unemotional and distant, he would sacrifice lives to win. He was described as being 'what monsters have nightmares about'.

The Pit presented perhaps the lowest point of this dark characterisation. In this, the twelfth novel in the series, the villain is a Gallifreyan named Kopyion who has been responsible for the deaths of millions of people on seven planets. The Doctor, controversially, makes no attempt to stop or even condemn his actions; it seems he is unable to take the high moral ground as Kopyion is a reflection of what he himself could become if his character were taken to extremes. The Doctor's development from *Remembrance of the Daleks* to *The Pit* was born out of the culture of the antihero such as in the *Terminator* and *Alien* films; the authors now realised that his character was ultimately self-destructive. This was highlighted in the twenty-first novel, *The Left-Handed Hummingbird*. Then in the twenty-third, *No Future*, the Doctor finally becomes aware that his actions are not only self-destructive but also hurtful to his companions Ace and Bernice.

THE HUMAN ALIEN

Even after the events of *No Future* the Doctor remains aloof, carrying the dark legacy with him. He becomes distant and detached, his alien nature being emphasised as something incomprehensible (*Sky Pirates!*). After Ace departs at the end of the thirty-fifth novel, *Set Piece*, he discovers a need to develop a sense of empathy and humanity. In the thirty-eighth novel, *Human Nature*, he strips all aspects of his Time Lord self away, including his physiology and memories, and becomes the human Dr John Smith. While this allowed author Paul Cornell to set up the Doctor's discovery of human values it also, more importantly, enabled him to explore what it meant to be the Doctor. It firmly established a broader conceptualisation of the Doctor as a whole person comprised of seven distinct personalities: he was not only the seventh Doctor but also *the* Doctor. This idea had been foreshadowed in the earlier novel *Transit*, the tenth in the series, when Ben Aaronovitch had poetically described him as 'all things to all cultures'.

THE EIGHTH DOCTOR

With the arrival of the eighth Doctor on television and imminent loss of Virgin's *Doctor Who* fiction license, plans were made to bring the New Adventures to a conclusion. The last few novels in the series emphasise the Doctor's redemption. He has carried the burden of blaming himself for the tragedy of his lifetime; he has sacrificed friends and companions, manipulated lives, betrayed friendships and trust, all in the cause of fighting and winning. He is conscious that he looks at the big picture at the expense of the important details (*Bad Therapy*) and knows that he cannot regenerate until he has faced up to the mistakes he has made.

THE HOUSE OF LUNGBARROW

In the penultimate novel, *Lungbarrow*, which picks up on events in *Time's Crucible*, the Doctor is forced to return to Gallifrey and rediscover his neglected family, the people of the strange House of Lungbarrow. *Lungbarrow* sees the Doctor learning of the power of the Hand of Omega and the nature of his identity. He has to accept and come to terms with his past and his family in order to move on. The truth is frightening but it defines the Doctor and, in doing so, heals him.

Commenting on *Lungbarrow* in Issue 14 of the fanzine *Broadsword*, Jonathan Blum wrote: 'Care as he does about what he believes in, fight as he does to do what he sees as right, he is never a tyrant, never in love with his own power, never out of touch with the small beauties and disappointments of life.'

Throughout the course of the New Adventures, the Doctor underwent a far more radical process of change and development than had ever been attempted on television. The novels also bequeathed a legacy of myth and theme that authors and readers alike have delighted in picking up and developing further. The seventh Doctor became an essentially tragic figure imbued with the compassion and eccentricity that can be found only in *Doctor Who*.

OVERSEAS

AMERICA
By Robert D Franks

Doctor Who's popularity in the United States was on the wane by the mid-Eighties, having hit its peak earlier in the decade with frequent airings of the Tom Baker episodes by PBS stations. John Nathan-Turner, realising the potential of the American market, was keen to reverse this trend, and actively sought out publicity opportunities. On 28 February 1987, a mobile *Doctor Who* trailer exhibition that had been touring the country for nearly a year made a scheduled stop at Mercer University in Georgia. Here, Nathan-Turner, accompanied by Jon Pertwee and Sylvester McCoy, joined it to announce that McCoy had been cast as the new Doctor. This occurred three days before the official BBC announcement in the UK.

Lionheart commenced distributing the McCoy serials toward the end of 1987 as television 'movies' – the episodes of each story being edited together into single 'feature length' adventures. *Doctor Who* was now saturating the American market, with over one hundred PBS stations carrying the series. Around this time, the newly formed Friends of *Doctor Who* group held several 'Day with the Doctor' mini-conventions which, although not on the same scale as the earlier Chicago events presented by the commercial Spirit of Light organisation, still attracted a large turn-out.

In 1992, with *Doctor Who* no longer in production and its future up in the air, the fledgling cable Sci-Fi Channel tried to negotiate with BBC Worldwide for exclusive American rights to transmit the series. It ultimately managed to secure a set of Tom Baker episodes. This however had an adverse effect on the PBS stations; when they found that they were no longer able to bill the series as 'exclusive', many started dropping it from their schedules.

Coinciding with this decline in the series' coverage of the American market there was, paradoxically, a revival of the large scale conventions both on the East coast and on the West. Two of these annual events – the Visions convention in Chicago and the Gallifrey gathering in Los Angeles – continue to attract a large number of fans each year.

CANADA
By Michael J Doran

The McCoy era marked a change in the way *Doctor Who* was seen in Canada. From 1976 until 1988, the provincial Ontario-only network TVOntario (TVO) had aired selected Jon Pertwee episodes (several of which, including *The Claws of Axos*, *The Curse of Peladon*, *The Mutants* and *The Time Monster*, were returned to the BBC as 525-line two-inch recordings in the early 1980s as the only broadcast-quality colour versions in existence), all but a couple of Tom Baker stories, and all Peter Davison and Colin Baker stories. With a Saturday evening time slot, the show had been able to develop a following similar to the one it enjoyed in the UK. The first local fan clubs had started up in 1978, and this activity had formed the basis for the *Doctor Who* Information Network (DWIN), established in 1980 and now the longest running *Doctor Who* fan club in North America. The twenty-fourth season was aired on TVO in the usual way, on Saturday evenings with a repeat the following Thursday evening. The run started with *Time and the Rani* Part One on 9

January 1989 and concluded with *Dragonfire* Part Three on 10 April 1989. In July 1989, however, it was announced that TVO had lost the *Doctor Who* rights to the recently launched nationwide youth-orientated cable network YTV. For the first time since 1965 (when the Canadian Broadcasting Corporation had aired the first five William Hartnell serials), *Doctor Who* would be available right across the country for Seasons 25 and 26.

One TVO insider put this development down to the network simply forgetting to renew the rights in time and YTV snatching them up. Nevertheless, it is unlikely that TVO would have been able to continue much longer as a broadcaster of *Doctor Who*, as it had been showing the series in blocks of approximately twenty-six episodes, its 'seasons' bearing no relation to the originals, and with the BBC now producing only fourteen episodes per year, this would soon have become impracticable. As it was, the twenty-third and twenty-fourth seasons were linked together for broadcast in Canada and the latter was aired only seventeen months after its UK transmission, whereas the gap in the past had generally been more than two years.

The twenty-fifth season premiered on YTV on 3 September 1989, in a 7.00 pm Sunday time slot, with *The Happiness Patrol* Part One, the stories being shown out of their UK transmission sequence. Due to a programming error (transmission of *The Greatest Show in the Galaxy* Part Four was delayed by a week as *Remembrance of the Daleks* Part Four was mistakenly rerun in its place), the run lasted fifteen weeks and finished on 10 December. Viewers had only a short time to wait for more new episodes, as the twenty-sixth season went out during the spring of 1990, in a 5.30 pm Saturday time slot. Again the stories were shown out of their UK sequence.

Between September 1989 and August 1994, YTV also aired, in a variety of afternoon, evening, and late night time slots, all the other complete stories that still existed in the BBC archives at the time. Fan reaction to YTV was often negative, particularly in Ontario where many viewers disliked the fact that – unlike on TVO in the past – the episodes were interrupted by commercials. The station nevertheless managed to bring *Doctor Who* to many Canadians who had never seen it before or who had previously had to depend on American PBS border stations. Their screenings were also the first opportunity that Canadian viewers had to see most Hartnell, any Troughton and many Pertwee serials.

Edmonton, Alberta TV station CITV was the first broadcaster anywhere in the world to air the Fox/BBC/Universal *Doctor Who* television movie (which had been filmed in British Columbia, Canada). This was transmitted on Sunday 12 May 1996 at 10.00 pm Canadian Mountain Time. The movie was also aired by CHCH Hamilton on 14 May at 9.00 pm Canadian Eastern Time. Both stations are available on a variety of cable systems across Canada.

SELLING THE DOCTOR

In 1998, *Doctor Who* was once again on cable in Canada. 'SPACE: The Imagination Station' purchased a run of episodes and aired the series commercial-free from Monday to Friday. The McCoy episodes were scheduled to follow on from this.

AUSTRALIA
By Damian Shanahan and Dallas Jones

The arrival of Sylvester McCoy as the Doctor coincided with a change in the way that *Doctor Who* was handled by the Australian Broadcasting Company (ABC). Instead of being dealt with by the Drama Department and screened in a 6.30 pm time slot, as had traditionally been the case, the series now formed part of *The Afternoon Show*, run by the Children's and Education Department, and went out an hour earlier. This change was made for two reasons. First, the ABC under the helm of Controller David Hill now had a policy of competing with the commercial networks, and *Doctor Who* was seen as lacking in audience-pulling power in an early evening slot dominated by the networks' current affairs programmes. Secondly, many viewers had actually requested such a change.

The new season was announced in September 1988 and commenced with *Time and the Rani* on Monday 31 October at 5.30 pm, running five nights a week. An ABC spokesperson indicated that the series would receive no publicity and would be cancelled if acceptable ratings were not achieved – a decision that shocked but did not entirely surprise Australian fans, given the new policy that had been adopted. The ABC declined to indicate what it would consider to be acceptable ratings, but there is no doubt that *Doctor Who* had never been particularly popular with the general viewing public in Australia. Its previous best performance had been an 8% share of the viewing audience for the 20th anniversary special *The Five Doctors*. Repeats of Tom Baker's stories, as movie length compilations on Saturday afternoons at 1.00 pm during this period, had received only between 3% and 5% – although this may have understated the series' true popularity, judging by an article in the *Sydney Morning Herald* on 27 February 1988 in which a spokesperson for the ratings company AGB McNair was quoted as saying of the new 'people meter' assessment devices: 'Some mothers tended to conceal the fact that their children were watching *Neighbours* or *Doctor Who*'.

Unknown technical difficulties resulted in a loss of vision for the opening titles of one episode of *Delta and the Bannermen*, but otherwise the transmission of the twenty-fourth season proceeded uneventfully, concluding with *Dragonfire* Part Three on Thursday 17 November.

Surprisingly, however, the run then continued with the following season's opening story, *Remembrance of the Daleks*, which aired from Friday 18 to Wednesday 23 November. This was a one-off advance screening arranged – apparently at the behest of *The Afternoon Show*'s host James Valentine – so that the ABC could properly celebrate *Doctor Who*'s silver anniversary. The remainder of the twenty-fifth season was not purchased at this stage, even though the twenty-fourth had won a significant increase on the poor ratings for the Saturday afternoon repeats and the previous 6.30 pm weekday transmissions – *Time and the Rani*, for instance, had gained a 6%-7% share of the viewing audience.

As in the UK, the anniversary period saw the release of the Timelords' 'Doctorin' the TARDIS' single, which entered the Australian music charts on 21 August at No. 8, rose the following week to No. 4, spent the next four weeks at No. 3 and then on 2 October peaked at No. 2. The later 'Gary in the TARDIS' remix failed to enter the Australian charts.

After *Remembrance of the Daleks*, the ABC recommenced screening repeats of the Tom Baker stories. It was not until August 1989 that premiere dates were confirmed for the remainder of the twenty-fifth season, which was to be preceded by a second run of all the earlier McCoy episodes. Originally the ABC planned to start this run on Tuesday 24 October, so that the first episode of *Silver Nemesis* would be transmitted on 23 November – enabling Australian viewers to see the start of the series' 25th anniversary story on the 26th anniversary! It was then realised however that a screening of cricket and golf would interfere with this (sporting events routinely being given priority over Children's and Education Department programmes), so, following consultation with the Australasian *Doctor Who* Fan Club, the ABC brought the start date forward to Friday 20 October and screened the stories in production order rather than UK transmission order. In this way, the first episode of *Silver Nemesis* still went out on the anniversary date, and the season eventually ended with *The Happiness Patrol* Part Three on Monday 4 December 1989. Some regional viewers had the last five episodes of the season delayed by the screening of a cricket match, but only by a few days.

The last three stories of Season 25 were repeated in a run that began on Tuesday 16 October 1990 and led directly on to the premiere screening of Season 26, publicity for which had been planned at a special meeting, as the ABC had viewed all the episodes and been very impressed with their quality. The season began with *Battlefield* Part One on 29 October and ran, as before, five nights a week, Monday to Friday at 5.30 pm, as part of *The Afternoon Show*. It concluded with the final episode of *Survival* on Friday 16 November.

SELLING THE DOCTOR

NEW ZEALAND
By Paul Scoones

The first the New Zealand television audience saw of Sylvester McCoy's Doctor was during Television New Zealand's *Doctor Who* 'Silver Jubilee' week of special screenings in November 1988 on TV2. *Silver Nemesis* was broadcast as an omnibus edition of all three episodes on Friday 25 November 1988. Part One had been transmitted for the first time in the UK just two days earlier, but New Zealand was the first place in the world to screen Parts Two and Three. The story was scheduled in a ninety minute timeslot from 4.30 pm to 6 pm, with commercial breaks and, between Parts Two and Three, a five-minute break for news headlines. Part One's opening titles were used at the beginning of the story and Part Three's closing credits at the end, and although the other opening and closing titles were removed, Parts Two and Three retained their opening reprises and episode numbers. Part One was cut, with about a minute missing from the point at which a commercial break occurred, although it is unknown whether this was an intentional timing edit or an accidental omission caused by the insertion of the commercials. Viewer ratings started at 7% for the first quarter hour of the story, then dipped to 6% and remained steady up until the last quarter hour when they dropped to 5%.

After experiencing the world premiere of *Silver Nemesis*, New Zealand viewers then had to wait more than a year to see further McCoy stories. The regular screenings (which had reached *Time-Flight* by the time of the 'Silver Jubilee' week) finally caught up to the McCoy era when *Time and the Rani* Part One screened 23 January 1990 on TV2. At this point, episodes were being transmitted Monday to Fridays at around 4.30 pm. This was the timeslot for the Season 24 episodes however from *Remembrance of the Daleks* Part One onwards *Doctor Who* was moved to Sunday mornings, beginning 18 February 1990, with episodes initially starting at 10.20 am and then, after the first two weeks, at 9.35 am. *Remembrance of the Daleks* Parts Two and Three were screened a fortnight apart to accommodate coverage of the Commonwealth Games.

Season 25 stories were screened in their production order, so *Remembrance of the Daleks* was followed by *The Greatest Show in the Galaxy*, *Silver Nemesis* (this time complete and in its original three-part form), and *The Happiness Patrol* in that order. Season 26 was however screened in its correct story order. An alternative version of *The Curse of Fenric* Part One was screened that lacked on-screen subtitles for the Russian soldiers' dialogue in the opening scenes, but otherwise the episodes were unedited.

The six-and-a-half-year run of *Doctor Who* episodes on New Zealand television, which had begun with The *Mind Robber* in April 1985, finally reached its conclusion with *Survival* Part Three on 16 September 1990. This was coincidentally the same weekend that New Zealand's first national *Doctor Who* convention with guests from the series took place in Christchurch. WhoCon 1990 was run by the New Zealand *Doctor Who* Fan Club and featured guest appearances by Jon Pertwee and Mark Strickson.

The 1996 television movie made its New Zealand debut on Wednesday 30 October 1996 at 8.30 pm on Television Two. TVNZ was offered both the uncut US version and the edited UK version of the movie, and opted to screen the former. It was watched by 13.2% of the potential viewing audience, which placed it higher than the programmes screening opposite on either of the other two channels and eighth in the top ten television movies and miniseries screened on New Zealand television throughout 1996.

The TV Movie was repeated on 3 July 1999, screening on a Saturday night on TV2 at 9 pm. The audience rating was 10.5%, which was consistent with ratings for other movies screened in the same timeslot.

FANDOM
By Ian Wheeler

The *Doctor Who* Appreciation Society (DWAS) had been at the centre of fan activity in the UK since its formation in 1976 and was still going strong when the seventh Doctor arrived in 1987. Its long-running newsletter *Celestial Toyroom*, now edited by Neil Hutchings, was a lively and well-presented mixture of news, comment and rather overt humour. Hutchings was succeeded by Brian J Robb in 1988, and although the layout became somewhat untidy, the contents still made for a satisfying read. The next permanent editor, following a short stint by Andy Lane and Andrew Martin in 1989, was Michael Proctor, who arguably inherited the newsletter at the worst possible time, as *Doctor Who* was no longer in production, news stories were hard to find, and the Society's membership seemed reluctant to contribute articles or features. Although Proctor made a brave attempt, it was not until Martin Kennaugh took over in 1990 that things began to improve and *Celestial Toyroom* once again became essential reading. Kennaugh remained as editor for four successful years. His assistant Keith Hopkins then took over, and the newsletter continued to go from strength to strength. Eventually, however, Hopkins left, and a succession of short-term editors then followed before Steve Haywood took over on a permanent basis in 1997. The DWAS's flagship magazine, *TARDIS*, also returned to regular publication in 1997, having made only sporadic appearances during the late Eighties, but somehow lacked the professional and authoritative edge that it had once enjoyed.

The DWAS had been irregularly beset throughout this period by problems in the running of its Membership Department, which had a knock-on impact on the distribution of *Celestial Toyroom* – members frequently received issues late and occasionally even in the wrong order. Another difficulty faced by the Society in the late Eighties was increasing competition in the form of glossy, independent fanzines. *The Frame* was one of the best examples, and contained a lively mix of rare photographs, interviews, features, fiction, artwork, humour and behind the scenes articles. Created and published by David J Howe, Mark Stammers and Stephen James Walker, it began in 1987 and ran until 1993, when the editorial team reluctantly decided that they could no longer produce the fanzine at the same time as writing their two series of non-fiction *Doctor Who* books for Virgin Publishing. *The Frame* took a balanced approach toward criticism of *Doctor Who*, not least because all three editors had a great affection for the series. *Doctor Who Bulletin*, on the other hand, was probably the most opinionated *Doctor Who* fanzine ever to be produced. Edited and published by Gary Levy (who later changed his name to Gary Leigh), it had been launched in 1983 but became increasingly critical of the series during the Sylvester McCoy years, and was particularly negative about the work of producer John Nathan-Turner.

While the opinions expressed by Levy and his contributors were often extremely harsh, they were not entirely unrepresentative; fandom was deeply split over McCoy's first season in particular. There were indeed some fans who had doubts about McCoy's suitability for the role of the Doctor right from the very beginning, and it was not only in the pages of *Doctor Who Bulletin* that negative comments appeared. After *Time and the Rani* Part One was broadcast, DWAS Co-ordinator Andrew Beech wrote an article for the *Daily Mail* in which he expressed the view that McCoy 'showed the glimmerings of a believable performance [but] the sight of the Doctor grinning inanely, prancing about and doing pratfalls over non-existent obstacles, uttering lines such as "absence makes the nose grow longer" and making a cheap joke of the role does not inspire confidence'. As McCoy settled into the role, however, he gradually began to win over his critics, and by 1989, his popularity was such that he was able to romp to victory in the 'favourite Doctor' category of the *Doctor Who Magazine* readers poll for that year.

Doctor Who Bulletin, or *DWB* as it was called on its masthead, was to remain highly outspoken throughout its long run. In 1989 it transformed into *Dreamwatch Bulletin* (which conveniently also abbreviated to *DWB*) and broadened its coverage to include a whole range of fantasy films and television programmes; then in 1994 it evolved into *Dreamwatch*, a successful, professionally published news-stand magazine.

While *The Frame* and most other glossy fanzines, including *Private Who*, *Proteus* and *NWE* (*New Whovical Express*), slowly faded away in the early

Nineties, a handful – most notably *Skaro* and *Matrix* – continued. There was also something of a revival of more modest, photocopied fanzines produced on a tiny budget and supported by a small readership and lots of enthusiasm.

Conventions and other special events remained an important part of the fan scene during the late Eighties and the Nineties. Dominitemporal Services Ltd on behalf of the DWAS continued to hold its large-scale PanoptiCon gatherings, generally on an annual basis, but here too faced increasing competition from independent fan groups organising their own successful events. Smaller-scale gatherings took place under the auspices of an ever-growing network of DWAS and independent *Doctor Who* local groups.

Other fan activities during this period included a number of campaigns to try to persuade the BBC to put *Doctor Who* back into production. These included the 'Target Who' letter-writing campaign directed at *Radio Times* and *Points of View* (a BBC viewers' feedback programme), which failed to make an impact as not a single letter was either published or broadcast. One group of fans even campaigned for funds to mount a legal challenge against the BBC's decision to drop the series, but this was ultimately abandoned.

Off-air audio recordings of Sixties *Doctor Who* episodes, including all those subsequently wiped by the BBC, had long been in circulation amongst the series' fans. In the Nineties, however, much clearer copies became available, mostly from the respective collections of Graham Strong, David Holman and David Butler. These have since been used by a number of fans to create video 'reconstructions' of the missing episodes (the picture usually consisting of a mixture of still photographs and video images, sometimes accompanied by captions describing the action and dialogue), and also in a few instances by the BBC itself, to replace poor quality soundtracks on episodes held in their archives.

The period beginning in 1987 and continuing into the 1990s was, overall, something of a golden age for fandom. Rather than withering away after the demise of *Doctor Who* as an ongoing series, it arguably became stronger and more focused than ever before.

VIEWER REACTION
By Ian Wheeler

Press coverage of McCoy's first season may have been far from enthusiastic, but it would be wrong to say that reaction to the arrival of the new Doctor was entirely negative. The response from the general viewing public – arguably those whose views mattered the most – was often very different. *Radio Times* ran a number of letters of comment from readers who had seen the new Doctor's debut adventure and enjoyed it. S Lancaster from Stoke-on-Trent wrote: 'The real Doctor is back ... For the first time in six-and-a-half years, I can't wait to see the next episode ...' Michael Proctor from Hertfordshire was equally impressed, referring to McCoy as 'an inspired choice'. In Scotland, the *Sunday Post* had some equally positive feedback. 'Sylvester didn't do much for me in the first episode', wrote Miss J Napier of Glasgow, 'but now I have to admit he's got me hooked'. J Robertson of Aberdeen appeared to agree: 'Sylvester is a good new Doctor and the story is fine. The series has definitely improved from last year.'

It wasn't all plain sailing for the series, however, and Margaret Francis of Bristol expressed some strongly negative opinions in the pages of the *Eagle*, the long-running British adventure comic, in January 1989: 'Sylvester McCoy must be the most wimpish Doctor Who ever, as he looks more like something out of a *Carry On* film than what is supposed to be science fiction. *Doctor Who* used to be a super series, but now it's like watching a pantomime, which is a shame'. The comic's fictional editor, a cheerful computer by the name of Max, responded: 'A jokey science fiction series is okay by me. Personally, I preferred *Red Dwarf*, but anyone who takes *Doctor Who* seriously should see a Dalek Doctor!'

Viewers' letters were not the only indication that the BBC had of viewer reaction to *Doctor Who*. They also had hard statistics in the form of an Appreciation Index, or AI, for each individual episode. In much the same way as ratings are compiled by studying the viewing habits of certain households, AIs are an attempt to gauge audience enjoyment in the form of a simple percentage. The higher the percentage a programme gains, the better it was received by those who watched it. The average AI for the twenty-fourth season was 60, with a high of 64 and a low of 57. These figures would generally be considered disappointing, but fortunately things improved over the next two years: Seasons 25 and 26 both gained an average AI of 68. This was still some way below the typical figure for BBC drama – which during the period of Season 26's transmission was 76 – but it should be remembered that *Doctor Who* had always appealed to a somewhat specialist audience and its AI figures were arguably 'diluted' by the reactions of casual viewers with little interest in the series. The AIs for the McCoy stories were, in fact, generally higher than those for the earlier Doctors' eras, although as methods of collecting the data had changed over the years, such direct comparisons can be misleading.

Other forms of statistic were collected by the BBC for Television Audience Reaction Reports. These included 'personal ratings' for the stars of programmes, based on surveys completed by a viewing panel. McCoy's rating was low to begin with, but rose after the twenty-sixth season, when 78% of those questioned found him 'likeable'. One viewer remarked that McCoy was '... naturally charming, not a mannered Doctor'. There were also three 'audience profiles' compiled during the seventh Doctor's era, giving a general picture of viewers' age, sex and social status. These were for *Time and the Rani, Remembrance of the Daleks* and the twenty-sixth season as a whole. From these, it would appear that an even greater percentage of *Doctor Who*'s viewers than in the past were adult – 74% for *Time and the Rani* and 78% for both the Dalek story and the twenty-sixth season. There also existed a very even balance between male and female (an exact 50/50 split for the twenty-sixth season). If any conclusion can be drawn from this information, it would arguably be that few programmes have brought together people of different ages, sexes and backgrounds in quite the way that *Doctor Who* managed in the late Eighties.

In 1989, when rumours started to spread that *Doctor Who* was coming to an end, the public were as determined as ever to have their say. The *Radio Times* letters page was once again a forum for debate. 'I hope that Jonathan Powell gets the sack as soon as possible as Controller, BBC1,' wrote Alan Dobbie from London. 'His decision to axe *Doctor Who* at the end of its present series shows that he doesn't understand what people really want. We want *Doctor Who* to continue'. Similar concerns were expressed by a contributor to the BBC's *Points of View*, who was told that there were in fact no plans to cancel the series.

It would be a long time before a new *Doctor Who* project would come to fruition, and viewer reaction to the 1996 Paul McGann television movie is covered elsewhere in this book. Later the same year, however, *Doctor Who*'s many followers finally had a real opportunity to show their appreciation. As part of the celebrations to mark the BBC's sixtieth year of television broadcasting, a telephone poll was held to determine the nation's 'Favourite Popular Drama'. There were twelve nominees to choose from, including such popular successes as *Bergerac, Casualty* and *EastEnders*. To the apparent surprise of many, *Doctor Who* won, and McCoy and Peter Davison collected the award as part of the televised *Auntie's All-Time Greats* birthday party. This spectacular victory subsequently attracted some sniping in the press, particularly from disgruntled *EastEnders* cast members, and suggestions were even made that well-organised *Doctor Who* fan clubs had rung in *en masse* to influence the outcome. In fact, there had been no such organised fan campaign to try to influence the vote. In the hearts of many, and by a simple majority vote, the award had gone to the series that most deserved it.

RATINGS
By Ian Wheeler

When considering the viewing figures for McCoy's time as the Doctor, it is important to place the raw numerical data in context. From 1987 to 1989, *Doctor Who* was scheduled against the toughest possible opposition in the form of Granada's *Coronation Street*, the UK's oldest and mightiest soap opera. The ratings were thus bound to be lower on average than for earlier eras of the series' history. It should also be borne in mind that many families are likely to have watched *Coronation Street* and recorded *Doctor Who* on video, a factor not allowed for at this time, as only those viewers who had seen a programme on transmission were counted for ratings purposes.

The ratings for Season 24 were modest but consistent. All the episodes fell within a relatively small range, with a minimum of 4.2 and a maximum of 5.5 million viewers. A notable fall occurred between the first and second episodes of the opening story, but this was nothing new: it had happened on many previous occasions in the series' history, as numerous casual viewers tuned in out of curiosity to see how the season began and then lost interest. The average figure for the season was a somewhat disappointing 5.0 million viewers (although this was still higher than that for the previous run – consisting of the single fourteen part story *The Trial of a Time Lord* – which had had the advantage of a traditional Saturday evening time slot). There are five factors that would seem to account for this rather low figure. First, and most importantly, the scheduling of the series opposite *Coronation Street*. Secondly, the actual transmission time of 7.35 pm, which was rather late for some children and also gave *Doctor Who*'s opponents on other channels a five minute advantage (shows tending to start on the hour or half-hour). Thirdly, McCoy had a relatively low public profile (certainly in comparison with, say, Peter Davison, who had already acquired a major following on *All Creatures Great and Small* before coming to *Doctor Who*). Fourthly, after the hiatus of 1985 (when the series had been taken off the air for eighteen months by BBC1 Controller Michael Grade), people had got out of the habit of watching *Doctor Who* and in many cases simply did not bother to tune in when it returned. And finally, the season itself was arguably of a relatively poor quality, with high levels of humour resulting in negative press reviews. Poor publicity has been cited by some commentators as an additional factor, but this is not entirely valid as *Radio Times* coverage of the series was good, and numerous on-screen trailers were shown.

The ratings for Season 25 were far more respectable, averaging 5.4 million viewers and peaking at 6.6 million. McCoy had by now established himself in the role of the Doctor, and the season had the added advantage of beginning transmission in October rather than September, which was when many new shows made their debut and competition for viewers was more fierce, and running on into January, when ratings are traditionally higher. The combination of an important anniversary and the return of the Daleks and the Cybermen created a considerable 'nostalgia factor,' and the season itself was of a high quality, receiving supportive reviews in the press. Unusually, the second episode of the opening story, *Remembrance of the Daleks*, gained a higher rating than the first, suggesting that there may have been good 'word of mouth' about the quality of the latter and its exciting 'hovering Dalek' cliff-hanger.

Season 26 did less well, and in fact received the worst viewing figures of the McCoy era. *Battlefield* Part One was seen by only 3.1 million viewers, *Doctor Who*'s all-time lowest rating. The figures for *Ghost Light* and *The Curse of Fenric* hovered around the four million mark, but only *Survival* gained what could be described as a healthy rating, with five million viewers for Parts One and Three. This time, there can be little doubt that a major factor accounting for the season's relative failure was a lack of publicity. There was virtually no effort made to promote the series in the *Radio Times*; and, although there had been some press coverage of the stories at the time of their production, a press call (with John Nathan-Turner, Sophie Aldred and Jean Marsh) on 16 August 1989 to publicise their imminent transmission failed to generate any significant interest, and a second one (with Nicholas Parsons) did not take place until 19 October, by which point only *The Curse of Fenric* and *Survival* remained to be transmitted. Given that the viewing figures had been steadily rising during the course of the season, it is tempting to wonder how much more successful it would have become had it continued for a few more episodes. Looking at these figures alone, however, it is perhaps not entirely surprising that *Doctor Who* was taken off the air at this point.

The series bounced back in 1993 when the *Children in Need* special *Dimensions in Time* achieved an average viewing figure of 13.7 million. This, however, was somewhat misleading, as the annual charity telethon had by this point become consistently popular, and the ratings quoted were only for the quarter-hour segments in which the *Doctor Who* skit happened to be transmitted. Rather more impressive was the 9.08 million figure won by the 1996 *Doctor Who* television movie. This placed it ninth in the top one hundred most watched programmes that week, the second highest position attained by a drama show. This was, by any standard, a remarkably good figure, and showed that many of the viewers who had deserted *Doctor Who* in the late Eighties had returned, along with a whole new audience of youngsters.

SEVENTH/EIGHTH DOCTOR STORIES
IN ORDER OF AVERAGE VIEWING FIGURES
(Figures in millions of viewers)

Doctor Who	9.08
Silver Nemesis	5.50
The Greatest Show in the Galaxy	5.43
Remembrance of the Daleks	5.35
Delta and the Bannermen	5.27
Dragonfire	5.07
The Happiness Patrol	5.07
Survival	4.93
Paradise Towers	4.93
Time and the Rani	4.63
The Curse of Fenric	4.13
Ghost Light	4.07
Battlefield	3.65

www.ingramcontent.com/pod-product-compliance
Lightning Source LLC
Chambersburg PA
CBHW071113080526
44587CB00013B/1325